Power at Sea

Power at Sea

VOLUME 2

The Breaking Storm
1919–1945

Lisle A. Rose

UNIVERSITY OF MISSOURI PRESS

COLUMBIA AND LONDON

ISBN-13: 978-0-8262-1702-8
ISBN-10: 0-8262-1702-8

Designer: Kristie Lee
Typesetter: Phoenix Type, Inc.
Typefaces: Adobe Garamond, URW Antiqua, Arsis
Book Club Edition

For Robert H. Ferrell

IN GRATITUDE FOR HIS MANY
YEARS OF SUPPORT

CONTENTS

MAPS

BETWEEN 1939 AND 1945, a storm that had been gathering for twenty years broke across the world ocean with a force and violence that no one had adequately foreseen. Every form of naval warfare—carriers and convoys, invasions and intelligence, wolf packs, wireless, and so many others—was employed by four major sea powers fighting desperately for survival. For two decades, men of goodwill but often foolish minds had grappled with disarmament at sea, knowing full well that if it was not achieved and maintained, the aggressive appetites of nations laboring under economic stress and scarcity could not be contained. As with all wars, every potential participant condemned the resort to arms, but some would make war in the name of national survival and the others would accept war rather than perish. And the war came.

When the blizzard of blood and steel had at last blown itself out, the global landscape was transformed. In the spring of 1939, a geopolitician placing the point of his or her compass on the Rhine and drawing a circle some five hundred miles in diameter would have included within its circumference all of the historically great capitals of the modern world: London, Paris, Rome, Berlin, Amsterdam, Brussels, even Madrid and Lisbon. The early twentieth century had brought only modest changes to the global power equaton. Far-off Tokyo was busily engaged by fair means and foul in creating an imperial "Greater East Asia Co-Prosperity Sphere," while on the European peripheries, governments in Moscow and Washington, D.C., struggled to master vast problems of political control (the USSR) and economic impoverishment (the USA).

Six years later all had changed. Europe and its great capitals lay more or less in ruins, its empires either gone forever or tottering toward extinction. Japan was defeated and devastated. In their place, the two formerly weak peripheral powers had, from Moscow and Washington, D.C., amassed unprecedented power. While the Soviet Union now dominated all but the western and southern edges of the vast, sprawling Eurasian landmass, power on the world ocean lay entirely in the hands of the United States, a relative newcomer to the international scene, an upstart that would need to employ sea power, along with many other forms of strength available to it, to create and shape the kind of open and generous political system anathema to the men of the Kremlin.

In the war just passed, the U.S. fleet had incorporated every major advance in combat, tactics, and strategy fashioned in the twenty years since the last great world cataclysm: aircraft carriers; amphibious warfare; replenishment at sea; advanced long-range submarines; strong, powerful, and swift, if not always nimble, ship-based aircraft capable of dueling on an equal basis with land-based planes and pilots; and, last but far from least, effective logistics. This one great fleet, and no other, could expect as a matter of course to maintain and indeed improve upon both its qualitative and its quantitative superiority in the coming years, even as American sailors watched their exhausted British allies—the only possible though inconceivable rival—send ship after ship to the breaker yards while the empire staggered on its way to collapse.

As in volume 1, I have many people to thank for their help and support, including George Thompson and Randall Jones at the Center for American Places in Harrisonburg, Virginia; the research staffs at Suzzalo and Odegaard Libraries at the University of Washington, Seattle; the National Maritime Museum in Greenwich, England; the Nimitz Library at the United States Naval Academy at Annapolis, Maryland; the Naval Historical Center in Washington, D.C.; and the Naval Undersea Museum at Keyport, Washington.

Edward J. Marolda, David Alan Rosenberg, and Kenneth Kohlstedt placed in my hands critically important materials and information that I might otherwise have missed. Edwin Finney Jr., photographic curator at the Naval Historical Center, spent several hours with me by phone tracking down essential photographs. Laura Weavers made them available to me with gratifying swiftness. Robert Ferrell and several anonymous readers have gone through various iterations of the manuscript over the years with great care and insightful chapter-by-chapter advice on revision that saved me from numerous sins of omission or commission. Once again, John M. Rose has made the maps that are so critical to a proper telling of any maritime story, while my wife, Harriet Dashiell Schwar, has again brought her skills as a professional historian to her reading of portions of the volume's final version. Finally, the editorial staff at the University of Missouri Press has transformed manuscript to book with admirable speed and professional skill. I am, of course, responsible for whatever errors of fact or interpretation that remain.

I would like to gratefully acknowledge the use of ESRI's data and map collection and its third-party vendor ArcWorld for providing the data used in the creation of the maps in this volume.

The Pacific War, 1941-1945

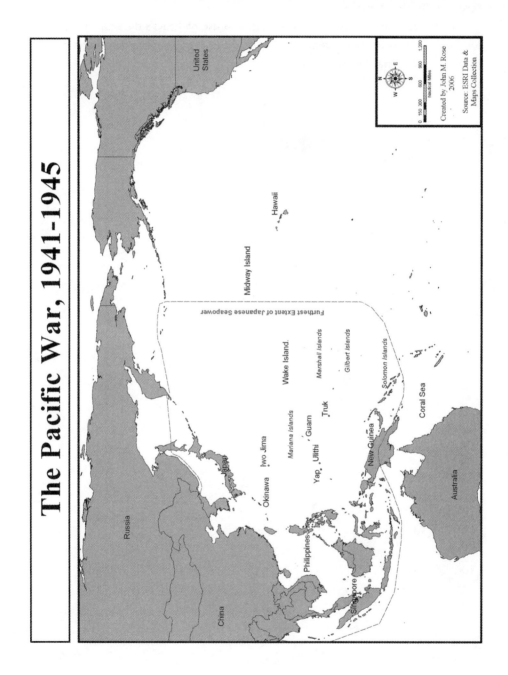

United States

Hawaii

Midway Island

Furthest Extent of Japanese Seapower

Wake Island.

Marshall Islands

Gilbert Islands

Solomon Islands

Mariana Islands

Truk

Guam

Iwo Jima

Yap. Ulithi

Coral Sea

Okinawa

New Guinea

Japan

Russia

Philippines

Australia

Singapore

China

Created by John M. Rose
2006

Source: ESRI Data &
Maps Collection

0 150 300   600   900   1,200
Nautical Miles

The Atlantic Lifeline, 1939-1945

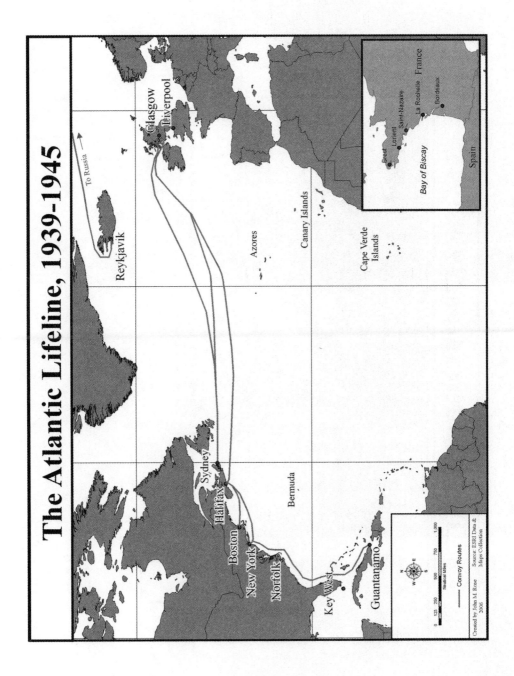

To Russia →

Reykjavik

Glasgow
Liverpool

Sydney
Halifax
Boston
New York
Norfolk

Key West

Guantanamo

Bermuda

Azores

Canary Islands

Cape Verde
Islands

Brest
Lorient
Saint-Nazaire
La Rochelle
Bordeaux

France

Bay of Biscay

Spain

Convoy Routes

0 125 250   500   750   1,000
Nautical Miles

Created by John M. Rose
2006

Source: ESRI Data &
Maps Collection

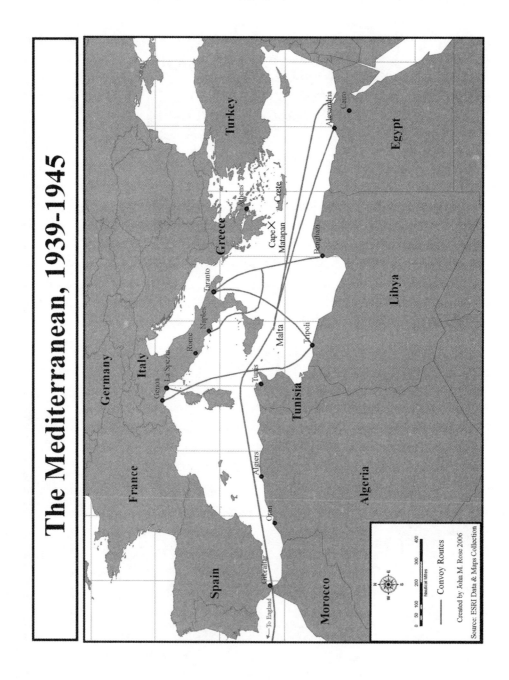

The Mediterranean, 1939-1945

Power at Sea

CHAPTER 1

The Containment of Sea Power

Washington, 1921–1922

DURING THE LAST WEEKS of 1918, with the stroke of a pen, at the bark of an order, in furtive, tearful farewells on a train platform, European monarchy skulked from the scene of its shame. It took with it all the dignified proceedings of kings at arms, all the monstrous pageantry, the blazonry and armor of rulership, all the dreams of the heroic life that for centuries had given a sense of meaning and purpose, however near or distant, to the exalted and simple folk of the Continent. The kaiser fled to melancholy exile in the Netherlands; the czar and his family were hustled from St. Petersburg to oblivion somewhere in the East; the Austro-Hungarian emperor disappeared along with his empire. Even where monarchy clung to power, as in Britain, its sun was wintry, weak, and withered.

In its place came a motley collection of the formerly despised outcasts of European politics—democrats, communists, liberals, socialists, and trade unionists—proclaiming a bright new day for Everyman. Armies and navies were no longer the playthings of kingly and princely autocrats, but rather the servants of parliaments and publics. The hideous cost and gruesome ambiguities of warfare at sea as well as ashore had swept away the boisterous navalism that had characterized the years immediately preceding 1914, and though navies retained a pride of place in public opinion, people now objected to the menacing size and great expense of modern fleets.

Throughout the first postwar decade the politicians and their visions of a brave new world jarred and jostled each other for power. At Versailles in 1919, at Washington two years later, and at Locarno in 1925, the masters of the new order tried to put the world back together.[1] Versailles was meant to fashion a European security system that would last for decades; Washington would do the same for Asia and the Pacific while creating a just and fair balance of world naval power; Locarno would correct the defects and failures of Versailles. These conferences, wrote a contemporary, "marked the first attempt of Democracy to reorganize the Old World in accordance with its own principles."[2] But what kind of peace did the democratic statesmen and diplomats want? What kind of peace could they obtain? Versailles created the League of Nations, but millions refused to believe that collective security was anything more or less than a sham and a fraud perpetrated by the satisfied powers on the rest of the world. The United States simply refused to join the League. Germany, absent until 1926, walked out in 1933, followed immediately thereafter by Japan. The peoples of both nations were filled with revulsion for international life and convinced that a postwar world of moral decay and widespread physical squalor could be redeemed only by a secular messiah. And the messiahs soon appeared. If the peace finally failed, what kind of war would military and naval statesmen have to wage? In this turbulent, often hostile new environment, worried admiralties and navy departments constantly adjusted their perspectives and policies, all too conscious of the fact that the agendas of the remaining great sea powers had not changed and that contests for regional or global supremacy continued unabated.

The war had bled Britain white. The treasury was exhausted, and the lords of politics and of the Admiralty knew that the war bills were coming due and that they would be staggering. An average of eight million pounds had been spent on battle *each day* between August 1914 and November 1918. "We had lent two thousand millions to our allies," a British journalist recalled in 1938, "none of which we should see again." England had been transformed from a creditor to a debtor nation. Two million unemployed, many of them veterans of the western front, shuffled the streets of London or sang for pennies in city parks. Meanwhile, the German fleet had disappeared. France and Italy possessed moderate-size fleets, but neither nation had completed a single battleship or fast cruiser in five years.[3] There seemed to desperate millions little or no reason for a huge navy. And the Royal Navy was huge. During four years of war it had expanded from a fleet of perhaps four hundred vessels to more than thirteen hundred combat ships of all types. Although most of the new additions were small craft—destroyers, minelayers, and armed trawlers—the British fleet of 1919 included forty-two first-class dreadnought battleships and battle cruisers.[4]

Sir John "Jacky" Fisher, prewar first sea lord, architect of the British dreadnought fleet, and a hero to millions then and later, told anyone who would listen that "half the Navy wants scrapping and the other half will be equally useless in a few years because of the internal combustion engine and oil." Retired admiral Percy Scott, another prewar naval genius (in gunnery), argued that the battleship itself was doomed as a weapon of war, asserting that "at an early date this country and its interests will be defended by aircraft." Fisher concurred. Aircraft and submarines together had doomed the battleship, and for those reactionaries in the navy who persisted in defending a surface fleet, he had but one reply: *Sack the lot!* In letter after letter to the *Times,* Fisher explained and defended his position.

> It's as clear as daylight that future war at sea absolutely precludes the use of any vessel of war that can't go under water because aircraft will compel it. . . . All you want is the present naval side of the air force!—that's the future navy. . . . By land and sea the approaching prodigious aircraft development knocks out the present fleet, makes invasion practicable, cancels our country being an island, and transforms the atmosphere into the battleground of the future.

There seemed nothing for it but to scrap dozens of the old battleships and to break up countless cruisers. Eleven months after the Armistice nearly two hundred ships had been stricken from the lists, and the Admiralty canceled nearly the entire existing building program to the point that by the end of 1919, *"there will not be a single war vessel—large or small—on the stocks in this country."* Hundreds of dedicated and blooded naval officers were "axed." They "became garage owners, poultry keepers or farmers until they went bankrupt, as mostly they did."[5]

Yet global realities could not be ignored. In 1921 the Admiralty submitted a somber appreciation to the imperial cabinet, concluding that defeat of one portion of the worldwide empire "implied defeat of the whole; there could be no question of 'buying off' an acquisitive enemy by ceding to him" one or more colonies.

> The strategic situation has undergone a complete change as a result of the late war. With the elimination of Germany as a naval power, and little fear of rivalry from either France or Italy, British waters and the Mediterranean

have ceased to be areas in which we are likely to be seriously engaged. . . . The formidable naval Powers of the present day, are the United States of America and Japan, both of whom are rapidly expanding their fleets. Thus, instead of the North Sea, British waters, or the Mediterranean, the oceans round the widely separated coasts of the U.S.A. and Japan have become the foci of naval interest.[6]

The Admiralty was especially uneasy about Washington's continued determination to build a navy second to none. Against whom would this great sea force be employed and for what purposes?

Washington was no less alarmed at the world scene. The notion that had taken hold in the months immediately preceding entry into the Great War, namely, that the international community was a nest of vipers against whom the United States needed to be well armed, continued to fester under the surface of genuine amity that working sailors had achieved at Queenstown and Scapa Flow. In a mere nineteen months of war, the United States had placed on the building stocks a sizable merchant marine. It never got to sea to carry men and cargo to the battlefronts during the nation's brief involvement, but it now lay ready if need be to challenge war-weary Britain for economic superiority on the world ocean. For a variety of reasons, then, the U.S. Navy's General Board in 1920 recommended completion of the massive shipbuilding program begun four years before, reshaped somewhat by wartime imperatives but reconfirmed in 1918 by both Congress and President Wilson. No fewer than a dozen twenty-three-knot battleships and sixteen thirty-five-knot battle cruisers should be laid down. Against whom would these ships be deployed? Did the United States Navy possess a coherent postwar strategic vision? It did, or at least the Planning Section of the navy's "Forces in European Waters" over in Paris did. The planners' strategic vision went well beyond the generally assumed notion then and now that the United States was preparing for a postwar commercial showdown with Britain on the high seas by building a superior navy. Even before the guns fell silent on the western front, the planners began dispatching a series of memorandums to Washington. France and Italy, they wrote in October 1918, were eager to "take over" a substantial proportion of the German and Austrian war fleets. Thus, "there can be little doubt that an understanding exists" between the two countries and Great Britain. "In other words there have been counsels on this subject of vital interest to us from which we have been excluded." Moreover,

It should not be forgotten that we have strong evidence of an agreement between Great Britain and Japan by which not less than five British dreadnoughts are to be transferred to Japan after the Peace. . . . Assuming the distribution [of enemy ships] made as indicated the United States with seventeen modern capital ships would be faced at once with an alliance between Great Britain and Japan controlling a total of sixty-seven capital ships. Even with Japan left out Great Britain would face us with *three* times the number of capital ships that we have. This in itself is an intolerable situation.

So much for Allied unity. However much Billy Gob and Jack Tar enjoyed working with each other, calculating heads at the strategic level were already assessing America's postwar national security at sea and finding it wanting. "Four Great Powers have arisen in the world to compete with Great Britain for commercial supremacy on the seas," the planners continued, "Spain, Holland, France, Germany. Each one of those powers in succession have been defeated by Great Britain and her fugitive Allies." Perfidious Albion, indeed! Now a fifth commercial power, "the greatest one yet, is . . . arising to compete for at least commercial equality with Great Britain," and "already the signs of jealousy" in London toward the United States "are visible," at least to the American planners. "Historical precedent warns us to watch closely the moves we make or permit to be made." The planners thus concluded that all enemy submarines— German and Austrian—"should be destroyed" and that no German or Austrian naval vessels should be used to augment the fleets "of any power whatever." They then took a further, shocking, step by urging maintenance of a powerful German fleet after the war "to exercise a distinctly conservative influence on the application of British sea power." Finally, "the United States should never permit the transfer of British capital ships to Japan, as the move would be distinctly hostile to American interests." Human nature being what it is, it is doubtful that the planners managed to keep either their prejudices, suspicions, or proposals from totally escaping the attention of their Anglo-French colleagues on the Allied Naval Council at Paris.[7] If they had to this point, the British soon smoked them out.

That same month, Rear Admiral Sydney Fremantle argued on behalf of the Royal Navy that the surrender of the German fleet should be made an article of the Armistice terms. Germany must be disarmed at sea as on land, lest it be tempted to a "recommencement of warlike operations." Since Britain's future security "depends upon that of our sea communications," destroying or sequestering the German navy was a high priority. Asked to comment, the Planning Section dismissed the admiral's arguments out of hand; they represented British proposals only and were probably meant as a shield behind which the High Seas

Fleet would be "distributed among the powers now at war with Germany. . . . Viewing the position from a strictly American view point, if the German Fleet were destroyed, Great Britain would be at liberty to do with our new merchant marine as she saw fit, since her naval power would so far outbalance our own as to make it practically impossible for us to oppose her, no matter how arbitrary her methods might be." To consider the German navy an ally was, of course, unthinkable. But to view it as a counterweight to a haughty power that had consistently trampled on neutral rights throughout the war in prosecuting its blockade was only prudent.

> It may be right and proper that Great Britain should have a greater naval force than other European Powers, since she must, by the very nature of her insular position, assure to herself the opportunity to live by the importation of food. It is not, however, right for Great Britain to occupy as commanding a naval position that she may by the mere exercise of her will and the employment of her Fleet, stop the importation of food equally necessary to all the countries in Europe.[8]

In other words, His Majesty's government could not be allowed to employ the Royal Navy in an ongoing blockade of Germany to force a harsh and unrealistic armistice through hunger. The question of disposition of the German navy should be left to the Peace Conference.

When, several weeks later, the Admiralty in London circulated a draft of "Naval Armistice Terms" for comment, the U.S. Naval Advisory Staff to the Allied Naval Council again emphasized American opposition to either the permanent surrender or the destruction of "all German, Austrian, and Turkish vessels being built. . . . We believe it unwise," the staff paper read, "for reasons already given, to prohibit Germany from building or possessing a Navy." In that spirit, the fortifications and harbor works on Heligoland, Germany's outpost on the North Sea and shield against enemy forces raiding the Bight, and the naval towns of Wilhelmshaven and Cuxhaven should be preserved, not destroyed, as the British urged. "The Island of Heligoland is a defensive position for Germany. . . . We believe the future ownership of Heligoland should remain with Germany."[9] And so it did.

Stephen Howarth has argued that, in fact, the Americans—or at least Woodrow Wilson, who was taking a hard tone with Britain at this time—were bluffing. "While his naval planners fully anticipated another war (and accepted that Britain might just as easily become an enemy as Japan), Wilson believed he was moving close to his deepest desire: the establishment of an era of lasting global peace."[10] Whether all this was true is questionable in light of Wilson's later willingness to disrupt the conference and go home over the issue of future Anglo-American naval construction. That the British were bluffing—or at least huffing and puffing with little behind their insistence that they would spend the last farthing to maintain naval supremacy—is incontestable. As early as 1905, the Colonial Defense Committee warned Canada that the Royal Navy had lost naval supremacy in the western Atlantic to the expanding U.S. fleet. Moreover, "the greatest interest of this country," that is, Great Britain, lay in "maintain[ing] friendly relations with the United States." A memorandum by cabinet secretary Maurice Hankey to the Committee of Imperial Defense in July 1919 stated bluntly:

> The United States of America is the most powerful nation in the world.... It is quite out of the question that we could make a successful war against her, and it is doubtful if all Europe combined could do so.... Fortunately, such a war is almost unthinkable. In the main, American ideals are our ideals. If there is antagonism to the British Empire among important elements in the United States, that is not generally realised in Great Britain, where there is no corresponding antagonism.[11]

In the early postwar months, then, British naval officials and observers resurrected the same arguments they had employed in 1916–1917 when American appetites had first become manifest. The United States was a vast continental imperium in its own right that required no navy to guarantee either national prosperity or security. Britain, on the other hand, was a comparatively small island nation that survived and prospered through a network of global dependencies. Not only did the British Empire stimulate jealousy and envy among the lesser powers of the world, but Britain's strategic position on the sea approaches to Europe was also a constant source of irritation to continental powers. Germany was defeated, but for how long? Britons remembered Prime Minister Arthur James Balfour's prewar observation that without a superior fleet Britain would no longer count as a great power, whereas without any fleet at all Germany could remain the greatest power in Europe. Having all but beggared itself outbuilding Germany before 1914 and then having plunged into near bankruptcy to win the Great War, Britain simply could not engage in another naval race of the kind contemplated, however innocently, by the United States. "What is needed at this juncture in our fortunes," wrote the prominent naval analyst Archibald Hurd in the autumn of 1919, "is a policy of reasonable reduction and far-sighted consolidation. The country is rightly determined upon

a policy of national economy, and that policy must apply to all the departments, not excluding the Admiralty, the War Office, and the Air Ministry." Let
the United States and Japan build as they would, Hurd maintained; their ships
could be no better than those Britain already had on hand. Britain should
maintain a construction holiday for five years, and then determine whether a
new arms race would be in its interest.[12]

The lords of the Admiralty could not accept such a magisterial view of developments. They either knew or sensed that by the U.S. Navy's own reckoning, the "32,000 ton *New Mexico* class battleships, approved in 1914, were 25
per cent stronger than Germany's 28,000 ton *Bayern* class and a remarkable 38
per cent stronger than Britain's 27,500 ton *Royal Sovereign* class, both of which
were approved at about the same time." The editor of *Jane's Fighting Ships* remarked on the American determination to build and deploy "everything" ships.
With such power in hand, the British Admiralty wanted to know why their so
recently cherished allies were behaving as they were. The vast U.S. naval building program of 1916, which promised even bigger and better ships than the
New Mexicos, had been modified under wartime conditions to emphasize the
destroyers needed for successful antisubmarine work. But Wilson and Congress had never abandoned the goal of building one of the world's two largest
navies in order to enforce Washington's definition of freedom of the seas and to
protect what was fondly believed to be a forthcoming rebirth of American maritime power. The U.S. wartime shipbuilding program had turned out huge
numbers of merchant vessels with extraordinary rapidity, stimulating great interest in Congress and among the public in reviving the long-moribund U.S.
merchant marine to compete with those of Great Britain, Japan, France, and
Italy. At times the United States seemed determined not only to match British
sea power but to become the world's leading maritime and naval state as well.[13]

In the summer of 1918 Congress had passed a naval bill amplifying the
1916 program. During a period of six years more than a thousand additional
combat ships would be constructed. The General Board of the navy justified
the program in a memorandum of September 18, which reconfirmed the
American fleet had to be at least the equal of any other sea service in the world.
A vast U.S. navy would be "adequate" to provide "due weight to the diplomatic
remonstrances of the United States in peace" or to enforce the nation's policies
in times of war. Construction of a fleet of perhaps as many as sixty-nine capital
ships, more than any other navy including Britain's forty-two, would keep
American yards busy for years. Ten weeks later the General Board amplified its
argument in a lengthy memorandum for the chief of naval operations (CNO),

which was submitted on December 2, just two days before Wilson sailed for the Paris Peace Conference, and which reached the president within twenty-four hours. Overriding strategic reasons demanded that the United States acquire former German holdings in the Pacific, including the Mariana and Caroline Islands, and the United States should not shrink from its naval expansion program, since large navies, not small, would enforce the power of Wilson's cherished postwar League of Nations. Just before sailing from Hoboken for the Paris Peace Conference in early December, the president granted an interview to the three trusted news correspondents he was taking with him. Pressed about military and naval matters, he emphasized the dangers of "militarism." "No one power," he argued, "no two powers, should be supreme." Wilson added that "if it came to a point of England refusing to reduce naval armaments, 'the United States should show her how to build a navy. We would be in a position to meet any program England or any other power might set forth.'" With those thoughts in mind, Wilson went on deck to receive a tumultuous send-off from hundreds of ships large and small amassed in New York Harbor, together with the battleship *Pennsylvania* lying just off the coast and several dirigibles and airplanes.[14]

When Wilson (and Congress) showed no signs of backing off from the commitment to build a navy second to none, the Admiralty at last lost its poise.[15] As the Paris Conference staggered toward a conclusion the following March, Secretary of the Navy Josephus Daniels found himself peremptorily accosted by Britain's first sea lord, Admiral Rosslyn Wester-Wemyss, who called without appointment to demand to know why the United States was so determined to increase its fleet. Wester-Wemyss bluntly told Daniels that Britain must have the "largest navy afloat." The next day Wester-Wemyss met formally with Daniels and the chief of naval operations, Admiral William Benson, and asserted Britain's case. England was an island nation, "with colonies all over the globe, making the greatest navy essential to Great Britain's existence."

Benson would have none of it. No nation from then on should be supreme at sea. The United States had imperial responsibilities from the Philippines to the Virgin Islands and was required to enforce the Monroe Doctrine from Alaska to the Strait of Magellan. "Equality with the British Navy" was the minimum standard that Washington would accept. A further meeting between the Americans and Walter Long, lord of the Admiralty, brought forth further British concerns. In its current desperate financial condition Britain simply could not rebuild its merchant marine to match proposed American construction, nor could the Royal Navy match the American naval building program. Long was "alarmed" and added that it was intolerable that Britain, having suffered tremendous losses in men, money, and ships during the recent war, should now "become a second-rate sea power commercially or otherwise." Daniels tried to reassure. The United States had no desire for global naval or maritime supremacy; there was "no purpose in any naval program to replace Britain as 'mistress of the seas.'" But the peace of the world did demand naval parity between Britain and the United States.

The navy secretary set the matter before his president with brutal clarity on April 7: "Admiral Benson feels strongly that we should go on building until our Navy is as strong as Great Britain's, which of course would mean that we would have to ask for a big appropriation for new ships in the next Congress." But British prime minister David Lloyd George was "very earnest and very strong in saying he would not give a snap of his finger for the League of Nations if we keep on building."[16]

Daniels was less than candid in his assurances to the British, for the U.S. Naval Advisory Staff at the conference was strongly urging on Wilson a policy of naval superiority. Two days after Daniels wrote the president, Benson sent the latest staff memorandum to Wilson through Daniels. U.S. naval policy, the staff asserted, involved promotion and guardianship of national interests "in every way consonant with justice" together with assisting in the promotion of global welfare. A sober examination of America's "world situation in the new order of things" led to the realization that "all of our important international relations and all of our important international questions hinge upon matters relating to the sea and sea communications. We cannot advance our external interests, nor can we influence world policy, except by way of the sea. . . . Under present conditions," the Royal Navy "is strong enough to dominate the seas in whatever quarter of the globe that domination may be required." Kaiser Wilhelm had in fact done the United States a favor with his High Seas Fleet that had tied down the bulk of the Royal Navy in home waters and checkmated possible British designs on global domination. But the German fleet had now "disappeared" into Scapa Flow where, it was assumed, the rotting vessels would be parceled out to the victors as spoils of war. Moreover, the staff paper continued baldly, "We are setting out to be the greatest commercial rival of Great Britain on the seas," and because the United States was a young, vibrant, growing nation, it might well in the near future excite the jealousy and animosity of fading Britain. Finally, the staff considered the argument that a large U.S. naval building program in fact threatened the legitimacy and authority of Wilson's cherished League of Nations. Quite the contrary. A Royal Navy bestriding the world's sea-lanes uncontested constituted the real threat to a League. "As long as Great Britain insists on retaining her overwhelming naval force, the only answer for the purposes of the League is the building of an equal force by some nation capable of constructing and maintaining a fleet of equal strength and efficiency," and in the conditions prevailing in the spring of 1919, only the United States was in a position to do this. "With two navies of equal strength," the U.S. Naval Advisory Staff concluded, "the world would breathe free from the fear of a naval domination that has the power at any moment of threatening the economic life of any nation." Only at the very close of the paper did the staff suggest a possible way out of the prevailing impasse. If *both* Britain and the United States reduced their naval armaments substantially and in a way to balance forces, the world would truly breathe free. Once reductions were achieved, the British and Americans could "determine jointly from time to time what the strength of the two fleets shall be."[17] In other words, a joint Anglo-American naval condominium to rule the world ocean.

The British anger at American intransigence reached such proportions that at one point Wilson cabled the White House to have the liner *George Washington* sent back across the Atlantic to Brest to fetch him home. As both sides seethed, the president's chief adviser, Colonel Edward M. House, and Robert Cecil, one of Lloyd George's inner circle, at last reached an agreement. Cecil cultivated the image of the sophisticated, world-weary British diplomat continually surprised and amused by the propensity of others to become excited. As the navy staff paper wended its way up the U.S. naval and civil chains of command, Cecil wrote Colonel House a lofty note that began, "I have found in exalted quarters that some of the recent utterances by high officials connected with the United States Navy have produced a very unfortunate impression." Cecil suggested that it was time to knuckle down to business and hammer out a compromise, which he and House proceeded to do. Britain would support the League of Nations in toto in exchange for an American pledge not to build beyond the 1916 program. As for the fate of the rapidly deteriorating High Seas Fleet, Germany's sailors took it upon themselves to resolve that problem. In a last gesture of defiance, the German crews scuttled their ships in protest over the forthcoming treaty. Just days before the Paris Conference concluded with what nearly every German (and some Western Allies) considered a brutally punitive peace, British Tars lounging on the decks of their ships at Scapa Flow were startled, then astonished, then alarmed to see nearly every one of the German ships in their care suddenly sag over on its beam ends and begin to sink. Only a handful of the once splendid sixty-six battleships, battle cruisers, and lesser vessels were saved by the belatedly aroused British naval security forces, and they were of no use to anyone but the Americans, who would later use their share of the remaining ships as aerial bombing targets. Admiral Wester-Wemyss pronounced the act a blessing. He was undoubtedly right.[18]

In the immediate aftermath of the House-Cecil agreement, Secretary Daniels poured analgesic on the widening Anglo-American wound. Daniels and a delegation of senior American naval officials visited London during the final week of April and the first week of May, which Daniels characterized to his British hosts as "two of the most delightful, informing and happiest weeks of our lives," including "interesting conferences" with their opposites in the Royal Navy. During the course of his visit, Daniels assured an appreciative London audience that his country would do nothing "to add to the naval burdens of this [that is, Britain] or any other Power... that international developments do not strictly require us to do." Washington harbored no aspirations "to possess such strength at sea that we can impose our decrees arbitrarily on other free peoples," and he assumed—to hearty "Hear! Hear!"s—Britain did not either. But should the forthcoming League of Nations fail to achieve and maintain global security, "then, regrettable as the choice will be, repugnant as it will be to the American people, it will be essential, from the dictates of elementary national interest, that they shall build and maintain a fleet commensurate with the needs of national defense" that embraced both the Atlantic and the Pacific. Here was a warning not only to Britain but to Japan as well. The British press interpreted Daniels's remarks as positively as possible, noting the secretary's further observation that it would be "a calamity worse than a crime if the British people and the American people ever entered into a competition in Navy building."[19]

Benson, however, did not share Daniels's comparatively optimistic view of international affairs. "There will at all times," he wrote President Wilson from London, "be an European and an American interest which will always differ. It must be quite evident to you," the chief of naval operations added, "that in practically all questions that have come up Great Britain has been able to maintain her position and carry through her claims largely through the dominant influence exercised in consequence of her tremendous naval superiority." That superiority had to be whittled down. "Everything should be done to decrease or at least prevent an increase in the naval expenditures of Great Britain, France and Japan" while increasing that of the United States "in order to stabilize the League of Nations and to have it develop into what we intended it to be." Wilson was unable to get suitable language into the Treaty of Versailles but assured Benson that "the same result" could be obtained through appeal to public opinion.

Certainly, the taxpayers in Europe and Japan would not "consent to bear the burden of a larger naval establishment."[20]

Lost in all the chatter was the fate of the German navy. Now nearly devoid of ships, its sailors suddenly discovered that the triumphant Allies would allow their service to continue as a coastal-defense force. As with the army, Germany's remaining handful of seamen instantly formed a powerful, dedicated core of professionals that, as we shall see, schemed and intrigued as best they could throughout the 1920s and early '30s to stay abreast of naval developments and technologies and stood ready to rearm when Adolf Hitler came to power.

Anglo-American naval tensions soon escalated again, this time over the question of oil, which had now become the only feasible means of propelling warships large and small. In the summer of 1919 aggressive American business interests appeared in the Middle East, actively seeking oil concessions in an area long considered a British preserve. Alarmed British naval authorities in the region protested to the Foreign Ministry in London about concessions issued to Standard Oil by Syrian and Palestinian authorities; they also asserted that American relief efforts in Armenia were being used to cloak the nefarious activities of sharp-trading Yankee merchants. His Majesty's government reacted in the same insensitive manner that it had exhibited in enforcing the wartime blockade, the memory of which still caused many American shippers and navy men to see red. The prompt efforts to block the activities of American oil interests on the eastern shore of the Mediterranean created widespread alarm in Washington. The navy's General Board rather lost its head and complained to Secretary Daniels that Britain's actions reflected an increasing jealousy of the fledgling U.S. merchant marine. In the past, the board added erroneously, Britain had gone to war on every occasion in which it perceived its interests to be threatened by its former colonies. Historian Charles M. Melhorn has suggested that Anglo-American tensions became so acute so swiftly in 1919 that there was a genuine possibility of a naval war in the Atlantic that year. This is clearly a highly speculative conclusion. The close relationships on both working and senior levels between the American and British fleets in 1917–1918 clearly precluded a conflict just two years later. Indeed, the wartime Anglo-American naval partnership had reached the point where fledgling naval-aviation enthusiasts on both sides exchanged data and observations, some of which became critical to the development of American aircraft-carrier design and doctrine.[21]

Moreover, it should have been clear to knowledgeable Britons that the focus of American attention had shifted decisively after the Armistice from Europe and the Atlantic to Asia and the Pacific. Whatever aspirations Congress and the business community may have harbored for challenging British maritime supremacy paled before White House and Navy Department concerns for the fate of American interests in the Far East. After 1918, diplomats, sailors, and excitable public opinion makers could produce a broad catalog of concerns and impressions that seemed to point directly to Japanese designs to dominate the entire East Asian–Pacific region, possibly including even the establishment of clandestine naval bases on the west coast of Mexico.

President Wilson became outraged over Tokyo's steadfast refusal to withdraw from the former German concession at Tsingtao (Qingdao), China, and the adjacent Shantung (Shandong) Peninsula. By 1919 Japanese commercial and military presence in Manchuria and Shantung "aimed at Peking [Beijing] like a great pincers."[22] But Washington's major concern focused on the Yangtze River valley, China's heartland. The Western trading companies, minus Germany, returned to the area after the Great War stronger than ever and "determined to be their own policemen" in the midst of the near anarchy that had gripped the region since the overthrow in 1911 of the ancient imperial government. The U.S. Asiatic squadron grew larger than at any time since 1899. Four elderly but still fast and moderately powerful armored cruisers patrolled the downriver area out of Shanghai under the command of Albert Gleaves, a four-star admiral who flew his flag on the *South Dakota*. A vice admiral commanded the other three ships collected into Cruiser Division 1. Upriver, strung out in port cities from Nanking (Nanjing) to Chungking (Chongqing), were a half-dozen gunboats. Two more were moved to Hong Kong and Canton to show the flag. Britain, Japan, and even France all strengthened their China fleets accordingly.[23]

American sailors realized that control of the country's formidable resources could make Japan "invulnerable." The imperial government was becoming more convinced than ever that it must be the arbiter of China's destiny. Along the Yangtze Japanese agents were already dickering with warlords once friendly to Western gunboat captains and business interests. Amid a confusing welter of interests and a dynamic, fluid political atmosphere, the American naval attaché in China was convinced that Sun Yat-sen at Peking and a rival government at Canton were "working hand in glove with the Japanese." Gleaves asked for and got congressional appropriations for four new shallow-draft gunboats to expand the American presence and influence on the river.[24]

Because he favored an early withdrawal from the Philippines, Wilson was somewhat less concerned over Japan's determination to permanently assume the old German claims to the Mariana, Caroline, and Marshall Islands. Since

France and Britain had accepted Japanese expansion in a secret agreement of February 1917, the president was in no position to oppose and at Paris he deferred to Tokyo's demands. Possession of the midocean island clusters provided the Imperial Japanese Navy with the in-depth defense system that its strategists had long insisted was essential to repulse a possible Anglo-American air and sea drive across the Pacific. At the same time U.S. military and naval leaders charged with responsibility for the defense of Manila Bay and with attempting to enforce the long-standing policy of the Open Door in China realized that in the event of war Japanese aviation and submarine forces operating from Saipan could neutralize Guam, thus destroying the integrity of the Midway-Wake-Guam island chain that linked Hawaii with Luzon. Whatever naval forces and military garrisons were stationed in the Philippines would thus be cut off and easy to destroy. The generals and admirals made these concerns known publicly, and in 1921 British naval critic Hector Bywater incorporated them in his influential book, *Sea Power in the Pacific*.[25]

Yap compounded America's mid-Pacific problems. The tiny island, a former German holding five hundred miles southwest of Guam, controlled alternative transpacific cable routes to China, the East Indies, and the Philippines. Everyone knew it was impossible to guarantee the integrity of government or commercial communications on cable lines that passed through foreign territories.[26] But since the European powers had already given away so much to Japan in East Asia and the Pacific, Yap also fell into their lap at Paris as a League mandate. Washington opposed the decision, and the matter dragged on in diplomatic correspondence and international communication conferences for several years, further clouding American-Japanese relations.

Wilson nonetheless managed to checkmate Japan in its moments of victory. He forced Tokyo to agree to honor long-standing German commercial rights in Shantung and to express a willingness to consider handing back the area to China at some unspecified date. Moreover, Saipan, the Carolines, and the Marshalls (the latter only two thousand miles southwest of Hawaii) would be given to Japan only as League mandates, which meant they could not be fortified.

Fears of Japanese designs in China and the mid-Pacific did not exhaust the litany of Navy Department concerns. Tokyo had contributed by far the largest contingent to the postwar international intervention in Siberia, which was ostensibly meant to keep order but in practice supported the opponents of bolshevism. American naval men were convinced that Japan was scheming to detach Russia's Maritime Province or at least incorporate it into an economic sphere that would soon include Manchuria and the Yangtze River valley.[27]

At the same time Washington and the nation continued to be deeply disturbed over rumors and allegations of continued Japanese activities in Mexico and throughout the rest of Latin America. In the spring of 1921 the naval attaché in London reported that Britain might be selling some of its older battleships to Japan through Chile and other Latin American countries (a charge the Admiralty promptly denied). Naval intelligence files now "bulged" with tales of clandestine Japanese bases in Mexico's Magdalena and Turtle Bays, while an alleged Japanese-Mexican-Spanish commercial treaty was supposed to contain a secret clause like the German proposal in the Zimmermann telegram to return the lost provinces of Texas, New Mexico, and Arizona to Mexico in the event of a Japanese-American war. The attaché reported the wildest stories. In late 1921 a destroyer from the Pacific Fleet was sent into Mexican waters to disprove his assertion that the Japanese were secretly shipping whole sections of submarines to the Las Tres Marías islands for reconstruction and presumable use by the tiny Mexican navy. Some months before, the Office of Naval Intelligence had obtained information that the entire former German Latin American intelligence service was now in the pay of a "third power"—which could only be Japan— to destroy the Panama Canal. Convinced a conspiracy was afoot, the Navy Department kept in daily contact with the embassies in Buenos Aires, Panama, Valparaiso, and other southern points, trying to "follow the movements of the supposed conspirators." Although the canal remained undisturbed, the director of naval intelligence, Captain Luke McNamee, insisted that the former German agents had been "absorbed" by the Japanese, British, Mexicans, Chileans, and Argentineans.[28]

Washington immediately mounted a diplomatic and intelligence counteroffensive in Berlin that yielded top-secret German charts of the former Pacific-island holdings and an assertion by German naval authorities and industrial interests that they would much rather work with the United States than with Japan. But when Washington showed little interest in a long-term arrangement, the Germans turned once again to the Japanese. Krupp, Goertz, and Zeiss sold Tokyo naval machinery, optical equipment, steel plates and ingots, wireless materials, airplane motors and parts, and diesel engines. The Japanese also contracted with Swiss and Italian firms for the largest diesel engines in the world, and by the summer of 1921 three British missions had arrived at the Yokosuka naval base to begin "a crash program to make Japan self-sufficient in aeronautics."[29]

But the most convincing proof to American civil and naval authorities of Japan's aggressive intentions was Tokyo's determination in the summer of 1920 to at last fund and initiate the "eight-eight" naval building program initially called for in the 1907 Imperial National Defense Policy. Eight of the most powerful battleships and eight of the most modern battle cruisers should be at sea no later than 1927. Naval analysts Harold Sprout and Margaret Sprout, writing in 1940, claimed that these sixteen vessels would not be ordinary capital ships. The battlewagons would be "super-dreadnought[s]"; the battle cruisers would be "giants." The postwar records of the Mitsubishi Shipbuilding and Engineering Company, which was to build several of these vessels, corroborate the Sprouts' suspicions. At a time when the largest and newest battlewagons in the U.S. fleet displaced 32,500 tons, mounted eight 16-inch guns, and steamed at 21 knots, battle cruisers *Tosa* and *Kaga* were to be 40,000-ton ships mounting ten 16-inch guns and capable of 26.5 knots. The planned but unnamed hull number 12 was to be a battle cruiser of 41,200 tons carrying ten 16-inch guns and able to steam at 30 knots, and ship number 15, one of the two pièces de résistance of the program, was a fast battleship of 47,500 tons mounting eight 18-inch guns and also capable of 30 knots.[30]

The construction of sixteen massive capital ships in Japanese yards quickly proved to be more than a slumping postwar national economy could possibly bear. The harried vice minister of finance told navy minister Katō Tomosaburō early in 1921 that the national financial situation was "fast becoming hopeless; whether it will be ruined or not is up to you Navy people."[31] Yet to many Japanese naval men gazing east across the Pacific and southward beyond Taiwan (then, and for many years after, called Formosa), the eight-eight plan was the least the country could do to ensure national survival, for the view from Tokyo during the first years of the postwar era was as disturbing, if not more so, than the view from Washington.

America's persistent racial insensitivity was a continual source of bitterness and tension. At Paris Wilson had steadfastly refused to support Japan's yearning for a clause affirming racial equality in the forthcoming League of Nations. The following year Californians placed a referendum on their ballot imposing even more stringent prohibitions against "alien" landholding in the state. The naval attaché in Tokyo reported that the resultant anti-American campaign was the most bitter to date. Even the prompt and generous American aid following the great Tokyo earthquake three years later could not wholly suppress Japanese outrage at repeated expressions of American racism.[32]

Only two months after the Armistice of 1918 word leaked out of Washington that at least half the American battle fleet would be moving to the Pacific. The year before, American naval planners had concluded that the United States should "exercise...a commanding superiority of naval power" in that region while retaining "a defensive superiority against all potential enemies" in the Atlantic. America's destiny in the western ocean, proclaimed by many since the cruise of the Great White Fleet a decade before, was now about to be made manifest. The decision was formally announced in June 1919, and the reason given for at last dividing the U.S. fleet was to stimulate a spirit of professional rivalry in the service and thus "promote the efficiency of the Navy as a whole." Other considerations were adduced, including the winning of California votes for the Democratic Party in the forthcoming national elections. Only a few observers mentioned Japan, but Japanese diplomats and intelligence experts at the embassy in Washington and at home in Tokyo could not have been pleased to read in the *New York Times* that all six of the big battle cruisers currently being laid down in American yards were designated for duty in the Pacific, where their "speed and long cruising radius" made them "peculiarly suitable to conditions" in that ocean. In July 1920 Secretary Daniels formally reorganized the U.S. Navy into three fleets: the Atlantic, Pacific, and Asiatic. The newest 14- and 16-inch-gun battleships, he announced, would be sent west to California ports. Early in 1921 the Atlantic Fleet passed through the Panama Canal to engage in joint fleet maneuvers. And in June the new Republican administration formally stated that henceforth "most" of the U.S. Navy would be permanently stationed in the Pacific.[33]

The many proponents of Alfred Thayer Mahan's doctrine of a concentrated fleet for decisive action might complain about the folly of dividing naval forces, but the Japanese knew what the move portended. Not only was the American fleet now in the Pacific, but it was also, potentially, in the mid-Pacific, for in August 1919 the first battleship-size dry dock was commissioned at Pearl Harbor, and Hawaii suddenly became a potential midocean bastion for the United States.[34] With routine maintenance and upkeep facilities available for the biggest capital ships, the U.S. fleet not only shielded the American West Coast from sudden assault but was also now just thirty-four hundred nautical miles away from Japan. True, the fleet would remain stationed at San Pedro and San Diego for years, limiting its annual fleet exercises to brief cruises to the Panama Canal, out to Pearl, and back to California.[35] But the great Hawaiian base was there, ready for permanent occupation anytime world events warranted.

The construction of Pearl Harbor, in fact, changed the entire strategic situation in the Pacific to Japan's detriment. A glance at the map reveals how peculiar is the geography of that ocean. Both above and below the equator, the western portion is honeycombed with island archipelagoes that point like stepping-stones to the Asian mainland and Japan. East of Hawaii the twenty-four hundred statute miles to southern California are bereft of any landmasses whatsoever. Even an enemy occupation of Hawaii could not substantially menace the west coasts of the United States or Mexico if a powerful fleet and air force were available for defense. Looked at from Tokyo, enemy occupation of Hawaii (including its farthest outpost, Midway, more than a thousand nautical miles beyond Pearl Harbor) would provide a launching pad for an island-by-island advance to the doorstep of Japan either by a southern route through the Marshalls, Marianas, and Palau to Formosa and beyond or north via Marcus, the Bonins, and the Ryukyus.[36]

American development of Pearl Harbor did not exhaust the catalog of Japanese concerns. By 1921 it was clear that, despite London's dispatch of yet another mission that proved critically important to Japanese naval development, Britain was tiring of the 1902 Anglo-Japanese alliance.[37] Japan's wartime condemnation of the British alliance in the midst of Allied setbacks on the western front and Tokyo's several semisecret wartime dalliances with Germany were coming back to haunt the Tokyo government.[38] From its perspective, British coolness was discernible as early as 1909 as a result of the Russo-Japanese War, Japan's growing trade with China that progressively infringed upon the sales of costlier British products, London's alliance with Moscow to contain Germany, the increasingly cloudy relations between Japan and the United States, and, not least, the consequent growth of pro-American and anti-Japanese sentiment throughout the British Dominions.[39] But if the alliance lapsed, so would ready Japanese access to the most advanced Western naval and aviation technologies. Moreover, the accord conferred prestige that was desperately necessary to Japanese self-esteem. By its own exertions Japan had worked its way up to great-power status, the first assuredly non-Western nation in modern times to do so. In the early years of the century it had enjoyed some cautious applause for this achievement; even enlightened American opinion had been appreciative. Had not Teddy Roosevelt unofficially lauded the Japanese as yellow Anglo-Saxons? But now it seemed to Tokyo that the entire Pacific area had turned against it simply because of its efforts to rescue China from Western influence. The Australians and New Zealanders cordially hated the Japanese; so did the citizens of California, Oregon, and Washington. Japanese designs on Manchuria, China, and Siberia had created grave frictions with London and Paris. The peoples of Asia—Chinese, Malays, Filipinos—looked with apprehension on a nation that had arrogated to itself the destiny of the region. If Japan lost the British alliance, it would be truly isolated; worse, it would suffer, in the striking phrase of Stephen Howarth, "a kind of humiliating demotion," one that would seemingly prove that the Japanese "could not hold their own in the world."[40] For the eighty million Japanese who fervently believed that their nation had the moral imperative to uplift the international community to their level of sophistication—by force if necessary—such a humiliation could not be endured.

As time came to renew the alliance, powerful interests worked to destroy it. American sailors thought the Tokyo-London accord "sinister," for it encouraged both Japan and Britain to expand their Asian interests at China's expense. From Shanghai, Admiral Gleaves cabled that the British and Japanese contemplated nothing less than the total dismemberment of China between them. London was aware of American displeasure and was by this time desperately eager not to further antagonize its battleship-happy cousins. The tireless American naval attaché in London reported that only a few politicians there favored renewal of the ties with Japan as a means of protecting India. Most Britons believed the liabilities of the alliance far outweighed its advantages. In fact, the Admiralty and Foreign Office were unhappily aware of Japan's disaffection during the darkest months of the war. They were also suspicious that Japan might well use British preoccupation with a future European war to fall on Australia and New Zealand. Whatever else British diplomacy might accomplish, it had to achieve some sort of arrangement, agreement, or understanding with the United States if the postwar world was to be stabilized and the integrity of the empire east of Suez guaranteed. London hoped to replace the Anglo-Japanese alliance with a tripartite accord including both Washington and Tokyo that would stabilize not only naval rivalries but also the political situation in Asia and throughout Oceania. Even if such a tripartite agreement should be achieved, Britons believed they had to stiffen the defense of their own substantial imperial interests in the East, and this meant building up Singapore as a great naval, military, and air base.[41]

In 1919 Admiral of the Fleet Sir John Jellicoe of Jutland fame was dispatched on a tour of the eastern empire to consult with dominion authorities and plan for imperial defense. Upon his return he formally recommended stationing a large fleet of capital ships and support craft in eastern waters. Captain Stephen Roskill has argued that Jellicoe specifically sought "to combat Japanese plans"; Russell Grenfell, another solid historian of the period, insists that Jellicoe actually wanted the ships based in Sydney in eastern Australia, which would be somewhat close to the Japanese mandates in the Marshalls and Carolines, but far enough from strategic Japanese interests in East Asia and the adjacent seas so as not to antagonize Tokyo. In fact, Roskill was correct. The Admiralty did not wish to antagonize Australian opinion and so downplayed Jellicoe's conviction that Singapore, not Sydney, was "undoubtedly the naval key to the Far East."[42]

Some accounts have stated that Jellicoe specifically asked for eight battleships and eight battle cruisers in the Far East, a perfect match of the proposed Japanese building program. Others have asserted only that he asked that thirteen capital ships be sent east, with Australia and New Zealand each supplying one battleship of its own.[43] Certainly, an eight-eight formula could not have escaped Tokyo's notice. Nor could the Japanese look with equanimity on Britain's intention to shift a major portion of its battle fleet to eastern waters just as the United States was dramatically shifting its fleet westward through the Panama Canal.

Equally disconcerting to Tokyo was the Admiralty's decision in 1921, reached only after much argument and the greatest reluctance, to follow Jellicoe's advice and construct the main eastern fleet base at Singapore, not Sydney. The decision was almost immediately ratified by the British Imperial Conference. Such a bastion at the tip of the Malay Peninsula would command one of the crucial choke points on the world ocean (the straits of Molucca) and dominate the sea approaches to the mineral-rich East Indies and their great oil fields. True, Jellicoe's proposal to station a permanent battle fleet in the East had fallen "on stony ground" at the Admiralty and the Foreign Office, both of which had already gloomily concluded by this time that Britain could no longer retain its "two power standard" (the Royal Navy remaining larger than the two closest fleets combined) but would have to accept either the United States or Japan as coequal. That decision was also ratified by the 1921 Imperial Conference. Nonetheless, Singapore like Pearl Harbor would presumably be ready soon to receive and support a major fleet against Japan if Tokyo's policies and aspirations continued to antagonize the Western powers.[44]

As Japanese military and naval authorities looked out on the world in the early twenties, therefore, they could be pardoned for thinking that the military, political, and even economic tides seemed to be running against them everywhere except on the adjacent continent of Asia. For four years, as warfare had raged all across Europe, Japanese warships had patrolled hundreds of thousands of square miles of the Pacific and Indian Oceans without let or hindrance. Japan had cooperated with Britain in successfully besieging the German bastion at Tsingtao, and at the behest of Whitehall the Imperial Japanese Navy had steamed out into the Pacific to help in the search for Maximilian Graf von Spee's squadron, using the cruise as a pretext to seize German-held islands in

Oceania. In a third "unheralded" campaign, a division of Japanese destroyers entered the eastern Mediterranean in the spring of 1917 to help hard-pressed British antisubmarine forces battle the German U-boats. None had gone to the bottom under Japanese depth charges, but Tokyo had proved to be a loyal partner in the Anglo-Japanese alliance.[45] Now Japan was once again to be compressed by the great powers into a very narrow sphere of operations and influence. It was Asia's great indigenous power, but the rest of the world seemed determined to rob it of its rightful destiny.

These disheartening developments fractured the Imperial Japanese Navy into what would become "Fleet" and "Treaty" factions. The former, led by senior Admiral Katō Kanji and including "Japan's Mahan," Satō Tetsutarō, insisted the nation must push ahead vigorously with its massive eight-eight construction program. Others argued for a more cautious and fiscally realistic course. Should the Americans and British continue to outbuild the Japanese fleet in terms of sheer numbers, Japan must respond with fewer but finer and more powerful capital ships. Initially, four fast battle cruisers of 41,400 tons mounting 16-inch guns would be laid down together with four 47,500-ton monster battleships carrying ten 18-inch guns apiece. After rejecting an eight-eight bill, a reluctant parliament (the Diet) approved the four-four plan. There were several good reasons to do so. Tokyo was well aware of postwar Anglo-American tensions over the Middle East; surely, the rivalry would resume in China as well once peace came again. One scholar of the period has concluded that "caution and perhaps confidence born of successful maneuvering in domestic politics" inclined Japanese political leaders to the belief that in East Asian affairs, at least, Tokyo might become an honest broker and arbiter between Washington and London.[46] The Fleet faction, however, clung steadfastly to its eight-eight vision as a solution to all Japan's problems. "Big guns" and "big ships" guarding the approaches to the Home Islands were the keys to national survival. Satō Tetsutarō and his colleagues at the Naval Staff College had long since concluded that sixteen mighty capital ships would ensure Japan of a 70 percent parity with any attacking fleet, which would provide the margin of victory. The 70 percent ideal was itself expressed in a variety of ways. Before the opening of the Panama Canal 70 percent meant that either the United States or Germany could afford to station only half their fleets in the Pacific because of persistent tensions in Atlantic waters. Thus, 70 percent would in fact become a seven-to-five ratio in Japan's favor. With the end of the Great War, the opening of the Panama Canal, and the advent of the submarine, Japanese planners estimated that although an enemy (that is, the

United States) could dispatch its entire navy toward Japan, determined submarine attacks would so whittle down the advancing fleet that by the time the climactic battle was fought, the ratio would be no worse than seven to seven.[47] Anything less than 70 percent parity with the Western navies, however, was unacceptable. In July 1920, after nearly a decade of unstinting lobbying, the Fleet faction finally won out when the Diet reversed the earlier four-four legislation and passed an eight-eight bill.

But even with sixteen capital ships on hand, the great American naval buildup threatened after 1916 would overwhelm Japan's ability to maintain 70 percent parity, particularly if there arose a combination of sea powers against Nippon. Here was where the prospect of losing the British alliance became so fearsome and the need to build capital ships of superior size and capability so critical. Moreover, Japanese strategy by this time was utterly divided. The 1907 Imperial National Defense Policy, which was never significantly altered, formally designated Russia as Japan's prime hypothetical enemy, "and the Army's forward position on the Asian mainland was made Japan's basic strategy." The army would almost certainly require some naval assistance to fulfill its mission whether against Russia or China. At the same time the navy was allowed to identify the United States as its chief opponent and successfully resisted efforts to create a single national command structure under army control. Japan thus might well find itself fighting a two-front war with wholly inadequate resources and a chaotic command structure.[48]

Short of a suicidal conflict, however, there was little that Japan could do to arrest events. If the Fleet faction did not understand this, navy minister Katō Tomosaburō did. Katō, in office from August 1915 to May 1923 and "one of the strongest leaders in the history of the Imperial Japanese Navy," soon became identified by friend and increasingly bitter foe alike as head of the Treaty faction within the service, allied with the diplomatic corps in pursuing a policy of restraint and international accommodation as the only rational course for Japanese development and national security. Early in January 1921, Katō's vice minister, Ide Kenji, told a New York newspaperman that if the other powers reduced their naval armaments, "Japan would not necessarily" insist on pursuing its eight-eight construction program "to the bitter end." Two months later, Katō himself made a similar commitment, stating to an Associated Press reporter that Japan would not insist on completing its eight-eight building program if a "dependable" agreement to limit international naval power could be found. Katō Kanji and his Fleet-faction allies were enraged. From the outset of

Katō Tomosaburō's ministry, the younger Katō Kanji "was extremely upset by" the older man's "despotic" manner, resolving critical issues "without adequate consultation with his subordinates."[49]

In fact, the Japanese were already cheating with regard to their own naval building program. The battleships *Nagato* and *Mutsu,* completed in 1920 and 1921 as the first elements of the eight-eight program, were supposed to be 32,600-ton vessels with eight 16-inch guns and only 23 knots' speed. The truth was that they were 35,000-ton ships with a maximum speed of 27 knots, a full 5 knots faster than the most recently commissioned U.S. battlewagon, *Maryland,* which also carried eight 16-inch guns. "Nor was the world told about the 1,345-ton *Shimikaze,* the new wonder destroyer. She was armed to the teeth with four 4.6-inch guns and six torpedo tubes, and could speed at 40 knots." Meanwhile, the Japanese yearly sent two decrepit old cruisers from the Sino-Soviet war a quarter century before crawling unpretentiously around American and European shores on goodwill cruises, impressing the foreigners with Japan's outmoded technologies and limited naval capabilities.[50]

Unfortunately for the Japanese, the world began catching on to their schemes soon after the end of World War I. In 1919 Oscar Parkes and Maurice Prendergrast, coeditors of the authoritative *Jane's Fighting Ships,* congratulated the Japanese Navy Department for "once again verif[ying] all the technical details of this [Japanese] section." As a result, the editors reported deadpan, "a considerable number of Japanese Minelayers and Fleet Auxiliaries, hitherto unheard of, have been added."[51] Since cruisers and destroyers continued to be identified as "fleet auxiliaries," it was clear that the Japanese had previously concealed from the world much of their naval strength.

Not only were the sizes and capabilities of warships steadily escalating in the early postwar years, but so were the sizes and power of guns. During the first two years of the peace the Americans successfully tested a 16-inch 50-caliber gun, which they soon placed on their three new *Maryland*-class battleships; ordnance men were also working on an 18-inch rifle. The French started work on a 17.7-inch gun and the Japanese on two monster 19-inch cannons (one of which burst during trials).[52]

By the summer of 1921 it was clear that international naval developments were spinning out of control. London had reinstituted a modest rebuilding program centering about two 16-inch-gun battleships that would eventually materialize as *Nelson* and *Rodney.* The French and Italians had thirty-three and twenty-four vessels, respectively, under construction, and although none were capital ships, "there could be little doubt that a new generation of battleships was in the offing" throughout the world from Britain to Japan, "displacing around 50,000 tons and armed with 18-inch guns."[53]

But naval rivalries had far outdistanced public opinion. To a stunned world still gasping from the terrible exertions of 1914–1918 and contemplating the beginnings of a postwar economic slump, another arms race seemed nothing less than criminal. With capital ships costing about thirty-two million dollars apiece, Britain, Japan, and the United States had by 1921 committed themselves to battleship and battle-cruiser construction programs that alone would have cost well over one billion dollars—a prodigious sum for the time.[54] Yet who would step forth to declare a halt? Certainly not the French, who remained obsessed with a German revival. Italy, now uncertain where it stood in the European security and political system after an unhappy experience at Paris, wished to expand its navy because its chief Mediterranean rival, France, was doing so. But Britain, Japan, and the United States all had good reasons to bridle their navies if their individual agendas could be met. Indeed, the British Imperial Conference early in 1921 formally accepted "the principle of the equality of navies," which formally translated into a "one power standard" in which the Royal Navy would allow a single competitor (well known to be the United States) to match it in size and power.[55] William E. Borah of Idaho had already introduced a resolution in the U.S. Senate calling for naval arms reduction, and it was clear that the American public was solidly behind the idea. So, of course, were Katō Tomosaburō and the Treaty faction within the Imperial Japanese Navy. Unbeknownst to all the foreign powers, however, was a top-secret American intelligence capability that began paying huge dividends just as Secretary of State Charles Evans Hughes issued his call for an international disarmament conference in Washington, D.C.

Deep within the U.S. Army Signal Corps resided a small "Black Chamber" of cryptanalysts led by Herbert O. Yardley. By early 1921 the chamber had broken the chief Japanese diplomatic code and begun "reading" Japanese embassy cables from around the world. The Americans soon learned that London and Tokyo—both deeply concerned by the American naval building program and unresolved questions regarding the fortification of various Pacific islands— were in agreement that a "Pacific Conference" between the great powers should be convened. Not wishing to lose either the naval or the diplomatic initiative, Hughes promptly issued his invitations. Because of the Black Chamber the Americans could not lose by calling and participating in such a conference. As

Yardley recalled a decade later (after being dismissed because his work disturbed Secretary of State Henry Stimson): "The Black Chamber sent to Washington . . . some five thousand deciphered Japanese messages which contained the secret instructions of the Japanese Delegates."[56] If the Americans indeed read five thousand messages, they learned far more than just Tokyo's instructions to its delegation. They must have also learned of the Japanese reaction to the proposals of the other delegates from Britain, the United States, France, Italy, and several lesser powers. And they undoubtedly learned everything about Japanese participation in those invariable and informal "corridor conversations" that often constitute the most important part of an international gathering.

The Washington Conference (November 11, 1921–February 6, 1922) thus constituted a stacked deck against every naval power in the world except the United States, which already held the best cards. When the delegates at last convened it remained only to determine specifically how the Americans could or would translate their secret advantage into a set of naval agreements suitable to their national interests.[57]

As naval statesmen and experts looked back on the Great War, many concluded that capital ships had proved to be expensive failures. Fletcher Pratt, a long-serving U.S. naval officer and authoritative commentator on naval matters, vividly summarized their opinion: "Some 121 first class vessels of the battle line, costing from ten million to forty million dollars apiece, had been under the flags of the fighting nations during the war. In four years they had appeared in actual combat only during about four hours of the misty afternoon of May 31, 1916, and then for an exchange of pawns which decided nothing but that battleships were too valuable to be risked in any more such experiments."[58]

Battleships had proved "brittle," and "a huge investment in minor craft was consumed in protecting the blubbering giants from such enemies as submarine and torpedo boat." Ironically, Britain had almost lost the war because of these crude leviathans; they required so many escorts to protect them that it proved impossible for the Admiralty to supply sufficient destroyers to convoy merchant shipping. Advancing technology was also the enemy of the battleship. *Dreadnought* had rendered scores of pre-dreadnoughts obsolete at a stroke, yet these vessels could not just be scrapped. They were employed on a variety of duties during the war and when hit invariably proved to be "useless death traps," capable of being sunk by "cheap, diminutive craft they never saw." Each of these fragile victims took to the bottom nearly a thousand men.

Not only was the battleship vulnerable to the torpedo and the mine, but many authorities maintained that it could also be easily bombed to death from the air. In the summer of 1921, as Yardley's Black Chamber produced the first results of its code-breaking efforts and Hughes sent out his invitations, a number of crude first-generation bomber aircraft under the command of General Billy Mitchell of the U.S. Army Air Service sensationally destroyed the 22,800-ton battleship *Ostfriesland,* anchored off the Virginia Capes. Mitchell's "demonstration" seemed to confirm prejudices that were as strong within as well as beyond international naval circles.

Experts then and now realized that the feat was far from professional. One authority has called it a "farce." Mitchell's pilots had to borrow radios, compasses, and bombsights from their naval colleagues just to accomplish their mission, which was to assist U.S. Navy and Marine Corps pilots in assessing the impact of aerial bombing on dreadnought battleships. Mitchell's men broke the rules in subjecting *Ostfriesland* to a sudden massive raid from low altitude with eleven hundred–pound bombs that damaged the vessel so badly that only a boarding party could keep it afloat. A similar attack by Mitchell's men the following day with eighteen hundred–pound bombs sank the vessel almost immediately, before naval explosives experts could inspect the damage pattern. Several smaller vessels, only one of which appears to have been in decent condition, were bombed from the air by U.S. Navy and Marine Corps pilots as well as Mitchell's men and eventually went down. Each survived single or multiple hits by small bombs, but succumbed to those of three or six hundred pounds. Every ship, including *Ostfriesland,* required many hits to sink. Each was stationary and unmanned, thereby offering no resistance in terms of antiaircraft fire, speed and maneuverability, or damage control. Responsible naval authorities also emphasized one final point: the most modern of the sunken vessels, *Ostfriesland,* although a veteran of Jutland and a first-class battleship by Great War standards, was in fact in horrendous material condition at the time Mitchell's fliers hit and sank it. The High Seas Fleet had, of course, declined precipitately in terms of upkeep after Jutland. Months of internment at Scapa Flow (*Ostfriesland* was one of the few ships captured by British Tars before it could be scuttled) accelerated material deterioration. Yet it required a multitude of eleven hundred– and eventually eighteen hundred–pound bombs before the vessel finally gave up the ghost and slipped beneath the waves.[59] But to aviation enthusiasts and budget cutters in Washington—and London—Mitchell's controversial "tests" provided all the ammunition they needed. "The experience of the war appeared to indicate that the battleship had reproduced the history of the dinosaur to the point where a law of diminishing return began to operate against size," Pratt wrote some years later. "The brute was already having difficulty doing enough useful work to keep itself alive, yet unit sizes continued to increase and no one dared build small battleships while there were larger ones afloat."[60]

Critics of the battleship were not confined to the fledgling aviation community. Proponents of surface and subsurface warfare were also asking what kind of naval conflict World War I had truly been. With the exception of the useless standoffs at Dogger Bank and Jutland, had it not been essentially a commerce war, a throwback to the old *guerres de course* of the eighteenth century? And what vessels were best equipped to fight such wars? Certainly not expensive, lumbering battleships but instead swift cruisers, darting destroyers, and especially stealthy submarines. The Great War just past had provided many an example. At the Battle of the Falkland Islands the ancient British cruiser *Kent,* escorting two British battle cruisers, made more speed than on its trials, sinking a fast and rather new German commerce destroyer in the process. The German cruiser *Emden* was "hopelessly obsolete" when it began its short raiding career in 1914, yet "accomplished more than any other ship of the Kaiser's navy." During the attempt to force the Gulf of Riga in 1917, "other old German cruisers were the mainstay of the attack," supporting the German army's thrust eastward that helped knock out czarist Russia and create the Soviet Union. "An old submarine" sank the three British cruisers in 1914, and "a division of American destroyers dating from the Spanish War voyaged half round the earth from the Philippines and did yeoman service in the Mediterranean."[61] Could not the world's navies divest themselves of most of their obsolete mastodons for the sake of international disarmament? Could not Britain accept parity with the U.S. Navy in battleships alone without compromising the safety and security of either realm or empire? Could not Japan accept a 60 percent ratio in capital ship strength vis-à-vis the two greatest powers without compromising either its honor or its safety? Mutual destruction of battleships and a general appreciation that naval warfare had changed and would continue to change proved the key to achieving general, if sharply limited, naval reductions. The territorial settlements that accompanied the naval agreement conformed to the vision of a new day in international affairs.

To be sure, no one at Washington was prepared to sink *all* the world's battleships. Old ideas die hard, and old loves die hardest. The world's three great navies would retain at least ten modern capital ships apiece, enough to form an impressive battle line or naval review. As late as 1939 Pratt emphasized that a future war at sea between two or more of the great powers would climax in another Jutland-like duel—a "battle of desperation"—between lines of battleships. "But in any case, only one such battle. One will be enough." But a climactic conflict between capital ships would be prefaced and surrounded by months, perhaps years, of mutual hit-and-run commerce raiding by squadrons of Japanese, Italian, British, French, and U.S. cruisers and submarines in such vital areas of the world ocean as the North Pacific, the Mediterranean, the Malay straits, and even the North Sea.[62] The age of the ironclads was over; indeed, it had never truly materialized. A war of the "tin clads"—fast, heavily armed, but weakly protected cruisers—was anticipated.

And so, after weeks of hard bargaining, the diplomats and sailors at Washington came to a rough agreement that whittled down the enormous battleship fleets of the prewar and war years to manageable proportions and encouraged navies to pursue the new technologies that the conflict had brought to fruition above and below the seas. There would be a widely hailed ten-year "holiday" on the building of battleships and battle cruisers, which could mount at most 16-inch guns on a 35,000-ton hull. Of course, having achieved this remarkable reduction in global arms, the delegates immediately rushed to make the inevitable exceptions and reservations. All five powers—Britain, the United States, Japan, France, and Italy—could upgrade their existing capital ships. Moreover, Japan could complete *Mutsu*, the United States the three ships of the *Maryland* class armed with 16-inch guns; Britain could keep the new 42,100-ton battle cruiser *Hood* (which mounted only eight 15-inch guns) and finish building the 35,000-ton *Rodney* and *Nelson* (nine 16-inch guns, 23 knots) to replace four older dreadnoughts. Deference was also paid to the recent Italian and French sacrifices on behalf of the Allied cause, which had prevented the two nations from completing their prewar dreadnought fleets. France could lay down two new battleships or battle cruisers during the ostensible ten-year moratorium to ensure that its naval power continually matched that of Italy, which was allowed 70,000 tons of new capital-ship construction. This latter provision would prove to be the fatally weak joint in the international naval edifice, though no one suspected it at the time.

Overall, Britain would agree to share a "10–10" power parity with the United States in capital ships, Japan would surrender its cherished 7 ratio and settle for 6, and France and Italy would each have a 3.67 parity. These percentages translated into fifteen operational battleships for the United States and Britain, nine for Japan, and five each for Italy and France. In practice the exceptions and reservations agreed to at Washington meant that between 1921 and 1939 the Royal Navy would operate seventeen to twenty-two battleships and battle cruisers, the United States fifteen to eighteen, Japan ten, France ten, and Italy seven. But three of the American battlewagons (*Florida*, *Utah*, and *Wyoming*)

were so obsolete that by the end of the decade they had become auxiliary ships or
target vessels. Of the French and Italian big ships of 1921, only two (the Italian
Conte di Cavour and *Giulio Cesare*), when rearmed and repowered, really measured up to their Japanese, U.S., and British counterparts. All the Italian vessels
were lightly armed and all the French dreadnoughts poorly armored. Moreover,
throughout the twenties neither Rome nor Paris exploited the opportunity provided by the Washington agreements to lay down one or two modern vessels.
Thus, none of the "big three" naval powers felt threatened in allowing their
Italian and French junior partners to operate a larger number of weak, obsolete
ships than the Washington agreement provided.[63]

But if a future naval war would in fact center around commerce raiding and
destruction by cruisers and submarines, then the Washington Conference
achieved no disarmament whatsoever, for the delegates quickly agreed that
there were to be no restrictions on the construction of what had traditionally
been considered fleet "auxiliary" vessels. Britain, Japan, the United States, France,
and Italy were free to build as many ships carrying 8-inch guns and below as
they liked, so long as a 10-10-7-3.67-3.67 parity was maintained among the
five signatories in the 6-inch-gun "light" cruiser category and a 10-10-6-3.67-
3.67 parity in "heavy" 8-inch-gun cruisers. Perhaps Washington was not, as
Pratt later contended, "a swindle on the people of the world," a "wrapper in
spectacular colors placed around a present [restrictions on capital ships alone]
which the admiralties would in any case have been forced to lay before their
taxpayers." He was probably closer to the truth in observing that "the delegates
simply found themselves beyond a meeting of the minds on so many points
that they discovered with delight a point on which all could agree—namely,
that the battleship had not paid for its keep in the past, and that its future was
doubtful."[64] Whether hypocrisy was a conscious element in the deliberations
and decisions, no one can say. But the result was not naval disarmament per se
so much as a nudging of sea power into new, less expensive, and possibly less
intimidating channels.

Having diminished the power of the big gun at sea, the conferees turned to
the disposal of the new weapon systems. The British, for obvious reasons, had
tried to introduce resolutions outlawing the submarine, but no one else was
interested. The Japanese, for equally obvious reasons, wanted to station a substantial submarine force in the Pacific. The French appreciated the submarine's
capability as a commerce destroyer in any future Mediterranean war. The Americans, with their priceless ability to read the internal deliberations of at least one
foreign delegation, fashioned a compromise that simply reaffirmed international

law regarding the drastically limited role of the submarine in commerce warfare, that is, it must surface and give fair warning before it sinks an enemy merchant ship. But after the experience of 1915–1918 no one truly thought that submarines would be bridled in a future conflict.[65]

The aircraft carrier presented problems of its own. It could not be ignored, but unlike the submarine it had been almost completely untried in combat. Moreover, confusion remained over definition. There were a handful of true floating airfields and a half-dozen seaplane tenders in commission by 1921–1922, but the only floating airfield of any great size was Britain's hybrid monstrosity *Furious*, a converted light battle cruiser with a "fly off" deck forward and a landing deck aft separated by a superstructure. *Argus*, a converted passenger liner with an unobstructed flight deck 565 feet long and 68 feet wide, had been with the fleet since 1918; the almost equally small and unsatisfactory *Hermes* and *Eagle* were in the final stages of construction. Japan had the new small ten-plane carrier *Hosho*, which it had developed in conjunction with the recent British Sempill aviation mission, and the Americans possessed the equally small and new carrier named *Langley*.[66] But with many nearly completed battleship and battle-cruiser hulls on the stocks in shipyards from Yokosuka to New York to Glasgow, the temptation soon became overwhelming to siphon off the admirals' wrath at losing their big guns by giving them airplanes. Each of the three great navies would be permitted to convert a handful of almost finished battleships to large floating airfields.

The United States and Britain were allocated 135,000 total tons of conversion and new construction, Japan 81,000 tons, and France and Italy 60,000 tons. Nations could convert or build such ships over the next decade up to each country's agreed tonnage quota. Carriers would be limited to 27,000 tons' maximum displacement and could carry a maximum battery of 8-inch guns. No limits were placed on the number of aircraft any ship could carry. But the large U.S. battle-cruiser hulls on the stocks exceeded the displacement limit by several thousand tons, and similar Japanese vessels were nearly as large. In deference to the sacrifices the two nations were prepared to make in battleship tonnage, the Americans were allowed to convert two battle-cruiser hulls to the 33,000-ton carriers *Lexington* and *Saratoga*, and the Japanese two hulls of almost similar size that became *Akagi* and *Kaga*. The British lacked such potential monsters but did have two half-sisters of the *Furious* (soon to be converted to a clear deck carrier) on the way, and by 1930 they had been completed to the full-fledged carriers *Glorious* and *Courageous*. None of the three, however, came close to matching the two huge American and two big Japanese flattops, each of which normally carried seventy-two planes (the Americans could actually deploy more than a hundred if they chose). The three smaller British flattops were capable of handling only forty-two aircraft.[67]

So large were the Japanese and especially American ships in relation to the size of their embarked aircraft that they became invaluable test beds for the growth of naval aviation. For many years their spacious decks provided more than ample room for a steady stream of ever newer, larger, and better aircraft that emerged from the factories on both sides of the Pacific.

As in so many other areas of Japanese naval technology, the rise of aviation closely followed developments in the West. Naval aviation had come of age during the Great War, as seaplanes were employed in tactical bombing raids against enemy zeppelin sheds, and aircraft of all sorts were employed aggressively on antisubmarine patrols. Soon the requisite visionary appeared in Japan as well in the person of Lieutenant Commander Yamamoto Eisuke of the navy's General Staff—who as early as 1909 began touting the limitless possibilities of aviation. The inevitable missions to the West followed, and just before war in 1914 the first flimsy naval aircraft appeared over Japan. Thereafter came the equally inevitable debates and discussions as to whether seaplanes or wheeled aircraft embarked aboard dedicated "aircraft carriers" were the most efficient weapon systems. When war broke out and the fleet moved to bounce the Germans out of their enclave at Tsingtao, the Navy Ministry hastily arranged to have a merchant vessel converted to a seaplane tender, and the handful of imported aircraft that operated from *Wakamiya* proved the inestimable value of aircraft reconnaissance to fleet units. Strenuous efforts to employ the planes as bombers, however, proved futile. As war intensified to horrific proportions on the other side of the Eurasian landmass, remote Japan slipped into relative somnolence, though a handful of aviation theorists—"extremists" in the opinion of historian Mark Peattie—continued to press the notion that those nations that could control the airspaces of the earth would dominate the seas and continents as well. Moreover, the imperial government made sure that observers with the British fleet spent some time on its new carriers, especially *Furious,* while back home daring pioneers pushed the few aircraft they did have—mostly Farnum seaplanes—to new speeds and heights. By 1919 aircraft from *Wakamiya* were included in the annual fleet exercises, and one of them from the Blue Fleet found the main body of the enemy Red Fleet far over the horizon and flew back to drop a reporting marker on the deck of the Blue Fleet flagship. This achievement was understandably considered a major advance in sea warfare, but naval authorities realized that the four years of combat on the western front had taught the victorious Allies, as well as the defeated Germans, invaluable lessons that Japan simply had to absorb.[68]

The Royal Navy still considered itself a mentor to the Japanese fleet, and when Tokyo requested a British mission to improve the proficiency of the Japanese naval air arm London responded quickly. In little more than a year's time, Baron Sempill and his handful of fellow aviators imparted a "quantum jump" in training and technology to Japan's aspiring naval aviators. Initially, mission staff concentrated on flight instruction, providing its eager pupils with more than five thousand hours of rigorous training. Then the Western tutors expanded instruction to include aerial combat—dogfighting, high-level bombing, and torpedo attacks—together with aerial reconnaissance and photography, plus the handling and maintenance of various types of aircraft. Critical as was the training, it composed only half of a comprehensive package, for the British brought with them not only the most advanced guns, bombs, torpedoes, cameras, and other aviation technology but also more than a hundred aircraft, "comprising twenty different models, five of which were then in use" in the Royal Navy's soon-to-be virtually disbanded Fleet Air Arm. Not surprisingly, the Japanese soon felt comfortable enough with their emerging pilot-training program and the aeronautical engineering learned from the British mission to begin construction of their own aircraft. The government ordered Mitsubishi to design and build both fighter and torpedo planes for the Imperial Japanese Navy; the company prudently turned to British technicians and pilots for aid and assistance. By the end of 1921 the first fighter was completed, and two years later a full-fledged, modern technical research laboratory had been established near Yokosuka for the development of both land-plane and seaplane technology. Nakajima and Kawanishi joined Mitsubishi in designing and building aircraft for the fleet, and in 1927, acknowledging aviation's growing value, the Navy Ministry gave the flyers their own separate bureau.[69]

Across the Pacific, Congress in 1926 approved a five-year program to build one thousand planes of specialized rather than multipurpose type for the U.S. Navy. These scout, patrol, bombing, torpedo, and fighter aircraft would not only be placed on carriers, battleships, and cruisers at sea but operate from land bases as well. Japan struggled to build half the number of similar-type aircraft, which was still far more than the aircraft complement of the Fleet Air Arm of the Royal Air Force (RAF). The Americans even found an inadvertent bonus in their carriers. Because *Lexington* and *Saratoga* were built on slim battle-cruiser hulls, they were narrower than desired, and consequently their hangar decks were much too small. At least two-thirds of the air group thus had to be stowed on the flight deck. "The situation unintentionally led to the deckload strikes and quick turnaround cyclic operations that proved so effective in World War II, Korea, Vietnam, and the Gulf War."[70]

Once again the international naval and diplomatic communities tacitly accepted certain evasions in order to retain American goodwill. As completed, *Lexington* and *Saratoga* were 888 feet long and 3,000 tons beyond the 33,000-ton displacement that the conference allowed as an exception. The Americans blithely announced that the additional tonnage was defensive in character, and the rest of the world accepted the explanation with varying degrees of humor and disbelief.[71]

Finally, the conferees turned to the problem of political stabilization in Asia and the Pacific. Everyone agreed to preserve the territorial integrity of China; few took the commitment seriously. Fortification of the Pacific islands was another matter. Japan agreed to a six-ten capital-ship ratio with the United States in exchange for an American pledge to suspend further fortification of the Philippines and not to fortify Guam. Washington expected a corresponding concession from Japan: nonfortification of the island screen stretching southward from the Home Islands through the Ryukyus and Bonins to Taiwan. The militarization of these islands would give the Imperial Japanese Navy "an even tighter grip on the sea communications of the far western Pacific. It would move the strategic frontier of Japan several hundred miles nearer to the Philippines," rendering that archipelago still more vulnerable to attack, especially from the air.[72] Once again Tokyo was forced into concessions it did not wish to make. Reading the Japanese cables and knowing chief delegate Katō Tomosaburō's bargaining position as soon as Katō did, the Americans, with their unwitting British allies, placed brutal pressure on their Asian colleagues. Katō, committed to international cooperation, was consistently conciliatory. His genuine desire that Japan not be isolated not only made him a man of stature in the conference but also played right into Anglo-American hands, even as it infuriated the growing Fleet faction in the Imperial Navy as well as important elements within Japan's diplomatic and military circles. Katō Kanji, who was also on the Japanese delegation and already head of the emerging Fleet faction dedicated to carrying through the eight-eight construction plan, interpreted the American proposals as a brazen effort "to deprive the Imperial Navy of its supremacy in

the Far East" and impose Yankee "hegemony" over the entire world ocean. Perhaps he was not far wrong. In the wake of the Great War, America's admirals had
become arrogant and overbearing. Katō Kanji was particularly—and understandably—incensed by the comments of Atlantic Fleet commander Hilary P.
Jones that "the United States absolutely requires keeping Japanese naval forces
below a 60 per cent strength to be able to bring Japan to her knees over the
China question."[73]

With Tokyo's grudging approval, Katō Tomosaburō conceded to British insistence that Singapore in fact lay in the Indian rather than the Pacific Ocean
and that its fortification should not be considered with respect to Asian-Pacific
affairs. Pearl Harbor and the airfields on Hawaii were also not to be an issue.
Beyond that, Britain, Japan, and the United States should agree on a strict status
quo with regard to the fortification of their Pacific possessions. Katō Tomosaburō
and his superiors accepted all these provisions, but did stand firm on one point:
if Japan was not to develop the Kuriles north of the Home Islands, then the
United States should agree not to build up the Aleutians, which aimed at the
Home Islands like a dagger from the northeast. The U.S. Army and Navy had
hopes of establishing a great fleet and air base at Dutch Harbor on the eastern
end of the island chain but backed down.

The international diplomatic corps left Washington reasonably satisfied, but
few sailors were. The diplomats envisaged the Washington agreements as the
foundation of a system of gradualism in which the world's great powers, linked
by their adherence to the gold standard, would undertake an evolutionary stabilization of both Far Eastern and European affairs beyond the limits and structure of the League of Nations. American rejection of the League had rendered
necessary this rather awkward arrangement, but the agreement at Washington
to maintain the political and territorial integrity of China, followed by Locarno
and the 1928 Pact of Paris (the so-called Kellogg-Briand Pact) outlawing war as
an instrument of national policy, suggested that a new era of general international
peace and progress was at hand.[74]

Admirals and captains were unconvinced. American naval men remained as
morbidly suspicious of the Japanese as they were determined to ride roughshod
over their British colleagues with regard to fleet parity. Few in the Navy Department or the fleet believed that the Japanese would actually forbear from
fortifying all of the islands in their possession from the Marshalls to the
Ryukyus. If Tokyo armed its Pacific possessions, the ability of a U.S. fleet to
fight its way westward to either liberate or lift a siege of the Philippines would

be extremely risky. American naval circles viewed the decision to drastically reduce their own as well as foreign battleship strength as nothing short of idiotic:
the United States had practically forfeited its ability to win a Pacific war.[75]

To Britons, the loss of superior status at sea after several centuries of undisputed rule was a wound in the heart that has never completely healed. Andrew
Cunningham, the destroyer captain and future first sea lord, remembered "a
good deal of uncertainty and discouragement" in the Royal Navy after the
Washington Conference. "We were no longer the first Naval Power." In fact,
the Admiralty had acknowledged that fact to the dominions before the conference opened. But a further "drastic pruning" of the officer corps that promptly
took place under the "axe" wielded by First Lord of the Admiralty Eric Geddes
caused widespread gloom together with "numerous cases of extreme penury
and hardship." Professional naval people were already dismayed by the government's 1919 decision that in view of the recent victory over Germany and an
impending League of Nations to keep the peace, no major war need be expected for ten years. This ten-year rule was reconfirmed every year throughout
the twenties, leaving the Royal Navy "beginning to suffer from senile decay."[76]

Beyond the fleet, opinion was mixed. The Washington Conference had certainly curtailed naval armament in a dramatic fashion, and anyone who favored
peace had to applaud the achievement. Many did. Initially at least, the accords
"provided a badly needed triumph for Britain's faltering coalition government,"
which was urgently seeking postwar international economic recovery and political cooperation.[77] But outstanding opinion makers like Archibald Hurd, now
coeditor of the influential *Brassey's Naval and Shipping Annual,* and former first
sea lord Sir Rosslyn Wester-Wemyss could never forgive Whitehall for dipping
the White Ensign in acknowledgment of American co-supremacy on the world
ocean. At Washington, British diplomacy had been guilty of "humiliating acquiescence in the arms proposals of the United States." Moreover, Wester-Wemyss
warned prophetically that the "check" to Japan's rising naval power might bear
bitter fruit. "If events should prove that [Japan's] limited navy is insufficient for
the purpose for which it was created, there will arise in Japan a spirit of bitterness which may prove a serious peril to the future of the Four Power Pact" regarding China.[78]

The Washington accords split Japanese naval opinion bitterly. British historian H. P. Willmott has fairly appraised the conference as "a package deal that
left the Japanese bruised and resentful." The conflict between the Treaty and
Fleet factions that had been smoldering for months over the issue of fulfilling
the eight-eight dream now burst into flame. Katō Tomosaburō returned to

Tokyo convinced that his intransigent subordinate, Katō Kanji, outraged at abandonment of the sacred ten-seven power ratio, had tried to sabotage the work of the conference. Certainly, the conference had been no fun for the navy minister himself. Described by one American delegate as a self-styled "samurai gentleman whose eyes lit up as he spoke of the samurai traditions and songs," Katō Tomosaburō hinted at several points during the long, detailed, tedious discussions that if he could not return home with a guaranteed 70 percent ratio in capital ships, he would have to commit suicide, and a Japanese historian states that rumors flooded Tokyo as Katō was on his way home that he had in fact done just that in Washington. Indeed, as the conference progressed, the two Katōs clashed bitterly. In late-evening discussions, the unrelenting Kanji stood up to Tomosaburō. One night, the two men quarreled so harshly that a "worried" Tomosaburō quietly looked into Kanji's bedroom to make sure the younger admiral had not killed himself. Despite his choleric efforts, Kanji could never shake his navy minister's resolve or control.[79]

Knowledgeable observers glimpsed a more powerful if less tangible consideration behind the angry reaction to the Washington accords. "Japan's naval leaders have interpreted the lower ratio . . . as implying a stigma of national inferiority," globetrotting commentator William Henry Chamberlin wrote in 1939. "Once this argument was put on this emotional plane there could be only one issue, for a people as proud and sensitive as the Japanese. No Navy Minister, no Premier, could have survived the storm of nationalist denunciation."[80]

Chamberlin was wrong in one respect. For many long years, the conciliatory course that Katō Tomosaburō charted at Washington did survive. Katō Kanji returned home expressing bitter complaints that quickly resonated among younger officers in the service and the public at large. As time passed the Fleet faction engaged in elaborate mind games, ostensibly proving that ten-six, when carried to certain arithmetic or geometric lengths, actually translated into one hundred to thirty-six, and that even ten-seven could guarantee a practical fighting ratio of only one hundred to forty-nine.[81]

Katō Tomosaburō and the Treaty faction nonetheless defied their opponents and with great difficulty stifled opposition to the Washington agreements. He and his allies continually emphasized that Japan had attained dizzying heights; it was now universally and formally recognized as the world's third-greatest naval power and as such a great deterrent force. In the brief year remaining to him, Tomosaburō reduced the Japanese navy by fully one-half. But he died in 1923, and everything he worked for soon unraveled. To millions of proud folk living marginal personal existences in order to lift their nation up to great-power

status, the requirement to scrap modern vessels like the nearly completed 39,900-
ton battleship *Tosa,* "built as it were with the blood and sweat of the Japanese
people," was intolerable. By 1925 Katō Kanji's Fleet faction, with its growing belief that the U.S. Navy had become "*the* arch-antagonist with whom hostilities
were unavoidable," threatened to dominate opinion within and beyond the
Imperial Japanese Navy. Washington had been "a case of pure power politics
which resulted in a terrible defeat for Japan." Many were reminded of the anti-
Japanese immigration laws in California, which were widely assumed to have
"caused the abrogation of the Anglo-Japanese alliance." No one yet dreamed of
going to war with the Americans, but young cadets like the future destroyer
captain Tameichi Hara, not long out of Eta Jima and terribly impressionable because of the brutal training, did not know what to make of the growing fanaticism of their superiors, who "drummed into us daily" the "theory" of American
perfidiousness.[82]

In terms of security, the Washington Conference created no winners and
many losers. The Americans did achieve their cherished goal of co-supremacy
on the world ocean, but in order to gain a symbolic triumph the White House
and State Department had sacrificed a fleet of sufficient size to ensure effective
power projection in both the Atlantic and the Pacific. Whether or not the Japanese *would* fortify their island barriers (and evidence seems to indicate they did
not before the late thirties), they *could* fortify them much sooner than the
Americans could build a large-enough squadron of new battlewagons to break
through. At the same time, the British Admiralty surrendered for the life of the
agreement (that is, practically until 1935) buildup of the Singapore base, thus
leaving the Royal Navy "without a berth east of Malta capable of accommodating and refitting a capital ship." The practical result of the Washington Conference, then, was to leave any future initiatives throughout the western Pacific
firmly in Tokyo's hands.[83] The Japanese, meanwhile, lost their long-cherished
ten-seven power ratio in capital ships and failed to pry either the Americans out
of Hawaii or the British out of Singapore. If in coming years Japan for any reason felt a compulsion to expand south or east beyond the Asian mainland, it
might well face weakened but determined opposition from the Anglo-Saxon
powers, absent a crisis in Europe.

But it was Britain that lost the most. Never again would Britannia dominate
the global sea-lanes that were so vital to its domestic and imperial security. The
Imperial Conference of 1921 might have practically ratified Washington in advance, but no matter; the pain of mastery surrendered at the conference table
rather than at war at sea never quite abated. Of course, emasculating the war-

making capabilities of its participants was exactly what the Washington Conference was all about, and, with one exception, the agreements did succeed in taming serious international naval rivalries for nearly a decade.

The exception lay in Anglo-American relations. The United States pushed Britain hard from the end of the Great War of 1914–1918 down to the mid-thirties when the rise of Nazi Germany and samurai Japan forced a rapprochement. There was some desultory talk within British naval circles during the early twenties of war with the United States, until the cabinet put an end to it. Conventional wisdom, even within the Royal Navy, was summed up by Admiral Sir Barry Domville, who stated that "anyone who is not a congenital idiot must realise that the greatest guarantee for world peace is that lasting friendship should exist between the British Empire and the United States." Every effort, every policy, should have as its objective "increased cordiality" between the two English-speaking peoples.[84]

America's pugnacious sailors were not so certain. If the United States maintained its pace of maritime shipbuilding, it would eventually reach a point—sooner rather than later—when U.S. global commerce would equal, then surpass, that of Great Britain. Were the cousins willing to forgo the improvements in comfort and lifestyle that such a change would bring? America's admirals thought not, and so some rather desultory planning occurred involving an American invasion of Canada if war came, followed possibly by a blockade of the British Isles. There was nothing particularly serious or urgent about all this, but it did reflect lingering tensions between London and Washington, if not the peoples they led.

Slowly, Whitehall and Downing Street were beginning to appreciate the limits of sea power in the industrial age. Airpower now largely canceled out the close blockade as a decisive weapon of war; in a future European conflict, the Royal Navy could not impose victory in and of itself but only in conjunction with the Royal Air Force and British army. American strategists, too, accepted the new realities. The primary mission responsibility of the United States Navy remained the first line of defense for a continent whose sheer size and diverse topography served as deterrents to foreign invasion. Power projection *across* the sea would be pursued only in a Pacific war in which the fleet would be expected to steam to the western Pacific in search of the climactic naval battle with the Imperial Japanese Navy.[85]

Three factors kept the world ocean generally calm throughout the mid- and late twenties. First, the huge U.S. merchant marine that the wartime building program promised and Congress insisted on dreaming about never materialized. True, the American president and United States Lines continued to show the flag on the Atlantic, and the Dollar and Matson Lines did the same in the Pacific. But there was no vast postwar expansion of either merchant or passenger vessels. Shipbuilding is costly, and without wartime subsidies American private enterprise in the 1920s discovered that there were far more lucrative ways to invest than in a chancy competition with established British and French international shipping firms. Monies that might have been invested in getting the new cargo ships and passenger liners into the world sea-lanes were instead funneled into radios, automobiles, the Hollywood film industry, textiles, and even airplanes. While America's merchant marine atrophied, Britain's retained both its pride of place and its practical control of world trade throughout the interwar years. The second factor that kept international rivalries and hostilities in check until 1933 was the unwillingness of Congress to build the U.S. fleet up to practical parity with the Royal Navy or, indeed, much beyond the size of the Imperial Japanese Navy, thus reducing British jealousies and Japanese fears. The third factor was Britain's inability to place a major fleet back in the Far East. It had been almost twenty years since Jacky Fisher had hauled his predreadnoughts back to home waters. Jellicoe's postwar proposal to re-create a major fleet east of Suez was ruled out by the drastic reduction of the Royal Navy at the Washington Conference. The restrictive building formulas and warship ratios agreed upon there whittled down an imperial fleet past the point where it could efficiently and effectively implement its many duties in both European and Far Eastern waters. Britain had to confront a potentially hostile United States in the Atlantic and Japan in the Pacific and keep in mind that "the postwar fleets of France, Italy, Baltic Russia, Spain, and so on might not be individually imposing; but all together they added up to quite a few ships. Even the severely restricted German Navy of Versailles proportions counted for something."[86] In the future Britain could dispatch a "main fleet to Singapore" only in times of guaranteed calm in European affairs. After 1929, there was precious little calm to be found anywhere in the international community.

CHAPTER 2

The Race Resumes

THE WASHINGTON NAVAL agreements were to run until 1936. Had they been left alone, it is possible that the world might have been spared another war. But the Japanese decision to build up to and cheat on the accords, together with the uncontested reemergence of German sea power, precluded such restraint. As a consequence the fragile postwar international naval consensus upon which world peace depended fell disastrously apart.

Throughout the mid- and late twenties, London and Washington watched uneasily as Tokyo steadily increased its sea power through both new construction and a steady growth and expansion of its naval air arm. World War I had proved an enormous boon to Japanese shipbuilding and naval technology. Between 1913 and 1919, the annual launching of merchant ships increased a dozenfold from 55,000 to 636,000 gross tons. The half-dozen commercial shipyards grew to 57, the number of workers in the shipbuilding industry from 26,000 to 95,000. By the latter date, the Japanese shipbuilding industry "could at last obtain machinery—turbines, boilers, reciprocal engines and other propulsive equipment—from indigenous suppliers," while the navy itself achieved "near technological sufficiency," and by the 1920s, when another round of naval construction was undertaken, "the skills available at both naval and commercial dockyards made Japan capable of turning out a range of warships that in design and construction were equal or superior to those of any navy in the world."[1]

The Imperial Navy would have it no other way. Frustrated by the six-ten parity with Britain and the United States in capital ships, the Japanese were determined to produce warships in every other category that "would be individually superior to those of the enemy, even by a single gun or torpedo tube, or by a single knot of speed."[2] The commissioning of the light cruiser *Yubari* as early as July 1923 signaled the inception of the new policy. Officially described as an "experimental" ship, *Yubari* was designed by naval constructor Hiraga Yuzuru "to test the concept of a cruiser of high speed and relatively high firepower on the smallest possible displacement." For the next decade and more, Japanese yards turned out both light (six-inch-gun) and heavy (eight-inch-gun) cruisers, plus destroyers, that ranged from superior to far superior to their contemporaries in the West.[3]

The purpose of these new vessels would be to fulfill a newly conceived third aspect of a war of attrition against a future American naval foray into the western Pacific. With the advent of the first true ocean-spanning submarines, Japanese naval doctrine expanded the U-boat's role to include surveillance and ambush of the enemy fleet even as it left its Hawaiian base. Thereafter, the approaching fleet would be assaulted not only by submarines but also by cruiser-destroyer forces that would launch night torpedo attacks against the enemy's capital ships. Either the battered U.S. fleet would turn back to Hawaii in defeat, or it would plow on to be destroyed by the main Japanese battleship line in a decisive mid-ocean duel. In order to press home a successful attack against the advancing enemy battle line, Japan's new cruisers and destroyers would have to be ton for ton the best ships of their class in the world—big, fast, rugged, and festooned with both guns and torpedoes. Naval architects like Yuzuru met those requirements brilliantly. They created a dozen heavy cruisers of the *Myōkō* and *Takao* classes—splendid and extremely powerful ships that could churn up thirty-three knots in even large seas—and the huge two thousand–ton *Fubuki*-class destroyers whose armament rivaled that of many light cruisers.[4]

The Washington accords had stipulated that although there would be no limit on the number of eight-inch-gun cruisers so long as construction remained within the six-ten parity structure, such vessels could not exceed ten thousand tons. All of the *Myōkō*s and *Takao*s, however, displaced well over that figure, though Tokyo never admitted it. The Japanese vessels mounted a ten-gun main battery, carried eight twenty-one-inch torpedo tubes, and were more heavily armored than their tin-clad American counterparts, all of which weighed in at substantially below ten thousand tons and all but two of which mounted only a nine-gun main battery. The dozen British *Town*- and *County*-class heavies, built in the mid- and late twenties, were even more inferior to the Japanese vessels, carrying only six to eight guns in their main batteries, with maximum speed a knot or two slower than their Japanese and American counterparts. With its superb new cruisers, the Japanese navy by 1930 was thus beautifully positioned to wage either a defensive war against an advancing enemy fleet or an offensive *guerre de course* against enemy commerce across the length and breadth of the Pacific. If there was one point on which the Fleet and Treaty factions within the Japanese navy seemed to agree, it was that the seven-ten ratio in 6.1-inch-gun cruisers must never be surrendered at future conference tables.[5]

The few foreign visitors privileged to visit the new Japanese vessels were suitably impressed. When the brand-new *Kent,* which had just become the flagship of the British Far Eastern Fleet, visited Yokosuka in 1929, its officers were invited to visit *Myōkō.* The Britons were bowled over. "Now *this* is a real warship," one gushed to his hosts. "*Kent* is a luxury liner by comparison!"[6]

As Japan's splendid cruisers began appearing in the late twenties, American authorities pressed the British for a formula that would favor construction of a comparatively few "replies" to keep the Japanese in check. Whitehall, however, favored quantity over quality, arguing that Britain required more, not fewer, cruisers to patrol the imperial sea-lanes and ensure the protection of trade. Although His Majesty's government also constructed a few eight-inch-gun cruisers, it continually pressed Washington to support an international agreement terminating construction of such vessels in favor of less costly light cruisers. An unsigned and undated draft memorandum, or perhaps speech, from this period summed up the British position—and British exasperation—perfectly:

> General [Charles Gates] Dawes [the American financial and disarmament expert] says "The reduction of Naval Armaments is the next step to be taken towards World Peace." A reduction in the wholly unjustified scale of U.S. Naval Armaments is certainly called for and if it were followed by Japan, would justify some reduction of our... destroyers and submarines, but not appreciably in the one element that is most absolute, viz. Cruisers, for we have seen that they form our only protection to the most dangerous form of attack that—if properly planned beforehand—can be launched and prosecuted with small means by an inferior power."[7]

Whitehall and Downing Street agreed to a naval conference at Geneva in 1927 in an attempt to clarify some of the ambiguities and in hopes of fully correcting some of the felt wrongs committed at Washington. It went nowhere. Foreign secretary Austen Chamberlain berated himself for not making a more careful preconference assessment: "I confess that I did not foresee in any way the rigidity of the American attitude." Britons were just as rigid. In the melancholy aftermath of the conference, First Sea Lord David Beatty made it clear that whereas the Royal Navy was prepared to accept parity in capital ships,

"Britain could not commit herself to the same principle in cruisers," to which the U.S. Navy's General Board promptly replied that "equality with Great Britain is the sole basis on which a just treaty limitation can be imposed."[8]

The view from an increasingly bedeviled Admiralty was that the Americans just didn't get it, despite Lord Balfour's attempt a few years before to make them see the light:

> Suppose for example, that your Western States were suddenly removed 10,000 miles across the sea. Suppose that the very heart of your Empire was a small and crowded island depending upon oversea trade not merely for its luxuries but for the raw materials of those manufactures by which its superabundant population lives, and for the food upon which they subsist. Suppose it was a familiar thought that there was never a moment of the year when within the limits of your State there was more than seven weeks' food for its population, and that food could only be replenished by oversea communication.[9]

Japan's steadily growing sea power shocked the Royal Navy. By the summer of 1933, Whitehall had laid "down the basis of our Naval Preparations as being a war in the Far East." At the end of September, Admiral William Fisher submitted a letter to the secretary of the Admiralty in response to the new policy. Fisher had just assumed command of Britain's Mediterranean Fleet, traditionally a stepping-stone to first sea lord, the highest service position in the Admiralty, roughly conforming to chief of naval operations in the United States. The new fleet commander began by visualizing two separate future wars at sea. The European contest would involve enemy "attacks on our harbours, naval and commercial, . . . all forms of attack on our sea-borne commerce and expeditionary forces in transit, but which will not include a General action at sea." The other contest would be "*distant,* e.g. Western Atlantic [presumably against the Americans] or Far East, in which all forms of attacks on our sea-borne commerce must be expected, with the *possibility* of a general action to decide the mastery of the sea in the theatre of war." Naval operations in Europe would not greatly involve *"fleet"* cruisers, "since their most useful role would probably be the screening of the Battle Fleet at night against destroyer attacks, which duty could be largely entrusted to our own destroyer flotillas." But combat in the distant seas of the western Atlantic and Far East was a much different matter. "Both the U.S.A. and Japan have powerful, modern and efficient battle fleets which will be used in conjunction with all the usual ancillary forces." In particular, these putative enemies would mount "serious attacks on our trade routes . . . carried out by 8-inch gun cruisers—that such—acting in pairs or greater numbers will be strategically disposed to cover operations of 6-inch cruisers and armed raiders, and that all will make every possible use of aircraft for locating trade and destroying it." As a "broad principle," therefore, "endeavours should be made that whenever the battle fleet proceeds to sea in the expectation of a general engagement, it should do so in superior strength of all arms." Fisher was satisfied that the most recently designed and built British light cruisers of the *Leander* class were more than a match for comparable Japanese ships, but if Japan should build light cruisers with a ten- or twelve-gun main battery, then Britain would have no choice but to follow, "for though the advantage of that type is not apparent when used as a *Fleet* cruiser (i.e. to screen the battle fleet), it is very definitely so when used as a commerce destroyer and its opponent must not be inferior. I am of opinion that vis a vis Japan and bearing in mind the value of air reconnaissance if a saving is to be made in any portion of the Grand Fleet it can most safely be done in the number of *Fleet* cruisers."[10]

British naval strategy in the postwar age of cruiser and commerce warfare was thus clear: the greatly reduced battle fleet would be employed in distant waters to engage the enemy grand fleet and to disrupt enemy attempts to destroy imperial commerce. Since enemy heavy eight-inch-gun cruisers could sweep aside or destroy Britain's legion of light six-inch-gun cruisers protecting the imperial lifeline, an international moratorium on the construction of the bigger ships (which were too expensive in large numbers for the Royal Navy to build and operate) became an essential objective of British foreign policy. But the U.S. Navy's General Board, looking west, not east, had become enamored of long-range eight-inch-gun cruisers that could ply the broad Pacific with ease, even though such vessels were "tin clads" as far as protective armor was concerned in order to remain within the ten thousand–ton displacement limit. Britain then possessed fifteen such vessels; the United States wanted to complete the twenty-three authorized under its 1924 and 1929 building programs. Indeed, so anxious were the Yanks to build up their heavy-cruiser flotilla that the last vessels were designed before the first ones had completed their trials.[11]

The tiny German navy of the early and midtwenties was a harmless and docile force. According to one authority, it "floundered leaderless, unable to escape involvement in [a series of right-wing, anticommunist] political imbroglios, which threatened its existence." Important policies were often left to subordinates "who enjoyed an inordinate measure of independence from the usual administrative and fiscal controls."[12] Admiral Hans Zenker and his predecessor, Admiral

Paul Behncke, entertained no vaulting ambitions, and the handful of officers remaining in the Kriegsmarine during the 1920s sailed their few obsolescent ships when and where they could and somberly pondered the fate of the High Seas Fleet. Erich Raeder, Franz von Hipper's staff officer at Dogger Bank and Jutland and a rapidly rising star, argued that Germany must never again go to war with Britain and that to further this policy the navy must forever remain essentially a coastal-defense force. The chief theoretician of the Kriegsmarine in these years, Vice Admiral Wolfgang Wegener, reached essentially the same conclusion. The British distant blockade of 1914–1918 had amply demonstrated the crippling weakness of a North Sea fleet, no matter how large or initially enthusiastic and efficient. Since Britain could never again permit the development of a large continental navy, it would be folly to build one. If an effective German navy were somehow rebuilt, it would require the kind of bases in western Norway and France that would permit sudden and flexible deployments directly into the Atlantic. No matter how the matter was looked at, a future German navy would be the direct cause of a future European war, and no sane individual in the 1920s could bear to contemplate such a catastrophe.[13]

But beneath its high-command structure, the navy was honeycombed with individuals willing and even eager to court disaster as the price of rebuilding national greatness. Submarine veterans provided the essential link between the imperial and Nazi eras. The German submariner of 1914–1945 proved a fanatic champion of his weapon system and the cause of Germany. After 1918 he was desperate to find again the "unique spirit of comradeship engendered by destiny and hardship . . . where every man's well-being [is] in the hands of all." Many U-boat veterans shared the views of young Karl Dönitz, who in 1919 discovered that "the naval profession was attractive only if there was some hope of going to sea in a U-boat again." He was assured by the Personnel Desk of the Navy Office that his hopes would soon materialize. By the early twenties the young submariners were scheming with right-wing allies on the fringes of the military, industrial, and political communities to discredit and subvert the Weimar Republic. They proved devious, cunning, and blindly loyal to those who would resurrect their careers. Good Nazis in embryo, after 1933 they enthusiastically marched into Hitler's ranks.[14]

Perhaps no individual in the early postwar years did more to maintain the morale, the strength, and the hope of the German navy in eventual resurrection than the former submarine commander Wilhelm Canaris. A rather sinister figure with a taste and flair for intrigue, Canaris would eventually become one of the most ambiguous figures in recent German history. As head of naval intelligence during World War II, he dallied clandestinely with the Allies for purposes that remain essentially obscure. But in the desperate days of 1919–1920 when an impoverished Germany lay helpless before its countless enemies, his heart and soul were devoted to the rebirth of German sea power. Working out of the now drastically reduced Navy Office, Canaris began building up a secret, or "black," personnel reserve within extreme conservative groups and employed "well directed propaganda to keep alive the idea of a powerful and combat-ready fleet." In 1920–1921, when national fortunes were at their lowest, the Canaris-led cabal managed to find secret caches of small arms all over Germany that it either used to equip a secret naval reserve or sold to Danish arms dealer for money to keep the tiny but financially starved fleet in some sort of operation.[15]

The Canaris cabal was not the only element in the small, struggling postwar German navy to dabble in intrigue. Raeder, despite an ostentatious aversion to any movement or impulse that might lead down the road to another war, became an "ardent" supporter of the various free-corps bands that sprang up all over Germany in 1919–1920 to maintain the eastern borders against Poles and Balts. In the spring of 1920 one of these groups, the infamous Ehrhardt Brigade, managed to occupy Berlin and installed Dr. Wolfgang Kapp as chancellor. Raeder openly urged his superiors to throw the weight of the navy behind Kapp. When the putsch failed in the face of a general strike by German workers, Weimar authorities forced Raeder into a two-year "retirement."[16]

With the survival of the republic seemingly ensured after 1924, Raeder turned away from domestic politics to concentrate on helping to rebuild the surface fleet within the confines of Versailles, while Canaris and his fellow intriguers schemed to evade and subvert the prohibition against German submarines.[17] The navy and various business circles had already discovered the advantages of dangling the possibility of advanced technology transfers before foolish or greedy foreign firms and governments in order to promote German interests. Foiling the "close meshed network of informants employed by the Allied Disarmament Commission," naval officers and civilian designers had already begun "sneaking off to foreign countries where, far beyond the inspector's range of vision, they embarked on plans for a new U-boat arm—to begin with, only on paper."

As early as 1922, the Navy Office acquired an interest in a Dutch design company at The Hague that promptly signed on thirty of the best submarine designers from the drawing offices of Germany's two most important wartime U-boat yards, Kiel's Germania and the Vulcan Company of Hamburg. In 1924 Germania got a secret contract from Kawasaki Shipbuilding Company in Osaka, and Canaris was dispatched to the Far East to oversee construction and the transfer of submarine technology to the Japanese through drawings and blue-prints.[18] Thereafter, the submarine cabal within the German Navy Office expanded its activities brazenly. Even as Canaris sailed off to Asia, one of the designers from Vulcan or Germania appeared in Finland where he oversaw the building of several submarines for the Finnish navy that were the prototype for the German U-boats of 1935–1939. The following year the German design team at The Hague provided the plans for two 500-ton U-boats for Turkey that also closely approximated the first generation of undersea craft built for Hitler a decade thence. Other German technicians in the late twenties supervised the construction of submarines for Sweden, Holland, and Spain. Since the Versailles Treaty did not expressly forbid German experts acting on behalf of other nations in neutral countries, the German technicians and drafters stood on legally unimpeachable ground.

At the Nuremberg trials it was revealed that funds for such enterprises were provided by the Defense Ministry of the Weimar Republic and dispersed by a Captain Lohmann of the navy, who was simultaneously engaged in other, even more shadowy and disreputable, activities. When, as part of the secret accords with the Reichswehr, Soviet officials came calling on German maritime firms in 1926 asking for assistance in designing a new class of coastal-defense submarines, they were eagerly obliged. German designers and naval officers worked closely with their Russian counterparts to design a large number of medium-size and small U-boats that took to the Baltic and Black Seas between 1930 and 1938.

Raeder and Canaris never got along, and when the former at last became admiral of the fleet in 1928, he bridled the activities of the Canaris cabal both at home and abroad. More than personal animosity was involved in the decision. Having been compromised in the Kapp Putsch, "Raeder saw the navy's major problem as a political one—the danger of being dragged into party politics." And the experience of war had convinced him that the navy had become "too involved with the other branches" of the German armed services. As a consequence, he worked diligently and successfully to "make the navy a self-sufficient organism with all reins of administration firmly in his hands." Raeder did, however, continue the practice of assisting foreign nations in building submarines and, according to Anthony Martienssen, even "secretly placed orders for U-boats" in Spanish, Finnish, and Dutch dockyards. He also allowed subordinates to dally with the despised communists, sending at least one naval mission to Moscow in 1926 where, without giving away much information or making any commitments, the Germans learned a good deal about Stalin's typically grandiose ambitions for the creation of a major navy. A later Soviet mission to Germany won a brief visit to the then new *Deutschland* but nothing more.[19]

Raeder's heart lay with surface ships, not submarines, and in that sentiment he was at one with the rest of the international naval world. Conventional wisdom held that "submarines did not translate into sea power, and that technological developments since 1914–18," most notably the asdic underwater listening device, had largely rendered submarines "obsolete."[20] Under the provisions of the Versailles Treaty, Berlin was permitted after 1928 to replace one of the half-dozen old pre-dreadnoughts that constituted the Weimar navy with a new vessel. Within several years two other superannuated ships could be replaced. Zenker and Raeder evidently experienced a sudden change of heart. They refused to consider replacing the pre-dreadnoughts with slow ten thousand–ton *Monitors* whose construction would confirm the navy's status as nothing more than a coastal-defense force forever tied to the army. For all their protestations of peaceful intent and moderate ambition, Zenker, Raeder, and their colleagues could not accept such a humiliating role. What they needed was a powerful and fast heavy ship that could either dominate the Baltic or deploy on the world's sea-lanes as a commerce destroyer. When plans for *Deutschland* and two sisters were unveiled, the Reichstag was appalled at both the concept and the cost of the new vessels. But uneasy over the resurgent power of the armed forces, the legislators reluctantly gave way.

To calm world opinion the Germans never classified *Deutschland* and its later sisters as anything other than *Panzershiffes*—armored ships. But indeed they were much more. When *Deutschland* appeared in 1933 (to be followed by *Scheer* a year later and *Graf Spee* in 1936), astonished British naval journalists promptly dubbed them "pocket battleships." They were not far wrong. *Deutschland* and its sisters were at the cutting edge of the Versailles provisions: six 11-inch guns in two turrets (one forward and one aft) were mounted on a 609-foot hull, ostensibly displacing the requisite ten thousand tons and capable of a top speed of twenty-six knots. In fact, even with the 3-to-5½-inch welded iron sheath (accounts of thickness vary) and the use of aluminum whenever possible, the three vessels at nearly twelve thousand tons each (some accounts go as high as thirteen thousand tons plus) were grossly overweight. Indeed, they had to be in order to satisfy basic structural demands. The two 11-inch-gun turrets were massive for a cruiser-size vessel meant to sail the often gale-lashed seas of the North Atlantic while enjoying at least minimal anti-shell and -torpedo protection. The Germans airily dismissed the ships' size (as had the Americans at the Washington

Conference with *Lexington* and *Saratoga*) as of little consequence, arguing that the increased weight went into defensive arrangements (armor and internal subdivision). The *Deutschlands*, driven by diesel power rather than conventional engines, were designed to outrun any ship they could not outshoot and out-shoot any ship they could not outrun. They were also given a then incredible cruising range of nineteen miles at fifteen knots. With eight big 5.9-inch secondary batteries and torpedo tubes on the stern, the *Deutschlands* were very formidable ships indeed; in fact, they could properly be defined as the most powerful ships for their size ever built.[21]

But perhaps the most stunning feature of the *Deutschlands* and one that enhanced their impression of incredible, compact power was their appearance. Together with the 8-inch-gun American cruisers that began appearing in 1929 and, to a lesser extent, the new Japanese heavies of the same period, the German pocket battleships were visually stunning vessels. Prior to the 1920s the world's steel warships large and small all looked as if they had been turned out of the same ugly boiler factory. Funnels were usually tall and spindly, superstructures were low and blocky, and guns appeared to have been haphazardly strewn about weirdly shaped hulls that had been hammered together with thousands if not millions of rivets. Few if any capital ships, cruisers, and destroyers pos-sessed any hint of elegance or grace. Only Britain's last battle cruisers, *Repulse,* commissioned in 1916, and *Hood,* commissioned in 1920 as the world's largest warship, could be called truly beautiful.

All that began to change in the late twenties and early thirties. Warships acquired an almost yachtlike grace that reached its epitome in the German capital ships of the interwar and early war period (*Bismarck, Tirpitz, Gneisenau, Scharn-horst,* and the "pocket battleships"), the Japanese superdreadnoughts *Yamato* and *Musashi,* and the American *Augusta*-class cruisers followed later by the *South Dakota*– and *Iowa*-class battleships and (arguably) three *Yorktown*-class carriers.

Superstructures acquired a flowing elegance that in the battleships was epito-mized by a tall control tower either incorporating the bridge (and, in the Ameri-can *South Dakotas* a single funnel as well) or just aft of it. All main batteries were mounted centerline, and hulls (with the exception of the German pocket battleships) were built with clipper bows and often gracefully curving sterns. Like the great new ocean liners of the day, capital ships and cruisers were not clumsily riveted together but smoothly welded, giving hull and upper works the same sleek sense of power.

The exact nature and dimensions of *Deutschland* were not known when in October 1929 British prime minister Ramsay MacDonald traveled to Washington in search of a permanent solution to the cruiser issue. The North Atlantic community was poised at the very crest of postwar prosperity; no one could imagine the abyss into which the economies of the West were about to fall. Presumably, Weimar was not building beyond the Versailles restrictions. But it was clear that once Germany completed its fast modern "cruiser," it would possess a powerful commerce destroyer that could at least theoretically disrupt the balance of European naval power. The fact that *Deutschland* would be closely followed by at least two and perhaps as many as five sisters added to international unease.

With Germany and Japan looming as possible future threats to Britain's dramatically diminished sea power, MacDonald was determined to come to a permanent agreement with the Americans on cruisers that would pave the way for another international conference on naval disarmament. In October 1929, on the very eve of the great Wall Street crash that would pitch the world into a new age of crisis, MacDonald sailed to the United States. The seriousness of his intent could be gauged by the fact that no other leader of the British government had ever visited the former colonies. The prime minister was a pacifist, and when he arrived in the United States he found a willing ally in President Herbert Hoover, a lifelong Quaker.

The British had previously insisted on possessing at least seventy 6.1-inch-gun cruisers, each displacing no more than seventy-five hundred tons, to serve as commerce protectors in a future war. Now MacDonald offered to reduce the number to fifty. Hoover promptly accepted. "On the American side," recalled Henry Stimson, Hoover's secretary of state, "there was perhaps no equivalent concession; since the British had conceded the principle of [overall Anglo-American naval] parity, and since the American cruiser fleet was mostly still on paper, it was the size of the British cruiser requirement that determined the major lines of agreement." Matters were not quite as simple as Stimson believed, however, because while the United States subsequently agreed to cut its 8-inch-gun cruiser flotilla from twenty-four to twenty-one, that would have given Japan under the ten-six formula sixteen heavy cruisers to Britain's existing fifteen, which was unacceptable to the Admiralty.[22] But discussions had progressed far enough that MacDonald could return home in triumph, and he promptly issued an invitation for another five-power naval conference to meet in London in February 1930. All the invitees—France, Italy, Japan, and the United

States—accepted. No one, apparently, thought to invite Germany. It proved a dreadful oversight.

London was the last harmonious international disarmament conference to convene for a half century. The ultimate impact and dimensions of the recent Wall Street crash were not yet perceived. Government confidence and public morale in all five countries remained high after six years of general prosperity. The Royal Navy was eager for an agreement. The United States Navy was divided, with the General Board still unhappy with any restrictions on 8-inch-gun cruisers, while the chief of naval operations, Admiral William V. Pratt, remained a single-minded advocate of Anglo-American friendship.[23] As at Washington nine years earlier, the Japanese arrived in London without detailed instructions. Isoroku Yamamoto, a dynamic and brilliant young officer with a limitless future and an insatiable taste for poker and women, would recall that as discussions got under way, the head of the delegation, Tsuneo Matsudaira, felt impelled to ask for so many clarifications and so much guidance from home that close to a million yen was spent in cables between London and Tokyo. Nonetheless, the two men basically adhered to the beliefs of the Treaty faction within the Japanese fleet that set international cooperation above all other considerations. Yamamoto in particular had spent some time in the United States and had visited the automobile assembly lines in Detroit and the oil fields of eastern Texas. He had become convinced, he told a wide circle of acquaintances, that for Japan to engage in a shipbuilding race with the United States would be an act of incredible folly that would strain the national economy to the breaking point. Yamamoto and his colleagues in the Treaty faction argued that intense conversations within the navy notwithstanding, a mere 10 percent difference in various warship ratios between the United States and Japan meant very little. "They could not believe, in fact, that the seventy percent for which the hawks called could ever enable Japan to feel secure in its defenses where America was concerned." Yamamoto understood that if the two nations ever went to war, the United States would be able to concentrate its attack on Japan, whereas the Japanese counterattack would have to be widely dispersed among its opponent's vessels. Of greatest importance, however, was the fact that once war began, U.S. industrial capacity would simply overwhelm Japan. "Thus even with a seventy per cent navy Japan would still be obliged to stick to its policy of avoiding a conflict with the United States."[24]

Matsudaira, Yamamoto, and their fellow delegates seemed to represent dominant opinion, for Japanese elections held during the conference returned Prime Minister Yuko Hamaguchi and his moderate Minseitō Party cabinet to power with a comfortable margin in the Diet. Nonetheless, the Japanese proved hard bargainers, and the discussions on the cruiser question between Matsudaira and the chief American negotiator, Republican senator David Reed of Pennsylvania, were long and tedious. The Japanese demanded a flat 70 percent ratio with Britain and the United States in 8-inch-gun ships. Reed demurred, arguing that such a concession would arouse a storm of anti-Japanese sentiment at home. "The British were perhaps even more categorical," maintaining that any increase in Japanese heavy cruisers would force additional British building in that category "and so destroy the Anglo-American agreement." Reed at last crafted a complex formula that Matsudaira grudgingly accepted. In exchange for continued Japanese acquiescence to a 6–10 ratio for 8-inch-gun cruisers, the United States agreed to stretch out its cruiser-building program to 1936, at which time expiration of the London accords would allow all parties to reopen the question. In fact, the Japanese did derive a 7–10 formula (indeed, a 7.5–10 formula) from the conference, since their first four 8-inch-gun ships (the *Aoba*s and *Kinugasa*s mounting only a six-gun main battery) had been well below the ten thousand–ton limit. Thus, while their *tonnage* ratio in 8-inch-gun cruisers would be 60 percent, the *number* of such ships in the Japanese navy would be 75 percent of those in the U.S. fleet until after 1936. Moreover, as an apparent sop to Japanese concerns, the Washington agreement was reconfirmed with respect to Japan's 7–10 parity in 6-inch-gun cruisers and its absolute parity with the two great powers in submarines. This latter concession seemed significant to the Anglo-Americans, for once again at London the British delegation pushed strenuously, if with utter lack of success, for a total ban on undersea warfare. This time the Americans were with them. But because of continuing French and Japanese insistence on undersea boats, the conferees were able to agree only on a clause prohibiting unrestricted submarine warfare, a provision that eventually every nation in the world violated with a greater or lesser degree of hypocrisy.[25]

As finally written, the London Naval Treaty of April 22, 1930, extended the "holiday" on battleship and battle-cruiser construction for another five years (but with a continuation of the seventy thousand–ton exception for France and Italy) and established two classes of cruisers: type A, "heavy" 8-inch-gun ships, and type B, "light" 6-inch-gun ships. The cruiser balance within world navies was to be decisively shifted from 8-inch- to 6-inch-gun ships, though each signatory could transfer a small percentage of tonnage from one category to the other. As with the Washington accords, the London treaty allowed replacement of overage vessels. The formula agreed to was sixteen years for ships laid down before January 1, 1920, and twenty years for newer craft. Since the

numerous seventy-five hundred–ton American *Omaha*-class light cruisers had
proved wholly unsatisfactory, they could be replaced beginning in 1936. Admiral
Pratt and his colleagues in the American delegation strenuously resisted efforts by
the British, Japanese, and French to restrict light cruisers to seven thousand tons.
Pratt realized that a ten thousand–ton light cruiser could be a very formidable
ship, capable of carrying a large battery of 6-inch guns in a well-armored hull and
turrets, while possessing engines that could drive it at speeds well in excess of
thirty knots for very long distances. Moreover, 6-inch guns were capable of far
higher rates of fire than 8-inch batteries and could thus employ a "smothering"
effect on enemy battle lines, though admittedly requiring much closer ranges
for effect.[26] The London Naval Conference also limited tonnages on destroyers
and submarines, and the powers also agreed to further reduce their stocks of
battleships (Britain by five, the United States by three, and Japan by one).

The conference failed in only two respects, but they would eventually prove
fatal. The French and Italian delegations flatly refused to place their cruiser
fleets under any restrictions whatsoever regarding either numbers and size of
vessels or size of guns. Stimson, offering his services as honest broker, could not
remember when he had seen "three grimmer and less compromising faces than
those of the French leaders as they insisted upon their full naval program."
The other three delegations spent long hours and days cajoling, coddling, and
soothing their continental colleagues, but to no avail. Paris simply did not trust
Mussolini who, without doing anything about it, had been rattling his saber for
years over Italy's need for living room in North Africa. All Frenchmen knew that
Italian expansion across the Mediterranean could come only at their expense.
As Stimson later recalled: "No Frenchman could give parity to Italy and survive
in public life." The German pocket battleships also posed a new threat. France
prepared to meet it by invoking its seventy thousand–ton exemption clause in
capital ships to build two fast, powerful battle cruisers—*Dunkerque* and *Strasbourg*. When they appeared in the late thirties, the two handsome vessels were
the only ships in European waters, except the British battle cruisers and perhaps
the *Queen Elizabeth*-class fast battleships, that could run down and outshoot
Deutschland and its two sisters. With Germany now an active menace to the east
and Mussolini posturing belligerently to the south, French delegates rigidly defended their position.

Thus, only Japan, the United States, and Great Britain signed the London
accords. Among the signatories, only Britain expressed concern about the Franco-
Italian impasse. France was clearly straining all its resources to maintain its

huge army against Germany, and broad areas of Mussolini's Italy were mired in poverty. It appeared highly unlikely that Italian or French naval building programs over the next five years would be of sufficient size to threaten the Royal Navy in the Mediterranean and thus destabilize the cruiser agreements.[27]

The Americans came away from London ecstatic. They knew their own "big ship" people at home would be upset with restrictions on heavy cruisers, but the Japanese (to say nothing of the British) had been so accommodating and further reductions in naval armaments seemed so promising that there appeared little to worry about. The navy's General Board was as unhappy as Stimson and others predicted, but Pratt, the maverick chief of naval operations, readily convinced a parsimonious Senate to ratify the agreement.

Stimson later enthused over Japanese "frankness and friendliness": they had been "continuously fair and conciliatory." Confronted by the same "noisy big-navy opposition at home," Matsudaira had nonetheless brushed it off "in the same manner as the British and American leaders." Granted, the Anglo-American front had pushed Matsudaira hard to obtain the overall ten-six heavy-cruiser ratio, but the Japanese had seemed to take it well. They had achieved full parity in submarines and their cherished seven-ten ratio in light cruisers. There seemed little for anyone to worry about.[28]

The official Japanese reaction seemed to bear out the optimism of the West. On the occasion of Japan's formal ratification on October 27, 1930 (Navy Day in the United States), Prime Minister Hamaguchi delivered an international radio address in which he claimed that the London treaty "has opened a new chapter in the history of human civilization. We have once for all escaped from what I may call the 'pioneer stage,' in which every nation's hand is actually or potentially against every other. We have entered on the sane and friendly 'settlement stage,' in which every one is united to suppress intrusions by any one in another's sphere."[29]

Both Americans and Japanese moderates totally miscalculated the mood not only in Japanese naval and military circles but among the general public as well, for when the text of the London agreements reached Tokyo, it ignited a firestorm of protest. The West seemed determined to impose an eternal ten-six ratio on Japanese naval strength, which was "an insult to Japan's status as a first-rate power and a grave threat to its defenses." Indeed, "while the overall tonnage allowed to Japan . . . amounted to 69.75 percent of the tonnage allowed to the Anglo-American naval powers, much of this was in categories of secondary importance to the Japanese." At Washington, Japan's battleship fleet had been emasculated; now, at London, the perfidious Americans and Britons had accomplished the same goal with regard to both 8-inch-gun cruisers and submarines. What seemed to the Anglo-Americans a gracious concession on undersea craft was to the Japanese no concession at all. Japan already possessed nearly 78,000 tons of U-boats, about a three-to-two ratio each over the British and the Americans. Matsudaira had fought hard to set the submarine limit at 78,000 tons. Instead, the Western powers had insisted on a 52,700-ton limit, which approximated the current size of the submarine flotillas in both the British and the U.S. navies. "The Naval General Staff in Tokyo was enraged." War games had demonstrated that such tonnage would leave Japan short by two full squadrons—sixteen boats—of what planners considered necessary to wage a successful war of attrition against an advancing enemy fleet during a future Pacific war. As for 8-inch-gun cruisers, the Japanese delegation was obliged "with considerable bitterness" to accept a ratio of 60.23 percent, a limit that Japan had already reached by the time the treaty was signed, leaving the American and British navies free to build up to their collectively overwhelming ratios whenever they wished. Indeed, "the real source of aggravation for the Japanese Navy" in the London Naval Treaty was that its provisions "resulted in not merely an inferior ratio in Japanese naval strength across the board, but an actual reduction in that strength" vis-à-vis Britain and the United States. Tokyo convinced itself that the Washington Naval Treaty "essentially reflected the actual relative strength of the three major naval powers," whereas under the London accords, "Japan was obliged to halt her construction of heavy cruisers, a category in which, during the past decade, it had labored with effort and skill to obtain a lead."[30]

The "highly incensed" Naval Staff Board, in an almost unheard-of breach of etiquette in the web society, publicly censured the Minseitō cabinet for its determination to have the treaty ratified in opposition to the navy's wishes. The cabinet's decision to cling to foreign friendship no matter the cost in national security, prestige, and domestic popularity proved to be a Pyrrhic victory. Tameichi Hara, the future destroyer ace and in 1930 an obscure young lieutenant, recalled his colleagues and superiors reacting "in a frenzy" to ratification of the London Naval Treaty. They were "infuriated" that the despicable Americans had simply forced their terms down the throats of Matsudaira and his timid colleagues. A decisive change came over the Japanese navy after October 1930 as the prestige of the Treaty faction abruptly declined and that of the Fleet faction came to predominate. From now on most Japanese naval men "came . . . to consider the United States not merely a potential enemy, but a probable enemy."[31]

Clumsy Anglo-American behavior elsewhere further fueled Japanese resentment, suspicion, and hostility. Back in 1925 Washington had deemed the time appropriate to reconfirm and recognize the identity of interests between the United States and Britain's Pacific dominions that had first become evident during the cruise of the Great White Fleet seventeen years before. On July 1 forty-five U.S. warships, including the best battleships, steamed out of Hawaii and swept southward through the central Pacific to spend roughly a month in Australian and New Zealand waters. According to one jingoistic account, written in 1943 but undoubtedly faithful to the spirit of the earlier year, the Yanks received "a most enthusiastic welcome." As in 1908, their hosts expressed deep appreciation for the appearance of a war fleet that "was, in substance, partly their own, certainly their sole bulwark against the teeming yellow hordes to the north."

Tokyo informally made known its disapproval of the American initiative; Whitehall was apparently silent. But six years later, in February 1931, Britain ostentatiously squeezed one of its two newest battleships, Nelson, through the Panama Canal to join the USS Texas and other elements of the American battle fleet on the Pacific side of the Isthmus. The message was clear; Britain's large Atlantic Fleet was not necessarily confined to the Atlantic.[32] It could move through the canal to join forces with the Americans should Japan prove obstreperous in either East Asia or the western Pacific.

The London treaty and apparent Anglo-American efforts to intimidate Japanese sea power not only radicalized the Imperial Navy and its public but also helped fuel the anger that sent the army careening down the road of uncontrollable aggression against China. Japanese army and civil officials believed they had many other pretexts for war in September 1931: conflicting and complex interpretations of almost impenetrable treaty clauses regarding respective Chinese and Japanese economic and governing rights in Manchuria, the stationing of armed guards along Japanese railroad rights-of-way, and the murder of Captain Shintaro Nakamura and several companions by Chinese soldiers near Taonon in June 1931. The crisis was ignited by a mysterious explosion on a Japanese railroad just north of Mukden (Shenyang) during the night of September 18, 1931. Japan's local Kwantung Army promptly erupted out of its encampments and spread throughout the region. The Tokyo government steadfastly supported and sought to justify this act of aggression, though it cost Japan world opinion. According to two knowledgeable observers writing in the late 1930s, "There is reason to suspect that the hasty action of the supreme command of the Japanese Army" in deferring to the Manchurian Incident in September 1931 "was in part a reaction against the constitutional methods which prevailed in 1930" when the civil authority for the last time overrode the wishes of the armed forces and ratified the London naval agreements.[33]

When hostilities expanded briefly to Shanghai the following January, it was at the instigation of the Japanese fleet commander on the scene. "That the idea was a naval one," the *New York Herald Tribune* reported, "is borne out by Tokyo dispatches saying that the Cabinet meeting on January 23 ... realized the possible gravity of the situation, but 'decided to leave the matter to the Minister of the Navy.'"[34]

A boycott of Japanese goods and a street incident involving Chinese students and some Japanese monks led the Naval Office in Tokyo to order in a division of marines to clear the International Settlement of Chinese troops. The United States, Britain, and France promptly reinforced their small garrisons in the settlement, and for a brief time tensions rose to a level not seen since the war years.

The whole incident was in fact very complex, but it did result in a brutal Japanese land and air assault on civilian sections of Shanghai and Chinese airfields on the adjacent coast. The Japanese first employed seaplanes from the tender *Notoro* in the nearby Yangtze River and later carrier aircraft from *Kaga* and *Hosho* offshore. One contemporary account claimed that "a giant carrier"— presumably *Kaga*—in fact launched aircraft while lying directly off the city's famed Bund. Wherever the assaults came from, they were witnessed not only by Western residents but by a growing corps of international newspapermen who rushed to the scene as well. While the bombing attacks and dogfights provided the Imperial Japanese Navy with some invaluable initial experience in the employment of naval air, Western citizens were confronted with the violent face of battle for the first time since 1918, and they were horrified by Japan's unlimited and relentless brand of warfare.[35]

However shocked the United States might have been by the Japanese behavior at Shanghai, no one in the government was prepared at this stage to forcibly contest Japanese aggression. In a series of tense cabinet sessions in the autumn of 1931, President Hoover made it clear that he supported international condemnation of Japan by word but would not reinforce it by deed. With the Manchurian Incident just weeks old, the president considered proposing either a unilateral or an international economic boycott of Japan but recognized that such an act could escalate to war. He called in his military and naval advisers and asked them how the United States would fare if it found itself alone in a conflict with Japan. Chief of Naval Operations William Pratt correctly prophesied that Japan believed its "existence as a nation is at stake" and that it would "leave the League rather than submit to League intervention." The United States with its current five-to-three ratio in naval power could defeat Japan, but the navy was far from full strength and a portion would have to remain in the Atlantic to safeguard U.S. interests in Europe and the Americas. To win a war with Japan, both the battle and transport fleets would have to be materially strengthened and a great army would have to be raised, trained, and equipped to fight in either Japan or China. Victory would take anywhere from four to six years, as Japan would undoubtedly use the pretext of war to expand as far as possible into Southeast Asia and the adjacent archipelagoes. Hoover later rationalized that the undoubted suffering of several million Filipinos would have to be set against eventual freedom for several million Manchurians.[36]

Hoover decided to do nothing beyond signaling Japan through Secretary of State Stimson that the United States would not recognize any territory taken from China by force or in violation of the Washington treaties. Much to Tokyo's chagrin, the League ultimately adopted the "Stimson Doctrine." But the gesture was worse than meaningless. In the words of Stimson's later collaborator, McGeorge Bundy, the doctrine was a "bluff," and all parties to the Manchurian crisis knew it.[37] In the end, the U.S. government joined the European democracies in strongly signaling Japan that it would suffer no practical consequences as a result of its aggression. But Stimson and the democratic West had shamed and humiliated Japan without restraining it, and the Japanese left Geneva in 1933, following on the heels of the German delegation summoned home by the Nazi government in Berlin.

Japan fell into a very dangerous mood. "Independent diplomacy" and "armed isolation" were the new realities, together with a right-wing politics of coup and assassination. The people gave power in the 1932 elections to the strident if badly divided Seiyukai Party, whose right wing was eager to give the army and navy carte blanche. The emperor's most influential advisers now "determined to keep their lord safe by appeasing the military." The army, suddenly confronting the Soviet Union along lengthy borders acquired with the occupation of Manchuria (soon renamed Manchukuo), proposed construction of "a greater Japanese Empire" on the adjacent mainland that would provide Japan "with both the strength and the security of a major world power."[38] Nationalist rule in China remained weak and uncertain. By playing off one local warlord against another, Japan could squeeze Nationalist influence from North China and eventually integrate its economy with that of Manchukuo. The navy, still bitterly divided between the Treaty and Fleet factions, could neither speak nor act with a

single voice, but its more radical elements began toying with a dramatic possibility to secure and maintain Japan's dominance in Asia and the western Pacific.

The use of carrier planes at Shanghai reflected the efforts of forward-looking
elements in the Imperial Japanese Navy to integrate airpower into every aspect
of warfare. Yamamoto in particular, after briefly commanding the big, brand-
new carrier *Akagi* in the midtwenties, became convinced that aviation would be
the decisive factor in any coming conflict. Soon after returning to Japan in 1928
from an embassy staff assignment in Washington, D.C., Yamamoto became
acquainted with a plan for attacking Pearl Harbor from the air. Satō Tetsutarō's
strategy for killing enemy navies in their home waters was being revived. Author
of the daring proposal was an obscure lieutenant commander just out of the
Naval Staff College named Kusaka Ryunosuke, who was obviously one of those
rare individuals able to see when an emperor had no clothes. He addressed a
question that everyone in Japanese naval and military circles had steadfastly
ignored for years: what would happen if American behavior in a Pacific war
refused to conform to Japanese expectations and its Pacific Fleet could not be
lured westward for a decisive battle? Ryunosuke's answer was simple and obvious: if the Americans would not come to Japan, then Japan would have to go
to the Americans. Somehow, someway, the U.S. fleet would have to be neutralized, and if it remained in Hawaiian waters, it would have to be assaulted there.
The only means of doing so was with aircraft launched from carriers. Japan
would have to bomb Pearl Harbor.

Thirty copies of Ryunosuke's report were printed, and it prompted a burst
of interest in the upper circles of the Japanese navy. The high command went
off for a week's retreat to bone up on the still relatively new science of aviation.
Soon thereafter, Yamamoto was shown the report, which was more a speculative essay on how to start and prosecute a war few hoped would happen than a
meticulous plan for a preemptive strike against Pearl Harbor. Nonetheless,
Ryuonosuke's effort reflected the Imperial Navy's steadily growing interest in carrier aviation and its possibilities. The 1930 fleet exercises emphasized the employment of naval aircraft in a wide variety of roles, including carrier strikes
against well-defended ground targets. As the power and range of carrier aircraft
began to increase dramatically in future years, carriers

> became recognized above all for their ability to strike at targets beyond the
> range of surface guns and . . . torpedoes. Gunnery staffs as well as airmen
> became convinced that carrier planes should be used for a preemptive
> strike against the enemy's carriers to achieve air superiority in the vicinity
> of the [climactic] surface battle. . . . By mid-decade, with the improved

performance of bombing aircraft, particularly the dive bomber, the destruction of the enemy's carrier force became the focus of Japan's carrier forces.[39]

Such thinking, however, was subordinate to Japan's continued emphasis on a defensive naval war. Yamamoto himself belonged to the moderate Treaty faction within the Japanese navy. While steadily declining in numbers and influence, the moderates continued to hope for peace with the United States. Yamamoto clung to the belief that Japan's mission in the world was essentially peaceful and progressive; the idea of assassinating the U.S. Navy at its Hawaiian anchorage was repugnant to him. The navy's task was to uphold legitimate—even predominant—Japanese interests in Asian waters and to defend the empire from attack by aggressive enemies. He therefore embraced the fundamental Japanese—and American—scenario for a great Pacific war in which Japan would be the defensive fleet. But now Japan's arsenal would include not only the battle fleet, submarines, and fast, powerful cruisers and destroyers but aircraft as well. Yamamoto shrewdly perceived that "where small carrier-based aircraft were concerned, at least, both sides were roughly equal in the ranges at which they could hunt out and attack the enemy; there was no guarantee, therefore, that Japan could deal a one-sided blow to the American fleet." The comparative handful of carrier-strike aircraft would surely contribute to the progressive weakening of the advancing enemy, and their fighter aircraft would help protect the emperor's ships against air attack. But according to this doctrine, carrier aviation could never be a decisive element in defense strategy. The "South Sea islands" mandated to Japan by the League in 1919, however, were "unsinkable aircraft carriers," capable of supporting scores if not hundreds of long-range aircraft of superior performance. "Shifting from one land base to another," these planes "could hunt out and mount a preemptive attack on the American fleet." Land-based aircraft thus "provided the bulk of Japan's naval aviation up to the eve of the Pacific War." As late as 1937, out of a total of 895 Japanese naval aircraft, 563 were based ashore. Most were designed specifically to protect the Home Islands should the enemy somehow break through or avoid Japan's fleet and island barriers.[40]

However much Yamamoto and his colleagues in the Treaty faction yearned for peace, the army in Manchukuo and the equally radical naval leadership at Shanghai were rapidly undermining the American relationship. Christopher Thorne, the most careful and dispassionate student of the affair, concluded that the Shanghai incident of 1932 induced a sea change in American thinking toward Japan, especially within the navy. British and French thought was much slower to change. People, press, and governments in western Europe insisted either that Japan was perfectly correct in upholding its commercial rights against the heathen Chinese or that, even if it was wrong, it was both a nominal and, through League membership, a formal ally of the West and did not deserve censure.[41]

In the spring of 1933 the new Roosevelt administration dramatically changed the course of U.S. naval policy and in the process completed the estrangement of the Imperial Japanese Navy from its Western allies in the still recent Great War of 1914–1918. In one of his first acts as president, Franklin Roosevelt asked Congress for funds to slowly but steadily bring the American fleet up to existing treaty standards.

The material deterioration of the fleet since 1922 was as striking as that of Great Britain's, and the navy's chief aviator, Admiral William Moffett, and Congressman Carl Vinson, chairman of the House Committee on Naval Affairs, put their own, nearly identical, spin on the issue. Anyone could play the statistical game of comparative naval power, and if British experts and observers like Archibald Hurd and Lord Beatty saw matters one way, Moffett, Vinson, and the United States Navy drew other conclusions. Moffett claimed that the United States, not Britain, had been the big loser at both the Washington and the London naval conferences. The United States had scrapped 842,000 tons of warships, whereas Britain had scrapped only 448,000 tons and Japan 193,000 tons. France and Italy had not broken up a single unit. As a consequence, "Uncle Sam lost everything but his shirt tail." Moreover, throughout the 1920s the United States had built only forty warships, "less than one-fourth of the building done by Japan and a little more than one-fourth done by England. The British and Japanese programs have comprised practically every class of combatant ship, and have maintained their navies very nearly up to full treaty strength."[42] In an age of growing international tension and crisis, the time had long passed for America to reassert its naval might.

London and Tokyo reacted with incredulity and alarm to the U.S. construction program, which by January 1934 included three carriers, seven heavy and four light cruisers, thirty-two destroyers, and a half-dozen submarines. British foreign secretary John Simon was reported to be "much displeased" with the American decision to achieve practical equality with the Royal Navy. Britain hinted that it might build whatever ships it needed to remain numerically ahead of the United States. Rumor had it that London and Paris would formally request Washington to suspend its construction plans in the interest of international disarmament.[43]

The Japanese were even more unnerved. Roosevelt's initiative promised to thoroughly unhinge a barely acceptable status quo. Much as Tokyo detested the London Naval Treaty, it could live with it so long as the fleet remained at or near full treaty strength while the Americans remained substantially below it. By early 1933 the Fleet faction, led by navy minister Mineo Ōsumi, was insisting that "the smallest ratio that the navy would consider" was seven to ten in capital ships, eight to ten in heavy cruisers, and complete parity in all other warship classes. When Roosevelt came into office, the entire Japanese fleet was roughly 80 percent the size of its American rival, "and the Japanese expected to maintain that level" until the expiration of the current London naval agreement in December 1936. Now the Americans had seemingly thrown over all restraint. Osaka's *Asahi* newspaper argued that an American buildup to treaty limitations would place the world back in the anarchic environment of 1921 where the hand of each navy seemed to be against its neighbor. "It is to be hoped that the Roosevelt administration will listen to reason and halt a policy which would doom efforts at disarmament when the present limitation treaties lapse."[44]

When the Roosevelt administration showed no inclination to back off (naval construction was an integral part of the domestic New Deal recovery program, prompting one caustic critic, Senator Gerald P. Nye, to characterize the naval legislation as "a bill for the relief of the munitions makers of the United States"), the Fleet faction within the Japanese navy seized the initiative, and moderates like Yamamoto were overwhelmed and at least temporarily silenced. Katō Kanji and the others were buoyed by the general demand that quickly arose within the country for complete naval equality with the rest of the world. At the end of May 1933, the Foreign Ministry announced that Japan now regarded the London treaty as "unstable," and Japan formally notified its fellow signatories in the United States and Britain that "at the expiration of the London naval treaty in 1936 Tokyo will no longer be content with the naval ratio of 5:5:3." According to authoritative Western sources, "The Japanese capital lets it be known that . . . it will ask for parity in fleets with Washington and London." The following September the Japanese Naval Office made its position unmistakably clear: Japan would "build a Navy up to the limits of the London Naval Treaty, irrespective of cost," if the United States continued to build up to treaty specifications.[45]

Within the Japanese navy, the Fleet faction easily routed the rapidly waning Treaty faction. One report had it that Katō Kanji and his protégé, Admiral Nobumasa Suetsugo, "were holding meetings in the Akasaka geisha district and 'seducing' fleet commanders to their view." The press fell in line behind the Fleet faction. So, apparently, did the army, as it concluded a tacit quid pro quo deal with its service rival in which the sailors would support a continental imperial policy in exchange for army backing for a large—and costly—naval building program. With these victories in hand, a now fairly united navy went after the government. Minister Ōsumi used the threat of resignation to get his way: Japan now demanded total naval equality with all other powers; anything less was unacceptable. In August 1934 some senior officers went much further, insisting that "opinion in the combined fleet was united" behind a policy of treaty abrogation and return "to an independent defense." Just before Tokyo formally announced that it would not consider extending the Washington and London accords past 1936, the shrewd and knowledgeable Netherlands ambassador to Tokyo told his American colleague, Joseph Grew, that the Imperial Navy had become "imbued" with "patriotic and chauvinistic fervor and with a desire to emulate the deeds of the Army in order not to lose caste with the public." The Japanese fleet, the Dutchman added, "would be perfectly capable of descending upon and occupying Guam at a moment of crisis, or, indeed, at any other moment, regardless of ulterior consequences."[46]

Some months later Commander Takagi of the Imperial Navy submitted an article to the most prestigious British defense publication warning the world that ever since Matthew Perry's incursion eighty years before, "the people of Japan have an inherent and ever-present fear of outside interference." Takagi reminded his readers that the West had denied Japan the full fruits of victory in its wars with China and Russia and had generated "difficult problems" for Tokyo in the early postwar era before betraying Japan once again at the London Naval Conference. Great Britain and the United States together currently enjoyed a 170 percent advantage in warship tonnage, "yet there are some who contend that Japan's naval strength is excessive. Unless there is a readiness on the part of nations with superior navies, or which face few difficulties or dangers, to make voluntary sacrifices, the lesser Powers will be left in a state of such constant restlessness and insecurity that whatever benefits might otherwise accrue from disarmament would be lost."[47]

The Japanese Naval Ministry announced that nearly half the 1935 national budget would be expended on warship construction, amounting to at least fifty thousand tons per annum. Ōsumi boasted that Japan's newest light cruisers, like the rest of its naval arsenal, were superior to all comparable vessels in the West, "because the Japanese Navy has sacrificed comforts and the size of its crew quarters to obtain greater gun power and defense armaments." Exploiting the loophole in the London Naval Treaty that allowed Japan almost unlimited expansion in six-inch cruiser construction, naval strategists and architects, bewitched by the promise of night combat against an advancing enemy fleet, came up with the *Mogami* class, a powerfully armored set of four ships carrying no fewer than fifteen six-inch guns in five turrets, three forward and two aft. Laid down between 1931 and 1934 and completed between 1935 and 1937, the *Mogami*s were to be "capable of slugging it out with" the American and British eight-inch heavy cruisers. Moreover, these ships, like all Japanese cruisers and destroyers of the interwar period, carried a formidable number of torpedo tubes. Reflecting this sense and spirit of qualitative over quantitative superiority, the commander of the Combined Fleet, Admiral Sankichi Takahashi, told the National Defense Institute at the end of May 1935 that "the conviction must be implanted in the mind of every officer and man in the Japanese Navy that Japan will be the inevitable victor in any international conflict."[48]

Suspicion of American motives and objectives had become entrenched in the Japanese psyche. Whatever the Americans said or did was considered a direct threat to Japan. When the U.S. battle fleet temporarily transferred to the Atlantic in 1933 for what was officially described as training maneuvers and showing the flag along the East Coast, Tokyo denounced the move as a "trick to block appropriations for Japanese naval increases in 1935." A story in the Washington press in early November 1933 asserted that Japanese "propagandist agencies" had already begun to "deluge the interior" of the country with reports that the United States sought to block Japan's naval expansion in order to ensure naval supremacy "in view of our potential enmity."[49]

By this time, knowledgeable people sensed the inevitability of another and even more terrible world war. "You have this year to do in what you like," Ernest Hemingway wrote in September 1935 with barely concealed bitterness and cynicism. War would not even come "next August, nor next September; that is still too soon; they are still too prosperous from the way things pick up when armament factories start at near capacity; they never fight as long as money can still be made without." So the reader could plan that fishing or hunting trip, make love to his or her spouse, make a bet, take a drink whenever he wished, go to a ball game, have a picnic. "But the year after that or the year after that they fight. Then what happens to you?"[50] It was a question that was also being asked with increasing urgency in admiralties and navy departments across the globe.

CHAPTER 3

A Lion in Winter

BY THE EARLY THIRTIES, the British fleet was in deplorable condition. Although its battleships still looked impressive on parade or steaming in and out of harbor, its cruisers and destroyers were often in terrible shape. A few aged vessels had been replaced by a handful of successors, some, like *Kent,* inferior, and some, like the new six-inch-gun *Leanders*, of excellent design. Other flotillas, however, were filled with decrepit ships such as the nineteen C-class cruisers that had been hastily thrown together between 1913 and 1918 and had seen strenuous service in the Great War. Mounting four or five six-inch guns at best, they were poor sea keepers, and their material condition rendered them almost useless.[1]

Nor were many of the big ships any better. A Fleet Committee report of December 7, 1931, concluded that none of Britain's capital ships should be retained in service more than twenty-seven years, "and this is especially true of ships which were designed before the war or were built during the war to serve some special purposes" (the latter reference presumably to the handful of slow monitors with a few big guns designed solely for shore bombardment). The Admiralty committee concluded that it would be "very unsafe to contemplate replacement at a rate of less than one ship a year. But this involves an increase in [annual naval] Estimates of (say) four or five million pounds a year." Britain's position with respect to cruisers, destroyers, and submarines was stable, the report concluded in the face of powerful evidence to the contrary, "provided that we adhere steadily to our present [modest building] programme." But "if any further postponement of replacement" of capital ships "takes place in 1932 or 1933, it is impossible to say what large sums may not have to be spent in order that the old and in some cases semi-obsolete ships may be kept capable of continuing in service. Such a course would prove most unsatisfactory and most uneconomical."[2] But at a time of deepening economic crisis due to the extension of America's Great Depression internationally, the money for replacement of capital ships was simply not available. The five *Royal Sovereigns,* which had been laid down just before and during the Great War as follow-ons to the *Queen Elizabeth* class, and were comparably armed, continued in frontline service until the last months of World War II.

The December 1931 committee report warned of other potentially crippling deficiencies as well, noting "our present serious position in regard to reserves of war material—i.e. Anti-submarine booms, Oil Fuel reserves, new and improved anti-aircraft guns for the Fleet, mines and mining stores, minesweeping stores, ammunition for auxiliary vessels of all descriptions, anti-submarine equipment for auxiliary patrol vessels, etc." The committee urged that such deficiencies be "ameliorated" by an annual program "of replenishment and upgrade." British naval experts and enthusiasts were in equal despair. The London accords may have delighted the Americans, but many in England viewed them with as much alarm as did the warlords of Tokyo. An early reaction came from David Beatty who in July 1930 submitted a motion in the upper house of Parliament stating that "the one nation to whom sea power meant its existence was the only power to make any disarmament or any reduction, and that to such an extent to render us impotent and incapable of protecting that which we have, and of maintaining control over the connecting links of our varied and far-flung Empire."[3]

The following spring Archibald Hurd, long the dean of British naval analysts, told a gathering of naval architects that, thanks to both the Washington and the London naval agreements, British naval tonnage would have been reduced by nearly half (more than 46 percent) in the twenty-two years between 1914 and December 1936 (when the London agreements expired). Personnel would decline by more than 37 percent. "On the other hand over the same period, the fleet of the United States will show an increase of tonnage of 30.1 per cent and that of Japan an increase of 36.7 per cent, while Italy will reach a strength of 18.7 per cent greater." Moreover, under the new London treaty, Great Britain would have to scrap five older capital ships that "otherwise would have remained on the active strength till December 1936." Two years later Oscar Parkes, the editor of *Jane's Fighting Ships,* abandoned his publication's traditional international orientation and Olympian calm to castigate His Majesty's government, and the following year, 1934, the editors of the equally prestigious *Brassey's Naval and Shipping Annual* expressed equal alarm, though in a more restrained fashion.[4]

After noting the rapid naval expansion of both the United States and Japan together with the darkening scene in Germany, Parkes concluded that "a further whittling down of the British Navy" could no longer be tolerated as a sop to maintain the peace. "That we have allowed our naval strength to diminish to the danger point has been stressed by the First Lord [of the Admiralty]." Parkes took exception to the navy's belief that Britain possessed a sufficiency of cruisers and light forces so long as the London treaty was generally adhered to. "In point of fact the Navy could no longer guarantee the safety of our overseas supplies of food and oil in case of war, as the cruiser forces available are pitifully inadequate both in numbers and strength." Because British politicians had been so eager to maintain the peace and the capital ship–building "holiday" that seemed to guarantee it, "our representatives at the London Naval Conference" had made "one-sided concessions . . . with the result that our constructors have been faced with the very disagreeable necessity of providing us with ships definitely inferior to their 'opposite numbers' abroad." Britain's hope that it could lead the world to smaller cruisers by example had failed utterly. Parliament had agreed to a modest replacement program that included the construction of two big nine thousand–ton cruisers and a host of smaller *Leander-* and *Orion-*class ships, all mounting six-inch guns. But Britain would have to do far more, Parkes warned. "The desire for Peace may be worldwide, but rapidly growing and virile Nations" demanded new markets and fresh territories for their restless surplus populations. Peace in Europe might be preserved by further pacts and treaties, but the situation in the seas and lands beyond the Continent remained perilously uncertain.

Not only was Britain woefully deficient in both numbers and capability of traditional warships, as Parkes maintained, but it had also failed to keep pace with the breathtaking advances in naval air that even at this early date gave promise of one day revolutionizing the war at sea. Britain had pioneered in placing aircraft on floating airfields. But by the time *Argus* and *Furious* took to the waves during the last year of the Great War, British naval aviation had already suffered a series of catastrophic reverses from which it never fully recovered. When the Germans mounted two effective daylight air raids against London in 1917, the cabinet panicked in the face of significant civilian casualties and promptly established a commission under South African general Jan Smuts to hastily review national security policies and objectives. Two months later Smuts and his commission produced a report that transformed British strategic thought. "The day may not be far off," Smuts warned, "when aerial operations, with their devastation of industrial and population centres on a vast scale, may become the principal operations of war, to which the older forms of military and naval operations may become secondary and subordinate."[5] Following so soon after the unprecedented German air raids, Smuts's report suddenly made "strategic air power" the rage in government circles and among a wide segment of the public. At a moment when national resources had shrunk alarmingly, it was inevitable that the intense competition for pilots and planes between the Royal Naval Air Service and the Royal Flying Corps (RFC) must result in a victory on one side or the other.

Early in 1918 a series of counterraids against German towns by British aircraft in France carried the war to the enemy in the way that no battleship or machine gun ever could. His Majesty's government was readily convinced by Hugh Trenchard and other zealots within the RFC that the quickest way to end the war was to place all aviation resources in the hands of the strategic bombers. The government quickly established an Air Ministry and a Royal Air Force to carry out Trenchard's vision. The ministry promptly placed enormous pressure on the flyers within the Royal Naval Air Service to transfer to the RAF. Most did, killing the impetus for an independent and assertive naval air arm. After several months of trying to accommodate the new order, elements in the navy familiar with the Air Service argued strenuously for its return. "If Air Units are to effectively work for and with the Navy," wrote Admiral Stanley Colville, commander in chief at Portsmouth, "it is most necessary to keep up the Naval atmosphere and continue to carry out the purely Naval and seafaring work necessary with Seaplanes, Airships, Kite Balloons, and even Aeroplanes which are carrying out anti-submarine work, in a Naval and seamanlike manner." Whereas Air Service personnel, air and ground crew alike, had grown up and learned to operate in a "naval atmosphere," the Royal Air Force "has . . . adopted methods that are very much more military than they are Naval, so that it is now necessary to control and administer these Naval Operating Air Units in an almost entirely military manner." Colville had a point. Flyers either at sea or flying over the sea had to develop and sustain a "seamanlike" attitude; this would become ever clearer as seaplanes and their tenders metamorphosed into full-fledged aircraft carriers with a mix of several thousand sailors (ships' company) and air-group personnel. The brand-new Royal Air Force would have none of it. "The changes of environment and duties between the various branches of Royal Air Force work is no greater than the change from Submarines to Battleship life, or from a Gunboat on the China Station to the Grand Fleet," riposted Royal Air Force general R. M. Groves, newly transferred from the Naval Air Service.[6]

Once in control, the air force promptly began whittling down its naval component. An Admiralty memorandum to the War Cabinet on August 31, 1918, complained that "after discussion with the Air Ministry, a reduction of the original Admiralty estimate (to a total of 130 squadrons) was agreed upon, but it is feared that the further reduction now proposed (to a total of 95 squadrons) will render it impossible to deal adequately with the submarine menace."[7]

For a time thereafter, it appeared that the fledgling RAF might be broken back down into the Royal Flying Corps (land) and the Royal Naval Air Service. But Trenchard and his colleagues fought strenuously against such a prospect, and they were helped immeasurably by the sailors—led by Beatty—who consistently and stupidly asserted the continued primacy of the battleship, thereby implicitly negating the need for a naval air corps.[8]

Not until 1924 did the Admiralty at last awake to the realization that although the navy possessed a half-dozen small and medium-size carriers, it had no dedicated aircraft to place aboard them. In April a government committee under Lord Arthur Balfour induced the RAF to establish within its ranks a small Fleet Air Arm. But even here the navy once again unwittingly conspired in its own ruin. In the midtwenties the RAF Fleet Air Arm formed a Torpedo Development Unit at Gosport, England, where for a number of years a handful of flyers took a rigorous four-month torpedo training course. By all accounts the training was excellent and the flyers quite enthusiastic. But in the mid- and late thirties, the concept of aerial torpedo attacks at sea was bitterly contested and contemptuously dismissed in private meetings and the public press by the insistent advocates of the battleship. Capital-ship designers believed they had taken fully into account the at best ambiguous lessons derived from Billy Mitchell's antics. Battleship champions argued that the new capital ships on the world's drawing boards were not only sufficiently armored to withstand both aerial bombing and torpedo attacks but also sufficiently armed with small, deadly, rapid-firing antiaircraft guns to beat off or break up any aerial attack before it could fully materialize.[9]

Farsighted naval officers who grasped the frightening potential of aviation both as a seaborne weapon and a land-based threat to battle fleets were appalled. Andrew Cunningham, the 1918 destroyer captain who would become Admiral of the Fleet Viscount Cunningham and first sea lord during World War II, later wrote of the "ghastly failure" of placing naval aviation within the confines of the RAF and the Air Ministry. "As the Air Estimates . . . were ruthlessly shorn" in the late twenties and early thirties, "the Naval Air Arm became a sort of Cinderella, starved, neglected, and nearly forgotten. It was not until 1937, after a severe and protracted struggle on the part of the Admiralty . . . that ship-borne aircraft again came under the full operational and administrative control of the Royal Navy with whom they would work in war. It was only just in time."[10]

In fact, it was too late. Throughout the twenties and early thirties, the RAF controlled aircraft design and procurement, and although it experimented with torpedo planes and attacks, it refused to develop a dive-bomber for the navy or a carrier-based fighter plane capable of effectively dueling with enemy land-based aircraft off the Atlantic and Mediterranean coasts of Europe. In the early thirties RAF designers at last produced a torpedo-scout plane, but it was already obsolete. The Swordfish could stagger through the air at little more than a hundred miles an hour at best, slower than U.S. and Japanese aircraft that had been in the air for a half decade. British pilots were forced to fly these pathetic "string bags" throughout much of World War II. Indeed, as late as 1942, bi-planes constituted the bulk of the attack-aircraft complement aboard British carriers.[11] Thereafter, the Royal Navy procured ever larger numbers of U.S.-designed single-winged fighter, bomber, and torpedo planes to bring their carrier air groups up to modern standards.

The British response to the new medium of airpower was not so much misplaced as it was too limited. To maintain its predominant power position in the world, Britain required both a strategic air force based in England and a powerful air arm based on large fleet carriers to guard British communication and transportation lines across the world ocean. It got one but not the other.

Perhaps Smuts, Trenchard, and such postwar zealots as Italian general Giulio Douhet and American Billy Mitchell were too extreme in their championship of the bomber as the supreme weapon of war. But there could be little doubt after 1917 that both the dirigible and the airplane had destroyed Britain's formerly impregnable position off the coast of Europe. "Already on the morning after Jutland the entire gun-power of the British battle-fleet had proved insufficient to drive off a single German Zeppelin," Fletcher Pratt wrote in 1938, "and compared to the airplane the Zeppelin was a thing of gossamer, ready to burst into flames at a touch."[12] All of Britain's expensive battleships and cruisers could do little to prevent an enemy air assault against Britain's towns or an enemy parachute invasion of British soil.

But if airpower had destroyed Britain's invulnerability, it had also enhanced the island kingdom's strategic position. A powerful long-range bomber force based in Great Britain posed an ever present threat to ambitious continental powers. Without landing a single soldier on French or Dutch beaches, Britain would always be at the back of a European aggressor, ready to project devastating amounts of airpower onto continental battlefields and into continental cities. Indeed, if Trenchard and Douhet were correct, and many thought they were, Britain could achieve victory in a future war through airpower alone. This new possibility at once transformed and dramatically diminished the role of the Royal Navy. It now seemed that the Admiralty's only task would be to shield British shores from direct invasion (and even here a defending air force might do a better job) and to protect the imperial lifelines in the western approaches and out on the world ocean to ensure the continued flow of supplies and matériel that Britain required to sustain a devastating aerial offensive over Europe.

This scenario served as a deadly justification for the further decline of the navy. Britain's beaches could be just as readily defended from invasion by many cruisers, destroyers, and land-based fighters and bombers as by ponderous battleships and expensive, mission-duplicative aircraft carriers. A fleet might be needed out in the Far East against Japan, critics admitted, but it could be properly protected by land-based aircraft deploying from aerodromes at Hong Kong and in Malaya. And the chief role of the navy in any future conflict, such critics argued, would clearly be the suppression and destruction of enemy U-boats along the imperial trading routes from Canada, South Africa, and Australia. Even here the RAF's Coastal Command would presumably be an equal partner in the western approaches. Under the circumstances, the notion of deploying large, fragile aircraft carriers with their comparatively limited capabilities and great development and operating costs seemed a criminal indulgence to the RAF and its many friends in British society and the government. In the fourteen years after the Washington Conference the Royal Air Force fought viciously and successfully against any efforts either to build new aircraft carriers or to develop a distinctive carrier doctrine. As the ten-year rule fastened an ever tighter grip on British strategic thought and fiscal policy in the late twenties and early thirties, naval aviation languished and the Royal Navy stumbled along with its half-dozen carriers of dubious quality and a mere handful of carrier aircraft that were far below even that standard.[13]

Lingering international reputation and public affection at home might have allowed the Royal Navy to maintain a global empire with aging ships and a wholly inadequate air arm had it not been for the "mutiny" at Invergordon that exposed the rot at the heart of an ostensibly mighty sea service.

Even during the final stages of the war, despite the terrifying example of the 1918 mutiny within the German High Seas Fleet, the Admiralty had paid little attention to legitimate complaints from mess decks and dockyards about low pay and poor conditions. In the first years of the peace, British sailors failed to share proportionately in the meager pay raises accorded to government workers but did suffer disproportionately from periodic government pay cuts. In September 1918 Lionel Yexley, the longtime seamen's champion on "civvy street," dispatched a memorandum directly to the cabinet begging for official recognition of the prewar lower-deck societies as official avenues for dialogue and redress of grievances. He was ignored. With the Red revolution in Russia just completed, Britain's comfortable classes once again spied radicalism everywhere in society and the armed services.[14]

In January 1919 serious unrest broke out in the minesweeper flotilla of the Grand Fleet when several crews refused to go to sea, and by the next year the lower-deck societies, which remained in legal limbo, began quietly reaching out to the radical elements in the civilian trade union movement and elsewhere. Radical veterans' groups like the National Union of Ex-Servicemen began buttonholing sailors on the streets of London and the dockyard towns, and there was much subdued talk on mess decks, fantails, and superstructures of strikes for better pay and working conditions. A substantial number of "electrical artificers" openly joined the Electrical Trade Union. The alarmed commander in chief of the Atlantic Fleet wrote that the lower-deck movement "was becoming more centralised, more powerful," and Lord Beatty openly expressed the fear of many in the service that loyalty was being undercut by revolution.[15]

The Admiralty struck back quickly. An official Order on Discipline was published in the autumn of 1920, and agents were sent into the mess decks and shoreside canteens to spy. Thereafter, an occasional example would be made of someone, "even when only on suspicion, to keep the rest in line." In 1921 two ratings (the equivalent of U.S. Navy petty officers) on the new battle cruiser *Hood* were court-martialed for mutiny for allegedly displaying red bunting in their mess. Six years later an ordinary seaman was discharged as a radical agitator after having been seen visiting a communist bookstore, even though a search of his person and effects turned up no communist literature.[16] By this time conditions on civvy street were known to be grim, and however awful the navy might be, it at least provided a job and shelter. Yexley backed away from support of the sailors, torn between ancient allegiances and a newfound belief, generally shared throughout Britain, that any impulse for significant social advancement had to be inspired by the newly installed "Bolshies" in Moscow.

Throughout the mid- and late twenties, authorities did little beyond intimidation to address seamen's grievances. There were persistent rumors of impending pay cuts that kept the lower deck in turmoil. With the war over, rental rates for navy families ashore were uncontrolled by government regulation, as were railroad tickets. Pay was still incredibly low at a time when the Royal Navy, like all the other sea services, was becoming increasingly "brainy," as technology and machinery steadily grew more complex. Key ratings and their families suffered abominably from often desperate living conditions. When rumors of a proposed pay cut reached the lower decks in August 1923 and the seamen's societies reacted angrily, the authorities cracked down hard. Admiralty representatives appeared at society meetings at Devonport and Chatham, the citadels of agitation, and, dismissing expressions of grievance, proceeded to read out Article 11 of the Articles of War and the Order on Discipline, warning the radical sailors "to keep within the bounds of King's Regulations."[17] When this failed to dissuade the most militant leaders of the sailors' movement, several were arrested and thrown out of the service after doing hard time.

Matters did not improve significantly in the following years. Anthony Carew, the closest student of the Royal Navy's lower ranks in the twentieth century, recounts two incidents from 1930:

> In the Mediterranean Fleet the battleship *Revenge,* previously a happy ship, became a very unhappy one overnight when a new captain, J. A. G. Troup, took command. . . .
>
> From the onset he presented himself as a strict disciplinarian and told the crew in effect that he would make them or break them. He worked the hands exceptionally hard, and defaulters were punished severely, especially leave-breakers. When the ship was at Golfe Juan men who had broken leave during the previous six months were not granted the twenty-four hours general leave that was customary when visiting Riviera ports. The up-shot, in the time-honored tradition of the service, was a deliberate mass breaking of leave. Some men deserted, and Troup was jeered when he went ashore. As the men had hoped, the incident led to an Admiralty inquiry, something which complaints through the regular channels were unlikely ever to achieve.
>
> A more celebrated case occurred a few months later on the submarine depot ship *Lucia.* The *Lucia* had long been an unhappy ship. Though she was away twice a year on cruises, leave was only given as though she were a harbour vessel; in general, less leave was granted than in other Devonport ships. She had little in the way of recreational facilities. The crew were subjected to many petty annoyances: just before the incident an order curtailing the hours for smoking on the upper deck had particularly annoyed them, and meal hours were often foreshortened. The men were worked hard, and the day they refused duty was the fourth successive one of extra work. It was a Sunday, normally a rest day. Weekend leave had already been

cancelled but they expected leave on Sunday afternoon. When, instead, they were piped to turn to and clean ship in readiness for painting they stayed below and closed the hatches. Twenty-seven were arrested. Leading Seaman William Carter was dismissed from the service and four others were court-martialed, with sentences of up to six months hard labour.[18]

The public reacted with a storm of protest, and the officers involved were sacked. The seamen's prison terms were commuted, though the navy insisted on making an example of Carter and his dismissal stood. But the officers of the King's Navy never understood in these years that with the lower-deck societies suppressed, there were simply no avenues available to intelligent and often highly articulate men to protest injustices or vent their anger over occasionally intolerable conditions.

Indeed, the upper levels of the officer class refused to believe that there *were* intolerable conditions. Admiral Ernle Chatfield had entered the Royal Navy as a thirteen-year-old cadet in 1886. Son of an admiral, he was, in Andrew Gordon's felicitous phrase, a member of the Royal Navy aristocracy that "could take good appointments more or less for granted." He first attracted the attention of senior staff when he took a destroyer up the Thames at twenty knots for a cricket match at Greenwich. Chatfield had been Beatty's flag captain in World War I but had escaped the turmoil and wrath over Jutland that destroyed his colleague Flag Lieutenant Ralph Seymour. Thereafter, the good appointments kept coming. Chatfield was made commander in chief of the Atlantic Fleet in 1929 and the following year moved on to the Mediterranean, where he served for two and a half years as William Fisher's predecessor before taking the inevitable next step up to first sea lord in February 1933. Chatfield was, by the standards of the day, a decent as well as indubitably competent man whose personal and official correspondence reflects a deep mistrust and dislike of the Americans based on the uneasy realization that they could outbuild, though not outsail or outfight, the Royal Navy.[19]

At the end of October 1930 Chatfield wrote the first lord in London, expounding at great length on the high morale and professionalism both within his old (Atlantic) and new (Mediterranean) commands. All this talk of turmoil and unhappiness on the lower deck was the work of troublemakers ashore, especially in the press. He condemned newspaper attacks that emphasized the high desertion rate aboard *Revenge* following its Riviera visit and "the malicious and unjustified attack on Captain Troup" that constituted nothing less than a "general studied insult to H.M. Navy." "When the general conduct of the Fleet is so fine," Chatfield added, "and the state of zeal and discipline is so high, a strong feeling of resentment is apparent" against "a quarter [that is, the press] where the Navy is always entirely ignored except when an opportunity occurs to insult it."[20]

The long-simmering crises on the lower decks over discipline, working conditions, and pay at long last burst to the surface in September 1931 when His Majesty's government, under pressure from the private sector to cut costs in the face of mounting economic distress, announced a broad pay reduction for civil servants and the armed forces. In an act of stunning insensitivity, the Admiralty decided that naval pay and allowances were to be reduced immediately, severely, and disproportionately. The lowest-paid seamen would suffer the most—a full 25 percent cut—while officers' pay would be reduced an average 11 percent. "The cuts were regarded" by the lower deck "as a breach of contract, a repudiation of the oft-repeated assurance by politicians and the Admiralty that the 1919 rates would remain." Good men who had served valorously with the Grand Fleet at Dogger Bank and Jutland and who then had suffered a dozen years of scorn and neglect had had enough.[21]

Agitation for public-sector pay cuts had been circulating in England for some time when the Atlantic Fleet reached its various home bases in late July and officers and men were detached for their traditional one-month summer leave. Sailors and ratings were thus able to follow the unfolding story at home, without any intimidating interference by their officers. For weeks, rumors flooded the country about the cuts, but the authorities remained quiet. When the cuts were at last announced in early September, the men were back aboard their ships at Invergordon, preparing for autumn maneuvers. With inexcusable stupidity, the Admiralty, which had been fully warned of impending lower-deck agitation by knowledgeable observers (including, perhaps, several seamen's wives), had allowed the news to become public first through the press rather than the regular channels of Fleet Orders. Moreover, when the Fleet Orders were finally issued, a supplementary Admiralty letter of explanation "was not happily worded, and in ships whose Captains tried to use it, in conjunction with the Fleet Orders, to explain the cuts the effect produced on the men was not persuasive or tranquillising."[22]

The mess decks of His Majesty's ships and the naval canteens ashore erupted in protest. Angry informal meetings were held on nearly every battleship and cruiser in the fleet, and knowledgeable officers realized that trouble was brewing. Matters swiftly got out of hand as agitators brewed up a storm of fury. "The real significance of the Invergordon story," wrote one enlisted man who was there, "is simple enough to put into two short sentences. The day the Atlantic Fleet assembled at Invergordon (Friday, 11 September 1931), mutiny was as far from any man's mind as the idea of flying to the moon on a bat's back. But within two days the whole Fleet was ready to mutiny—or to stop work. It makes no difference what one calls it, it amounted to the same thing."[23]

Andrew Cunningham, then ashore at Chatham, later argued that the unrest was centered in the big ships and was the result largely of their comparative size and impersonality where officers simply could not know their men well. "In the destroyers, where officers lived at close quarters with the men and knew them much better, the ship's company was usually a happy family and no trouble occurred." This was beside the point, and, however reluctantly, Cunningham and his colleagues knew it. Even twenty years later he could only grudgingly admit that "the men were labouring under a grievance which was not without some justification."[24]

At Invergordon on Cromarty Firth in the Scottish Highlands, which had become a major fleet anchorage after the 1914–1918 war, the big ships were due to get under way for sea between 0800 and 1000 hours on Tuesday, September 15, 1931. Individual meetings of petty officers held on the various ships and ashore the previous weekend had reached agreement that if the flagship *Valiant* refused to sail, "the rest would 'chuck their hand in.'" At dawn on the fifteenth, the normal time for seamen to turn to and scrub the decks, only *Hood* and cruisers *Norfolk* and *York* could report a full muster. "In *Valiant* the petty officers and a few leading seamen presented themselves for duty, but no seamen turned to. Only seventy-five of *Rodney*'s seamen were present. Sixty of *Nelson*'s were absent from duty. Fifty-seven were missing" in the cruiser *Dorsetshire*, "while in *Adventure* the hands fell in reluctantly."[25] As Anthony Carew notes, the men of Britain's Atlantic Fleet had demonstrated a remarkable collective inclination to strike.

At morning quarters before the beginning of the forenoon watch, some captains attempted to address their crews in an effort to restore order and discipline. They failed. All eyes remained fixed on *Valiant,* whose anchor party refused to work and whose small-boat crews claimed to be experiencing "difficulty" bringing their tiny vessels aboard. As 0800 passed and *Valiant* continued to remain at anchor, a ripple of cheering echoed throughout the anchorage. What might have charitably been labeled a strike had now become a mutiny. In the next hour and a half, some ships did sail, but at 0931 they were recalled to the anchorage while the men waited to see what would happen.

The Admiralty simply waited out the malcontents, while the cabinet flatly refused to consider rescinding the pay cut. For thirty-six hours the fleet lay immobilized. On the evening of September 16 the crew of *Valiant* at last fell in for orders, and the mutiny was for all practical purposes over. Less than thirty-six hours later, on the other side of the world, agents of the Kwantung Army would set off the blast on the railway line to Mukden that began the Manchurian Incident and the world's march to another great war.

The men of the Royal Navy had hoped to make a point: that a work stoppage, or mutiny, "call it what you will," in Len Wincott's phrase, "was their only alternative to allowing the cuts to become operational and thereby reducing the Navy to the level of a fleet of Greek raisin boats and their families to poverty." Wincott, a rating aboard the cruiser *Norfolk,* added that the Admiralty had, "without the least protest, thrown to the wolves ninety thousand men, the bulk of whom had signed their lives to the service at a very tender age and for whose care and welfare they [the Lords of the Admiralty] were responsible."[26]

The purblind bureaucrats of Whitehall refused to take the point. Even as the fleet steamed out of Invergordon, deliberately dispersed to separate anchorages, First Lord of the Admiralty Austen Chamberlain told Parliament there would be no victimization of the men involved in the protest. In fact, some two dozen ratings were subsequently dismissed, along with several commanding officers of the big ships, some of whom Captain Roskill suggests were deliberately sacrificed. In the crisis atmosphere of the time when any popular protest was instinctively defined as a conspiracy, the navy's intelligence service worked feverishly to infiltrate the lower decks and seek out agitators. Soon the inspectors had compiled a list of 120 men throughout the fleet who they charged had played a major part in the sit-down. Some were pressured immediately to leave the service. Len Wincott was one of them. Radicalized by the Admiralty's policies, he went ashore in 1932 and two years later emigrated to the Soviet Union, where he lived for the next forty years, eleven of them spent in a Stalinist labor camp. The sincere efforts of Cunningham and a handful of other fundamentally decent officers to defuse the crisis by inviting seamen and ratings into their offices and cabins to air grievances and purge emotions were undercut by "the blind reaction of the Admiralty," which steadfastly refused to make firsthand contact with the ratings and seamen who for more than three centuries had served it so well.[27]

Invergordon led to a few very modest improvements in the lives of Jack Tar and his struggling family. Pay reductions remained in force, along with the sporadically and whimsically harsh discipline. Despite occasional complaints from isolated elements in Parliament, most notably Lady Astor, that certain commands within the navy were *"neglecting the sailor's wives,"* the seamen and ratings who served George V, Edward VIII, and George VI struggled to survive on reduced wages for four years before the national economy improved sufficiently to allow the government to restore some of the cuts. By 1938 efforts had been made to increase enlisted men's allowances, especially marriage allotments, as well as the amount of home leave granted to the men of the overseas fleets.[28] But naval intelligence never let up its relentless pursuit of alleged wrongdoers on the lower decks. Its agents scoured the fleet right down to 1939 looking for malcontents and provocateurs, further reducing morale and efficiency. After years of resistance, a reluctant Admiralty was at last induced to conduct a thorough review of enlisted life in the autumn of 1936 based on a "persistent fear that, despite the regulations" put in effect after Invergordon, "men might combine to present a united front." When it finally came, the review attracted no fewer than five thousand requests for relief, but it was undercut by the government's decision that major economic issues such as pay and allowances were not topics for negotiation. Admiralty responses to the lower-deck requests were slow in coming; the first grievance was not addressed until February 1937, and "the process was still not complete on the eve of war in July 1939," despite some sanctimonious utterances by the comfortable classes and their spokesmen within the navy that "the British sailor of to-day must be treated as a human being capable of thought and feeling."[29]

The senior officers of Britain's senior service were horrified by Invergordon, though they tried to present a front of business-as-usual to the public once the immediate crisis had passed. Chatfield addressed a circular message to his Mediterranean Fleet sailors a month after the mutiny expressing his "high appreciation of your conduct at a time of severe trial." They had not joined their radical mates at home in defying authority, and he commended them for maintaining traditional "loyalty and discipline," especially with respect to the airing of grievances (that is, sending complaints formally up through the chain of command). But Chatfield did not try to disguise from the fleet his sense of "the very serious occurrences in certain ships at Invergordon." Although "the Petty Officers, Noncommissioned Officers and Men" of the Mediterranean station

> have just cause to pride themselves on their conduct during a difficult occasion, we must all, as part of the personnel of the Navy, share the discredit that has fallen upon it. . . . It is our task, together, to shorten the period of loss of trust in us, to redeem our good name, to restore our Service to the high place it has previously deservedly held, and to prove that the confidence of the Country in the British Navy, which has been so severely shaken, can be renewed.[30]

After the praise, reassurances, and exhortations came the inevitable recrimina-
tions. Who had been responsible for this appalling collapse of morale? Chatfield was flooded with letters from colleagues charging the civilian bean counters
(to use a term from a later era) within the Admiralty for being so coldly insensitive to Jack Tar's needs. Chatfield absorbed these arguments, then burnished
them and passed them on to Whitehall in a seven-page letter of his own. The
Admiralty had allowed itself to be stampeded into announcing pay cuts by a
panicky cabinet responding to a worsening national economy. Civilian drudges
in the Accountant General's Department and Naval Branch had compounded
the felony by working out an inequitable "scheme," then failed to warn the Admiralty Board of its inevitably unhappy consequences. "Between you and me,"
Chatfield wrote to the deputy chief of the Naval Staff, "and as I have said to the
First Sea Lord, there is a strong feeling afloat that the *Admiralty* are unsympa-
thetic." The first sea lord and the Admiralty Staff would have to stand up to
civil authority, and especially the Treasury, if the financial burdens on the fleet
were not to continue to worsen.[31]

Finances were only part of the problem. Relations between the upper and
lower decks of the Royal Navy were equally to blame. Chatfield attempted to
meet this problem head-on, and in doing so revealed just how wide was the
chasm between officers and men. He wrote to the deputy chief of the Naval
Staff:

> I think the [Admiralty] Board are mistaken in the notion you imply that if
> officers had been in closer touch with their men this would not have hap-
> pened. I do not believe any closer touch could exist between officers and
> men in this Fleet, and probably all Fleets abroad, than is the case. There *is*
> close touch and that is the advantage of 2½ year commissions [that is, ser-
> vice in overseas fleets] with no [home] leave periods. The touch is proba-
> bly as close as it ever can be between *Englishmen* of different classes. We
> are not a confiding race and never shall be, and even officers know little of
> each other's private affairs.

Matters were different but no better in the "Home Ports and Atlantic Fleet."
"With ships broken up for leave periods for three months annually, with the
Welfare Committees, with their very doubtful influence on discipline and
contentment, the Barracks with no real touch at all between officers and men,
young Divisional Officers haven't a dog's chance." In a subsequent message
responding to an Admiralty circular letter, Chatfield argued that "Cadets *must*

be given some technical training and become much better acquainted with life on the Lower Deck before being rated Midshipmen." Past that point he would not go. When Lieutenant Commander Kenneth Evans's book *The Mutiny at Invergordon* appeared in 1937 with its emphasis on the loyalty of Jack Tar to his officers and the "deplorably handled" matter of the pay cuts, Chatfield (by then first sea lord) and his subordinate fleet commanders became dreadfully upset, believing that the book would give aid and comfort to Britain's rivals not only in Germany and Italy but in France, Scandinavia, and the United States as well. The Admiralty tried to suppress the book but failed. It also flatly refused to open its files or records to the author, whom Chatfield characterized as a mere "journalist."[32]

Chatfield's colleagues were less charitable. Several months after the mutiny, Admiral William Fisher, then Chatfield's chief subordinate in the Mediterranean, complained that Invergordon would never have happened except for the "Gentle Annieism" approach that too many officers had shown their men, especially the many incompetent petty officers. "The result of this mental attitude on the part of some Senior Officers," Fisher continued, "shows itself in the increasing tendency of the men to imagine they have a legitimate grievance if they are called upon to carry out any orders outside the ordinary accepted routine, or if their leave is curtailed for service reasons." Fisher advocated a sharp tightening of the petty officer's course at Portsmouth Barracks to prepare the men to really lead. They, not the officer class, should have control and real command over the nonrated men, with whom they should no longer be allowed to "hob-nob."[33] Fisher succeeded Chatfield as commander in chief of the Mediterranean Fleet in early 1933 and promptly began implementing several of the proposals he had made to his predecessor, in particular elaborating and enforcing the responsibility of division officers to see to their men's welfare and morale.

The Atlantic Fleet was a different matter. In mid-May 1932 Admiral Sir John Kelly, who had assumed command, wrote to the secretary of the first lord of the Admiralty that he was "now satisfied, generally, with the discipline in Ships, though individual Ships and 'Ship Spirit' vary directly with the leadership and interest shown by the Officers." Kelly warned, however, that the Admiralty should be "under no illusions that the Atlantic—or Home—Fleet is as if Invergordon had never happened. Invergordon *has* happened, and—as well as making a blot on the escutcheon—has left a wound which has barely cicatrized, and which, if not handled very firmly here, tenderly there, will be liable to ooze, if not break down, for a very long time to come." While the Royal Navy might not be standing on a precipice, it was "at the top of a hill whose slope was formed by the success, in the Men's point of view, of the Mutiny. On shore, discipline still falls short, by a good deal, of the standard I require."[34]

As late as the summer of 1937, Dudley Pound, who had assumed command in the Mediterranean, wrote to the Admiralty of his unhappiness "about reports of unrest in 'Warspite' [then with the Home Fleet] getting into the papers, although it is denied in the next paragraph, it doesn't do the service any good. It is a rotten start for a ship [that had just come out of a prolonged period of overhaul] and I do not think [Captain] Crutchley is quite happy about some of the men, but he and [Executive Officer] Everett will know how to deal with them."[35]

As the correspondence of Fisher and Pound suggests, leading political circles in England and the higher echelons of the naval and military high commands counted absolutely on the fact that Jack Tar and his Missus together with the enlisted people of Britain's small army retained a touching loyalty to Crown and country during all the years of abuse and neglect.

Deficient in ships, leadership, morale, and vision, Britain confronted ever more formidable problems after Invergordon. Chief among them was Japan, though many in the Royal Navy wondered whether the Yanks with their own rebuilding program and their steadfast unwillingness to understand Britain's cruiser problem were any better friends. Could London allow Far Eastern events to dictate a permanent rift with the old Japanese ally? Whitehall's Defence Requirements Committee thought not, and in its report of early 1934 urged that "every effort" be made to "resume former cordial relations with Japan." One committee member argued that "entanglement with the U.S.A." constituted "the worst of our deficiencies." Sir Warren Fisher, the permanent undersecretary at the British Treasury, boldly urged his colleagues not only to "sacrifice American friendship" if need be but even to "include, if necessary, preparations for hostilities against America—in order to regain the more valuable friendship of Japan." The ambassador in Tokyo, Sir F. O. Lindley, urged the same course. Britain's Far Eastern policy, he cabled home, "should be based, as in the past, on the principle of friendship with Japan. Any other policy imperils our whole Eastern possessions." His Majesty's government should be under no illusion of the costs of such a policy. Japan would come first in British calculations, the United States second. Moreover, Lindley concluded, Japan was probably, even then, looking for a possible alliance with Nazi Germany, even as it struggled to maintain cordial relations with London and Washington. Eventually, whatever chances there were to forge the new kind of policy favored by Lindley and Fisher foundered on the rocks of irresolvable Anglo-Japanese conflicts over international trade.[36] But Anglo-American relations had reached a nadir not seen since the grim days of 1919–1920. International collective security was breaking down and a new age of anarchy loomed, one in which the Royal Navy might find itself bereft of any significant allies at sea. And then Adolf Hitler appeared with an apparent solution.

The Western democracies understandably panicked when Germany openly announced rearmament in the spring of 1935. France, still with the largest European army by far, abruptly compromised its Little Entente alliances in eastern Europe designed to hem Germany in and dallied with the bitterly hated and feared Soviet Union in an ultimately feckless effort to contain surging Nazi power. The French also extended military conscription from eighteen to twenty-four months to cover manpower shortfalls at a time when the birthrate was in decline. Hitler immediately picked up on these gestures to claim that Germany was being humiliated and bullied and now must rearm to the teeth for simple national survival.

Britain's foreign secretary, Sir John Simon, thought he saw a better course—unilateral appeasement. He was strongly encouraged to pursue this policy by the leadership of a Royal Navy now steeped in gloom and despair. Chatfield, first sea lord and chief of the Admiralty's Naval Staff after February 1933, was "'the dominant personality in the formulation of British strategic policy' before World War II," and he became obsessed with the idea that His Majesty's fleet was on the brink of assuming impossible security burdens in both Europe and the Far East. To Chatfield and his colleagues, the 1922 Washington naval accords had set the scene "for a game of poker in which the stakes were the [British] Empire itself and the bluff could be called by Japan declaring war concurrently with Germany." From Hitler's rise to power in 1933 onward Chatfield persistently warned that "Japan would surely strike south" to seize British and European imperial holdings in the Far East "if the Royal Navy became detained elsewhere." With both Germany and Italy busily building warships, that fear was clearly well founded.[37]

Chatfield set forth his ideas on British naval policy in a June 1934 letter to Warren Fisher that deserves extensive quotation. "We are in the remarkable position of not wanting to quarrel with anybody," Chatfield began, "because we have got most of the world already, or the best part of it, and we only want to keep what we have got and prevent others from taking it away from us."

The best way, in my view, to do that is to look after our own defences, both East and West, and so make it less likely that our dominant position in the world, geographically, shall not be challenged.... The last thing I want to do is threaten Japan. The most we can hope for in the East is to have a sufficient Navy that it can go there in an emergency, not to threaten her, but to prevent her threatening us, and Australia and India. I do not see how we can ever prevent Japan, ourselves, from dominating China, so long as the Chinese are so feeble as to let them do it, and if that is the menace we are looking at then I think we can do very little and it is much better to try and settle our differences over China by diplomatic means.... But if we are looking at the other menace, the aggrandizing of Japan generally in the Pacific when it is a menace to our Dominions and India, then I think we can do a great deal by merely having a sufficient Fleet, recognized by Japan as able to go out to Singapore, which at once secures the strategic position. While, therefore, I am all in favor of being as friendly with Japan as possible and *letting her know it* I do not want that looked upon as a reason for reducing our Naval world power. Whatever we may be able to do with our Army or Air Force in preventing our own country from being invaded or attacked, it will never reduce our Naval responsibilities of maintaining our Empire, sea communications and Mercantile Marine, on which our wealth finally depends.... Our Royal Navy, in conjunction with those of the Dominions, should always be adequate to secure the safety of our seagirt Empire.... [W]e do not wish to propitiate Japan at the expense of a hostile and jealous United States. At the same time I am entirely with you that we do not want to tie ourselves as we have done in the past to the United States, because she is unreliable and does not know her own mind and her statesmen do not know the mind of their own Country. Nothing that is said by the President or any of their Statesmen can ever be accepted at more than its face value, as we all know.... The one thing which causes all the trouble is the endeavour to make military agreements to limit arms. That is why I should like to see the attempt to make Naval agreements abandoned and substitute for them political understandings, leaving each Nation free to build what she wants. If Japan will not agree to her 5:3 ratio the best thing is to beg to differ and to part company on that attempt without quarreling over it.[38]

Chatfield not unnaturally concluded that Britain's global dilemma could be resolved by pressing Berlin for the kind of "political understanding" on naval armaments that it was clear that neither Italy nor Japan would give. Unfortunately, it was not clear that Erich Raeder was prepared to give way on naval armament either. In March 1934, a year before formal German rearmament,

Raeder boldly proposed a "Replacement Shipbuilding Programme" of eight battleships, three aircraft carriers, eighteen cruisers, forty-eight destroyers, and seventy-two submarines to be completed in fifteen years, that is, by 1949. The German Naval Ministry blandly stated that the reason for such an audacious program, in total violation of the Versailles Treaty provisions, was "parity with France." In fact, as Holger Herwig has observed, Raeder was "reasserting" nothing less than "Tirpitz's claim to maritime greatness," though the admiral firmly believed his führer's repeated assertions that there would be no war with Great Britain for at least a decade. Even under those restrained circumstances, the German naval construction program constituted a bluff, though it is uncertain whether Raeder fully understood how much of a bluff it was. Germany simply did not possess the financial and material resources to build a modern fleet in addition to a large modern army and air force. Those restraints would become evident soon enough, but one stood out boldly from the outset. The old High Seas Fleet had run on coal, of which Germany had a great plenty. But the new-model battle fleets of the thirties ran on oil, and oil was a very precious commodity in a nation suddenly and quite publicly committed to forced draft rearmament of all its armed forces. The prospect that in addition to creating the kind of huge air force and mechanized army required to subdue Europe Germany could afford to field a powerful blue-water fleet that might come close to matching the Royal Navy was foolish beyond measure.[39]

Six months after Raeder announced his "replacement" program, Chatfield convinced His Majesty's statesmen and diplomats that only another international naval conference, in advance of the scheduled expiration of the Washington and London naval accords at the end of 1936, offered Britain a way out. Provision had been made in both accords to convene a conference in 1935 to reach new agreements while the old were still in force. Such a conference might yield political understandings that would advance British interests rather than further sweeping naval disarmament. Talks designed to outline a new set of international naval agreements were held throughout late 1934, but though they were cordial, they revealed a widening rift among the three leading naval powers, for Japan was now demanding absolute naval parity. Germany, of course, was not a member of the disarmament club because the provisions of the Versailles Treaty should have rendered the question of reaching any sort of naval agreement with it moot. But it had openly violated the treaty with Raeder's announced replacement shipping initiative. His Majesty's government, in consultation with France and other European nations, should have strangled the German naval initiative in its cradle. Instead, the British Admiralty, hoping to lure nascent German naval power to its side, queried Berlin about attending a new international conference. The Nazi government promptly replied that Germany would do so only if granted "equality of rights."[40] Hitler was playing on British (and French) fears brilliantly; Raeder's Replacement Shipbuilding Programme was obviously a straw in the wind, designed to determine the strength of Anglo-French resolve to maintain both the Versailles and Washington treaty structures. The following month, the German ambassador in London informed Hitler of Parliament's growing concern over the clear evidence of German rearmament. The führer replied shrewdly that he had "earnestly sought and would continue to seek effective armaments agreements," especially in the naval sphere, where he was prepared to accept 35 percent parity with the Royal Navy. Raeder had evidently convinced Hitler that he could safely push for such a ratio, and perhaps go as high as the 50 percent that the admiral now dreamed of.[41]

In February 1935, following intensive Anglo-French consultations on the matter, London and Paris informed Hitler he could rearm with British and French blessings only if he would subscribe to a new agreement in which Germany would guarantee the borders of all existing eastern European states and would agree to enter binding international arbitration in case of conflicts with those countries. The führer promptly countered with an olive branch of his own: a public pledge that German naval rearmament would reach only 35 percent parity with Britain, leaving German naval tonnage some 15 percent less than that currently possessed by France. At this point, London blundered. Before the Foreign Office could reply to Hitler's proposal, the War Office on March 4 published a white paper recommending "judicious rearmament" in response to the growth of German military power. A calculatingly infuriated Hitler countered two weeks later by announcing total German rearmament—on the ground and in the air as well as at sea, including construction of huge bomber and submarine fleets.[42]

The führer now pitilessly exploited Simon—and the Royal Navy—for all he could get. Just before the release of the embarrassing British white paper, Hitler had invited His Majesty's government to send a cabinet minister to Berlin, and Simon was picked to go. The Foreign Office hastily summoned their French counterparts to London and got them to drop the notion of a new eastern security pact in favor of a mere regional "consultative" arrangement, thus paving the way for whatever agreement Simon might reach with Hitler that could preserve the mobility and reduce the security burdens of the Royal Navy. Then came the white paper and Hitler's fervent announcement of rearmament to an ecstatic nation, which prompted His Majesty's government to anxiously query

Berlin if the Simon visit was still on. When the ever eager foreign secretary was assured that he would be well received, he raced off to Berlin where his hosts were waiting to humble him.

On the eve of the Anglo-German meetings, Ambassador Leopold von Hoesch in London cabled his Foreign Ministry that "the key to a satisfactory solution" that would safeguard German rearmament "is held by Britain. As regards the other important Powers, they appear to observers here, too, to be united in their growing hostility towards us. I hear from a reliable source that, in Italian Embassy circles here, Germany is always openly described as the country which Italy must always regard as her true opponent." France remained "the centre of hostility towards Germany," despite "a few signs of sympathy in certain circles." Moreover, judging from experience, France could be "expected to become the more unapproachable the more she feels herself supported against Germany by other Powers." The United States, the ambassador sniffed, "in her well-known ignorance of European affairs, has completely misunderstood" Germany's intentions.[43] If there ever was a time for Britain to speak firmly to a still highly vulnerable führer on behalf of a loosely united Europe, it had come.

Instead, Simon let Hitler bully him unmercifully. When the foreign minister and his undersecretary, Anthony Eden, arrived at Templehof airfield on March 24, they were confronted with the pomp of Nazi Germany's new military power. Stepping from the plane, they were met by a company of stunning, six-foot-tall, blond, blue-eyed, clean-featured SS troopers, who were attired from head to foot in black except for gleaming white gun belts and gloves and the red, white, and black swastika armbands. Their commander saluted with drawn sword and cried, "Sir! The Standarte Adolf Hitler is at attention and at your orders." " 'Ah, yes,' " Simon replied with "an uneasy sidelong glance at the bayonets, 'yes, indeed,' and made haste to his motor car." Matters went downhill from there.[44]

For two days Simon, Eden, and Hitler and his henchmen roamed broadly over the landscape of continental problems. But a naval agreement remained at the center of attention. The flavor of the naval discussions was best caught by the führer himself who on March 27, as Simon was flying back to London, told Raeder that he had demanded 35 percent parity from Simon. When the British foreign secretary replied that such a demand would have "repercussions" in France, Hitler bluntly replied that that was no concern of his; he would recognize British naval supremacy because of the needs of the British Empire, but such a consideration did not apply to France. When Simon added that, of course, Germany would be invited to the forthcoming world naval conference where Britain would certainly be willing to talk about "new construction programmes rather than about ratios," the führer replied that such a proposal "was unacceptable to Germany since Germany as a disarmed nation must naturally, in order to achieve equality of rights, have very large construction programmes." This thinly veiled threat of another unlimited naval race that might match or even exceed the destructive building programs of 1908–1912 was one of two frightening possibilities that Hitler laid before his British guests.[45] The other involved Germany's growing power in the air and the likelihood of future terror raids against English cities.

Simon returned home determined to conclude a bilateral naval agreement with Germany that would symbolize the continuing friendship between the two nations, a "friendship" that could be likened only to that between a tired old lion and a famished young snake. He had Chatfield with him. "The Admiralty's purpose was to forestall the development in European waters of a threat so serious as to paralyze the fleet's capacity to act elsewhere," namely, against Japan in the Far East.[46] Naval leaders convinced themselves that a 35 percent parity formula would preserve British freedom of action beyond European waters.

But before Simon could keep the diplomatic momentum going, Mussolini stepped in. The duce had one more card to play against the man who would soon become his firmest, indeed his only sure, ally. In 1934 the duce and the führer had clashed over Austria, and Hitler had won the race to decisively influence affairs in that weak and unhappy country that lay as a buffer between Germany and Italy. Early in April of the following year, Mussolini called for a three-power conference at the northern Italian resort city of Stresa in an effort to create a united Anglo-Italian-French alliance against Germany. But the so-called Stresa Front never had a chance once Simon and his prime minister, the ailing and soon-to-be-replaced Ramsay MacDonald, made it clear to the assembled delegates that Britain would not go to war to stop Hitler from re-creating German militarism. Let the Nazis defy, indeed destroy, the Versailles sanctions: His Majesty's government "would not consider the possibility of sanctions in the event of treaty-violation." As Winston Churchill later sardonically observed, Simon's intervention "naturally confined the Conference to the region of words."[47] Mussolini heard Simon's remark as clearly as did Hitler. The duce was through with the democracies who, he now realized, would never try to stop him from carving out his cherished overseas empire in the wilds of East Africa.

Having survived the Stresa scare thanks to Simon, Hitler on May 21, 1935, reconfirmed his previous offer: a German fleet no more than 35 percent as strong as that of Britain. Germany, he said, did not have either "the intention or the necessity or the means to participate in any new naval rivalry." He was right, of course, but the purblind British did not really hear what he was saying. His Majesty's government promptly rushed into Germany's arms. Nazi foreign minister Joachim von Ribbentrop was invited to London in June for naval talks. "Vain and tactless, he told the British that Hitler's offer was not subject to negotiation; they must take it or leave it. The British took it." They took it because they thought there was no other choice: "Germany would build a fleet whether recognized by Britain or not," and the best thing to do was "to agree formally to such a fleet at the lowest limit possible." Moreover, the German proposal was not devoid of appeal. Hitler promised to maintain the 35 percent level no matter what further developments occurred in international affairs; an Anglo-German naval agreement, his representatives at London insisted, would be "final and permanent."[48]

What the British got was an agreement that not only allowed the Germans to build five modern battleships "whose tonnage and armament would be greater than that of anything the British had afloat," together with twenty-one cruisers and sixty-four destroyers, but also allowed Hitler the right to build submarines of any type up to 60 percent of the total in the Royal Navy, and, should "exceptional circumstances" demand, up to 100 percent. But again, the Germans practiced shrewd diplomacy to get their way. If the Kriegsmarine were to build up to parity in submarines with the Royal Navy, construction would have "to be obtained through the transfer of tonnage from other categories," that is, without an overall increase in the 35 percent ratio.[49]

In fairness to British negotiators, the implications of the enormous giveaway in submarine tonnage were not at all clear in 1935. Astonishingly, "widespread opinion prevailed in all navies, including the German, that the U-boat had lost the role it had achieved in the First World War as one of the most effective naval weapons."[50] Several explanations come to mind as to why. First, the U-boat had been defeated, and largely in the narrow choke points and close-in waters around the British Isles. With the development of the asdic acoustic sensor, it was believed the U-boats would be even more easily subdued in a future war. Admiralties did not anticipate further developments in U-boat technology that might permit even relatively small boats to operate in the open reaches of the Atlantic. If Hitler should gain control of the entire western European coastline, then the U-boat, even one not especially advanced technologically from its 1918 precursor, would have wide, deep waters in which to roam. And with the development of the wolf pack . . . In any case, when the Anglo-German Naval

Agreement was publicly unveiled just weeks before preliminary discussions began leading to a new international naval conference, Japan, the United States, and Italy expressed no objection. France was furious, but could do nothing.

The catastrophic nature of the Anglo-German Naval Agreement of 1935 is almost beyond measure. It is a reflection of the utterly deluded and demoralized state of British officialdom at the time that old David Beatty, the dashing battle-cruiser commander of 1916 and now fleet commander Earl Beatty, rose in the House of Lords to offer the "opinion that we owe thanks to the Germans." Hitler had come to Britain "with outstretched hands and voluntarily proposed to accept" the 35 percent ratio. "If they had made different proposals," Beatty continued, "we would not have been able to stop them. That we do not have an armament race with one nation in the world at least is something for which we must be thankful."[51]

If Britain's political leadership was timid and tired, Germany's was at once enthusiastic and frustrated. Hitler pronounced June 18, 1935, the happiest day of his life, for he was convinced that the signing of the Anglo-German naval accord signaled a new day in Anglo-German relations, merely "the preliminary to a firm Berlin-London political tie" (dare we employ the term *axis*?) that would guarantee Germany a free hand on the Continent. Incredibly, many German naval officers expressed dismay at being bridled so by the agreement with Britain. The führer should have bargained for more! Germany would remain 15 percent behind France. According to one authority, Hitler expected such an outcry, telling the senior naval officer on the Ribbentrop delegation to London, Admiral Karlgeorg Schuster, that he would be criticized for not demanding even stronger parity with the Royal Navy, but that he, Hitler, "knew from experience how much to demand."[52]

Raeder appreciated how much Hitler had obtained. During the summer of 1935 he had a subordinate draw up a memorandum, which was circulated throughout the *Kriegsmarine,* that concluded, "The Agreement is entirely satisfactory for years to come. Any substantially larger figure . . . could hardly be reached in the next decade." The accord "will give us the opportunity of creating a modern fleet which is appropriately constituted and in accordance with our maritime needs."[53] With that, the German navy more or less fell into line.

Critics then and later would enumerate exactly what Britain had to be "thankful" to Hitler for. First, the führer had openly broken the provisions of the Versailles Treaty, and with British connivance. Second, 35 percent parity gave the führer free rein to build up a navy "as fast as was physically possible." German naval yards would be set working nonstop for a decade.[54] Third, and most devastating, a close reading of the treaty (which historians have generally *not* done) made clear to contemporaries that what Hitler was demanding was not 35 percent parity with the British Home Fleet but 35 percent parity with the entire Royal Navy. Sensitive observers at the time immediately did a statistical analysis and concluded that if built up to complete treaty limits, a German navy would constitute 400,000 tons to the Home Fleet's current total of 351,000 tons. In a time of general world crisis, with the Royal Navy stretched to the breaking point covering imperial commitments in the Mediterranean, the Pacific, and South American waters, Hitler's navy might well defeat Britain in detail by first destroying the Home Fleet and then annihilating the individual units or small squadrons that came rushing home piecemeal from the far corners of the empire. If the führer could keep the peace long enough to develop a navy firmly within the limits of the Anglo-German accord, Britain would find itself in a catastrophic position.[55] Fourth, in dealing so directly and cravenly with the most menacing figure the twentieth century had so far produced, Simon, with the enthusiastic support of the Royal Navy, had betrayed every ally and neutral in Europe. If collective security had been on its last legs at Stresa, it was dead after His Majesty's government formally ratified the implicit Simon-Hitler naval agreement reached at Berlin. Never again would Paris and London completely trust each other or act in full concert against Nazi aggression. Hitler would exploit the anxieties of each capital in coming years as he tore Old Europe to shreds. Finally, Hitler had taken Britain's measure, and nothing would stop him short of war. His ambassador in London had been right: Britain held the key to any sort of firm and long-lasting leash on German expansion. When Simon supinely threw over nearly twenty years of British naval and diplomatic opposition to the submarine in his eagerness to cut a deal, the führer realized the kind of men, and the kind of nation, with whom he was dealing. At Nuremberg in 1946 the chief British prosecutor, Sir David Maxwell-Fyfe, supposedly "brought out" in his cross-examination of Raeder that the 1935 naval agreement "was intended to curb German submarine production."[56] This was casuistry of the worst sort. The Versailles Treaty had flatly forbidden Germany from constructing offensive U-boats. That treaty was still in effect as international law. All that was required was enforcement. Instead, Simon and his colleagues aided and abetted Nazi lawlessness, then blamed the Nazis for being lawbreakers. Hitler could appreciate such hypocrisy. He also knew how to exploit it.

So did Benito Mussolini. The last, but by no means least, disaster produced by the Anglo-German Naval Agreement was its confirmation of Mussolini's own rapidly crystallizing belief in the softness of the democracies and his conviction that they would never again stand up to aggression. He, too, had been given an implicit green light to expand where he wished. Chatfield and his colleagues in the British Admiralty may have thought that Simon had preserved Britain's dwindling naval power and declining naval reputation, but within a matter of weeks after the Anglo-German accords were signed the duce completely disabused them of that idea.

The origins of the Abyssinian or Italo-Ethiopian war of 1935–1936 lay in nothing more than Mussolini's determination to redress an old insult (in 1896 a small Italian garrison had been wiped out in the disputed border area between Abyssinia and Italian Somaliland) while carving out an overseas empire. The little East African country held few resources, and its frontage on the Red Sea was of only modest strategic value. Because the majority of its population and its capital were located on a four thousand–foot-high inland plateau, Abyssinia would be difficult to defeat, even by a modern army. Mussolini's army had become highly mechanized, and its engineering corps would prove to be possibly the best in the world at that time. But Generals Pietro Badoglio and Rodolfo Graziani and their troops confronted formidable barriers of terrain and climate that would require bulldog courage to overcome. The Abyssinian army was, by all accounts, a crude and premodern institution. But like all peoples under unprovoked attack, the Abyssinians were prepared to fight valiantly.[57]

The duce announced as early as 1934 his determination to attack Abyssinia; Europe was well warned. Moreover, Abyssinia was the only African member of the League of Nations; its emperor, Haile Selassie, and his diplomats were well regarded when the international diplomatic corps bothered to think about them at all. Simon and his French colleagues could not have been ignorant of the implications for Italian policy of the collapse of the abortive Stresa Front and of the Anglo-German Naval Agreement. Almost immediately after the naval accord was signed in the summer of 1935, Mussolini began assembling the troops and ships for his Abyssinian expedition.

Here was the point, nearly a year before the Rhineland crisis and long before Austria or the Sudetenland, when the democracies could have stopped the dictators cold, for Mussolini could not get at Abyssinia without passing his troops and their supplies through one of the great strategic choke points on the world ocean, the Suez Canal. The Royal Navy controlled Suez from its large adjacent base at Alexandria. London could have prevented Mussolini from sending his troops through the canal at the outset. Or Britain could have let the duce's men and equipment pass through, then slammed the canal door behind them, cutting off essential resupplies and causing the duce's splendid army either to die on the vine in East Africa or to retreat home in shame via the Indian Ocean, the Cape of Good Hope, and the South Atlantic.[58] Such action would undoubtedly have given a powerful shot in the arm to the European democracies and might even have caused the collapse of Italian fascism. Hitler and his gang would have been isolated in a suddenly rejuvenated Europe willing and able to keep Nazism under the closest scrutiny. Certainly, Mussolini waged the conflict in East Africa with sufficient brutality (there were well-reported incidents of the aerial gassing and bombing of undefended native villages) so that His Majesty's government, to say nothing of the League of Nations, could have justified closing the canal after the war began on the pretext of Italian atrocities. Indeed, the world was revolted by Italian excesses, but the European democracies did nothing.

They remained paralyzed for several reasons. First, Abyssinia *was* a non-Western country, and therefore in the prevailing racism of the time really not worth risking another general European war over. Second was the hope (it never really became a conviction) that the "grim 'geography' of the central Ethiopian plateaux may prove too much even for the huge modern army of 400,000 men, with heavy artillery, 'climbing' tanks, bombing-planes, chemical aids [that is, poison gas] and the rest." Third, and most important, was the rapidly crystallizing international fear of airpower, a fear that by 1935 was reaching almost frantic proportions. For all his adolescent and grotesque posturing, Mussolini was no fool. He had fashioned his military machine well. Knowing that Italy was poor and without an overseas empire would forever remain so, he did not try to match the Royal Navy at sea, nor the French army on land. Instead, the duce concentrated his nation's attention on "the one department of military strength in which no nation had yet established such a commanding position . . . in which labor counted for more than material resources" — the air. With a sufficiently large air force, Mussolini could strike swiftly across the Alps or the Mediterranean without directly confronting either the French army or the British fleet.[59]

By 1935 Italy's Regia Aeronautica was the talk of Europe. The previous year, Commander Italo Balbo had led a long-range mass flight of giant torpedo-bomber seaplanes from Rome across western Europe and the Atlantic to the United States. The RAF might have done as well; the Americans would do so the following year when a similar mass flight flew nonstop to Hawaii. What filled Europe with a thrill of horror was an event that took place as Balbo's Savoias swept over Paris on their way west. As these heaviest and slowest aircraft rumbled above the French capital, a flight of French fighters — "pursuit planes," in the language of the time — rose to escort them. At altitude, the

French pilots discovered that they could not hold speed with the Italians. "The demonstration showed that France had nothing that could stop the Italians if they would a-bombing go. That fall the Italian fleet manoeuvres were held off the coast of Sicily, and airplanes played the most prominent part." From that moment forward, Fletcher Pratt wrote in 1939, "Italian strategy... [was] based on the intimate cooperation of shore-based aircraft with ships."[60]

Any effort by the Royal Navy to stop or stifle the Italian army in East Africa might well call forth the wrath of the Regia Aeronautica in the skies over Malta, Alexandria, and perhaps even London as well. Indeed, at the height of the Abyssinian Crisis, as it was forever known, the Prince of Wales—soon to be King Edward VIII—privately informed his old drinking and polo-playing companion Lord Louis Mountbatten, then in command of a destroyer in the Mediterranean, that there was a "fifty-fifty chance of the Italians bombing Malta."[61]

In throwing down the gauntlet to the world community in Abyssinia, Mussolini implicitly challenged the Royal Navy's traditional control of the Mediterranean. Suddenly, after fifteen years of uneventful steaming, frequent exercises, and visits to the many lovely spots that dotted the great inland sea from Gibraltar to the Gulf of Corinth, the British Mediterranean Fleet abruptly found itself once more on the edge of war.[62]

It was not ready; or, rather, Ernle Chatfield and the Admiralty concluded that it was not ready. As war clouds gathered in August 1935, the joint armed forces Planning Staff in London prepared for war with Italy. At the end of the month, as Mussolini's army clearly prepared to embark for the Horn of Africa, the Royal Navy was directed to make "all preparations short of war." The Home Fleet assembled on August 29 and was ordered to remain in readiness to sail for the Mediterranean. The Mediterranean Fleet was to be immediately reinforced with an aircraft carrier and two flotillas of destroyers and one of submarines. But Whitehall was also hesitant. Mussolini had been preparing his army for months; the Italian navy had grown in numbers and strength over the past several years. The fleet would be operating from Malta and Alexandria where antiaircraft defenses were weak if not nonexistent. Moreover, supporting any British ground or air effort in the Mediterranean would be extremely difficult. Italian air strength commanded the Central Basin, forcing a rerouting of supply convoys around the Cape of Good Hope, but as the British approached Suez from the south, they would encounter significant Italian naval strength in the Red Sea. All in all, prospects of an Anglo-Italian war, or even an Anglo-French war against Italy, looked grim. Britain (and France) would triumph, but at a possible cost so high as to jeopardize the Royal Navy's future ability to control the North Sea against the new German navy or to favorably affect future events in the Far East where Japan continued to build and bluster as it maintained its threat in China with the additional possibility of an extension to Western imperial holdings in Southeast Asia. "Moreover," the writer of the official *United Kingdom Military History* of this period adds, British "naval strategy so far—and for all practical purposes for some time to come—was based on the assumption of complete freedom to use the Mediterranean to transfer the Fleet, if need arose, to the Far East." The most that London and Paris believed possible were weak economic sanctions against Italy (the still formidable U.S. industrial plant lay beyond League control) with the nervous hope that Mussolini would not be driven to war.[63]

As the first detachments of the Italian army finally left home ports in September 1935, Sir William Fisher, then commander in chief of the Mediterranean Fleet, received an astounding document from London that concluded with "a very pessimistic, if not to say defeatist, view of the Mediterranean Fleet's capacity to deal with the Italians." Years of underfunding, of steaming with inferior ships, of laboring under the realization that legally Britain could not ever again rule the waves, and, perhaps most important, the awful legacy of Invergordon, which must have caused every captain and admiral to wonder if he could trust his sailors, had at last undermined the world's greatest sea service. Nonetheless, and to his eternal credit, Fisher reacted with outrage. The very embodiment of the feisty British sea dog, he informed a subordinate that he had "sent a signal to Their Lordships telling them I disagree with every word of this pusillanimous document. The Mediterranean Fleet is by no means so powerless as is here set out."[64]

Nonetheless, Fisher promptly dispersed the fleet from its anchorage at Malta, only sixty miles from Italian airfields on Sicily, scattering his ships to Alexandria and to Gibraltar in what one naval critic later characterized as "a flight that was called a 'strategic concentration.'" Throughout September and October 1935, the fleet was steadily reinforced from all over the world as Mussolini's troops continued to pour through the Suez Canal. A battleship and cruiser plus the carrier *Courageous* steamed into the Mediterranean from home waters. Two cruisers came from South America and two more from China.[65] The Royal Navy was still the world's greatest sea service when it chose to be.

Certainly, the Italian navy thought so, as did representatives of the world press. "You are sending us to our death," the Italian admirals reportedly screamed at Mussolini when he warned them they might have to fight Britain. At the time, Mussolini's own naval-rearmament program was just getting under way, and all that Admiral Domenico Cavagnari had were "two obsolete dreadnoughts at his disposal" to confront the Mediterranean Fleet. Mussolini was undeterred. "Are you afraid of the British Navy?" he contemptuously sneered to his admirals. "I can give the King of England a slap in the face and get away with it." An American newsman watched Fisher's ships, "Britain's mightiest men of war... all England's heaviest and toughest looking bulldogs of the sea," slam salvo after salvo of one-ton shells into a constantly heaving ocean. The fleet, headed by flagship *Queen Elizabeth* and its four sisters, contained "50 thousand men and 400 thousand tons of steel-clad dynamite waiting here with guns loaded and steam up and decks cleared for action. It's certainly going to be hell if it's ever turned loose."[66]

But the Royal Navy was facing a new and unprecedented situation, one that it would confront all too soon again off Norway, Crete, and Malta and that the United States Navy would have to deal with during the early weeks at Guadal-canal: a surface fleet, with insufficient air cover, was being menaced in narrow seas by superior airpower. London—and Fisher—did what could be done. When back in 1933 it had become clear from intelligence sources that Mussolini might one day provoke an international crisis over Abyssinia, Fisher asked that the fleet remain at Malta as a check upon Italian appetites. To ensure fleet safety, he requested that the island be massively reinforced with aircraft and antiaircraft guns. The Naval Staff wanted to help, but there were neither funds nor resources. "So all Fisher got was the discouraging reply that there were 'even more serious defence commitments elsewhere.' Presumably the Admiralty had Singapore chiefly in mind."[67]

As it became obvious toward the end of August 1935 that the crisis was at hand, Fisher insisted that with suitable reinforcements, he could handle "any situation at sea... provided that France was friendly." Fisher had developed a bold plan. "It was known to all the Flag Officers," Andrew Cunningham later wrote, "that if war came it was not the intention of the Commander-in-Chief to wait tamely at Alexandria or anywhere else. The moment the flag fell he was determined to strike at the Italians on their very doorstep." The night following the declaration of war, Fisher would send a strong force of destroyers and several of Britain's newest light cruisers up the east coast of Sicily and into the southern entrance to the Strait of Messina. "We were to bombard harbours and port installations, and generally to make ourselves obnoxious. As the senior Rear-Admiral of the force detailed," Cunningham continued, "I was to be in command of the operation," although Fisher made noises to the effect that he would not miss the show and would somehow hitch a ride on one of the destroyers.[68] Fisher's imaginative operation never came to fruition, but six years later his senior rear admiral, now in command of the Mediterranean Fleet, would concoct an even more breathtaking enterprise that would utterly demoralize Mussolini's sailors and revolutionize naval warfare.

The Admiralty soon realized that Italian forces could be stopped not only at Suez but in the Red Sea as well. As late as September, Mussolini had dispatched only two cruisers and a half-dozen destroyers through the canal toward the Abyssinian coast. British and Australian naval units east of Suez were poised to rush into the Red Sea and confront the duce's sailors if ordered. Britain seemed ready for war. "By the middle of September all the draft messages for the Admiralty to assume world-wide control of merchant shipping were ready," and a "Mobile Naval Base" centered around heavy antiaircraft batteries was about to depart for Malta to ensure that that island did not fall in case of an Anglo-Italian war.[69]

But at the moment of crisis, the fighting sailors at Alexandria were done in by their superiors at home. Chatfield simply was not willing to risk the Royal Navy in chancy combat with both the Regia Aeronautica and the Italian fleet, even though by this time three aircraft carriers had been sent to Fisher. There seemed at least one compelling justification for inaction: the Royal Navy still did not possess either an adequate carrier-based dive-bomber or fighter plane capable of taking on the high-performance land-based counterparts.[70] Given the advanced state of Italian aircraft and the excellence of Italian pilots, the Regia Aeronautica could presumably brush aside any British carrier aircraft protecting the surface fleet and sink any of Fisher's ships found in the narrow seas during daylight hours. Whether this would in fact be the case, the Admiralty was not disposed to discover. Nor was His Majesty's government willing to risk a war with Italy that might result in devastating air raids by the Regia Aeronautica against London and other English towns.

Here was the result of the RAF's shortsighted and high-handed insistence that the navy be given no significant airpower. Preoccupied both offensively and defensively with the prospects of strategic bombing, Britain's Air Ministry completely forgot the Royal Navy's long history as a deterrent force in global politics. For nearly three centuries, Britain had not only created a steadily expanding world empire but also sustained it largely on the Royal Navy's capability to intimidate all potential rivals anywhere on the world ocean and its adjacent seas and coasts. But after 1919 the Air Ministry and its allies within His Majesty's government deliberately withheld from the British fleet the one advanced technology—airpower—that it required to maintain its deterrent capability. Shorn of that, the timid souls like Chatfield who regrettably rose to power in the Admiralty during the interwar years had the excuse to do nothing in the face of naked aggression.

In the crucial autumn of 1935 when the totalitarian bluff could still have been called, the first sea lord indulged in dramatic lamentations over the general decline of his service and the stupidity of the civil authorities. He wrote an old friend, "It is a disaster that our statesmen have got us into this quarrel with Italy, who ought to be our best friend because her position in the Mediterranean is a dominant one." The "miserable business of collective security" had "run away with all our traditional interests and policies," and "we now have to be prepared . . . to fight any nation in the world at any moment." As for Abyssinia, Chatfield added that he had "no objection to the Italians being established there" because it would soon prove a weakness rather than a strength to Mussolini so long as Britain kept command of the sea.[71] But, of course, Chatfield had just practically forfeited Britain's command of the seas to Mussolini—a fact that Captain Roskill does not seem to appreciate in his otherwise excellent account of the Abyssinian Crisis.

The behavior of the Admiralty in the autumn of 1935 had little grounding in reality. It is highly doubtful that Mussolini would have risked a general European war over Abyssinia had the democracies stiffened their backs and closed Suez to him. Hitler remained a very new, very uncertain, and still very weak ally. The Italian navy, though a powerful force and becoming stronger yearly through new construction, remained deeply fearful of the British fleet, and despite Balbo's dramatic long-range flight, London was a long way from Italian airfields. But above all, with the bulk of its comparatively small army in East Africa, Italy would have been wide open to invasion by either French forces attacking through the Savoy region or British forces coming in from the sea. Had London stood firm and closed Suez, Mussolini would have found himself in an impossible situation, able to rely only on an air force that whatever its demonstrated technical competence had never been tried in long-range battle or short-range defense.

In the event, Chatfield and the British Foreign Office were taken off the hook by the French, although Gallic behavior should not have been a barrier to British action. While the question of closing Suez to the Italians was never presented to the Paris government because it was never considered at London, French army staff officials reinforced British timidity at the end of October by reminding their British colleagues that most of the theoretically powerful French army was, in fact, demobilized and that mustering it for an Italian war would consume many weeks. Perhaps it would be better for France to stay out of a Mediterranean conflict until fully mobilized, leaving Britain to fight Mussolini alone. After all, John Simon had destroyed the Stresa Front, then signed the disastrous naval agreement with Hitler. Let the British Foreign Office and Royal Navy take this problem in hand also.[72] Soon thereafter, with the Italo-Abyssinian war now under way, French authorities provided the British naval attaché at Paris with particulars of the disposition and material conditions of French warships in the Mediterranean together with details of French docks and oil reserves in the region. But French naval authorities in North Africa proved sufficiently grudging or unwilling hosts to the few British naval units that called so that Chatfield was able to use Gallic foot-dragging as a further excuse to urge a do-nothing policy on his diplomatic colleagues in London. So insistent was the first sea lord in pushing his views that the Foreign Office did not even demand the one other action that might have shut down Mussolini's African offensive: an international oil embargo. By April 1936, with the Italian army at last approaching Addis Ababa and with Hitler's entire army of two divisions safely ensconced in the Rhineland, the French clearly indicated their "willingness to pay Italy's price rather than to run risks *vis-à-vis* Germany."[73]

Thus, twice within a year the British Admiralty was instrumental in sabotaging policies and actions that could have brought the fledgling European dictators to their knees long before they became so powerful that only a global coalition could stop them. The Royal Navy deferred to (and thereby encouraged) German rearmament; the Royal Navy deferred to (and thereby encouraged) the savage and brutal aggression of Italian fascism. Fifteen years of the profoundest demoralization within the service, caused by constant turmoil and decline, blinded the Admiralty to the fact that naval power remained the fulcrum of twentieth-century history and that Britain still possessed it in sufficient quantity to decisively influence the course of global affairs. Had Britain stood firm and slammed the door at Suez behind the Italian armies after they reached East Africa, it would have been a classic demonstration of sea power that would have impressed the entire world. Instead, Chatfield and His Majesty's government allowed the threat of the Japanese navy in the Far East and the Italian air force in Europe to defeat the British fleet without firing a shot.

Fisher's sailors were reduced to impotent fury as they watched Italian transports steam past Alexandria heading for the canal and south to Abyssinia, their decks packed with troops shouting "Duce! Duce!" as they passed the British warships.

One day during the dinner-hour a large transport crammed with two or three thousand soldiers arrived, all cheering defiantly at our two ships. As they passed, they broke into the Fascist anthem "Giovinezzia"; but were considerably put out by the loud cheers of "Encore!" from the hundreds of sailors on the forecastles of the *Despatch* and *Resolution*. It is impossible to describe the withering contempt the British bluejacket can put into his applause if he dislikes the entertainment or entertainer, and on this occasion their sarcastic shouts penetrated even the thick hides of the Italians.[74]

Unfortunately, the duce's troops were not the only ones who suffered "withering contempt" as a result of the Abyssinian Crisis. At Geneva, Anthony Eden pushed through the rapidly dying League a limited embargo against Italy. But it was a joke from the beginning. Many of the items on the list were tangential to war making, and citizens of those powerful nations that had either never joined the League or just left it—the United States, Germany, and Japan—were perfectly willing to ignore sanctions and give the duce what he wanted.[75]

After 1935 the entire British defense establishment fell into a state of dread as all three British armed services now faced the nightmare of nothing less than a three-front war: in western Europe, in the Mediterranean, and in the Far East. Twenty years earlier Britain could count on Japan to do what little naval policing had to be done in Asian and Pacific waters while the French largely took care of the Mediterranean. No more. As the Axis powers grew steadily in strength, confidence, and truculence, Chatfield and the secretary of the Committee of Imperial Defence, Sir Maurice Hankey, begged the Foreign Office to initiate some sort of démarche toward either Italy or Japan to relieve the intolerable pressure on the fleet. With Hitler now menacing the peace of Europe, would it not be best simply to ignore Mussolini's new African empire and "placate" Japan by recognizing its Manchurian conquest? Chatfield "became desperately worried" about the prospect of having to send a major fleet to the East after war had broken out in Europe. All of the Admiralty's ancient bitterness toward the bumptious Americans broke out anew. Who was truly responsible for this new world crisis if not the United States? Was it not the Americans who had insisted in 1919 on collective security through a League of Nations, then walked away from their own creation, leaving Britain and France to shoulder the entire responsibility? Was it not the Americans who had insisted in 1922 that Britain cut itself loose from its Japanese ally as the price of naval parity? Now the chickens were coming home to roost, and the United States stood aloof, eventually (in October 1937) insisting that it was up to Britain and France to somehow, someway, "quarantine" the dictators.[76]

The dominions would be of no help in a future naval war in the East. In 1914 Churchill and Whitehall could at least count on a battle cruiser apiece from Australia and New Zealand and moneys from Canada for the partial construction of several capital ships. Twenty years later, with the world in the midst of economic depression, the New Zealand squadron of the Royal Navy comprised but 2 cruisers, while the Royal Australian Navy possessed only 3 cruisers, 3 destroyers, 2 sloops, and a survey ship. The Royal Canadian Navy was little more than a coastal-defense force.[77]

To Chatfield and the lords of the Admiralty, appeasement seemed the only way out of the terrible dilemma. In January 1937 the first sea lord petitioned the Foreign Office: "As we cannot fight simultaneously in the East and the West, can we make an agreement in one area or the other, not necessarily a permanent agreement, but one which will give us greater security than we have now during our slow period of rearmament?"[78] The Foreign Office demurred. Surely, Britain could rearm against the dictators and face them down with the help of France and the United States. But it quickly became "painfully obvious to both the Treasury and the Admiralty only a few months into rearmament [that] existing programs had taken up all of Britain's available industrial capacity, leaving no scope for" further acceleration in the teeth of Nazi, Fascist, and Japanese programs. Those charged after 1935 with rearming the United Kingdom proposed "an entirely new standard of naval strength." According to the long-standing Defence Requirements Committee, a fleet would be placed in the Far East "fully adequate to act on the defensive and to act as a strong deterrent against any threat to our interests in that part of the globe." At the same time, a Home Fleet would be maintained capable of defeating its German opposite "in all circumstances." This new "Two-Power Navy Standard" was to be enforced by the "New Standard Navy" composed of old and new vessels that would total 20 battleships, 15 carriers, no fewer than 100 heavy and light cruisers, and 198 destroyers, together with 82 submarines.

Instead, the navy got roughly two-thirds of what it asked for, and the British fleet retained a distinctly elderly cast of 15 battleships, 8 carriers, 70 cruisers, 144 destroyers, and 55 submarines, all to be in place by 1940. In the event, not even this program would be fully met by new construction. Now at last, the terrible price of "victory" in the Great War of 1914–1918 became manifest. Britain simply had not the funds or the resources to undertake another great naval race like that of 1908–1914. Moreover, in those now distant days it had had to build against only one navy; after 1936 it would have to build against three.[79]

Chatfield was filled with despair and defeatism. The empire upon which the wealth and glory of Britain rested could not be held. In his January 1937 petition to the Foreign Office, Chatfield condemned His Majesty's government for "drifting along in our Imperial policy without a sufficiently definite aim." He continued: "Our present League policy and our frequent advocacy of collective security have led the people of this country to feel that they are not masters of their own destiny, but that, owing to some idealistic principle to which we have subscribed publicly, we may be drawn into some European crisis in which we have no vital interest and for which we are militarily totally unprepared at the present time." Britain had no friend it could trust and, in the case of both Italy and Japan, had lost friendships recently regained. The basic, essential, unavoidable fact was that "it is exceedingly doubtful, even if we increase our Naval and Air strength to the utmost possible limit under voluntary conditions of service, whether we can maintain the Empire if engaged simultaneously East and West."

Britain's only recourse, as Chatfield perceived it, was to abandon its foolish, unlimited commitments to collective security under the League of Nations and strike out on its own, rearming as rapidly as possible while pursuing a policy of appeasement toward the predator powers.

> We should be prepared, as Sir Robert Vansittart [chief diplomatic adviser to His Majesty's government] recommends, as part of a comprehensive effort to give reasonable satisfaction to the German people after a penalising Versailles Treaty, to restore, *as part of a general settlement,* some of the overseas territories that were taken away from her, such as the Cameroons [which Chatfield earlier hinted could be neutralized by British sea power whenever Germany became obstreperous]. We should endeavour to make as good an agreement with Japan as we can and as early as possible, because with such an agreement we should be much more likely to receive a reasonable response from the German people.[80]

Would appeasement and rearmament be enough to save Britain and its empire? Would the navy be up to its historic responsibilities? By this time, English shipbuilding, along with so many other aspects of the national industrial system, had experienced a marked decline. John Brown, Cammell Laird, and the other yards could still turn out some of the best small ships in the world, as the fast and powerful *Tribal* and *Hunt* classes of destroyers and the splendid

Dido-class light antiaircraft cruisers amply demonstrated. But the six-inch-gun ships of the *Arethusa* class were unremarkable in either power, speed, or protection. Even the big nine thousand–ton light cruisers of which Britain was now building several more were not dominant ships.

The greatest embarrassment to British arms at sea were the five new battleships authorized in 1936–1937 and completed over the next four to five years. Destined to form the backbone of Britain's modern capital-ship fleet in the coming war, the *King George V* class (or *KGV*s, as they were popularly known) simply did not measure up to prevailing international standards. Determined to remain within the Washington-London thirty-five thousand–ton sixteen-inch-gun restriction, the Admiralty ordered ships that were only 750 feet long, with a maximum speed of twenty-seven to twenty-eight knots. Their hulls were divided by a double lateral bulkhead, "an ill-conceived design feature" that in the case of torpedo hits prevented incoming waters from spreading evenly across the entire beam. Piling up on one side of the ship or the other, the waters would soon cause such an unbalance as to induce a capsize. But the worst and most obvious weakness of the *KGV*s lay in their main armament. Oppressed with memories of weakly armored capital ships blown to bits at Jutland, Britain's designers were determined to construct the most powerfully armored vessels possible. But there would be the inevitable sacrifice. Whereas every other major navy in the world had already advanced to fifteen-, sixteen-, and even eighteen-inch guns, the Royal Navy found that it could place no larger than fourteen-inch batteries on its new ships. This was a regression not only from the nine sixteen-inch guns of *Nelson* and *Rodney*, which displaced slightly less than thirty-five thousand tons, but also from the fifteen-inch main batteries of the *Queen Elizabeth*s that had been laid down a full quarter century before. Winston Churchill, long out of office but still keen on naval affairs, was deeply perturbed. But there was nothing he could do. Great Britain would enter the second great war of a still young century with either very old or grossly inadequate ships. (A remobilized veteran of the Great War, reaching Scapa Flow in September 1939, remarked that it was as if time had stood still since 1918: "A lot of the ships were even the same, too. Ruddy uncanny, I can tell you.")[81]

His Majesty's fleet suffered from other crippling weaknesses as well. As late as 1939 the navy had done little, either in the laboratories or in the shipyards, to prepare for a renewal of an undersea war with Germany. Correlli Barnett has written that the most serious charge against the Admiralty in the interwar years was that, "with eyes focused on the battlefleet, it ducked until too late the enormous operational and quantitative problems of once again having to set up a

complete convoy system and defend this against the U-boat." A touching faith in
the new but limited asdic technology led to a deplorable lack of antisubmarine
escort vessels, and as late as 1937–1939 the Admiralty put six-inch guns and
rapid-fire light antiaircraft batteries aboard as many merchant ships as it could,
called them armed merchant cruisers, and prepared in the event of war to send
them out into the sea-lanes as convoy escorts.[82]

Gunnery provided the greatest example of the steady decline in professional
competence within the service during the interwar years. The successors of Jacky
Fisher and Percy Scott simply were "not properly trained in scientific design
and armament engineering." Worse still, they exhibited a classic pigheadedness
in seeking expert advice from outside the service. As a result, the Royal Navy in
1939 (and for some years thereafter) lacked sophisticated precision equipment
for antiaircraft defense, such as had been developed in both the German and
the U.S. navies. Britain's sailors would enter World War II "firing at enemy aircraft with the hopeful wildness of aim of a tyro shot trying to bring down fast
flying grouse." The Mediterranean Fleet in particular would be cruelly hampered in forthcoming battles with both the Regia Aeronautica and the Luftwaffe as it expended vast amounts of ordnance without significant result.[83]

Finally, Whitehall had allowed the navy's splendid intelligence system to
stagnate. Soon after World War I, Blinker Hall's Room 40 was closed, and all
intelligence activities were transferred to civilian agencies. As the prospects of
war emerged in the midthirties, a naval intelligence office known as Room 39
was resurrected at the Admiralty. After January 1939 it was run by the immensely
able Captain John H. Godfrey whose people set out energetically to gather information from as many sources as they could, including intercepts and decoding
of German radio traffic, aerial photography and sightings of German shipping
by aircrews, the reports of agents abroad, the reading of German communiqués,
and interpretation of monitored German propaganda. Upon the outbreak of
war these sources would be supplemented by prisoner-of-war interrogations
and intercepted directives sent to German agents in Britain who had been
identified and quietly "turned." But for long months before and after the commencement of hostilities, the British could not break into either the German or
the Japanese naval or diplomatic codes. As late as 1935 the Admiralty had devoted little research to cryptanalytic technologies or to enciphering machines,
despite the frequent importunities of young fleet wireless officer Lord Louis
Mountbatten. The Royal Navy was thus restricted to a crude and outmoded
form of hand ciphering. "During Mussolini's Abyssinian campaign and perhaps
during the Spanish Civil War British vessels on active duty used these ciphers so

ineptly that BDienst [German naval intelligence] cracked them comfortably."
In 1939 BDienst's commander, Heinz Bonatz, produced a document titled *The
System of British Wireless Communication* based on nearly five years of inten-
sive study.[84]

Britain did succeed in keeping generally abreast of international trends in
one crucial area: aircraft carriers. For many years after 1918, the question of
airpower at sea remained a highly contentious issue. Yes, critics conceded, long-
range aerial reconnaissance and gunfire spotting aloft, together with fighter,
bomber, and torpedo planes, might *in theory* be vital components in any future
fleet engagement. But such engagements would themselves be irrelevant in to-
morrow's warfare where land-based strategic bombing would rule supreme. In
1922 the British writer W. S. Brancker argued that "aviation has become, par
excellence, the weapon of offense. No war can be won except by offensive action; and consequently the Navy and the Army must give way to the new [air]
arm in national importance, and in their claims on national expenditure."
Three years later Billy Mitchell made a more sweeping argument against big,
costly, labor-intensive floating airfields, an argument that would become gospel
in much of the international aviation community for nearly two decades: carrier aircraft were intrinsically inferior to land-based planes, and the carriers
themselves were fatally vulnerable to surface, subsurface, and aerial attack. Moreover, "As airplane carrying vessels are of no use against hostile air forces with
bases on shore, and as they can only be of use against other vessels or hostile
fleets that are on the surface of the water, and as these fleets will be supplanted
by submarines, there is little use for the retention of airplane carriers in the
general scheme of armaments."[85]

By 1937, however, the wars in China, Africa, and Spain had demonstrated
beyond all doubt the multifaceted capabilities of warplanes, and the Admiralty
had become as air-minded as the RAF. A new generation of admirals, including
Andrew Cunningham, led a prolonged fight to regain control of naval flying.
Ironically, the RAF was ready to surrender. Guernica and other examples of the
terrifying effectiveness of indiscriminate aerial bombing convinced the air force
that this should be its primary mission in the war that all now saw coming. The
RAF did not wish to be burdened and distracted with having to serve the needs
of the fleet at sea.

Nonetheless, improvements in the Royal Navy's air arm came slowly and
hesitantly. They were largely restricted to administration and recruitment and,
significantly, did not include any upgrade of the pitifully few and obsolete aircraft that the Fleet Air Arm possessed. On May 20, 1935, Lord Eyres Monsell,

then first lord of the Admiralty and by all accounts a weak reed, was at last induced by unremitting service pressure to approach Prime Minister Ramsay MacDonald (then in his last month of office) and ask that he appoint a cabinet committee to explore the navy's unhappiness with the eleven-year-old Fleet Air Arm arrangement. The air arm was a composite body of RAF and Royal Navy officers and men. All maintenance personnel were RAF, and units came under the operational, administrative, and disciplinary control of the navy only when those units were embarked aboard ship. Ashore they reverted to RAF control. A committee chaired by Sir Thomas Inskip was eventually appointed by the new prime minister, Stanley Baldwin, after intense bureaucratic maneuvering and politicking by both services and their civilian champions.[86] Chatfield developed a series of draft talking points to be used with Baldwin should that prove necessary to move the Inskip Committee in the right direction and flog it along. He also retained correspondence and memorandums as the issue was hotly debated over the next two years. The entire fleet was exercised with a sense of "anxiety" and "injustice" about the issue, Chatfield wrote in 1937.

> The fact is that the efficiency of the Navy and the safety of the country is at present being jeopardized. There is a serious deadlock between the Admiralty and the Air Ministry which is doing incalculable harm. . . . The Fleet feels that having loyally made every endeavour for 13 years to make the Balfour Scheme [that is, the RAF with a small Fleet Air Arm component] work and having represented that it will *not* work, they should not be compelled to continue it unheard. . . . We are dangerously short of personnel, both pilots and observers [penciled marginalia reads 50 p(ilots) 360 O(bservers) short, 20 catapult A(rtificers?) paid off 105 short next April 1938] not only because our petty officers are not allowed to join the Fleet Air Arm as Pilots, but also because the system of dual rank is objectionable to our officer Pilots and in many cases acts unfairly on them, and our Observers have no status recognized by the Air Ministry. . . . Further, our material is not what we feel it should be but we have little to say in the matter of provision.

Earlier, Chatfield had written to Winston Churchill, then a member of Parliament, "We are now in a position where we have not even got enough pilots in the Navy to man the miserable quota of aircraft which have been allotted to us."[87]

Chatfield and the navy found two ready and increasingly influential patrons in Parliament: Churchill, just beginning in 1936–1937 to emerge from the wilderness into which he had cast himself a decade earlier, and Sir Roger Keyes,

the naval hero of World War I turned politician. By the spring of 1937, farsee-
ing statesmen and commentators in Britain realized that Hitler had become a
great menace. Of equal importance, Baldwin appointed Samuel Hoare, a most
able and experienced bureaucrat, to head the Admiralty. "As far as the Navy
that floats on the sea and dives under it are concerned, I think you have done
splendidly," Keyes wrote to Chatfield on March 1, 1937, "and I am sure that
Hoare is of infinitely greater value to the Navy than Eyres Monsell. I can never
forgive the latter for letting the Navy down so badly over the air question,"
Keyes continued. "I suppose that he was afraid to tackle Baldwin, at any rate
judging by the latter's remarks to me last Summer Monsell had completely
failed to bring home to him, how bitterly the Navy resents the Air Ministry's
control over one of the Navy's essential arms. I think Baldwin recognizes it now,
but he is an extraordinarily obstinate person, as he once told me, and he won't
give way more than he can help." Progress was thus slow, and the Inskip Committee dawdled amid bureaucratic infighting and intense politicking. Keyes
wrote to Chatfield again on July 5 that until quite recently both Parliament
and the nation had lost interest in the navy—"the Air would provide for all
defence"—but now matters had changed and everyone had taken "the keenest
interest in Naval matters. Everyone realizes the immense importance of restor-
ing British Sea Power and Parliament is prepared to vote whatever is necessary
to ensure Naval security," provided that "they think the money is being wisely
spent and it is *very important* that they should trust the Board of Admiralty."[88]
Such parsimony would prove tragically shortsighted as the predator states rushed
to rearm.

In the summer of 1937 the Inskip Committee at last recommended that the
Fleet Air Arm be given over to full Admiralty control, and Baldwin duly announced on July 30 that this would take place immediately. Meanwhile, His
Majesty's Treasury had found funds in 1934 to build Britain's first truly modern
aircraft carrier, the 22,000-ton, 31-knot *Ark Royal* that came into service in 1939,
just before the outbreak of war.[89] The 1936 Naval Estimates contained funds
for two 23,000-ton, 32-knot ships, and by the eve of war Britain had more fleet
carriers completed (seven) or being built (five) than any other navy, though all
but one of those in service were marginal vessels.

As early as 1926 there had been informal discussions within the Admiralty
over the use of inexpensive auxiliary aircraft carriers to defend trade against
both surface raiders and submarines. A 1931 discussion of future convoy warfare led to the suggestion that some merchantmen be fitted with catapults and
a recovery deck while retaining their centerline-funnel arrangements. Four

years later attention had shifted to diesel-powered merchantmen that could be converted to a full flight deck, and the concept of the escort carrier, or CVE, began to take shape as an all-around "trade protection carrier." The Admiralty began to look about for suitable diesel-powered merchantmen in the 10,000- to 20,000-ton range with a speed of 14-plus knots that could be rapidly converted in wartime. But then, just before the outbreak of war in 1939, the Admiralty suspended its CVE studies, believing that the newly commissioned *Ark Royal* and its successors would provide sufficient airpower for the fleet to perform both its offensive and its escort functions. Perhaps the sea lords were led to this disastrous conclusion by pride and overenthusiasm once the Fleet Air Arm at last came back under Admiralty control. Britain's new naval airmen put on an impressive display above the international fleet gathered for George VI's 1937 coronation celebration. With Germany's small surface and subsurface fleet, was Britain's air supremacy at sea not guaranteed?

But Britain's practical experience with modern fleet aircraft carriers was in many ways unsatisfactory. Unlike their U.S. and Japanese counterparts, British fleet carriers would have to operate in the narrow seas directly off the northwestern and southern coasts of Europe, where enemy air attacks could be expected at any moment with little or no warning. Moreover, the Royal Navy was just as obsessed with protecting aircraft carriers as battleships from enemy gunfire. Finally, Britain's sailors remained bedeviled by the lack of modern aircraft that could tangle on at least somewhat equal terms with the advanced land-based fighters and bombers of the Luftwaffe and Regia Aeronautica. To survive and to continue to function, therefore, British carriers would have to be much stronger in terms of both armor and internal subdivision than U.S. or Japanese ships. Moreover, they could not "spot"—or park—any portion of the embarked air group on deck for fear of having them blasted to pieces (perhaps taking the entire ship along with them) during a sudden air attack. The entire air group aboard British carriers would thus have to be accommodated on the hangar deck. As a consequence, the capacity of British carriers vis-à-vis their American and Japanese sisters was drastically reduced, and British carrier operations and tactics had to be radically adjusted.

Ark Royal was designed to carry seventy-two aircraft in a rather clumsy two-hangar arrangement; in fact, it seldom carried as many as sixty. The *Illustrious* and *Implacable* classes that followed it in swift succession after 1936 reverted to a single hangar that could usually accommodate no more than thirty-six aircraft, though later in the war this was sometimes increased to more than forty.

All the vessels did possess extremely well-armored flight decks that, as the main strength deck, were faired naturally into the hull. The hangar decks below, especially in the *Illustrious* and *Implacable* classes, were, in effect, armored boxes.

Because of the necessarily small air group, attack planes had to predominate by a wide margin to ensure any offensive punch whatsoever. Most British air groups were composed of torpedo and high-altitude bomber aircraft at a five-to-one ratio over fighter planes. With only a half-dozen outclassed Skua mono-wing aircraft available (whose 195-knot top speed placed them 40 knots slower than enemy Heinkel 111 bombers and nearly 100 knots slower than the ME-109), continuous combat air patrols were difficult to maintain, and the development of fleet air defense suffered accordingly. The Skuas would only slowly be replaced by more suitable Grumman Martlets following the outbreak of war. *Ark Royal* and the *Illustrious* and *Implacable* classes therefore mounted large and powerful antiaircraft batteries. This strategy would fail spectacularly on several occasions during the coming war, but as *Illustrious* would demonstrate in the Mediterranean in 1940, and its sister ships much later in the Pacific, British carriers could survive and in some instances even continue air operations after absorbing amounts of punishment that would cripple or sink a U.S. or Japanese flattop.

Britain's small carrier fleet was bolstered with several striking operational innovations just before and after the outbreak of war in 1939, including radar, the installation of small combat-information centers, and the development of air-control operations. But as an American admiral later noted, although "all of these wonderful things came from the British . . . they have never had the funding to really implement them to the extent they would like."[90]

The development of more or less effective carrier designs and operational procedures constituted the Royal Navy's only substantial deference to modernity in the interwar period. Unfortunately, carrier operations would have to be carried out by a comparative handful of grossly inferior and long-obsolescent aircraft. According to naval air historian David Hamer, "At the outbreak of the Second World War the Royal Navy had a total strength, ashore and afloat, of 232 operational aircraft—85 per cent of which were biplanes with fabric-covered wings, constant-pitch propellers, no flaps, fixed undercarriages and no voice radio."[91] The slow rate of rearmament paced by a Parliament determined that every pound and pence be well spent and accounted for kept Chatfield in despair. And if that were not enough, tensions in the Mediterranean and Far East never diminished, demanding every resource the navy could muster.

The outbreak of the Spanish civil war in August 1936 and Hitler's almost immediate decision to aid the Franco insurgents with guns, aircraft, and "volunteers" galvanized Benito Mussolini to join his fellow dictator, while Joseph Stalin sent his own volunteers and equipment to support the legitimate Republican government in Madrid. As Europe fell into emotional turmoil over a conflict that many interpreted as a clear-cut struggle between fascist aggression and peace-loving peoples (it was far more complicated than that), Britain and France strove to maintain a neutral front. A year after hostilities broke out, with Franco temporarily in check, his intelligence people reported that five Soviet freighters headed toward Republican Spain and carrying no fewer than twenty-six hundred tanks and three hundred aircraft had just cleared the Turkish Straits, escorted by three submarines. Mussolini's people could not confirm, and in fact the report was wildly exaggerated. But Il Duce believed that his navy could choke off supplies to the Republicans and thus precipitate an early Nationalist victory. Beginning on August 6, 1937, Italy seeded the Aegean and Spanish Mediterranean coasts with submarines while erecting a barrier of cruisers, destroyers, and auxiliary warships in the Sicilian Strait. The patrols, unmarked and operated mostly at night, had orders "to attack any Republican ship, any Soviet merchant ship, and any merchant ship under a Republican flag." Over the next month Italian submarines and surface vessels made 438 attacks on suspected targets, firing more than forty torpedoes at twenty-four ships, sinking four merchantmen and badly damaging a Republican destroyer.

An immediate hue and cry arose from Europe's progressive centers, and there were demonstrations on Parisian boulevards (the city was a key recruiting ground and transportation point for Spanish Republican forces). Mussolini denied all, while extolling ever growing Axis unity. In London the Admiralty's own intelligence identified the "pirate submarines" attacking Soviet and Republican shipping as Italian almost from the beginning. But the Royal Navy was preoccupied at the moment with the Japanese rape of Nanking and consequent bombing of British and American warships on the adjacent Yangtze River (which destroyed the American gunboat *Panay*). Fearful of outright war with Japan, which would, among other things, necessitate maintenance of the sea-lanes to the Far East via Gibraltar and Suez, the Admiralty simply "disregarded its own intelligence and lobbied for a peaceful solution of the new Mediterranean crisis." British policy could not even be moved when an Italian U-boat accidentally attacked one of His Majesty's destroyers; unofficially, however, London let it be known that Mussolini's secret air and naval blockade of Spain had become "intolerable." The duce seemingly relented when Prime Minister Neville Chamberlain followed the message with the dispatch of a destroyer division to Gibraltar. Nonetheless, for the next year and a half, British diplomacy sought by every legitimate means and stratagem to woo Mussolini back into the fold. The duce countered by quietly maintaining the Spanish blockade right down to the death of the Republic in March 1939.

Only when the increasingly irrepressible duce brazenly sent his marines rushing across the Adriatic to conquer poor little Albania the following month was His Majesty's government at last moved to review its policy priorities. The post-Munich world was clearly careening toward war, though Chamberlain insisted that he "had no intention of starting" it over the Balkans. Many in the British Foreign Office "believed that Italy's attack on Albania proved Mussolini to be a 'gangster' determined to revise the Mediterranean status quo." They also agreed with Permanent Undersecretary Alexander Cadogan that "we can't *do* anything to stop it." Nonetheless, guarantees were extended to Greece and Romania, and in mid-May, while the Royal Navy began working "on the details of a possible war against Italy," His Majesty's government joined Turkey in issuing a "declaration of common interests in the eastern Mediterranean." No one, however, wanted to fight a three-front war, and so it was left to Mussolini to determine the time and circumstance in which he might wish to throw down the gauntlet.[92]

The United States constituted the one bright spot for an Admiralty confronted by a steadily darkening world scene. The Western democracies, so craven at Geneva, did not need further crises in the Far East. Tokyo was now adamant on naval parity, but perhaps another international conference could bring Japan to its senses. It did not. Preliminary negotiations at London in the autumn of 1935 followed by the conference itself yielded nothing but despair. Japan would accept nothing less than full equality with those powers whose global empires or extensive coastlines (or both) required significantly larger fleets. Tokyo was willing to make only two ostensible concessions. One was to Britain's insistent request for a significant, then modest, increase in light-cruiser tonnage to cover its imperial commitments. The other was a wholly unrealistic proposal that all but a handful of the world's existing warships, from battleships and aircraft carriers to destroyers and submarines, be destroyed. Everyone recognized the transparent folly of the idea, which, among other things, would leave even a drastically reduced Japanese navy more secure in its region and thus suggestive to further aggression.

During preliminary talks and in the early stages of the conference itself, the Western delegations were understandably leery of breaking up the international naval regime by confronting Japan's proposal for a common upper limit. The British at first played an infuriatingly coy role, or so Washington believed. For much too long, Foreign Minister John Simon and his people toyed with the Japanese, invoking memories of the old treaty of friendship, listening attentively to the possibility of a nonaggression pact, and reacting appreciatively to Japan's willingness to allow the Royal Navy the increase in light cruisers it so desperately wanted. Foreign Minister Koki Hirota shrewdly played on wounded British sensitivities on this latter point, because even a modest increase in tonnage would restore that predominance in sheer size that the Royal Navy had forfeited to their American cousins at Washington fifteen years before. When Roosevelt learned at one point from his chief negotiator, Norman Davis, that Prime Minister Ramsay MacDonald and his people were "discussing a new building program arrangement and a tripartite non-aggression pact with the Japanese," the president erupted in fury. The British "Tories" had better be told that if they were "even suspected of preferring to play with Japan to playing with us, I shall be compelled, in the interest of American security, to approach public sentiment in Canada, Australia, New Zealand, and South Africa, in a definite effort to make these Dominions understand clearly that their future security is linked with us in the United States." Despite diplomatic to-ing and fro-ing that did them no good in international circles, neither Simon nor Mac-Donald could, in the end, either surrender a sizable portion of the Royal Navy to the scrap heap or accept Tokyo's insistence that Japan's honor and destiny demanded complete naval equality.

The American position was as clear as that of the Japanese. The naval-disarmament agreements worked out in Washington had secured international peace and stability for the past fifteen years. No international developments or crises since then required their revision—quite the contrary.

So positions were maintained, formal negotiations and some corridor conversations notwithstanding, and in early January 1936 the Japanese delegation cabled home to Foreign Minister Hirota that "there is nothing to do but withdraw." Under instructions, the delegates asked for a final vote on the fifteenth, declaring that if their position was not accepted they would leave. It was not and they did.[93]

At the rump conference including Britain, the United States, France, and Italy, the Americans at last gave way to British supplication and agreed on a five-year building holiday in heavy (that is, 8-inch-gun) cruisers. Between January 1, 1937, and the end of 1942, cruisers would be confined to eight thousand tons in displacement and a 6.1-inch-gun caliber. Norman Davis and his fellow American delegates insisted that after 1942 they might well embark on an unlimited heavy-cruiser program, but for the moment financially strapped Britain got its way. The Anglo-American rapprochement so tentatively begun at London continued in the summer of 1936, as Chatfield mounted his fight to improve and expand the Fleet Air Arm. American and British naval officers began exchanging visits on each other's aircraft carriers, and several British naval officers, including now captain Louis Mountbatten, visited Pensacola Naval Air Station. During these visits both sides informally shared a significant amount of technical and operational data. As in 1917–1918, British and American sailors had no problem getting along on the working level; it was the lords of the Admiralty and the Navy Department who continued to feud. The shared dangers of the Yangtze River Patrol during the Japanese advance upriver in 1937–1938 and shared horror at readily observable Japanese barbarity further developed mutual respect and understanding between the two navies. In this instance cooperation extended all the way up to the senior command and ambassadorial levels. When British ambassador Sir Hughe Knatchbull-Hugessen was accidentally shot by a strafing Japanese aircraft, a U.S. Marine supplied blood for the transfusion. In November 1937 Admiral William Leahy, the chief of naval operations, sat down with Britain's naval attaché in Washington, D.C., to explore the possibility of a joint naval demonstration somewhere off China or Japan. Nothing came of it, but another de facto naval alliance between the two great English-speaking peoples was becoming a possibility.[94]

Such a possibility did little to ease Chatfield's mind. He would step down in September 1938 to be succeeded, in the normal course of the Royal Navy's politics of promotion, by Dudley Pound, coming up to London from command of the Mediterranean Fleet. At the end of December 1937 Chatfield in a long, rambling letter to Pound marked "Most Secret and Personal" revealed just how badly stretched the Royal Navy had become in a full-blown age of crisis, where world-shaking incidents in Europe and Asia seemingly occurred monthly if not oftener and the nightmare of a three-front naval war with wholly inadequate resources loomed ever larger.

The situation in East Asia was obviously playing out as Chatfield had foreseen in his letter to Warren Fisher at the Treasury back in June 1934. A "Main Fleet to Singapore" might be necessary, requiring substantial portions of the Home and Mediterranean Fleets be sent east as a show of force against a Japan that was now obviously threatening imperial interests. Pound was the evident candidate to take the bulk of the Royal Navy beyond Suez. Yet Chatfield was hesitant about how to proceed.

The whole situation as regards the Fleet going East is at present very uncertain; naturally I am averse to sending it if it can be avoided but I am
making all preparations as far as I can. Neither am I forgetting the difficult
questions of maintenance, ammunition, etc. Obviously the Fleet that you
will have to take out is not very satisfactory, but if it did go out, I think we
should be certain to have the American Fleet as well and that will make a
great difference. Of course in that case everything would be arranged beforehand as regards strategical movements and you will be fully informed.

Some pressures had been ameliorated, if not removed, by the growing Anglo-
American naval rapprochement. Yet others remained, and Chatfield was still
skeptical of what practical help Washington would be willing to extend in the
case of an Anglo-Japanese crisis on the Yangtze River or in the East China Sea.
"I have had some pressure put on me to send out 'reenforcements,'" Chatfield
continued,

but I have stated that nothing less than a Fleet equal to the Japanese
would be sufficient. Actually, of course, as you will have seen in my teleprint
to you the Fleet that we could send out would in many respects not be
equal to the Japanese, but the HOOD would make up in some way for the
inferiority in 8" Cruisers and anyway the Americans have plenty of those.
All talk, however, of any action by the United States is taboo and highly
secret, but we won't mention it to anybody else. Anyhow one can never be
sure what they will do and we cannot rely on them absolutely. I wish I
could send the REPULSE as well but as it is there will be only three [capi-
tal] ships left at home and with the DEUTSCHLANDS to prey on our trade
routes I have had strong pressure on me to keep both HOOD and REPULSE
at home, but this I have resisted, as the Japanese have some fast battleships
which you will not have. A difficult question will arise about the WAR-
SPITE. . . . Naturally if the WARSPITE went out I should have to keep another ship back. A good deal might happen and change might be made
also as a result of staff conversations with the United States. It is quite possible of course that now the Japanese have had such a warning of the danger they are running to [presumably a reference to President Roosevelt's
"Quarantine Speech" of the previous October 5], they will be more careful
and their military offensive will be less inclined to run amok and endeavour to confine the war to the East and Centre of China. If they decide to attack Canton, [just sixty miles from British-held Hong Kong] danger of incidents will increase.[95]

Strapped for money (though not attention after 1936), opposed every step of the way for years by the Royal Air Force whenever service needs or interests collided, demoralized by loss of status, riven from within by discord between the upper and lower decks, paralyzed by European and imperial commitments that seemed overwhelming, and instinctively hostile to the modern world of incessant invention, innovation, and change, Britain's senior service under the new and uncertain leadership of the dogged but uninspired Dudley Pound would face war in 1939 against enemies who, though no more technologically advanced than the Royal Navy, were both determined and inspired.

CHAPTER 4

Preparing for Armageddon

Germany

HISTORIANS HAVE LONG asserted or assumed that the German navy was the unwanted stepchild of Nazism because Hitler and his henchmen feared the sea and were thus intrinsically at odds with their sailors. "If Adolf Hitler ever looked out over the sea and marveled, no one remembers it. If ever while young he thought of going to sea and finding out what lay beyond, he never said so.... To him the sea remained alien and awesome.... He had no use for the sea in the north above the English Channel or in the south between Europe and Africa." The führer openly derided as preposterous Kaiser Wilhelm's faith that Germany's future lay upon the world ocean.[1]

Although such assertions are correct, it is also true that Nazi militancy embraced and sought to make productive use of all the armed forces of the state. Just a week after gaining power, Hitler took his navy chief aside after a military conference to assure him that "the Navy would not be neglected," adding that, of course, the expansion of the German fleet "was to be in conformity with the requirements of German continental policy." Recognizing that his navy chief was a careerist and an opportunist, Hitler played on Erich Raeder's vanity and aspirations. He raised "complicated questions of naval construction and showed a surprising knowledge of technical details." The führer discussed "naval personalities" and with disarming candor "freely admitted his ignorance of naval strategy." At that time, Adolf Hitler was a charismatic younger man of forty-four.

The slightly older Raeder, basking in his reputation as a strategic thinker, could not help but be overwhelmed. Right up to the spring of 1939 Raeder exhibited a touching faith in his führer's assurances that he would be given the time and resources to build a powerful navy that could, in effect, intimidate Great Britain's increasingly elderly fleet without necessarily having to fight it.[2]

During the first three years of the Hitler regime, a flood tide of navalism spread across Germany rivaling that set loose by the kaiser and Alfred von Tirpitz thirty years before. Veterans' groups and youth associations were taken over and supported by the party. A knowledgeable British observer noted that "space was demanded in all newspapers for pro-naval propaganda; innumerable books and pamphlets for old and young were produced, glorifying the Imperial Navy and publicizing the new one; money for men and material was to be had in abundance." In accordance with Nazi "educational" practice, "the past, even unto the dim days of Viking raiders, was combed for exploits to build up a tradition of German sea power." Hitler even traveled to Kiel sometime in the late thirties to dedicate a Naval Memorial. And his young sailors recited a grim poem for their führer that closed with the words: "But then comes the darkness and raw winds blow. / A Fleet lies sleeping in Scapa Flow."[3]

In the late twenties Hans Zenker and Erich Raeder had managed to build three fast 6-inch-gun light cruisers that might operate alone as raiders or together as a single raiding squadron. In November 1932, as the first of the three "pocket battleships" was about to appear, General Kurt von Schleicher, chancellor of the rapidly expiring Weimar Republic, first openly violated the terms of the Versailles Treaty by approving construction of sixteen small U-boats. When Hitler came to power two months later, he immediately approved orders for two light cruisers and numerous armed merchant vessels. One powerful element in Raeder's 1934 Replacement Shipbuilding Programme that did take rapid shape on the building stocks was a "26,000 ton" battle cruiser to be named *Scharnhorst,* which sacrificed armament rather than armor for speed. When completed, the vessel would mount a main battery of only nine 11-inch guns on a 31,800-ton hull. But it was capable of more than thirty knots and enjoyed protection closer to that of a battleship than a cruiser. Raeder and his admirals and captains were laying the foundations for the kind of vigorous commerce war against Britain and France that naval experts in the 1930s confidently expected to define the next conflict at sea. As early as 1927, ambitious factions within the navy had contacted former members of the overseas supply organization that had flourished throughout the 1914–1918 war, and four years later the system was again up and operational.

Another battle cruiser (to be named *Gneisenau*), folded quietly into the 1934 building program, would be rushed to completion in order to join *Scharnhorst* in neutralizing the two French replies—*Dunkerque* and *Strasbourg*—to the pocket battleships. Construction of two 10,000-ton heavy cruisers *(Admiral Hipper* and *Blücher),* armed with eight 8-inch guns, was also given priority, as were the beginnings of a formidable destroyer fleet of fifteen 1,650-ton vessels (which actually displaced well over 2,000 tons upon commissioning) armed with 5-inch guns and eight 21-inch torpedo tubes. Nazi Germany also strengthened its coastal defenses with the construction of the first of a class of very powerful motor torpedo boats. The war minister, General Werner von Blomberg, had already given his consent to a navy request for the establishment of an "anti-submarine" school at Kiel that in fact quickly became a training academy for U-boat crews.

The fledgling Kriegsmarine did not forget another crucial element of naval power: intelligence. Well before Hitler came to power, Raeder and his colleagues had revitalized their own "Room 40." The Beobachter Dienst, or "Observation Service," known to friends and foes alike as BDienst since its establishment in World War I, came under the energetic leadership in 1934 of Lieutenant Commander Heinz Bonatz, who immediately began a systematic study of the characteristics of British wireless transmissions, "their customary pattern, periods of special intensity, mode of delivery, wave-lengths most often used," and so on. Over the years, Bonatz and his faceless analysts developed a "fair enough" insight into British signaling procedures and techniques as to pinpoint with acceptable accuracy the location of most British fleet units. The Germans also immediately turned to deciphering British merchant-shipping codes with spectacular results that would become terrifyingly evident after 1939. And BDienst took on one other crucial task: that of analyzing and drastically improving and complicating a small, electric keyboard coding machine called Enigma, whose plugs, wires, reflectors, and three (eventually four) alphabet-ringed rotors could be arranged in such a complex and complicated fashion that it was believed no enemy cryptanalysts could ever break the frequently changing code patterns that the machine produced.[4]

But Raeder's yearning for a second High Seas Fleet was impossible to fulfill. Hitler not only feared the sea but was also contemptuous of sea power, dismissing Tirpitz's *Hochseeflotte* as a "parade piece." Moreover, the führer wanted no part of a maritime war pitting Germany against Japan and Italy, which by 1935 were becoming attractive as potential allies; he especially did not want to fight Great Britain. From 1933 until well into World War II, Hitler fancied making a world-shaking deal with England whereby His Majesty's government would give resurgent Germany a free hand on the European Continent in exchange for a German pledge not to seek subversion or destruction of the British Empire. And finally, there was the matter of resources. An oil-powered Nazi High Seas Fleet on the scope and scale that Raeder dreamed of would have sucked up every drop of petroleum every day throughout the country.[5]

Falling into line behind their führer and doubtless wishing to lull putative enemies as well, naval propagandists after 1935 publicly disavowed any suggestion that Germany intended to rebuild Tirpitz's High Seas Fleet. Fregattenkapitan F. O. Ruge, writing in a British defense publication two years later, was able to mingle bravado with restraint. Within the terms of the 1935 agreement with Britain, "Germany is free in the choice of the types [of ships] to be built, their displacement, the calibre of their guns, etc." Nonetheless, the agreement with Great Britain did "fix" the size of the German fleet "and shows better than words could do the firm will of the Leader of the Reich not to compete with Great Britain in naval armament."[6]

While Ruge and others wrote and spoke one way, Raeder continued to take quiet steps to rebuild Germany's sea machine. Just before Christmas 1937, the admiral added no fewer than six battleships to his "replacement" program, together with two aircraft carriers, in addition to the two that had been contracted twenty-five months before. Raeder had earlier dismissed carriers as "dangerous 'gas cans'"; now he began to grasp their enormous potential as Atlantic commerce raiders in company with a fast battleship or battle cruiser or two.[7]

Raeder's capital ships, no less than those of the earlier Hochseeflotte, were designed to at once rally and comfort the large German populations that remained abroad. His vision of a fleet upholding and symbolizing the mythical notion of "Germandom" was not incompatible with the dreams of his Nazi overlords to rule the entire world ultimately, if not by physical occupation at least by politico-military intimidation. By 1939 Englishmen were aware that "the main duty of the German Navy in peace was—and is—the linking of overseas Germans with the homeland." As soon as his fledgling service was sufficiently large and efficient, Raeder instituted world cruises by individual units and small squadrons of light cruisers, "and the first duty of a German warship in a foreign port is to establish close contact with the local colony." The influence of such visits on lonely and sentimental exiles was nearly unimaginable. In the late thirties British journalist Frank Clements traveled to Portsmouth in the company of a German girl to visit the *Graf Spee*. As she walked the decks, the young lady "suddenly exclaimed with an intensity which would have been ridiculous in an Englishwoman: 'Oh, how fine it is to be on German soil!'" Clements was struck by the fact that the enraptured girl was not in far-off "Malay but within a stone's throw, so to speak, of Germany."[8]

When he became grand admiral in 1928, Raeder had introduced a "policy of sound discipline and morale" based "on humane and intelligent treatment of all subordinates, and a respect for the dignity of the individual." He enjoyed the backing of the entire service, for "every superior officer in the Navy silently swore that there should never again be a *November, 1918.*" The veterans of Tirpitz's navy understood that under the Weimar Republic Germany had made the transition from a nation of classes to a democratic state, and "the position of the enlisted man within the community had likewise changed" for the better.[9] Obedience, dependability, and a sense of duty had to be instilled, not imposed.

Raeder and his captains thus found it easy to adapt to the Nazi system of enforced comradeship. By 1939 not even most reactionary captains could stand against it. At Christmastime that year the American radio correspondent William L. Shirer was invited to Kiel to inspect the fleet, and he witnessed a series of incidents that demonstrated how far the German navy had moved from the days of the kaiser. Shirer first visited *Gneisenau.* "I was surprised at the spirit of camaraderie between officers and men on the ship and so was—I soon noticed—my monocled *Oberleutnant* from the World War." As Shirer and his hosts, senior officers all, moved through the battle cruiser and entered the crew's quarters, "there was no jumping up, no snapping to attention as I had expected." The captain noticed his guest's surprise. "'That's the new spirit in our navy,' he said proudly." The men on all German warships got exactly the same kind and amount of rations as the officers, and *Gneisenau*'s captain quoted a Nazi proverb "to the effect that the same food for officers and men puts an end to discontent and helps win the war." Shirer then visited a submarine. "We sat around a long table, officers and men intermingled in a manner that shocked my *Oberleutnant,* singing and talking."[10]

After a time Raeder began timidly and not so timidly challenging Nazi mores and the Nazi lifestyle. He made no secret of his dislike for Hermann Göring and other extremists who reciprocated his feelings. Raeder was proud of his Christianity and of the fact that he was able to keep the surface fleet reasonably devout and reasonably free of Nazi fanaticism. He once told a navy pastor that he would not wage political warfare against Nazism but would show himself to be a true disciple of Christ. Göring snickered to Hitler about the admiral's ostentatious churchgoing, which was so un-Nazi-like as to suggest a whiff of treason.[11]

Raeder also chafed under the Nazis' ostentatious programs of self-denial. The admiral was a "stiff disciplinarian, an intense worker, and extremely practical thinker," but he was no ascetic, believing that living well was a prerogative of superior rank. At one point during the war he was publicly embarrassed when authorities identified him as one of a handful of obstructionists who had dealt in the black market in foodstuffs to obtain good wines and beef for his table.[12]

While Raeder yearned to re-create the imperial surface navy, he quickly found that his new fleet was as riven with jealousy, division, and strategic uncertainties as was the old. Karl Dönitz was convinced that the submarine, not the battleship, must be Germany's weapon of choice in any future conflict. Whereas Raeder's relations with Hitler became increasingly distant after 1939, Dönitz gave the despicable Wilhelm Keitel a good run for the honor of being the führer's chief lickspittle. A rabid anti-Semite who on a visit to Cape Town in 1934 reported on the efforts of the "Jewish Mayor" and "the strongly-influenced Jewish press" to whip up anti-German sentiment, the admiral's "beliefs in Germany and its world mission, in the Fuehrer, and the creed of National Socialism were . . . fervent." Peter Padfield cites a passage Dönitz wrote in a war diary following an entry by a staff officer who pronounced Hitler less than brilliant: "The huge force the Führer radiates, his unshakable confidence, his far-sighted judgement of the situation in Italy have made it plain during these days what very poor little fry [Würstchen] we all are by comparison with the Führer, and that our knowledge, our vision of things outside our limited sphere is fragmentary. Anyone who thinks he can do better than the Führer is foolish." After succeeding Raeder in 1943, Dönitz often stayed at führer headquarters, sometimes for days at a time. At the end, he seemed Hitler's chief ideological soul mate, and in April 1945 the falling Hitler tossed him the torch of leadership. Grossadmiral Karl Dönitz became the second—and last—chancellor of the Third Reich.[13]

Dönitz's character and temperament had been forged in the crucible of the 1915–1918 undersea war, and he later wrote almost lyrically of the experience.

> I had been fascinated by that unique characteristic of the submarine service, which requires a submariner to stand on his own feet and sets him a task in the great spaces of the oceans, the fulfillment of which demands a stout heart and ready skill; I was fascinated by that unique spirit of comradeship engendered by destiny and hardship shared in the community of a U-boat's crew, where every man's well-being was in the hands of all and where every single man was an indispensable part of the whole. Every submariner, I am sure, has experienced in his heart the glow of the open sea and the task

entrusted to him, has felt himself to be as rich as a king and would change places with no man.[14]

The legacy of stealthy, pitiless, and indiscriminate undersea combat waged by a close-knit community of sailors melded comfortably with Hitler's "New Germany" of youthful true believers. Nazi Germany and Fascist Italy thrived because each regime successfully responded to the most fundamental challenge of the 1930s: serving the needs of ambitious young people "bewildered by the perplexities of this strange and terrible world in which they find themselves."[15] Beneath all the adolescent posturing and puerile assertions of Hitler, Mussolini, and their propagandists about the superiority of the Aryan or Italian folk, about racial purity, destiny, blood, soil, and the need for redemption, "living room," and violence, lay a bedrock desire to create immortal national monuments to themselves on the shoulders of the spirited, aggressive, and unquestioning young. "It is the era of youth," wrote the notable English journalist Philip Gibbs in 1938.

> The first article of the Fascist faith is intolerance. And the second article of the Fascist faith is that youth is more important than old age because it is not hostile to new ideas and can be converted to new loyalties. It is for youth to make the Brave New World. It is for youth—Fascist youth, fit and splendid and high spirited—to push out the old maunderers, the old gabbers, the old compromisers, and to take charge of life. These are good words to hear by healthy young men full of self-confidence and self-conceit, eager to show their mettle. Given a leader, the right coloured shirt, and plenty of machine guns, and the power is theirs. All the rebels, eccentrics, faddists, theorists and little "intellectuals" go down before the Fascist battalions. Is not that how the world goes?[16]

German and Italian youth would be served. Out of a world of mass poverty, want, and frustration they would be enlisted into young people's groups. They would wear elaborate and attractive uniforms and march with their garish flags behind blaring bands and beating drums in vast parades. They would spend their summers on Baltic or Mediterranean beaches and their springtimes and autumns in forests and hills contemplating the grandeur of "mountain and cloud." They would attend distant annual party rallies gratis, standing proudly in vast, anonymous ranks almost hysterically eager to catch a glimpse and hear the words of the supreme leader who was magically transforming nation and folk from privation and humiliation to material power and political respectability. Above all, they would belong to a great, thoughtless, swelling tide of power and action defined by a charismatic champion: "Fuehrer, befiehl, wir folgen!" (Leader, order us, we will obey!).

As the Hitler regime steadily escalated its anti-Semitic crusade in the wake of the 1935 Nuremberg Laws, the German navy largely fell into line. Raeder retained a handful of "non-Aryans" on his headquarters staff and intervened privately when he could to save old friends and acquaintances who had fallen victim to Nazi barbarism, but he went no further. On the one occasion when he timidly protested violence against the Jews in the aftermath of Kristallnacht near the end of 1938, Raeder easily allowed himself to be deflected by Hitler's assurance that Göring and the others had acted on their own and that "the excesses of the regime were occurring against [the führer's] will and without his knowledge."[17]

The sudden growth of a somnolent and obsolescent coastal-defense force into a small but powerful navy three times its former size forced Raeder and his subordinates to find junior and midlevel officers where they could.[18] The academy at Flensburg was immediately expanded, and training was shortened. In a move that would have horrified the officer corps of the *Hochseeflotte,* Raeder permitted a substantial number of promotions from the enlisted ranks. Retired officers were recalled, and merchant sailors were offered or simply given commissions.

The navy enlisted structure was drastically reformed. Under the provisions of Versailles, the coastal-defense fleet had been manned by long-serving professionals—enlistments were usually for a dozen years. This system was "not suited to German conditions," a Kriegsmarine officer observed stiffly in 1937, since the navy was so small that promotions were impossible. The Nazis reduced enlistments to four years to accommodate thousands of eager applicants who, despite the melancholy history of 1914–1918, still viewed the naval service with awe and romance. After serving the universal apprenticeship in the Nazi labor corps, youngsters between the ages of seventeen and twenty-three enlisted for four years. Their enlistments might run a few months longer should they desire advanced specialist training in a given rate before going aboard ship. Once the enlistment was over and the young men returned to civilian life, they were given job preferences and a modest stipend to tide them over until their first paychecks arrived.

For those who wished to make the navy a career, petty officers were chosen after two or three years' service. The selectees were given an intensive six-month training course at the Petty Officer's Training Establishment ashore that mixed infantry training (three months) with either three months in a sailing ship for the deck rates or specialist courses for other ratings. "They receive general instruction in everything necessary for a petty officer and get practice in teaching, giving orders, handling men, using small arms, etc. Great importance is attached to the creation of a strict sense of duty and honour and of a vivid *esprit de corps*." Having completed the six-month course, the petty officers were sent back to the fleet. "In due course and after some more special training they are made chief petty officers, and later *Feldwebel* in which rank they wear fore-and-aft rig." *Oberfeldwebel*—specially picked and trained chief petty officers—fulfilled the old specialist duties of the warrant officers of the *Hochseeflotte*.

Once Dönitz became head of the navy in 1943, its Nazification accelerated rapidly. "Over and over again Doenitz made ringing addresses to the German sailors and to the nation, praising everything about Hitler—his peerless leadership, his infallibility." In December 1943 the newly appointed commander in chief told the navy leadership "how deeply he believed in the ideological education of the German soldier, the holy zeal and fanaticism with which the country must fight." Several months later he addressed his immediate subordinates again on this point, emphasizing that "the whole officer corps must be so indoctrinated that it feels itself co-responsible with the National Socialist state in its entirety." The officer was the exponent and symbol of the Nazi state. "The idle chatter that the officer is non-political is nonsense."[19]

Not surprisingly, Raeder and Dönitz did not get along well. Years later, at Nuremberg, Dönitz spoke to an American psychiatrist of the time when Raeder "was the big chief and I was just the little man in the navy." To the fanatic youngsters of the U-boat arm, their commander was "unser Doenitz," the "lion" of the service who could do no wrong. Why did the accursed Raeder have to pine for huge, expensive battleships when everyone knew that Germany could defeat Britain at sea by U-boats alone? "The little man in the submarine service summed things up in his own way when he said bitterly: 'Our Commander-in-Chief (Admiral Raeder) doesn't want any U-boats, and for why? Because we can't put a band on the upper deck and receive 'im with trumpets and drums!'"[20]

By 1937–1938 the German navy was again weighing the question of a North Sea–North Atlantic war versus concentration on the Baltic. Raeder had initially argued for the development of a modest fleet to confront France. After 1936, however, as Hitler accelerated rearmament, increased diplomatic pressure on the other European powers, and intervened in the Spanish civil war, Raeder realized that conflict with Britain was unavoidable.[21] How would the potential Soviet colossus respond?

Raeder formed two naval group headquarters, East and West, which battled each other continually. Eventually, the "western" headquarters responsible for the North Sea and North Atlantic won out, and France, then finally Britain, was duly labeled as Germany's chief antagonist. But the "eastern" headquarters made several powerful arguments for a naval concentration in the Baltic before being overwhelmed. Swedish iron ore from Arctic mines had become essential to the burgeoning German war machine. In peacetime winters it could be transported down the Norwegian coast, whose waters were sufficiently warmed by the North Atlantic Current and whose screen of offshore islands provided sufficient protection against attacks by the Royal Navy. But in wartime Norwegian waters would presumably be closed, and a Baltic passage would have to be established. Better to keep the fleet in the Baltic against a sudden British thrust than to dash it to pieces fighting the enemy in the North Sea. And if Soviet Russia should menace Germany's eastern frontiers, then surely the navy would once again play a major role supporting army groups on the Baltic shore as it had done in 1917. Such spirited debates over strategic and tactical planning reflected the growing pains of an uncertain young service suddenly bursting with a large number of young, energetic people and in need of bold ideas that would appeal to them. The fact that Raeder and Dönitz held sharply differing views of the course German naval expansion should take served to open up rather than stifle communication between senior officers and an impatient younger generation.[22]

Raeder proved a better man than the impatient Dönitz. He had picked Dönitz to lead the U-boat arm, and thereafter he steadfastly supported his often fractious subordinate. Moreover, Raeder was far more conscious of the submarine potential than the restless and dismissive youngsters in the U-boats realized. He sought, as he later said, a balanced fleet whose "component ship types should be both complementary and interdependent."[23] Germany must have both submarines and battleships if it were ever to wrest control of the North Sea, if not the world ocean, from the Royal Navy. Raeder remembered that the German ships at Jutland had been far tougher than their British opposites, that the fighting qualities of Franz von Hipper's battle cruisers and Reinhard Scheer's battleships had been superior to those of John Jellicoe and David Beatty. He also knew of, and apparently believed, British claims that the new underwater sound device called asdic could detect U-boats over a wide area on the edge of a convoy and that the escorts could then defeat them. Raeder was nonetheless more than ready for another go at Britain both on and beneath the ocean surface if only Hitler would give the German navy time to rejuvenate, to become at least a *Hochseeflotte* in miniature.

Certainly, he proved more willing to risk his ships than had his predecessors. At the time of the Austrian crisis in 1938, for example, he sent his still minuscule

navy, headed by the brand-new *Gneisenau,* into the North Sea to challenge
Admiral Sir Charles Forbes's fifty ships led by *Nelson.* According to a contemporary account, Berlin had first informed the British that German warships would
go no farther north than a line approximately between Flamborough Head and
the Danish coast. Quite soon, however, an "alarmed" British Admiralty was
told by its German opposite that the *Gneisenau* task force would be moving
closer to Scapa Flow "but without saying exactly where." The Royal Navy feared
a "frontier incident" at sea that could lead to war—an incident resulting possibly
from "secret tactics, smoke screens, or code-signal mixups." As a consequence,
battle cruiser *Repulse,* battleship *Royal Oak,* and the Fourth Destroyer Flotilla
remained at Portsmouth to guard the English Channel. The mighty *Hood* remained at Gibraltar either to close the western Mediterranean should Mussolini
send his navy out to join that of the führer or to race up to home waters should
that become necessary.[24]

Dönitz proved as bold a leader of the undersea fleet as his superior was of
the heavy surface forces. By the spring of 1939, light surface elements of the
German navy accompanied by about twenty U-boats cruised to Lisbon, Cueta,
and far into the western Mediterranean, reflecting not only the German Admiralty's unprecedented boldness in deploying the fleet but also its growing interest
in the strategically critical Mediterranean region. During maneuvers off Cape
St. Vincent, the U-boats maneuvered into attack formation and assaulted a
force of German ships composed of supply vessels and fleet destroyers. This was
Dönitz's long-held theory of the "wolf pack"—a collection of U-boats assaulting
enemy convoys en masse—transformed into deadly reality. The results of this
mock attack "justified Doenitz's belief in his own theory of tactics and training.
After the severest analysis he was satisfied that the '[wolf]pack' tactics had accomplished and in wartime would accomplish all that was expected of them."[25]

The British naval-rearmament program of 1937 and after ensured that the
Royal Navy would remain comfortably ahead of the rebuilding German fleet
for some years in terms of quantity though not quality of ships. Whitehall also
received invaluable aid from Hermann Göring. Military and naval politics under
Hitler were as vicious as in the kaiser's day, when Tirpitz fought the imperial
army for the nation's soul. Like Tirpitz, Raeder was eventually checkmated by
his opponents, for he had not only an army to fight but an air force as well.
Göring commanded the Luftwaffe and also controlled the allocation of resources
and finances throughout the Third Reich from his position as deputy for the
Four-Year Plan. He was delighted to make common cause with Wilhelm Keitel
and the army high command to deprive the navy of the materials it needed for

its battleships and cruisers. But his most stupid blunder was to ensure that even submarine construction had low priority. When in 1935 Hitler publicly declared German rearmament, he stated that the "latest designs for foreign countries" would serve "as the basis for the first new German submarine models."[26] But although the Germans had maintained their submarine technology, they had not been able to materially advance it. The boats designed and built for foreign governments in the 1920s and early thirties were essentially replicas of those constructed in 1918 and designed to operate in the waters around the British Isles rather than in deep ocean. By the late thirties, Dönitz's strategic thinking had advanced far beyond the crude conceptions of World War I. In the age of the airplane, it would be folly to try to clamp a close-in submarine blockade on Great Britain. U-boats in the western approaches surfacing to recharge batteries or racing to stay in surface contact with fast-moving convoys would be sitting ducks for an air attack. Dönitz's idea was to cut Britain's shipping lanes out in the open Atlantic, destroying its commerce on the high seas between the Old World and the New. Prosecution of this distant pelagic strategy required that much research and development be devoted to developing U-boat technology. Yet beyond a substantial upgrade in the operational range of German submarines, little or nothing was accomplished in this vital field before the outbreak of war. The U-boat "pack" that operated so effectively against the defending "convoy" off Cape St. Vincent in early 1939 was composed of small, cramped 500-ton boats of limited endurance, incapable of reaching midocean and waging the kind of sustained battles against enemy cargo ships and tankers that might tip the balance at sea in Germany's favor. The best that Germany could send out to midocean the following September was the 750-ton Type VII submarine, possessing greater operational range but in other ways little different and not as good as the U-boats that had prowled the western approaches twenty-two years before. Too few in numbers and too modest in capability, Germany's submarines in 1939–1940 would be unable to fully perform the commerce- and fleet-destruction missions essential to victory at sea.[27]

Göring also frustrated Raeder's insistent demands for a separate naval air force. The admiral's experiences in the Great War and especially at Jutland had made him realize the supreme importance of aviation for an inferior fleet seeking either commerce warfare or battle with an inferior portion of the enemy navy. Raeder was no Yamamoto or Halsey. He apparently never grasped the concept of naval airpower as a unique and potentially dominant force in the war at sea. His airplanes would fulfill the traditional role conceived for them as scouts and fire-control spotters. But in 1936 he did ask for a separate fleet air arm comprising eight hundred aircraft in sixty-four squadrons. He never got it, but his good mind and flexible temperament might have expanded his conception of carrier aviation's role once war came. The ships that his designers envisioned were as much cruisers as aviation ships, with heavy casemated guns placed low in ungainly hulls. But Raeder knew that without airpower his new navy would be wholly at the mercy of the British enemy. Moreover, Raeder insisted that his navy needed land-based aircraft trained in overwater operations that could harry the English fleet in the North Sea and the Channel.[28]

Like his RAF counterparts, however, Göring was determined not to surrender any aspect of airpower to a rival service. Unlike his British counterparts, he never changed his mind. German squabbles over naval aviation between 1935 and 1939 closely paralleled those that had just concluded in Britain, and with the same unhappy results for the navy. A single carrier, *Graf Zeppelin,* was launched in 1938 but never completed. The Luftwaffe retained control of overwater operations in the seas adjacent to Germany and the Continent, with ultimately disastrous results for the surface fleet.[29]

Just after the Austrian crisis and while Germany was agitating for the return of the Sudetenland, Hitler informed Raeder that he had changed his mind and that Britain must now be considered a future enemy, though the führer continued to insist that the navy had time to build up a formidable fleet before war came. Seven months later, with the Sudetenland in his pocket and the rest of Czechoslovakia poised to fall, Hitler invoked the proper clause in the Anglo-German naval treaty and notified London that Germany would increase its submarine tonnage to match that of Great Britain. Andrew Cunningham, now an admiral, was sent to Berlin to remonstrate. After a brief handshake with Raeder ("a fine-looking man who made us a pleasant speech of welcome"), he was turned over to one of Raeder's subordinates, Admiral Otto Schniewind, who formally notified him of German plans. Cunningham responded that there were no "special circumstances" justifying application of the 100 percent clause, "but though the Germans gave the impression of great friendliness we soon realized we were up against a blank wall," and the mission ended in failure.[30]

Pursuant to Hitler's decision to designate Britain as a prime enemy, Raeder late in 1938 adopted an ambitious program of warship construction named Plan Z drawn up by Commander Helmuth Heye of the Operational Section of naval headquarters. The plan envisaged an unbalanced fleet in which U-boats and battleships predominated. Historians differ somewhat over the precise dimensions of the plan, but by February 1939 Hitler had approved a nine-year building program that would comprise, in addition to the existing 2 battle cruisers

(Scharnhorst and *Gneisenau)* and 3 pocket battleships *(Deutschland, Admiral Scheer,* and *Graf Spee),* 4 fifty-six thousand–ton battleships, 2 forty-two thousand–ton battlewagons already being built *(Bismarck* and *Tirpitz),* 8 heavy cruisers, 17 light cruisers, 4 aircraft carriers of from nineteen thousand to twenty-seven thousand tons, and 221 coastal and seagoing submarines. The plan may also have included a dozen small twenty thousand–ton battleships. Even at this late date, Hitler assured his naval chief that no war with Britain could be considered until at least 1944, when the bulk of the surface force would be completed and ready for sea. Whether in fact it would ever be able to put to sea as a single powerful unit, given Germany's chronic fuel shortages, was another matter entirely.[31]

Raeder had no cause to rejoice, however, for the formidable fleet he wished to build remained largely on paper. By this time he had in hand *Scharnhorst* and *Gneisenau* together with the three pocket battleships, a handful of weak light cruisers, and roughly a score of large, fast, powerful destroyers with the initial Type VII submarines and the first of the splendid *Hipper*-class heavy cruisers about to enter service. But despite priority construction, the battle cruisers had taken four long years to build; the first two authentic battleships, *Bismarck* and *Tirpitz,* were at the fitting-out dock and still on the building ways, respectively. The entire naval building program was months if not years behind schedule.

By the end of 1938 an increasingly impatient and domineering führer would no longer give Raeder six years to prepare his new and uncertain fleet for war. By this time German naval planners had developed a "temporary objective" of 10 battleships, 15 fast battleships, 5 heavy and 24 light cruisers, 8 aircraft carriers, and 249 submarines. Raeder and his subordinates hoped to have such a fleet ready by midcentury. Hitler, demanding an impossible acceleration of construction in order to cover his own grandiose plans, would give them little more than six years.[32]

The entire new High Seas Fleet conception died in absurdity. In considering future deployment of "the 'Z' fleet," Commander Heye had concluded that "a German cruising fleet could remain at sea no longer than three months before problems of resupply, repair, refuelling, and restaffing would become insurmountable." Meanwhile, Dönitz's pleas for a dramatically accelerated U-boat construction program that could have brought Britain to its knees continued to fall on deaf ears.[33]

When war came on September 3, 1939, Raeder felt "bitterly betrayed." "The naval forces," he wrote, "are so inferior in number and strength that they can do no more than show that they know how to die gallantly and thus are willing to create the foundations for later reconstruction." The grand admiral was being

more than a bit melodramatic. Although Germany was flatly incapable of implementing Plan Z (assuming Britain and France would allow it), it did possess a
powerful squadron of surface ships and a significant, if much too slowly growing,
U-boat arm. A great deal could be done with such a force, if boldly employed.
The official naval historian and curator of the German Navy Archive, Kurt
Assmann, wrote no less than three strategy papers as war approached in 1939
articulating the importance of a German sea war against British commerce in
the Atlantic. *Economic, trade,* and *"tonnage" warfare* became the new buzzwords
around the German Admiralty in the final days of peace. A Nazi squadron
composed of a fast battleship, a battle cruiser, and an aircraft carrier, rampaging
across the North Atlantic for ninety days, could keep enemy merchantmen,
and maybe even enemy sea warriors, penned up in their ports for as long as it
took to starve Britain out. Whether or not this was so, Hitler's grand admiral
was determined that this time the German fleet would die at sea, not swinging
'round its anchor chains.[34]

   As was the case in 1914, Germany could count on one lesser ally at sea. But
the Italians of 1939–1943 would prove as deficient as the Austro-Hungarian
sailors that had been easily penned up in the Adriatic by Allied forces a quarter
century before. The Italian navy of the late thirties was an anomaly in many
ways. As the Abyssinian Crisis suggested and the coming war would prove,
Italian sailors continued to hold their British counterparts in the same kind of
awe that had impelled the monarch back in 1897 to order a twenty-one-gun
salute from the entire fleet as a gesture of honor for the Royal Navy during Vic-
toria's diamond jubilee. Italian shipyards completed the first two of four fine
fifteen-inch-gun battleships that Mussolini had ordered, with the other two
coming into service in 1940. By 1942, when Mussolini was prepared to join
Hitler in any general European war, Italy would possess no fewer than eight new
or completely refurbished battleships, more than enough, if properly handled,
to overwhelm the enemy, particularly since the Italians also outnumbered the
British Mediterranean Fleet in the categories of very fast and well-armed six-
and eight-inch-gun cruisers. Despite such advantages, Mussolini's sailors told
their German allies that "even a numerically inferior English fleet would have
many advantages because of its experience and traditions, over an Italian fleet
superior in numbers."[35]
   Admiral Domenico Cavagnari was determined to keep his fleet out of the
eastern Mediterranean where the British ruled from Alexandria, and he thought
the Italian army's plan to descend on Suez sheer madness. In case of war, Cav-

agnari proposed to send his ships west. Huddling under the protective air and sea cover provided by Franco and, he hoped, a German battle squadron in the nearby Atlantic off Gibraltar, he could successfully bring the French navy to battle. Thereafter, his fleet could steam proudly out into the ocean and have a "decisive influence on the outcome of the conflict" against Britain's badly stressed fleet, presumably depleted by German air and naval forces.[36]

Recent history may have played a major part in shaping this mood. In general, the Italian navy had not played a sterling role in the Great War of 1914–1918, and on more than one occasion the prime minister and cabinet had openly expressed their dissatisfaction with the fleet. Britain had been an ally and therefore an observer of these shortcomings. In any future war the Royal Navy would be certain to exploit whatever weaknesses remained.[37]

Italian strategists were preoccupied with their country's exposed position. Mussolini yearned to build an empire that would ultimately stretch from North Africa around to Abyssinia and on to Oceania. Fascist spokesmen proclaimed that Italy must, therefore, have a great navy not only to police *mare nostrum* (our sea) but to parade and posture out on the world ocean as well. But Italy was perilously exposed, a peninsula in an inland ocean. All of the nation's sea-lanes, east to Suez, the Red Sea, and beyond and west toward Gibraltar, were easily menaced, while its coasts and those of its larger island possessions were exposed to assault from both sea and air. At any moment a French fleet could swoop down from Toulon to devastate the Italian shoreline from Genoa to Sicily. In the Adriatic, Italian naval spokesmen professed to fear a fast-growing Yugoslavian navy that was in fact little better than a coastal-defense force. Beset as it was, Italy was determined to rely on the fascist spirit to fulfill its destiny.[38]

Laboring under a lingering sense of inferiority, most of the navy entertained few illusions about fascist destiny and deeply resented the regime. Shortly before the war Andrew Cunningham visited the big naval base at Livorno where the naval academy was also located. "Certainly the Italians appeared to give their young officers a good training," Cunningham recalled, though "according to our ideas the discipline was unnecessarily harsh, imprisonment in a cell being awarded for quite minor offences." He found the navy as a whole to be as royalist as he remembered from earlier days and angry over the incessant spying of the fascist regime and its crude indoctrination of the creed of blood and steel.[39] When war came, the deep divisions within Italian naval circles would become manifest.

The Italian fleet suffered from deeper and more crippling weaknesses that were not known or only dimly guessed at in the years immediately before the war. Ashore, its leaders had little access to or influence over Mussolini and his war staff, who remained oriented toward land and aerial warfare. The navy possessed no fleet air arm and had to rely exclusively on the Regia Aeronautica. In fact, Mussolini's law forbidding the Italian navy to possess independent air capability—enacted as early as 1923—remained on the books almost to the end of the twentieth century.[40]

At sea, Italy's incredibly fast cruisers were true tin clads, possessing little or no armor, and all warships from the smallest destroyer to the latest battleship sacrificed strength and internal integrity for luxurious officer accommodations, including, in the words of one caustic critic, such "cosseting features" as enclosed bridges "to afford shelter from the moderate Mediterranean climate." The pampering of Italian naval officers with luxurious accommodations, fittings, furniture, and the finest wines and food contrasted sharply with the spartan quarters and life of the enlisted men. "A gulf existed between officers and men which discipline did nothing to bridge. Punishment for minor offenses was severe," and officers cared little for the welfare of those in their charge. Such deficiencies might have been made up at least in part by the kind of rigorous training regimen that existed in the kaiser's *Hochseeflotte* in the years before 1914. But Mussolini's lazy sailors disdained to prepare for serious warfare. "Night exercises were sketchy. Daytime exercises were abandoned if bad weather intervened or heavy seas were encountered." The result was an utter lack of toughness and team spirit—of any degree of real professionalism—that would lead to frequent panic in battle. When war came, the Italians would find themselves pitted against possibly the greatest English sea dog since Horatio Nelson, Andrew Cunningham. Cunningham's experiences in World War I, and after, "taught him that war was won by defeating the enemy's mind." With desperately few resources and exhausted men, he would defeat the Italian navy every time.[41]

CHAPTER 5

Preparing for Armageddon

Japan

AS WAR CLOUDS GATHERED over the Pacific after 1935, Japan and the United States marched in virtual lockstep, developing the necessary tools and techniques to wage war across vast distances. While they did so, Japanese sailors and intellectuals made one final effort to justify to the world their nation's responsibility for the collapse of the international naval accords and its apparently unlimited expansionist appetites. All the old arguments were trotted out. Western critics, wholly "unfamiliar with the mentality of the East," tried to pin the label of "imperialist" upon Japan. Westerners were the true imperialists, however, because they were caught up in a wholly selfish ideal of the rugged individual, constantly out to remake his world for his own gratification. The peoples of the East had developed a more beneficent conception of the political state and its mission based on "the universal stream of life without beginning or end" whose visible symbol was the Japanese emperor. "The state must be guided solely by laws, by cosmic laws that fit the stream of life." Japan understood these laws and was in the process of applying them to the benefit of all East Asia. Manchuria, for example, had long been "an apple of discord in the hands of generals jealously fighting each other, an object of exploitation for robbers and highwaymen." For decades, "Russia" had cast a "greedy eye" on the area in its "insatiable lust for power." Japan had had to move into this intrinsically beautiful land in order to restore it. Now it was performing the same service for China. This was not Western-style imperialism; it was Oriental destiny. If the Western powers truly wished Japan and the peoples of the East well, they would stand aside and let Tokyo have its way.[1]

One thought that floated around Tokyo in 1936 proposed that after Japan achieved absolute naval parity with Britain, and the United States, the three nations should divide the world into regional blocs—Europe, Asia, and the "Western Hemisphere"—with each of their navies responsible for maintaining peace in its respective bloc. According to this argument, Japan was responsible for the future development of a huge area stretching north to south from the Kurile Islands through Formosa to the South Pacific and west to east from Manchukuo through Korea out to the Bonin Islands and New Guinea. "The Navy intends to have control of a section of the western Pacific stretching from the Sea of Okhotsk to the South Seas for the purposes of strengthening the national defense and promoting the tendency toward overseas expansion." Of course, Japan's intentions were only peaceful; "it is unthinkable," Tokyo writer Tadao Yanahara said in 1936, "that there is any intention of carrying out the South Seas policy by military operations." The government of neither the Dutch East Indies nor Australia was developing its lands as it should. It was time for them to abandon their "chauvinistic policies, remove discriminatory restrictions against Japanese goods, investments, and immigrants, and cooperate with us in the work of developing the South Seas territories." Seeking to dampen the effects of such bluster, navy minister Mitsumasa Yonai raised his voice in seeking to placate the Western powers regarding Japan's peaceful intentions. "The Imperial Navy," he told the Diet the following winter, "has no force to match the combined strength" of Britain and the United States. "It has no intention of building its strength to such a level."[2]

In fact, it was in the process of trying to do just that in the still crucial battleship category. During the 1930s Japanese capabilities and foresight were not widely appreciated in the West. Despite the splendid look of its warships, the Imperial Navy appeared to many to be a paper tiger. Japan needed some dramatic stroke to reverse the Anglo-American naval buildup that seemed to threaten it. Battleship admirals drew on the ancient dream of a superior "eight-eight" fleet for the answer. Japan could no longer afford such a fleet, given the rapid advances in shipbuilding technology and cost. But it could build several super capital ships that would totally outclass any battlewagons then in or planned for the Western arsenals. As early as 1933 ambitious junior officers in the navy's ship-construction division, bewitched by the sudden dramatic decline in U.S. economic strength relative to that of Japan, began inundating their superiors, including the head of the now triumphant "Fleet faction," Admiral Katō Kanji, with plans for two to four superbattleships mounting 20-inch guns together with four big, fast battle cruisers carrying a dozen 12-inch guns that would neutralize the U.S. Navy's tenuous superiority in heavy cruisers. With ships such as these, Ishikawa Shingo and others argued, Japan would be impregnable. As war with the United States became increasingly probable after 1935, navy planning became somewhat more realistic. It appeared that five 70,000-ton superbattleships armed with nine 18.1-inch guns could be built. In the event, Japan could afford to build only three, one of which, *Shinano,* was converted in wartime to a carrier that was torpedoed and sunk on its first voyage. The sudden appearance of such ships, no less than double the size of the Washington Naval Treaty limits and armed with the largest naval guns in the world, was meant to intimidate and demoralize Western admiralties and navy departments to the point that Japan would be given the free hand in East Asia and the western Pacific that it insisted upon. Or, failing that, should war come, the superbattleships would represent "the apotheosis" of the Imperial Japanese Navy's "fixation on quality as a battle winner." If the West reacted irrationally and sought to build "replies" to the monster vessels, they would be so large that they could not pass through the Panama Canal, and the two-ocean commitments shared by London and Washington might well keep such vessels in the Atlantic forever.[3]

The dream was foolish, of course, if for no other reason than that its fulfillment demanded drastic curtailment of every other warship type, especially the destroyers and destroyer escorts essential to protecting from the large submarine flotillas possessed by both Britain and the United States any future sea-lanes that Japan might develop. But the superbattleship concept was tantalizing. Somehow, in some way, Japan had to neutralize the West's limitless industrial capabilities. A quick intimidation might work, might induce the Americans in particular to practically surrender the Far East rather than ruin themselves in a naval race. Certainly, the increasingly isolationist mood of Congress after 1935 offered the Japanese some encouragement.

The moderates within the Imperial Navy, steadily dwindling in number, were appalled. The eight-eight fleet dream had proved impossible of realization in 1912 and 1920; why would it suddenly work now in a different form? Moreover, rumors of such ships sent a shock wave of disappointment and anger flooding through Western naval circles. When journalist Masanori Ito traveled through Europe and the United States in 1937, he heard criticisms everywhere of Japan's rumored leviathans. "The building of battleships may be a plus for Japan's naval strength," a British colleague told him, "but I am afraid it will end up as a minus for her in international relations." Hanson W. Baldwin, the respected military correspondent for the *New York Times,* told Ito that the time for talking about arms reductions was over. "We may have to have another war before there can be a real disarmament conference." Japan's master shipbuilders nonetheless pressed ahead. First conceived in the autumn of 1934, the design of the three monsters was not finalized for two years, during which time the fleet during annual maneuvers suffered losses and damage to even big ships from heavy weather. Was it possible that in their determination to build the most powerful and fastest vessels in the world, Japanese designers had inadvertently incorporated fatal structural weaknesses? In fact, they had and were forced to "almost superhuman efforts" to build sufficient strength stability into what became the superbattleships *Yamato* and *Musashi.*[4]

Japan and its navy were clearly overstressing themselves to meet real and imagined missions. After 1937, war in China would strain the country and its sailors still further. But Japan pressed ahead. As many as fifty experimental ship models were tested, and no fewer than twenty-three design plans developed, before the keels of *Yamato* and *Musashi* were laid in 1937 and 1938, respectively. Each displaced 67,000 tons light and roughly 71,700 tons fully loaded with stores and ordnance. The ships' propulsive efficiency was high, their armor plating was completed only after a decade of "earnest study," and their gigantic but graceful bulbous bows designed for maximum speed were "of a size of which few other naval architects had ever planned."[5] Nearly three thousand men were required to man the 863-foot vessels, whose 127-foot beam could accommodate the nine huge 18.1-inch guns of the main battery in three turrets, two forward, one aft, each of which weighed more than a modern destroyer. Nearly a hundred smaller guns for both surface and air defense were festooned about the somewhat cramped and compressed midships superstructure. Only there could they and their crews be protected from the terrible blast of the main batteries.

Not only were *Yamato* and *Musashi* huge, but they were also beautiful. As Russell Spurr noted, no one who saw one or both of them could ever forget them. The weather deck undulated gently from bow to stern without a break. Designers had repeatedly "modernized" Japan's battleships in the late twenties and early thirties by piling one bridge, fire-control center, and lookout station on top of another, creating tall, seemingly unstable pagoda towers that looked— and were—ungainly and top-heavy. But in *Yamato* and *Musashi* the builders had created a powerful and aesthetic silhouette composed of one smooth and graceful multideck control tower in front of a single monster stack stylishly raked back at twenty-five degrees.

The two ships were deficient in only two respects. Their original designed speed of thirty-one knots was premised on a 75,000-ton light ship displacement. But such a vessel could not fit into Japan's relatively shallow harbors; a 67,000-ton vessel could barely be squeezed in. But the drop of 8,000 tons required a sacrifice in propulsion machinery, and the two *Yamatos* were reduced to twenty-seven knots. Some critics have seen this as a major flaw.[6] But in fact Japanese seamen and builders were correct in noting that the Americans were not generally moving above this speed. Both the two *North Carolinas* and the four *South Dakotas* begun in 1937–1938 were rated at twenty-seven to twenty-eight knots. Only the four *Iowas* ordered in 1938 and completed in 1943–1944 were truly "fast" battleships readily capable of the thirty-three-knot speed required to maintain station within a carrier task force. The projected but never built five-ship *Montana* class of 1940, designed as replies to the still mysterious *Yamatos*, was designed to carry a dozen 16-inch guns on a 58,000-ton hull whose maximum speed identically matched that of the Japanese ships.[7]

The second design flaw would prove fatal. Japan had borrowed from Britain the idea of the double-lateral bulkhead running from stem to stern as a strengthening device. But as noted earlier, such a structure inhibited the free flow of water, thus threatening a rapid capsize from torpedo hits. *Yamato* and *Musashi* did contain a complicated system of valves that could pump water in and out of the antitorpedo blisters on either side of the hulls, but this was known to be of limited effect if the ships were badly flooded on one side or the other.

In Western but not Japanese estimation, the two great vessels suffered from several other deficiencies. As with every other Japanese warship built after 1907, neither *Yamato* nor *Musashi* carried life rafts or even life belts. The crude medical facilities aboard both ships "were incapable of dealing with heavy casualties." Historians and naval architects provide differing information on habitability. Mess decks and sleeping compartments were apparently unknown aboard *Yamato*. Men ate and slung their sleeping hammocks anywhere they could find room. Architects and admirals designed Japanese ships to show the nation's might and to prosecute a desperate war; the Imperial Japanese Navy was not in the business of providing social services, amenities, or even survival capabilities for its crews. Notwithstanding, a partial air-conditioning system in *Yamato* did make that vessel for a time "the most comfortable ship in the Japanese Navy." *Musashi*, "Battleship Number 2," represented a quantum leap forward. The ship was surprisingly roomy, with comfortable spaces for the entire crew. Not only was there a crude central air-conditioning system, but each enlisted man also enjoyed a bunk rather than a hammock and three times the amount of personal space found aboard the cramped destroyers. The captain's quarters were palatial, exceeding the finest accommodations in the best civilian hotels ashore.[8] Despite imperfections, the *Yamatos* were a remarkable testimony to Japan's coming-of-age as a modern industrial nation. Only a quarter century lay between construction of its first battleship and the keel laying of *Yamato,* a ship whose physical size and complexity (it contained well over 1,100 compartments) would be exceeded only by the American nuclear carriers of the mid-1970s. Japan was thus able to match the United States, Germany, and certainly Great Britain in the application of advanced industrial technologies to the building of a modern fleet.

While the *Yamatos* absorbed the attention of Japan's surface sailors, the flyers continued to press for the integration of airpower both offensively in the fleet and as a basic component of the island defense perimeter out in the Pacific. As Tokyo began to fortify its Pacific-island possessions after 1936, naval air units were sent in growing numbers to this outer defense perimeter. After Pearl Harbor they became the bedrock of the island defense strategy. Isoroku Yamamoto had joined the aeronautics division of the navy's Technical Department upon his return from the 1930 London Naval Conference, and thereafter he and his colleagues and successors concentrated as much or more on the development of medium-size and large land-based scout and attack aircraft as they did on carrier planes. The Kawanishi and Mitsubishi flying boats and the twin-engine Nell and Betty bombers that would become all too familiar to American pilots and sailors during World War II were developed along with the Claude, Zeke, and Zero carrier-based fighter planes; the Kate carrier attack bomber; and the Val carrier dive-bomber.[9] If all these aircraft ultimately proved inferior to their American counterparts, especially in protection and engine power, they were still formidable weapon systems when flown by skilled and dedicated pilots like Saburo Sakai. Japan's greatest fighter pilot of World War II spent his first month in the fleet in 1937 qualifying as a carrier pilot. But once he had mastered the approaches, touchdowns, and landings, he became a land-based flyer. "I never took off or landed on a carrier in combat. All my combat flying was done from land installations."[10]

The problem was that Japan always possessed far too few such men to fill carrier squadrons and island air bases. Superb pilots that they were, the flyers of the Imperial Japanese Navy all too often proved to be unstable characters who went to absurd and ultimately self-defeating lengths to prove their superiority. Unfortunately, their naval training reinforced such behavior. Sakai had already experienced the excessively brutal life of a Japanese seaman and even petty officer aboard the battle cruiser *Kirishima* and other ships. He simply did not believe that the navy harbored any more refinements of torture. He was wrong. In the first weeks of flight school, the cadets wrestled each other, and the loser had to stay on the mat and fight with ever diminishing energy new and eager foes. If he could not defeat one of his comrades, he was thrown out. As a consequence the matches took on a desperate and savage character, much to the delight of the training staff. Later, the men were told to shimmy to the top of a tall pole where they were ordered to balance themselves by one hand for at least ten minutes. They were expected to remain underwater for at least ninety seconds and to swim fifty meters at a fantastic pace. "The training course demanded perfection," Sakai recalled, "and a trainee could be dismissed for even the slightest infraction of the rules." On one memorable occasion, a cadet was thrown out on the eve of his graduation for celebrating too early and shamefully in an off-limits saloon.

This regimen, may well have been due to the fact that up to 90 percent of Japanese naval aviators were enlisted men. In a service and a society based on hierarchical structure and a "rigid seniority system," they could expect to be treated both harshly and capriciously. The lack of a strong officer cadre proved disastrous for Japanese naval aviation. Not only was there little opportunity for frank up-and-down-the-line exchanges of views that might have led to the development of effective tactical doctrines, but prospects for promotion to high command were limited if not nil as well. Thus, as late as 1942, when the already thin ranks of Japanese naval aviation began to be drastically reduced by combat, Japanese naval pilots were directed largely by commanders who were not air-qualified.[11]

As late as 1937 the Japanese navy graduated no more than one hundred aviators from flight school each year. Sakai's class was typical: seventy men had been picked for training out of fifteen hundred applicants. Of the seventy, only forty-five survived the barbaric training regimen. The few who staggered through such training were expected to be the greatest fighter and bomber pilots in the world, fearless young men who would sweep a soft and decadent enemy from the skies. In the earliest days of the program, the graduates of the Navy Fliers School at Tsuchiura, north and east of Tokyo, behaved with the brashness and boastfulness of the anointed and the elect. Once in the fleet, their flying often bordered on the insane, as they foolishly courted death in the name and for the sake of the emperor. "The navy's flying men in those days combined the pride of highly trained specialists with a kind of daredevilry fostered by the ever-present danger involved. There were many, even among the non-commissioned officers and men, who wore their hair long . . . and reporting late for duty and breaking barracks were both common occurrences."[12]

Yamamoto had tried to put a halt to such foolishness as early as 1924 when he briefly became second in command of the Kasumigaura Aviation Corps. He told his flyers they were slobs, and he worried that the fearsome training they had endured had turned them into hooligans possessed of an inflated sense of their own importance and capabilities. He was right, and many a good young pilot would lose his life due to either recklessness or shock in the first moments of combat over China. Even those who would become some of the best flyers of the Pacific war became, in their own words, "upset" and behaved "stupidly" when they first met a competent enemy. Throughout the late twenties and early thirties, a handful of keen Japanese planners and tacticians used *Kaga* and *Akagi,* together with *Hosho,* the light carrier *Ryujo,* and a number of shore stations, to steadily enlarge the scope and skills of Japan's naval aviators, who became increasingly proficient in carrier operations, fighter tactics (both offensive and defensive), dive-bombing, and torpedo attacks, while remaining disturbingly deficient in aerial reconnaissance and scouting.[13] But Japan's Achilles' heel remained the relative smallness of its naval-aviation community. Obsessed with quality rather than quantity, fatally prone to embody the axiom that the best was the enemy of the good, the Japanese naval air corps was setting itself up for ultimate disaster.

The incorporation into the world's navies of new, largely untried, but constantly advancing weapons like the *Yamato*s, the airplane, and the submarine suggested a possibility of power projection on a scale and in dimensions hitherto undreamed of. The vastness of the Pacific with its archipelagic structure made such projections mandatory. But the new technologies were themselves neutral, favoring neither the advancing nor the defending fleet. It was their intelligent use that would determine the outcome of battle.

It was in China, between the July 1937 Marco Polo Bridge Incident (which served as a pretext for Japan to launch a new round of aggression) and Pearl Harbor, that Japan would hone its impressive arsenal of war skills, especially amphibious operations and long-range air strikes. Decades earlier, at Weihaiwei (Weihai) during the Sino-Japanese War of 1894–1895, and in Korea and on the Liaotung (Liaodong) Peninsula in the Russian war, the Imperial Army and Navy had demonstrated a remarkable ability to hurl thousands of troops ashore quickly and with maximum safety. The soldiers and sailors of the emperor never let the many and often bitter tensions that frequently divided them get in the way of efficient and often imaginative joint planning for combined operations. Naval analyst Hector C. Bywater wrote in 1925 that because landings on hostile coasts had been practiced "year after year as a regular feature of Japanese army manoeuvres, this operation was one with which officers and men were perfectly familiar." All necessary equipment—boats, barges, pontoons, portable docks, and jetties—had been developed and had been in readiness in military depots for years. "In the same way the tactical problems of co-operation between an invading army and its supporting fleet had been thoroughly worked out." Admiral Richmond Kelly Turner, the United States Navy's most extensive and capable practitioner of amphibious warfare in the Pacific, later emphasized that "no one service invented amphibious warfare" and that while the United States Marine Corps contributed much in the way of doctrine and technique, they derived much of their initial information and insights from the Japanese.[14]

In China and later in the Pacific, Japanese amphibious assaults were marked by surprise landings, often at night, at several spots simultaneously or in rapid sequence. Air and naval superiority were always present at the point of attack. Japan had no marine corps as such. The army was responsible for amphibious warfare and the navy for getting the troops to the invasion beaches and supporting the landings with gunfire and aviation. But Japan did possess an elite corps of "debarkation commandos," special forces whose mission was loading the landing craft, moving them to the beaches, and returning the empty craft to the transports offshore. One keen student of Japanese warfare has observed that the nation's warriors had a tendency to overplan, and "the more detailed the landing guidelines, the more difficult it became to hold to them." This was the case when unexpected bad weather, high winds and surf, or unanticipated enemy resistance was encountered. As long as unforeseen difficulties did not occur, Japanese amphibious operations "ran like clockwork. But once a problem arose, confusion ensued," and Japanese troops were likely to respond with foolish daring such as human-wave assaults in order to "win back full freedom to act."[15] Nonetheless, Japan conducted a series of major amphibious operations in China and the Pacific between 1937 and 1942 that rivaled in size and success those later undertaken by the Americans in North Africa, the Mediterranean, and the Gilbert, Marshall, and Mariana Islands between November 1942 and June 1944.

Japan's preference for land-based naval aviation as an essential component of defensive warfare was given impetus by the war in China. Japanese forces followed up the Marco Polo Bridge Incident with a heavy air and land attack on the native sections of Shanghai. Within days, the army began a major thrust up the nearby Yangtze River valley toward Nanking and beyond, as Chiang Kai-shek's steadily retreating government lured the Japanese farther and farther from the coast.

Because of the vast distances involved, China inevitably became an air war— a strategic bombing campaign that in conception and scope if not scale pre-figured those undertaken by the Allies over Europe after 1942. Such a campaign required the use of every plane and pilot in the Japanese arsenal. From the beginning, the navy consistently outperformed its army opposites in long-range bombing, often under terrible conditions of weather and terrain. Naval aircraft proved superb; the new Nell land-based bombers flew missions of up to 1,250 miles from Formosa and Kyūshū against targets in and around Shanghai, Nanking, Hankow (Hankou, now part of Wuhan), and other river cities. "The elation which swept the Japanese populace with the announcement of the bomb-ing[s] was understandable," a Japanese historian recalled with chilling satisfac-tion. "We had a powerful, long-range, fair-and-foul-weather, day-and-night bombing force" with which to terrorize and kill thousands of civilians. Japanese casualties, however, were severe, especially during the first four months of the war, and until the end Japanese naval bomber aircraft, often unaccompanied by fighter escort until the advent of the Zero in 1939, were subjected to periodic savage maulings. Only in the crucible of battle did Japanese pilots learn the necessity of close-formation flying and at last master the art of dogfighting against skilled Chinese and Soviet pilots.[16]

Carrier aircraft began making significant contributions to the Japanese offensive at Shanghai in August 1937 and continued to do so as the campaign moved up the Yangtze valley. The first generation of ship-based aircraft proved incapable of carrying out their missions, and the aircrews suffered terrible casu-alties. As late as the previous May, the fighter, dive-bomber, and attack aircraft aboard the *Kaga* were all biplanes. On August 17 the carrier launched its first strike against Chinese targets beyond Shanghai. A dozen Type 89 torpedo-bomber biplanes led by Lieutenant Commander Iwai roared down *Kaga's* big flight deck and headed toward Hangchow (Hangzhou) to blast Chinese airfields. Only one plane returned. The bomber squadron failed to rendezvous with its fighter escort and had attacked alone.[17]

The Japanese learned quickly from their mistakes. A year later *Kaga* had been joined by the smaller *Hosho* and the second-generation light carrier *Ryujo,* while *Akagi* completed a modernization program. From the beginning, the car-rier air groups flying off *Ryujo* and *Kaga* were in the thick of the war. In late 1938 *Akagi's* flyers joined the melee. The first carrier-based Type 89 attack bombers and then the Type 96 carrier-based fighters (Claudes) were badly mauled by the Chinese air force, increasingly manned with foreign volunteers and stocked with the best foreign aircraft. In response, Japan hurried new land- and carrier-based naval aircraft into production. "By importing many foreign aircraft and weapons," two Japanese veterans of the campaign later wrote smugly, "we in Japan were able to gauge approximately what these weapons could and could not do. By keeping our planes and other armament within our borders and free from prying eyes, we led the world seriously to underestimate the combat strength of our naval aviation," until the "China Incident" forced the Japanese to reveal how far their capabilities had advanced.[18] In 1938–1939, Type 97 carrier attack bombers (Kates), Type 99 carrier dive-bombers (Vals), and the apex of Japanese aviation technology, the Zero fighter plane, all joined the fleet. As the Japanese army moved up the Yangtze beyond Nanking, chasing the always elusive Chiang and his forces, the carrier air wings moved ashore, following the army and bombing ahead of it in conjunction with the army air corps. By early 1940 land-based Nells, often escorted by Zeros or Claudes, were bombing Chungking, Chiang's last haven of safety beyond the river gorges of the upper Yangtze more than a thousand miles west of Shanghai.[19] Other bomber-fighter formations staging off carrier decks or, later, from advanced bases in Indochina ranged far and wide over southern China, ultimately closing down the vital Burma Road supply corridor.

The navy always boasted that its aviators were tougher and more adaptable than those in the army. Flyers and aircrew who trained ever more intensively for attacks against enemy surface fleets as the international situation shifted from Japan's advantage in the late thirties nonetheless demonstrated from the earliest days of the China Incident an ability to strike land targets effectively. "Conversely, it was also determined that pilots trained specifically for maneuvers over land experienced great difficulty in over water operations, even in merely flying long distances over the ocean."[20]

In the midthirties as the carrier *Ranger* came into the U.S. fleet and *Yorktown* and *Enterprise* took shape in East Coast shipyards, the Imperial Navy bestirred itself to keep in step. Scarce funds were found to upgrade and modernize *Kaga* as well as *Akagi*. Training and war games had demonstrated that the best defense a carrier had was its own planes, and the unwieldy eight-inch batteries on both ships were removed. The crude three-deck hangar arrangement was abandoned, and the single flight decks were extended fore and aft to cover nearly the entire ship. As a result, *Akagi*'s and *Kaga*'s plane capacity increased from 60 to 90 (though both would normally carry about 72 planes in combat). At the same time, Japan pushed ahead with two ships roughly comparable to the American *Yorktown* class: the 34-knot *Hiryu* and *Soryu,* each 16,000–18,000 tons and capable of carrying at least 63 aircraft.[21] A disastrous typhoon at sea in September 1935 damaged the fleet sufficiently to force designers to pay greater attention to strength and structural integrity. Both new Japanese carriers were built with higher hulls and forecastles.[22] The carrier faction won an even greater victory in 1937 when it was able to place in the Fleet Replenishment Program orders for two superb 25,675-ton, 34-knot vessels to be named *Shokaku* and *Zuikaku.* Each ship embarked 72 aircraft, and each would be completed in 1941 in time to take part in the opening offensive of the Pacific conflict.[23] On the eve of Pearl Harbor, Japan possessed six splendid frontline carriers—*Akagi, Kaga, Hiryu, Soryu, Zuikaku,* and *Shokaku*—that operating together as a fast mobile strike force, the *Kido Butai,* could deploy more than 350 aircraft. The *Kido Butai* displaced more than twice the tonnage allotted Japan by the Washington Conference.[24]

Doctrinal and administrative progress kept pace with new construction. Experience in China had finally convinced Japanese carrier and fleet commanders that the attack aircraft at their disposal could best be employed—and protected—as a massed group. "Extending these realities to air war at sea slowly but inevitably led to the conclusion that carrier forces must be concentrated," and by late 1940 the navy's tacticians had hit upon the box formation as the best way to deploy carriers in a task-force configuration. Within months, Rear Admiral Jisaburo Ozawa had come up with another advance. Scattered as it was throughout the Pacific islands and on carriers, naval aviation in time of war would inevitably be employed incoherently and ineffectively. He convinced Yamamoto to create an air fleet within the Combined Fleet structure and to split it into land- and carrier-based components for maximum effect. At the end of 1941, the Eleventh Air Fleet, comprising eight land-based groups, was ready to lead the navy's thrust southward toward the Philippines, Malaya, and the East Indies that would win Japan an empire within a few months. The First Air Fleet, encompassing all the aircraft deployed on the three carrier divisions, plus two seaplane divisions, composed "the single most powerful agglomeration of naval air power in the world," including the U.S. Pacific Fleet. Just as each of Japan's warships had to be qualitatively superior to fleet units in putative enemy navies, so Japanese naval aircraft had to possess greater speed, maneuverability, and, above all, range than comparable American—and British—planes. Japanese carrier aircraft were designed to deliver the critical first strike, to find and hit an enemy fleet before it could come in range to deliver aerial and surface blows of its own. Japanese carrier aircraft would have be lighter and more vulnerable than their U.S. opposites to achieve this objective, but as early as 1936 staff planners at Imperial Navy headquarters concluded that the key to success in any coming conflict "was to be mass attacks" by carrier aircraft "delivered preemptively because of the advantages of surprise and of 'outranging' the enemy."[25]

Mindful of America's industrial superiority, Japanese authorities realized that any protracted war, even if waged defensively, would require as many aviation resources as the empire could muster. The solution lay in building fast, medium-size merchant and passenger ships that could be quickly converted to effective auxiliary carriers. Soon after Japan formally withdrew from the naval limitation system in 1935, its architects began planning for the construction of the appropriate ships. The NYK Line was given a substantial subsidy to build two 24-knot vessels designed specifically for conversion to carriers. Laid down in early 1939, both ships possessed greater height between decks and a stronger main deck than normal in merchant ships and more wiring than a passenger liner needed, together with better subdivision and a longitudinal bulkhead in the engine spaces. The design allowed for the quick construction of hangars, elevators, and provision for extra fuel and aviation gas tanks.[26]

But the superbattleships absorbed so much matériel and funding that Japanese fleet construction, no matter how imaginative, had to suffer somewhere, and the sacrifices eventually fell upon the destroyers and destroyer escorts needed to keep Japan's huge merchant navy safe from enemy submarines. After 1940, as the final bills came due on *Yamato* and *Musashi,* the construction of small combatants virtually ceased. Japanese shipyards built no destroyer escorts between 1941 and 1943, whereas the Americans built well over three hundred. "The importance of merchant shipping was simply not appreciated" by a naval high command that in the last analysis could think no further in assessing command of the seas than a climactic Jutland-like battle between two lines of battleships heavily supported by airpower.[27]

This modified Jutland model led to further crippling follies. The *Yamato*s, the *Zuikaku*s, and their scores of support ships that Japan rushed onto the building stocks after 1935 would require thousands of new sailors and hundreds of new officers to effectively operate, but the elitist nature of the Imperial Japanese Navy fatally hindered rapid and efficient expansion. The Jutland scenario gave no consideration to the manpower and, above all, training needs involved in waging and surviving a prolonged war of numerous battles stretching over the vast distances of East Asia and Oceania.

A "solicitous" promotion system designed to guarantee every graduate of the naval academy at Eta Jima, no matter how marginal, at least a captaincy during his career meant that the naval officer corps had to be kept deliberately small. Moreover, the number of officers accepted at the academy as well as the number of personnel enlisted (and ultimately drafted) into the ranks were based on the size of the fleet at hand; thus, personnel requirements were determined only *after* naval construction and armament budgets had been approved. "In a navy that supposedly took ten years to develop a truly capable lieutenant and twenty years for a commander, training should have anticipated the numbers of officers and men required by the level of armaments ten years on." It did not. In the midthirties, as the fleet began to expand, there were fewer than ten thousand officers and not quite ninety-eight thousand enlisted men to crew not only a rapidly growing surface fleet but also dramatically expanding submarine and air forces, the naval landing force, and the shore establishments. According to historians David C. Evans and Mark R. Peattie, the navy went to war in December 1941 against the United States and Britain "short at least two thousand combat and engineering officers." Manpower swiftly reached crisis proportions in 1942–1943 when new-construction manning needs were increasingly undercut by widespread casualties and fatalities among the most experienced officers and men in the fleet. Fatally bound to a lengthy and rigorous training regimen for all, the Japanese navy never did develop a coherent program for effectively training thousands of new officers and recruits in a short period. New officers and men proved increasingly unqualified for their responsibilities "and thus generally lowered the navy's efficiency." Not until the end of the Solomons campaign in 1943 did the Personnel Department of the Navy Ministry reconsider its manpower and training policies, and "by then, the ministry realized, it was already too late to do anything effective about the problem."[28]

As the 1930s waned the Japanese army moved farther and farther up the Yangtze and along the China coast, fruitlessly seeking the final great battle that would bring the enemy to his knees and to his senses. In the process the army and navy learned how to integrate ground troops with gunfire-support ships, land- and sea-based aviation, and even on occasion submarines in devastating "triphibious" assaults against enemy coastal positions. Japan became the first nation to effectively meld sea and airpower in action, thus dramatically increasing the mobility, impact, and general effectiveness of its fleet.[29] But the Japanese never found the conclusive battle they were looking for. As with another foreign power in Asia years later, their high command continually searched for the light at the end of the tunnel, and commanders on the ground constantly asked for just that one more division or two that would finally resolve matters once and for all. All too soon, mounting frustration triggered unmitigated and repeated barbarism. Troops and airmen bombed, pillaged, and slaughtered indiscriminately and unmercifully. Tokyo never understood that the behavior of its troops in China forfeited all claims to international respect and understanding.

Japan could not conceal its atrocities. There were too many Westerners to witness them. Chief among the observers was a remarkable community of sailors. For nearly a decade after the first battle for Shanghai in 1932, Western cruiser and gunboat crews lying off the city or steaming up and down the Yangtze had a front-row seat for conflict. At one point in 1937, the men of the American gunboat *Panay* became victims of that conflict. The Yanks—and their British and French colleagues—quickly acquired a profound distaste and contempt for the Japanese that was in no way mitigated by the frequent cowardice and incompetence of Chiang Kai-shek's Nationalist Chinese government and its troops. The sailors, and the reporters who followed them into the Chinese cauldron, conveyed their attitude toward the Japanese to the international community, further amplifying long-standing cultural and racial animosities that would inform the great global conflict that loomed ever larger.[30]

In November 1938 Prime Minister Prince Fumimaro Konoe issued the famous—or infamous—"New Order" declaration in which the Japanese government formally pledged itself to the task of "fundamentally rectifying" nearly a century of Western imperial depredations in China:

> [Nazi] Germany and [Fascist] Italy, our allies against Communism, have manifested their sympathies with Japan's aims in East Asia. . . . It is necessary for Japan to not only strengthen still further her ties with these countries but also to collaborate with them on the basis of a common world outlook in the reconstruction of world order. It is high time that all of us should face squarely our responsibilities—namely, the mission to construct a new order on a moral basis—a free union of all the nations of East Asia in mutual reliance, but in independence.[31]

Two years later, with Europe back at war and its own armies still slogging up the Yangtze, Admiral Sankichi Takahashi, former commander in chief of the Combined Fleet, confirmed that Japan's proposed "new order in Greater East Asia" stretched from Manchukuo to Australia and eastward to the International Date Line. The new imperium would be "constructed in several stages. In the first stage, the sphere that Japan demands includes Manchukuo, China, Indo-China, Burma, Straits Settlements [that is, British Singapore], Netherlands Indies,

New Caledonia, New Guinea, many islands in the West Pacific, Japan's mandated islands and the Philippines." Australia and what remained of the East Indies "can be included later." Western observers noted that these statements were made not in advance of aggression, but in the midst of it. On the other side of the Pacific, fresh fictional accounts of an impending Pacific war had already appeared in American popular literature. A fuse had been lit.[32]

U.S. battleships maneuvering in formation sometime in the 1920s. USS *Pennsylvania* is the lead ship. (U.S. Naval Historical Center, NH 63346)

Grand Admiral Erich Raeder, commander in chief, German navy, 1928–
1943. Portrait taken June 23, 1936. (U.S. Naval Historical Center,
306-NT-112042)

Admiral Karl Dönitz, commander in chief, German navy, 1943–1945, and second and last head of the Nazi German state, April 30–May 8, 1945. Photographed sometime during World War II. (U.S. Naval Historical Center, 208-PU-52P-1)

Admiral Isoroku Yamamoto, head of the Imperial Japanese Navy Combined Fleet, 1941–1943. Portrait photo taken either just before or just after Pearl Harbor. (U.S. Naval Historical Center, NH 63430)

FDR and Churchill at the January 1943 Casablanca Conference. Army Chief of Staff George C. Marshall is standing directly behind Roosevelt, flanked by Chief of Naval Operations Ernest J. King (to the president's right) and Sir Dudley Pound, first sea lord of the Admiralty (to FDR's left). (U.S. Naval Historical Center, 80-G-35135)

Yalta Conference, 1945. White House Chief of Staff Admiral William D. Leahy stands behind the president. Admiral Sir Andrew Cunningham, commander in chief, British Mediterranean Fleet, 1940–1943, and thereafter first sea lord of the Admiralty, is behind Churchill's right shoulder, being chatted up by British Air Chief Marshal Charles Portal. (U.S. Naval Historical Center, USA C-543)

Admirals Raymond A. Spruance (pith helmet) and Pacific Fleet commander Chester W. Nimitz (hands at belt) pose with Admiral Ernest J. King and General Sanderford Jarman at Saipan, August 1944. (U.S. Naval Historical Center, 80-G-307861)

Battle in the Denmark Strait, May 1941. Shell splashes from the German battleship *Bismarck* fall near HMS *Prince of Wales,* while burning oil and the final, sinking remains of HMS *Hood* are to the left. Photographed from *Bismarck*'s escort, the cruiser *Prinz Eugen,* which separated from the doomed battleship shortly thereafter and made port. (U.S. Naval Historical Center, NH 69731)

Pearl Harbor from the air, October 30, 1941. Under air attack, the narrow "death-trap" nature of the fleet anchorage is clearly evident. (U.S. Naval Historical Center, 80-G-182874)

Battleship Row, December 7, 1941. The stricken vessels are USS *West Virginia* and USS *Tennessee*. (U.S. Naval Historical Center, NH-94378)

Battle of the Coral Sea, May 1942. USS *Lexington* is rocked by the explosion that seals its fate, blasting a plane off the flight deck in the process. (U.S. Naval Historical Center, 80-G-11916)

Battle of Midway, June 1942. Japanese heavy cruiser *Mikuma* photographed from an aircraft from USS *Enterprise* on the afternoon of June 6, 1942, after having been bombed by planes from *Enterprise* and USS *Hornet.* (U.S. Naval Historical Center, 80-G-414422)

Tanker SS *Robert C. Tuttle,* burning and sinking off Cape Henry, Virginia, after being torpedoed on June 22, 1942. (U.S. Naval Historical Center, 80-G-14047)

North Atlantic convoy. Lookouts on the escorting destroyer USS *Greer* watch merchantmen steaming in heavy seas, June 1943. (U.S. Naval Historical Center, 80-G-42023)

Battle of the Atlantic. German Type IX submarine attacked by American patrol planes southwest of the island Ascension, November 5, 1943. (U.S. Naval Historical Center, 80-G-208282)

The attack continues. Note U-boat crew cowering on the low conning tower near their guns. U-848 was sunk soon thereafter. (U.S. Naval Historical Center, 80-G-208284)

U.S. Marines resting on Guadalcanal before battle, late 1942. (U.S. Naval Historical Center, 80-G-20683)

D day, June 6, 1944. LCVPs (landing craft vehicle personnel) race to put troops ashore on Omaha Beach. (U.S. Naval Historical Center, 26-G-2337)

Invasion of Iwo Jima, February 19, 1945. Initial landing wave heading for the beaches on the island's southeast coast at about nine in the morning. USS *Tennessee,* long resurrected from the mud of Pearl Harbor, is providing close-in gunfire support. Photographed from an aircraft launched from the escort carrier USS *Makin Island.* (U.S. Naval Historical Center, 80-G-310951)

Aircraft carrier USS *Bunker Hill* burning after a kamikaze attack off Japan, May 1945. (U.S. Naval Historical Center, 80-G-274266)

U.S. destroyer *William D. Porter* sinking off Okinawa after a kamikaze attack, June 1945. LCS 122 is standing by. (U.S. Naval Historical Center, 80-G-490027)

American Revolution

WHILE CHINA PROVIDED Japan with further combat experience in a limited context, American preparations for a Pacific war necessarily remained theoretical, grounded in War Plan Orange with its emphasis on defeating Japan by means of a single triumphant fleet action somewhere in the western Pacific followed by a crushing blockade of the enemy's Home Islands. Yet within that planning structure and in pursuit of its objectives, the United States Navy transformed itself during the interwar years. While the battle fleet continued to symbolize American sea power as "the first line of defense," planners, theorizers, and activists prepared for a much different kind of war, one that emphasized projection, distance, and mobility. Such a war would require a navy that could fight in four dimensions—not only on, beneath, and above the sea but also onto Pacific islands and, perhaps, East Asian coasts. To fight successfully, the navy would need its own soldiers, called marines, its own air force, and its own Construction Battalions. It would have to steam vast distances and remain at sea for long periods. Only a nation that combined wealth with technological sophistication and the ability to organize and administer great corporate enterprises could afford such a war machine. Remarkable Japan, with its narrow resource base in all categories, was doing so on a modest scale, straining every sinew to the breaking point in the process. The United States, with its enormous and technologically literate population, vast industrial plant, and increasingly isolationist population, created the framework for such a machine but would go no further until war was forced upon it.

War Plan Orange depended absolutely upon the ability of the U.S. battle fleet not only to steam several thousand miles to the Far Pacific but also to remain there indefinitely, either as it sought out the enemy fleet or as an effective blockading force. Depending upon where the climactic, Jutland-like fleet action would be fought, Guam might not be close enough to serve as a fleet anchorage and repair and replenishment center. Wake and Midway were much too small for such purposes. Capture of suitable enemy islands might not occur when and as needed. Underway refueling and replenishment therefore might well be critical for victory at sea. The only model for lengthy sea keeping readily to hand was, of course, the Great White Fleet of 1907–1909 that had demonstrated the critical importance of ongoing replenishment to effective long-range power projection.[1]

Washington had chartered foreign "colliers," as coal vessels were known, to rendezvous with Robert "Fighting Bob" Evans's and Charles S. Sperry's battle-ships at various points around the globe, but the foreign ships did not always arrive in a timely manner. With the navy's widespread conversion to fuel oil after roughly 1915, young lieutenant Chester W. Nimitz, an expert on early diesel engines, expanded his expertise to fueling techniques. Using the navy's first oiler, *Maumee,* as a test bed, he developed new gear and towing rigs for over-the-stern refueling. When the United States entered the Great War in the spring of 1917, Joseph Taussig's six new destroyers steamed across the Atlantic on their own. But later reinforcements for the antisubmarine war were often smaller, older ships, and so *Maumee* was sent to the mid-Atlantic where it oper-ated for months as a mobile fueling station for the destroyers that followed Taussig "over there."

A decade after the Armistice, the demands of War Plan Orange had grown so immense that the navy's director of war plans reminded the chief of naval operations that the limited number of bases in the western Pacific required replenishment as well as refueling operations at best speed if the fleet was to operate effectively over long distances and long periods of time. In the face of enemy air and submarine threats, a modern fleet could not be immobilized for long periods while it refilled itself. By this time cumbersome over-the-stern refueling techniques had given way to more practical and rapid alongside pro-cedures. By the 1930s refueling pairs of destroyers alongside increasingly fast-moving fleet oilers had become routine. Abeam replenishment rigs had been developed for "high-lining" food, medical supplies, and mail between moving ships at sea. Underway refueling and replenishment of battleships and carriers soon followed, and the "big boys" were themselves modified to reprovision their escorts, assuming an increasing "service station" role in the aftermath of the *Lexington's* experience in 1937 as it spent several weeks at sea heading a naval task force searching fruitlessly for aviatrix Amelia Earhart. During that time the carrier serviced the accompanying destroyers and cruisers on several occasions.

As underway refueling and replenishment became ever more sophisticated, rapid, and routine in the United States Navy, the Japanese upgraded their capabilities accordingly. By the midthirties, both navies were constructing fast (16.5- to 17.5-knot) replenishment vessels capable of alongside servicing, and in 1939 the U.S. fleet welcomed *Cimarron* and *Neosho,* large tankers capable of steaming at 20 knots. Two years later, Vice Admiral Chuichi Nagumo's Pearl Harbor strike force, including six carriers, two battleships, three cruisers, nine destroyers, and three submarines, was refueled twice on its way to target by eight tankers, some of which then returned to Japan while the rest took up station to refuel the fleet on its way back to home waters.[2]

However routine it became for both navies, refueling of ships at sea always remained a hazardous business, demanding the highest standards of seamanship from all hands. Refueling of the big carriers and battleships was an especially demanding and daunting task.

> The two vessels are required to steam on exactly parallel courses at identical speeds within twenty to seventy feet of one another for hours while all the material to be transferred is passed across the fast and narrow river between them. Quick, skilled hands and precise judgment are necessary, especially on the receiving ship. The captain in most cases assumes control himself, his best helmsman is at the wheel, his most efficient talker at his side ready to relay his commands. In the engine rooms picked men are at the throttles, and out on deck chief boatswains mates direct the men that handle the heavy lines and hoses. Line handlers must wear life jackets because they work along the extreme edges of the deck and the sea has a way of boiling up between the steep sides. The dynamic forces involved when a 25,000 ton carrier and a 15,000 ton oiler are maneuvering at eight to twelve knots within fifty feet of each other are difficult to compute or imagine.[3]

When ships brushed against each other in heavy seas, as they occasionally did, steel structures were torn and mangled as if involved in a major automobile accident. Manila lines or heavy fueling hoses were known to snap and break, lashing back to maim or kill men. But by the earliest days of the Pacific war, refueling at sea had become routine. In the Atlantic, Dönitz was already experimenting with "milch cows," large submarines that could refuel and replenish the U-boats to maintain them on distant stations.

If underway refueling was one critical element in the anticipated long-range projection of sea power, amphibious operations were another. Japanese capabilities in this area were well known and appreciated within restricted naval circles in the West, but the one major amphibious effort in recent times familiar to all—Gallipoli—had been a calamity. Americans have always been confident in their ability to reverse others' disasters, and in the early 1930s a renewed interest and even faith in modern amphibious warfare seized the United States Marine Corps. As elsewhere, the army had long dominated planning. The 1927 *Navy Landing Force Manual* stressed that "the organization, drill, and combat principles are based on those of the Army." By 1940 the U.S. Army Transportation Service possessed eight troop transports and seven freighters of its own, and both services for many months after Pearl Harbor had overlapping functions in both the overseas movement of troops and the assault phases of amphibious operations. It was not until March 14 and April 10, 1942, that the navy created amphibious-force commands for the Atlantic and Pacific Fleets, respectively.[4] Thereafter, it was the navy that took the lead in organizing the assault phase of amphibious operations. Although the Marine Corps would stage dramatic island assaults in the Pacific from 1942 to 1945, they were on several important occasions (Kwajalein and Okinawa, to name but two) accompanied ashore by army infantry divisions. And the great landings in North Africa, Sicily, Italy, and, of course, Normandy were all-army operations.

Such essential caveats aside, the United States Marines devoted themselves to amphibious warfare in the interwar years to an extent unmatched by the other two services, and they developed policies, plans, and procedures that all three services would employ with great effect in both the European and the Pacific theaters of operation. As usual in the freewheeling and intensely competitive American military culture, such developments did not come easily or without cost.

From 1849 to the end of the nineteenth century, the Marine Corps had been limited primarily to providing detachments to the ships of the fleet, and in the years following Appomattox critics in both Congress and the military establishment seriously questioned the need for its services. But the Spanish-American War; the conquest of the Philippines; the U.S. occupation of Guam, Wake, and Midway; the subsequent development of War Plan Orange; and the award to Japan in 1919 of Germany's former Pacific-island holdings forced strategists to consider the implications of a future Japanese-American conflict. Planners expected Guam and Wake to fall, dooming the Philippines. Thus, to come to grips with the enemy, the Americans would have to fight their way back west across the vast ocean and seize at least some of its archipelagoes. Such a conflict would require seagoing soldiers to hit the beaches and destroy the local garrisons, while heavy Construction Battalions (formally established in April 1942 and in service within weeks thereafter) would build advance bases that might well need to be defended against a determined enemy counterattack. The Marine Corps was the logical choice to fulfill the amphibious assault responsibility, as the General Board of the navy recognized in 1900.[5]

In 1910 the corps established a school for formal instruction in defensive amphibious operations at New London, Connecticut, and two years later, the commandant of the Marine Corps issued the first outlines to guide the curriculum. By 1914 more than seventeen hundred officers and men had been trained and had conducted their first exercise at Culebra, a small island near Puerto Rico. The notion of a defensive rather than offensive role for the marines' advanced base units continued to prevail. The 1914 exercise at Culebra was conducted in the broader context of naval warfare between an advancing "red" fleet (Germany) and the American "blue" fleet. The marines landed at Culebra and set about rapidly fortifying the island. Two weeks later the red fleet appeared, and its landing force was repelled by the marine "Advanced Base Force." Shortly thereafter, red-fleet units were defeated by the blue fleet, which then steamed north to take up defensive positions off the East Coast of the United States.[6]

Following intense immersion in the last battles of the western front, the Marine Corps returned in 1919 to its earlier interest in developing amphibious warfare concepts and doctrines. The postwar political climate in Washington, D.C., however, was poisonous, and the corps was riven by personal feuds and rivalries, even as its now long-standing role as enforcer of American foreign and colonial policies in the Philippines and the Caribbean came under bitter and growing public criticism. At the same time, the Washington naval agreements, which were widely interpreted as dramatically diminishing American sea power in the Pacific, forced a reconsideration of War Plan Orange. Fortunately for the marines, capture of at least some midocean islands and their transformation into advanced support bases for an advancing U.S. fleet remained essential doctrine in planning for a future conflict with Japan. The corps remained the obvious candidate to fulfill this mission responsibility. All of these swirling factors and considerations coalesced in 1920–1921, compressing and focusing strategic thought within the corps toward amphibious warfare.[7] Recalling Gallipoli, senior staff people swiftly concluded that the British disaster was due to "faulty doctrine, ineffective techniques, poor leadership, and utter lack of coordination between the services." But planners had also learned other lessons. While in London in 1917–1918 as U.S. Naval representative, Admiral William Sims, who grasped the implications of every new wrinkle in modern warfare, had appointed a marine colonel, Robert H. Dunlap, to study amphibious operations. Dunlap concluded from his analysis of a proposed Allied landing in the Adriatic that "the balance between a defender and attacker was a dynamic relationship based on relative strength and tactical doctrine, not an absolute advantage to the defender." Even the stoutest shore defenses could be overcome by the intelligent as well as ruthless application of force.[8]

Major Earl H. "Pete" Ellis took up the task of defining Marine Corps amphibious doctrine in a future Pacific war. Ellis, a strange, tormented man and a drunk who marched to his own drummer, doubtless took up his task at the direction of Commandant John A. Lejeune, who himself possessed a formidable intellect. Ellis would die under mysterious conditions in the Pacific in 1923 and thus never live to see his ideas come to fruition. But he, more than anyone else in the United States, could claim to be the father of modern amphibious warfare. Ellis was both a synthesizer and a creator. He drew upon and logically expanded ideas that had been in the Marine Corps portfolio since the turn of the century. An "Orange" war against Japan could be won only by a successful advance of the battle fleet into the Far Pacific. Hawaii was the natural launching pad for such a venture, which would require establishment of a series of support bases farther west. It was hoped that Guam and Luzon could fulfill those roles if they were sufficiently fortified so as to withstand enemy assaults. Earlier doctrine had assumed that even if those islands fell, others needed to support a fleet advance would be there for the taking. This idea had informed the first amphibious exercise at Culebra in 1914 when the leathernecks had stormed an empty island and transformed it into a stronghold. But as a result of Versailles, the Japanese now occupied those midocean island groups—the Marshall, Caroline, and Palau islands—deemed essential to the navy's Pacific offensive. The marines would have to fight their way onto hostile beaches and destroy a determined enemy where he lived, thus fulfilling their basic mission as "the Advanced Base Force of the Navy." Ellis had studied at the Naval War College in 1911–1912 and concluded that the Japanese fleet would remain in home waters until the advancing Americans forced an engagement.[9] With this overall strategic consideration in mind, Ellis submitted a detailed operations plan to the commandant in July 1921. The initial phase would involve the seizure of the Marshalls, in particular the islands of Enewetak, Wotje, and Jaluit. Next, the Carolines were to be occupied as far west as Yap. Palau would follow. Then would come the relief or recapture of the Philippines. At some point in this process, the Imperial Japanese Navy would feel compelled to come out and fight, thereby losing the war.

One salient fact must be kept firmly in mind: neither Ellis nor anyone else absorbed in preparing for a Pacific war ever contemplated the need to invade Japan proper. With the loss of its fleet, American strategists believed, Japan would be rendered powerless. If Tokyo did not sue for peace after the climactic naval battle, then U.S. forces would impose an ever tightening blockade of the Home Islands from even more advanced bases seized in the Bonins, Ryukyus, and perhaps even on the China coast. As early as 1922, army planners exploring the necessity and costs of a Japanese campaign reached the sobering conclusion that an invasion attempt offered "almost no prospect of success." Five years later, another army team stated that chances for a successful invasion of Japan were "extremely doubtful . . . regardless of our greater potential man power and munitions, because the enemy can always concentrate forces greatly superior to the successive expeditions into which our land forces must be organized for overseas transportation." The Army War College staff added that the fanatic ferocity of the Japanese fighting man rendered the Home Islands "almost invulnerable."[10]

Tactically, Ellis argued that night assaults against enemy beaches should be rejected as too dangerous and confusing, though small reconnaissance parties could be put ashore. The invasion fleet of fire-support ships and transports should approach under cover of darkness, but landings should be made at dawn or soon thereafter to make use of the maximum amount of daylight. The gunfire-support ships should be positioned on the flanks of the landing so as to sweep the beaches during the ship-to-shore movement. Aircraft should be employed not only for preliminary reconnaissance but also as ground support once the troops were ashore, strafing enemy trenches and defensive positions in front of the advancing U.S. troops. The invading force should be landed in ships' boats towed to the beaches by power craft equipped with bow guns. At least two waves of tows should be sent in, "each tow composed of not more than three boats, properly dispersed to avoid concentrated fire from the beach."[11] The landing force should be composed of infantry, machine gunners, signalmen, and field artillery. Each regiment of field artillery and machine gunners should comprise two thousand men and each infantry battalion five hundred. In addition, special underwater demolition teams should be trained to destroy beach obstacles by wire cutter and explosives.

Perhaps Ellis's most striking contribution was his insistence that the corps reorient its thinking with regard to size and mission. In the war just past, the marines had essentially fought as part of an army engaged in large-scale ground maneuvers on the European Continent. Ellis implicitly told colleagues and superiors to forget Belleau Wood. In the next war—a Pacific war—the marines would be transformed into an elite corps of shock troops, bursting suddenly and violently onto enemy beachheads to overcome with superior spirit and firepower a determined and entrenched foe.

Many marines bitterly rejected Ellis's vision. The corps had won new battle honors in France. To depart from what had worked so recently was difficult to accept. Fortunately, Ellis and the growing band of zealots he left behind after 1923 could always count on the support of Lejeune and theorist Major General Eli K. Cole. Moreover, Ellis had embedded his strategic and tactical vision so firmly within the context of War Plan Orange that it was almost impossible to argue against it.

To a remarkable degree, then, Ellis's plan, which Lejeune approved soon after submission, provided both the sound strategic rationale and the tactical guidelines for a future amphibious war in the Pacific islands—a war that had to be waged if the United States was ever to defeat Japan. But funds remained scarce throughout the later 1920s, and opposition to the Ellis scenario remained too strong to translate ideas into policy. Moreover, the navy was distracted by its own problems in trying to develop a coherent strategy with too little resources.

The onset of the Great Depression threatened to destroy the Marine Corps entirely. By 1930 Herbert Hoover and his secretary of the navy, Charles Francis Adams, were preaching naval and military retrenchment as one antidote to mounting economic distress. Soon they enjoyed the support of army chief of staff General Douglas MacArthur and chief of naval operations Admiral William V. Pratt. The following year, Hoover and Adams seriously contemplated disbanding the corps and transferring it to the army. Only the stout resistance of Commandant Ben Hebard Fuller and the presidency of naval champion Franklin Roosevelt rescued the corps from obliteration.[12]

Under FDR, with many a setback, the marines began to make substantial headway in developing effective amphibious warfare tactics and doctrine. The breakthrough came in 1934, a year after the corps was at last unburdened of its three decades of occupation duty in Central America. Assistant commandant Major General John H. Russell was able to obtain the necessary funds and authority to establish a staff at Quantico to develop plans for a marine strike force that "could mobilize rapidly for service with the fleet." Within a year, the

Fleet Marine Force was in being, with Quantico its headquarters. An amphibious warfare school was established, and a *Tentative Manual* based on Ellis's ideas was quickly prepared that broke operations down into a half-dozen categories: command relations, naval gunfire, aerial support, ship-to-shore movement, securing a beachhead, and logistics. Four basic senior- and junior-level courses were developed from the manual. At last, the United States Marine Corps was committed "unequivocally" to amphibious warfare as its primary mission responsibility.[13]

Armor and aviation would become the essential components of modern amphibious operations. The marines employed their first tanks during the 1924 exercises at Culebra. The following year aircraft were employed during exercises on Oahu.[14] Conventional wisdom insisted that "close air support was an unprofitable—even a wrong—undertaking for an air force. The Marine Corps refused to accept this doctrine." So did the German Luftwaffe. Together, the two services would revolutionize modern war. As early as 1919, the handful of Marine Corps flyers on duty in Haiti began successful experiments with dive-bombing suspected insurgent positions. Eight years later, in Nicaragua, marine pilots put "the new art of dive bombing and strafing" into practice while supporting the Second Marine Brigade against dissident forces. "There, for the first time in combat, aircraft strikes were directly controlled by the man on the ground" through radio communication between forward fire-control men and the aviators above. "Simultaneously, combat air transport had its baptism of fire. Combat patrols in the field were supplied with food, ammunition, and emergency equipment by air delivery." That same year marine fighter squadrons accompanied the Sixth, Tenth, and Twelfth Marines to China to help the ground troops maintain communications between and security within each of the far-flung American diplomatic posts and commercial entrepôts in the country wracked by civil war. During the several months in which the marine flyers maintained communications between Tientsin (Tianjin) and Peking (Beijing), "they brought aerial photographic interpretation and reconnaissance to a new high in development, keeping the ground commander completely informed of all movements of potentially hostile forces."

Throughout the interwar years, as the U.S. Army Air Corps sought to sever its connection with ground forces in order to pursue strategic bombing, the marines welded their aviation units and ground forces ever more tightly. Every marine absorbed the essentials of ground warfare, including formal and informal training in weaponry and tactics, before becoming eligible for flight training. The flyers lived in the same barracks and quarters, ate at the same tables, and slept in adjacent bunks with "ground Marines." As they honed their skills in close air support, the fliers also took time to learn how to operate from the navy's handful of aircraft carriers, the obvious platform for close-in support of amphibious operations. Soon the marine flyers joined their navy colleagues in designing and developing suitable aircraft for carrier-based air support of amphibious operations, culminating in the dual-purpose F4U fighter-bomber of World War II designed both to strafe and bomb the enemy on the ground and to clear him from the skies above.[15]

Following years of unstinting effort, "the Fleet Marine Force embarked upon its combat role in World War II as a completely integrated air-ground team, with an air component unequaled anywhere else in the world for its equipment, its technique, and above all, its complete subordination and devotion to the needs of the ground component it was to support." From Guadalcanal on to the Persian Gulf, the kind of close air support that the marines pioneered would be a prime ingredient of U.S. amphibious and ground warfare. Naval aviation was just a step behind the marines in developing the art of close-in air support, and the Army Air Corps was forced to become reasonably proficient under the demands of ground combat in North Africa and northwest Europe during World War II. But at their Wake Island Conference in October 1950, Douglas MacArthur told Harry Truman that "ground support is a very difficult thing to do. Our Marines do it perfectly. They have been trained for it." The superiority of marine aviation was due to a connection between pilot and infantryman that "was intimate and constant." Marine aviators possessed "an understanding and appreciation of infantry problems that a mere airman could not possibly acquire."[16]

As World War II burst upon the United States, the Marine Corps steadily expanded and elaborated its techniques and equipment. While the navy developed new types of ammunition to increase the striking power of onshore bombardment, the corps trained invasion beach specialists to bring order out of the inevitable chaos of landing under intense enemy shellfire. The specialists were given the responsibilities of marking the various assault beaches, establishing communication centers, controlling incoming seaborne traffic, directing labor parties, evacuating the wounded, and expediting troop movements off the beach. Once the beachhead was secured, the specialists turned to the formidable logistics problem of directing vast quantities of ammunition, food, gasoline, and water inland to support the advance.

After Pearl Harbor the corps turned to the nation's laboratories and manufacturing centers for the vessels needed to mount large-scale amphibious attacks. The LCVP (landing craft, vehicle, personnel) "was developed by trial and error from a retractable boat of shallow draft and protected propeller which Andrew J. Higgins built originally for the use of fur trappers in the Louisiana marshes." With Marine Corps funding, Higgins designed a landing craft with a bow ramp for the discharge of troops and small tanks. "An amphibious vehicle invented by Donald Roebling for rescue work in the Everglades was the inspiration for the LVT (Landing Vehicle Tracked)." Generally known as the "amtrac" and mission capable on both land and water, it could carry up to thirty fully armed troops. The LST (landing ship, tanks), known not so lovingly to those who manned or rode it as "the Large, Slow, Target," became the mainstay of operations in both Europe and the Pacific after mid-1943.[17]

At-sea replenishment and amphibious warfare were two of three means by which a modern navy could project its power across the world ocean. But the most effective agent of all proved to be carrier-based aviation employed in a sweeping strategic role against enemy fleets, island bastions, and even homelands.

America's civil and military postwar leadership, unlike its British counterpart, refused to be stampeded into defeat on the issue of airpower at sea, even though at least one prominent publicist dismissed carrier aviation as of little account in a future U.S.-Japanese conflict. Journalist Hector C. Bywater's influential fantasy, *The Great Pacific War,* published in 1925, reflected prevailing thinking. In the novel, which takes place in 1931, Japan provokes a war with the United States by temporarily crippling the Panama Canal by means of a bomb set off in a Japanese freighter passing through. Naval airpower triumphs initially when a small Japanese force built around a submarine and a seaplane tender raids the American West Coast. Enemy seaplanes bomb San Francisco indiscriminately from twenty thousand feet, starting fires and filling hospitals. After recovering its aircraft, the enemy task force sails away unscathed. The success of this raid (which in some ways anticipates the 1942 Doolittle raid on Tokyo) is overshadowed, however, by the miserable failure of American carrier attack aircraft in the climactic fleet action later in the novel. Planes from *Saratoga, Lexington,* and two fictional carriers are wiped out by a combination of the guns of the Japanese fleet and the enemy's combat air patrol. "How different now were the circumstances from those which aviation enthusiasts, deceived by artificial peace tests against helpless targets, had pictured! From the ships below, turning and twisting at high speed, came a veritable stream of shell, the incessant detonations of which caused the planes to rock as if in a gale of wind." As the desperate Americans in their biplanes dive down on the enemy, they pass through a cloud of poison gas emitted by the enemy fighters and are all but obliterated. Not one enemy ship is hit.[18]

By the time Bywater wrote, battleship proponents had come to accept the airplane's essential role as a gunfire spotter, opening the door to carrier proponents.[19] Whereas battleships and even heavy cruisers could catapult spotter planes, such aircraft required protection by powerful fighter aircraft against the enemy's defensive air patrol over his battle line. Moreover, the enemy could be expected to send out swarms of aircraft to protect his own planes seeking to plot fall of shot against the U.S. battle line. As early as the spring of 1918, the chief of naval operations made the Office of the Director of Naval Aviation part of his staff. Six months later, naval aviators returning in triumph from Europe urged the CNO to request the secretary of the navy to press Congress for a bureau of aeronautics. Hearings before the navy's General Board soon followed and revealed that no matter how deeply fliers might be divided over the future shape and direction of naval aviation, they were nearly unanimous in advocating for their own bureau that could fight for appropriations, equipment, and personnel policies on par with other branches of the service. The senior officers on the board strongly supported their younger colleagues, concluding that aircraft had become "an essential arm of the fleet," requiring the development of fleet aviation and the creation of an independent naval air service. "Fleet engagements of the future will probably be preceded by air engagements. The advantage will lie with the fleet which wins in the air."

Congressional support, a sympathetic White House (President Warren G. Harding was an able and enthusiastic reformer, a fact that has been obscured by the rampant scandals of his administration), and firm backing from the National Advisory Committee for Aeronautics carried the day; the Navy's Bureau of Aeronautics ("BuAer") came into being in August 1921. American naval aviation had won a position of administrative impregnability that sailors in Britain's Fleet Air Arm could only envy, for among other responsibilities that Admiral William Moffett was able win for the bureau was the sweeping authority for "all that related to designing, building, fitting out, and repairing Naval and Marine Corps aircraft." Moreover, the bureau had authority to recommend to the Bureau of Navigation and the commandant of the Marine Corps "how pilots would be selected, assigned, and promoted." BuAer was also to supply the chief of naval operations with every bit of information required for "all aeronautic planning, operations, and administration," which practically translated into full autonomy for naval air to select which direction—or directions—it chose to move in defining and fulfilling its mission responsibilities.

From the dawn of airpower at sea there were always two alternatives to the aircraft carrier: seaplanes and flying boats (the former equipped with pontoons rather than wheels, the latter with boat-shaped hulls for direct water landings) and dirigibles. Those within and beyond the United States Navy who felt compelled, however grudgingly, to accept the logic of Billy Mitchell and others regarding the eternal vulnerability of *any* surface ship, including aircraft carriers, looked to these other two weapon systems to sustain naval aviation.

British seaplane operations in the Great War, no matter how ambiguous in outcome, fired the imaginations of many in the United States Navy who believed the "hydro-aeroplane" was the weapon of the future. Captain Washington Irving Chambers became convinced of the superiority of seaplanes within minutes on a warm San Diego morning in January 1911. Several weeks after witnessing the first-ever launch and landing of an aircraft on *Pennsylvania* in San Francisco Bay, Chambers traveled to southern California and saw Glenn H. Curtiss land his seaplane near the same big cruiser, which promptly swung the aircraft aboard with its crane, then immediately swung the aircraft back onto the water, where Curtiss quickly took off again. Chambers marveled at the superiority—what the navy would call the "relaxed tolerances"—of seaplane operations compared to Eugene Ely's daring landing and takeoff in a wheeled aircraft. *Pennsylvania* did not have to be stationed into the wind to launch and recover Curtiss's aircraft, and the launch and landing runouts of seaplanes were unlimited. Takeoffs could be safely aborted without plunging off a ship's bow.[20]

Seaplanes possessed two other characteristics that Chambers believed made them unbeatable as the prime aviation weapon at sea. First, small numbers of them could be catapulted off existing power-projection vessels—battleships and large cruisers—and could return to land alongside. This meant that existing fleet units could themselves carry out essential scouting and, it was argued, fleet defense missions.[21] Chambers himself developed the first workable catapult as early as 1912 at the Washington Navy Yard. By 1916–1917 he had overseen installation of fixed-track types on several of the navy's large armored cruisers, including *Seattle* and *Huntington*. Second, and most important, seaplanes and flying boats could be built bigger and heavier than carrier-borne aircraft and thus could carry a much larger and exponentially more deadly payload. The British, it is true, developed the world's first carrier-borne torpedo planes near the end of the war. They were designed to be launched from the hybrid carrier cruiser *Furious* with the specific mission of attacking the High Seas Fleet. But in 1918, and for more than twenty years thereafter, naval planners and aviators worried that torpedoes and bombs capable of being lifted off carrier decks and flown several hundred miles were simply too small and light to seriously damage a large modern warship, be it a heavy cruiser, battleship, or aircraft carrier.

By the early thirties fledgling navy aerial strategists like America's Logan Ramsey were writing learned articles in which the relative merits of bombs versus torpedoes were discussed in detail but without much resolution.[22]

In 1919, just ten years after Louis Blériot had managed to stagger the twenty air miles across the English Channel, Lieutenant Commander A. C. Read made the first transatlantic flight from Long Island to Portsmouth, England, via Newfoundland, to the Azores and Portugal in his NC-4 flying boat.[23] Although his plane was the only one of four to complete the journey, his success could not be denied. Seaplanes and flying boats could deploy anywhere in the world there was water. Seventy percent of the planet was immediately available to them, and every inhabited continent save Australia (where population was largely confined to the coasts) possessed numerous lakes of sufficient size to accommodate them. The strategic importance of such aircraft seemed illimitable. The true aircraft carrier, many maintained, was what had been developed during the Great War, a mother ship for seaplanes or flying boats.

By this time most of the features of the aircraft carrier as a floating airfield had been put in place, and it was clear that such a vessel would have to be large and costly. There was a flight deck and often two, for until the midthirties the British and Japanese preferred one deck above the other in order to provide simultaneous launchings and landings in times of emergency. There were one or two elevators and one or two hangar decks complete with small maintenance and repair shops on each side. There were landing cables that incoming aircraft, throttled back to minimum flying power, hooked onto. There were catapults to launch heavily laden aircraft more efficiently and safely. Finally, there was general agreement that some sort of "island" structure should be placed on one side of the flight deck to provide funnel vents for exhaust fumes as well as navigation and fire- and flight-control facilities. Floating airfields obviously had to be sizable (at least fifteen to twenty thousand tons), lengthy (eight hundred feet would be optimal), and speedy (twenty-eight to thirty knots) to be able to deploy an acceptable number of defensive and offensive aircraft efficiently. Size and speed became especially important as bigger and heavier carrier aircraft capable of carrying greater payloads materialized. Flight decks had to be long enough and the wind across the deck great enough (demanding even higher ship speed) to obtain sufficient lift.

What was the value of such a comparatively expensive vessel when set against the other forms of naval aviation? By 1919 Chambers was a power in the small U.S. aviation community, and Read's daring seaplane flight across the Atlantic seemed to point the way to the future of sea-air operations. John Towers, naval aviator number 3 and now a full commander, told the navy's General Board, "I am one person who does not believe that the use of the airplane from an airplane carrier will last very long."[24]

Beyond seaplanes were the dirigibles, successors of the huge zeppelins that had finally shown substantial promise during the last stages of the Great War as terror bombers. Indeed, before 1914 many predicted that the future of mankind in the air belonged not to propeller-driven airplanes, but rather to propeller-driven airships. Even twenty years later, many continued to share this belief. Capable of a large load-carrying capacity, great range, and high altitude, airships seemed untouchable aerial bombers. In 1908 H. G. Wells had published his sensational futurist novel *War in the Air* in which scores of German zeppelins suddenly appear over New York in the dead of night and bomb the city to rubble in a preemptive raid designed to deter Americans from developing "flying machines 'of the Wright model.'" When the Great War broke out in August 1914, the airplane was still "a frail toy and the Zeppelin was the undisputed master of the skies."[25]

The zeppelin lost little of its luster in the next four years, and with the Armistice, Allied technicians were as eager to learn Germany's airship secrets as those of its submarines. The British, French, and Italians seized the German navy's remaining dirigibles and literally flew most of them into the ground before turning to their own generally unsatisfactory designs. The Americans approached airship technology from a different angle. Rather than seizing half- or fully completed airships, the U.S. Navy sent its technicians to the building sheds at Friedrichshafen to carefully study German designs and construction techniques. In 1923 the United States Navy built *Shenandoah,* an almost exact replica of one of the German navy's last zeppelins, L-49, which had crashed in France during the war. But the Americans made one crucial change: they employed helium for their lifting agent rather than hydrogen. Helium was far less volatile than hydrogen, but it was also less effective.[26]

Unfortunately, naval authorities wanted a bigger ship than the L-49 design and so added extra frames to *Shenandoah* to support the many more helium bags required. The change resulted in a structurally and aerodynamically weaker vessel, and in 1925 the airship was ripped apart in a heavy storm over Ohio. But its brief life sparked a surge of interest in zeppelins within the small American naval-aviation community. Throughout the early twenties, Britain and France continued to insist that Germany be banned from constructing zeppelins. But the European powers could not prevent private American companies from importing German talent to construct dirigibles in the United States, and in 1924

German designers went to work for the Goodyear Zeppelin Company in Akron, Ohio. At this point, London and Paris capitulated, and the German zeppelin industry sprang back to life. To bridge the gap before the American-built airships were completed, the United States Navy contracted with the Germans to provide one airship to supplement the doomed *Shenandoah*. The 5,066-mile, eighty-one-hour flight of LZ-126 from Friedrichshafen to Lakehurst, New Jersey, where it was rechristened *Los Angeles,* was deemed one of the most notable events of the autumn of 1924.[27]

By the late twenties the Americans were experimenting with dirigible aircraft carriers as long-distance scouts for the fleet. Up to a half-dozen small planes could be stored in a hangar in the bellies of first *Los Angeles* and then *Akron* when it appeared several years later. The planes were launched from a bay next to the hangar to zoom over enemy fleets and determine their precise size and composition. Returning to the airship, the planes attached themselves to a hook, or "trapeze," as it was called, and the pilots turned off their engines. The hook ran to a derrick that pulled the planes back into the airship's belly for restorage in the hangar and relaunch down the bay. "Since the airships by then had a range of nearly 10,000 miles, and air speeds about three times as fast as either cruisers or aircraft carriers, the combination of airship and airplane appeared to be devastating in the American war games."[28]

But Richard Byrd's dramatic flights to the poles in 1926 and 1929, together with his and Charles Lindbergh's dramatic flights across the Atlantic in 1927, suggested that airplanes far faster than dirigibles could be constructed to fly several thousand miles, through often poor weather, and that the future belonged to the heavier-than-air craft.[29] In the end, the lighter-than-air ships signed their own death warrant. In 1930, after airship R-100 flew successfully to Canada and back, the British sent its sister, R-101, off on what was to be a triumphant tour of India. The "R"s proved to be badly designed and handled ships, however, and 101 got no farther than a French wheat field, where it met its end in a shattering explosion that killed all aboard, including the British air minister. Three years later, *Akron* went down in a violent storm off New Jersey, carrying to their doom seventy-three men. Undaunted, the Americans completed *Macon* in 1933. But it proved a disaster from the first. Even before it broke up off Point Sur, California, during the annual naval maneuvers in 1935, the giant airship had been put back in the sheds at least once for major structural repairs. *Macon* crashed due to failures that had done in both *Shenandoah* and *Akron*. Seventy-nine of eighty-one men were rescued, but the Americans at last gave up on the airship as an offensive weapon.[30]

The ultimate unsuitability of both seaplanes and dirigibles as offensive weapons of war was far from clear as late as 1930. The man who may have saved the aircraft carrier in the American fleet was none other than that aging enfant terrible William Sowden Sims, who, with his equally obstreperous, reform-minded colleague Admiral Bradley A. Fiske, swung into line behind naval airpower even before the Mitchell tests. Sims shared the opinion of his old friends in the Royal Navy Jacky Fisher and Percy Scott that the age of the battleship was over. Fiske, who had been the last "head" of the U.S. Navy (1913–1915) before creation of the post of chief of naval operations, went even further. As early as 1911 he had grasped aviation's limitless possibilities ashore and at sea, arguing that the future defense of the Philippines could best be guaranteed by building four airfields sheltering one hundred planes apiece. By the middle war years, Fiske had enumerated every task that naval aviation could possibly accomplish, from bombing enemy ships and shore installations to delivering important messages to protect communications between ship and shore and ship and ship. Throughout 1917–1918 he agitated for the development of seaborne torpedo and bombing aircraft to attack German U-boat bases.[31] About the time that Sims assumed command of the Naval War College in 1921, a fleet air-defense study group concluded that large, mobile floating airfields precisely met the needs and fulfilled the demands of War Plan Orange. Assuming fortification of Japan's island mandates, including the deployment of submarines and aircraft, "any westward passage of the U.S. fleet to the Orient would have to be attended by a formidable force of naval aircraft." Moreover, in the first days or weeks of a Pacific war, Guam would inevitably fall to the enemy, who would immediately convert the island into a powerful base for both offensive and defensive operations. The "Orange" (Japanese) fleet would shelter there under the umbrella of a powerful air force, and "the oncoming U.S. fleet must inevitably accept battle within that area of cover." It was therefore imperative that the American fleet carry with it large numbers of aircraft that could win the battle in the skies over the contending fleets. Heavy, slow seaplanes encumbered with pontoons, floats, and aerodynamically misshapen hulls simply could not stand up to attacks by swift, maneuverable enemy land-based aircraft. Nor could they press home their own assaults against enemy island installations. Dirigibles, of course, would be out of the question, even carrying a handful of defensive fighter planes. A fleet air force capable of rapid response to impending enemy attacks or to any and all opportunities to assault enemy shipping and shore installations could be composed only of fast, nimble, wheeled aircraft, and such planes could be efficiently embarked and deployed only from large

aircraft carriers.[32] When Sims took command at Newport he promptly incorporated aircraft carriers into the detailed elaborations of War Plan Orange that
were annually worked and reworked on the Naval War College gaming tables.
He also apparently led a doomed crusade to convert some if not all of the
seventy-five hundred–ton six-inch-gun *Omaha*-class cruisers then on the builders'
stocks to light carriers.

Soon he was able to reach a much larger audience through the writings of
another flag officer, retired admiral William F. Fullam, who, under the pseudonym
"Quarterdeck," wrote frequently for the New York press. As soon as *Ostfriesland*
slipped beneath the waves off the Virginia Capes, Fullam began a vigorous campaign to make "the aircraft carrier, not the battleship, . . . the backbone of the
fleet." Fullam understood the implications of the new aviation and submarine
technologies for the future of warfare in general and the battleship in particular.
Combat at sea would not require carrier-based aircraft to sink enemy battleships; if the planes could obliterate the screening destroyers, the battleships
would be utterly defenseless against submarine attacks. "Battleships and surface
ships alone," Fullam intoned, "can 'command' only one part of the sea—the
bottom!"[33]

Naval and public opinion was undoubtedly swayed not only by Fiske, Sims,
Fullam, the fleet air-defense study group, and a generation of young carrier
enthusiasts just emerging from Pensacola but also by the fact that both Japan
and Britain were or soon would be operating carriers of their own. The United
States had no choice but to follow. This was certainly the view of Admiral
William A. Moffett, BuAer's first director and rightly considered the "architect"
of American naval aviation. Moffett was in many ways an indiscriminate enthusiast for airpower. He supported the development of floating airfields, but he
also championed seaplanes and especially dirigibles, which he believed could
provide the fleet with the kind of advanced, long-range scouting capabilities
that aircraft simply were incapable of. Moffett never lost his belief in airships
and at the time of his death aboard *Akron* in 1932 was pressing for no fewer
than ten of the great dirigibles.[34]

Moffett firmly believed that airpower at sea would strengthen but not sup-
plant the battle line. He was smart enough to be impressed by the Mitchell
demonstration, which he witnessed. According to Moffett's biographer: "The
sinking of the *Ostfriesland* had a catalytic effect, convincing Moffett that the
best course for the Navy was to build a well-balanced fleet, with a mix of heavy
and light ships, 'all of which are to be coordinated in their activities and protected by aircraft.'" Carriers together with catapult-carrying battleships and

cruisers were the essential means of getting planes to sea quickly. Shortly after Mitchell's stunt, Moffett went to Capitol Hill and told Congress about aircraft carriers: "We need no less than eight big ones, because a Navy today without aircraft protection and the search-patrol, scouting-patrol, and shot-spotting facilities which aviation provides, is fatally weak when it puts to sea."[35]

The fights with Billy Mitchell and the Army Air Corps, together with a persistently parsimonious Congress, frustrated efforts by Moffett and his colleagues to create a significant carrier fleet. Although there was some talk in 1919 and 1920 about building a "dedicated" 20,000-ton, 800-foot, 28–30-knot ship from the keel up, postwar budgetary considerations forced the navy to accept a converted ship that proved as thoroughly unsatisfactory as Japan's first small carrier, *Hosho.* When it emerged in 1922, the former naval collier *Jupiter,* now renamed *Langley,* like *Hosho* sported a flush deck, a navigation bridge below and forward, and hinged side funnels. The design, together with the vessel's slow speed (15 knots) and small size (11,500 tons and 542 feet), made for a distinctly unsatisfactory prototype. Thus, when the Washington naval conference opened the door to the construction of much larger carriers that would save some capital-ship hulls, both the American and the Japanese naval communities leaped at the opportunity.

Several factors contributed to the emergence of the aircraft carrier as an important component of the U.S. fleet in the 1920s. One was the striking advance achieved in aircraft design that transformed the carrier from essentially an auxiliary vessel of the battle line, that is, a scout, to a full-fledged offensive weapon with its own unique tactical if not strategic potential. Moffett and the Bureau of Aeronautics spent almost a decade after the Armistice developing an efficient radial engine. They finally achieved the breakthrough technology with the 1927 Curtiss F8C, powered by a Pratt and Whitney "Wasp" engine. By this time biplane airframes had been strengthened sufficiently so that extraordinary stress could be imposed without danger of structural failure. Even before the appearance of the F8C, U.S. Navy as well as Marine Corps fighter pilots had begun experimenting with dive-bombing. By the end of 1925 the Navy Department began to throw its weight behind the notion of steep-angle attacks against enemy ships and even shore installations by carrier aircraft. Commander Kenneth Whiting, an early enthusiast of fixed-wing wheeled aircraft onboard ships, told the navy's General Board that current fighter planes provided with twenty-five-pound bombs could deliver a potentially devastating attack against enemy carriers. A then obscure young officer named Marc Mitscher joined Whiting in urging the General Board to consider and emphasize the aircraft carrier's offensive potential against all types of enemy ships. Both Whiting and Mitscher were careful not to claim too much for this new dimension of naval warfare. Although aircraft could now for the first time reliably hit rapidly maneuvering targets, dive-bombers were not sufficiently fast nor their bombs sufficiently heavy to permit penetration of heavily armored decks. Battleships and large cruisers were still immune from destruction from the air. But carrier decks could be disabled, thus denying future enemies the opportunity to provide advanced gunnery control for their own battle line. And although neither Whiting nor Mitscher referred to earlier arguments, the notion that carrier planes could destroy an enemy battle fleet's destroyer screen, thus opening the way for devastating submarine assaults, was still fresh in many minds.[36]

But while the big 33,000-ton carriers *Lexington* and *Saratoga* allowed by the Washington Naval Treaty steadily grew on the stocks and the first flyers and flight-deck crews on *Langley* pioneered effective launch and landing techniques (including night operations), the carrier still seemed to many an expensive luxury. Jutland remained the prime model of future naval warfare and even at Newport received the lion's share of attention. As late as 1930 young lieutenant Logan Ramsey, who would become a prominent World War II staff man and commander of an escort and fleet carrier, respectively, argued that a future naval war would still center around a climactic encounter between battleships. Since both capital-ship types were hideously expensive to build and operate, and since it was necessary for an advancing fleet to have total control of the air above, the only solution would be to divest the aircraft carriers of most if not all of their offensive capabilities, that is, bomber and torpedo aircraft, in order to fill their decks with fighter aircraft to defeat the waiting enemy's carrier- and land-based aerial assaults.[37]

Opinion about the carrier's role and mission had already begun to slowly change when *"Lex"* and *"Sara"* joined the fleet in late 1927 and began demonstrating the carrier's unmatched capability to project sea power far over the horizon. Fast floating airfields carrying up to eighty or even ninety bomber, fighter, and torpedo-carrying aircraft could expand the reach of naval power perhaps ten times farther than the twenty-two- to twenty-four-mile range of a battleship's main battery. If enemy battle lines could not be destroyed, they could be disrupted. Most impressive was the ability of aircraft carriers to approach vital enemy shore installations unseen and to smash them with one shattering blow.

This was first demonstrated dramatically in 1928, when Rear Admiral Joseph Mason Reeves, newly promoted commander of aircraft squadrons, U.S. Battle Fleet, took *Langley* through the Panama Canal to test Naval War College game-board conclusions about the offensive capabilities of aircraft carriers. Reeves sailed his slow little carrier north of Hawaii, and one quiet Sunday morning while no one was paying attention, he launched the ship's forty-odd aircraft in a sweep over Pearl Harbor that caught the entire shore establishment napping as well as the few Pacific Fleet units then in port. The next year in fleet maneuvers off Panama, Reeves, now aboard the brand-new thirty-four-knot *Saratoga*, stationed the big carrier and its light, fast escort of cruisers and destroyers beyond the Galápagos Islands, then sent the small task force charging at top speed toward the canal and the screen of battleships, cruisers, and carrier *(Lexington)* defending it. *Sara* and its single escort (a light cruiser) slipped right past the defenders in the middle of the night, and at dawn the carrier launched its entire group in a mock bombing and strafing attack that observers unanimously admitted would have put the Pacific end of the canal out of operation for months. Battleship admirals protested that their defensive screen would in fact have sunk *Saratoga* before it launched its attack, and their insistence tended to obscure *Saratoga's* achievement. But the implications of the *Langley* and *Saratoga* raids for a successful prosecution of War Plan Orange were not lost on the navy's more farsighted planners and strategists. The carrier people refused to give up. Twice more, in 1932 and 1938, carrier aircraft staged successful mock bombing raids on Pearl Harbor. According to Alan Schom, Japanese spies in Honolulu took due note and sent their observations home to Tokyo.[38]

From 1928 on, *Lexington, Saratoga,* and later *Ranger, Yorktown,* and *Enterprise* played important roles in the annual fleet exercises, while ship- and air-group commanders constantly shuffled the mix of bombers, scout planes, fighters, and torpedo aircraft in their arsenals, seeking the right combination for maximum offensive power against an enemy fleet. Behind the fleet stood the Bureau of Aeronautics, whose administrative structure and function not only protected U.S. naval air from outside interference but also produced "a huge quantity (by comparison with Great Britain and Japan) of qualified pilots, mechanics, and plane handlers" who were provided with a clear professional promotion path. Within this institutional structure, innovation through ceaseless, often daring, experimentation could be safely indulged. As analysts Thomas Hone and Mark Mandeles have written, BuAer fostered a particularly effective set of innovative techniques that reflected the nature of American society as a whole. Failure was tolerated so long as it yielded productive results and precise information and accurate analyses about system performance. Patience with the rate of desired change was "combined with a vision of the future which force[d] change." And differing priorities were carefully balanced, "particularly in peacetime, when lack of sufficient money to meet all the legitimate demands" compelled senior officers to make essentially political decisions about expenditures.[39]

Nonetheless, big-gun conservatism died as hard in the United States Navy as in any other sea service. Throughout the 1930s, battleships and battleship admirals continued to dominate strategic and tactical thinking. The one glaring fact that no carrier advocate could deny was that their ships fitted awkwardly at best into standard fleet maneuvers and as a consequence were terribly vulnerable. Carriers required at least thirty-knot speed to conduct air operations into the wind. No true battleship afloat prior to 1939 could make more than twenty-five knots; America's Pacific battle line was five knots slower. When operating independently, carrier captains and admirals were forced to rely on swift cruisers and destroyers. They rapidly came to conceive of carrier operations in terms of speed and flexibility as opposed to the slow, blundering battle lines. The outlines of the Japanese and U.S. fast carrier task forces of 1941–1945 could be discerned in embryo nearly a decade before.

Despite its undoubted promise, America's small carrier fleet remained on the fringes of strategic and tactical thinking as late as 1941. That spring the author of an award-winning essay on the future of American sea power wrote that although "no one denies that some completely new tactical considerations have been injected into [national] defense as the result of the airplane . . . it is strongly doubted whether any new strategic element is involved, particularly with regard to the defense of this continent." Defense of the United States was the battleship navy's supreme task. Its proponents could not deny that advanced aircraft could now damage and perhaps even sink their mighty leviathans, and to that extent the aircraft carrier had achieved a certain coequal status with the battleship. But "while mutual dependence was recognized, the carrier was to support the battleship and not the other way around." To be sure, such support was to be achieved offensively, not defensively. Carrier operation manuals of 1938 and 1941 stated flatly that it was "highly improbable that control of the air can be gained by employing aircraft to shoot down enemy aircraft. The surest and quickest means of gaining control of the air is destruction of enemy carriers . . . by bombing attacks." But because the aircraft carrier was, of necessity, lightly armored, with huge bomb magazines and fuel bunkers highly vulnerable to surface gunfire, the battleship admirals had good reason not to detach them and their protective air screen for independent offensive action. The burden of proof that such actions might yield decisive tactical if not strategic results fell upon the air zealots, but, unable to escape the dominance of battleship strategy and doctrine, they could not demonstrate convincingly that carrier airpower could decide a naval battle in and of itself. As a consequence, carriers remained tied to the battle line or the scouting force "within gun protection range of the battleships and cruisers."[40]

Thus, no great sea power with the possible exception of Japan was ready for war when Adolf Hitler in the late summer of 1939 pushed Nazi Germany and its profoundly reluctant Anglo-French antagonists into a corner from which there was no escape. The first great war at sea had really settled nothing. The second would settle everything.

CHAPTER 7

Contours of Conflict

WHEN IN 1939 and again in 1941 their masters cried havoc and let slip the fleets of war, the world's great navies leaped at each other's throats without hesitation. For six long years they held nothing back. Whereas a great battle in a single afternoon in the waters off northwest Europe largely defined both the naval war of 1914–1918 and the fleets that waged it, World War II constituted one long series of engagements large and small across the entire breadth of the world ocean. To the very end, victors and vanquished alike convinced themselves that the issue remained in doubt.

The Second World War was so vast, its battles so varied and immense, that in the end one is left—always—with mystery. The play of contingency, accident, chance, experience, inexperience, boldness, invention, and innovation was a critical element in every action large or small. No prewar plan based on theory or assumption played out perfectly in the crucible of battle. World War II was no simple *guerre de course*. Nor was it decided by great lines of battleships blazing away at one another. The commanders on all sides were as much the prisoners as they were masters of events and developments. In the violent shock of combat, leaders often relied on hastily devised tactics that failed dismally or succeeded brilliantly. From time to time new leaders rose above the organized hysteria of combat to impose form and texture upon conflict. However an engagement ended, no two participants ever experienced or reported it exactly alike. More than a half century later, with the smoke long cleared, the passions long cooled, it is possible to see how commanders might have perceived and acted differently, how corners could have been cut, unnecessary engagements or commitments avoided, decisive encounters forced long before they were. But the veterans will tell you—as veterans always do—that victory at any given moment in any given battle simply went to those who committed the fewest blunders.

From the beginning the war at sea was at once multidimensional and industrial. Behind the fighting fronts—in Washington and Berlin, London and Tokyo—sat the masters of logistics, the movers of industrial output. Production proved the critical element in global war. As the link between factory and front, "the logistic process is at once the military element in the nation's economy and the economic element in its military operations. And upon the coherence that exists within the process itself depends the successful articulation of the productive and military efforts of a nation at war." Logistical conditions and capabilities largely determined what was strategically available and tactically feasible. Soldiers, sailors, military analysts, and historians may wish to dwell on the drama, follies, and triumphs of battle, but logistics is always the indispensable servant of victory, and, "like any indispensable servant, it is frequently the master."[1]

While others fashioned the most pertinent instruments of destruction and ensured their production in sufficient quantity, the logisticians supervised transportation from factory to port and across the seas to a hundred different destinations in the most efficient and expeditious fashion. Seaborne transportation was the key; without a sufficient amount, the Allied war effort would grind to a halt. As Philip Pugh has observed, the wartime alliance between Britain, the United States, and the Soviet Union "did not come from any comprehensive pre-arranged pact but, rather, from them being flung together by the common experience of Axis aggression. Hence, there was ample scope for divergence of interests."[2] The most remarkable aspect of World War II was not the fragility and strain of the "Grand Alliance," but its existence at all, and for a time sufficient to complete the task of defeating the Axis.

During the first twenty-seven months of combat, the burden of carrying on the essential commercial activities fell almost exclusively on Britain, whose shipbuilding industry was a shambles. Because of deliberate government retrenchment policies during the Great Depression, the capacity of British shipyards between 1930 and 1937 had fallen from 3.5 to 2.5 million tons; it could not readily or rapidly revive to meet wartime emergency. Moreover, the Royal Navy's call on British yards for a modest naval rebuilding program sharply restricted the recovery of Britain's merchant marine. When war came in September 1939, "the weak foundation of British planning for wartime tonnage gradually became evident." Over the next nine months during which the Grand Alliance was confined to Britain and its soon-to-be-defeated western European associates, British negotiators tried, with little success, to reimpose the same restrictions on neutral shipping and shippers while providing the same guarantees as had obtained between 1915 and 1918. With the fall of western Europe to the Germans, most of these merchant marines sailed over to Britain, but negotiations on how those vessels would be used and the remuneration for their use—and loss—consumed hours of tedious negotiations.[3]

The solution, of course, was to seek new shipbuilding sources outside the United Kingdom, and in the final months of 1940, at the height of the first "disturbingly effective U-boat offensive," London dispatched a "Technical Merchant Shipbuilding Mission" to North America to do just that. Whereas Canadian capabilities had eroded nearly as badly as those in Britain, American yards were beginning to flourish under the Merchant Marine Act of 1936, a typical New Deal economic stimulation program that was organized and directed by the Maritime Commission. With the war generating business for neutral shipping, American shipyards delivered 47 new vessels by October 1940, and the commission had awarded contracts for 130 more. Here was the foundation for Allied victory that the British mission exploited fully.[4]

The final, essential, element was the creation of a standardized ship design capable of being mass-produced quickly and relatively cheaply on both sides of the Atlantic. The British Admiralty's director of merchant shipping, Sir Amos L. Ayre, had already produced one, a 441-foot-long vessel with a 57-foot beam and a deadweight capacity of 9,300 to 10,100 tons. Ayre's objective was cargo-carrying efficiency, economical operation, and, above all, rapid construction. Variations to accommodate the needs and capacities of various shipyards could be readily incorporated into what was essentially a modular design. Britain built the prototype vessel at the North Sands Shipbuilding Yard and named it *Empire Liberty.* Soon, with the prefix dropped to assuage Yankee distaste for anything imperial, "Liberty ships" formed the nucleus of the enormous Allied cargo-carrying capacity of World War II. In the United States contracts were let for several hundred such vessels even before Pearl Harbor, and on February 19, 1942, Roosevelt called Maritime Commissioner Emory Land to the White House and told him that he wanted 9 million tons of ships constructed that year and an additional 15 million tons in 1943. It could not be done, of course. The United States possessed neither the shipyards nor the building ways in what yards there were for such a mind-boggling undertaking. But it was done. Land began a fierce scramble to find the necessary space, while fighting off the navy, which was in the midst of its own remarkable expansion. Production geniuses like Henry Kaiser were encouraged to do the job, and they did. As Liberty ships in their several variations began pouring out of British, Canadian, and American yards after mid-1942, any real chance that Hitler's U-boat commanders had of cutting the Atlantic lifeline went glimmering.[5]

Not only did Liberty ships stock the Allied merchant marines, but roughly one hundred were painted haze gray, turned over to the navy, and became "AKA"s or "attack cargo ships" that supported the conquest of more than a dozen key Pacific islands from Tarawa to Okinawa as well. In the late summer of 1945, they stood ready to support the invasion of Japan. (In the midfifties I served briefly aboard an AKA that had seen action not only at Iwo Jima and Okinawa but also at Inchon during the Korean War. It was still an effective ship and remained in commission for several years thereafter.)

As Allied production genius built hundreds of ships to transport the sinews of war, thousands of logistics experts—supply officers and combat-loading specialists—in California, Hawaii, New Zealand, Virginia, New York, London, Plymouth, Liverpool, and Algiers (and early on in the Pacific war in Japan, Malaya, Manila, and Rabaul as well) continually received, inventoried, measured, and loaded the millions of tons of bullets, beans, bandages, black oil, and other indispensable items that arrived on their docks or in their storage tanks for the next Pacific, North African, Mediterranean, or European campaign.

Behind the great convoy battles in the North Atlantic and Mediterranean and the grand carrier actions and amphibious assaults in the Pacific sat hundreds of code breakers and intelligence specialists at Bletchley Park and Pearl Harbor, teasing essential secrets out of enemy messages and behavior, then advising navy and war departments where to sail or not to sail their ships, where to land or not to land their troops. At Liverpool, Halifax, and New York other hundreds of staff people manned large operations rooms, dueling with enemy commanders and communication specialists who directed the U-boat war from the French coast. In Hawaii and Australia staff teams pried operational secrets from Japanese signals, and fleet- and amphibious-force commanders positioned their units accordingly.

Victory and defeat were starkly defined on all sides, and every effort was directed toward a single objective: the achievement and maintenance of a consistently favorable statistical balance. If over a prolonged period Germany's airmen and submariners could sink more Allied ships on the North Atlantic than could be replaced by hard-pressed British and later American yards, then Britain would succumb, America would be isolated, and the Soviet Union, pulled into battle by Hitler's invasion in June 1941, could be readily driven behind the Urals and forever contained. Germany would be master of the Continent. This was the dream in Berlin—and at Admiral Karl Dönitz's U-Boat Command Headquarters in France—and it was not wholly infeasible if the Nazi warlords played their excellent but limited resources both carefully and imaginatively.[6] Should the Imperial Japanese Navy seize enough territory in Asia and Oceania and destroy enough American warships and airplanes to sweep the U.S. fleet from the Pacific, Tokyo might establish a ribbon-defense line from the Aleutians to the Solomons so firm that the American will to battle might break and Japan could exploit the riches of an Eastern empire at will. This, too, was possible if the Japanese were as careful yet bold as their German allies. Conversely, if enough men and cargo could be fought through to England and Malta, Allied bomber fleets staging from Britain and North Africa could pulverize German and German-held cities, factories, and oil fields, while Allied forces could be built up in preparation for a series of forcible lodgments on the Continent. If the United States Navy could hang on in the Pacific for eighteen to twenty months after Pearl Harbor while helping maintain the North Atlantic supply routes, then the necessary time would have been bought for America's incredible industrial might and manpower to be brought fully to bear against the Axis. Once the Allies took the offensive, they would still require soldiers and supplies to be poured onto enemy beaches faster than the entrenched and determined foe could destroy them. But each Pacific island assaulted and seized, each European bridgehead obtained and enlarged, created a new fighting front on which Axis power could be inexorably bled away.

Men might freeze and drown by the thousands across the length and breadth of the North Atlantic; they might be blown to pieces along with their ships in mournful, steamy nights off Java, the Solomons, and the Philippines or die on bullet-lashed beaches or in dugouts, caves, and machine-gun nests from Tarawa to Normandy to Iwo Jima; they might be bombed to death off Crete and Malta or be suddenly assassinated in their anchorages at Scapa Flow, Alexandria, Taranto, Pearl Harbor, Truk (Chuuk), and Kōbe. But in the end, the statistics were all that mattered. In every skirmish at sea, on every island or continental beachhead, offensive power had to overcome defensive force. Karl Dönitz knew it; so did Churchill and his admirals. Chester Nimitz and "Bull" Halsey realized it, and so did Isoroku Yamamoto and his successors.

The sea war off Europe could at least be maintained by British and later Allied shore installations at either end of the Atlantic and the Mediterranean. England and North Africa were natural jumping-off points for a return to the Continent and decisive battle with the Wehrmacht. The Pacific was a different matter. Here vast fleets had to haul their supplies with them over thousands of miles in the form of huge "trains" of cargo and ammunition ships, oilers, and tenders. For the Okinawa campaign, the apex of the American march across the Pacific,

> the logistic support arrangements for [Admiral Raymond] Spruance's fleet were awesome. The monthly consumption of oil was 750,000 tons, which had to be met by commercial tankers bringing oil from the American West Coast to the advanced base at Ulithi. From there a shuttle service of 40 fleet tankers brought the oil to the operating area off the Ryukyus. Four converted escort carriers brought replacement aircraft from Guam and Ulithi to the carriers in the operating areas, while seventeen more escort carriers shuttled aircraft between the West Coast and the forward bases. Provisioning at sea had long been provided, but replenishment of ammunition at sea had first been seriously attempted during the Iwo Jima campaign, and by the Okinawa campaign had become standard. The result of all this support was that the fighting ships could remain in the operational area for unprecedented periods.[7]

Defeating enemy fleet units was not enough. Key islands and archipelagoes had to be conquered if Japanese dreams of security were to materialize or American dreams of victory were to be realized. Enormous three-dimensional amphibious operations were required that demanded the organization of men and matériel on an ever mounting scale. How many troops, guns, and tanks would have to be hurled onto this atoll or against that island? How heavy and prolonged would the preliminary shore bombardment by ships and planes have to be? What were the conditions of the surf, on the beach, on the island as a whole? How long would the operation take? How many landing craft, amphibious vehicles, miles of communication wire, and tons of food, ammunition, blood, and bandages would be required? How many casualties would have to be dealt with, and how many replacements would be needed? How many scalpels, sutures, doctors, and nurses would be available? When could ships, troops, medical personnel, and planes be freed up for the next offensive operation?

Here was industrialism at its peak. And no other peoples, however courageous, brave, or even imaginative, could match the Americans in its employment. In 1946 Chester Nimitz likened the American logistics effort to the work of a caterer "who estimates the needs of a large party, orders the necessary items, sees that they are properly dished up, and then stays on after the party to clean up the mess." During World War II the United States devoted an astounding

80 percent of its logistics appropriations to new construction, only 20 percent to upkeep. Long before a specific operation, logistics specialists sat in conferences with the long-range strategists to determine what and how many supplies would be needed, where, and when. Even an individual sailor, airman, or marine was a "logistic" until he was trained and delivered to the spot where he was to function. Nimitz employed metaphor with telling effect to describe his country's enormous efforts in successfully prosecuting a two-ocean war:

> In most households supply and demand are fairly constant. Sunday's roast beef is Monday's hash; Monday's washing is Tuesday's ironing. But logistics specialists must be ready for roast beef on Sunday and a huge barbecue on Monday! Consumer demand shifts as the tide of war flows from one area to another, usually more quickly than anticipated. In the household, and in industry, there is an established pattern of operations. The grocer's wagon makes deliveries on schedule, the wholesaler's and manufacturer's trucks run on routine.
>
> In wartime, the Navy's housekeeping is subject to all sorts of interruptions. Supply lines are under constant threat. Design of ships and weapons must be changed to meet new conditions.

American productive capacity was so enormous that despite countless inefficiencies and periodic bottlenecks, logisticians during the latter stages of the Pacific war were flooded with a cornucopia of goods, allowing them, when necessary, to resemble the hyperefficient housewife who expects two guests for supper and at the last moment has to prepare a seven-course dinner for nine. By 1944 requirements and demands were worked out in such detail that "a commanding officer setting up an advance base could order his components and supplies out of a 'mail order catalogue' which would rival Sears Roebuck's famous tome for completeness. Everything from quarter-inch screws to many-ton cranes and big guns was listed."

As just one example of the enormous demands placed on logistics and supply officers, Nimitz cited the recapture and conversion of Guam to an advanced base. Initial plans called for a force of 12,501 officers and men using 157,524 measurement tons (cubic feet) of matériel. "That material had to be assembled from all over the United States. It had to be loaded in exactly the reverse order, so that the first-wanted articles would be on top of the cargo." But when the job came to be done, Nimitz and his subordinates employed 52,785 officers and men consuming 1,271,148 measurement tons of supplies—a 422 percent increase in personnel and an 807 percent increase in matériel. The changes were required not by enemy opposition, but by the decision to enlarge Gua-manian installations to include "CinCPac" (commander in chief, Pacific Fleet) headquarters.[8]

Never again would war be prosecuted with such a passionate prodigality of life, effort, and matériel. Control of the world ocean was the central ingredient of this mighty endeavor. America's industrial arsenal was the engine that could drive the Allies to ultimate victory. But if the physical and human products of the American effort could not be gotten to every corner of the globe where battle raged or critical supply lines ran, the war could not be won. Every tank deployed on a North African desert or a European plain; every jeep and truck delivered to an Iranian or Soviet Arctic port; every shell and bullet expended in a French orchard, in a German river valley, or on a Pacific atoll; every bomb dropped on a Nazi town or a Japanese city was brought to the delivery point by ship across broad seas or narrow channels contested by a determined antagonist.

The pressures on commanders and their strategic and logistical staffs were appalling and unremitting. "Global war strains geographic knowledge and understanding," cartographer Francis Brown wrote in 1943.

> Not only does it demand specific knowledge of the location of countries, of seas and rivers and mountain ranges; it requires appreciation of strate-gical relationships, of how a blow struck in one quarter of the world can affect military operations in another quarter thousands of miles away. Commanders in global war are faced with the dilemma whether to con-centrate their strength in one vital area or to distribute it around the earth. Vast distances acquire new meaning in terms of supply, and before the instruments of modern warfare the traditional isolation of nations evapo-rates. All become potential battlegrounds.[9]

The "instruments of modern warfare" themselves expanded exponentially between 1939 and 1945. Older technologies like the airplane and the submarine were dramatically improved; promising young technologies like radar, sonar (a drastic improvement of the British asdic system), and various radio direction-finding devices were elaborated and applied in all three spatial dimensions. Exotic new technologies emerged from wartime laboratories and testing fields: long- and short-range self-propelled rockets, jet engines, the proximity fuse, and, finally, that ultimate doomsday weapon, the atomic bomb.

We can begin to grasp the dimensions and dynamics of World War II at sea by asking if there was ever a time when the numerically and technologically inferior Axis navies could have secured victory for their regimes, and, if so, when, where and how? Any such inquiry must begin with a reminder that the Axis navies were regional, not global, in character. The strategies of each great naval power—Allied and Axis—varied dramatically. What is crystal clear in retrospect is that a certain—perhaps substantial—degree of cooperation and coordination of plans was required if the Japanese and German fleets were to inflict decisive defeat on their enemies. This never happened. "From the very start of political convergence" in the 1930s, Hans-Joachim Krug and his colleagues have observed, "both Germany and Japan were intent on making use of the other party just to support their own power politics." Following a few striking exchanges of technical information regarding aviation and submarine engineering in the interwar years, neither side revealed its plans or capabilities to the other. Once war broke out, the widely separated "allies," if such they were, pursued their own interests and policies, "with only temporary periods of limited coincidence of interests."[10] The mutual suspicion of totalitarian states whose social systems and political structures were deeply divided by cultural differences, racial animosities, and diplomatic rivalries (in China, for example, German officers advised Chiang Kai-shek prior to World War II) prevented the kind of close cooperation that, in the spring and summer of 1942, just might have brought victory to the Axis. Allied victory in World War II absolutely depended upon the combined efforts of the United States, Britain, and the Soviet Union. Should any one of these three powers be knocked out of the war, Axis victory, however limited, would be ensured. Thus, it was entirely possible that either of the Axis regional navies could have a decisive impact on the course of battle.

Sir Dudley Pound, who led his beloved Royal Navy from the outbreak of war to the autumn of 1943, never precisely articulated a grand strategy. But Britain's aims at sea were clear enough. The task, as always, was to keep open the global sea-lanes of transport and communication, which would ensure Britain's survival and eventually permit an Anglo-American invasion of Nazi-held western Europe. This meant neutralizing if not destroying the German U-boat menace at all costs and by all means, while sweeping the Atlantic and Indian Oceans clean of Erich Raeder's handful of battleships, battle cruisers, pocket battleships, and marauding armed merchant cruisers. Pound's one clear strategic innovation was to stubbornly hold Malta as a springboard for counterattack when Italy erupted into the war in June 1940, followed by the German invasion of the Balkans and the establishment of Erwin Rommel's Afrika Korps on the south shore of the Mediterranean. By the time Pound left office in 1943, ultimate victory over the European Axis was in view.[11]

A keen student of German naval affairs has argued that Pound's counterpart, Erich Raeder, never developed a coherent strategy for the conduct of the war. Keith Bird maintains that Raeder, like Alfred von Tirpitz, determinedly and foolishly pressed forward with the construction of a fleet "without formulating a grand naval strategy which would incorporate Germany's needs or capabilities." The only result of a Nazi navy, like its imperial predecessor, was to frighten potential enemies without gaining firm allies. Such an argument rests, of course, on the assumption that Raeder, in fact, firmly controlled the Nazi navy, that "after 1928 the navy became Raeder and Raeder the navy." But as we have seen, such was not the case. From the outset, Dönitz was a formidable competitor for the allegiance of a service badly split between the battleship sailors (Raeder) and the U-boat men (Dönitz). When Nazi troops marched to the Channel, the Bay of Biscay, and the Norwegian coast, the triumph of the U-boat over the battleship was ensured. Nonetheless, neither man ever enjoyed the resources required to make Germany preponderant at sea. Both were left with no choice but to wage an unrelenting, increasingly futile, war against Allied supply lines by every means possible.[12]

Pearl Harbor was the response of the Japanese naval high command to the impossible strategic problem that the nation had created for itself in invading China four years before. By the end of 1940 it was clear that only the United States posed a practical obstacle to Tokyo's unhindered pursuit of a "Greater East Asia Co-Prosperity Sphere" that would ensure its hegemony over the region for decades if not centuries. Pearl Harbor disrupted habitually cautious thought within the Imperial Navy and sent it careening in all directions in an effort to secure the broadest possible flanks for the new Japanese empire. And when the Americans responded at Guadalcanal, Yamamoto and his admirals proved fatally slow to react. Nonetheless, Japanese strategy during World War II was clear enough: strike hard and wide, obtain as much territory and resources as possible, then defend them with growing fanaticism as the enemy counteroffensive gains momentum and approaches Nippon's shores.

America's admirals—principally Ernest J. King and, in the Pacific, Chester W. Nimitz—held a clear, if flawed, vision of how to win a two-front global war. According to historian Robert Love, King, a turbulent, suspicious man who disliked most people, "viewed Germany and Japan as posing radically different problems for the Allies. If Germany could defeat Russia and hold England at bay, it could win the war. . . . On these grounds, he supported sending Lend-Lease material to Russia." On occasion he lent heavy naval units to the Royal Navy when reinforcement of the north Russian convoys was required by the appearance of Germany's dwindling number of capital ships in Norwegian waters. He also agreed to army chief of staff George C. Marshall's plan for the establishment of substantial bases in the Persian Gulf through which lend-lease supplies could flow through Iran into southern Russia. But King believed the Soviets were incapable of defeating Germany alone—a questionable assumption, as it turned out—and by 1943 he may well have concluded that it was not in the U.S. interest to have that happen. That year, he readily accepted plans to employ the increasingly powerful Atlantic Fleet in the impending invasion of Normandy.

Matters were much less clear in the Pacific and remained so to the end. Though Love argues that "no American military leader, least of all Admiral King, ever questioned the capacity of the United States to bring Japan to book," Pearl Harbor and the subsequent Japanese rush south and eastward clearly frightened many in Washington and Hawaii. One analyst warned early in 1942 that "Japan's demonstrated . . . capacity for powerful mobility" was, for the moment at least, "beyond anything we are prepared to offer." In line with that thinking, King cabled Nimitz, "Our primary concern . . . is to hold Hawaii and its approaches (via Midway) from the westward and to maintain its communications with the West Coast. Our next care in the Pacific is to preserve Australasia [Australia and New Zealand] which requires that its communications be maintained—via eastward of Samoa, Fiji, and southward of New Caledonia." From there, "we can drive north-west from the New Hebrides into the Solomons and the Bismarck Archipelago after the same fashion of step-by-step advances that the Japanese used in the South China Sea."[13] Such thinking, understandable in the immediate aftermath of the shocking attack on Hawaii, became less so as time wore on. Victory at Midway provided both the opportunity and the pretext to strike directly at Japan once more, as had been done with the Doolittle raid just weeks before. It is clear from Japanese records that the April 1942 raid on Tokyo and other Japanese cities induced Yamamoto and his admirals to keep their sizable and efficient fleet tied down in home waters. Further bold raids against the Home Islands and a reeling Japanese fleet might have kept the war largely confined to the western and northern Pacific, on a line running from the Gilberts to the Philippines and up to Japan. Instead, King (and Roosevelt) allowed himself to be deflected into a long, costly campaign in the Solomons and Bismarck Archipelago, far from the enemy's metropolitan area, that in its early stages nearly resulted in a further, possibly catastrophic, defeat at Guadalcanal. The campaign was justified as a defense of

Australia and New Zealand, neither of which was in imminent danger of invasion at the time.

Moreover, the navy was forced to share the Pacific with Douglas MacArthur, whose ego matched that of King and whose theatrics surpassed anyone in positions of authority save George Patton. Not surprisingly, King hated MacArthur, while Nimitz allowed himself to be outmaneuvered by the general, whose fixation on recapturing the Philippines placed the Pacific campaign in a strategic vise from which it never recovered.

With these points in mind, then, it is evident that there were four occasions when the Axis leaders might have gained at least a stalemated victory by an active—or more active—use of sea power: if Hitler had successfully crossed the English Channel to invade Britain in the autumn of 1940; if the Japanese attack on Pearl Harbor had been expanded to include an attack on the Panama Canal that would have closed the U.S. global transportation and reinforcement system for many months; if Japanese and German forces had been able to forge a linkup or a near linkup somewhere in the Middle East in the summer of 1942; and if the Japanese had been able to stifle and decisively defeat the first U.S. wartime offensive at Guadalcanal, thereby regaining the initiative in the Pacific and possibly destroying the American will to go on. Admittedly, all of these scenarios are, in the felicitous words of historian Ikuhiko Hata, "little more than a bundle of hypotheses."[14] But they do illuminate the possibilities open to as well as limitations upon all of the great sea powers who waged global war in the 1940s. They also pitilessly reveal the fatal unwillingness of one prominent enemy commander—ostensibly a daring gambler—to wield the might at his disposal with the dash and imagination that could have brought victory to his morally bankrupt cause.

CHAPTER 8

The Axis

Lost Victories

THE MOST OBVIOUS point at which sea power might have turned the tide of World War II decisively in the Axis favor came in the summer of 1940, following the fall of France when Britain stood alone and nearly defenseless against a German invasion. Had Hitler and his admirals been able to successfully push several armies across the narrow waters of the English Channel, onto the beaches of Kent, and into the streets of London, World War II would undoubtedly have ended with the United States and the Soviet Union isolated, besieged, and with no common interest.

Much of the credit for Britain's plight in 1940 could be claimed by the German navy. Little more than two months after the commencement of hostilities, Winston Churchill, newly reinstalled at the Admiralty, wrote that "the naval war alone has opened at full intensity." In a shocking reversal from its habits of a quarter century before, Germany was carrying the battle to Britain on as well as beneath the seas, and "we are being driven day by day into an absolute defensive by far weaker forces." Nine months later, now prime minister Churchill wrote the Admiralty complaining that control over the crucial northwest approaches to the United Kingdom could be lost at any time. "The repeated severe losses . . . are most grievous."[1]

From the autumn of 1939 to the spring of 1941 Erich Raeder's sailors, with the inestimable aid of Göring's bomber offensive against English ports, savaged Britain's sea power. Commerce was battered, and the British fleet was progressively whittled down across the farthest reaches of the world ocean by submarines, aircraft, cruisers, motor torpedo boats in the Channel, battleships, armed merchant cruisers, and mines. Statistics tell the story. In the first 120 days of combat alone, Britain lost a total of 222 merchant ships. From January to March 1940 it lost an additional 181, from April to June 299 more, and from July to September 297. In the first year of the war, Britain's merchant navy was thus reduced by a grand total of 999 freighters, lighters, tankers, and transports. In the last three months of 1940 and the first three months of 1941, when Britain stood most alone, it lost another 599 merchant vessels.[2]

Grand Admiral Erich Raeder, master of the German assault at sea, might have been a careerist, but initially he was a bold careerist, who had learned his lessons as a battle-cruiser sailor standing at Franz von Hipper's elbow at Dogger Bank and Jutland. "I personally gave the Admiral every tactical message that came in, along with suggested action in conformity" therewith. Twenty-three years later, the subordinate exceeded his superior by every measure of audacity and success. Germany's grand admiral was not without flaws. Pitting a small, untried, and unready service with a questionable past against what the world continued to believe was the greatest navy on earth placed increasing strains upon his nerve and character, and as time passed he grew increasingly timid and erratic, taking on all the attributes of what later generations might label a control freak. He often issued ambiguous orders, tampered with them, and eventually sacked successful seagoing commanders like Admiral Wilhelm Marschall who did not carry out his directives as he thought they should have. He never believed his views were properly understood, yet in one-on-one interviews he confused subordinates as often as he enlightened them.[3] Nonetheless, it was Raeder's boldness that drove the German navy to largely define the contours of World War II in its initial phase.

Raeder's strategy from the outset was to throw every resource he possessed at Britain. In September 1939, *Scharnhorst* and *Gneisenau* were ready for sea, as were all three pocket battleships, the new heavy cruiser *Hipper*, a half-dozen light cruisers, perhaps a score of destroyers, and another twenty or so submarines. Several other heavy cruisers were about to be commissioned, together with a handful of U-boats. But battleships *Bismarck* and *Tirpitz* were at least a year and two years away, respectively, from commissioning.

Despite the limitations of a small if growing navy, Raeder possessed two precious advantages that had been denied his predecessors a quarter century before. First, he was not distracted by a nervous supreme commander constantly at his shoulder and elbow as the kaiser had hovered over Friedrich von Ingenohl, Hugo von Pohl, and Reinhard Scheer, inquiring anxiously about the fate of precious sea toys. The führer's ignorance and mistrust of the world ocean were notorious. He often quipped to his naval adjutant that the sea was "only for adventurers." At the apex of his power and influence over world affairs when Britain lay prone at his feet after Dunkirk, Hitler told his army chiefs, "On land I am a lion, but with the water I don't know where to begin." As long as he produced satisfactory results Raeder enjoyed a measurable influence over Hitler. The führer might have recognized Raeder as essentially someone who could be bought. But he came to appreciate the man's strategic and tactical sense. "Hitler had considerable respect for Goering and Raeder," General Walter War-limont recalled. As a member of the Operations Staff of the Oberkommando der Wehrmacht, the supreme command of all German armed forces, Warlimont was a close and constant participant in the upper-level decisions of the Nazi war machine, and he later remembered that Raeder was treated "with marked cir-cumspection. In contrast to the Army, both Services [that is, the Luftwaffe and Kriegsmarine] were able to preserve a considerable degree of independence.... [I]n the case of the Navy, apart from certain isolated instances, this persisted throughout the war." As we shall see, Warlimont overstated the case, but it is true that prior to 1943 Raeder enjoyed a fair working relationship with his führer, and Raeder's successor, Karl Dönitz, always did. Second, Raeder initially enjoyed an intelligence advantage over his enemies. Beobachter Dienst—the German naval Observation Service under Commander Heinz Bonatz and com-monly referred to as BDienst—remained comfortably ahead of its often wildly scrambling British counterparts in Room 39 of the Admiralty. "During the Nor-wegian campaigns and at other critical stages of the early war at sea it was... BDienst that dominated." After August 1940, when the Admiralty changed its signal codes, BDienst was able to decrypt only about 10 percent of British naval traffic in "real time," that is, with sufficient rapidity for it to be practically applied by Germany's sailors or airmen. Nor was BDienst ever able to master the ciphers used by the commander in chief of the Home Fleet or his flag officers. But prior to the late summer of 1940 and especially during the Nor-wegian campaign, Commander Bonatz's analysts regularly read 30–50 percent of enemy naval traffic. Although "only a small part of this was in time for op-erational use it was enough to provide useful estimates of the location and movement of the Home Fleet." Moreover, Bonatz's men were as effective as their later American and British counterparts in employing "inspired guesswork" to fill in badly needed gaps in hard knowledge. Raeder, Dönitz, and the commanders at sea were thus reasonably certain of the disposition of most British fleet units and could maneuver around or confront them as conditions warranted with relative impunity. In his sweep through Norwegian waters in early June 1940, for example, Marschall with *Scharnhorst* and *Gneisenau* went specifically looking for the two British carriers operating there and caught and sank *Glorious*.[4]

Within significant limits, then, Raeder could fight the kind of war he wanted.[5] Days before the outbreak of hostilities, he dispatched two of Germany's three pocket battleships *(Deutschland* and *Graf Spee)* equipped with primitive, short-range, but reasonably efficient radar sets out into the Atlantic as part of a concerted three-pronged effort to destroy enemy commerce and disrupt the British battle fleet by submarine, surface ship, and mine. Shortly before and after the departure of *Deutschland* and *Graf Spee,* various supply vessels were sent out to support the pocket battleships during what was anticipated to be long weeks if not months of cruising. Hitler ordered the pocket battleships to lay low for a time as he sought to entice Britain and France to the peace table. But by mid-October it was clear that London and Paris were determined to maintain hostilities, and the word went out from Berlin to commence raiding.

In November 1939, while *Graf Spee* was marauding through the South Atlantic and Indian Oceans, upsetting sailing schedules from Dakar to Bombay, Raeder sent *Scharnhorst* and *Gneisenau* into the convoy lanes between Britain and Canada. Room 39 proved unable to detect German sailings from radio intercepts as its predecessor occasionally had done in 1914–1916. As a consequence, the two battle cruisers were able to sail from Wilhelmshaven undisturbed. Hugging the coasts of Jutland and Norway in the gloom and darkness of early winter in northern latitudes, they sailed toward the North Atlantic through the Iceland-Faeroes gap, becoming the first German capital ships ever to appear on the world ocean in wartime. The RAF's woefully undermanned Coastal Command failed as dismally as Room 39 to detect the sortie, while BDienst kept Marschall, commanding the two battle cruisers, apprised of British fleet movements. Unfortunately for Marschall and his men, *Scharnhorst* and *Gneisenau* were unable to completely evade the British surveillance line in the gap, and just before a brief winter North Atlantic day closed, *Scharnhorst* was spotted by the armed merchant cruiser *Rawalpindi*. A brisk battle ensued in which the woefully undermanned Briton managed to land several shells aboard *Scharnhorst* before falling out of the fight ablaze. The chivalrous Germans stuck around to rescue what enemy crewmen they could and were spotted by the cruiser *Newcastle*. Marschall immediately broke off operations and returned to Germany via the Norwegian leads. Raeder was furious, but Marschall defended himself with the observation that no capital ship should be placed in harm's way with night coming on and enemy ships in the vicinity capable of launching torpedo attacks.[6] Marschall also made the indisputable point that the two big raiders had fulfilled their basic mission, which was to send the British fleet kiting over the entire North Atlantic in a vain search while convoys nervously tiptoed their way across the seas from Halifax to Liverpool and back again, their commanders and sailors peering anxiously across the watery horizons for the glimpse of a German fighting top.

Deutschland was able to cruise unharmed if quite frustrated for several weeks before returning home with only two enemy merchantmen to its credit and an American vessel, *City of Flint,* erroneously seized. But the strain on Churchill's elderly heavy ships began to tell as the battleships *Warspite, Resolution,* and *Revenge,* together with several old cruisers, were detached from Home Fleet anchorages to convoy duty as guards against enemy surface assaults. The 1918 nightmare of a German battle-cruiser breakout into the North Atlantic had materialized.

Not until mid-December 1939 did the gloomy prospects of the Royal Navy temporarily brighten. On the thirteenth, submarine *Salmon* torpedoed the light cruisers *Nuremberg* and *Leipzig* in the North Sea as both vessels were moving to support the return of several German destroyers from mine-laying operations off the English east coast. *Leipzig* was so badly damaged that forever after it could be used only for training purposes. That same day, nearly eight thousand miles to the south, Commodore Henry Harwood, with a small eight-inch-gun cruiser and two swift light cruisers, intercepted and defeated *Graf Spee* early on a sunny morning off the Uruguayan coast, forcing the German warship to seek the dubious sanctuary of Montevideo Harbor, where after seventy-two hours it was blown up by its crew to avoid either destruction in a further sea fight or humiliating internment.[7]

Despite the embarrassing loss of his newest pocket battleship, Raeder kept up the pressure during the first full year of the war. From the spring to the early autumn of 1940 he dispatched seven armed merchant cruisers into the world's sea-lanes. *Atlantis, Orion, Widder, Thor, Pinguin, Komet,* and *Kormoran* sailed scores of thousands of miles to wreak indiscriminate havoc on Allied shipping. *Pinguin* even penetrated Antarctic waters to raid the Norwegian whaling fleet, while *Kormoran* died off the coast of Australia, taking with it the Australian cruiser *Sydney.* Another British cruiser, *Cornwall,* was badly damaged by *Pinguin* in the Indian Ocean before the German raider blew up and sank. Altogether, the German merchant cruisers sank more than a half-million tons of Allied shipping before either returning home or perishing under British guns. By November 1941 the Royal Navy had at last rid the seas of most of these tormentors, though the last German auxiliary cruiser, *Michel,* was not sunk until October 1943.[8]

Raeder kept sending out his precious battleships and cruisers against the British lifeline. The pocket battleship *Admiral Scheer* replicated *Graf Spee's* earlier effort while avoiding its sister's tragic fate. Breaking into the Atlantic in October 1940, *Scheer* encountered the British armed merchant cruiser *Jervis Bay,* which promptly threw itself against the German raider, allowing a convoy to scatter. *Scheer* eventually sent *Jervis Bay* to the bottom but was able to run down and sink only five of the widely dispersed merchantmen. The pocket battleship then turned south and, sustained by no fewer than a half-dozen strategically placed support vessels, went on to log fifty thousand miles in the Atlantic and Indian Oceans, sinking more than one hundred thousand tons of British shipping before sailing home to Kiel on April 1, 1941. At one point, the cheeky skipper, Theodor Krancke, ordered a radar set sent out from Germany on one of the support ships, and he had it fitted to the mainmast in the South Atlantic before starting his successful race back to port. The most successful German raiding cruise of the war began in February 1941 while *Scheer* was still at large. Admiral Gunther Luetjens took *Scharnhorst* and *Gneisenau* on a voyage that extended from the Canadian coast to West Africa. Never before had the Royal Navy had to contend with such a powerful German presence on the world ocean. Luetjens found several unescorted convoys, and his two battle cruisers sank a total of twenty-four ships. *Hipper* was not so fortunate; its three abortive raiding cruises in the Atlantic during 1940 and 1941 yielded comparatively little.[9]

Altogether, the surface raiders accomplished exactly what Raeder had wished. From the Denmark Strait to Madagascar to the northern coast of Australia, they ran the Royal Navy ragged, stretching and straining the Admiralty's limited resources to the uttermost. Most of Britain's handful of battleships spent many long weeks tethered to either slow (seven- to nine-knot) or fast (ten- to twelve-knot) convoys, with only a few remaining with the Home Fleet in order to respond to German breakouts and bring the enemy fleet to battle. Most important, the presence of *Scharnhorst* and *Gneisenau* in the Atlantic "had for a time completely disrupted the whole complex cycle of convoys with a consequent serious drop in vital imports to Britain."[10]

While German commerce raiders roamed the world ocean, U-boats, mines, and surface ships mounted an equally ferocious offensive against the Royal Navy itself, accounting for the loss of two of Britain's precious half-dozen aircraft carriers *(Courageous* and *Glorious)* and one of its equally precious few battleships

(*Royal Oak*). The loss of *Courageous* in the first weeks of the war was due entirely to British folly. In an effort to overcome the paucity of convoy escorts,
Churchill unwisely instituted a favorite but totally ineffective antisubmarine
tactic from 1917–1918—the hunter-killer group. This time the groups were
composed not only of destroyers but also most of Britain's few aircraft carriers,
which to the dismay of Home Fleet commander Admiral Sir Charles Forbes
were detached for antisubmarine duty. But in the absence of advanced surface
and subsurface detection gear (to say nothing of intelligence intercepts), the
hunter-killer group remained a notion ahead of its time. Even worse, such
groups were potential sitting ducks for Nazi submarines because German naval
intelligence was able to read a portion of British communication traffic. On
September 14 Britain's single truly modern carrier, *Ark Royal,* was attacked by U-
39 west of the Hebrides and would have been sunk had not the torpedoes exploded prematurely due to faulty magnetic firing pistols. Three days later U-29
was directed to the Bristol Channel where the *Courageous* hunting group was
conducting operations. After two hours of tense maneuvering, Kapitänleutnant
Otto Schuhart was in position and rammed two fish into the side of the
22,500-ton carrier, which went to the bottom in fifteen minutes, carrying with
it the captain and 518 others. As was so often the case throughout the war,
Schuhart escaped in the resulting confusion. On September 26, nine days after
Courageous went down, *Ark Royal* was almost bombed to death by the Luftwaffe off Heligoland as it covered the retreat of a wounded British submarine.

Royal Oak was sunk at its anchorage in Scapa Flow just weeks after the opening of the war by the daring young submarine ace Gunther Prien who accomplished what no British sailor believed was possible. Prien's audacity once again
bounced the Home Fleet from its strategically placed base in favor of temporary havens twenty-four hours farther from the North Atlantic sea-lanes, which
proved a critical factor in the inability of the Royal Navy to hunt down marauding German battle cruisers and pocket battleships.

As the number of British heavy ships was steadily reduced in the first weeks
of the war, Raeder—and Göring working on his own agenda and schedule—
also launched a major mining offensive against Britain. Many of the mines were
of the new magnetic type, against which British industry could and should have
developed countermeasures long before the war. In the six months between
September 1939 and March 1940, German destroyers, trawlers, U-boats, and
long-range Luftwaffe aircraft laid fields in or immediately off Loch Ewe, the
Clyde, Liverpool, Swansea, and the Bristol Channel on the west coast of Britain;
Falmouth, Portland, Weymouth, Portsmouth, and Dover on the Channel coast;

and Cromarty Firth, Invergordon, Dundee, the Firth of Forth, Newcastle upon Tyne, Great Yarmouth, and a dozen other ports and harbors on the east coast. Almost immediately the offensive paid substantial dividends in both merchant and naval sinkings and damage. Between September and the end of December 1939, seventy-nine British merchantmen went to the bottom due to mines.[11] The battleship *Rodney,* returning to Loch Ewe for a brief refueling visit after vainly chasing *Scharnhorst* and *Gneisenau,* struck a mine and was severely damaged. It would not return to active service for nearly nine months. Since battle cruiser *Hood* had been struck by a bomb that revealed its need for an extensive refit, the Royal Navy was at one point in the winter of 1939–1940 reduced to but nine effective battleships. For several days in December, the not-yet-damaged *Hood* was the sole unit in the Home Fleet battle line, as the other heavy units were either on convoy duty in the Atlantic or being rushed home from the Mediterranean.[12] Even before *Rodney* was stricken, the new 10,000-ton cruiser *Belfast* had its back broken in the Firth of Forth by a magnetic mine and had to be virtually rebuilt. Commander Lord Louis Mountbatten's destroyer *Kelly* had its stern blown off. Not for many months did the Admiralty Research Laboratory come up with an effective antidote to the magnetic mine, the "degaussing" cable or coil, which rendered ships' hulls magnetically neutral. In the meantime, the Germans pressed their mining offensive ruthlessly by submarine, aircraft, and, as the winter nights grew longer, surface ship as well. In the first six months of 1940 another 103 British merchant vessels were lost to enemy mines. Unfortunately for Hitler's admirals, there were not enough of the new weapons to inflict fatal damage on British shipping before effective countermeasures were introduced. In the summer of 1940 British losses to German mines declined precipitately as more and more ships were fitted with degaussing cables. Moreover, German torpedoes, especially the most advanced, the Mark G7a and Mark G7e, often proved defective in the early months of the conflict, as their magnetic explosive pistols often went off prematurely. Had such weapons worked well, there is no doubt that *Ark Royal* would have fallen beneath the waves in the first month of the war and other British warships would have undoubtedly perished in the spring of 1940 off the coast of Norway. Once more, German industrial failures and a lack of planning foresight on the part of the navy negated the impact of what could have been two decisive weapons.[13]

Nonetheless, by the summer of 1940 Germany had mounted one shockingly successful amphibious invasion, supplemented by a limited airborne assault. The conquest of Norway reflected the triumph of the "western," or North Atlantic, faction of the Kriegsmarine over its "eastern," or Baltic, opponents.

When in the autumn of 1939 Raeder began pressing Hitler to risk the entire navy and much of the Luftwaffe in a series of sudden, rapid assaults by air and sea to capture western Scandinavia, he gave as the ostensible motive protection of the Swedish iron-ore supplies that Allied planners—apparently erroneously—thought were essential to Germany's war effort.[14] But Raeder and many others in and out of the navy had a much stronger motive for pressing their Scandinavian strategy. They had also absorbed the lessons of World War I when Britain's Home Fleet had kept the *Hochseeflotte* largely bottled up in the Heligoland Bight. Norwegian coastal ports commanded ready access to the Greenland-Iceland-U.K. "gaps" from which German warships could reach the critical convoy lanes between the Old World and the New. They were worth gambling the entire surface fleet to obtain. In the event, although no major surface units were destroyed in the operation, the Germans lost at least a quarter of their light surface forces.

In his meeting with Hitler on October 10, 1939, Raeder warned that the British might have imminent designs of their own on neutral Scandinavia. Should they stage a coup de main and capture Norway, "the northern part of the North Sea would then be flanked on both sides by the British Fleet and Air Force, which could definitely deny it to our use except for submarines. Our surface ships would no longer have any chance of reaching the Atlantic, and with enemy mine barriers set like those in World War I, the exit even for submarines would be extremely hazardous." Furthermore, any occupation of Norway by Britain "would put tremendous pressure on Sweden" to join the Allies, thus denying Germany its ore supplies.[15]

Hitler was at first resistant. Determined to attack France and the Low Countries the following spring, he did not wish to stretch his commitments further. Moreover, seizure of a nation whose coastline extended nearly eight hundred miles would be a staggering undertaking for Germany's minuscule navy, no matter what help could be expected from the Wehrmacht and Luftwaffe. But Raeder returned to the Reichschancellory in mid-December with further arguments, and the appearance in Berlin of a Norwegian named Vidkun Quisling who was eager to do the Nazis' bidding served to turn the führer's mind. Hitler was further made uneasy by Churchill's invitation on January 20, 1940, to all "northern neutrals" to join the Allies. Although the first lord's call was rejected, it certainly indicated the direction of British thinking, and in German eyes British seizure of the supply ship *Altmark* in a Norwegian fjord several weeks later confirmed the impression that London would never allow Norway to remain truly neutral. According to a source within the German supreme command, "Hitler chose to solve the [Norwegian] problem by military methods."[16]

Staff planners from all three German services worked with greater closeness, harmony, and imagination than ever before or again to craft orders for a sudden assault to seize Oslo and all of Norway's North Sea and Atlantic coast port towns from Kristiansand to Narvik.[17] For the first time in history, warfare would be integrally conducted in all three dimensions: air, land, and sea. Norway would set the pattern for later Allied operations in North Africa and Europe and Japanese and American activities in the Pacific. Then, days before "Operation Weser" was to take place, Raeder suddenly got cold feet. His entire surface navy would have to be dedicated to the enterprise, and the prospect that it could be sunk in toto could not be dismissed. The grand admiral therefore begged his führer to try to ensure continued Norwegian neutrality by diplomatic means alone. But as Raeder soon realized, preparations were too far advanced to be reversed. With a somewhat heavy heart he therefore recommended invasion day as April 7 (when the moon would be full). Hitler decided to wait a further forty-eight hours.

Enjoying interior lines of communication, the Germans mounted the Norwegian campaign primarily from the sea, supplemented by limited parachute assaults.[18] The navy embarked more than ten thousand troops on cruisers, destroyers, and small merchantmen and successfully landed them at Oslo, Kristiansand, Stavanger, Bergen, Trondheim, and Narvik. The task forces assigned to seize Trondheim and Narvik in northern Norway were given distant support by *Scharnhorst* and *Gneisenau,* which acted as decoys to keep the Royal Navy away from the Norwegian coast. To ensure air control over the Norwegian battlefields and adjacent seas, the Wehrmacht invaded Denmark and seized several airfields. In its opening stages Weser proved a stunning success. Interservice cooperation among the assaulting forces was outstanding. Only at Oslo did the invasion fleet suffer stiff opposition, with the brand-new heavy cruiser *Blücher* going down before the guns and torpedoes of the outer fortresses. In the first twenty-four hours, the Germans seized all their objectives before the Anglo-French could react. Thereafter, the navy's job was simply to keep the enemy sufficiently off balance to allow the army to complete its work of subduing two million widely scattered Norwegians. With essential support from the Luftwaffe, the navy performed its task brilliantly.

Hitler had, in fact, beaten his Anglo-French enemies to Scandinavia by less than a day. The British War Cabinet, and especially Winston Churchill, had been as mindful of Norway's importance as Raeder had guessed. Churchill was determined to reverse the unhappy trend at sea, and throughout late 1939 and early 1940 he pondered several schemes to get the Royal Navy on the offensive. The first lord not only contemplated an attack against Norway but also pondered forcing the Skagerrak and Kattegat with a powerful battle fleet to control the Baltic. Correlli Barnett has sneeringly dismissed Operation Catherine as belonging to "the same category of Churchillian cigar-butt strategy as his 1915 brainwave of capturing the Friesian island of Borkum, or even the Dardenelles expedition itself: glibly attractive when arrowed broadly on a map of Europe, but a nonsense in terms of the technical means and military forces available." Certainly, the poor showing of the Home Fleet off Norway lends credence to Barnett's biting skepticism. And aviation historian Allen Andrews has argued that the Luftwaffe would have massacred any warships that Churchill might have sent to the north German coast.[19] But a quick British thrust into the Baltic in the first days or weeks of the war to disrupt German naval exercises and perhaps bombard the Hanseatic towns might have been worth the gamble (even with the loss of a precious battleship or two) in stiffening Scandinavian resolve to stand up to Hitler. Instead, Denmark and Norway remained strictly neutral (though clearly sympathetic to the British), while Sweden continued to supply Berlin with iron ore.

As in the past, Churchill was frequently his own worst enemy when it came to developing and implementing strategies. He remained bitterly disliked within the Conservative Party and government right up to the shattering events of May 1940. In late March, while the first lord appeared to be pressing simultaneously for approval of Operation Catherine, the mining of the Norwegian coast, an outright invasion of southern Norway, or all three, Oliver Stanley, the secretary of state for war, told a colleague that Prime Minister Chamberlain was "head and shoulders above everybody in Cabinet. Winston becoming very interfering and discursive. Handled splendidly by Neville." The colleague added that Stanley "dreads idea that Winston may ever be PM." Churchill's tense relations with his fellow cabinet members extended to his beloved Admiralty as well. According to Captain Roskill (who was intimately involved with the matter), Churchill never trusted the naval planning staff, a legacy of World War I. According to Roskill, Churchill failed to see that the Admiralty administration of 1939 was far better educated and sophisticated than that of 1914. Perhaps. Certainly, the record of British naval behavior during the 1930s leads to much skepticism on this point. In any case, Churchill did bring with him to the Admiralty his own team of advisers, headed by the notorious—and widely resented and disliked—professor F. A. Lindemann, "which apart from the duplication and confusion it caused, was hardly a fair assessment of the ability of the staff and scientists already available."[20] Thus, Admiralty planning through much of World War II was in as great an uproar as during Churchill's tenure a quarter century before. The problem was, of course, that Churchill was an often impulsive meddler. He was as much a control freak as Raeder, and as both first lord of the Admiralty and prime minister he could never keep his mind or hands off the most detailed aspects of the war in general and the Royal Navy in particular.

But the opportunity to deny Germany its iron-ore supplies at a moment when Hitler's designs on western Europe were quite clear slowly turned Chamberlain's War Cabinet in Churchill's direction. Throughout the terribly cold and then snowy months of late autumn and early winter 1939–1940, while Europe and the world waited tensely for the "Phony War" in the West to explode into violence, Churchill developed the notion of mining the Norwegian leads. He dropped the matter for a time, then returned to it on March 21. After that, the plan, dubbed Operation Wilfred, dominated Churchill's thinking, though he and the cabinet also devoted a great deal of time to pondering if not preparing for the anticipated German blow against Belgium and France.

As finally approved, Operation Wilfred provided for mining the inshore waters from Narvik southward, covered by powerful elements of the Home Fleet. The exercise would begin on April 8. But surely Hitler would not allow the British to scuttle the shipment of his precious iron ore uncontested. To successfully mask the mining operation, it would be necessary to land troops at Bergen and Stavanger, and a supplementary plan to Operation Wilfred, dubbed R4, was also approved. Norwegian neutrality had already been breached in the *Altmark* affair; it would be further breached by the mining of the leads. Churchill and His Majesty's government were now prepared to take the final step and simply invade southern Norway itself. Not only would the mining operation be protected, but should R4 proceed according to plan, Britain could establish the air and naval bases in southern Norway that would directly menace German activities in the Baltic with the same practical effect as if Operation Catherine had been carried out. One is reminded of Churchill's impetuous 1913 thoughts of invading portions of the Low Countries in order to obtain bases against Wilhelm's High Seas Fleet.

The British scheme in terms of schedule, objective, and means was thus almost identical to Operation Weser. On April 8 British army units coming ashore from four cruisers supported by elements of the Home Fleet would seize Stavanger and Bergen while the mining force covered by the Home Fleet would commence its operation. Fate had seemingly set the stage for a decisive Anglo-German clash and the first great naval action of the Second World War.

It never happened, because Churchill and Forbes took what may have been deliberate bait set by Raeder. As the German fleet departed Wilhelmshaven on April 7 for their Norwegian objectives, Room 39 apparently got wind of the sortie. Under clear skies but in a steadily mounting gale, a force of British bombers was sent into the North Sea and attacked the enemy force without success. The Admiralty promptly ordered Forbes to sea several hours in advance of the Home Fleet's scheduled sailing to cover the assaults on Bergen and Stavanger. But neither Churchill nor anyone else in London had an inkling that the departure of the German heavy ships was prelude to an enemy invasion of Norway. *Scharnhorst* and *Gneisenau* had already staged one disruptive foray into the Atlantic. The Admiralty and War Cabinet concluded that those ships and *Hipper* were embarked on another cruise and that the numerous destroyers attending them were there to assist in the breakout. According to Captain Roskill, Churchill on his own initiative ordered the disembarkation of troops from the British cruisers at Rosyth so that these ships could join the Home Fleet in the hunt for the three German vessels. Forbes, his mind equally settled on the notion of a German raiding cruise, set course to intercept the three enemy heavy ships several hundred miles off the Norwegian coast. Whether or not Raeder had actually intended his two big ships and *Hipper* to lure Forbes and the British fleet away from the Norwegian invasion, this was what happened. At a stroke, the erroneous reactions of Churchill and Forbes had deprived the British and French of contesting the initial German assault either at sea or ashore. Once ensconced in Oslo, Kristiansand, and the Atlantic port towns, the Germans lost no time in spreading out across the snowy mountainous hinterland like some malignant stain.

The Anglo-French forces reacted as swiftly as they could, but it was too late. By the time ships could be again combat-loaded and sent north, the Germans were ashore and well entrenched and the Allied riposte proved too little and too late. A daring British naval thrust up the Vest and Ofoten Fjords led by battleship *Warspite* destroyed a half-dozen German destroyers and bounced the small Nazi invasion force out of Narvik for a time, permitting an Allied counterlanding in the area. But the Luftwaffe kept British reinforcements, including carriers and their aircraft, from effectively supporting the shore party, and Forbes was so intimidated by initial German air attacks against his ships that he kept his fleet far at sea. *Gneisenau* and *Scharnhorst* periodically lurked about to keep the British further off balance without subjecting themselves to a decisive naval engagement. Churchill meddled disastrously in the arguments between the senior army and navy commanders at Narvik, while the Luftwaffe, "using bombers, transports and seaplanes with the utmost flexibility," had demonstrated brilliantly that "a country could be laid open for occupation by ground forces although the attackers were faced by a superior naval power." The overall result was to neutralize whatever effect the Royal Navy might have had on the campaign. When Hitler unleashed his offensive in the West a month after the Scandinavian invasions, Anglo-French forces were promptly pulled out of northern Norway, but as they left Narvik the always aggressive Admiral Marschall, in *Scharnhorst* and *Gneisenau,* fell upon the unsuspecting carrier *Glorious* (having just missed *Ark Royal*) and blew it out of the water, despite gallant and futile attacks by the carrier's destroyer escorts that previewed the actions of American small boys at Leyte Gulf four and a half years thence. Barnett is caustic about the Allied disaster. Although Norway portended the vast amphibious operations of 1942–1945, "those later maritime operations were thoroughly prepared and planned beforehand." Combined task forces "working together to cover and support major expeditionary forces ashore . . . were organised and rehearsed for their roles in good time." In contrast, Churchill "precipitately" threw the fleet and British army into a campaign that neither was prepared to wage.[21]

Yet it is possible to interpret Churchill's rashness and impetuosity—his "Whitehall map warfare" and "cigar-butt strategy"—more charitably than either Barnett or Roskill has seen fit to do. A new war of unprecedented mobility was breaking upon the world, and the scope, scale, and nature of the violence had yet to be understood and absorbed by cautious minds. To argue or suggest that the British should have understood and known well how to exploit the new warfare is asking too much. They had modestly rearmed; they had not built a Hitlerian war machine with all that that implied in terms of ruthless tactics, disciplined planning teams, and well-trained troops operating within the context of a garrison-state mentality. No one in the early spring of 1940 could tell how good the Germans were likely to be either in the air, on the ground, or at sea. No one could tell where they would place the emphasis of their endeavors (submarine warfare excepted) or how effective that emphasis and those endeavors might be. In battle, as in so many other activities, people learn by doing, by making mistakes and miscalculations and learning from them. There was something to be said for British rashness in the early stage of a war in which the foe had seemingly neutralized one's superiority at sea. If dash and daring might lead to the imposition of a moral superiority over the enemy, it must be tried. Raeder, after all, was willing to risk Germany's entire surface fleet on one campaign.

Until Britain and its current or putative Allies could learn to think again in terms of truly ruthless professional warfare, they would remain forever on the defensive. Churchill seemed to understand this and sought a forced-draft advance in British behavior through a policy of deliberate audacity. On the morrow of another melancholy defeat in Crete a year later, he summarized his bulldog reaction to the repeated enemy victories at sea in 1940–1941. Hitler and Raeder might have seized the initiative, but the prime minister would never admit it.

> There are some who say we should never fight without superior or at least ample air support, and ask when this lesson will be learned. But suppose you cannot have it. The questions which have to be settled are not always questions between what is good and bad; very often it is a choice between two very terrible alternatives. "Must you, if you cannot have this essential and desirable air support, yield important key points one after the other?" The further question arises as to what would happen if you allowed the enemy to advance or overrun without cost to himself the most precious and valuable strategic points. . . . Where would the Germans be now?[22]

Students of the Norwegian campaign from Moulton to Macintyre to Barnett all agree on one point: German mastery of the air over the battlefield and surrounding waters was the decisive element in the defeat of the Allies. In Norway for the first time, airpower came into its own. Churchill and his French allies could get small armies ashore at Namsos, Aandalsnes, and Narvik. But so long as German aircraft continually harried and preyed upon supporting supply ships and warships as well as troop movements, it proved impossible to sustain the ground forces, much less use them for a major counteroffensive. Forbes could have used his carriers, the modern *Ark Royal* and the elderly *Glorious,* more aggressively than he did. But their air groups were small and unbalanced toward cumbersome, slow-flying attack planes, and he was understandably concerned for the safety of his fleet, whose size was far less than John Jellicoe had enjoyed twenty-five years before. Forbes chose caution over daring, and it would eventually cost him his job.

If airpower at sea as well as on land was to prove decisive, then the one ruthless move that Britain made in the closing stages of the Norwegian campaign would eventually pay immeasurable returns. On May 6, 1940, reacting to the German capture of the Norwegian coast, Britain for all intents and purposes invaded and seized neutral Iceland. It is a measure of the desperation that had now gripped the Chamberlain government that the prewar appeaser of Hitler committed an act against international law that had brought Churchill great censure when he had suggested seizure of a coastal strip of the Low Countries in 1913 and the conquest of southern Norway just weeks before. But the great rocky, glaciated midocean island dominated the entire upper North Atlantic. From Iceland's harbors and the airfields laboriously carved out of volcanic powder, the Royal Navy and Air Force could, with sufficient time and resources, extend the range of protection over the convoy lanes between the New World and the Old to substantial proportions.

The Norwegian campaign was a critical turning point in the Second World War, for with the conquest of western Scandinavia and the subsequent seizure of France and the Low Countries, Hitler's writ ran from Cape Finisterre to the Arctic Circle. The Baltic supply line from Sweden was now secure, and the great landlocked sea could be used as a training and staging area for the Kriegsmarine without any fear of enemy disruption. But of far greater importance was the fact that the German navy had suddenly acquired the most immediate and broadest access to the North Atlantic. No longer would German U-boat or surface sailors have to face the daunting prospect of forcing Channel minefields or sailing the long miles around the northern tip of Scotland to escape home waters. Within a matter of a few breathless weeks the world ocean was suddenly lapping at their feet as they stood on the shores of Norway and France. One of the great ironies of history had come to pass: what had eluded a kaiser obsessed with a global vision had fallen into the lap of a führer preoccupied with a continental strategy. One hundred and thirty-five years before, another potential conqueror had stood on the shores of France and gazed across the twenty-mile Strait of Dover at England sleeping in the sun. "Let us be masters of the Strait for six hours," Napoléon had said, "and we shall be masters of the world."[23] Now it was Hitler's turn to try.

Popular belief has long held that the invasion of England never went anywhere because the German air force lost the struggle to command the skies over Kent and Sussex to the RAF the following August and September. As is so often the case, popular belief is at best half right.

Hitler's heart was never behind the invasion of England, no matter what the circumstances; neither were most of those in the German armed services. Invading unsuspecting Norway with its two million widely scattered people possessed of no significant military force, while brilliantly conceived and executed, was a far easier prospect than trying to force a lodgment on isles harboring forty-five million aroused and determined antagonists. Moreover, Hitler's foreign policy centered about wooing England, not conquering it, which is undoubtedly why he ordered his commanders to stop and let the Franco-British armies escape from Dunkirk. Even before he became Reichschancellor, Hitler hoped to come to some sort of grandiose world-sharing agreement with the British, and from 1938 on to the fall of France two years later this was a central theme in his policy. By early July 1940, when the führer at last (and reluctantly) ordered the Wehrmacht, Luftwaffe, and Kriegsmarine to begin planning for an amphibious and airborne assault, time was running out. Churchill had rallied his forces and people for a prolonged and desperate struggle. Of almost equal importance, the Royal Navy had laid extensive minefields off the northern French and Dutch coasts that would force the Kriegsmarine to engage in at least limited sweeping operations before any invasion fleet could reach the Channel.

The prospective German operation was code-named Seelöwe (Sealion). On August 1 the führer issued his first general directive on the subject that emphasized the need to obtain aerial superiority over the Channel and southern England and discouraged Luftwaffe attacks against the Royal Navy as diversions from the main objective. In fact, Germany's inability to mount a serious amphibious operation, together with a gross exaggeration of the size and effectiveness of the British army awaiting the Wehrmacht in England, proved to be the decisive factors in discouraging Hitler from implementing Sealion, whose basic "problem was purely that of transport across the sea." Colonel General Franz Halder, the army chief of staff, recalled that from July to late September 1940, most of the German navy and much of the army worked intensively in the estuaries of the Rhine, Meuse, and Scheldt, hastily constructing or converting other vessels to transport and landing craft. Armored forces trained for a cross-Channel assault in the Frisian Islands, while on the French and Dutch coasts the Ninth and Sixth Armies were engaged in "special courses for... assault troops." But these activities were surrounded by an air of unreality and profound confusion. "Even at the time," Halder later admitted, "it was hardly possible to form a clear picture of all these preparations." The confusion was compounded by a constant alteration in details so that in the end, "plans only remained consistent in their broad outlines."[24]

General Gerd von Rundstedt, the acerbic army commander who was picked to lead Sealion, was even more caustic and precise in his criticism. His two-paragraph dismissal of Sealion is devastating:

> The proposed invasion of England was nonsense because adequate ships were not available. They were chiefly barges which had to be brought from Germany and the Netherlands.
>
> Then they had to be reconstructed so that tanks and other equipment could be driven out of the bows. Then the troops had to learn how to embark and disembark. We looked upon the whole thing as a sort of game,

because it was obvious that no invasion was possible when our navy was not in a position to cover a crossing of the Channel or carry reinforcements. Nor was the German air force capable of taking on these functions if the navy failed.[25]

As finally conceived, Sealion would require three phases. According to Halder, Phase I, the landing on beaches between Dover and Plymouth, was to take place in several waves that would ultimately place twenty-six infantry and armored divisions on British soil.

> The first wave was to be formed of fast landing craft, some crossing under their own power, others lowered from sea-going ships outside the coast defense zone. The second wave was to consist of the main body of landing craft some of which could move slowly under their own power, some of which had to be towed. The third wave was to consist of large sea-going vessels which would carry the bulk of the troops as well as their supporting tanks, engineers, signal unit, etc. Phase II provided for the crossing of the panzer and motorized divisions from Holland and of further infantry divisions from the French coast. Phase III provided for the crossing of further infantry divisions and of large supplies to form a supply base. The details of Phase II and Phase III could be worked out only after it had become clear to what extent sea-going vessels would be available after the completion of the initial phases.[26]

In other words, Sealion would be mounted on a shoestring by a comparative few very slowly moving and thus highly vulnerable landing craft, with the prospect that an adequate supply base could not be accumulated for at least several days and possibly several weeks. Given its terms and conditions, it is doubtful that Sealion would have been mounted even if Göring's flyers had seized control of the skies over Britain. Not only was complete air superiority essential, but so was control of the flanks of the amphibious assault, and that would have required both extensive countermining and employment of every warship that Raeder could muster. Had such control been attempted from the air alone, it would have required the Luftwaffe to destroy virtually every ship in the British fleet either before or during amphibious operations. Although it may be fairly stated on the basis of air-sea battles off Norway and later Crete that the German air force was capable of inflicting great damage on the Royal Navy, it is also true that the German flyers did not come away from their battles with the enemy unscathed. Nor, of course, did they face the entire Royal Navy, as it was assumed they would have had Sealion been attempted. A successful invasion of England would have required the entire German navy and air force, plus a large portion of the German army. This was simply too big an enterprise and too costly a gamble for a führer and his generals fixated on control of continental Europe.

Or so it seemed. In fact, British power was more fragile and German prospects consequently more promising than the führer and his commanders realized. In 1914 the *Hochseeflotte* had refused to immolate itself in the Channel in order to seal off the western front from British reinforcements. Twenty-six years later, according to one naval veteran of the time, the British fleet suffered the same lack of nerve. The whole system of British home defense from the time of the Armada through the Great War of 1914–1918 had "depended ultimately on a battle-fleet even though it might not be used to defeat [an] invasion directly. The British naval dispositions to oppose invasion in 1940 were initially in accordance with these principles. A flotilla of some forty destroyers and over a thousand auxiliary patrol vessels was available to patrol the Channel and the southern North Sea," while the Home Fleet remained stationed at Scapa Flow "with six cruisers further south ready to support the flotilla."

But "the new factor of airpower altered this concept fundamentally." Beginning in July 1940, the Luftwaffe, newly established on frontline French and Dutch airfields, began assaulting English Channel shipping in the Strait of Dover. While the Ju.87 dive-bombers suffered heavily from the Hurricanes and Spitfires of RAF Fighter Command, "even with fighter protection, it was soon found too expensive to operate ships in the Channel by day and [the flotilla] patrols were confined to the hours of darkness." As the Battle of Britain reached a climax in the skies over southern England in August and early September, "no one now seriously believed that if the Royal Air Force was defeated by the Luftwaffe the [naval] flotilla would be able to operate for long in the Narrow Seas. After its experience in Norway it was clear that the Home Fleet could not help either. It had been reluctant to face a single Fliegerkorps in that campaign and would have still less chance against the five Fliegerkorps now in France." Forbes obviously believed this to be the case and opposed stationing any of his battleships or cruisers near or in the Channel. "He even went so far as to say that whilst the R.A.F. was undefeated he believed that defence against invasion should be left to them and the Army." This shocking conclusion "could only be taken as an abdication from the Navy's traditional role and a belief that the fleet was only of use against an invasion as a last ditch suicide force."[27]

In fact, there was something rather peculiar about the Royal Navy in the early war years. On the big ships, at least, it was as if there was no war. Late in 1940 Lieutenant Commander Joseph H. Wellings, the assistant U.S. naval attaché in London, joined the Home Fleet for a time. His first service was aboard a destroyer, HMS *Eskimo,* whose ship's company he found both keen and agreeable. The battle cruiser *Hood* that he joined near the end of the year was filled with the same pleasant chaps, but it was as if they were members of a yacht club. At a time of steadily growing stringencies in the civilian sector, the food aboard ship was nothing short of sumptuous, with huge, well-cooked breakfasts including fruit, cereals, fish, eggs, kidneys, mushrooms, and so on, goods that the civilian sector would hardly see again until 1949 or '50. Lunch was the same: at least seven kinds of cold meats, vegetables, sweet butter... There was both dinner and supper, plus tea. And there were drinks—pink gins or excellent martinis before both lunch and dinner. Wellings wrote his wife on several occasions that he really had to watch his weight.

For all its flaws, John Jellicoe's Grand Fleet had been a hardworking outfit. But in 1939–1941 there were no repeated sweeps by the heavy ships of the upper North Sea. When intelligence was received that one or more of Raeder's handful of big surface ships, a cruiser, pocket battleship, or even *Scharnhorst* or *Gneisenau,* might be preparing to sail against the Atlantic convoys, one of the Home Fleet's World War I–era battleships or battle cruisers, *Ramilles* or *Repulse,* for example, would leave Scapa Flow to serve as escort over to Halifax and back. But, presumably, the German menace from above and below the waters was too pronounced for extended fleet operations under any conditions short of extreme emergency such as the Norwegian campaign when, in fact, the fleet remained largely out of action. So the massive forty-two thousand–ton *Hood,* the largest warship in the world at that moment, spent quite a bit of time swinging around its anchor chain. On New Year's Eve 1940, everyone remained in the wardroom after dinner for drinks—even the youngest "snotties"—and near midnight the captain appeared together with the admiral and his entire staff. One of the younger officers drew out his bagpipes, and as the gin continued to go down, men and boys began to dance. Five months later everybody in that compartment with the exception of Wellings and all but three of *Hood's* thirteen hundred–plus company would be vaporized together with their ship under the guns of Germany's newest and most powerful warships, battleship *Bismarck* and cruiser *Prinz Eugen.*[28]

Had the Germans but known or suspected the indolence of their enemy's heavy units, then two compelling invasion scenarios might well have come into play. John Lukacs's research suggests that the best time for Hitler to have conquered Britain was during or immediately following Dunkirk. In the desperate ninety-six hours following the evacuation, Churchill, knowing full well the defeatism that now gripped his beloved fleet, feared that Hitler might be able to put several thousand superbly trained and disciplined shock troops ashore in Kent or East Anglia from small, fast motorboats (presumably at night) together with several regiments of paratroops who might even descend on London itself, thus creating a major disruption as several hundred thousand demoralized and largely disarmed Allied troops sorted themselves out amid no little chaos after returning to England. Had the führer abandoned his not implausible policy of seeking a general peace with His Majesty's government during the earliest stages of the French campaign and ordered emergency planning for an immediate, dramatic coup de main against England as soon as the British and French armies were neutralized in Belgium, the operation might have permitted a much larger follow-up effort to succeed in the coming weeks.[29]

Military analyst Hanson W. Baldwin has argued that Sealion itself could have worked as late as August or September 1940 if the plan had been revised and prosecuted under precisely the right circumstances. "At night a large airborne and amphibious force might have spanned the Strait of Dover and the Channel and probably could have forced a landing on British soil despite the intervention of the British Navy and the RAF. . . . It is entirely conceivable, too, that the Germans could have won a localized air superiority over the invasion area—the only kind that mattered."[30] Certainly, the Germans' need to sweep at least a narrow corridor through the British minefields off the northwest European coast would have given London some warning that an invasion was imminent. But we now know from Admiral Arthur Hezlet that had the Luftwaffe defeated the RAF's Fighter Command, the Royal Navy probably would not have moved from Scapa Flow to the Kent and East Anglian invasion beaches until too late. Indeed, once Hitler forced a major lodgment in England, his soldiers and sailors might well have been spared *any* intervention by the Home Fleet. Churchill's repeated assurances to FDR and others that should Britain go down the navy would sail to the New World suddenly take on portentous meaning. The prime minister clearly assumed that his ships and sailors would not immolate themselves seeking to forestall a Nazi invasion, but would sail away to fight another day. Baldwin's compelling scenario of a sudden, violent blow against England of the sort that had been embraced as truth by a hysterical public in the months and years immediately preceding 1914 just might have worked a quarter century later in the face of the Royal Navy's almost flagrant defeatism.

Such thoughts, it is clear, never enticed Hitler and his generals—indeed, they probably never entered their minds. Fearful and ignorant of the water—even such a narrow body of water as the Channel—and mistrustful and dismissive of a navy that had just performed so superbly in Norway, they drew back (as they had at Dunkirk) from seeking a knockout blow. It was a decision that only cost Hitler the war. Germany's lack of familiarity with or experience in large-scale amphibious operations meant that it would not—and perhaps could not—project its power to the point that national security could be guaranteed. After the spring and summer of 1940, Germany was, with its conquest of the western European coast and its handful of battleships and submarines, a modest high-seas power at last. But Britain remained not only to bedevil it from the air and challenge it on the waters but also to serve as the physical and political linchpin of the future Grand Alliance and the springboard for an eventual Allied return to the Continent.

Pearl Harbor was the second point at which an inferior sea power might have decisively turned the tide of battle. As many writers have observed, the raid represented a great blunder for the Japanese who destroyed an obsolete battle fleet but could have practically driven the Americans back to California. Had Pearl Harbor's clearly identifiable oil-storage facilities been obliterated, together with its formidable fleet-repair and -support facilities, the three carriers then at sea, representing the only striking power the United States had left in the Pacific, would have become floating hulks within days if not hours and thus ready targets for Admiral Chuichi Nagumo's flyers. As it was, not only did the Americans retain their few precious flattops, but Pearl Harbor remained open to serve them as an advance base as well. Beyond the irreplaceable loss of more than twenty-four hundred servicemen, the Japanese did their enemy a positive favor by in effect junking not only an obsolete fleet but an obsolete strategy as well.

When Nagumo's flyers begged him for permission to mount a third attack, he supposedly replied that he feared Japan had aroused a sleeping giant. Whether the admiral actually made this remark, his actions in turning back to his homeland unscathed clearly reflected a crucial fact about the Pacific war: even at the outset and in nominal defeat the United States had gained a moral advantage over Japan. The sailors who had leaped to their guns at Pearl Harbor and the handful of flyers who had raced their few planes skyward from the adjacent airfields achieved far more than they would ever realize.

The blunders at Pearl Harbor reflected a profound flaw in Japanese strategic thinking. Isoroku Yamamoto and Nagumo believed that they might lose up to half their fleet, for they could not be sure that Tokyo's duplicitous diplomacy would work. When it did work—brilliantly—Combined Fleet planners had no contingency plan to truly exploit the Hawaii attack.

For twenty years after Pearl Harbor, the notion that the "sneak" Japanese attack was nothing more nor less than "murder with a toothy smile" dominated American thinking. Tokyo's "peace mission" to Washington had been nothing more nor less than a deceitful effort to lull Americans into believing that Japan wished to settle its outstanding differences with the United States short of conflict, even as the warlords of Tokyo prepared to spring their deadly assassination on the Pacific Fleet. But as Japan became a reliable cold-war ally and Asia's democratic workshop, a more sympathetic appraisal of Pearl Harbor began to emerge from America's college and university faculties. In fact, it was argued, evidence indicated that the Tōjō government had been prepared to give Washington its declaration of war nearly an hour before Nagumo's flyers were scheduled to appear over Oahu. The envoys, Kichisaburo Nomura and Saburo Kurusu, were directed to deliver the dramatic final part of the Japanese war message at 1:00 P.M. Washington time (7 A.M. in Hawaii). But embassy interpreters and typists, ostensibly hungover from Saturday-night partying, failed in their responsibility to translate the message rapidly and efficiently. As a result, Nomura and Kurusu did not deliver it to Secretary of State Cordell Hull until 2:20 P.M., by which time the attack on Hawaii was well under way.

But in December 1999 a Japanese scholar, Takeo Iguchi of the International Christian University in Tokyo, dramatically resurrected the traditional argument, not by citing new documentation but by rereading the old. Foreign Ministry archives and the wartime diary of Japan's General Staff revealed that the Tōjō government had pursued a policy of deliberate deceit regarding the Pearl Harbor attack: President Roosevelt, his advisers, and the American military and naval leadership were meant to be lulled into the belief that Japan had no hostile intentions toward the United States in December 1941. A December 7 entry in the *Japanese War Diary* (December 6 in the United States) "notes approvingly that 'our deceptive diplomacy is steadily proceeding toward success.'" Iguchi has concluded that the war diary "shows that the [Japanese] army and navy did not want to give any proper declaration of war or indeed prior notice even of the termination of negotiations." He has further concluded that the delay in delivering the war message "was probably the result of deliberate planning" in Tokyo, since the message contained a number of "heavy garbles" that "set it apart from most of Tokyo's [previously] clean transmissions."[31]

So Japanese diplomacy brilliantly set up the U.S. Pacific Fleet at Pearl Harbor. Had Nagumo destroyed the oil-storage facilities on Oahu and had Japanese flyers then moved on to bomb an even bigger target—the Panama Canal—the United States would have been closed out of the Pacific for many months while the imperial fleet could have steamed, bombed, shot, and invaded as it pleased.[32] Japan could quite possibly have established that impenetrable "ribbon-defense line" down the middle of the ocean from the Aleutians to the Solomons of which its strategists had long dreamed. Such a line could conceivably have bridled the United States for years to come and perhaps driven Washington to seek the kind of negotiated peace that would have made East Asia and half of Oceania a Japanese imperial playground. Nagumo had with him the refueling and reprovisioning ships to mount such an attack (Panama lies five thousand miles southeast of Hawaii) and a vast ocean in which to disappear after the assault. Panama did not possess significant aviation or military defenses at the time.

The canal was (and is) one of the crucial choke points on the world ocean. It is also a very fragile passageway. As Hector C. Bywater emphasized in his 1925 fictional account of a great Pacific war (which was widely read on both sides of the Pacific), it can be knocked out of use for months if just one part is damaged. Had the Japanese bombed the entire length of the Panama Canal heavily, American repair crews would have been faced with rebuilding ruined installations in both Hawaii and the Isthmus simultaneously, probably delaying the rehabilitation of both for months. Critically needed naval reinforcements from the Atlantic (including the carriers *Yorktown, Hornet,* and later *Wasp,* all of which played crucial roles in the early Pacific war) would have been forced to spend many further weeks reaching the Pacific either through the Strait of Magellan (a perfect ambush spot for Japanese submarines) or around the southern tip of Africa and across the southern Indian Ocean to already-besieged Australia.

The canal's greatest importance lay in its role as an expeditious conduit for the products of U.S. industry. Every day between early 1942 and the summer of 1945 its artificial lakes and sophisticated locks were filled with ships proceeding in both directions. East Coast shipyards from Boston to Norfolk were just beginning to turn out the first units of a huge, modern battle fleet, most of which was needed in the Pacific. West Coast shipyards (especially the Kaiser facilities in California and Oregon) were building the vast numbers of freighters, cargo vessels, and transports needed to convey millions of men and supplies to distant battlefields in Europe as well as the Pacific, together with the numerous escort carriers that played such a crucial role in winning the Battle of the Atlantic over Hitler's submarines. Moreover, America's industrial plant and rail system were keyed to ship war goods to Atlantic as well as Pacific ports from whence they would be disbursed to battlefields worldwide. If the canal was knocked out, American flexibility in fighting a massive two-front war in Asia and Europe would be destroyed. The buildup of men and supplies at distant jumping-off points that required weeks or months with the canal in operation would have required years if American men and arms had to be sent around the southern tips of Africa or South America. With a drastic reduction of U.S. bottoms to carry the sinews of war to Britain, and far fewer escort carriers to harry Dönitz's U-boats, the Battle of the Atlantic might very well have tipped decisively in Hitler's favor in 1942 or 1943.

Yamamoto knew all about America's industrial strength and geography from years of residence in the 1920s. He had also presumably read, or was roughly acquainted with, Bywater's scenario of a shattering blow against the canal to open a great Pacific war. For a long moment between December 1941 and the following spring, with the U.S. battle fleet in ruins, Yamamoto had the entire Pacific to do as he pleased. But the admiral and his fleet planners never conceived of following up Pearl Harbor with an attack on the Panama Canal. In the final analysis, their strategic vision was strangely limited, even timid. "For Yamamoto, as for the rest of the Japanese high command, the attack on the U.S. Pacific Fleet at Hawaii was a secondary operation whose purpose was to ensure the security of the main Japanese objective: Southeast Asia."[33] The Pearl Harbor attack and the subsequent establishment of a mid-Pacific ribbon-defense line were apparently as far as Japan's essentially defensive-minded sailors could allow themselves to think. Certainly, the continental United States was unconquerable, at least as far as Japan's limited military and naval capacities were concerned. The Japanese high command certainly knew this. Yet like the kaiser and his admirals twenty-seven years before, Yamamoto and his colleagues refused to use the formidable naval power at their disposal to the very limits of its promise. Granted, the destruction of even half of the Imperial Japanese Navy's carrier strike force at the outset of the war, had the small U.S. carrier fleet been somehow able to find and sink it, would have been far more strategically catastrophic than Germany's loss of most of its High Seas Fleet a quarter century earlier. Japan's was a seaborne empire guaranteed by sea power, Germany was a land power. But Japan's failure of strategic and tactical imagination at a crucial point—Nagumo's failure to risk his fleet one more time on a third raid against the oil facilities at Pearl Harbor followed by Yamamoto's disinclination to go after the Panama Canal immediately after December 7—ultimately cost Japan the war and, for a time thereafter, much of its national life as well.

There remained yet another point at which enemy sea power might have won World War II. Had the Axis powers coordinated their resources in the spring of 1942 so that the Japanese irruption into the Indian Ocean coincided with a major German naval breakout into the Atlantic, Anglo-American sea power, then at its nadir, might well have been overwhelmed before the rapidly building new U.S. fleet could have been brought to bear.

In the four months after the attack on Hawaii, Japan swept south, east, and westward, overwhelming Allied garrisons in Micronesia, the Philippines, Hong Kong, and Southeast Asia with comparative ease. Japan had been at war for four and a half years when it began its Pacific lunge, so its forces were battle hardened and well trained. Nonetheless, expansion across vast stretches of Oceania and Southeast Asia confronted both the army and the navy with new and formidable strategic and logistical problems. The Western garrisons at Hong Kong, Singapore, the Philippines, and the East Indies immediately felt the brunt of Japanese power and succumbed sooner or later. Estimates vary widely, but it is probably safe to say that at a minimum one hundred thousand Western troops and Western-trained native soldiers were killed or captured in the process. The Malayan jungles were considered impregnable (so all of Singapore's great naval guns were pointed to cover the sea approaches), but the Japanese knifed through them on foot and bicycle to deal the British their most humiliating defeat ever at the hands of a non-Western foe. The vulnerability of unprotected capital ships to air attack was settled once and for all when *Prince of Wales* and *Repulse* fell before the land-based planes of the Japanese navy. Churchill had rushed the two capital ships eastward as evidence mounted in the autumn of 1941 that Japan was about to enter the war and attack Western holdings in Asia. It was a measure of how far the Royal Navy had fallen that the battleship and battle cruiser—one new, one elderly—were all that could be mustered to constitute that "main fleet to Singapore" that Whitehall had promised the Eastern dominions in the anxious years between the wars.

American forces in the Philippines mounted a gallant and prolonged defense, but the issue was never really in doubt, and the disruption of Japan's timetable of conquest proved minimal. In roughly 150 days Japan threw the West completely out of Asia and seized for itself the tin, rubber, oil, manganese, and other precious resources of a vast empire. To complete the process, Japanese amphibious operations captured the American-held midocean islands of Wake and Guam, seized large portions of New Guinea, and even established a small base on a very obscure island in the southern Solomon Islands called Tulagi.

Behind this stunning performance was a mastery of operations and logistics that was truly remarkable. As W. D. Puleston wrote soon after VJ day, the Japanese army and navy had learned during the war in China "how to integrate ground troops and ships with land and sea aviation, and the navy learned how to combine its ship-based and land-based planes with surface ships and submarines." The two services collaborated in the construction of specially designed landing craft for amphibious operations, "and the High Command united land, sea and air forces in one highly efficient triphibious combat team."[34] Japan had never before moved beyond the immediately adjacent China coast, the Yangtze River valley, and portions of nearby Northeast Asia, although it had had plenty of time in the late thirties to modestly build up its island mandates out in the Pacific. To suddenly embark on a series of military conquests over thousands of square miles of oceans and islands in a short time demanded an almost super-human efficiency in matériel procurement and distribution, data processing, inventory control, combat loading and unloading, the development of realistic shipping schedules, and a hundred other details. Japanese logistics specialists obviously met the challenge and consistently matched needs and requirements to available resources; the smoothly executed amphibious operations in Malaya, the Philippines, Borneo, and the Dutch East Indies proved it.

Ahead of the great amphibious fleets steamed *Kido Butai,* Japan's striking force of six big fleet aircraft carriers with their accompanying screen. Japanese and American historians have traditionally emphasized Nagumo's unfamiliarity with carrier tactics and warfare prior to his command of *Kido Butai* at Pearl Harbor (he had been trained in torpedo warfare) and his instinctive conservatism that often shaded into timidity. One recent Japanese authority has written of Nagumo's loss of both "vitality and fighting spirit" even before the outbreak of war. He "had begun to appear quite neurotic." Certainly, the admiral exhibited unwonted restraint at Pearl Harbor, and, understandably, Midway appears to have induced permanent apprehension in the man. But during the six months between those events, his determined, even audacious, use of the carrier force at his disposal cannot be disputed. As with the U.S. enemy, carriers were not Japan's weapon of choice; they were its weapon of necessity. No other warship type was capable of projecting power over the vast distances that needed to be conquered or neutralized with sufficient speed to complete the midocean ribbon-defense line before the enemy could properly react. As the arc of conquest continually expanded, *Kido Butai* was forced to split up into its component divisions to cover all commitments, and one or sometimes two of the brutally overworked ships were forced into the yards for brief but essential overhauls. But operations never slackened. From Pearl Harbor to Wake Island, Darwin, Colombo, Trinco-malee, the Coral Sea, and Midway, the Japanese carrier fleet was ever on the move during the first half year of the war, operating, the most recent British official naval history reminds us, "across one-third of the globe." During that time it destroyed the U.S. battle fleet and drove the British from the Indian Ocean. In the process it sank innumerable merchantmen and warships, strafed or shot down several hundred Allied planes, and blew apart countless installations, storehouses, and the like. All this was largely accomplished in stealth. Nagumo's force was scarcely seen. For weeks on end, American, British, and Dutch soldiers, sailors, airmen, and civilians went about their peaceful business with war seemingly hundreds of miles away. Then, suddenly, the enemy was there, his planes sweeping in over harbor and hill to bring terrible damage. Nagumo proved to be one of the great authors of carrier warfare.[35]

Beginning in February 1942 when boats formerly operating off Hawaii and the American West Coast were added to the mix, the Japanese submarine command rushed its units into the Indian Ocean, where they promptly sank nearly eighty-three thousand tons of Allied merchant shipping at almost no cost. In early April, *Kido Butai,* minus *Kaga,* sent home for repairs, entered the Indian Ocean in order to neutralize whatever British sea power and airpower remained on the western flank of Japan's new Southeast Asian empire.[36] Thousands of miles away, the American battle fleet remained smashed in the mud of Pearl Harbor, while the handful of U.S. carriers had begun hastily devised "pinprick" attacks on the eastern and southern perimeters of Japan's imperium.

The British Admiralty, meanwhile, had hastily assembled a new "Eastern Fleet" in the waters near Ceylon (Sri Lanka) under Admiral James Somerville. On paper the fleet looked powerful enough: battleship *Warspite* and no fewer than four sisters of the *Royal Sovereign* class, plus two large modern carriers, *Indomitable* and *Formidable;* the old and small carrier *Hermes;* seven cruisers; and sixteen destroyers. But the force was much weaker than it seemed. The battleships, all veterans of Jutland, were poorly armed against antiaircraft attack and were known to be floating coffins. *Hermes* could deploy only a dozen obsolete fighter aircraft, while the two big carriers together embarked only fifty-eight slow biplane strike aircraft and thirty-three fighters of markedly inferior quality. The fighters could be wiped out in either the strike-escort or combat–air patrol mode by Nagumo's fast and nimble Zeros, and the biplanes would be easy prey should they try to attack the Japanese task force. Once a British carrier strike was brushed aside, Nagumo's superb torpedo planes and dive-bombers could go after the Eastern Fleet with impunity, and Somerville knew it. Not only were his battleships vulnerable to air assault, but so were his carriers. Built to withstand extensive bomb hits and to survive even devastating damage above decks, the *Illustrious* class had not been provided with similar protection against torpedoes. *Indomitable* "nearly sank after being hit by a single aircraft-launched torpedo in the Mediterranean in 1943."[37] Its sister *Formidable* was doubtless just as fragile, while *Hermes* had no protection at all.

Even before Nagumo appeared, Somerville had made the decision to employ his venerable and vulnerable vessels merely as a "fleet in being." When *Kido Butai* devastated Ceylon and sank two British heavy cruisers and *Hermes,* Somerville, in a complicated series of maneuvers, evaded battle and then withdrew temporarily all the way to Mombasa in East African waters, while a small enemy task force under Vice Admiral Jisaburo Ozawa, built around the light carrier *Ryujo,* raided the Indian coast in the Bay of Bengal, destroying twenty-three merchant ships and leaving Indian coastal trade paralyzed for weeks.

Churchill was in despair. There seemed no way to stop the Japanese from dominating the entire Indian Ocean basin. On April 7 the prime minister wrote President Roosevelt that five and possibly six Japanese battleships—two or more armed with sixteen-inch guns that could blow the *Royal Sovereigns* to pieces— were lurking near Ceylon in company with Nagumo's carrier task force. Somerville's fleet would surely be overwhelmed in any battle with the enemy who had just completed the first of what would be two shattering air raids against the island. "The situation is therefore one of grave anxiety," and the prime minister begged the president to order some sort of demonstration by the U.S. Pacific Fleet (which "must now be decidedly superior to the enemy forces") in the Indian Ocean. Roosevelt, of course, could offer nothing, and Churchill arranged to land a hastily gathered invasion force on the northern tip of Madagascar, convinced that the Japanese were coming that way.[38]

A young American naval officer who had escaped the cauldron of the Philippines expressed the attitude of perhaps exaggerated respect that unprepared Western Allies came to hold for their Oriental enemies in those first desperate months of the Pacific war when Nagumo's *Kido Butai* was running wild:

> Nobody knows anything about a war until it begins. Just two years before the Polish air force had been blown to hell on the ground. The French caught it the following spring. In spite of that, the same thing happened to our planes at Pearl Harbor. And yet two days later, in spite of all of it the Japs catch our air corps [at Clark Field] on Luzon with its pants down. Only that wasn't the end. Months later, on my way out through Australia, I pass a big American field, and there they are, bombers and fighters parked in orderly rows, wing tip to wing tip. "Hell," they told me, "The Japs are hundreds of miles away." Except that's where they're always supposed to be when they catch you with your pants down, and I thought to myself, Jesus Christ, won't these guys ever learn?[39]

Churchill was very nearly right in his own panicky assessment of Japanese intentions and capabilities. As historians H. P. Willmott and Hans-Joachim Krug and his team have demonstrated, the warlords of Tokyo were experiencing a prolonged crisis of victory. Pearl Harbor had seemed a smashing success, and their timetable for the conquest of all Southeast Asia and much of the Southwest Pacific region was proceeding on or ahead of schedule (only the American-Filipino garrisons at Bataan and Corregidor would heroically disrupt Japanese plans, but without measurable impact). The wide-ranging *Kido Butai* had ravaged Western air- and naval power from Hawaii to northern Australia, the Dutch East Indies, and Ceylon without the loss of a single ship and only a handful of aircraft and pilots.

Should Japan slacken its offensive pace, consolidate its gains, and wait for an eventual and inevitable counterattack from the Anglo-Americans? Or should it maintain the pressure of a constant offensive, and if so, where? Key elements in the navy led by Yamamoto and his chief of staff, Rear Admiral Matome Ugaki, strongly advocated a prolonged thrust west into the Indian Ocean once the conquest of Southeast Asia was completed. These politically astute officers realized that India itself was a hotbed of discontent under native leaders Mahatma Gandhi and Subhas Chandra Bose. (The latter would be invited to Tokyo in November 1943 to participate in the Greater East Asia Conference as head of the "Provisional Government of Free India." He went on a German U-boat.) An invasion of Ceylon could tip the scales decisively against the small British garrison on the subcontinent. The implications were enormous: "India was the anchor of the British war effort in both the Middle and Far East, yet given the state of nationalist opinion within India and the British loss of Malaya and Singapore and her [subsequent] defeats [at the hands of the Japanese] in southern Burma, there was every chance that further British reverses [such as the loss of Ceylon] might well result in the collapse of her authority on the subcontinent." With India either neutralized or even conquered by Japanese forces, and with the Imperial Navy operating westward from Ceylon, the entire tier of flimsily held British colonies from the Persian Gulf to East Africa might well tumble and Japan would gain oil reserves to last it for generations. Indeed, a Japanese thrust toward India and the Middle East had even greater implications: it could link up with a German offensive out of the North African desert toward and beyond Suez. On February 18, 1942,

the German naval attaché in Tokyo reported back to his superiors that the Japanese had sounded him out on the matter of a joint German-Japanese move to secure Madagascar, after German pressure on [the puppet French government at] Vichy had made the French amenable to the 'suggestion.' This report came one day after the General Operations Division of the German navy had passed on to the Japanese all the information it had about possible landing sites on Ceylon.[40]

Three weeks later, Raeder reported to Hitler:

> The Japanese have recognized the great strategic importance of Madagascar for naval warfare. According to reports submitted, they are planning to establish bases on Madagascar in addition to Ceylon, in order to be able to cripple sea traffic in the Indian Ocean and the Arabian Sea. From there they could likewise successfully attack shipping around the Cape. Before establishing these bases Japan will have to get German consent. For military purposes such consent ought to be granted.[41]

A month later the Axis situation seemed even more promising. Erwin Rommel was about to launch his last great offensive against Cairo and Suez. To support his attack, German naval officials insisted to the Japanese members of the "Tripartite Military Commission" in Berlin that "a strong fleet be sent to the [western] Indian Ocean from the Japanese side." The "operational focus" of immediate Axis activity "had to be Egypt." This was all fine, Admiral Nomura responded. Tokyo, too, seemed to agree that the moment to break the British Empire—and the Allied cause—had arrived. But Tokyo's interest was India. Foreign Minister Tōgō Shigenobu had already begged German ambassador Eugen Ott "to make a joint declaration" supporting native uprisings for independence on the subcontinent and in adjacent Burma. Hitler had demurred, instructing his diplomats to issue a "cautious and passive" reply. Undeterred, Prime Minister Hideki Tojo declared before the Diet in mid-February Japan's "steadfast" support of the Burmese people to "build a nation of their own" and thereafter to "march" with Japan "as comrades-in-arms toward Great East Asian co-prosperity," adding that his government was similarly prepared to help India. But as Captain Hans-Joachim Krug has observed, "Japan could not take on India alone," despite the strident demands from Gandhi that Britain quit the subcontinent. The fact was that although both Berlin and Tokyo wanted to bring down Britain, German attention was fixed on Suez while Japanese attention was focused five hundred miles to the east. That five hundred miles proved just too far for Japanese and German arms to stretch. When the moment came for joint action, neither Hitler nor his Japanese opposites could summon the requisite resources. Thus, Admiral Nomura "decried" to his hosts in Berlin "the lack of progress toward a simultaneous offensive and emphasized the necessity for a simultaneous attack on the British Middle East position, with Germany and Italy coming from the Mediterranean and the Caucasus and Japan from the Indian Ocean." Japan seemed poised to dispatch at least some submarines and armed merchant cruisers into the Red and Arabian Seas to attack "British supply traffic." But the Japanese high command cabled their nominal allies at the other end of the Eurasian landmass that they, in turn, must be prepared to launch simultaneous land offensives not only against Egypt but deep into southern Russia as well. Alas, such demands proved mere empty gestures. Berlin and Tokyo had signed the Tripartite Pact in 1940 (along with Rome) to forestall a massive Soviet assault against their respective positions in Europe and East Asia. Neither was interested in or capable of any coordinated action beyond that point. On April 7, even as Nagumo was running wild off Ceylon and Churchill was cabling Roosevelt of his desperate need for some sort of U.S. naval demonstration east of Suez, the Japanese naval staff told its opposites in Berlin that "the Japanese Navy's main theater [of operations] was still in the Pacific" and its main objective the destruction of the U.S. fleet.[42] Within days *Kido Butai* had left the Indian Ocean—back to Japan to prepare for Midway, where it met its doom. When Rommel reached the gates of Cairo in May, suddenly inflaming Japanese army interest in invading Ceylon and bringing Britain to its knees, the imperial fleet was nowhere near, and after its crushing defeat in the central Pacific all thoughts of a major Japanese amphibious offensive in the Middle East went glimmering.

But the disarray in the enemy camp was far from obvious to anxious Western intelligence analysts and naval planners throughout the somber spring of 1942. In the West, Axis naval fortunes were, if possible, even more favorable than east of Suez, and if the German surface and submarine fleets had been able to tie down American and British naval resources in the Atlantic while Rommel burst out of North Africa toward the Middle East and the Japanese moved to consolidate their hold on the Indian Ocean basin all the way to the shores of East Africa, Ernle Chatfield's 1935–1936 nightmares of an overwhelmed British fleet might well have come true, and London, if not Washington, could conceivably have had to sue for peace. A joint German-Japanese pincer offensive in the Mideast would undoubtedly have been a major stretch for both Axis powers, but it was doable at this point in the war, so long as both sides concentrated on implementing the policy. Anxious analysts in Washington and London had no way of knowing that the Axis partnership was in fact a chimera. As *Kido Butai* ravaged Ceylon in early April, spreading terror across the entire Indian Ocean basin, a renewed Nazi submarine offensive was in high gear both off the American coast and in the mid–North Atlantic. Of transcendent importance was the sudden loss by the Allies of access to the German naval cipher system. Due to a series of fortuitous circumstances supplemented by deliberate action, British sailors in early 1941 had seized and British code specialists had subsequently analyzed enough of the German Enigma system to re-create it through a series of machines known as *bombes* that were located at the central British (and after January 1942 Allied) deciphering center at Bletchley Park, north of London.[43] After May 1941 the dreadful shipping losses to U-boats and especially U-boat wolf packs that marked the period from July 1940 onward had been reversed. Whereas Nazi mines, aircraft, U-boats, and surface vessels had sunk an astounding 1,239 British merchantmen in the ten months following midsummer 1940 (the U-boats alone accounting for 548 vessels), in the six months after British cipher analysts successfully broke into the enemy's Enigma system, German mines, submarines, and aircraft accounted for only 326 British and Commonwealth sunken cargo vessels and steamships, as the convoy control rooms at Liverpool and Halifax simply maneuvered their charges out of the way of known U-boat ambush positions and enemy minefields. Moreover, the Royal Navy (with increasing help from its American cousins) was rapidly expanding its convoy system, the number of escorts in that system, and the advanced weapon systems needed to bring the U-boats to heel.[44]

But the sudden loss of access to the most highly classified operational orders from Admiral Karl Dönitz to his U-boat commanders denied British code breakers and sailors not only an understanding of near- and long-term enemy intentions and capabilities but also the information that BDienst had at long last broken the British convoy codes and was reading up to 80 percent of that traffic, thus providing Dönitz and his U-boat commanders with almost complete information on convoy sailings, routes, number of escorts, and so on. The Enigma blackout (based on a shift from a three- to four-rotor system) lasted throughout 1942, until capture of another German top-secret cipher book from a sinking submarine revealed to the wizards at Bletchley that "the four letter indicators for regular U-boat messages were the same as the three-letter indicators for weather messages that same day [which Bletchley had continued to crack from the old three-rotor system] except for an extra letter. Thus, once a daily key was found for a weather message, the fourth rotor had to be tested only in twenty-six positions to find the full four-letter key."[45]

In the interim the U-boat war on the North Atlantic again swung decisively in Germany's favor. Between January and March 1942, a total of 533 Allied merchant ships were sent to the bottom, 242 by U-boats alone, with another 203 lost to "unknown causes," many of which must have been by submarine. In April–June 1942, another 456 Allied merchant vessels were sunk, 343 by Dönitz's "gray wolves" operating largely off the American coast and in the North Atlantic "black gap"—a broad area extending perhaps a thousand miles roughly south and east of the southern tip of Greenland where Allied land-based air cover for convoys and independently sailing vessels did not extend. In July, August, and September, as the British began the first of many Arctic convoys to the Russian port of Murmansk, 365 additional merchantmen were lost to German arms, 302 being accounted for by U-boats. In the October–December 1942 quarter, another 308 Allied merchantmen joined their brothers on the floor of the Atlantic, 272 killed by enemy submarines.[46]

Moreover, the fortunes of the Allied surface navies, at a very low ebb throughout 1942, reached their nadir in the first six months of the year. All of the handful of U.S. fleet carriers, save the old and slow *Ranger,* were earmarked for the Pacific, whereas the two newest battleships—*North Carolina* and *Washington*—were just completing their shakedown cruises before heading for duty in the Pacific and with the British Home Fleet, respectively. The follow-on *South Dakota* was placed in commission only in March, its very near sister *Massachusetts* (the first of a three-ship class) not until May. The Royal Navy was in as bad a shape or worse. Of the five *King George V* battleships ordered under the 1937–1938 rearmament programs, *Prince of Wales* lay thousands of miles from home waters at the bottom of the South China Sea. *King George V* itself and *Duke of York* were with the Home Fleet to stiffen the seven or eight older, slower World War I–vintage battleships, but the last two units of the *KGV* class, *Howe* and *Anson,* were still being built. Of the seven modern fleet carriers that took the Royal Navy through the war, *Ark Royal* was already gone, torpedoed off Gibraltar in November 1941. *Illustrious* was still in Norfolk, Virginia, completing its rebuilding after being fearsomely bombed off Malta the previous year. *Formidable* and *Indomitable* were essential to the Mediterranean–western Indian Ocean area. *Implacable* and *Indefatigable* would not join the fleet until 1944. Only *Victorious* was available to the Home Fleet.[47]

Had the Germans preserved and consolidated their surface fleet for such a moment as this, they could have undertaken a major naval offensive in the Atlantic, coordinating U-boat wolf-pack attacks against Allied convoys with a sweep of their four splendid heavy ships, *Scharnhorst, Gneisenau, Bismarck,* and *Tirpitz,* escorted by *Hipper, Prinz Eugen,* and a destroyer screen. In light of all the forces it took just to track down *Bismarck* in the spring of 1941, it is difficult to see how the Royal and United States Navies would have managed to defeat such a German surface squadron. Certainly, they would not have been able to do so without suffering the kind of catastrophic losses that would have doomed the lifeline to Britain. At the same time, *Kido Butai* and the Japanese army could have moved against India and then the Persian Gulf as Rommel broke out of North Africa.

But, of course, nothing of the sort came to pass for a variety of reasons. The Japanese army finally refused to support a strong naval advance into the Indian Ocean, and Yamamoto's chief of staff, Admiral Ugaki, admitted at one point early on that three days of war games on maneuvering tables had suggested that "the idea of the operation in the Indian Ocean was not good." Although Japanese forces got ashore on Ceylon, "we missed the main force of the enemy fleet and were hindered by the local enemy air strength. We need further study for its actual execution." Thus, Nagumo's carrier thrust toward Ceylon in April 1942 represented little more than "the lame remnant" of the original plan of February "for a powerful thrust into the Indian Ocean, which, in turn was only a substitute for the original plan to conquer Hawaii."[48]

Not only had the Japanese grossly overestimated the extent of British air- and sea power on the western, that is, Indian Ocean, flank of their southern advance, but they were also fatally smitten with the idea of sweeping east to neutralize Australia through the conquest of New Guinea and the Solomons. At this point, the Japanese simply overreached themselves. Yamamoto and his enthusiastic planners had wanted it all, and they had very nearly gotten it. Just a month after Pearl Harbor, Ugaki exultantly recorded in his diary: "We shall be able to finish the first-stage operations [that is, the conquests of Hong Kong, the Philippines, Malaya, the Dutch East Indies, and the weakly held American outposts in mid-ocean, Wake and Guam] by the middle of March. What are we going to do after that? Advance to Australia, to India, attack Hawaii, or destroy the Soviet Union at an opportune moment according to their actions?" The entire Asian-Pacific world seemed suddenly at Japan's feet. But Ugaki was no fool. He added that the eventual military and industrial recovery of the United States was certain, as was the prospect of renewed British pressure on the western (Indian Ocean) flank of the new Japanese Empire.[49] Yamamoto and the Combined Fleet were truly caught in a crisis of victory, and their solution was to simply continue advancing everywhere until eventually confronted by strong enemy forces.

The first serious check upon Japanese expansionism came in the form of continuing assaults by America's three Pacific Fleet carriers *(Lexington, Yorktown, and Enterprise)* and their handful of cruiser and destroyer escorts against enemy bases in the central and Southwest Pacific. These "tip and run" raids, especially those conducted between February 20 and March 10 by Vice Admiral Wilson Brown, first with *Lexington,* then with *Lexington* and *Yorktown,* against the Japanese bases at Rabaul on the island of New Britain and Salamaua and Lae in New Guinea, awoke Yamamoto and the Japanese high command to the fact that even this early in the war, U.S. aviation technology was selectively superior to that of Japan and that the Americans would use whatever weapons remained in their naval arsenal as aggressively as possible to regain a measurable balance of power in the Pacific. As long as Admiral Shigeyoshi Inoue had seemed able to seize objectives in New Guinea on his own, there was no great importance attached to operations in what was clearly a secondary theater of operations. But the failure of Japan's southwest-Pacific commander

> to carry out his mission in the face of enemy carrier activity... had the effect of raising the question of future operations in the southwest Pacific from a matter purely of local concern to one of national attention.... If Inoue needed carrier support—and the scale of the 10 March attack, which revealed the presence of two enemy carriers in the southwest Pacific, indicated that he did—then the whole question of how, when and where Japan was to make her main effort in 1942 had to be rethought.

Committing Nagumo's carriers to Inoue's support made it virtually "inevitable that the Japanese effort in the southwest Pacific would have to be a major one, perhaps the major one for 1942."[50]

Just as Japan was deflected from a possibly decisive Indian Ocean offensive, so the Germans were unable to mount the kind of complementary naval blitz in the Atlantic that might have brought Britain crashing down. The fault was far from Raeder's alone: Germany might have won the Battle of the Atlantic *if* it had mounted a coherent and sustained air, submarine, and surface offensive against British convoys. But Göring actively disliked the navy, and the Luftwaffe offensive at sea was sporadic, depending always upon whatever slender resources could be spared from the Battle of Britain and later the prolonged air war in Russia.

Forced to work alone with an unbalanced fleet of many submarines and a handful of splendid surface units, German naval strategy in World War II was always opportunistic. Chances for favorable surface action were few and of

short duration; Raeder came to believe that they had to be seized the instant
they appeared. This meant throwing the most precious surface ships out into
the Atlantic piecemeal the moment they were in hand. No serious effort was
made at fleet concentration, nor did Raeder's planners ever develop a strategy
linking the surface fleet with the U-boat war. Raeder got away with his strategy
and tactics in the first two years of the war as his surface sailors won some brilliant victories, but then his luck and that of his admirals abruptly melted away.

By ordering Gunther Luetjens to bring *Scharnhorst* and *Gneisenau* into Brest
in the spring of 1941 after their second raiding cruise, Raeder at once placed
the big ships under the thumb of Royal Air Force bombers and divided the
German battle fleet between the Channel and the Baltic at just the time that
new construction cried out for a concentration of forces. Luetjens could have
returned to Germany through either the Denmark Strait or the Iceland-Faeroes
gap and then down the Norwegian leads. By bringing the two biggest and most
experienced warships in the German navy into Brest, where frequent bombing
attacks from nearby England kept them immobilized for long, critical months,
he put them practically out of the war. The battle cruisers, joined for a time by
Hipper, were periodically bombed at their French docks by a determined RAF
shuttling almost daily over the short distance from England. The ships were
unable to get under way for home waters for an entire year.

Instead of being placed at the head of a small but powerful and growing battle
fleet, *Bismarck* found itself alone with the equally new heavy cruiser *Prinz Eugen*
when working-up exercises were concluded in the Baltic at the end of March
1941. (Of the two remaining pocket battleships, *Deutschland* [renamed *Lutzow*]
was still under repair, and *Scheer* was returning after its long and exhausting
cruise, and in any case both older "armored ships" were at least three to four
knots slower than the new battleship and heavy cruiser.) What should be done
now with this splendid new giant? Raeder agonized over the problem. *Bismarck*
was to have been the capstone of a grand naval campaign against Britain—the
culmination of two years of raiding and harassment against British sea power.
Raeder's strategy was to have the battle cruisers at Brest race back out into the
Atlantic simultaneously with the breakout of *Bismarck* and *Prinz Eugen* from
the Denmark Strait. The whole operation would be "bulk[ed] . . . with numerous submarines."[51] The continued immobilization of *Scharnhorst* and *Gneisenau* frustrated the plan. Raeder was disturbed but not deflected. This stressed
and impatient sailor felt time pressing in upon him. He had to keep the drumbeat of surface action going if the Royal Navy was to continue to be strained to
the utmost and the credibility of Germany's surface fleet was to be maintained.

Moreover, Raeder had great confidence in Luetjens. The man had just conducted a most bold and successful cruise with the only two big ships Germany had then possessed. He had not turned back, as had Wilhelm Marschall, at the first sign of the enemy.

Yet when the two met on April 25, just a month before the scheduled beginning of Operation Rhine—the breakout of *Bismarck* and heavy cruiser *Prinz Eugen* into the Atlantic on a prolonged raiding cruise—Luetjens frankly advised Raeder to postpone the exercise until at least one of the bomb-damaged battle cruisers at Brest could be gotten ready for sea, or until *Bismarck*'s sister, *Tirpitz*, had completed building and working up. Raeder politely rejected the advice. "Wars do not wait," he later wrote, "and the general strategical situation did not permit our deliberately withholding such a strong combat unit." To pause until one or both of the repeatedly bombed and damaged battle cruisers was ready for action "might mean forever renouncing the opportunity to use the new battleship in the Atlantic."[52] Waiting for *Tirpitz* was an even worse suggestion since, as it turned out, it would not be fully ready for sea for at least eight months.

The reaction of his mercurial führer should have given the admiral pause. Hitler was not enthusiastic about Operation Rhine, though he did not forbid it. Raeder's dismay may have deepened in early May when Hitler paid a sudden, brief visit to *Bismarck* at its Baltic home port of Gotenhafen. The excited crew, proud of their ship and enamored of their führer, gave the Nazi dictator a quick tour of the monster vessel.[53] At that time Luetjens expressed directly to the führer his strong reservations about the feasibility of the upcoming operation based on the most recent voyage of the battle cruisers; Luetjens especially emphasized the danger from British carrier aircraft.[54] But Raeder was determined, and at 0200 local time on May 19, 1941, *Bismarck* left its anchorage in Gotenhafen roadstead and steamed down the Baltic, headed northwest toward Norway, the Atlantic, and immortality.

The brief history of Operation Rhine—the wild, improbable tale of the short cruise and violent death of *Bismarck* in vast, lonely, windswept seas under gray and rainy skies—is too well known to be fully retold here.[55] But the breakout, pursuit, and eventual killing of the great German battleship, which in its brief life managed to take *Hood* to the bottom with it, had as decisive an impact on the war and subsequent world history as the voyage of another German capital ship, *Goeben,* nearly twenty-seven years before.

First, and foremost, the death of *Bismarck* abruptly ended what had up to then been a major sustained and successful offensive at sea by the German surface fleet. In insisting upon Operation Rhine, Raeder was proved desperately wrong. With *Bismarck* under the waves, *Scharnhorst* and *Gneisenau* still bottled up in Brest, and *Tirpitz* months from commissioning, the German navy was abruptly reduced to its submarine component. For Hitler, the sinking of *Bismarck* was shattering. This self-professed coward of the sea had just visited the vast and splendid ship with its beautiful flowing lines and great guns. How much larger, how much more formidable, was a battleship than a panzer division or a squadron of Heinkels! Yet this giant had been shot to pieces and sunk on its first cruise. Raeder tells us, "From a climax of glee over the sinking of the *Hood,* Hitler was ... in little more than three days, dropped to the depths of despondency."[56] From that moment on, Hitler distrusted the surface navy and, Walter Warlimont's observations to the contrary, clearly distrusted Raeder as well.

Raeder's flawed leadership was now open for all to see. Clearly, Luetjens should have turned heel after killing *Hood* and returned to Germany. He had won a stupendous victory, destroying what was believed to be the largest warship in the world (in fact, in terms of both tonnage and overall physical dimension, *Bismarck* was clearly the larger as well as stronger vessel). But Luetjens had before him the example of his predecessor. Wilhelm Marschall had turned back with *Scharnhorst* and *Gneisenau* after destroying *Rawalpindi,* and over a period of time Raeder had literally hounded him from command. Who would wish that kind of an end to his career? So Luetjens—clearly Raeder's man—had foolishly pushed on to lose his ship and his life, humiliating his country and his führer at precisely the moment when German arms were triumphant everywhere else.

The loss of *Bismarck* also revealed the fragile state of morale within the German surface fleet. So long as things went well, spirits were high. But inevitable mistakes and reversals swiftly bred a sense of defeatism. *Bismarck,* it is true, fought as well as could be expected in its last battle with the British heavy units on the misty morning of May 27. But indications are that Luetjens certainly and Captain Ernst Lindemann possibly had by this time become demoralized to the point of paralysis. The collapse of discipline and morale aboard *Bismarck* quickly became known in the West when the handful of survivors were interviewed in British internment camps. As quickly as possible, gleeful British naval authorities set forth the facts as they saw them, and shortly after Pearl Harbor, Edwin Muller, a freelance writer who had traveled to and written often about prewar Germany, published a powerful little article in an American journal about the last days aboard the doomed battleship. The victory over *Hood* and *Prince of Wales* had raised morale to an impossible high, and Captain Lindemann had begged Luetjens to turn back and allow Hitler and Germany to savor the triumph. But

Luetjens refused, and as the British knot began to tighten, the admiral allegedly went to pieces. He devastated the crew with a succession of dark messages, stating first that they must prepare for the worst and then that they might all die. In the last hours, according to British authorities, Luetjens could be heard behind his closed cabin door shouting hysterically: "Do what you like. I'm through." The handful of *Bismarck's* crew plucked from the icy seas before U-boat-sighting reports forced suspension of rescue efforts "were haggard and hollow-eyed, as if they had gone through months of torture. Days later, when they had been put to bed, rested, given restoratives, they were still dazed. They hardly spoke, even to one another. They reminded one observer of the legend of the Zombies, the living-dead of the West Indies who walk without souls." A half century later, *Bismarck's* fourth gunnery officer and senior survivor of the dead battleship, Burkard Baron von Müllenheim-Rechberg, substantially confirmed the collapse of morale aboard the Nazi warship during its last days of life.[57]

In fact, such reactions to the traumas of violent defeat and chancy rescue at sea were common throughout the war and, indeed, are in all wars. But the image of the young Nazi Superman had been so indelibly imprinted on the minds of people throughout the Western world that to see the German boys react as they did brought great comfort to many an anxious heart in the Allied camp. Neither the führer nor his immediate entourage could disguise the fact that morale in the surface navy was not the highest.

Bismarck's loss shattered Hitler's fragile faith in the navy. When the führer insisted in early 1942 that the battle cruisers and *Prinz Eugen* (who had separated from *Bismarck* after the initial action and later successfully crept into Brest) "dash" up the Channel, he was not anticipating that they resume their careers as midocean commerce raiders. He wanted them solely for the defense of Norway, which he was convinced was about to be assaulted by an Allied expeditionary force.[58] Thereafter, Germany's battleship-cruiser force was confined to occasionally threatening the Arctic convoys, its ocean-raiding days forever ended. Not a battle cruiser, not a pocket battleship, not the *Tirpitz* ever again broke out successfully to raid the North Atlantic convoys or the southern trading routes as had *Scheer, Graf Spee, Scharnhorst,* and *Gneisenau.* Nor would the führer allow Raeder to risk the big ships against the British cruisers protecting the Murmansk convoys. The result was inevitable: during the infrequent sorties they did make, the Germans were invariably hesitant in the attack, while the increasingly confident British were resolute in defense. After a botched effort against a Russian-bound convoy in the Barents Sea at the end of December 1942 resulted in damage to *Hipper* and only minimal disruption of the British force, Hitler became enraged and during the course of a ninety-minute tirade ordered Raeder to scrap all the big ships. When the grand admiral refused, he was sacked.[59]

Despite personal and policy differences, neither Raeder nor Dönitz was fatally rigid in his outlook. At the outbreak of war Raeder had ordered construction of the advanced battleships, cruisers, and aircraft carriers suspended indefinitely in order to concentrate on the building of submarines. Dönitz upon appointment to supreme naval command managed to convince Hitler to spare both *Scharnhorst* and *Tirpitz.* But Hitler never allowed *Tirpitz* to undertake a serious sortie, and *Scharnhorst* was sunk in a wild sea fight north of the Arctic Circle at Christmastime 1943 after the führer permitted Dönitz to mount one more surface attack on the Russian convoys. From the code breakers at Bletchley Park and other sources, the British Admiralty was able to deduce that *Scharnhorst* was probably coming out to assault convoy JW55B coming up from Loch Ewe. Superb seamanship by Vice Admiral R. L. Burnett commanding JW55B's cruiser screen allowed *Belfast, Norfolk,* and *Sheffield* to press the unsuspecting German battle cruiser into a trap with the fast-approaching distant covering group under Home Fleet commander Sir Bruce Fraser in the battleship *Duke of York,* and *Scharnhorst* was pounded to rubble and sank in the night-blackened, gale-lashed seas. Only thirty-six men out of a total complement of more than two thousand were plucked from the icy waters.[60] Thereafter, the German surface navy practically ceased to exist except for a few forlorn operations during the spring of 1945 in support of retreating German forces along the south Baltic shore.

Finally, the *Bismarck* affair had another profoundly important influence on the course of World War II: it brought the Roosevelt administration and probably a majority of the American people measurably closer to belligerency, for it confirmed to the president the rightness of some very controversial steps—many of them highly secret—that he had recently taken or was about to take. From the outset of the war the United States had been pro-British, but sympathy did not in most circles extend to intervention. At the White House, however, it did. The fall of France and the appearance of German troops on the Channel twenty miles from England "thoroughly frightened the nation" and provided the president with his first opportunities to gear up what he would later describe as the "arsenal of democracy." At White House urging, Congress in the summer of 1940 passed a huge naval appropriation, the so-called two-ocean navy bill, designed to make the United States unquestionably the world's greatest sea power by 1943–1944. In September FDR offered direct aid to the beleaguered British (who had lost ten destroyers at Dunkirk and had another seventy-five damaged) in the form of the "destroyers-for-bases" deal in which the United States provided the Royal Navy with fifty "overage" World War I–era destroyers (most of which were in poor condition) in exchange for ninety-nine-year base leases on a strategic arc of British-owned islands stretching from Newfoundland to the Caribbean island of Antigua. Berlin was left to wonder if Roosevelt's gesture was defensive or offensive.[61] The answer came soon enough. In January 1941 Anglo-American-Canadian staff talks began in Washington, D.C., to forge common strategy for coalition warfare should matters come to that. The ABC-1 agreement two months later "gave unequivocal priority to the European-Atlantic theater with the primary aim of defeating Germany" before the coalition moved on to confront Japan in any significant way. The decision seemed irrefutable at the time. Germany was demonstrating a far more dramatic and successful military capability than Japan and exercised absolute control of western Europe and its coastline, while only Britain stood against it.

At the same moment, following strenuous lobbying from the White House, Congress passed the Lend-Lease Act. The legislation was designed, Roosevelt had breezily informed reporters the previous December, to "get rid of the silly, foolish old dollar sign" so that financially exhausted Britain could obtain unlimited amounts of vital war matériel without having to dip into its last reserves of gold and pounds sterling. "When the show was over," the president added, "we would get repaid something in kind." As New Jersey dockhands began loading the first seven billion dollars' worth of ammunition, armor, and aircraft aboard British ships, Roosevelt, his fellow Americans, and the Nazi warlords in Berlin suddenly confronted a dilemma. Lend-Lease had practically made the United States a cobelligerent with Britain and the Soviet Union. Hitler had no desire to expand the war in the West to include the Americans, at least until he had vanquished Stalin's Red Army. Yet the führer was loath to rein in his exuberant and effective U-boat commanders who were happily sinking British and neutral shipping all over the Atlantic. How could the United States ensure safe passage of its goods through the Atlantic without tripping over the German submarine net?[62]

Roosevelt and the group hawks around him (including Secretary of War Henry Stimson, Secretary of the Interior Harold Ickes, Secretary of the Navy Frank Knox, White House adviser Harry Hopkins, Chief of Naval Operations Harold Stark, and Admirals Ernest J. King and Richmond Kelly Turner) were determined to intervene at their own pace and on their own schedules. They would be stampeded neither by the increasingly desperate British nor by the always menacing Nazi U-boats. The president moved toward active intervention slowly and erratically as he sought to educate both public opinion and his own bureaucracy on the nation's duty. It was an arduous task. The isolationist movement in and out of Congress may have represented majority opinion in the country. It was, in any case, powerful, articulate, well financed, and quite aware of the implications of the destroyer deal and Lend-Lease. Isolationists fought furiously and steadily to deflect Roosevelt from the path to war. But the president's hawkish advisers kept him on course whenever he seemed to waver. In December 1940, after the president had won an unprecedented third term and notified the nation about his Lend-Lease plans, Stimson urged that the United States "forcibly stop the German submarines by our intervention. Well [Roosevelt] said, he hadn't quite reached that yet." But at an informal meeting with Knox, Stark, and Army Chief of Staff George C. Marshall shortly thereafter, Stimson found to his "very great relief" that "'they all agreed with me that the eventual big act will have to be to save the lifeline of Great Britain in the North Atlantic. There are a number of things to be done first in the Far East by way of stiffening up the brakes on Japan, but it is very apparent that nothing will save Great Britain from starvation if her supplies run out.'" Stark was already on record with a twenty-four-page memorandum outlining "Plan Dog"—which envisioned a strong naval offensive in the Atlantic while holding Japan at bay in the Pacific if war with that nation could not be avoided. Stark argued that the United States could not defeat Hitler by naval means alone. British manpower was insufficient to achieve victory in the West. "I believe that the United States, in addition to sending naval assistance, would also need to send large air and land forces to Europe or Africa, or both, and to participate strongly in the land offensive." When Knox saw the document, he wrote "True" in the margin next to the passage. After years of Orange, Black, and Rainbow plans designed, respectively, to develop and fix strategies for a war against Japan, war against a European power, and, after 1936, war against the Axis coalition in both Europe and Asia, Dog reflected the sudden impact of the Nazi U-boat on American strategic thinking. The British were soon notified of Dog's existence and provisions, and they reacted appreciatively.[63]

By the spring of 1941 Roosevelt's strategic thinking was far advanced. So was that of Adolf Hitler, who responded to the British occupation of Iceland by declaring in March 1941 a broad area around that island a war zone in which neutral shipping was liable to sinking by Dönitz's U-boats. In response FDR issued a series of orders that brought the United States to the very brink of a naval war with Nazi Germany. The president had already directed the re-creation of a full-fledged Atlantic Fleet in February, several weeks before Hitler's Iceland announcement. Roosevelt placed the hard-driving and humorless perfectionist "Ernie" King in charge of the new sea force (notified of his appointment, King commented, "When they get into trouble they send for the sons of bitches"). At the end of March a series of informal Anglo-American talks resulted in Washington's agreement to pursue a policy of "belligerent neutrality" and to conduct a number of "short of war" operations in the defense of Greenland and of convoys heading to or from the eastern Atlantic. The navy promptly organized a support force of destroyers, aircraft, and tenders under the command of Rear Admiral A. L. Bristol to operate out of Argentia, Newfoundland. Roosevelt then ordered King to draw up Hemisphere Defense Plan No. 1 that made provision for "aggressive action" by American warships against German submarines *and* surface raiders in the western Atlantic. Since *Scharnhorst* and *Gneisenau* had already appeared not far off Canadian shores and the U-boats were being forced by progressive extensions of the British convoy system to operate well within the president's prospective zone of "aggressive action," Hemisphere Defense Plan No. 1 could be construed as an act of war. But FDR did not stop there; he dramatically expanded hemispheric boundaries eastward to include Greenland, Iceland, even the Azores. Then King on April 18 issued Atlantic Fleet Operation Plan 3–41 that stipulated that "warships of any belligerent—except for powers having West Indian possessions—coming within 25 miles of the hemisphere were to be considered trespassers and dealt with as pirates." By the autumn of 1941 U.S. destroyers were openly engaged in the escort of British convoys as far east in the Atlantic as point "Momp" (midocean meeting point), about halfway between the British Isles and Canada.[64]

On April 14 Hopkins and Undersecretary of State Sumner Welles, with London's blessing, met with Icelandic consul general Thor Thors in Washington, D.C., and opened "extremely secret" negotiations that ultimately led to a "reluctant and tardy consent" by Iceland's prime minister that the United States dispatch the four thousand–man First Marine Brigade to Reykjavik "to supplement and eventually replace" the British troop garrison, "which [was] needed elsewhere." In a covering letter to the orders sending the marines to Iceland, Stark informed King and the commander of the brigade of his belief that "this is practically an act of war." Hitler and his admirals realized that the irrepressible momentum of their U-boat war was drawing the United States ever closer to active belligerency. The passage of the Lend-Lease Act just eight days before *Bismarck* sortied from Germany could only confirm their impression. The new legislation permitted

Roosevelt to sell, transfer title to, exchange, lease, lend, or otherwise dispose of war matériel to any nation that the president deemed vital to the defense of the United States. "From the very first," Raeder later wrote, "the anti-German bias of the American president... had been obvious, and his desire to support the Allies unmistakable."[65] The Nazi high command had no desire to get into a naval war with the United States, however, and surface and U-boat commanders alike were strictly enjoined to leave American shipping, including war vessels, absolutely alone.

But *Bismarck*'s sudden appearance in the Denmark Strait between Greenland and Iceland deeply disturbed the president and his military and naval advisers. Hitler seemed to be determined to bring war to the Western Hemisphere. When the great battleship destroyed *Hood*, severely damaged *Prince of Wales* (which had been sent out directly from the builder's yards), and disappeared into the Atlantic wastes, it caused a flurry of hysteria on the American East Coast not seen since those long-ago days of 1898 when another belligerent European admiral had set sail from the Old World toward the New. In the final years before long-range aircraft (and soon thereafter intercontinental missiles and spy satellites) transformed war and shrank the globe, the battleship was having its last moment of glory. Never again would eight big naval guns on a single hull so intimidate the world. Might the Nazi monster suddenly appear to shell Halifax, New York, or Norfolk? Would it appear in Rio to stage a propaganda display before the sizable German populations in Latin America, thus destabilizing the entire area for Berlin? Would it then round Cape Horn and sail on through the South Pacific and the China Sea to Japan, stimulating that nation to declare war on the United States?

Wild as these speculations seem today, they were not entirely implausible. Alfred von Tirpitz had, after all, defined the fundamental mission of his navy in terms of arousing and sustaining a patriotic sense of "Germandom" among the numerous émigré populations abroad. Raeder and a host of Nazi propagandists had reiterated the theme just scant years before. Roosevelt himself thought that Hitler had deliberately sent *Bismarck* into the western Atlantic as a warning to the United States to stay out of the war. The president believed it not unlikely the battleship would head for the Caribbean and perhaps take possession of the strategic island of Martinique. "Suppose she does show up in the Caribbean," he asked a group around his desk one blistering-hot late-spring day as *Bismarck*'s whereabouts in the stormy Atlantic were being debated. "We have some submarines down there. Suppose we should order them to attack her and attempt to sink her? Do you think the people would demand to have me impeached?" Someone quietly answered, "Only if the Navy misses."

Presidential speechwriter Robert E. Sherwood caught the mood of quiet horror emanating from the presidential desk.

> Here was the reality of one murderous ship, off on some wild, unpredictable career, guided by the will of one man who might be a maniac or genius or both, capable of converting one inexplicable impulse into a turning point of history. And here was the President of the United States, sitting in the White House in an atmosphere of oppressive calm, wondering what the next naval dispatch would tell him, wondering what he would be able to do about it.[66]

When *Bismarck* was at last found again it was the Americans who helped find it. Luetjens, believing that enemy radar beams had never left his stern, foolishly sent a lengthy situation report to Berlin. According to one rather sensational but generally reliable source, powerful radio direction finders on the American East Coast as well as those in Britain and Iceland picked up the signal. Washington promptly notified the British Admiralty, which placed the data from across the Atlantic next to information from its own stations, thereby obtaining a fairly precise fix on *Bismarck*'s whereabouts. Luetjens was obviously heading southeast toward Brest or one of the other French Atlantic ports. Unfortunately, navigators aboard *King George V* erroneously plotted the fixes given to them and headed the wrong way. *Bismarck* was again about to slip away when it was sighted by the U.S. Coast Guard cutter *Modoc,* which was cruising far away from its normal weather-reporting station. *Modoc* was in fact out searching for survivors from sunken British merchantmen when *Bismarck*'s fighting top suddenly appeared over the distant horizon and just as quickly swept on and away. The cutter sent a routine sighting report, and soon after an American-built Catalina patrol plane belonging to Coastal Command took off from Londonderry. The aircraft, and several others, had either been "lent" to the British before the two-week-old Lend-Lease Act had become law or had been dispatched to Ireland within hours thereafter. Most interestingly, the plane's crew was a mixed assortment of Yanks and Britons. Presumably, the Americans were not disposable war matériel but had been dispatched to show their English cousins how to fly the strange plane. In any event the "pilot adviser" aboard was Ensign Leonard Smith of Missouri. Hours after takeoff Smith and his mates glimpsed *Bismarck* through intermittent clouds and were almost shot down as they swept in for a closer look. The sighting report was soon transmitted to *Ark Royal,* which with the rest of Force H was steaming hard north from Gibraltar. The carrier's first strike at the German battleship was a disaster, but the second crippled *Bismarck,* sealing its fate.[67]

The *Bismarck* affair, together with the incessant Nazi submarine offensive that had now carried into the western Atlantic, completed Washington's move to outright belligerence. On May 27, just hours after the shattered hulk of *Bismarck* slipped beneath the gray-green waves of the North Atlantic, Roosevelt declared an "Unlimited National Emergency." War, he told his people, "is approaching the brink of the Western Hemisphere itself. It is coming very close to home. . . . It would be suicide to wait" until the Nazi aggressors "are in our front yard. We have accordingly extended our patrol in North and South Atlantic waters." Historian Michael Gannon has found evidence in the Ernest J. King Papers that as early as June 1941, the commander in chief of the Atlantic Fleet was interpreting Roosevelt's Hemisphere Defense Plan No. 1 in the most extreme terms. Warships on so-called neutrality patrol in the western and central Atlantic were placed under orders to *initiate* hostile actions "should enemy forces be sighted or sound-detected." In July "King issued a series of operations plans that contained such language as: 'Destroy hostile forces which threaten shipping of U.S. and Iceland flag.'" King was, in fact, merely reflecting his commander in chief's own thinking, for Roosevelt had just written Stark:

> It is necessary under conditions of modern warfare to recognize that the words "threat of attack" may extend reasonably long distances away from a convoyed ship or ships. It thus seems clear that the very presence of a German submarine or raider on or near the line of communications [between Britain and the New World] constitutes "threat of attack." Therefore, the presence of any German submarine or raider should be dealt with by action looking to the elimination of such "threat of attack" on the lines of communication or close to it.[68]

FDR's growing belligerence was based on secret information given to him by Churchill at the Argentia Conference in mid-August. Signals between Dönitz and his U-boat commanders over the previous sixty days clearly indicated that "so long as he was fighting his war of conquest against the Soviet Union, Hitler wanted at all costs to avoid incidents which might bring the U.S. into the war." One such incident had occurred on June 19, three days before Hitler moved against Russia, when U-203 encountered USS *Texas* in the eastern Atlantic and queried U-boat headquarters what to do. The response, as passed on by Churchill, emboldened Roosevelt to allow the Atlantic Fleet "to chase German raiders" whenever the Royal Navy was present or nearby to render assistance. American destroyers would also escort the fast Allied convoys from Halifax to and from a midocean point south of Iceland.[69] The president was quite unwilling, however, to place any of his navy under British command. Rightly so; the country would not have stood for it, and it might have been considered an impeachable offense.

The United States was clearly gearing up for war, and not the least because of a widespread impression in both public and private circles that the Royal Navy—and the country it guarded—was about to collapse. The year before, just after Dunkirk, FDR had raised with Ambassador Lord Lothian the fate of the British fleet should England go under, prompting the British Foreign Office to speculate on employing the fleet as a bargaining chip to lure the United States into an early declaration of war against Germany. Should Hitler gain control of British fleet units, he could treble or quadruple the size of his navy at a stroke, posing an ostensibly overwhelming challenge to the New World. Would it not be wise, British diplomats mused, to point this out to the president and his Congress as a means of getting them into the war? But "Churchill was fiercely determined not to permit any bargaining about the future disposition of the British fleet." Give us the tools, he famously broadcast across the ocean, and we will do the job. So he and Roosevelt and Congress settled down to an ultimately successful negotiation of the destroyers-for-bases deal and, later, Lend-Lease.[70]

This did not answer the problem of the Royal Navy's apparent exhaustion. Until the last incredible spasm of good fortune, the entire British Home Fleet had seemed powerless before *Bismarck*. Had the balance of power at sea—and thus on every war front—suddenly and decisively shifted to Germany? Eight weeks after *Bismarck's* destruction, Hanson Baldwin speculated on the future of the Royal Navy should England be brought to its knees. Would Hitler be able to seize the Home Fleet, and if so, with what results? Baldwin concluded that most of the British warships would be either too damaged or too stressed by repeated steaming to be of much use to the Germans, and, in any case, they were too complex for Hitler's sailors to master in a short time. But if the British fleet should fall into Nazi hands, American shipbuilding potential was becoming so pronounced that the United States could simply outbuild the Axis powers should that be required. The conclusion was obvious: the fall of the Royal Navy might well lead to "the emergence of the United States as the foremost sea power of our time. And in such a world we would need to be."[71]

In the months after *Bismarck's* death, the Battle of the Atlantic steadily intensified. Roosevelt enlarged the new Atlantic Fleet with both new construction and reinforcements from the Pacific, including three battleships and the carrier *Yorktown* (which raced back west through the Panama Canal as soon as Japan attacked Hawaii). As the president gave orders to extend destroyer, aircraft, and battleship patrols "from the blue Caribbean to the icy waters of Greenland" and on out into the central Atlantic to forestall a possible Nazi conquest of the Azores, "quasi-belligerency" gradually "shaded into war." FDR angrily charged that Hitler's young U-boat crews had become "the rattlesnakes of the Atlantic," and he laid down a stern warning: "From now on, if German or Italian vessels of war enter the waters the protection of which is necessary for American defence, they do so at their own peril." By now, British cryptanalysts were using their capabilities to read the German U-boat communication codes ("Ultra") so effectively that U.S.-escorted Allied convoys could be "cleverly routed" around the U-boat patrol lines, so incidents were few. But the Americans hunted Dönitz's boys so enthusiastically that one, U-552, turned on its tormentors and put a torpedo into the magazine of the old destroyer *Reuben James* and sank it just six hundred miles off the Irish coast.[72] A growing realization that command of the seas, not just neutrality, was the key to national security was inexorably drawing the United States into the climactic battle of the twentieth century.

There was, perhaps, one final point—Guadalcanal—at which a daring use of Axis sea power might yet have turned the tide of war decisively against the Allies. By the late summer of 1942 Japan had suffered three reverses, one of them staggering. The Doolittle raid against Tokyo in mid-April came about because Captain Francis S. Low, a brilliant operations officer on Admiral King's staff, noticed while flying into Norfolk shortly after Pearl Harbor that twin-engine bombers were making simulated runs on a carrier deck outlined on the runway below.[73] Low, who would soon become a rear admiral and make key contributions to the formation and success of the Tenth Fleet fighting U-boats in the Atlantic, immediately conceived the idea of staging some of the U.S. Army Air Corps light B-25 bombers from a carrier deck for a raid on the Japanese capital. He rushed back to Washington, D.C., and approached King with the idea. It was the darkest time of the war, and an air raid on Japan from either China or the Aleutians was already being actively considered at both the White House and the War Department. No one had thought of staging bombers off a short, narrow carrier deck, but after Low made his proposal, no one thought of anything else.[74] Risky as a carrier was, it stood a greater chance of success than a long-range assault from the always stormy, foggy Aleutians or from "Free China" whose dimensions continued to be constricted by repeated Japanese probes and offensives.

The Doolittle raid was developed, and carried out, in a matter of weeks, with *Hornet* steaming all the way from Norfolk through the Panama Canal to a point little more than six hundred miles off the coast of Honshu with only brief stops in California. Despite negligible material effects, the bombing of Tokyo and a handful of other Japanese industrial cities was a sensation in ways that its creators could never have imagined. Although it provided the hoped-for shot in the arm to the Allied cause, its chief effect was to abruptly catapult the aircraft carrier to the status of a major strategic weapon. Not even *Illustrious* at Taranto or *Kido Butai* at Pearl Harbor had achieved what *Hornet* had. Small as they were, Doolittle's B-25s were bombers, and the raid proved that even the relatively small fleet carriers of 1942 were big and efficient enough to launch major bombing raids (although the planes could not be recovered). Moreover, *Hornet* was mobile, whereas airfields in the Aleutians, China, and anywhere else were not. The *Hornet* task force (with *Enterprise* along to provide combat air patrols) stumbled into the Japanese picketboat line hundreds of miles off the coast, yet was able to launch the Doolittle flyers to successfully bomb the enemy capital while escaping unscathed. The notion of the aircraft carrier as a highly mobile strategic bombing platform took hold, never to be discarded.

For the Japanese, the Doolittle raid was an unendurable mortification. The homeland that had not been desecrated since the Meiji Restoration was again dirtied by the machines of barbaric Westerners. But the raid also legitimated at a stroke the insistent arguments of the Yamamoto faction within the Imperial Navy that the current expansionist policy must not be stifled but be accelerated. Their handful of carriers were all the Americans had left as an offensive force, and all that was required to secure Japan's ribbon-defense line in the Pacific was to hunt down and kill these ships. Within days, the handful of Doolittle's flyers who had failed to reach friendly fields in China or internment in the Soviet Union were having the truth tortured from them, and Yamamoto and the high command knew the Tokyo raid had been staged from *Hornet*. Japan was suddenly placed in a fearfully anomalous situation. What good would it do, Yamamoto argued, to seize and exploit the South Pacific and Southeast Asia if the Home Islands remained vulnerable to attacks by enemy carriers? Japan must deal with its two remaining problems at a single stroke. It must complete its mid-Pacific defense line by seizing Midway and use that operation to lure the enemy's last few carriers into decisive battle. With the defense line complete and the American carrier fleet destroyed for at least eighteen months (until replacements could be completed), the ships and aircraft of the imperial fleet could easily defend the approaches to the Home Islands while mounting probing attacks against Alaska and Hawaii that would force what remained of the U.S. surface navy to flee back to California, thus possibly breaking the American will to fight.

After the Doolittle raid, Yamamoto's arguments were unassailable. But first two of Nagumo's fleet carriers—the new *Shokaku* and *Zuikaku*—fell afoul of the aggressively probing Americans down in the Coral Sea, in what became not only the first carrier battle in history but also, arguably, the most confusing battle in all of naval history. The Japanese flattops had been detached from *Kido Butai* on its way home from the Indian Ocean to fulfill an impossibly complex set of assignments that reflected Japan's growing difficulty in completing its grandiose oceanic empire with limited forces. Admiral Chuichi Hara and his relatively inexperienced flyers of Carrier Division 5 were ordered to provide distant air cover for army landings far to the east on the island Tulagi across a narrow sound from a larger island in the lower Solomons called Guadalcanal, then immediately thereafter directly support landings at Port Moresby, New Guinea, hundreds of miles to the west, and conduct preliminary raids against enemy airfields in northern Australia to neutralize MacArthur's small bomber force. The latter mission would allow construction of a seaplane base in the Louisiade Archipelago just off the southern tip of New Guinea around the corner from Port Moresby. The "inverted triangle" formed by the occupations of Port Moresby, the Louisiade, and Tulagi "pointed firmly south to Australia," effectively isolating the northern and western sectors of that vast island continent. The construction of a landing strip on Tulagi, together with a small submarine as well as seaplane base, was also designed to complete the southern anchor of Japan's mid-Pacific defense line, while ensuring the isolation of the entire Australian continent and New Zealand by severing the sea-lanes north to Hawaii and the United States. *Lexington* and *Yorktown*, under the command of Frank Jack Fletcher, were serving as a desperate barrier against these possibilities.

Throughout the first week of May 1942, Fletcher and Hara chased each other around the Coral Sea, neither certain that the other was there, or in what force, or what he was up to. Fletcher, of course, enjoyed an enormous intelligence advantage: "Hypo" Station at Pearl Harbor had broken the Japanese naval code months before, and radio-interception units aboard both U.S. carriers contained Japanese-speaking officers. The Americans knew a heavy invasion force, covered by at least some of Yamamoto's fleet carriers, was bearing down on Port Moresby by way of the Louisiade. Hara enjoyed no such advantage. But Fletcher, a lean, trim fifty-seven, was an old-school admiral who before Pearl Harbor had spent his sea years aboard battleships, cruisers, and destroyers. His inclination was to dismiss intelligence information that was not immediately pertinent, and he tended to distrust intelligence that contradicted his inclinations. Nonetheless, fortune smiled upon him. When the first Japanese forces occupied Tulagi, Fletcher promptly ordered an air strike by *Yorktown,* which he had earlier detached from *Lexington,* thus committing the supposedly unpardonable sin of splitting his forces in the face of the enemy (Lee had done it several times during the Civil War with favorable results). Luckily, Hara's carriers were by this time four hundred miles away, refueling off Rabaul, having been delayed in launching the Zero reinforcements for Tulagi by bad weather. Had this not occurred, Hara with his two big modern carriers would have been near the island, ready to pounce on any enemy forces that might appear. At last, on May 7, with the two American carrier task groups reunited, scouting aircraft from both sides discovered enemy fleet units from afar, and thus began the first naval battle in history in which the contending surface forces never came within visual contact.

It is nearly impossible, sixty-five years on, to imagine or re-create the crude context in which the four great aircraft-carrier battles of 1942 (Coral Sea, Midway, eastern Solomons, and Santa Cruz) were fought. The Japanese had no radar, and limited intelligence at best. American sets were primitive, their intelligence superior, but still grounded in reading enemy radio traffic. There were no satellites to confirm and precisely locate enemy sea formations from thousands of miles on high, no secure high-speed data links to wing the information instantly from reception stations ashore or afloat to fleet commanders. All one knew was that the enemy was out there somewhere—maybe five hundred miles away, maybe three hundred, perhaps much closer. One launched one's scout planes from a carrier or a cruiser in a ceaseless search for visual evidence of the enemy's presence and location, fearful always that the enemy would find you before you found him. This was the terrible burden of command that weighed on Japanese and American carrier admirals alike during those desperate early months of the war. Once your scout sighted far-off wakes, it was difficult, if not impossible, to get close enough for positive identification before being shot down, which would negate the mission. So pilots and observers, dividing their gazes between what lay far below and what might suddenly come rushing at them from nearby clouds or a sun-filled sky, made hasty estimates and guesses about what they were seeing and with equal haste sent out fragmentary, partially correct, or even erroneous messages on the composition and strength of probable enemy units. "Discovered what appears to be large enemy force bearing 190 degrees" was a not untypical message during the 1942 carrier battles upon which a Japanese or American admiral would have to act, or not act, risking his precious few carriers either way. The fact that an even bigger portion of the enemy force might in fact still be lurking beneath often present curtains of clouds and squall lines, or that the report might be (and in the Coral Sea usually was) wholly incorrect, amplified the danger manyfold. Once reasonably firm or tantalizing messages regarding enemy whereabouts were received, commanders on both sides could not wait—or felt they could not wait—for corroborative or corrective information. It was "Flight quarters! Pilots, man your planes" and get to the enemy and sink his carriers before he gets to you. So daring American and Japanese boys rushed their planes off the flight decks and went hunting for an adversary whose last-known position was here, or there, twenty or thirty minutes ago when the sketchy information from the scout planes came in. But in the hour or more it took to get to that position, the enemy might have moved far enough away in any direction so as never to be found. Such were the conditions in the Coral Sea, at Midway and the eastern Solomons, and at Santa Cruz. The fact that either side found the other, even though at Coral Sea the two fleets at one point in the night passed within just fifty miles of one another, was little short of miraculous.

May 7 was a day of blunder, as both Fletcher and Hara sent out massive air strikes against phantom targets based on faulty intelligence or reasoning. Fletcher believed Hara was in front of him, screening the Port Moresby invasion force, when in fact the Japanese were at his rear, looking in the wrong sector to kill the small American carrier fleet that had struck Tulagi and that Hara knew had to be destroyed before the Port Moresby operation could be safely concluded. At one point a *Yorktown* scout pilot, Lieutenant John L. Nielsen, came racing back to report that he had sighted enemy light cruisers and two destroyers off the island Misima in the Louisiade. What he in fact sighted was part of the Port Moresby covering force. But his earlier on-the-spot message had stated the enemy comprised two carriers and four heavy cruisers, and that had prompted Fletcher to send out his entire striking force of dive-bombers and torpedo planes. Immediately hauled into the carrier's flag plot to explain the shocking discrepancy between what he had actually seen and what he had first sighted, Nielsen admitted to "an unfortunate coding error." An allegedly distraught Fletcher "roared" at the unfortunate boy, "Young man, do you know what you have done? You have just cost the United States two carriers!" In fact, poor

Nielsen was not at fault at all. His "coding device was misaligned and wrongly enciphered the all-important message." Fletcher may or may not have lost his temper, but disaster clearly loomed "with the realization that our [carrier] task forces had shot their bolt." But so had Hara, who thought the Americans were south and east, not west, of him. When he learned the truth, he sent his flyers out to sink a carrier and cruiser that turned out to be the fleet oiler *Neosho* and the destroyer *Sims* that had been ordered far out of harm's way. *Sims* went down under a hail of bombs; the oiler was left a drifting hulk. The Americans were luckier, for the Port Moresby invasion fleet that Nielsen had sighted and Fletcher had sent his planes to attack did contain the light carrier *Shoho*. Fletcher's pilots promptly bombed and torpedoed *Shoho* to death in one of the finest coordinated strike efforts of the Pacific war, leading Lieutenant Commander R. E. Dixon to radio triumphantly back to *Yorktown*, "Scratch one flattop!" the first of many Japanese carriers that would succumb over the next three and one-half years to the bombs and torpedoes of the United States Navy.

That night of May 7–8, 1942, the two commanders and their staffs, sifting through a small mountain of often contradictory data, at last began to get things right and the following murky dawn sent out aggressive patrols. The two fleets found each other at last, and both struck heavily. The Japanese bomb and torpedo attacks against the lumbering *Lexington* and the smaller, more nimble *Yorktown* were masterpieces of coordination. For just the third time in history, the long-imagined assault of carrier aircraft against enemy carriers was at hand, and the men of *Lexington* joined the boys of *Shoho* and *Hermes* in experiencing the heat and din, the flame, blood, and horror, of carrier warfare. Antiaircraft gun crews, pumping round after round into cloudless blue skies and along the wave tops found themselves as helpless to stop the onrushing enemy aircraft as had their allies aboard *Prince of Wales* and *Repulse*. Two torpedoes ripped into *Lexington,* and as the huge craft slowed dramatically, bombs ripped through its flight deck to add fire and carnage to the already terrible damage belowdecks. A bomb struck *Yorktown*, which caused it to momentarily lose power, but it was soon under way once more. Not *"Lady Lex."* After hours of heroic firefighting, sparks from a generator ignited fuel vapor from ruptured tanks nearby, and the carrier was wracked by a huge explosion that ignited uncontainable fires. Late in the afternoon, its hull glowing cherry red from the flames raging inside, the giant ship slipped beneath the waves, still burning and exploding as it went.

Meanwhile, Fletcher's pilots had found *Shokaku* and *Zuikaku*. Once more the story played out: small planes diving or jinking and weaving as they skimmed above the wave tops, frantic gunners trying to shoot them down by line of sight. Three planes were lost, but the same number of torpedoes slammed into *Shokaku,* flooding the flattop's bow and bending its flight deck so badly that no aircraft could be launched. *Zuikaku* escaped unscathed.

Despite dramatic discrepancies in ship loss, Coral Sea has rightly been considered an American victory. With loss of air cover from *Shoho* and with Hara's two big fleet carriers hightailing it for home, the Japanese had no option but to break off the invasion of Port Moresby, which was never rescheduled. Though losing *Lexington* (with *Yorktown* moderately damaged), Fletcher's airmen sank *Shoho* and mauled *Shokaku.* Moreover, the Japanese lost a significant portion of their planes and pilots. *Zuikaku's* air group was especially hard hit. Mischance and ill-luck cost the Japanese as many flyers and aircraft as did battle. A flight of twenty-seven aircraft sent out on the first day of battle failed to find the U.S. fleet, jettisoned bombs and torpedoes, and was heading home when it stumbled close to the American task force, which picked them up on radar. The surprised enemy was jumped and dispatched by Fletcher's combat air patrols. As the two fleets blundered close to one another hours later, another Japanese scouting squadron came across the two U.S. carriers in fast-deepening dusk and, thinking they were home, attempted to land. The astonished Yanks pulled themselves together and shot down several of the enemy aircraft while the others winged away desperately into the gloam. Only five aircraft made it home to their carriers.[75]

The whittling down of experienced and capable Japanese aviators had commenced. Not only was the badly damaged *Shokaku* knocked out of the forthcoming Midway operation, but so was *Zuikaku,* whose air group suffered a disproportionate number of casualties. Moreover, the Americans had begun to demonstrate a tactical dominance in fighting; the "Thatch weave" of Wildcat fighters, for example, proved capable of overcoming the superior performance capabilities of the more fragile Zero. But Frank Jack Fletcher demonstrated a disturbing propensity for lunging with all his forces at the first enemy carrier he saw rather than holding back at least some reserves in case larger, or at least other, carrier forces might be around. It cost him *Lexington* and proved to be a deep-seated flaw in leadership that would dog American naval fortunes at Midway, the Philippine Sea, and Leyte Gulf.

It was Midway, of course, that seemingly doomed Japan, and Midway was indeed a miracle.[76] But historians absorbed in the immediate drama of the battle have missed much of the larger context. Even if Japan had conquered the island, even if Nagumo's carrier fleet had survived more or less intact, its overall wartime position would have been little improved. At Midway the Japanese not only suffered from poorly conceptualized planning and wretched luck (to say nothing of the gallantry of American airmen) but were also the victims of geographic determinism and industrial inferiority. Japan's industrial capacity was at best 10 to 12 percent of America's; it simply could not build and sustain a fleet of sufficient size to eternally dominate half the Pacific. And if it could not dominate the western Pacific, it was ultimately doomed to defeat by an enemy possessed not only of a potentially unlimited industrial potential but also of a sufficient manpower base to adequately exploit the industrial and military capabilities it enjoyed. Geographically, as noted earlier, the Fates had condemned Japan to an impossible position. The island and continental structure of the East Asia–Pacific region guaranteed that it could be attacked from every point on the compass. At the same time, it was almost impossible for Japan or any other Pacific nation to effectively threaten the United States. The distances in the eastern Pacific were simply too great. Granted that Midway atoll was the farthest outpost of the Hawaiian Islands chain, it nonetheless lay a thousand miles west of the large American military, air, and naval bases on Oahu. To strike Pearl Harbor and Hickam Field often enough and with sufficient force to neutralize the Hawaiian Islands and soften them up for eventual invasion (which a truly impregnable *midocean* defense line would have demanded), the Japanese would have had to seize atolls much closer to Oahu. But June 1942 was the nadir of American fortunes; within months, long before Yamamoto could have contemplated moving on eastward from Midway, the first components of what would be an irresistible flood of American men, ships, planes, and matériel were beginning to reach the Pacific through that canal that Yamamoto had inexcusably left intact. And even if Yamamoto had been able to seize or neutralize Hawaii, he would have still been twenty-four hundred miles from the American West Coast, far beyond the effective range of either the strike aircraft of the day or amphibious operations. (Possible Japanese pressure against the American West Coast via the Aleutians and southern Alaska would have been even more problematic given the distances, weather, and terrain between Kiska and Vancouver islands.) But the Japanese would have had to directly threaten the continental United States to have any hope of winning the war outright.

Japan's only real hope lay in *not* moving so far out into the Pacific as to dilute its splendid but limited military and naval forces. Yamamoto and his partners would have been better advised *not* to draw a "ribbon-defense line" at Kiska, Midway, and Tulagi but rather to draw a steel cord around the Bonins, Philippines, Malaya, and the most readily defensible parts of the Dutch East Indies (Indonesia). Given the industrial, military, and geographic realities of the Pacific war, the Japanese needed to effectively concentrate, not disperse, their inferior forces to hold the Americans at bay while exploiting the riches of China and Southeast Asia. Instead, Yamamoto chose to sail out into the mid-Pacific, across the International Date Line where his regional fleet had never operated (except for the quick Pearl Harbor raid), to seize an island that could not be long held against a soon-to-be-superior foe. He was courting disaster, and he found it.

The fatal flaw in "Operation MI," Japan's plan to seize Midway, involved the use of *Kido Butai* in both tactical and strategic roles at a time when the U.S. carrier fleet remained substantially intact. Erroneously assuming that both enemy carriers had been sunk in the Coral Sea and that *Enterprise* and *Hornet* had been drawn so far down into the South Pacific that they could not immediately respond to the Midway invasion, Nagumo would employ the 261 aircraft aboard his four carriers on June 4, 5, and 6 to soften up Midway for invasion with the same kind of massive air strikes that had devastated Java, Australia, and Ceylon. While the Combined Fleet's main (battleship) force, headed by *Yamato* with Yamamoto on the bridge, came rushing up, Nagumo would rearm his aircraft on the afternoon or evening of June 6 to meet any enemy carriers or other fleet units that could be expected to appear no earlier than the seventh, the day Japanese forces would storm ashore at Midway. After destroying the enemy fleet, *Kido Butai* and the battleship force would render whatever last support might be needed at Midway before steaming off to Truk to prepare for the capture of Fiji, Samoa, and New Caledonia and the bombing of Sydney. These grandiose plans leaped from the brain of Captain Kameto Kuroshima, the Combined Fleet's senior operations officer, but they "reflected the ideas and personality" of Isoroku Yamamoto.[77]

Operation MI's disastrous infeasibility was apparent from the beginning. War games held in late April and early May clearly indicated that *Kido Butai* was vulnerable to air attack from Midway whenever its air groups were off attacking the island. And what would happen, it was asked, if enemy carriers were, in fact, in the area as early as June 4? Could they not launch disastrous flank attacks against Nagumo's carriers while the air groups were concentrating on Midway? Yamamoto's staff officers simply overrode or ignored such unpleasant possibilities, allowing the Operation MI scenario to continue as if *Akagi, Kaga, Soryu,* and *Hiryu* remained intact and in action at all times. In truth, the Japanese, from Yamamoto on down, continued to view *Kido Butai* not as the new, chief striking arm of the Imperial Navy, but merely as an admittedly important, but not crucial, adjunct to the battle fleet. Had Yamamoto used the powerful Japanese battleship force to escort *Kido Butai* from the beginning, its powerful antiaircraft batteries might well have saved most if not all of Nagumo's carriers from destruction.[78]

Of course, Yamamoto, Kuroshima, and subordinate staff planners could not know that their signals were being read, that *Yorktown* had survived, that *Enterprise* and *Hornet* rushed back from the South Pacific in time for all three carriers to be in ambush position north and east of Midway by the afternoon of June 3. But the lack of flexibility, foresight, and, above all, humility that characterized Japanese naval planning at this stage in the war was both striking and fatal.

The Japanese might still have been able to win the Battle of Midway by exposing the three American carriers lying in ambush to the north and east of the atoll. But Yamamoto dispersed his battleship-carrier fleet when he should have concentrated it, then permitted Nagumo to concentrate *Kido Butai* when its carriers should have been dispersed.[79]

In addition to *Kido Butai*, Yamamoto had in hand two light fleet aircraft carriers, *Ryujo* and *Junyo*, that could and should have been brought into the Midway operation. Instead, Yamamoto detached them to conduct diversionary raids thousands of miles to the north against Dutch Harbor in the Aleutians, thereby supposedly drawing off part of whatever defensive American fleet remained. *Ryujo* (sixteen fighters and twenty-one torpedo planes) and *Junyo* (twenty-four fighters and twenty-one dive-bombers) were formidable ships. Had they (and their escorting screen) been used at Midway, they would have increased Yamamoto's margin over the Americans to six carriers to three and provided Nagumo with the flexibility that the Midway operation absolutely required. *Ryujo* and *Junyo* could have been employed in advance of Nagumo's four strike carriers, aggressively probing for enemy warships. They might have detected the American fleet as early as the afternoon of June 3, rather than the following morning when a float plane from one of Nagumo's escorting cruisers at last stumbled onto the enemy carriers even as they were launching their first strikes. At the very least, the two Japanese light carriers or their planes would undoubtedly have been sighted by reconnaissance aircraft from Midway. In either instance, *Ryujo* and *Junyo* would have attracted and absorbed the initial attacks by Raymond Spruance's and Frank Jack Fletcher's own carrier pilots, since both American admirals consistently displayed a propensity to hit the first enemy forces they found with everything they had. Alternatively, Yamamoto could have ordered Nagumo to employ the two light carriers tactically, to strike Midway (perhaps adding one of the four fleet carriers to strengthen the air assault) while withholding three or all four fleet carriers in a strategic role to go after the American carriers when found. Freed of the need to think *and* act both tactically and strategically—to ensure the devastation of both Midway and the American carrier fleet—Nagumo and his staff would have had time to fully grasp and assess the situation and hit the Americans from their undamaged fleet carriers before the Americans could find them. Instead, Yamamoto forced Nagumo to employ his four carriers and their superb air groups in *both* tactical (that is, air strikes on Midway in advance of the planned invasion) and strategic (finding and destroying the American carriers) roles. Implementing these disparate assignments required the kind of close scheduling *and* equally close grouping of the four carriers within visual range of each other that at once left little or no margin to incorporate the inevitable uncertainties, confusions, and surprises of battle and left the big carriers highly vulnerable to enemy air attacks.

Later in the war, the Americans significantly modified the tactical and strategic role of carriers. Possessed of enough flattops of all sizes and types, Chester Nimitz let his admirals roam the Far Pacific launching hit-and-run raids from the big fleet and fast light carriers at enemy island strongholds while seeking out the Japanese fleet. Once the invasion of a specific island began, local air support was provided from the decks of a score or more escort carriers, while the fleet and light fleet carriers waited for a possible riposte by the Imperial Navy. The Japanese, on the other hand, based the Midway operation on two utterly false assumptions: that the Americans possessed one or two fewer carriers than they actually had and that what American carrier forces there were remained thousands of miles away in the South Pacific. The tactical-strategic burdens placed on Nagumo's carrier crews and pilots proved too great to overcome once the Americans brought their entire available carrier fleet into action days before they were expected. The organized chaos aboard the Japanese carriers in the midmorning hours of June 4, 1942, when flight decks had to be kept open for combat–air patrol refueling while Midway strike aircraft were hastily rearmed below for an attack on the newly discovered enemy carrier fleet amply demonstrated the tragic limitations of Yamamoto's thinking.[80]

At the same time, as Mark Peattie has cogently argued, Nagumo's four strike carriers were simply too small a force to keep tightly concentrated. "Expecting a straightforward attack against American base facilities on Midway and ignorant of the proximity of American carriers, the Japanese had no time to disperse their carriers before they were struck." *Kido Butai* was a magnificent weapon so long as it experienced no significant aerial opposition. Four, five, or all six Japanese fleet carriers steaming within visual range of one another could dispatch an air armada that descended on remote enemy garrisons in a hurricane of fire and steel, leaving behind devastation and demoralization. But emphasis on the all-out offensive meant a consequent slighting of fleet air defense. Once the enemy was able to muster substantial aerial strength of its own at Midway and send it onto a *Kido Butai* whose carrier strength was reduced by fully one-third with the absence of *Shokaku* and *Zuikaku,* the terrible vulnerability of Japan's carrier strike force stood revealed.

The Americans were somewhat more astute at this point in the war. When word came of the Japanese carriers, "*Hornet* sheered out of formation, forming a small, separate group" that with two heavy cruisers, an antiaircraft cruiser, and three destroyers operated at extreme visual range. Just that degree of separation kept *Hornet* from ever being attacked when the enraged Japanese flyers from the surviving *Hiryu* set out to avenge their dead comrades. By the time they reached the American fleet, *Enterprise* and *Yorktown* had also become separated by "several miles," and with comparatively few aircraft the Japanese chose to concentrate on the first carrier they came upon, which was the luckless *Yorktown.*[81]

One of the most striking aspects of the battle, however, has gone largely unnoticed, and that was the ability of *Kido Butai's* combat air patrols to successfully fend off for hours formidable attacks from supposedly superior land-based aircraft as well as from Spruance's carriers. Nagumo's four flattops were but moments away from utterly escaping potentially lethal assaults by long-range, high-altitude bombers (B-17s), low-level bombers, and torpedo planes from both the island and the lurking American carriers. Nagumo must have thought in those last moments before disaster struck that he and his command had escaped everything that a beleaguered and surprised enemy could throw at them. Then, and only by the sheerest good luck, dive-bombers from *Enterprise* and *Yorktown*—the last available elements in the American arsenal—arrived high overhead at precisely the moment when the highly efficient but undoubtedly exhausted Japanese combat air patrols had been pulled down to wave-top level to deal with *Yorktown's* torpedo planes. What Wade McClusky and his mates found were three of Japan's half-dozen frontline fleet carriers, their flight decks and hangars full of aircraft that over the past hour and more had been fueled, armed, disarmed, and rearmed again in an ever shifting response to fragmentary information about the presence of an enemy carrier fleet and the clear need to strike Midway's stubborn defenses one more time. McClusky's bomber pilots pushed over and came down, engines screaming, in a graceful waterfall of death, the flyers hanging in their straps until the very last moment, totally concentrating on release of their bomb loads to ensure fatal hits on the frantically maneuvering enemy carriers. When the last dive-bombers pulled up and away from *Akagi, Kaga,* and *Soryu,* they left behind blazing, exploding, sinking wrecks filled with the corpses of Japan's finest carrier crews and some of its most skillful and experienced carrier pilots. Nagumo's remaining carrier, *Hiryu,* managed to find and damage *Yorktown* (which later succumbed to an enemy submarine attack) before itself being overwhelmed by the same bombers from *Yorktown* (which had found a home on the *Enterprise*) and the *"Big E"* that had killed its sisters earlier in the day.

After Midway the Americans could and should have taken the last wind out of the sails of Japanese expansionism by mounting another carrier raid deep into the western Pacific. A further assault on the Home Islands was probably out of the question, as the air defenses around the Japanese coasts had been greatly strengthened since the Doolittle raid and were constantly on the alert. But a raid on Marcus Island, a thousand miles offshore, with the implicit threat of further air attacks ever closer to Japan (against the Bonins or Ryukyus, for example) would certainly have forced Yamamoto and the service high commands to suspend all further activities in far-off New Guinea and the Solomons in order to keep the fleet home. The whole Japanese rationale for the Midway operation, after all, had been to secure the sea approaches to the Home Islands. That objective had not been realized, and the approaches remained open to an assault from the east. They could be closed only by stationing the major portion of the battle fleet (including aircraft carriers) off Honshu and Kyūshū. Even if an American raid against Okinawa or Marcus had been detected and failed with the loss of a carrier or even two, the effect would have been the same: Japan could not have afforded to keep its fleet and air forces scattered over tens of thousands of miles of southern ocean, leaving the enemy with the initiative to strike at or near the homeland whenever it wished.

And it is important to realize that after Midway, the Japanese thought that the Americans *did* possess the carrier resources to strike even the Home Islands, perhaps many times. Following the carrier battle of Santa Cruz in the Solomons in late October 1942, just four months after Midway, the Japanese "Fleet Summary Action Report" stated that the enemy had mustered four carriers when in fact the Americans possessed only two, one of which, *Hornet,* was sunk. Japanese analysts, clearly confused and bedeviled by the enemy's policy of naming ships, nonetheless believed that Nagumo's flyers had destroyed a *"Saratoga* type" and a *"Yorktown* type" flattop. However, "the enemy builds and christens [a] second and third generation of carriers, as many as we destroy. No wonder they do not need to change the names."[82]

But Ernie King and Chester Nimitz failed utterly to appreciate the strategic opportunities that lay before them in the weeks and months immediately following Midway. American authorities never considered contracting Japan's badly stretched forces by occasional hit-and-run threats against Marcus or Okinawa. Instead, everyone in Hawaii and Washington played Japan's game. (And those of Australia and New Zealand as well. Historian Richard Frank notes that Churchill's and Roosevelt's agreement that "Australia and New Zealand must be held," even as some in the U.S. military establishment were prepared to write them off, "provided the ingredients for unanticipated campaigns in the South Pacific that began in April 1942.)[83] The South Pacific was where Japanese forces continued a modest expansion after Midway, and it was to this area that the Americans would go with whatever limited resources they could muster to confront the enemy.

At the end of December 1941, shortly after he became chief of naval operations, King told Nimitz of his strategic vision for the Pacific war. He erroneously assumed that the Japanese offensive was limitless, that its objective was not to establish a ribbon-defense line but to press eastward in the Pacific as far as possible, destroying the Allies' "vital flank" linking California and Hawaii with New Zealand and Australia. To guard this flank, Washington dispatched no fewer than 80,000 troops to the Southwest Pacific between January and March 1942, aiming at an eventual buildup of 290,000 men. As Ronald Spector observes, the initial commitment "was nearly four times the number" of soldiers "departing for Europe during the same period." So much for the ostensible Anglo-American strategy of "Europe first." King and the rest of the American military establishment cannot be faulted for their assumptions. Light Japanese naval forces had already penetrated eastward beyond the Gilberts and American bases on the island Johnston and Palmyra Atoll to shell the islands Ocean and Naru, and in the words of one biographer, "King thought these attacks presaged an advance against Samoa and the Ellice Islands." Therefore, the Japanese offensive should be blocked by "maintaining communications between the West Coast and Australia, chiefly by... holding the Hawaii-Samoa line."[84]

As early as February 5, 1942, the Navy War Plans Division had proposed an early counteroffensive in the South Pacific from bases established in the Ellice Islands (now called Tuvalu) with the initial objective being the capture of Tulagi in the lower Solomons. By mid-April, just before or after the raid on Tokyo, naval planners visualized a future advance against the Japanese in four successive stages: first, a buildup of forces in the Ellice and adjacent islands and in Australia–New Zealand; second, a combined U.S.-Australian–New Zealand amphibious offensive up the Solomon Islands chain and through New Guinea to capture the Bismarck Archipelago and the Admiralty Islands with "heavy attrition attacks...against enemy forces and positions in the Caroline and Marshall Islands"; third, a seizure of those two island groups; and, fourth, an advance into the Netherlands East Indies or the Philippines and from there on north to Formosa and an eventual blockade of Japan. As the historian of the Joint Chiefs of Staff observes:

> The long-established program [that is, War Plan Orange and the various Rainbow Plans of the late thirties and early forties providing] for an advance through the Central Pacific which was to open with operations in the Carolines and Marshalls remained unchallenged, but it was to be delayed while steps were taken to secure the islands of the Southwest Pacific. There is no record of opposition to this pattern within the Navy Department, and the Army planners, who seem to have had only a general idea of what their colleagues were contemplating, were more concerned over the timing of projected operations [so as not to interfere with the buildup for invasions in North Africa and the Mediterranean] than the objectives.[85]

The ultimate decision to concentrate on a limited offensive in the Solomons–New Guinea area reflected the fact that Washington considered the Pacific primarily a navy show, with the European theater the prime responsibility and playground of the U.S. Army and Army Air Corps. If King wanted to concentrate on dislodging Japan from the South Pacific, the army would not grumble too loudly, so long as the offensive would not consume too many precious men, supplies, and amphibious vessels needed in the Mediterranean and eventually for the cross-Channel assault on Fortress Europe. Once the initial troop commitment was reached, Chester Nimitz's Pacific and Douglas MacArthur's Southwest Pacific commands would receive a comparative handful of reinforcements. Less than a week after the Battle of Midway, Ernie King obtained George Marshall's concurrence "to a campaign in the Solomons leading to the enemy air base at Rabaul on New Britain in the Bismarck Archipelago."[86] The campaign that King so casually put in train would consume nearly two years of blood, sweat, and agony before the Bismarck barrier was breached.

King's proposals fitted in perfectly with army objectives, for it at once gave something for Douglas MacArthur to do yet isolated him from further major influence over strategic planning for the war as a whole. MacArthur and his publicity people had managed to turn the disastrous defeat in the Philippines into a one-man triumph for the general, whose reputation was now mortgaged to his pledge to return to the archipelago at the earliest possible date. No one in Washington, D.C., including Franklin Roosevelt, wished to confront Mac-

Arthur, whom the president had long considered one of the most dangerous men in the country for his ostensibly well-hidden but very real Caesarist political ambitions.[87]

MacArthur was now far away in Australia, but he had become the darling of the right wing of the Republican Party (and would garner a handful of votes at the 1944 Republican Convention). The best thing for all concerned was to keep him both distant and happy. The navy's decision that the Solomons campaign would be prelude to the long-assumed central-Pacific offensive envisioned in War Plan Orange fitted right into MacArthur's agenda, for an advance to and beyond the Bismarck barrier would lead straight to the Philippines. MacArthur's insistence on the primacy of the Southwest Pacific produced tensions with his Europe-first colleagues in the Pentagon and eventually also with Nimitz, who was impatient to get a central-Pacific offensive rolling. But no one dared question the general, whose arguments seemed to reflect sound military and naval strategy and whose political position was unassailable.

There is no indication in the formal history of the Joint Chiefs of Staff that the South Pacific strategy was ever reconsidered in light of the opportunities created by the Midway victory. "Shocked out of their delusions of invincibility by the defeat at Midway," one leading student of the Pacific war has written, "the Japanese abandoned their drive to cut off Australia."[88] But King and Nimitz pressed on with their South Pacific strategy. The result was to place a still badly damaged and only slowly rebuilding blue-water navy into a brutal, close-in war amid the densely packed islands of the lower Solomons, allowing the enemy to concentrate his forces and display his unique strengths—land-based airpower in conjunction with a slowly rebuilding carrier fleet, and especially supremacy in night surface fighting at sea with initially superior forces. The Americans unwittingly played right into prewar Japanese tactical and strategic thought.

Despite the shattering Japanese defeat at Midway, the situation in the Pacific when the marines stormed ashore at Guadalcanal on the morning of August 7, 1942, remained in balance. Yamamoto and Nagumo still possessed the big, new fleet carriers *Shokaku* and *Zuikaku,* now fully restored, as well as three or four powerful light fleet carriers with one powerful fleet carrier and a number of light carriers in final construction stages. The Americans could counter with *Enterprise, Hornet,* the oft-damaged *Saratoga,* and the comparatively small, slow, and breakdown-prone *Wasp.* The Japanese battleship fleet had not been touched, and included the giant *Yamato* with its brand-new sister *Musashi* about to enter service. Should these monsters be risked in the narrow and constricted waters around Guadalcanal, they would surely inflict decisive damage on any of the two or three new American battlewagons that might be encountered, to say nothing of the U.S. Navy's tin-clad cruisers and destroyers.

Moreover, the battles that occurred off Guadalcanal and up The Slot in 1942–1943 "had not been anticipated in U.S. naval planning; not, at least, if one is to judge by the amount of training for such combat conducted during the previous decade." The prewar United States Navy with its five-three superiority in capital ships over Japan had assumed a classic Jutland-style daylight conflict between columns of battleships "unfettered by the proximity of land and the uncontrollable chances of low visibility. Night brushes between the light forces accompanying" the two battle lines "were not expected to be decisive."[89]

Finally, the 1942 Pacific campaign remained in thrall to Washington's preoccupation with developing a second front against Nazi Germany as quickly as possible. Thus, the land, sea, and air forces available for the Guadalcanal invasion were woefully inadequate for the job at hand: a single marine division—fortunately "full to the brim" with seasoned officers and noncommissioned officers—together with three aircraft carriers (Saratoga, Enterprise, and Wasp) with another (Hornet) in temporary reserve at Pearl Harbor and roughly 280 mostly obsolete land-based aircraft and seaplanes in the Australia–New Zealand area. Moreover, Allied airfields adjacent to the Solomons area were few and far between. In contrast, Japan could deploy "overwhelming aerial might to bear on any Allied forces venturing into the Solomons" from distant but formidable air and naval bases at Kavieng, Rabaul, Lae, and Salamaua.[90] Not surprisingly, the undertrained and exhausted American sailors suffered a crushing defeat on the second night of the Guadalcanal operation when four cruisers (one of them Australian) and their accompanying destroyers that had been screening the unloading operations for more than thirty-six hours straight were caught with their guard down off nearby Savo island and massacred by Admiral Gunichi Mikawa's audacious cruiser-destroyer fleet steaming down from Rabaul for the express purpose of sweeping the Yankees away.[91] Frank Jack Fletcher promptly pulled his three carriers and escorting warships out of the area, while the now unprotected transports off Guadalcanal lifted anchor and also scurried away, leaving the marines ashore with less than half their supplies and none of their heavy equipment. The shocked commander on the beachhead, General Alexander Vandegrift, summoned his grim-faced unit commanders and told them that under no circumstances must Guadalcanal become another Bataan or Wake Island.[92]

From the beginning, however, the Japanese failed to both appreciate and exploit the opportunity that their opponent handed them. To many later critics within his own navy, Yamamoto had already committed a cardinal error by not keeping the fleet at Truk in the Carolines following Midway. Instead, the admiral had taken it back to home waters, nearly three thousand miles away from the Solomons. In fact, the admiral probably feared that the Americans would do precisely what they should have done: mount renewed carrier assaults in the western Pacific. Once news reached Tokyo of enemy landings on far distant Guadalcanal and Tulagi, the Japanese navy high command "racked our brains to contemplate countermeasures" and enthusiastically supported Mikawa's determination to strike the invasion beaches hard and quickly. ("The Eighth Fleet is going to surprise the enemy in Guadalcanal tonight. Come on, boys! Do your stuff!") But Yamamoto did not take the main fleet south until August 17, a full ten days after the American invasion.[93]

Indeed, Yamamoto appeared to believe that Mikawa's victory over the U.S. cruisers and destroyers off Savo had been sufficient to chase the Yankees out of the Solomon Islands. His chief of staff, Matome Ugaki, wrote on August 13 that "some enemies still remained in the Tulagi and Guadalcanal area, but now they are supposed to have been left behind with small craft when the enemy withdrew.... The most urgent thing at present is to send a troop there to mop up the enemy remnant, rescue the garrison, and repair the airfield."[94] All this was true, but incomplete. The enemy's demoralization was temporary, his determination permanent.

Vandegrift's marines hung on for the crucial middle two weeks in August during which they could have been pushed off the island or shattered on its beaches by determined Japanese counterattacks. On August 20 the first units of what would become the famed "Cactus Air Force" flew onto the muddy airstrip seized from the Japanese and renamed Henderson Field. Even then, a determined and coordinated Japanese air, sea, and land assault might well have destroyed either the American forces ashore on Guadalcanal or the small carrier-cruiser-destroyer fleet that provided distant and sporadic but essential support.

All that saved the United States Navy—and Marine Corps—from being thrown out of the Solomons with catastrophic loss of morale was Yamamoto's decision to inject his naval and airpower into the fighting piecemeal. The Japanese military and political leadership had concluded that the Americans could not mount an effective Pacific offensive until 1943 at the earliest, and Yamamoto ordered the main body of the Japanese fleet to Truk, still convinced that the enemy had assaulted Guadalcanal with a small raiding party that could be easily dislodged. Perhaps he also believed that the Guadalcanal landings were a feint to lure the Imperial Navy away from defense of the Home Islands. Whatever the motive, the Japanese fleet's trip down to Truk was quite leisurely, and it was not until August 20 that Yamamoto was at last jarred out of complacency by the news that at least one enemy carrier was in the Guadalcanal area. He at once placed a fifty-eight-ship task force, including fleet carriers *Zuikaku* and *Shokaku*, north of the Solomons under Admiral Nobutake Kondo and began sending a few reinforcements to Guadalcanal down The Slot from Rabaul. On August 24 the aggressively probing Japanese met an equally aggressive probe by the American carrier-cruiser fleet under Fletcher's command, which continued to provide Guadalacanal with distant air support. The Battle of the Eastern Solomons was essentially a stalemate. As at Coral Sea, Fletcher again allowed himself to be lured into launching his entire airpower against an enemy light carrier without waiting to see if heavier forces were in the neighborhood. (To his credit, he suspected they might be and briefly withheld his launch before giving way to temptation.) *Ryujo* was sunk, but planes from *Shokaku* and *Zuikaku* almost destroyed *Enterprise*.

Yamamoto was at once angered and energized by the results of the Battle of the Eastern Solomons as well as by the growing strength and menace of the Cactus Air Force at Henderson Field that chewed up Japanese transports and escorts as they steamed down The Slot toward Guadalcanal during daylight hours. He concluded that the loss of *Ryujo* was "most deplorable," and according to his chief of staff, "it is apparent that landing on Guadalcanal by transports is hopeless unless the enemy planes are wiped out. So the plan was revised to transport reinforcements by minesweepers and destroyers which would shuttle from our place [Rabaul] to that island at high speed every day" to appear off Guadalcanal in the midnight hours. Thus was born the famous "Tokyo Express" through which Yamamoto sought to exploit Japanese superiority in night fighting and navigation. But the admiral allowed himself to be lulled by army assertions that with just a bit more reinforcement, the Americans could be driven off the island. Victory was always just one battle away. With blind tenacity, the Japanese followed a rigid script of nighttime reinforcement and shelling of enemy positions on the island designed to shock the marines (and later army units) into surrender.[95]

The Americans countered with an initially inept employment of the limited air and naval resources at their disposal. Accounts of the Guadalcanal campaign suggest that coordination between the marine and navy fliers on Guadalcanal and the fleet offshore was usually sporadic at best.[96] Essentially, the airmen and sailors conducted separate campaigns, the sailors confronting the night-running Tokyo Express whenever and with whatever resources they could, the airmen rising each morning to battle enemy planes approaching Henderson Field and then bombing whatever enemy warships and transports remained within range from actions of the night or two before.

The fearsome conflicts with Japan's superb cruiser and destroyer forces off Guadalcanal in the autumn of 1942 forced the United States Navy to learn the art of night fighting in the crucible of battle. "Radar and voice communications would take much of the chance out of night fighting," particularly since the enemy had no radar and was often sadly deficient in radio equipment as well. But the new tools were "too recently acquired to have been mastered. The strengths and weaknesses of the new equipment and the best procedures for its use still had to be learned by those who used it."[97] American proficiency in night fighting grew only slowly and sporadically. Two months after the dreadful drubbing off Savo, Admiral Norman Scott's cruiser-destroyer force patrolling around Guadalcanal squandered an opportunity to wipe out a corresponding Japanese force screening the landing of reinforcements at Cape Esperance, and a month after that, Scott and Admiral Daniel Callahan were both killed in a wild melee between a Japanese battleship-destroyer force and American cruisers and destroyers in the same area. Radar clearly picked up the advancing enemy, but though Callahan was able to cross the Japanese T, he refused to open fire on the unsuspecting Japanese targets because he did not trust radar and feared that what was detected might be elements of his own fleet. Only after two onrushing enemy destroyers crossed his bows and disrupted his battle line did Callahan belatedly open fire. By this time, the fully alerted enemy was less than a mile away, and the U.S. force was subject to overwhelming short-range counterfire. In the ensuing melee the Americans lost two more cruisers and several destroyers. Fighting back desperately, they managed to shatter *Hiei*'s upper works with five- and eight-inch-gun fire and even punched a small hole in the battleship's hull that caused sufficient flooding to short out the big ship's electrical system. Badly afire, its crew depleted and stunned, *Hiei* staggered out of the fight and into the darkness, the rest of the Japanese force following in its wake. Barely able to sustain ten knots, the battleship was sunk the following day by the Cactus Air Force out of Henderson Field and aircraft from *Enterprise* before it could crawl away up The Slot. In the meantime, carrier *Wasp* had been blasted to pieces by three torpedoes in mid-September while on escort duty south of Guadalcanal, and at the inconclusive Battle of Santa Cruz on October 26, the Americans lost *Hornet* while continuing to whittle down the corps of ace Japanese carrier pilots.

Just when Japanese naval air reached the point that it could no longer compete qualitatively or quantitatively with the American enemy is unclear. Midway seems to have created a balance that lasted well into the Guadalcanal campaign. The battle for the lower Solomons that appeared at the time so frustrating and (for many long months) so inconclusive proved to be the anvil against which Japanese naval air and surface forces battered themselves to pieces. In combat around and above Guadalcanal, the Japanese began losing not only key elements of their surface navy but also large numbers of irreplaceable land-based pilots. While straining every industrial sinew to match American naval might on and above the sea, Japan had failed miserably to anticipate construction and engineering needs in its great offensive out into the Pacific. At a time when American naval Construction Battalions with their heavy equipment—bulldozers, graders, steam shovels, and the like—could carve an airstrip and support base out of the jungle in a matter of hours, the few Japanese construction units that existed "worked with picks, shovels, and wicker baskets." When the Americans stormed into the Solomons, Tokyo desperately needed intermediate air bases on the islands they firmly held in the central Solomons, several hundred miles from Guadalcanal. Instead, Tokyo rushed men and machines into Rabaul, 565 nautical miles directly west of Guadalcanal where day after day, without letup, Japan's best pilots flew three hours or more down The Slot through often turbulent and murky weather to engage the enemy for at most fifteen minutes of high-stress combat in his airspace. Rapidly dwindling fuel forced a breakoff and a desperate flight toward home, pilots often nursing heavily damaged aircraft through stormy skies without adequate radio bearings. Under such inhuman conditions, navigational errors even among the best pilots became the rule, not the exception. No one could stand up under the strain for long. "Had Japan possessed even one fifth of the American capacity for constructing air bases," Japanese writers commented bitterly after the war, the Guadalcanal air campaign might have ended differently. Just one effective intermediate base on the Shortland Islands, Choiseul, or at Munda where damaged planes could set down and exhausted pilots break off flying for a time would have made a crucial difference. But no such airfield was built in the six months between the arrival of the Imperial Japanese Navy in the upper Solomons and the American appearance at Guadalcanal.

> It was a terribly depressing situation. At the outset of the invasion [of Guadalcanal] our Zero fighters were superior in almost every respect to the American planes which they opposed, yet their combat effectiveness was constantly being sapped by the strain which the pilots suffered from too many hours spent in the cramped confines of the planes' cockpits. This disintegration of our effectiveness in air attack was enough to drive the combat commanders to the verge of insanity; they had spent years in developing their air units to peak efficiency, only now to have them shackled by strategic blindness.[98]

For want of perhaps a hundred bulldozers and men skilled in operating them, Japan lost its superb ground-based naval air force—and thus the war.

However misguided, the American offensive in the South Pacific critically abraded Japanese naval and airpower months before the vast new U.S. fleet arrived. Yamamoto must have sensed the swinging pendulum. But at the last possible moment when a show of nerve might have given Japan the stalemated victory it yearned for, its leading naval figure reacted in exactly the wrong way. Time and rising losses in cruisers, destroyers, and pilots together with violent and bloody battles ashore that steadily reduced the Japanese garrison exhausted Yamamoto's innate good sense, and this ostensibly most brilliant of admirals committed one final sin of omission. The fate of the American land and air forces on Guadalcanal depended absolutely on control of the adjacent waters. Nearly every night, Japanese naval forces resumed the command that American airpower exercised tenaciously by day. As late as mid-November, the issue remained as much in doubt as ever.[99] If the Americans were to be driven from the island or destroyed upon it, now was the time to do so. Their defeat could well be perceived on both sides of the Pacific as having turned the tide of war once again—and permanently—in Japan's favor. Midway would be viewed as an anomaly in an otherwise unstoppable Japanese advance that had successively overwhelmed American forces at Wake, Guam, Bataan, Corregidor, and now Guadalcanal.[100] Voices might have been raised in the United States to conclude a peace that would divide the Pacific among the Asian victors and the vanquished Americans.

Such a scenario was a very, very long shot to be sure, given both American outrage and industrial capacity. But it just might have materialized, especially if Hitler had already brought his powerful surface fleet together and allowed Raeder to send it out in one or two squadrons to prey on Atlantic shipping. During the somber autumn weeks of 1942, with Ultra in its last stages of impuissance and the Nazi submarine offensive beginning to crest, Roosevelt and King developed a fresh respect for the Japanese that bordered close to defeatism. As "the struggle for Guadalcanal assumed an importance that neither King nor F.D.R had anticipated," Roosevelt became, in his own words, "frankly. . . pessimistic at the moment about the whole situation." He "warned that the loss of Guadalcanal could devastate American public morale." King, who had hoped to conquer the enemy bastion of Rabaul farther up the Solomons chain at New Britain by the close of the year, "later confessed that he was thoroughly 'surprised by the violence and the persistence of the Japanese reaction to our movement into the Solomons.'" Surely now, in November 1942, while the fate of

Guadalcanal continued to hang in the balance, was the time to invoke traditional Japanese doctrine and risk a large portion of the fleet in combat with whatever American heavy and medium naval forces remained in the area. It was time, in sum, to risk *Yamato* and the just-commissioned *Musashi*.[101] The situation was what these monster superbattleships had been built for: to fight out in the islands of the Pacific, overwhelming advancing enemy surface forces and intimidating enemy morale. Only a badly damaged *Enterprise* remained to contest Japanese carrier power anywhere in the Pacific, whereas Yamamoto had an even dozen battlewagons in commission to confront America's three or four. Only *Yamato* and *Musashi*, however, could smother the equally new but much smaller 16-inch-gunned *North Carolina* and *South Dakota* classes.

But Yamamoto refused to commit his two greatest ships. Why? One undoubted reason was that Admiral Kondo believed he had destroyed or driven away all American naval forces in the Guadalcanal area on the night of November 12–13, as, indeed, he had. But he also knew, or should have been told, of the presence of new American battleships in the area. Fully two months before, *North Carolina* had appeared with the *Wasp* carrier task group only to be badly torpedoed. But *South Dakota* had been a major presence during the Battle of Santa Cruz on October 26 when Tom Gatch's boys had knocked twenty-six aircraft out of the sky. Yamamoto's best strategy—at once prudent and bold— would have been to send *Yamato* and *Musashi* down The Slot to cover the latest Tokyo Express against the possible appearance of new enemy battleships, then to chew up American positions with their massive 18.1-inch guns, whose explosive and concussive impact would surely have driven mad those Americans they did not kill.

Yamamoto may well have been intimidated by enemy airpower, ignoring the fact that *Yamato* and *Musashi* were warships of such size and strength as to constitute altogether different and vastly superior elements of sea power. The Cactus Air Force, no matter how gallant, did not remotely approximate in size the enormous air armada that Marc Mitscher was later forced to employ to smother the two ships with bombs and torpedoes off the Philippines and south of Kyūshū, respectively. The salient fact, however, that Yamamoto should have realized was that his superbattleships would be committed to battle at night when no battleship had ever been or ever would be destroyed by airpower.

Midway, however, had sapped Yamamoto's confidence, and thereafter *conservation* rather than *expenditure* of force became the watchword in the imperial fleet. On June 4, the admiral had sat on *Yamato*'s flag bridge digesting every morsel of the *Kido Butai*'s disaster with groans of anguish. Putting in at Truk several months later with his fleet on the way to the Solomons, Yamamoto seems to have had a premonition of impending personal as well as national calamity, writing to a friend, "I sense that my life must be completed in the next hundred days."[102] So Yamamoto, the supreme gambler, lost his nerve. Instead of throwing his two finest battleships into the fight for Guadalcanal at its climactic moment, he dispatched the old battle cruisers *Kirishima* and *Hiei*. The sea-air battles of mid-November that concluded with a dramatic night duel between capital ships sealed Japan's fate. *Hiei* was mauled by Callahan's gallant cruisers and destroyers on the night of the twelfth, then bombed to death the next morning. *Kirishima,* returning two nights later at the head of another cruiser-destroyer force, led by Vice Admiral Nobutake Kondo, found the fast new battleships *Washington* and *South Dakota* waiting along with four destroyers. The battle did not go all the Americans' way. The destroyer force was wiped out, and *South Dakota* suffered a massive failure to its electrical system that kept it useless for long moments while Japanese gunfire pummeled its upper works. But that left *Washington* free to shoot *Kirishima* to pieces, and the battle cruiser was scuttled the next morning. Kondo, on the bridge of the cruiser *Atago,* had had enough and rushed away. The Japanese would never again send a battleship force against Guadalcanal and Henderson Field.

Historians can profitably imagine what would have happened if Admiral Willis Augustus Lee on the nights of November 14–15, 1942, had confronted both—or even one—of Japan's superbattleships. Standing out of range of American 16-inch guns, *Yamato* and *Musashi* would have pounded *Washington* and *South Dakota* under the water before turning their huge 18-inch batteries on Henderson Field. With the Cactus Air Force ripped to pieces, the two Japanese ships could have returned night after night until the U.S. Marines and Army units would have either surrendered or evacuated. The battleship might well have resumed its place as queen of the seas. Instead, by refusing to risk his most precious ships in admittedly perilous circumstances, Yamamoto lost *Hiei, Kirishima,* the battle, the campaign, and whatever faint chance Japan might have had to keep its fledgling oceanic and East Asian empire through stalemate.

Yamamoto's faintheartedness reflected a peculiar aspect of the Japanese character that contributed to that island nation's defeat. To the people of Nippon, enmeshed in both a warrior culture and a scarcity economy, warships were sacred entities. Each of the big carriers and battlewagons carried a portrait of the emperor, and the loss of any one of these vessels was deemed a national disaster spiritually as well as economically. Crews believed their ships to be irreplaceable, and they fought those ships to the bitter end; the few who at last abandoned a sinking or burning vessel did so in tears. Not so the Americans. Ships, however much they might be a temporary or even long-term home, were, in the last analysis, pieces of machinery that were expendable. When they could no longer function, they were abandoned, with regret to be sure but with anticipation that a replacement would soon be on the way. Although a few men wept at seeing their ship go down or burn uncontrollably, the great majority seem to have taken the attitude of two sailors on the sinking *Hornet* at Santa Cruz. As they went down the lines from the fatally stricken carrier, one asked the other if he would reenlist. "Goddamit, yes," the other replied. "On the new *Hornet*."[103] The supreme irony of *Yamato* and *Musashi* was that their very existence as the world's greatest battleships precluded their effective use. By the end of January 1943, the Japanese conceded defeat, moved their fleet back to Truk, and over a two-night period removed the last of their by now starving and tattered troops from Guadalcanal.

The Imperial Japanese Navy was burdened by more than the low morale of its commander during the Solomons campaign. It simply did not possess the detailed intelligence of enemy strength and movement available to the Americans through the breaking of the Purple Code. Throughout the Pacific war, the Japanese navy fought blind in many ways on many fronts: its intelligence was poor to nonexistent, its radar belated and crude, and its antisubmarine instruments rudimentary. In technology as in so many other areas, the Japanese were simply overwhelmed, as Yamamoto surely understood.

Indeed, the entire Japanese war effort was grossly inefficient. In November 1946 the United States Strategic Bombing Survey issued a devastating report on Tokyo's failures and follies in mobilizing for total war.[104] Well before Pearl Harbor and on through the early months of the Pacific campaign, the Japanese should have planned for and carried out a dramatic increase in shipbuilding of every kind to replace expected battle losses and meet the dramatically increased demands for transportation and reinforcements created by the new Southeast Asian and oceanic empire. Instead, the warlords of Tokyo allowed themselves to become so "elated with their successes" that production bottlenecks "became practically uncontrollable." Although the navy did establish a unified merchant and naval shipbuilding control board that proved somewhat effective, the country was completely unprepared to undertake the kind of mass production in which the Allies and particularly the Americans excelled. Industrial administration and supervision soon became chaotic, labor shortages grew steadily due to the drafting of ever larger numbers of men into the armed services, and the quality of workers who remained in the shipbuilding industries deteriorated.

After August 1942 the American submarine offensive began to decisively affect the Japanese war effort, and Tokyo paid dearly for its prewar decision to concentrate naval construction almost exclusively on large offensive warships. Forced to expand construction of both merchant vessels and naval escorts, Japan's admirals discovered that delays in increasing and "rationalizing" production at the beginning of the war could not be overcome. Existing bottlenecks became more pronounced and complicated. According to the Bombing Survey, "Only makeshift countermeasures could be employed as the demand arose, since a fundamental solution had become impossible." Not only was Japan's industrial capacity a fraction of America's, but the steady bickering between the Japanese army and navy over allocation of funds, resources, and production, together with "inadequate production administration and poor production technique[s]," created major industrial crises that were never resolved. Ever growing shortages of steel, labor, oxygen (for steel cutting and repairing), copper, copper alloys, cutting tools, and overall shipbuilding facilities steadily slowed those industries devoted to naval construction and repair. By November 1943 conditions were exacerbated by steady declines in imports from the ever shrinking empire, by a decrease in truck and automobile production that crippled local land transportation and thus the flow of critically needed matériel from one industrial site to another, and by growing food shortages in the industrial cities. A year later naval and aviation construction and repair, like nearly all other aspects of Japanese industry, had been brought almost to a standstill. Japan's leadership fell into despair. Matome Ugaki wrote on November 9, 1944:

> Today a telegram from the chief of the Operations Bureau of the Naval General Staff informed us that 418 planes (all kinds combined) and 410 planes of replenishment were all the navy could muster by the 8th, 15th, and the end of this month. My God! Eight hundred planes! How can we manage with this strength? We have to ask the army for the rest. And when those reserves are expended, what are we going to do? It must be a reasonable request to ask the monthly production of five thousand planes, army and navy combined, today, three years after the outbreak of war.[105]

Manpower shortages were as debilitating as industrial shortages. The power of Japan, an archetypal twentieth-century warfare state, depended upon a comparatively small group of highly and intensively trained professionals possessing fanatic morale and will. There was no flexibility in this warrior-caste system that would allow for a rapid and effective buildup or replenishment of manpower. Throughout World War II Japan (and to a somewhat lesser extent Germany and Italy as well) depended on the men it possessed at the beginning. The highly trained flyers and sailors fought until they died or were seriously wounded. There was no routine rotation homeward, no provision for assignment of a select number of combat veterans to effectively train a next generation of warriors. Thus, every loss of a Japanese capital ship or the destruction of another carrier's aircrew (as occurred to *Shokaku, Zuikaku, Hiyo,* and *Zuiho* at Santa Cruz) was catastrophic. Every American loss, on the other hand, however heartbreaking, was eventually replaceable. By the end of 1943 the Imperial Navy had been sharply reduced in all categories of warship, including its splendid heavy cruisers and large destroyers. The empire had been thrown into a defensive posture that it could never surmount.

The fault could be laid at the feet of a naval service that failed to develop and prosecute the kind of daring strategic vision that might have saved it from disaster. Increasingly frustrated by American curbs on their aggression, Japan's sailors substituted contempt for thought in approaching the dangers of a Pacific war. Ugaki's diary entries just before and after Pearl Harbor read like a script from some dumb wartime Hollywood B movie about the Yellow Peril. "In my opinion," he wrote toward the end of October 1941, the Americans "must fully realize how foolish it would be to fight with us.... To beat such guys into bits will be good for our empire." A week before the Pearl Harbor attack he added: "The United States has not accepted a single demand of our empire. How they insult us! The only way is to make short work of the United States." Four days before Nagumo's flyers appeared over Hawaii, Ugaki rationalized: "It isn't unfair to assault one asleep. This ensures victory over a most careless enemy. No other means of frustrating this numerous and big enemy can be found but to baffle them at the start." (In this instance, Yamamoto did not share his chief of staff's sentiments: "It does not do to cut a sleeping throat," he observed after learning of *Kido Butai's* stunning success at Pearl Harbor.) And, finally, on December 6 (December 5 in the United States): "Hawaii is just like a rat in a trap. Enjoy your dream of peace just one more day!" And two days after Pearl Harbor: "Enemy consternation is beyond description. It is their breakfast time at 0320 [Tokyo time]. While they were at their breakfast table, great masses of Japanese airplanes like bolts from the blue. I can imagine their utter surprise." And, finally, on December 10, noting U.S. radio reports of possible widespread courts-martial among the top navy brass: "Shall we send our judge advocates there to defend these officers, saying that Japan should be accused instead, since it was Japan that attacked there? Ha! Ha!" As Japan spread over hundreds of thousands of square miles of Southeast Asia, the South Pacific, and the Indian Ocean, Combined Fleet staff planners went on an orgy of speculation. Rear Admiral Tamon Yamaguchi (who would lose his life at Midway) proposed the successive conquests of Fiji, Samoa, New Zealand, Australia, Midway, and Hawaii, in preparation for an invasion of California in 1943. Although the plan was understandably treated as "wild fantasy" by both naval headquarters and the Combined Fleet, it reflected the contempt for the United States that gripped Japanese ruling circles between Pearl Harbor and the Doolittle raid.[106] But beneath delight lay unease. The eventual recovery of the United States was "certain," Ugaki added in his January 5 diary entry, and Britain would someday reappear in South Asia in force.

Midway transformed the enemy into something akin to a devil, and an underlying tone of self-pity (matching that of many German military and naval officials) began to creep into Japanese discourse. There was simply no way to stand up to the prodigious industrial might of the United States. After Japan had been defeated in the great air-sea battles around Guadalcanal, Ugaki recorded a message from Tokyo warning the fleet that the Americans might be planning a "surprise landing" on Japanese soil from submarines in revenge for the Pearl Harbor attack of the year before. Ugaki added that "news from New York" picked up by Japanese shortwave-radio monitors indicated that the enemy was well aware of declining Japanese air strength in the Solomons and planned to exploit it. "I fear that the enemy will get more conceited and eventually we'll be overwhelmed by the enemy air might. The enemy doesn't care about losing battleships, cruisers, and destroyers, and is trying to beat us with its overwhelming air power."[107]

Many Japanese sailors lost faith. Isoroku Yamamoto is still widely regarded in the West as the finest strategist, tactician, and all-around battle leader that Japan produced in World War II; some might even rank him with Horatio Nelson and Chester Nimitz as a bold and daring naval commander. Certainly, he towered above everyone else in the Japanese fleet. Yet to subordinates he was increasingly perceived as possessing feet of clay. After the war Tameichi Hara, Japan's finest destroyer skipper, charged Yamamoto with a "grave blunder" in withdrawing the fleet to home waters after Midway and with a "great blunder" in committing his destroyer forces piecemeal to the Solomons campaign where they, along with the cruisers, were badly chewed up by the increasingly bold and effective enemy. Yamamoto's colleagues in the senior ranks were even more scathing. In the 1980s Professor Ikuhiko Hata organized a roundtable discussion among Japanese naval veterans from the rank of captain on up for a special magazine issue on the Pacific war and was shocked to find that "the entire conversation turned, from beginning to end, on reviling Yamamoto." Criticisms were many and varied, "but all of them shared the view that Yamamoto's fatal mistake had been the offensive strategy he adopted from Pearl Harbor onward, arguing that he should have followed the traditional defensive strategy" of somehow luring the American fleet to decisive battle in Micronesia. Former vice admiral Nakazawa Tasukuwho, who had headed the Operations Section and later the Operations Bureau in the Office of the Chief of Naval Operations, argued that it would have been much better if Shimada Shigetaro, a classmate of Yamamoto and navy minister in the Tojo cabinet of October 1941, had been given command of the Combined Fleet, "not because Shimada would have been a more brilliant commander than Yamamoto, but because Shimada's experience in the Operations Section would never have let him contemplate anything other than a defensive strategy of interception." A former naval captain and gunnery authority grumbled that "Yamamoto didn't know a thing about using battleships."[108]

In reviewing the increasingly melancholy life and reputation of Isoruko Yamamoto, which so closely paralleled the decline and fall of his beloved navy, one is inevitably reminded of the ancient observation that victory has a hundred fathers while defeat is an orphan. Yet the criticisms leveled at him after the war by subordinates and colleagues alike have the ring of truth. For all his impulsive gambling, Yamamoto simply did not possess the kind of killer instinct necessary to retain the initiative in the Pacific war. After Midway, the Imperial Japanese Navy—with the single exception of Gunichi Mikawa's swift and devastating riposte at Savo—lost its spirit as a live and attacking force. Had Yamamoto committed his superbattleships at Guadalcanal, they might have decisively turned the tide of battle, particularly since, for many months after the Battle of Santa Cruz, American fleet-carrier strength in the Solomons was down to one or at most two units, whereas Jisaburo Ozawa's carrier fleet, however shorn of frontline pilots, still possessed a numerical advantage.

In the end, one is left to contemplate Axis ineptitude as well as comparative weakness: the folly of fighting an uncoordinated war, the foolishness of holding back an inferior but powerful fleet from battle, and, in Japan's case, the terrible fragility of national character at war. Exultant and contemptuous in victory, particularly of the sneak-attack variety, Japanese morale swiftly deflated to a state of timidity and despair by defeat. After 1942 Japan's heart was no longer in the fight to defeat the United States but only in the effort to somehow and in some way contain its inexorable advance. Its warriors would defend what they had and what they had won with fanatic fury, backpedaling only slowly and bloodily across the Pacific—back up the Solomons to the Bismarck barrier, then beyond in 1943–1944, even as the enemy seized the Gilberts, Marshalls, and Marianas before moving on to the southern Philippines—all the while their leaders buoying themselves up as best they could by exaggerated claims of enemy losses.[109] The kamikaze attacks against the U.S. fleet as it approached home waters in early 1945 and the suicide sortie of *Yamato* that spring revealed the intellectual as well as moral bankruptcy of the Japanese armed forces.

Germany's failure was grounded as much in geography as in psychology. At the one moment in its history when the Reich desperately needed an amphibious-warfare capability, it was sadly lacking. Norway should have opened Hitler's eyes to the enormous possibilities of a limited seaborne assault across narrow seas and provided a crude working model of how to achieve it. A limited lodgment on the beaches of Kent or Sussex could have been expanded to victorious dimensions by a follow-on parachute assault that would have bypassed much of the static, layered defenses that the largely unprepared British hastily flung up after Dunkirk. General Franz Halder's comment that the preparations for Sealion were not only so confused but also so scattered that no one really knew what was going on must be placed against the prolonged, complicated, and meticulous Allied preparations between 1942 and 1944 for a forcible return to the Continent.[110] The Allies had to iron out procedural differences and personal conflicts inherent in coalition warfare. But by June 1944 they had become highly adept in the enormous complexities of amphibious warfare, mounting more than a dozen such operations, good and bad—including Dieppe—in Europe and North Africa alone. They learned the art of power projection from the sea and developed the capacity for swift innovation and exploitation needed to make such warfare work. Such daring was well beyond Adolf Hitler's conception. His fear of the sea precluded serious, sustained planning for amphibious warfare, leaving Erich Raeder to expand Germany's small but splendid surface fleet piecemeal in a feckless effort to force some sort of naval victory in the Atlantic. In the end, it was this piecemeal expenditure of *both* Japanese and German naval resources at climactic moments—around Guadalcanal and with *Bismarck* and the other major units of the German fleet—that doomed the Axis cause.

CHAPTER 9

Defending the Atlantic Lifeline

CLAY BLAIR HAS ARGUED that in the early war years, Churchill and his colleagues constantly overestimated the U-boat menace, a mistake, Blair claims, that historians have faithfully reflected ever since. "In a word, the U-boat peril in World War II was and has been vastly overblown." As a consequence, contemporary and subsequent impressions of the Battle of the Atlantic were "wildly distorted." In 1939 Britain possessed more than five thousand merchant vessels of varying sizes; its fallen French, Dutch, Norwegian, and Belgian allies sailed perhaps another several hundred or so to British ports after June 1940. During the first eighteen months of battle, Germany possessed at any one time no more than a score of operational submarines of limited size, range, and offensive power. The Nazi submarine effort did not reach its apex until 1942–1943, by which time the United States was in the war and U.S. shipyards were beginning to turn out merchantmen at an astonishing rate in an incredibly short time. To argue, therefore, that the German David could slay the Allied Goliath was unrealistic. The very nature of the convoy system meant that when Dönitz's assassins found one, losses could be appalling, but, as Blair maintains, the vast majority of Allied convoys during World War II were not found, instead sailing safely and undetected to their destinations.[1]

But Blair himself is guilty of some serious distortions. Britain lost nearly one-third of its prewar merchant marine (roughly sixteen hundred vessels) in the first eighteen months of the war, during a time when it was struggling to hold a worldwide empire that required maintaining its maritime resources on a global scale. And losses in the Atlantic were due to the *balanced* nature of the German assault against enemy shipping. Manageable as it might be by itself, the Nazi submarine threat became a frightful menace when combined, as it was, with airpower and surface raiders.

Moreover, the *quantitative* sinking of ships was only one measure—and not a particularly accurate one—of U-boat success. *Qualitative* sinkings were equally important. Although throughout the war Dönitz's lads happily attacked any convoy found and any ships in that convoy, there is circumstantial evidence that oil tankers were, properly, the prime targets. By 1939 oil in its many guises had become the lifeblood of the advanced industrial world. Sink enough tankers, blow up their cargo or send it spilling in flaming bursts onto the sea, deprive Britain—and later Anglo-British forces in North Africa, Italy, and northwestern Europe—of enough petroleum, oil, and lubricants, and the Allied war machine, on the ground and in the air, would come crunching to a halt, no matter whether the British public was hungry.

This strategy was invoked as soon as the United States entered the war and Dönitz could get his first five boats across the Atlantic. A disproportionate number of tankers sailing alone from the Venezuelan oil fields across the Caribbean, through the Straits of Florida, past the North Carolina Outer Banks, and on to New York for eventual dispatch to British destinations were destroyed by German U-boats during their passage up the U.S. East Coast. When the Americans at last got these invaluable vessels into proper convoys with decent air support, resourceful German skippers went after the convoys with a killer resolve. "Unmitigated disaster" befell TM(Trinidad-Mediterranean)-1 when this too lightly escorted convoy set sail from Port of Spain in January 1943 with nine good-size tankers filled with about thirty million gallons of fuel, "much of it high-octane aviation spirit" meant for the recently opened North African front. Spotted by U-522 shortly after departure and soon beset by a seven-boat wolf pack that overwhelmed the single destroyer and three corvettes in escort, TM-1 staggered across the central Atlantic in ever dwindling numbers, fighting for its life night and day. By the time the convoy reached Gibraltar on February 8, it had been whittled down to only two tankers. The seven others, comprising 56,453 gross tons and carrying nearly 22 million gallons of precious cargo, lay as shattered hulks at the bottom of the Atlantic, dispatched by Dönitz's determined U-boat sailors.[2]

While Karl Dönitz's U-boats *by themselves* did not come anywhere near cutting the Allied lifeline to Britain, as it was so deeply feared in 1941 and 1942 that they might, close examination strongly suggests that the total German effort at sea and against British ports by plane, mine, and surface warship as well as U-boat between 1939 and 1942 did indeed come as close to victory as those at the time feared. Moreover, the German effort proved extraordinarily disruptive to British domestic and economic life, with catastrophic consequences for the future international power and status of the nation and its empire.

All this was accomplished under terrible political constraint, for in fact Adolf Hitler *never* really settled in his mind whether he wished to destroy England or to embrace it. Indeed, he never indicated clearly to anyone exactly what his strategic vision was, or how far it extended. His most bloodthirsty public threats were often followed by quiet private reservations. Dönitz wanted to wage a pitiless trade war with his U-boats against Britain to starve it and bring it to its knees—and to the peace table. Erich Raeder stood right behind him, poised to use the small surface navy to the same effect. The führer's Directive No. 9 of November 29, 1939, reflected this policy, stating that "destruction" of the enemy's economy was the quickest way to victory. Once war came, Hitler made the U-boat an immediate priority, though it would take months if not years to translate into a plethora of wolf packs at sea.

Yet as late as January 1941, Hitler indicated to the Wehrmacht leadership that although the war would be prosecuted with vigor both in the air and at sea, he was "still ready to negotiate peace with Britain." Two months later he reversed himself, approving Raeder's insistence upon "a concentrated single-minded operation by U-boats and the Luftwaffe against British maritime transport capacity." He reversed himself again the following July as tensions and sinkings rose in the Atlantic following the U.S. occupation of Iceland. The Russian campaign seemed to be going well, and Hitler said that he was "most anxious to postpone the United States entry into the war for another one or two months." Perhaps the entire U-boat campaign in the North Atlantic should be shut down for a time. Opportunities to deal with the Americans could be seized once the eastern war was wrapped up. The following October, just weeks before Pearl Harbor, with incidents in the Atlantic now threatening overt and immediate U.S. intervention, Hitler made the remarkable assertion to the chief of staff of the Naval War Staff, Vice Admiral Kurt Fricke, that he was "even now ready at any time...to conclude peace with Britain, as the European space which Germany has secured for itself through the conduct of the war so far is sufficient for the future of the German people." In fact, Hitler had already lost the war in the East and thus the war in general. His last faint opportunity to defeat the entire Red Army had disappeared in August. But with advance elements of the Wehrmacht continuing to slip and slide toward Moscow through the late-autumn rains and sleet of the Russian steppe, neither he nor anyone else at the time could envisage such a thing.[3]

Political constraints on a successful trade campaign were nearly matched by technological constraints. It is well to recall how perfect a metaphor German submarine-design and -construction programs were for the entire forced-draft Nazi rearmament program of the mid- and late thirties. Born clandestinely in foreign yards, the U-boat program after 1933 was the frequent victim of a command economy struggling to create a vast war machine in a few brief years from a limited industrial and resource base. Corners invariably had to be cut, and ruthless priorities had to be imposed by men like Hermann Göring who were both inexperienced and essentially uninterested in the subtleties and complexities of military buildup. Moreover, that buildup was always subject to political assumptions and imperatives. Prior to mid-1938, Hitler and his senior military people assumed that, with the Anglo-German naval treaty in hand, France and the Soviet Union would be Germany's chief enemies in any future war. U-boat construction was oriented in that direction; small 500-ton vessels were built, suitable for operations along the shores of the Baltic and the French Atlantic coast, together with a handful of Type VII submarines somewhat larger than the conventional U-boat design of 1914–1918 in order to undertake distant operations against maritime trade around distant French colonies. Moreover, "substantial developments" had been achieved in overall U-boat capabilities: "better torpedoes with bubble-less ejection, trackless and with non-contact pistols; the ability to lay mines from all U-boats, to transmit and receive signals both surfaced and submerged, greater diving depths, and increased power of resistance through welded pressure hulls," according to one U-boat skipper in an essay written for the British Admiralty in 1945.[4]

With the formulation of Plan Z against England in June 1938, U-boat construction was quickly ramped up in anticipation of a war to seal off the western approaches to the British Isles and to cut the Atlantic lifeline between the United Kingdom and North America. But time was too short before the outbreak of hostilities the following year to create a substantial U-boat force. Germany simply did not possess the requisite productive resources to cover militarily every favorable, or unfavorable, political commitment, development, twist, and turn while creating a world-class army, air force, and navy. Between 1933 and 1945, the Nazi war machine lurched from one emphasis to another, proving far less formidable than it might have been had young Hitler (he was but forty-three when he came to power, the same age as John F. Kennedy) been patient enough to create balanced and mutually supportive military forces. Short of both time and resources, Hitler and Göring had to largely replicate rather than advance the highly promising submarine technology bequeathed by World War I. Dönitz had no choice but to go along. The Type VII boats that came into limited service in 1939 and formed the backbone of Dönitz's North Atlantic offensive down to 1944 were "reliant, resilient, and robust. But they were also refined examples" of the submarine technology with which Germany had fought World War I. About 220 feet long and 20 feet wide, displacing 769 tons, capable of a surface speed of 17.7 knots (7.6 knots submerged), and with an extreme range of a bit less than 8,000 miles and a maximum range submerged of 80 miles at 4 knots, the most advanced Type VIIC U-boat in no way could be compared to the big 1,500-ton U.S. fleet boats that roamed the Far Pacific at the same time. Not until 1942 was Dönitz able to build a handful of advanced Type IX boats that could dive to nearly 500 feet, with a cruising range of nearly 30,000 miles.[5]

Dönitz did what he could to overcome the situation. His 1943 *U-boat Commander's Handbook*—clearly a compendium of lessons already learned and informally disseminated to new U-boat crews—insisted that submarines had to be of small size in order to ensure "good general maneuverability" both above and below the seas. Should the size of the Type VII and IX classes be increased "in order, for example, to substitute for [their] proper use a greater suitability for minor (additional) operations, such as gunnery operations, [their] underwater *fighting power* is proportionately reduced."[6] But Clay Blair, then a young veteran of the highly successful U.S. submarine campaign in the Pacific, was appalled at his first close-up view of a German submarine shortly after the end of the war. Small and cramped, the U-boat was clearly inferior in size, maneuverability, structural integrity, and firepower to the American fleet boats. Above all, the kind of substantial upgrades in detection gear necessary to keep the U-boats abreast of continual Allied technological advances was simply not possible on such small hulls. Hitler might conceivably have made the Atlantic war a very close contest had he possessed not only more but bigger submarines. As it was, that conflict swiftly became, in Winston Churchill's words, a "war of groping and drowning, of ambuscade and stratagem, of science and seamanship" carried out on a particularly cruel sea of brutal winds; driving snows; massive, cascading waters; and bitter cold.[7] To perish or be cast adrift in such dreadful waters was an ordeal past comprehension.

Dönitz and his U-boat sailors were forced to fight Allied science with stratagem, seamanship, audacity, and total immorality. In thoughtful and well-
researched efforts Jordan Vause, Timothy P. Mulligan, and to a lesser extent
Eric Christian Rust have tried to provide at least a partial rehabilitation of the
German U-boat commanders of World War II. The submariners were not
stamped from a single simple Nazi mold, Vause, Mulligan, and Rust maintain,
but rather were often complex and contradictory young men caught up in an
age of crisis who shared a simple patriotism and a single trait: the desire to do a
good job and to survive. Werner Henke, for example, fourteenth on the all-
time list of World War II U-boat aces, defied "American stereotypes and his
own officer corps' self-image," emerging from the historical mist as an "impetuous, ill-disciplined, hot-headed and cosmopolitan" fellow, "a dare-devil and a
ladies' man; a U-boat commander with an extensive collection of American jazz
and Cole Porter phonograph records."[8]

Erich Topp, himself a U-boat commander at twenty-six, crushingly rebukes
such arguments. The average German sailor, at least those in the U-boat arm,
became a fanatic Nazi, though not, usually, a party member, with little sense of
individual consciousness or morality, no matter how much he may have liked
Cole Porter. His job was helping his U-boat mates torpedo and drown as many
Allied merchantmen as he could to ensure the survival, and for the greater glory,
of the Third Reich. That was what he did or was asked to do—nothing more,
nothing less. "Each submariner obviously enjoyed and profited from the élite
image of the U-boat arm. The image also brought a deep sense of obligation.
One was profoundly conscious of the privilege of being a member of *Freikorps
Dönitz*. This created morale that was strong enough to camouflage or mask the
overriding drive of every human being—to survive. That explains why, even in
March–April 1945, submariners still went on patrol," though the loss rate by
this time in crossing the Bay of Biscay and then seeking out enemy shipping
was 90 percent or more.[9]

Years later, a U-boat survivor speaking of the Nazi era could allude to only a
vague "apprehension" over the "rude methods of the SA."[10] The Hitler gang
and its Nazi regime in the last analysis revered war, power, and violence, and the
U-boat arm—the "U-boatwaffe"—was no more able to avoid the implications
of such an atmosphere than any other branch of the German armed forces between 1939 and 1945, and that included the German surface fleet. Hitler's submariners were burdened by another legacy—that of Walther Schwieger, U-20,
and the exultant reaction of the kaiser and his people to that slaughter of the

innocents aboard *Lusitania* and all that it said and portended about the early-twentieth-century German character.

Dönitz's *U-boat Commander's Handbook* states not only that a successful captain must be audacious, quick-witted, a cool and clear thinker, indomitable, resolute, steadfast, tenacious, and skillful but that he must also be clever, obstinate, prudent when absolutely necessary to save his command and fulfill his mission, and, above all, "unscrupulous." Dönitz hammered home the transcendent importance of the Nazi submarine campaign:

> In the destruction of the enemy's overseas trade, the submarine is a particularly suitable naval weapon with which to challenge the enemy's naval superiority. The continuous successful use of the submarine in the war on merchant shipping is, therefore, in the long run, of decisive strategical importance for the total course of the war, since the enemy, who is dependent on his overseas trade, is in the position that, for him, the loss of his sea communications means the loss of the war.[11]

Dönitz clearly had no thoughts of the submarine as a terror weapon. It was, merely, a supreme strategic tool whose greatest advantage lay in its "invisibility." The admiral preached that surprise and constant vigilance would bring victory. He impressed upon his young killers that whether engaged in great convoy battles in the Atlantic or seeking out the heavy elements of the British fleet in home waters, "he who sees first has won!"[12]

The young men of the U-boat arm did all they could for their adored leader, and for a brief time in late 1940 and again in 1941–1942 when there were at last enough submarines to form wolf packs and the British (and then the Americans) were still reeling from the onslaught of war, it was sufficient to give the Germans a temporary upper hand. Prior to Pearl Harbor, Dönitz and his intelligence people were aided immeasurably by the actions of American insurance companies that openly shared information on convoy compositions and sailings with Swiss and British counterparts.

Dönitz had drawn several lessons from the earliest U-boat actions, and the primary one involved C3I—or See Cube Eye—command, communications, control, and intelligence. "With only a very small number of U-boats available for any operation," it would be madness to dilute their strength by designating one as a command and control vessel. To function effectively in gathering three or more U-boats and directing them to the target, a command and control ship would have to remain far enough away from a convoy to be beyond reach of any escorting aircraft. And with their low freeboard and conning towers, submarines were in any case inherently unsuitable as command vessels, particularly in the often towering seas and gales of a North Atlantic autumn, winter, and early spring. "Finally, the subordinate commander who would be detailed for this duty was urgently required at home for the training of new boats and crews and supervising their final preparations for sea as soon as they became fit for service."[13]

Dönitz explored another possibility: that his submarines, either individually or collectively, could be effectively controlled from ashore. Following several "experiments" in this regard, he reached the conclusion he had probably been looking for all along:

> That I could myself quite easily direct the *whole* tactical operation against a convoy from my headquarters ashore. . . . My primary functions in this respect were to pass on to U-boats at sea all the information regarding the enemy which I had received from a variety of intelligence sources, to correct or clarify any wrong or misleading information sent by the U-boats themselves, to issue orders to individual U-boats or groups, to coordinate the duties of maintaining contact and to intervene in the event of contact with the enemy being lost. My control, therefore, extended *up to the moment of the launching of an attack,* but *not* to the actual attack itself.

Once a wolf pack had been assembled around a convoy, it was each U-boat commander for himself acting independently. "It was on the commanders and their crews that the burden of the fight lay, and it was to them therefore that the credit for any success should be given." In his handbook for the U-boat skippers, the admiral noted that the chief weakness and vulnerability of the submarine lay in its slow speed. The weakness could be overcome only by permitting—indeed demanding—each captain to operate on his own, for only he knew the unique characteristics of his ship and his crew, which were the decisive factors in waging "annihilating attack" on the adversary.[14] Little wonder that the U-boat service loved its commander with a blind devotion that never flagged. He would direct them to glory, then stand back and let them take the credit.

Given the technological constraints of 1939–1940, Dönitz's decision to gather the entire conduct of Germany's U-boat offensive in his hands was probably wise and perhaps even inevitable. But the fate of the entire enterprise rested, as the admiral realized, on the absolute security of communications. Should the enemy ever break into German naval codes and read the Enigma-machine traffic in more or less real time, the result would be disastrous. Dönitz therefore admonished his captains to keep their signals as tight and brief as possible. On the other hand, he identified a wide range of information, from weather reports to convoy sightings and surveillance, that he deemed of vital importance in directing a U-boat campaign across the length and breadth of the Atlantic. His skippers would have to fill the airwaves to keep him fully informed and abreast of the latest developments.[15] And that would prove to be the U-boat's Achilles' heel.

The tightly controlled and firmly directed wolf pack was one answer to the problem of upgrading U-boat capabilities to meet mission requirements. Once war began, German scientists and technicians provided a few other solutions. Periscopes aboard the German U-boats became "mechanical work[s] of art," trained right or left by means of pedals. The operator's right hand controlled an angling mirror that permitted vision from seventy degrees above to fifteen degrees below the horizontal. The left hand operated a compensating lever that allowed for the motion of the sea and the small movements of the boat itself. A handle allowed for correction of the lenses, providing an alternative magnification of from 1.5 to 0.6, with various degrees of shading against the glare of either the sun or enemy searchlights or rockets. A "Kontax," or movie camera, could be used with the periscope, which could also be warmed to prevent misting of the mirror. "Obviously, the view through the periscope includes crosswires, range-scale and bearing from a compass-repeater, while a glance upward or downward enables gunfire to be controlled with the aid of various graduated dials." The torpedo firing button was close by.[16]

Near the periscope and coupled directly to it and the ship's gyroscope was the main attack-table, a "triangle-solving . . . geared calculating apparatus" with various graphs and cams that made it possible to fire at five different targets in a convoy in the space of a few seconds. The attack-table was attached not only to the periscopes and gyroscopes but also to another apparatus called the attack-sight, a hyperpowerful binocular on the U-boat's bridge for use during surface attacks. The attack-sight was capable of withstanding pressures up to one hundred fathoms, or six hundred feet, and could thus be left on the bridge should the submarine have to dive suddenly to escape enemy escorts or aircraft.

Finally, German torpedoes could be set automatically to alter course up to ninety degrees away from the directions in which they were fired, providing even greater flexibility to the attacking U-boat. In World War I submarine captains literally had to aim at targets with their entire vessel since the torpedoes upon leaving their tubes continued on a course preset by automatic gyroscopic steering mechanisms. But in 1940 U-boat commanders were no longer committed to a fixed course during attack; with proper torpedo settings, they could plunge into the middle of a darkened convoy and start spraying their deadly fish all around, certain to obtain many hits so long as the torpedoes were properly set.

Heinz Schaeffer, a U-boat ace of the later war years, provides a graphic description of how a night submarine attack against a large enemy convoy worked. As the U-boat, its commander on the bridge, rushed through the darkness into the midst of a flock of enemy ships,

> the torpedo-officer at the attack-table reports "Lined up," and the switch is made by which the attack-table is connected with the gyro-compass and the attack-sight. The mechanism churns around and two red lamps indicate that the process of calculating the information which has been fed into it is not yet completed. The lights go out after a few moments, and the petty-officer at the attack-table reports the resulting settings to the torpedo-officer. From this point onwards our own alterations of course are of little importance, being allowed for automatically. The target must simply be held in the crosswires of the attack-sight in order that the apparatus can do its job. The torpedo-officer gives the order "Follow" to the attack-table. A lamp glows and the attack-table is now controlling the binoculars [that is, the attack-sight] on the bridge. Meanwhile, the constantly changing firing settings are being transmitted automatically to the torpedoes and set on their angling mechanism. With this system we can fire at any moment and on any course, provided that the 90-degree limiting angle is not exceeded. The torpedoes will run to a pattern that spread[s] roughly over a ship's length by the time they reach the range of the target. We turn to our attacking course.[17]

In an age on the verge of a revolution in *electronic* wizardry, Dönitz thus provided his sailors with the most advanced *mechanical* aids possible. For a long time those crude computers and the weapons they controlled made the German U-boat a terrifying adversary against the handful of British corvettes, sloops, and destroyers with half-trained crews that were ranged against it. Incredibly, "no studies had been made in the Admiralty" or anywhere else in His Majesty's government of the antisubmarine campaign of 1915–1918, or of the effect of the convoy system. The British Naval Staff history of the trade war between 1939 and 1945 is merciless on this point:

> In the inter-war period the Royal Navy never undertook any systematic examination and analysis of the *guerre de course* waged against Allied shipping in the course of the First World War. At no time was there any study

that related the number of operational U-boats to the number of merchantmen which they sank, and there was no analysis of the role of antisubmarine units at the time when they made kills. There was no attempt
to examine the loss of time and tonnage imposed by independent routing
of merchantmen, and there was no attempt to examine the implications of
the fact that in the First World War the number of ships sailing in convoys
and the number of U-boats sunk both increased at much the same rate,
the figures of one quarter excepted.

The development of the underwater sound-detection system "asdic" in the
midthirties had induced a fatal confidence among Britain's sailors that "the day
of the submarine as a weapon of trade destruction was over." After all, the vast
majority of enemy U-boats in 1915–1918 had operated near offshore of the
British Isles. Those of 1939 were just enough larger and possessed sufficient
communication capabilities to roam effectively far out in the deep, unrestricted
waters of the open Atlantic, and in packs, if necessary. The British lords of the
Admiralty failed to grasp this fact sufficiently, and, after all, had not Herr Hitler
publicly renounced (in 1936) "submarine attacks on merchant shipping"? When
the führer abrogated the promise in July 1939, "it was too late to build up an adequate force of convoy escorts" in the scant weeks before the outbreak of war.[18]

A few of the most successful U-boat commanders made their own substantial contributions to the submarine war. Throughout the first nine months of
1940, they operated individually in the unescorted zone south and west of Iceland where enemy merchantmen were plentiful, and kills beyond the enemy's
convoy-dispersal point often remained absurdly easy. The names of submarine
"aces" soon began to appear in the German press and propaganda announce-
ments, men who had sunk more than fifty or one hundred thousand tons of
enemy shipping. There was Gunther Prien, of course, the "Bulldog of Scapa
Flow," commanding U-47, who followed up his spectacular sinking of *Royal
Oak* with claims of a score and more of British cargo ships sent to the bottom.
Cool, photogenic young Otto Kretschmer, who had U-99, and Joachim
Schepke, captain of U-100, with their arrogant, blond "Aryan" good looks (and
Kretschmer's rakishly tilted cap), soon weighed in with record claims of their
own. All were somewhat exaggerated, and at least two historians of the Atlantic
war assert that Schepke was an out-and-out liar.[19] But there was little doubt in
either Berlin or London that the U-boat campaign was slowly but surely wear-
ing Britain down. In fact, it was the combination of the U-boats *and* the Luftwaffe *and* the German mining campaign that was placing England in mortal
peril. But whatever the precise causes, the führer was pleased.

When in the autumn of 1940 Germany's shipyards and the Baltic training grounds were at last turning out submarines and crews in sufficient numbers so that Dönitz could finally anticipate gathering them in packs and sending them against the enemy convoys, Kretschmer devised ruthless new tactics that rendered the U-boats virtually invulnerable to counterattack when they assaulted enemy convoys. During their year of working up, the German submariners had developed a cautious respect for British asdic. If properly handled, the instrument could indeed provide a destroyer with the information either to kill a U-boat or at least to keep it pinned down long enough for a convoy to escape. Germany lost twenty-five U-boats during the first nine months of the war, a third of which (eight) were sunk by convoy escorts (most of the remainder were either surprised on the surface and destroyed by Coastal Command's handful of aircraft or lost in enemy minefields).[20]

But Kretschmer soon discovered that if enemy shipping could be attacked at night with the U-boat hull running awash rather than submerged, conditions would be entirely transformed. Asdic could not detect half-surfaced submarines, which could operate at a surface speed and maneuverability equal if not superior to that of the escorting corvettes. Visual sightings of half-submerged U-boats were difficult enough by day; they were virtually impossible at night, especially during the chaotic conditions of a sudden attack. Moreover, Kretschmer employed his decks awash in attack strategy *within* the convoy, sneaking past the escorts to emerge suddenly among the columns of merchantmen to fire single torpedo salvos at close range. Not for him the traditional fan-shaped salvo that might or might not catch a ship or two in its belly. "One torpedo, one ship" was Kretschmer's motto. By the end of 1940, he had sunk more than 200,000 tons of shipping using his new nighttime attack method. Slowly, some of his colleagues, with greater or lesser enthusiasm, adopted the tactic. The remainder chose to continue to fire spreads of torpedoes at convoys from the periphery. Dönitz, who immediately embraced Kretschmer's methods, offered his submarine ace a staff job ashore that Kretschmer politely rejected; he liked killing ships, and he was very good at it.[21]

So were many of Dönitz's other young captains. In the third week of September 1940 alone, they sent to the bottom twenty-seven British and Commonwealth ships totaling nearly 160,000 tons, "the highest rate of loss since the beginning of the war, and . . . in fact greater than any we had suffered in a similar period in 1917."[22] In early October Dönitz at last sent the first of his wolf packs into the Iceland-Faeroes gap and the western approaches where they operated with devastating effect.

The blitzkrieg at sea began on the night of October 17, 1940, a year to the day after Dönitz had sent his first small, experimental wolf pack out against a British convoy off Gibraltar. The new and far more deadly pack ultimately comprised a total of eight boats. It sighted and quickly struck two British convoys, SC-7 and HX-79. That month Dönitz's youngsters destroyed an average of 60,000 tons of enemy shipping per U-boat; Dönitz's goal of a 600,000-ton sinkage rate per month that would destroy the Atlantic lifeline drifted into distant reach.[23]

Surface raiders helped. Early in November the pocket battleship *Admiral Scheer* began its incredible 161-day cruise against British commerce in the Atlantic and Indian Oceans with an assault on the thirty-seven-ship convoy HX-84, protected only by the weakly armed merchant cruiser *Jervis Bay.* In the rapidly gathering gloom of a late upper-Atlantic autumn afternoon, Captain Theodor Krancke and his crew managed to send five of the frantically scattering ships together with *Jervis Bay* and an independently sailing merchant vessel to the bottom, subtracting 48,000 more tons from Britain's maritime list. But *Jervis Bay* prevented a far greater tragedy. Like its sister *Rawalpindi* several months earlier against *Scharnhorst* and *Gneisenau,* the converted liner instantly leaped between its charges and the enemy. Captain E. S. F. Fegen sailed his ship, obsolete 6-inch rifles blazing as long as possible, into the mouth of the much bigger German cannon. Krancke's 11-inch main battery and 5.9-inch secondary guns shattered *Jervis Bay,* and eventually pounded it beneath the waves. But Fegen and his gallant men disrupted the Germans' plan to bag most if not all of the convoy.[24]

For the Nazi submarine crews, the autumn of 1940 was a time of exultant slaughter as they used the darkness to easily slip past the two or three small escorts, penetrate the ranks of merchantmen, select their prey, and let fly with their torpedoes. As the black seas and skies around them erupted in red flame and pink smoke, the U-boats either stayed close to a slowly sinking ship or fled with impunity to reload their tubes and prepare to attack again. When crews had been stretched to the limit with tension, the captains left the convoy to let them catch their breath, dive, and reload once more. Daylight hours were spent either on or beneath the surface, stalking the injured convoy and awaiting sunset to lunge in for another nighttime of deadly, pitiless work.

U-boat doctrine was forged in the crucible of these battles. Submarine captains were ordered to never, ever let go of enemy convoys. They must attack, and attack, and attack, as long as their torpedoes held out. Convoys emptied the ocean of independently steaming ships; under the best circumstances they were hard to find. Thus, "on meeting an enemy concentration, advantage must be taken of this rare opportunity, at night as well as in daytime, by utilizing to the full possibilities of the boat and the torpedoes. After the first target, a second and a third target should be attacked at once." Dönitz assured his lads that "the confusion among the enemy forces which usually occurs at night, after the launching of the first torpedo, will make this easier." In order to maintain the initiative, even under counterattack by enemy escorts, the U-boats had to remain as mobile as possible. This meant remaining atop the seas to the very last moment, for "on the surface, the submarine commander remains master of the situation. If the submarine submerges, it becomes blind and stationary, and must leave it to the enemy to bring about any change of the position on the surface."[25]

For the British it was an unforgettable ordeal. In tense darkness, ships suddenly erupted in fireballs and steam, oil spilled from bunkers to ignite on the sea, and as the explosions rolled across the ocean the skies turned a lurid red. The few bewildered escorts hurried this way and that, their asdic operators searching the depths vainly for submarines that were not there. Only once or twice at most would someone in the convoy spot the small silver conning tower of a U-boat lurking beyond or racing through the columns to vanish quickly again in the gloom. Captain Donald Macintyre, himself an escort commander at the time, describes the repeated sense of shame and frustration that gripped the escort commanders and crews as they failed utterly either to protect their flocks or to come to grips with their maddeningly elusive tormentors. Search efforts under the strange light of bursting rockets and burning ships were repeatedly interrupted by the demands of conscience as desperate, often mortally injured, merchant seamen called out of the freezing darkness and burning seas for rescue.[26] With dawn came the reckoning: an ocean littered with corpses, debris, and oil and great gaps in the columns of ships.

Beneath the mounting horror of the war at sea were the cold statistics and the grim charts. As Germany's Atlantic offensive reached its first apex in late 1940, a large graph adorned an entire wall of the Admiralty's Operations Room at Whitehall. "It was divided near the top by a thin red line—a permanent measure of the narrow gap between victory and defeat." By January 1941 the gap had narrowed alarmingly. British imports were less than half of what they had been a year before.[27] The Battle of Britain and the Battle of the Atlantic insensibly melded into one three-dimensional conflict, and it was this *cumulative* aspect of Germany's war that seriously menaced Britain's existence. As Dönitz's submarines and Raeder's battlewagons sank ships at ever accelerating rates, up to a dozen long-range Focke-Wulf 200 Kondor aircraft ranged far out into the Atlantic, not only spotting convoys for the U-boat arm but also attacking the enemy from the air with bomb and bullet. During March, April, and May 1941, German naval aircraft alone sank a half-million tons of British shipping, moving Churchill to lament "the disproportionate effect that German long-distance patrol aircraft were having" on the Battle of the Atlantic. At the same time, Luftwaffe bombers assaulted the big port cities of the east and west coasts—Plymouth, London, Liverpool, and Glasgow among them—and mined adjacent waters. The "Blitz" swiftly emptied London and other east and south coast port cities and towns of shipping, and the Mersey and Clyde became jammed with vessels waiting to unload, yet held up by the need to devote the increasingly exhausted manpower ashore to a daily clearing of bomb-damaged areas and the rescue of victims. As early as December 13, 1940, Churchill sent a longish memo to the minister of transport noting that the drastic reduction of oil imports in September and October had been due not to a shortage of tankers but rather to the partial shutdown of the east coast and southern ports because of enemy air raids. Two days after Christmas he bombarded the Transport Ministry with another message. "It is said that two-fifths of the decline in the fertility of our shipping is due to the loss of time in turning round ships in British ports. Now that we are confined so largely to the Mersey and the Clyde and must expect increasingly severe attacks upon them, it would seem that this problem constitutes the most dangerous part of the whole of our front."[28]

How long could Britain sustain such losses at sea and disruptions in port? How far could its critical imports of oil, of foodstuffs, of iron and steel fall before it could no longer stand and fight alone? How quickly could its tiny prewar fleet of destroyers, corvettes, and sloops be built up by new construction, and how should new construction be balanced between merchant ships and escort vessels? How long would it take for Coastal Command and the RAF to neutralize the Luftwaffe's bombing and mining campaigns of English ports and waters and drive Raeder's handful of Kondors from the skies over the North Atlantic? Never before had sea power been so obviously measured in fighter planes as well as lowly steamships and the number and strength of capital vessels. In 1940–1941 a tanker might be worth as much as a battleship, a twenty thousand–ton freighter worth as much as an aircraft carrier, and a modern destroyer and RAF fighter squadron worth more than them all.

Here was the crux of the Atlantic crisis, and a half century later Philip Pugh summarized it perfectly. Hitler's U-boats inflicted a consistently adverse if never crippling multiplier effect on the Allied war effort. From the beginning the U-boats were sufficiently "checked" by the convoy system "so that the sudden collapse of trans-Atlantic shipping was never in prospect; but on the other

hand there was no prompt means of ending their much increased and continual depredations.... With Germany now dominant throughout Europe, the
prospect thus arose of the war becoming so long and the shipping haemorrhage
so great that Britain might bleed to death." Never did this prospect appear so
imminent as in the "First Happy Time" for the U-boats between July 1940 and
March 1941. During that period, Britain, and the merchant marines from Nazi-
occupied western Europe that had taken shelter under British arms, lost an
average of 22 vessels for every U-boat sunk. "If the same exchange rate had
been maintained until the end of June 1943, then the 215 U-boats lost by
then would have accounted for 4,730 Allied merchantmen. This would have
wiped out the Allied merchant fleet." Instead, losses dropped to 1,980 vessels,
still a major disaster.

Because the U-boats together with the Luftwaffe raids on English east coast
ports were so effective during the early years of the war, Britain could not afford to devote much shipping to traditional commercial, that is, money-raising,
activities, and the concentration of vessels in slow convoys together with port
congestion at Liverpool and Glasgow translated into a significant loss of trade
and hence of traditional tax revenues to the British government, thus markedly
exacerbating its rapidly declining international financial strength after 1940.
And, of course, the simple loss of hulls meant that those remaining had to be
devoted largely to the transportation of military supplies and equipment necessary for Britain's defense. After Pearl Harbor the new hulls that came increasingly out of U.S. yards had to be predominantly employed on the same transportation mission, not to save Britain from defeat now but for the buildup
necessary to launch and sustain the great Allied counteroffensives first in the
Mediterranean and then across the Channel. The result was a continual decline
in the British domestic economy, greater and greater stringencies, and, finally,
during the last stages of the war, "a race between German military defeat and
British economic collapse." Moreover, as Pugh observes, losses on the North
Atlantic also reverberated throughout the world, where after 1941 the Anglo-
American Allies were fighting a global war that depended for success absolutely
on substantial as well as secure transportation. Despite the enormous capacity
of U.S. shipyards, lack of sufficient shipping remained a chronic problem and
bottleneck in the Allied war efforts in both the Atlantic and the Pacific right
down to 1945. The necessary ships were scraped together for the necessary
operations, but it was always a near-run thing. As in 1917, but over a much
longer period, the German war on trade by U-boat, aircraft, and mine between
1939 and 1945 proved catastrophic for Britain. A comparatively "small effort

of this sort" (that is, small during the opening years of the war because of the comparatively few U-boats available) "imposes disproportionate costs upon the victim." Fortunately, "such actions (although very cost effective for the attacker) are not, of themselves, sufficient to win the war."[29]

The Royal Navy could at first devote little attention to antisubmarine (or antiaircraft) warfare on the Atlantic and in the western approaches. Raeder's surface forces and armed merchant cruisers preoccupied Whitehall; shipyards were turning out new destroyers and *"Flower"*-class corvettes at too slow a pace, while demands on the fleet destroyer force in Norway and later at Dunkirk, on the British Channel coast in anticipation of a Nazi invasion, and then in the Mediterranean were immense. Destroyer losses in all four theaters of operation were horrific. Only the "destroyer for bases deal" with the United States provided Britain with the margin of resources necessary to sustain its Atlantic lifeline in the year and a half between the fall of France and Pearl Harbor. But the margin was very narrow indeed. Whereas the Americans suddenly acquired a broad shield from Argentia, Newfoundland, to British Guiana, the British obtained some rather dubious goods. Nearly three months after the transfer, Churchill informed Roosevelt that only "a very few of your fifty destroyers" had been brought into action "on account of the many defects which naturally develop when exposed to Atlantic weather after having been laid up so long."[30]

The Atlantic weather and the often mindless, even brutal, discipline of the Royal Navy served to make the common British sailor's life in the early days of World War II even more miserable than at the time of Invergordon. Aboard His Majesty's cruisers and destroyers as well as battleships at Scapa Flow or in the main Icelandic fleet anchorage at Heflavik, "bullshit" remained "the order of the day." After days and weeks at sea in the dark, cramped, ice-cold, and leaky fo'c'sle living quarters of a fleet destroyer, where six inches of freezing Atlantic saltwater sloshed about continually on the decks, the men had to appear topside in harbor in blue serge uniforms without the light-blue collar. "Most of us stayed below in any old rig," Tristan Jones recalled, "but with comparative ease of mind." Mental calmness was paid for, however, by "the high incidence of TB [tuberculosis] in the Home Fleet—Jack [Tar] was reluctant to get into the fresh air because of such stupid bullshit as having to be in formal uniform," despite the fact there was no one around to observe him except his officers. Flogging continued to be an acceptable form of punishment, especially for the youngest crewmen. Cruiser *London* had sixty "boys" aboard, "many of them from borstals [juvenile correction facilities] and tough communities. Some of the boys did very well during their time in the cruiser, but others were hard to handle."

According to the ship's surgeon, "the most serious offences committed by these tough nuts" were punished by "so many strokes with a thick and heavy cane. This was quite a performance and was enjoyed by nobody. . . . On the whole I doubt if these floggings did any good."[31]

Doggedly, the British hung on through the terrible winter and spring of 1941. Jack Tar, the despised or dismissed victim of upper-class loathing and snobbery, never forgot who he was or what he was fighting for, and his touching loyalty pulled the Royal Navy through. Jones recalled the grim life on the lower decks of a British destroyer in the early war years and the dogged spirit of the men who dwelt there:

> Imagine a world of metal and asbestos, of clanging doors, humming machinery, oil smells, sudden pipes and shouted orders on a tinny loudspeaker system, cooking odors, and dozens of men crowding in the messes and the darkened passageways, and at action stations all day and all night, four hours on, four off, each day and every day, at the ack-ack guns, the torpedo tubes, the main guns, the engines, the boilers, the Asdic compartment, the radar cubbyhole half-way up the skinny mast, in the cold North Atlantic weather and all the men eager and willing to do their level best for their mates, for the Skipper, for the ship, and for their family and country—and parading through the midst of this, appearing instantly and almost always unexpectedly, his shoulders crouched as if to spring, his dark eyes glowering from under black eyebrows, his hands clasped behind his back, Dartmouth style, a martinet who should by rights have been on a parade ground or in a mental hospital.[32]

Conditions were no better on the bigger ships. Aboard cruisers protecting the Arctic convoys to Russia after the autumn of 1941, "there was usually a thin film of ice on the insides of the bulkheads of living spaces." Four-hour watches amid monstrous seas, frequent blizzards, and deadly cold had to be reduced to a half hour, "which was as much as most men could endure." Extraordinary measures were taken to prevent gun mechanisms, machinery, and navigational instruments from freezing. Conditions for the crew jammed together in the dark fo'c'sle were nothing short of barbaric. One able seaman recalled "mess decks flooded, clothing, crockery, vegetables all floating about. Can't sleep even if you want to—merely hang on and hope for the best." A member of the engineering gang aboard the cruiser *London* wrote, "Normal routine like cleaning ship was a non-event: as the days passed so the ship became more and more untidy, spilt food on the mess decks remained there, cocoa and sugar were all over the decks. I can hear the sound of granulated sugar crunching under my feet to this day." In the toilets, "I remember seeing a line of white porcelain lavatory pans disgorging their contents in fountains every time the great ship put her bows into the deep Arctic troughs." Men vomited on the decks, while ladders and even machinery began to rust despite the best preventive efforts.[33]

Nicholas Monsarrat's fictional Captain George Eastwood Ericson, retread commander of the corvette *Compass Rose*, might marvel at the instinctive heroism and competence of his common sailors:

> "The sea is in their blood," he thought.... [T]he phrase meant something after all: it was not just a romantic notion left over from Nelson, it was not just a baritone rendering of *Heart of Oak*, with manly emphasis on "Jolly tars are our men." "The sea in their blood" meant that you could pour Englishmen—any Englishmen—into a ship, and they made that ship work and fight as if they had been doing it all their lives, catching up, overtaking, and leaving behind the professionals of any other nation. It was the basic virtue of living on an island.

Such maunderings were pleasing conceits at best, not wholly borne out in experience and totally unmindful of the enormous cost to the poor souls forced to incorporate the Royal Navy's lower deck as well as the cruel seas into their experience. Anecdotal evidence suggests that where the Royal Navy was most "professional," it was also most hidebound and inflexible. Captains and officers coming into the service from civilian life or the merchant marine, even with Royal Navy backgrounds, tended to be more reasonable and human. Monsarrat himself was a "hostilities only" officer, and he portrays Ericson as a retread from the merchant marine; so were real-life captains E. S. F. Fegen of *Jervis Bay* and Edward Kennedy of *Rawalpindi*, both of whom treated their charges humanely and with respect, earning near adoration from their crews as a consequence.[34]

The U-boats' ability to overwhelm single convoys and sink large numbers of ships could not be denied. But at key moments Dönitz simply did not possess either the submarines or the aircraft to find and then overwhelm enough British convoys. Christmastime 1940 found only one German submarine in the Atlantic, and vital replacements had not yet reached French and Norwegian ports in sufficient numbers. Even if they had, the great, smashing winter seas of the North Atlantic wore down the U-boats and their crews and made attacks on convoys, even when found, virtually impossible.[35]

At the turn of the year, however, Dönitz again dispatched his gray wolves to the convoy lanes, and in January and February 1941 the number of U-boats on patrol in the eastern and central North Atlantic gradually crept past ten, and the ocean was moderate enough to permit them to send more than 300,000 tons of British shipping plunging to the bottom. By March, as the winter storms began to abate, Dönitz anticipated a further happy time. New construction was now allowing him to maintain an average of no fewer than nineteen boats at sea during the coming quarter. By summer the number would rise to thirty-two.

Moreover, some of the new vessels were of the Type IXB and IXC designs of 1,050 and 1,120 tons, respectively. Compared to the 750-ton Type VIIs, they were somewhat cumbersome and unwieldy, slower to submerge and therefore easier to detect and kill. But to compensate, they possessed greater range, durability, and firepower than the Type VIIs and thoroughly unsuitable Type Is and IIs that were all that Dönitz had at the beginning of the war. At the same time, Germany had lost just thirty-two submarines in the first eighteen months of combat, and only seven in the period July 1940 to February 1941. New vessels were appearing at the Baltic training stations monthly, while German yards were becoming increasingly efficient at rapidly repairing damaged U-boats. As a consequence, Dönitz possessed in port and at sea fifty-four oceangoing boats in the spring of 1941, twice the number he had at the beginning of the war.

He now concluded that he had enough craft both to send a few south to the African coast as a diversionary tactic and to form a patrol line in the western portion of the Iceland-Faeroes gap from which wolf packs could be quickly gathered whenever an enemy convoy was spotted.[36] Dönitz and his staff divided the vast North Atlantic into a series of interlocking patrol squares for easier scouting and force concentration. The cryptanalysts at BDienst maintained their mastery of the British convoy codes while continuing to tap into U.S. commercial traffic to gain information incautiously being passed out by maritime insurance companies and brokers. The code breakers and intelligence analysts passed the word to Dönitz that with Icelandic anchorages, fueling stations, and airfields now in British hands, Whitehall was routing vessels and escorts farther north. Prien, Kretschmer, and the others were placed accordingly, and on March 6, 1941, Prien spotted westbound convoy OB-293 two hundred miles southeast of Iceland. He radioed France and awaited reinforcements. By the end of the day a four-boat pack had been assembled that included Kretschmer in U-99; that night it plunged in confidently to attack.

The British response was unprecedented. As one U-boat crash-dived after attack, it was rammed by the enraged tanker it had just torpedoed, then was subjected to such a pounding by depth charges that it went out of control and nearly sank to the bottom before shooting to the surface, where it was destroyed by two of the four British escorts. Kretschmer's boat was badly rattled by

repeated depth-charge attacks. But it was Prien and his famous U-47 who suffered the most dramatic fate of all. Staying with the convoy through the night,
the submarine was suddenly glimpsed at about one in the morning through curtains of driving rain close by the destroyer *Wolverine.* Escort commander J. M.
Rowland could actually smell the U-boat's diesel fuel and hear its engines. A
second destroyer, the nearby *Verity,* promptly lit up the scene with a star shell,
and Prien crash-dived as the two destroyers began pounding the seas with depth
charges. For three hours the determined Britons plastered the area where Prien
had disappeared until at last they glimpsed oil on the surface, which raised their
bloodlust further. After another hour of steady pounding with depth charges,
the hydrophone operator heard the sounds of breaking crockery in his phones,
which typically indicated a submarine in extremis. Suddenly, U-47 broke the
surface briefly and then forever sank from sight. *Wolverine* immediately swung
around and dropped another pattern of charges.

> The result was a manifestation of destruction the like of which was never
> seen before or after. The British sailors on the *Wolverine* saw an orange
> glow deep below the surface of the sea which may have burned for as
> much as ten seconds [undoubtedly the result of sea pressure compressing
> the last air pockets aboard the imploding U-47 and igniting them in a flash
> of fire]: some aboard swore that flames briefly flickered above the water. It
> was as if the mouth of hell had opened to receive the Bull of Scapa Flow.[37]

Prien and his forty-six crewmen were gone, and within a fortnight Schepke
would join them in equally horrifying fashion. U-100 was just turning away
from shadowing a night-shrouded convoy when it was discovered by the destroyer *Vanoc,* which promptly rushed over and heavily depth-charged the frantically diving submarine. U-100 was badly damaged, and Schepke took it to the
surface, where *Vanoc*'s alert crew quickly spotted and rammed it. In the frightful collision, Schepke on the bridge of the U-boat had his legs cut off at the
trunk. As his submarine died beneath him, the legless Schepke was thrown
into the nighttime sea. "His white-covered cap was still worn with all its rakish
dash as he thrashed wildly for a few seconds and then sank beneath the heavy
swell to be followed a few minutes later by U-100. Despite his weaknesses,
Schepke had died like an ace—on his bridge." Moments after Schepke and
U-100 perished, U-99 was blasted to the surface and destroyed. Kretschmer
managed to survive the sinking to become a prisoner of war. All three of Germany's U-boat aces had been accounted for in less than fifteen days. Dönitz was

momentarily shattered. Perhaps he realized even then that Germany's hopes to win the Battle of the Atlantic had forever disappeared.[38]

Prien, Schepke, and Kretschmer were the perhaps careless victims of a British antisubmarine program that had at last begun to move into high gear. Over the next three years, the Royal Navy and the United States Navy employed a variety of stratagems, countermeasures, and technologies to successfully subdue the U-boat menace, even as an enraged Air Marshal Hermann Göring flatly refused to allocate more Kondor aircraft to the navy, allegedly sniffing, "Everything that flies belongs to me."[39]

The deadly wolf-pack attacks of 1940–1941 revealed the total lack of teamwork on the part of the escorts; each one responded individually and separately to a common threat. What was required was disciplined cooperation and tactics. The escort vessels, new and old alike, should be collected into teams, trained collectively, and kept together to the extent that inevitable losses, damage, and overhaul schedules permitted. Once this lesson was absorbed, the Royal Navy, under the spirited direction of Admirals Sir Percy Noble and then Max Horton, moved with unaccustomed swiftness to put it into effect.

Noble, "the best dressed man in the Navy," moved antisubmarine operations and training from Plymouth on the southwest coast to Derby House at Liverpool. There, "Area Combined Headquarters," soon known simply as "the Plot," was established in more than three hundred rooms on four floors. Soon it was manned by more than a thousand people, including a few RAF intelligence people and hundreds of Royal Navy officers and Wrens. Together, they "created a smooth-running, highly effective organization which, although vast, still managed to retain the personal touch." The heart of the operation was a "vast, fortified, basement, protected by blast walls and a reinforced concrete 'ceiling' several feet thick." In this "fortress" or "citadel," inevitably called "the Dungeon," lay a huge operations room with great wall maps "overlooked by glass-fronted offices." Here, as in Dönitz's U-boat Command Headquarters in France, was the nerve center of the Atlantic campaign, where the war at sea "took on the character of a monstrous chess game." For its own immediate purposes, the Admiralty also established a submarine tracking room below a concrete blockhouse on the northwest side nearest the Mall in London. Command was given to a brilliant thirty-eight-year-old civilian turned hostilities-only officer named Roger Winn who, despite a body twisted from childhood polio, exhibited a decided flair for mastering U-boat tactics and a willingness to work to exhaustion to beat Dönitz every way he could. When Max Horton replaced Noble at

Liverpool, he established an antisubmarine school in Larne, Northern Ireland, and set about creating eight escort groups (the first of many) that trained jointly off Londonderry and later also off the Clyde and Mersey Rivers. A tactical school was established in Liverpool itself for the training of escort officers. "Ace" escort commanders were designated to lead the groups in hopes of matching and destroying Hitler's best submariners. "By late 1941 the ships of the Liverpool Escort Force were escorting convoys far and wide: north to Iceland and thence to northern Russia, west to Newfoundland and the United States, south to Gibraltar and the South Atlantic." By early 1942 no fewer than sixty escort vessels (largely destroyers and corvettes) were gathered into seven groups. Another sixty-eight escorts gathered into similar "groups" operated out of Londonderry, Ireland, and a smaller number out of Greenock, Scotland. Of equal importance, Coastal Command with its all-too-slowly-rising number of aircraft was at last placed fully under Admiralty control.[40]

British laboratories and industry began providing the fleet and Coastal Command not only with more and better ships and aircraft but also with the first modest products of a rapidly accelerating "wizard war." Britain entered World War II with its ocean-oriented aviation in a deplorable state. Coastal Command, on which would fall much of the burden of antisubmarine work, contained only 216 frontline planes and 200 reserve aircraft.[41] All too slowly, Britain's factories and the RAF began producing new "machines" for the war at sea. By 1941 Coastal Command's big Sunderland seaplanes and small Hudson bombers were equipped with aerial depth charges and Royal Navy destroyers and corvettes with more powerful and faster-sinking depth charges. Because asdic was useless in tracking submarines directly under an escort's keel, British science came up with the "hedgehog," a device for hurling depth charges well ahead of an attacking destroyer. Both planes and escorts were provided with very high-frequency radio-telephone communications for direct voice contact between the escorts and among ships and aircraft during coordinated searches and attacks. And although the substance of communications traffic between Dönitz and his submariners at sea remained absolutely secure through the early spring of 1940, obtaining a fix on the general direction of radio traffic between France and an individual U-boat was not difficult. British (and American) laboratories had developed "Huff Duff," a high-frequency radio direction finder (HF DF) that proved instrumental in pinpointing enemy transmission points. Shore-based direction-finder stations could locate the approximate position of U-boat transmitters and warn convoys and their escorts of the probable location of enemy wolf packs.

The packs moved and roamed widely and communicated as briefly as possible. What was needed to detect submarines preparing to attack the convoys were Huff Duffs aboard the escorts themselves, and by early 1941 suitably small Huff Duffs were being developed for placement on even the small corvettes. This equipment could pinpoint the location of a nearby U-boat within a quarter of a mile if the submarine happened to be receiving or sending messages very close to the convoy. Throughout the war, Huff Duff continued to provide escort commanders with essential intelligence on the presence and general position of the enemy and even some suggestion as to the imminence and probable direction of his attack.

The capstone of Britain's rapidly crystallizing antisubmarine technology was radar. The first Type 271 surface warning sets were installed in both ships and aircraft in the spring and summer of 1941. Now enemy submarines running awash could be located within as well as just beyond the convoy. Aircraft could detect surfaced U-boats stalking the convoy from astern or racing up into attack position. The first shipboard and airborne radars were crude and marginally satisfactory. But the bugs began to be worked out under battle conditions, and both the sets and their operators soon improved markedly.

As officers and men got to know the various pieces of new equipment at their disposal and the way each complemented the other, the convoy escort teams began to shift from reactive to proactive players in the great game of hunt and kill. As in the latter stages of World War I, each convoy became a potentially offensive rather than defensive element in antisubmarine warfare. The U-boat's best bet remained the murder of independently sailing vessels or the few stragglers and cripples that inevitably fell behind almost every convoy. If an entire convoy had to be struck, semisurfaced night attack remained the norm. But the risks were growing ever greater.[42]

Historian Dan van der Vat has likened the role of the new British escort commanders to that of "player managers" on a soccer or baseball team. It is an apt analogy. Whereas the restricted perspective of a submarine conning tower forced Dönitz to continue managing from the distant French sidelines—and only to the point of gathering his wolves and pointing them toward the attack—British teams with their new detection capabilities were now managed immediately on-site. In practical terms this meant that whereas before a three- or four-unit wolf pack enjoyed a three- or four-to-nothing advantage over dispersed and blind convoy defenders, now an eight-vessel escort team or even the more normal and less disciplined five-vessel group enjoyed at least an equal advantage, and often a two-to-one edge, over any attacking U-boat.

By mid-1941 Britain's wartime building program was at last turning out an ever growing number of small and limited corvettes and sloops for the Atlantic convoys, together with a far smaller number of destroyers. At the same time, escort groups sailing from Greenock in southwestern Scotland or Londonderry, Ireland, began shepherding their flocks more than halfway to North America through exploitation of the Icelandic anchorages. A typical escort group would herd its charges to Iceland, refuel there, and then proceed on to thirty-five degrees west, wait for an eastbound convoy, and take it into Iceland for refueling and then on to Britain. This procedure had several beneficial effects beyond the simple extension of protection. First, routing the convoys farther north forced the U-boats to extend their range at the cost of time on station. Second, the northerly route provided more hours of summer daylight, thus reducing the time of maximum danger from German night attacks. Of equal or greater importance, Coastal Command stationed a squadron each of Hudson light bombers (unfit for Bomber Command raids over France or Germany), long-range Sunderland flying boats, and modern Stirling bombers in Iceland to patrol the convoy lanes to the south, east, and west of the island. As a consequence, U-boats lost the long-enjoyed luxury of tracking convoys on the surface during daylight hours in preparation for night attacks. With reporting ships often driven beneath the surface, Dönitz's U-boat captains found it increasingly difficult either to find enemy convoys or to gather the packs necessary to attack them. The U-boats were lured progressively westward toward the coasts of North America in search of independently sailing ships or weakly escorted convoys.

Adding to Dönitz's woes was the appearance on the North Atlantic of a fresh crop of frighteningly efficient British antisubmarine warriors. Many were stolid, competent people from the prewar merchant navy, men like Monsarrat's fictional captain George Eastwood Ericson who had spent obscure years commanding nondescript steamers all over the world and who knew the sea as intimately as any mariner ever can. Some were weekend sailors, personified by the equally fictional Keith Lockhart, many of whom rose steadily through sheer ability from the lower echelons of the officer corps to eventual command of corvettes, sloops, and the later frigates. A very few were regular navy types who had languished unappreciated through the long, dreary years of peace with little opportunity to display their talents. Fewer still were successful career people, like Donald Macintyre. All shared one characteristic: they were mavericks in a service that too often prided itself on blind obedience to tradition; they all possessed an ability to learn, to innovate, to quickly respond to Dönitz's constantly changing tactics with successful countermeasures of their own.

Chief among this small cadre was Captain Frederic John Walker, and in many ways his is the story of Britain's eventual triumph in the Atlantic, the key to victory in World War II. Like so many of his compatriots, "Johnnie Walker"—a slender, pipe-smoking chap with a lean look both genial and dangerous—had come from a naval family and had enjoyed a brilliant academic career at the Dartmouth naval academy, graduating shortly before the 1914–1918 war. But somehow his career never quite took off, burdened as it was by various fitness reports from skeptical or hostile seniors who questioned his suitability for higher rank. By the end of 1938 he had been passed over for promotion to captain, and probably only the outbreak of war kept him in the service. Even then, the first eighteen months were comparatively uneventful as he held a shore post at Dover. Only when Walker took matters into his own hands in the spring of 1941 and lobbied personally for a command at sea was he given the new sloop *Stork* out of Liverpool.[43]

When he arrived the following September in the great, gray city along the grimy Mersey, so many of its buildings either smashed or smoke blackened from incessant bombing attacks, Walker "found himself among strangely assorted bedfellows. It seemed that by design or accident all the misfits of the Navy had congregated at Liverpool. Among his brother officers were many of his own kind—'passed overs' who at some stage or other had become red-tape rebels."[44]

To his intense pleasure, Walker was promptly given command of the nine-ship Thirty-sixth Escort Group of sloops and corvettes. Pleasure soon turned to necessary pain:

> The working-up routine had been skillfully devised by an expert in the art of driving both officers and men mad in the least possible time. All day they carried out anti-submarine and gunnery exercises; at night they sailed again to protect imaginary convoys. When the sleepless nights and days had stretched into weeks, and orders were given and obeyed automatically, they were allowed one night at anchor. Tired out, the Group collapsed into bunks and hammocks. But it was not to be. In the early hours, the energetic senior officer of the training school came alongside in a motor-boat.
> "Officer of the Day."
> "Yes, Sir."
> "You have been rammed forward, your stern is on fire and the enemy are preparing to attack the anchorage. Get cracking."
> Alarm bells rang and they were at it again.[45]

From the first, Walker was captivated by the problems of antisubmarine warfare. How *did* one counter a nighttime surface attack by trimmed-down

German submarines? And once having found the enemy, how *did* one kill him? Walker's first suggestion was "Buttercup," a combination of intense star-shell illumination of a convoy area in response to an initial submarine attack followed by the heaviest plastering possible of a U-boat's suspected position with depth charges. Buttercup was far from a perfect answer: intense illumination would light up a convoy as well as the attacking submarines, not all of whom conveniently appeared where Walker thought they should. But Buttercup was a first step and led to some results. Above all, it demonstrated to friend and foe alike that the days of simple one-on-one reaction to U-boat assaults were gone forever.

As Walker trained and pondered, his colleagues discovered another crucial fact about antisubmarine warfare: their depth charges were being set too shallow. On August 27, 1941, U-570, a type VIIC submarine, was captured south of Iceland and brought into Scapa Flow. The vessel was immediately subjected to rigorous tests that demonstrated that German undersea boats were more strongly built and capable of diving to greater depths than had hitherto been suspected. Primers on depth charges throughout the Royal Navy were immediately set for significantly deeper detonations.[46]

The following December, Walker, in command of only his second convoy, lost a destroyer and the first escort carrier, *Audacity*, but brought thirty of his thirty-two merchantmen triumphantly from Gibraltar into the Mersey and in the process destroyed four enemy U-boats, including obliteration of the entire three-boat pack that had first attacked. Walker received the Distinguished Service Order for this exploit; more important, he got a hearing. "His impact on the Atlantic battle had been sudden and successful and, through the reports of Sir Percy Noble and Captain [G. E.] Creasy [director of antisubmarine warfare in the Admiralty], more swiftly recognized by the Admiralty than was usual in that citadel of conservatism." Walker made four recommendations, three more or less highly controversial. First, he argued that aircraft were absolutely indispensable for antisubmarine work. There should be both land-based planes to hunt down U-boats and carrier-based aircraft to drive off or kill the Focke-Wulf bombers on "homing" patrols. Second, the Admiralty should bend every effort to provide convoys with both an inner and an outer protective screen of escorts. By day, the outer screen should roam the far flanks of the convoys, searching out and killing stalking U-boats. By night, the semisurfaced U-boats would have to run a double gauntlet of outer and close-in escorts, increasingly equipped with sophisticated and precise communication and detection gear. Third, *all* escorts should be on call during daylight hours "as striking forces for offensive lunges away from the convoy" against detected U-boats. Finally, Walker questioned the utility of his own Buttercup illumination scheme since it did demonstrably open up the convoy to greater attack. Their lordships took Walker's recommendations under advisement. The idea of greater air cooperation between convoys and Coastal Command was quickly passed to responsible authorities, though it would be many months before another British escort carrier would sail with a convoy. The question of inner and outer screens was interesting but regrettably irrelevant in view of the continued paucity of escort ships. British yards were straining every sinew to build the corvettes, sloops, frigates, and destroyers needed on the North Atlantic, but as late as the autumn of 1942 the average number of escorts for any given convoy was only five. Walker's criticism of Buttercup was rejected because of the example of only a single convoy. What got their lordships' back up was recommendation three: that escorts *not* remain tied to the convoy but roam the adjacent daytime seas in an aggressive search for the enemy. This would never do, Walker was told. The risks were too great. Walker departed the Admiralty determined to go his own way and prove the wisdom of his tactics by further example. He and his colleagues did so, repeatedly.[47]

As the Royal Navy began fighting the U-boats to a rough, brutal draw in 1941, logistics experts in London pored over their statistics and came to a remarkable conclusion: Britain's "normal" import of goods during peacetime was roughly sixty million tons per year, but even at war the nation could exist on forty-seven million tons. "More surprising was the realisation by 1942 that Britain could live and fight—just—on about 26 million tons, less than half the level of prewar imports."[48] The German war at sea was not only doomed— it always had been, thanks to the incredible pluck of the average British civilian who would accept and "carry on" under harsh conditions that no American family at the time, or since, could imagine.

The breaking of the German naval codes by Bletchley Park in May 1941 was the last critically important component in the ultimate defeat of the U-boats. Had the British (and later American) cryptanalysts been able to maintain their break-in to German signal traffic, the Battle of the Atlantic would undoubtedly have been won sooner. The loss of German signal traffic throughout most of 1942, together with German capture of a British convoy codebook from a sinking freighter off Norway and the growth in the number of U-boats from 91 at the beginning of the year to 240 a year later, prolonged but did not reverse the antisubmarine campaign.[49] Even in this darkest Allied hour on the North Atlantic, with the British and American navies wholly ignorant of U-boat dispositions while BDienst directed the wolf packs on to Allied convoys, Huff Duff, steadily improving radar, depth charges reconfigured to increase sink rate and reduce underwater drift, and increasingly competent escort commanders and crews led to the loss of 100 Nazi submarines.

Moreover, the Allies were also inestimably aided at crucial points by Hitler's own strategic and tactical blunders. By 1941 the führer had become as smitten with his U-boat supermen as Dönitz, and on two occasions when the submarine offensive in the Atlantic was achieving substantial, indeed spectacular, results, Hitler insisted on transferring a significant portion of the U-boat flotilla to other fronts to help resolve real or fancied crises. In September the führer ordered the transfer of a half-dozen submarines from the Atlantic to the Mediterranean where Malta's air- and sea-based forces were cutting the convoy lifeline to Erwin Rommel and the Afrika Korps. The British island, almost dead center in the Mediterranean and only sixty miles from Italian territory, depended upon the sea for life fully as much as did the German army on the sands of Africa. Cut the sea-lanes to Malta, and the island would starve within weeks (which as late as June–July 1942 it nearly did). When the first six U-boats were not enough to tip the scales, Hitler ordered six more submarines sent in November, and by Christmas Day "practically all Atlantic submarines were in the Mediterranean or to the west of Gibraltar in response to an order to have twenty-five submarines on station in the vicinity of the Rock." Then Hitler got it into his head that the British or Russians were about to launch a major invasion of Norway. In January 1942 he briefly demanded that the entire navy, surface fleet and submarines alike, be sent northward to make a decisive contribution to the security of the Norwegian area. An appalled Dönitz protested often and vigorously. The North Atlantic shipping lanes between the New World and Old were where the war would be won or lost, he told his führer. If an Allied invasion force was ever sighted in Norwegian waters, the war would already be lost. Moreover, the führer was told, Norway simply did not possess the port and docking facilities to support the entire surface and submarine fleet. Hitler first relented and ordered only twenty boats to Norwegian waters, then changed his mind again and ordered them all north, before at last agreeing to the dispatch of only eight to supplement the handful already permanently stationed there. But his dithering could not have come at a worse moment. Pearl Harbor had suddenly provided an incredible opportunity for a major U-boat offensive against largely unprotected American coastal shipping. But with his submarine fleet dispersed, Dönitz initially had to make do with only five boats, and at no time could he dispatch more than fifteen.[50]

The formal entry of the United States into World War II spelled the end of any faint hope that Germany could somehow master the Atlantic, though for many long months it did not seem that way. Washington swiftly established wartime shipping routes up the East Coast from Guantánamo, Cuba (where vessels coming from South America and the Caribbean gathered), through the passage between south Florida and the Bahamas, along the one hundred–fathom curve off Jacksonville, Florida, Georgia, South Carolina, and the Outer Banks of North Carolina, and then on into New York. But Chief of Naval Operations Ernest J. King could not be induced to create a close inshore convoy system. The navy was admittedly hard-pressed at the outset for escorts. Within weeks after Pearl Harbor, Japan was running wild in the Pacific, where King's heart and mind were always to be found but not enough destroyers were. In the Atlantic the handful of destroyers and oceangoing Coast Guard cutters were assigned quite understandably to the great transatlantic convoys in order to ensure an early and sufficient military buildup in England for the invasions of North Africa ("Torch"). The U.S. Army Air Corps sought to fill the breach but had insufficient planes and a predilection for sensational "sub hunting" rather than close escort of inshore shipping.[51]

During the opening weeks of the war, then, freighters and tankers traversing the coastal route up the eastern seaboard traveled individually, without escort, until they reached New York or Boston, where convoys were formed either to sail directly to England or to join even larger concentrations at Halifax. Farther north, the small port of Sydney on Cape Breton Island became the concentration point for vessels bringing Canadian war material and foodstuffs up the St. Lawrence. Convoys then sailed, as they had for the past two years, across the North Atlantic, around the north coast of Ireland, and into Glasgow or the Firth of Clyde, north of Liverpool.

Fortunately for the Allies, and unfortunately for Dönitz, Pearl Harbor could not have come at a worse time for the U-boat arm. Hitler's paranoia over the safety of Norway and his conviction that U-boats alone could destroy the critical Malta convoys created crippling restrictions on an offensive off the American East Coast. Germany possessed at this time ninety-one boats, a not insignificant figure. But more than one-third (thirty-three) were in for repairs and maintenance; twenty more were either on their way to or on their way back from operational zones in the Atlantic. No fewer than twenty-three were in the Mediterranean, six more off Gibraltar, and four in Norway. Initially, Dönitz would have to make do with five boats, though later he would dispatch a few more. But these were good, modern vessels, new Type IXs displacing more than a thousand tons and well built. And he had hard, dashing, daring men like Reinhard Hardegen and Ernst Kals to command them. So off they went, smashing through wintry North Atlantic seas in early January 1942, set to inflict "a second Pearl Harbor upon a country whose naval leadership knew they were probably coming but was wholly unprepared to meet them."[52]

Throughout the winter and into the spring of 1942, urban authorities along the American eastern seaboard kept their skylines shining at night, their supper and dancing clubs blazing with light as if there was no war. "Reprehensibly," Michael Gannon states, "not a single coastal commander—ESF [Eastern Sea Frontier], Naval District, or Army—seems to have called for so much as a dimout of waterfront cities as security against U-boats."[53] This criminal negligence together with the desire of less competent and confident merchant skippers to orient themselves after dark by readily identifiable positions ashore resulted in brightly lit kill backgrounds for Germany's unmolested marauders who began fatally torpedoing their first victims at midmonth, many of them tankers carrying fuel for the cold cities of the East Coast and the prospective battlefronts of North Africa.

As the first U-boat kills were confirmed at the new Eastern Sea Frontier Headquarters in New York City, sixty-two-year-old admiral Adolphus Andrews sent every vessel he possessed to sea to hunt the enemy, "including some ships never designed for anything beyond harbor traffic" but rigged up with a depth charge or two. As the depredations continued day after day and week after week along with King's stubborn refusal to devote precious destroyers to convoying, the U.S. Navy and Coast Guard scraped the bottom of the barrel. It was simply not enough. Starting off the New England coast, the U-boat skippers, operating independently, worked their way down the coast, past New York, on to the waters off Cape Hatteras, and eventually Florida, killing tankers and other merchantmen, often in broad daylight before appalled onlookers ashore. Across the Atlantic, Churchill became alarmed, then incensed. Those tankers going down were carrying Britain's precious lifeblood. After a month, in a memorable reversal of Lend-Lease, the prime minister sent a flotilla of antisubmarine trawlers across the stormy Atlantic to help his besieged new allies. After several weeks of necessary repairs, the little ships performed bravely and efficiently. Two were destroyed in battling the U-boats, and the bodies of four recovered crewmen were buried in a single little cemetery down a quiet tree-shaded path at Ocracoke Island, North Carolina.

By March the American public had had enough of seeing ships going down in front of its eyes; the oil men were particularly outraged and made their feelings known directly to Washington officialdom through the Tanker Committee of the Petroleum Industry War Council. Politicians and nightclub owners suddenly felt the blowtorch of outrage. Finally, in late spring the garish lights of the coastal cities began to dim or go out, while Churchill continued to bombard his friend Franklin Roosevelt with complaints about the unacceptable rate of shipping losses. The frustrated prime minister sent Roger Winn, the brilliant head of the Admiralty's Submarine Tracking Room in London, to Washington to brief the Americans on ways and means to develop intelligence and tracking capabilities. He was told by one of King's subordinates that the Americans would learn their own lessons about antisubmarine warfare and had the ships to do it, thank you very much. Winn, a lawyer in private life, exploded: "The trouble is, Admiral, it's not only your bloody ships you're losing: a lot of them are ours!" Winn was promptly ushered in to see King who directed that an officer be sent to England to learn the tracking-room business properly. Of more immediate help, the chief of naval operations transferred eight destroyers to the Eastern Sea Frontier, together with a host of small Coast Guard cutters, *"Eagle"*-class motor patrol boats of 1918 vintage, and other small craft that could be fitted with crude detectors and depth charges. About this time, the embattled CNO wrote his army counterpart, General George Marshall, rather plaintively that no one understood better than he the value of convoys: "The convoy is not only *a* way to protect shipping," King wrote, but "it is the *only* way." Frustrated civilians, eager to help, were gathered into a coastal patrol to report the presence of any U-boat that carelessly revealed itself. Together with the British trawlers, this hastily gathered scrub fleet began to find and even attack Hardegen and his mates who, with the American coast now dark or dim at night, were increasingly forced to attack shipping in daylight. The air corps, joined by growing numbers of naval aircraft, abandoned the usually fruitless search for U-boats and concentrated on protecting the increasing number of convoys, with which the U-boats would eventually have to deal if they expected to kill the number of ships Dönitz deemed essential to drive Britain, if not the United States, from the war.

The happy times did not end immediately for Dönitz's sailors. On the night of April 10, Hardegen's U-123 torpedoed a tanker less than a mile off still brilliantly illuminated St. Augustine, Florida. People onshore rushed out of homes, hotels, and movie houses to stand on the beach in shocked horror as the doomed vessel burned and spilled oil. "A rare show for the tourists," Hardegen wrote sardonically in his war diary. But the dramatic rate of sinkings was beginning to decline as convoy and patrol activity increased, while far to the north and east the Battle of the Atlantic reached a climax, requiring as many U-boats as Dönitz could muster. If King lacked resources in the early months of the American war, so did his German opposite; it was becoming an old story for Germany: too few submarines to exploit opportunities that soon vanished. By August 1942, with more patrol vessels at sea every week and American antisubmarine skills rapidly sharpening, the kill ratio on the Atlantic seaboard reversed. Dönitz admitted sadly in his "War Log" that "in the sea area off Hatteras successes have dropped considerably." Only two boats had enjoyed recent success. Three others had been destroyed and another badly damaged. "This state of things is not justified by the amount of success achieved." The boats were withdrawn.[54]

For a time the U-boatwaffe stood up determinedly to the onslaught of American and British industrial power, technical expertise, and tactical ability that gathered with ever accelerating force in the months after Pearl Harbor. But by the end of 1942 British and American destroyer skippers and escort-group commanders were broadly agreed on a basic doctrine for confronting U-boats. The limited capabilities of submarine warfare in the diesel era had at last become clear. Hitler and Dönitz did not possess true *submarines,* merely small, submersion-capable, and, above all, *slow* torpedo boats. Deny the U-boat surface mobility—indeed, the very surface of the sea itself—for even a limited time, and it was practically useless, either individually or collectively. Once a U-boat was detected by radar, sonar, Huff Duff, or, after late 1943, "aircraft sweeping around a convoy by day or night"—whether it was approaching the convoy singly or in a pack, or having initiated a successful attack—it was immediately counterattacked by one or more destroyers, frigates, or corvettes who drove it beneath the surface. The submarine was then "held down" for long minutes or hours, allowing the convoy to escape. With its limited surface speed, an individual U-boat or even pack might take hours to catch up, all the while on the surface and increasingly vulnerable to patrolling ships and aircraft. If there was a sufficient number of antisubmarine vessels (as increasingly there were by 1943–1945) to devote exclusive attention to the U-boat, one or more would remain over the twisting, turning vessel for hours or even a day and more if necessary, tormenting the submerged craft by sporadic depth-charge attacks and a constant presence until either the submarine and its desperate crew was able to finally get away or the U-boat became sufficiently damaged or its crew so exhausted and frantic by hours of pounding that they surfaced their craft and took their chances on a direct fight. In nearly every instance in which U-boats surfaced to fight it out with British or American destroyers or land- and later escort carrier–based aircraft, they were sunk and most if not all of their crew killed.[55]

In October 1942 the North Atlantic war turned decisively. Dönitz lost a dozen U-boats that month while sinking but 38 out of the roughly 725 Allied merchantmen at sea, which amounted to a German kill ratio of only 5 percent. Only 3 of the 16 Allied convoys were heavily attacked. Nine or 10 of the 12 Nazi submarines were sunk by British and American aircraft unassisted by surface ships. The growing influence of airpower in the Battle of Atlantic had become manifest.[56]

Typically, Dönitz and his captains could not believe that British industry could develop the kinds of delicate instruments in suitably small packages that the U-boats began to confront as early as 1941. Germany could never build such equipment. And if Germany could not, then its mortal enemy could not. There are no more pathetic passages in the *U-boat Commander's Handbook* than those brief paragraphs dealing with "principles of defence by means of sound location" and communications. As late as 1943 Dönitz was telling his captains that all they had to fear was asdic and very long-range high-frequency radio direction finders located at several points in England. British capabilities even in these long-outmoded technologies were rather airily dismissed. "The interference level of the sound-locating vessel depends on the magnitude of the sounds proceeding from it, and on the state of the sea," Dönitz assured his men. "Traveling at speed, and rough seas, as well as the proximity of other ships, greatly impair the efficiency of the sound locating instruments." The manual was silent about shipboard and airborne radar, high-frequency radio detectors, and the many other advanced products that were streaming out of British and American laboratories to bedevil and destroy Germany's undersea sailors. The entire Enigma issue was, obviously, so top secret that it could not even be discussed. Poor, foolish Dönitz was setting his beloved boys up for massacre.[57]

Nonetheless, there would be one last moment of glory in the winter of 1943, to be followed by an instant and irretrievable reversal of fortune in the spring. Devastating assaults on convoys ONS-165, -166, -167, HX-229, and SC-122 during February and March seemed to presage a German victory. German shipyards and the Baltic training grounds were producing U-boats and crews in such profusion that U-boat packs of up to fifty boats apiece were operating all over the North Atlantic, and "it seemed ever more pointless to base the routing of convoys on radio intelligence and evasive tactics. A convoy which had avoided the concentration of one U-boat pack was likely, shortly after, to fall into the jaws of the next." But close observers of the U-boat war could see positive results emerging. First, in a long-running convoy battle, the Germans did best on the opening night. Once surprise was lost, Allied escorts responded quickly and effectively to attacks. Second, escort carriers were beginning to appear in sufficient numbers in the U.S. and the Royal Navies that they could close the last air gap on the Atlantic as part of the traditional Ocean Escort Group or form the nucleus of wide-ranging Support Groups operating independently of the convoys to destroy U-boats before the Germans could mount convoy attacks.[58]

Even as German submarines reached an apex of lethal efficiency, there was something pathetic in the boast of one of the admiral's staff people, himself a former submarine commander, that in the first twenty days of March, "we sank 105 ships totalling over half a million gross register tons, equivalent to half the new British construction for an entire year." By this time American shipyards on both coasts were turning out Liberty ships and other transport and supply vessels at a rate that completely eclipsed the British effort. During its forty-four-month participation in World War II, the United States built 2,751 Liberty ships together with several thousand other types of freighters, cargo vessels, transports, and landing craft. One West Coast yard sent 16 Liberty ships down its slipways each month.[59] To match this prodigious production rate, Dönitz's young men would have had to maintain their 100 ship–plus kill rate of March 1943 for months on end to again place the Allied cause in jeopardy.

The steadily advancing efficiency of the convoy system (including land- and carrier-based airpower along and well beyond the convoy routes) and the fearful slaughter of U-boats in April and May 1943, not only in the Atlantic but also by the RAF at night in the Bay of Biscay transit zone, at last awakened Dönitz to the realization that "the enemy was using a new radar device in his aircraft which enabled him to locate the U-boats without betraying his own position." In a conference with Hitler on May 31, a despondent Dönitz asked that German industry be tasked with the rapid development of an effective radar search receiver "capable of registering the frequencies being used by attacking aircraft." The führer was sympathetic and promised to do what he could, but he told Dönitz that Germany's industrial capabilities were already being strained to the limit.[60]

The Germans never discovered Ultra, the most horribly effective weapon against them on the North Atlantic. In November 1942, with the capture in the eastern Mediterranean of a German U-boat and its weather codebook, Bletchley Park again broke into the Enigma system and thereafter never lost its ability to read German naval traffic in real time. Fourteen months earlier Dönitz had become "highly suspicious" about the security of his U-boat codes when two of his subs that had rendezvoused at a remote bay in the Cape Verde Islands in response to a message from headquarters were ambushed and nearly destroyed by a British submarine. How could the enemy possibly be right there at just the right moment? Dönitz acted on his anxieties, but unfortunately for him and his crews he made no attempt to have an independent assessment made of his cryptographic security system by scientists outside his immediate circle. Rather, "the investigation was conducted by experts who, because of their official duties, had been constantly occupied with their own and the enemy's cipher systems. They were so convinced of the superiority of their own system that they had largely forfeited their objectivity, failing to consider the possibilities of techno-logical development in the field of electronic computers." Reassured of the inviolability of his signal code system, Dönitz went on using the Enigma ma-chines, unwittingly sending more and more of his men to their deaths.[61]

The following spring British cryptanalysts were at last allowed to share the Ultra secret with their American allies.[62] But the secret remained hidden from even the frontline consumers of its information for decades after the war. U.S. admiral Dan Gallery, who was interviewed in 1974, thought that the informa-tion his antisub task force received each day at sea in early 1944 was the result of inspired guesswork that approached witchcraft.

> We would go out and hunt submarines as best we could. Of course, we relied very heavily on the daily broadcast from Washington from the Tenth Fleet: the estimate of the submarine situation in the Atlantic which they put out every day. . . . There was a Commander Ken Knowles in Washing-ton who ran this submarine estimate thing. He was just a soothsayer. He could put himself in the position of a German skipper and just figure out what the guy was going to do and where he was going to go. He was abso-lutely uncanny in his predictions.
>
> I treated this COMINCH [commander in chief] daily estimate as Bible truth every day and we based our operations on it completely. One reason why I did was that the very first thing that happened on this first cruise was we got a special message from COMINCH from the Tenth Fleet saying: "There is going to be a refueling rendezvous of submarines off the Azores at a certain point at sunset on a certain day." It just gave us that informa-tion. We were going to be reasonably close to it so I laid off about a hun-dred miles from that point until about four in the afternoon. Then we launched eight torpedo planes to search that area. And right at sunset we caught the refueler with a sub alongside, hoses stretched across, and another sub standing by waiting his turn. We caught them and we blasted the hell out of the refueler and the guy alongside of him.[63]

But, of course, Ultra would have been useless without suitable weapons to implement it.[64] The decisive ingredient in the defeat of the U-boats was not radar, sonar, or Huff Duff but airpower, and here the Allies at first blundered badly. Shore- and carrier-based aircraft improved the range of antisubmarine activities ten- to a hundredfold. With enough Allied antisubmarine ships and aircraft, there was literally no part of the North and central Atlantic where U-boats could hide, especially since their basic task was not to evade the enemy but to aggressively seek out and attack him.

Until the development of the *Schnorchel* near the end of the war, German U-boats had to spend a great deal of time on the surface recharging batteries and, as Dönitz improved German underway replenishment techniques, refueling. Indeed, the need to replenish and refuel brought even the *Schnorchel* boats to the surface periodically. Because of Enigma, U-boats were thus vulnerable to sudden, shattering air attack. But at the beginning of the war, Coastal Command remained a small, unprestigious force with a limited number of short-range aircraft operating exclusively out of bases on the west coasts of the British Isles. The RAF continued to control both production and allocation of all British aircraft, and for many long months it fed machines and crews into Coastal Command with what the Royal Navy thought was criminal slowness. In the spring of 1942, Rear Admiral Louis Hamilton, commander of the First Cruiser Squadron tasked with escorting Arctic convoys to Russia, wrote bitterly to his mother that while RAF's Bomber Command was beginning to mount thousand-plane raids over Germany, "Coastal Command was being starved of the aircraft it needed to mount long range anti-submarine patrols." Moreover, "German warships were sneaking from the Baltic to Norway without being spotted by the RAF." Winning the Battle of the Atlantic was "hopeless," Hamilton added, so long as Arthur Harris and the rest of the RAF high command continued to believe "we could win the war by bombing German women and children instead of defeating their Navy and Army. . . . I am afraid that there is a grave risk of losing the war unless it is realised: (1) That it is primarily a maritime war. (2) That wars are won by killing the enemy's soldiers or sailors. (3) That the aeroplane is just as much a naval weapon as a submarine or destroyer."[65]

The seizure of Iceland helped the British—and soon the Americans—immeasurably in extending the range of their antisubmarine air patrols, and the British concentrated on developing the very long-range Liberator antisubmarine bomber. But air patrols from land (save those over the Bay of Biscay from nearby British bases) involved long hours of tedious flying and the expenditure of vast amounts of fuel. As late as the spring of 1943, a "black gap" existed in the North Atlantic convoy routes halfway between Iceland and Newfoundland. Small, cheap aircraft carriers that could either sail with convoys or act as independent hunter-killer groups were the obvious solution.

If the Allies did not know the value of escort carriers before September 1941, they should have thereafter. In that month, HMS *Audacity*, the former German merchant ship *Hannover* hastily converted, became the first "convoy aircraft carrier" to ply the seas. It made two highly successful runs to Gibraltar and back that autumn, accompanying and protecting British convoys. The small carrier's six to eight Grumman Martlet fighter planes shot down several long-range German aircraft and strafed a number of U-boats attempting to penetrate the convoy screen by day. In December it accompanied Johnnie Walker's famous convoy HG-76 that came through with the loss of only two merchant-men while sinking four U-boats. *Audacity* was instrumental in Walker's success: its fighters protected the convoy, chased off Göring's Focke-Wulf 200 long-range bombers, and continually sighted and tracked shadowing U-boats, allowing Walker's escorts to drive in for the kill. Unfortunately, not even its commanding officer knew how to handle this new ship of war. *Audacity* was torpedoed and sunk near the end of the voyage when the captain took it off several miles to starboard of the convoy to assume what he thought would be a safe night-time steaming position.[66]

Audacity was unsatisfactory in many ways: it was quite small and had been hastily thrown together; it possessed no hangar, which meant that for a takeoff, all nonoperational aircraft had to be ranged as far aft as possible, and even then the 462-foot runway was frighteningly short; and aviation mechanics and armorers cursed as they were forced to work out on the small, open flight deck in the wild Atlantic weather and damp sea air, which jammed throttles, seized up guns, fouled firing circuits, and corroded gun wells, breechblocks and barrels, IFF (identification, friend or foe) switches, spark plugs, and contact breakers. "After dark they had to use torches [that is, flashlights] masked by flue filters, screened by hand or jacket." Later escort carriers, whether converted or built from the keel up, all possessed enclosed hangar decks, but they needed frequent refits, as neither the hull nor propulsion machinery was designed for the kind of treatment received as a warship. The aviation gasoline systems also proved to be highly vulnerable, and the addition of electronic and ballast systems meant additional delays in construction.[67]

Nonetheless, *Audacity*'s brief career had been so spectacular, its ability to successfully fend off close-in submarine and air attacks against the convoy so marked, that it seems criminal that Allied officials dallied so long in bringing forth successors. This was especially true of the British, who complained bitterly that the Americans were slow in closing the mid-Atlantic air gap with their own long-range antisubmarine aircraft. British author Martin Middlebrook has argued that although escort carriers did valuable work, they were not a complete answer. "Each carrier tied up a large number of destroyers in its close escort; there were many days in the North Atlantic on which their aircraft could not fly; the aircraft did not have a great range." Yet Middlebrook is forced to concede that between April and August 1943, the combination of Support Groups, escort carriers, the closing of the mid-Atlantic air gap, and the changing of the Allied convoy radio codes in response to knowledge received from decrypting German Enigma signals defeated the U-boats.[68]

Peter Gretton, himself an escort commander during the climactic U-boat battles of March–April 1943, later characterized the wide-ranging Support Groups coming into place at that moment on the North Atlantic convoy lanes as a "potent factor" in destroying the Nazi submarine menace. "Taken alone," the fast-moving destroyers and frigates "were important assets, and when they also included an escort carrier with its anti-submarine planes and its fighters they were very formidable indeed. Moreover, when the weather in Iceland or Northern Ireland was such as to prevent flying from the bases... the escort carriers could probably operate and thus help to keep the 'air gap' closed."[69]

The Americans began an active escort-carrier conversion and construction program soon after Pearl Harbor, but the first products were employed to supply close-in air support to the North African invasion in November 1942. The British were even more dilatory. *Audacity*'s successor, HMS *Avenger,* did not deploy for nine months after its predecessor. After its air group performed superbly in sub-Arctic and Arctic waters fighting off U-boats and Luftwaffe air attacks against convoys PQ-18 and QP-14 in September 1942, the carrier sank like a rock after being struck by a single torpedo on November 15 (just twelve months later the American CVE *Liscome Bay* would go up like a torch after a similar blow off the Gilberts), and HMS *Dasher* was destroyed by a gasoline explosion in the Clyde the following spring. The next British CVE on the North Atlantic convoy lanes, HMS *Biter,* did not appear until April 1943, sixteen long months after *Audacity* slipped beneath the waves. The Admiralty seems to have been content to wait for the Americans to supply the Royal Navy with CVEs, then complained about the quality of the ships.

There was obviously some merit to the British complaints. But in August 1943, the Allied Antisubmarine Survey Board charged the British with overcaution in retaining American-built CVEs in their shipyards for prolonged periods of overhaul and upgrade. A knowledgeable American critic charged the Royal Navy with incompetence and inefficiency in operating escort carriers. By the time *Biter* at last went to sea, uss *Bogue* had begun its spectacular antisubmarine career, and from then on escort carriers joined destroyers as the prime killers of Dönitz's ships and men.[70]

The Germans fought back as best they could against the advanced technologies thrown against them, but the Allies successfully countered every weapon system that Dönitz was able to place aboard his tiny undersea craft. The German acoustic torpedo was defeated for a time by a simple towed noisemaker. On the other hand, the Allied version of the acoustic torpedo, "Fido," killed more than a dozen U-boats in the central Atlantic between the summer of 1943 and the following spring.[71] The ever more advanced German radar detectors that Nazi industry did manage to produce, from Metox through Wanse, Naxos, and Fliege to Mucke, were readily countered by Allied ten- and then three-centimeter radar sets that produced such a narrow detection beam that even the most advanced German instruments could not pick them up. Late in the war the Americans produced MAD (Magnetic Anomoly Detector) for detecting U-boats just below the surface or in shallow waters.[72]

The decisive turn in the Battle of the Atlantic came in May 1943 when Germany's U-boat youngsters attacked Allied convoys with as great a verve and daring as ever, only to lose an incredible forty-one boats. The victory was largely British and Canadian, for the previous month Washington, Ottawa, and London agreed that the Americans would be responsible for both the central transatlantic route from New York and the West Indies to Gibraltar and the Brazil-Boston route through Guantánamo, while the Royal and Royal Canadian Navies would protect the northern transatlantic convoys. Dönitz's son, twenty-one-year-old Oberleutnänt Peter Dönitz, died as second watch officer with all his mates aboard U-954 as it went in to attack convoy SC-130. The loss seemed to quietly break Dönitz. Forty-one boats! And for what? No fewer than four wolf packs found and assaulted SC-130. Not one Allied warship or merchantman was hit, while five U-boats perished. At the end of the month, Dönitz temporarily withdrew his wolves from the North Atlantic sea-lanes to ponder his next step, though he continued to maintain a few boats off Brazil and the shipping routes along the West African coast.[73]

One German historian has argued, with great merit, that the decisive theater in the U-boat war was not the Atlantic but the Bay of Biscay, and according to Clay Blair no fewer than thirty U-boats were destroyed and another nineteen

damaged in the bay between April and September 1943 by RAF bombers and
Royal Navy hunter-killer groups operating in conjunction with Coastal Command. At first the U-boats sought to counter the menace by surface transitting
the bay at night. But the nerves of many a bridge crew were shattered by the
sudden, blinding appearance out of the murk of aircraft searchlights that illuminated their vessel for the kill. Once again, Allied advanced technology was
responsible. The airborne sets available to the RAF by mid-1943 could track a
surfaced U-boat only to a point about two thousand yards away before sea return blocked the image. Squadron leader Humphrey de Vere Leigh proposed
placing a high-powered strobe light aboard each plane tied into the radar system.
An aircraft approaching a radar-contacted submarine would cut its engines at
the point where the U-boat's image began to fade off the screen, and the pilot
would keep the plane on its glide path toward the interception point with the
unsuspecting U-boat. Some seven or eight hundred yards out, the pilot would
turn on his "Leigh Light" to illuminate the submarine and kill it with bombs,
depth charges, or concentrated machine-gun fire. At their May 31 conference,
Dönitz informed Hitler that no less than 65 percent of recent U-boat losses had
occurred from the air during transit, rather than by enemy surface-ship action
in the convoy lanes.[74]

By the time Nazi science was able to provide Dönitz with a truly revolutionary system that just might have turned the balance of force and power on the
North Atlantic, it was too late. The *Schnorchel* was neutralized as much by
plummeting morale within the U-boat arm as by enemy countermeasures. The
Schnorchel was simply a long, elaborate breathing tube protruding from a shallow-
running submarine that allowed the boat to take in the oxygen required to
recharge its electric batteries and refresh the air within the hull without surfacing. But whatever advantage this stealth system might have bestowed upon the
U-boatwaffe was negated by a growing sense of grim despair. The crunching
losses of April–August 1943 seem to have taken the heart out of Dönitz's sailors
and the admiral himself.

> In June 1943 I was faced with the most difficult decision of the whole
> war. I had to make up my mind whether to withdraw the boats from all
> areas and call off the U-boat war, or to let them continue operations in
> some suitably modified form, regardless of the enemy's superiority.
>   Germany was on the defensive on all fronts. The Army was engaged in
> a series of hard-fought defensive battles. The air-raids on Germany itself
> were becoming increasingly severe. Under these conditions what effect
> would the abandonment of the U-boat campaign have on our war situa-

tion as a whole? Could we afford to abandon it? Were we justified, in view of our inferiority, in calling upon our submarines to continue the unequal struggle?

In the end, Dönitz "finally came to the bitter conclusion that we had no option but to fight on. The U-boat Arm could not stand aside and watch the onslaught, of which it had hitherto borne the brunt, now fall in all its fury as an additional burden on the other fighting services and the civilian population."[75]

So the gray wolves dutifully continued to put to sea to perish in steadily growing numbers; they had little choice with the draconian Gestapo and SS around to enforce wartime discipline in the harshest possible manner. Dönitz was reaching the bottom of the manpower pool now. In January 1944 U-223 sailed from the Vichy French Mediterranean port of Toulon under the command of twenty-two-year-old Peter Gerlach, whose only previous leadership experience was a seven-week "spell" under the watchful eye of a senior U-boat captain at the Twenty-second Training Flotilla in the Baltic. Gerlach tried. He sank a British destroyer but was pinned down and depth-charged by several of its experienced mates until the young Nazi captain decided the game was up and he would surface to save as many of his men as he could. Sending his twenty-year-old engineering officer below to set the scuttling charges, Gerlach then set his boat at full speed and ordered his men to jump off. He was "no good without his boat," Gerlach told a colleague, and disappeared. Even in the end, Gerlach failed, for the empty, onrushing U-boat suddenly turned of its own volition (possibly due to a rudder malfunction when the scuttling charges went off), doubled back, and even as it began to sink killed a large number of its crew as it ran them down, its propellers thrashing the seas.[76]

By this time, many of Hitler's youngsters no longer sought battle. Samuel Eliot Morison dismisses as a "nuisance" and a "dim blitz" the assault of three Schnorchel-equipped U-boats on the American East Coast in the early spring of 1944. In May the wolves sank only five Allied merchant ships totaling a little more than twenty-seven thousand tons while losing twenty-two U-boats, a shocking, unacceptable loss-to-success ratio.[77] By this time, the Schnorchel's limitations had become familiar to both sides. The system was virtually inoperable in any sort of heavy seas that washed over and down the pipe, causing the Schnorchel to short out in several highly unpleasant ways that left the crew in great if temporary distress.[78] Moreover, by 1944 the Allies had developed radar systems that could detect even the small head of a Schnorchel protruding above the waves several miles away. The Sunderlands, Liberators, and superb Avenger aircraft operating both from shore and off the decks of escort carriers in the central and North Atlantic thus hounded the U-boats day and night with radar and searchlights across the length and breadth of the ocean as well as in the Bay of Biscay transit zone.

Clay Blair has summed up the Battle of the Atlantic in these trenchant words:

> Some historians . . . write that on January 1, 1944, the German U-boat force reached a peak wartime strength of 436 or 456 boats. Seen at a glance these figures imply an enormous threat to Allied shipping, but nothing could be further from the truth. Although personnel of the U-boat arm remained resolutely and famously defiant [a defiance that would erode dramatically in coming months if Admiral Morison is to be believed], its strategy, tactics, and weaponry had failed—indeed, had failed abysmally. The only hope of a comeback rested on the possibility—repeat possibility—of obtaining at the earliest feasible date an effective search radar and radar detector, improved sonar, a reliable, high-angle automatic 37 mm anti-aircraft gun, better T-5 homing and other torpedoes, small and big "electro boats," "Walter boats," and a big fleet of Luftwaffe JU-290's for long-range detection and escort duties. But, of course, by this time even a fraction of such a wish-list was well beyond the capabilities of the over-strained German wartime economy to provide.[79]

After D day, Dönitz's wolves lost their finest French bases and were forced to operate from Norway or even German ports. Despite the *Schnorchel* and the threat of extremely fast Type XXI U-boats to come, "Allied escort-of-convoy and air cover had been so much improved by the summer of 1944 that the snorkel [*sic*] skippers were extremely wary, took few chances, and fired torpedoes only at enemy setups. They avoided transatlantic convoys. . . . [S]hip losses were about a tenth of one per cent."

Early that year Dönitz, heartbroken and embittered, admitted that "the enemy has succeeded in gaining the advantage in submarine defence." But it would not last, he promised. The Type XXI would change everything, and the day would again come "when I shall offer Churchill a first-rate submarine war." Germany had not been broken by the "setbacks of 1943," the grand admiral insisted. Nineteen forty-four would be a hard but successful year. After that, "we shall smash Britain's supply with a new submarine weapon." Dönitz was fated for disillusionment once more. The few Type XXIs that appeared were victims of bungling German production priorities and Allied bombing of German industrial plants. They proved to be poorly designed and built. Their diesel engines were "ruinously underpowered." The hydraulic systems that controlled the diving planes, rudder, torpedo-tube outer doors, and antiaircraft guns on the bridge were actually placed *outside* of the pressure hull, guaranteeing that any serious depth charging would cripple a boat. The modular hulls hurriedly prefabricated in thirty-two different factories that had little or no experience in such construction were often poorly welded, threatening the structural integrity of the XXIs and drastically limiting their ability to operate at any but the shallowest of depths.[80]

No more damning indictment can be made of Germany's U-boat arm than the fact that in the end it failed utterly to seal Hitler's Fortress Europe off from an assault from the West. Despite their undeniable tenacity and even gallantry in the service of a vile cause, Dönitz's gray wolves could not halt the buildup of men and matériel in the United Kingdom for the decisive cross-Channel attack against occupied France. Nor had Hitler's sailors earlier prevented the opening of a second front in North Africa and the Mediterranean that deflected badly needed German troops and aircraft from the main battlefields in Russia. Perhaps the most striking aspect of the Nazi failure at sea is that although many cargo ships went to the bottom, and the bones of many an Allied sailor lie bleaching the floor of the North Atlantic, comparatively few American or Canadian soldiers were drowned on their way to Algeria, Italy, or France.

The Allied logistical problem in the Atlantic had been relatively simple from the start. Whereas the Germans derived "immense advantage" from possession of submarine bases up and down the Atlantic coast of Europe, the Allies on both ends of the Atlantic had well-developed ports and naval stations from which to bring the U-boats to immediate battle. The destroyers-for-bases deal extended the shield of U.S. naval facilities far out into the Atlantic and Caribbean, where the U-boats were readily found to strike and to kill.[81] Once the Luftwaffe threat to British ports lessened after the opening of the Russian front in June 1941, British dockhands and cargo dispatch specialists with three centuries of experience in a global imperial trade to draw on were able to absorb, direct, and accommodate the growing flood of men and matériel from across seas with increasing efficiency.

All this paid off in the gray dawn of June 6, 1944, on Normandy's beaches, when horrified defenders abruptly saw through the rising mist the greatest invasion armada in history rushing toward them.[82] The Germans were enveloped in a literal typhoon of steel from ships bloodied in a half-dozen amphibious operations in the Mediterranean. At Omaha Beach, where the defenders had the best chance of throwing the invaders back into the sea, thus splitting the entire Allied lodgment for a later roll-up, conditions for a time were as appalling as on any landing zone in the Pacific. Like Salerno, Tarawa, and Iwo Jima, Omaha was nothing less than an awful industrial accident created out of hours of sustained and unlimited violence between determined foes. By midmorning, some four hours after the initial landings, the issue was still in doubt, and the beach was littered with blasted and burning vehicles, wrecked tanks, and rows of corpses, among which were the screaming, groaning, or deathly quiet wounded. The noise level oscillated wildly between deafening sound and sudden, eerie quiet. As at Salerno nearly a year before, naval gunfire delivered from American and British warships that "ran their keels to within inches of the sand" was essential in securing and sustaining a foothold.

> At about 0800 individual destroyers began closing the beach to fire on targets of opportunity on their own responsibility. An hour later Captain Harry Sanders (Comdesron 18), who had done close-in fighting in the Mediterranean, entered Fire Support Area No. 3 and promptly sized up the situation. Concerned over the [carnage] ashore, he ordered all destroyers to move in as close as possible to the beach to support the troops. Admiral Bryant at 0950 called all gunfire support ships over TBS [the "talk between ships" circuit]: "Get on them, men. Get on them! They are raising hell with the men on the beach and we can't have any more of that! We must stop it!" Magnificently they complied.... In their eagerness to help they incurred the risk of running aground time and again; and several did scrape the bottom, but got off.[83]

Critics have since argued that at Omaha, "naval and air preparatory fires had failed to neutralize the German defenses," resulting in unnecessary and unacceptably high casualties. The villains, argues Adrian R. Lewis, were Generals Omar Bradley and Bernard Law Montgomery, who agreed to ignore what had become solid naval and military "doctrine" on the need for powerful and above all sustained bombardment of enemy beach defenses in favor of a diffused and ineffective combination attack from air (the Eighth Air Force) and sea. Lessons painfully acquired at Dieppe, Salerno, Tarawa, and Sicily were thus dismissed. "The naval force at Normandy lacked the time and resources necessary to destroy or neutralize enemy defenses at Omaha Beach. The Navy had less than 40 minutes of daylight in the U.S. sector to neutralize the German defenses" before the assault began. Moreover, bombardment forces were equally divided between the Omaha and Utah beachheads, even though the former was known to be a much tougher nut to crack than the latter. Bradley was on the point of withdrawing the Omaha forces and throwing them into the Utah beachhead when he received word that at least some of the enemy strongholds had been reduced by a combination of naval gunfire and heroic soldiering ashore and that the first troops were moving off the sands, up the draws, and on inland.[84] Such arguments overlook the felt need by the Allied leadership to mask the time and place of the Normandy landings until the last moment in order to seal the invasion beaches off from effective enemy reinforcements and counter-attacks during the critical first twenty-four hours. Although naval gunfire may have been tragically inadequate in the preparatory stage at Normandy, it was clearly crucial during the initial assault phase on all the beaches and remained a vital element in expanding the initial lodgments. Yet Lewis and other critics may have made an important if never clearly stated point. Given command of the air and especially the effectiveness of long-range and heavy naval-support bombardment, it might well have been wiser to advertise rather than obscure the Normandy objective in order to allow naval gunfire and airpower to break up and destroy enemy armor and infantry formations rushing toward the invasion beaches. Erwin Rommel had hoped to drive the Allied armies back into the sea by concentrated armor attacks against the beachhead. But all evidence indicates that if his plan had materialized, the initial German defeat would have been even greater, for the tank columns would have simply been ground to pieces by naval gunfire. Gerd von Rundstedt later complained that the piece-meal commitment of his handful of armored divisions around the critical stronghold of Caen was a great mistake. He had wanted to relieve his tanks with infantry divisions, he told Allied interrogators, but the panzers "were always too closely engaged and anyway were under fire from the Navy" ten miles away. Long-range naval gunfire and the steady flow of Allied troops and supplies onto the invasion beaches after D day thus prevented the Germans from mounting a strong and coherent defense that might have isolated the beachheads and led to a replication of Gallipoli (indeed, the topography of Omaha Beach more than roughly resembles descriptions of the Suvla [Anafarta] Bay and Anzac beachheads of 1915).[85]

Finally, offshore gunfire support was critical to the successful Allied assault at Cherbourg on June 25, 1944. Seizure of the great French port shifted the center of sea-power support from gunfire to logistics. Logistics dictated the Allied selection of assault sites reasonably close to a major port (Cherbourg) and drove initial strategical-tactical considerations once a lodgment was made and its expansion begun. As Roland Ruppenthal has emphasized, the Allies did not plan on fighting their major engagement with German forces west of the Seine, and when they in fact did so at Falaise, their entire set of tactical and logistic assumptions was thrown off, as the Anglo-American armies were suddenly free to race across France and up into the Low Countries. Logistical capabilities never truly caught up with tactical and strategic hopes and plans before the German surrender, and this led to much confusion and anguish. But the cornucopia of supplies and men from U.S. and British factories and training centers never faltered and was sorted out with enough efficiency at Cherbourg and, much later, at Antwerp, so that except for a frustrating period between September and December 1944, problems of sustaining and fueling the Allied advance in the West never became insuperable.[86]

Normandy was more than just a campaign; it was one of a handful of defining moments in the twentieth century. "D-Day began the great peace that began to civilize Europe," a British journalist and historian wrote fifty years after the event. "A kind of miracle emerged, in which the Europeans laid aside their martial pasts and adapted comfortably to the new role of an economic giant that chose—perhaps for the first time in history—not to spend that wealth on becoming a military superpower." The "essence of that European decision, whatever the inter-alliance squabbles along the way, was trust in the Americans as an honorable ally and a reliable custodian of the stability and the democratic hopes of Europe. And the real meaning of D-Day was that it symbolized the moment when that trust was earned in blood."[87] So the hinge of fate that was the Battle of the Atlantic closed irrevocably in decency's favor.

CHAPTER 10

The Allies

Foundations of Conquest

AS THE UNITED STATES edged tensely toward war after 1939, its navy remained essentially what it had been since the turn of the century: a tough, competent, and (except for 1917–1918) relatively small service filled with many dedicated and innovative professionals—Halsey, Lee, Nimitz, Spruance, Mitscher, Gatch, Burlingame, Ramage, Lockwood, O'Hare, Thach, Flatley, Widhelm, and others—who stood confidently ready to take the navy to four-dimensional warfare anywhere in the world. The men who would hold the line against the surging Japanese in 1942—Bruce McCandless, Frank Jack Fletcher, and Norman Scott among them—had won their first commands in 1917–1918, often of the tough little "flush deck and four pipe" destroyers that carried the brunt of the United States Navy's war effort.[1]

The enlisted men were of a surprisingly high quality. They were an interesting group, as anyone can attest who happened across them in the early postwar years when many had become warrant or chief petty officers. Tough products of a scarcity economy, the Depression-era boys fitted naturally into the astringent and highly conservative environment of a peacetime armed service. With the inevitable exceptions, they proved to be adept students and good teachers, fairly quick to learn and as their turn arrived in the pecking order surprisingly patient in instructing those beneath them, yet wholly intolerant of incompetents, slackers, and shirkers. In sum, they constituted a perfect cadre around which to transform their service to global proportions.[2]

Throughout the thirties the navy could pick and choose its people. In 1938–1939, for example, only 9 percent of applicants were enlisted. Two years earlier there were already six thousand men on the enlisted waiting list.[3] The eighteen, nineteen, and twenty year olds who signed on for a six-year "hitch" at twenty-one dollars a month quickly learned what to expect, and what was expected of them. Unlike the world's other great sea services, the United States Navy was not driven by fanatic devotion to a führer, a duce, an emperor, or even sentimental attachment to a constitutional monarch. It was a career where one served one's country, but also fulfilled oneself. It reflected and responded to the American character of rabid ambition, incessant competition, personal betterment, and scarcely concealed contempt for those who did not measure up completely. Recruits were admonished to "*Keep this always in mind.* You are being trained to be a future leader of men. The hardest workers among you may become chief petty officers, warrant officers, commissioned officers. The rest of you will get only as far as your work, study, and effort entitle you to."[4]

The anonymous authors of the message "To the Recruit" in the 1940 *Bluejacket's Manual* were not kidding. The best and brightest of the enlisted men could, if they served long and ably enough, become "mustang" officers, advancing through warrant and commissioned ranks to lieutenant commander. A handful of truly exceptional young seamen were plucked from the fleet each year and sent to the academy at Annapolis, where the prospect of becoming senior officers and even admirals was not beyond reason.

From the time they entered the gates of the training stations at San Diego and Great Lakes, recruits knew they would be tested throughout their careers. American naval culture revolved around personal capability, courage, fighting spirit, loyalty—to one's self, to one's mates, above all to one's ship—and a firm but surprisingly evenhanded justice. "Every shipmate was part of a community, and the officers and enlisted men who made up that community expected him to be a good citizen, to enjoy his life aboard [ship], to love his new home, to be proud of [the USS] *Tennessee*" or any other ship to which he was assigned. "There was no room for the obedient sailor who remained an individualist—he had to become part of the [ship's] team."

Junior officers upon entering the naval service were informed in no uncertain terms that their careers would prosper only if they demonstrated an intelligent but firm loyalty both upward and downward.

> If you hope to deserve the loyalty of the men under you, then you must earn it by giving loyalty upward. Take pains to let [the enlisted men] know

that you respect and honor the policies and motives of your common senior. Just as zealously, make sure that you are loyal to your men. Look out for them. Be jealous, for them, of their rights and privileges. If you show them in many little ways that their welfare is your concern, that you are always thinking of ways to better their lot, you will find that they will *give* you a loyalty which you could never *command.*[5]

This was wartime advice. Prior to Pearl Harbor, enlisted men did not know their officers and did not wish to. "In those days I stayed strictly away from the brass as much as possible," a prewar battleship sailor remembered. "So did everyone else if they could. If you ran into them, you just never knew what you'd get. You might get assigned new duties. And when they were around, you had all the formalities you had to take care of, saluting and all this business. If you felt like being a little sloppy, that was fine at other times, but you couldn't do it around them."[6] First- and even second-class petty officers ran the crew. A sailor looking for a favor or more liberty or leave went through these "senior petty officers" who took requests to the chiefs, who passed them on to the ensigns and lieutenants (junior grade) who ran the division for final say. Nonetheless, a decent devotion to the welfare of those one commanded, though all too often observed in the breach, did remain the bedrock of American naval discipline as the country drifted closer to war in the waning days of 1941.

Life was tough for those sailors who could not learn or who would not conform. If a boot consistently failed to tie his neckerchief properly, he might find it drawn tightly against his throat and held there for long moments on hot, sweaty summer days when the temperature on the concrete "grinders" of Illinois or California could reach well above ninety degrees. A boy who failed to keep the rim of his white hat clean might find his entire company of more than fifty men ordered to wipe their muddy feet on the hat, after which his chief would order him to cram the filthy sailcloth into his mouth and keep it there for an entire morning. Whole companies were turned out at midnight for an hour or two of drills if the chief heard one or two of the boys snickering in their hammocks after lights-out; the miscreants were invariably disciplined more harshly by their mates than by the chief. Under such a strict but understandable regimen, most young men fell into line sooner or later.

After six or eight weeks of basic training and, for some, another four to six weeks of basic schooling, recruits were sent to the fleet, where those who had no specialized schooling were arbitrarily assigned where needed in either the deck force or the engine room. There, as a seaman second class or fireman third class, they became a "striker" for various specialty rates—boatswain's mate, gunner's mate, torpedo-man, boiler tender, electrician's mate, radioman, machinist's mate, signalman, and perhaps fifty others, including the aviation rates on carriers and airfields ashore. Those who had been given some schooling were placed higher on the specialist striker ladder and usually attained the petty officer's "crow" much faster. The base pay of thirty-six dollars per month (twenty-one dollars for recruits) began to modestly increase as strikers slowly moved up the promotion ladder into the petty-officer level. The average sailor, "reenlisting at 25, with second-class rating . . . will very likely marry on the salary and allowances that now total about $100 a month. With this spur to ambition, he steers grimly on the course to the chief petty officer rating that will permit him to retire at 45, a master of his trade with a pension of $1,400" per year. Promotion was invariably slow, but with little or no work "on the outside," reenlistment rates averaged above 70 percent, and desertion was practically nonexistent.

Throughout the twenties and thirties "in spite of government neglect the American fleets carried out training programs unparalleled in naval annals." While the Fleet Marine Force probed the defenses of the Panama Canal and Pearl Harbor, the Battle Force of battleships, carriers, cruisers, and destroyers distributed among San Diego, Long Beach, and San Pedro staged yearly communication, gunnery, and engineering competitions to keep fleet personnel up to the highest possible standards. "The program culminated in an annual movement either to the East Coast of the United States, or to Pearl Harbor," then back home to California.[7]

Life aboard the navy's battleships was at once routine, tedious, but fulfilling for many. As late as 1940, most enlisted men slept in hammocks lashed at least six feet above the deck so petty officers and others roaming or passing through the compartment could move comfortably. If you were a quiet sleeper, the hammock was wonderful, because while the ship rocked underneath it in heavy swells, the hammock remained immovable. But "you don't roll around much in bed in a hammock," one sailor from *Arizona* recalled. "Too many times I'd be lying on my side looking at the deck." In the year before Pearl Harbor, most navy ships replaced the hammock with cots, and, eventually, bunks, which the chiefs and first-class petty officers had always enjoyed as a perk of rate. Reveille was at 0500 or, at times, 0530, "and you had until ten to six to put your hammock away, go in and wash up, brush your teeth and hair and come out and have a hot cup of coffee." Many boys never got to the coffee—"I can't move that fast in twenty minutes," one remembered, "even when I'm trying to catch up." For the next hundred minutes, the men either did "bible class"—cleaning wooden decks placed over steel with bricks of sandstone, called "holystones," a tedious task that involved bending over and moving the bricks with a stick in a hole. "We'd scrub that teakwood, and when it dried it was a brilliant white"— or shined the bright work even brighter. The work made a breakfast of "beans and cornbread taste wonderful."[8]

Battleships were big enough to be impersonal, like a small town. Although no one could conceive of the huge supercarriers that lay only fifteen years over the horizon with their crews of five or eventually even six thousand sailors, the interwar battleships of the U.S. Navy carried up to fifteen hundred men, rigidly divided into divisions and even functions, who slept, ate, and lived in tight groups of fifty or a hundred. It was hard for a "deck ape" to get to know a "snipe" (engineer) or an "airdale" (air group aboard carriers, battleships, and cruisers), nor was it easy to break into elitist rates and lifestyles. Getting accepted into a fourteen-inch-gun turret aboard a battlewagon was a real coup. "A man's name was presented by the senior petty officer to the whole gun crew," John Rampley remembered a half century later. "If any of them didn't like him or thought he wouldn't be compatible you didn't get in. So, if you did make it, you felt that you were part of a select crew." Even on the big ships, some of the men slept close to "admiral's country," which was strictly off-limits. "He was way up," a sailor recalled of Admiral Isaac Kidd, the battleship-division commander aboard *Arizona*, "and he had the Marines to guard him. He had his own staff, cook, steward, the works. . . . You rarely saw him, maybe once a year he might hold an inspection. You heard him being piped aboard or piped off, but you didn't want to be around him. Too much gold."[9]

Whereas the battle fleet spent the bulk of its time in the twenties and thirties swinging around anchor chains in southern California, a small squadron of cruisers and destroyers, designated "the Hawaiian Detachment," was based at Pearl Harbor. In January 1940, Floyd Beaver, a young signalman, found himself assigned to the cruiser *Indianapolis,* then finishing a routine overhaul at Mare Island Navy Yard in Vallejo, California. Within days, the cruiser set out for "Pearl" and resumption of duty as the detachment flagship. "The Hawaii we found when we arrived was much different from the tourist mecca it is now," Beaver recalled a lifetime later. Only three small three- to four-story hotels, the white-painted Moana, the blue-clad Surf Rider, and the famous pink Royal Hawaiian, faced Waikiki Beach. "Downtown Honolulu was a definitely low rise small town." Pearl Harbor, too, "was far less than it would become. The hard edges of Navy Yard shops and administration buildings were softened by shading trees and green lawns. Even the parade ground was soft green grass rather than the hard and hot" concrete "*grinders* of Stateside Boot Camps."

The air base on Ford Island, in the middle of the harbor, was almost equally pleasant. I remember rows of small green cottages with red roofs—officers' quarters we were told—ranged under spreading tropical trees along the shores of what would become Battleship Row.

Buses and *taxis* entered and left freely from Pearl Harbor and the Army's inland Schofield Barracks. What we called *taxis* were actually eight-passenger limousines, but they pulled up to the very foot of our gangway at Ten-Ten Dock, entering and leaving the Yard without challenge of any kind. They came into Honolulu along seedy Hotel Street with its stand-up *saimin* counters, raunchy bars, and assorted open-front stores, few of them any more than two or three stories high, selling shoddy goods to a largely native market. Soldiers and sailors were let off at an Army-Navy YMCA hotel, from which they fanned out in search of whatever fun they could find. . . .

Honolulu, because it was so small, was not a good liberty port by Navy standards. But, since there were so few sailors there, it was not bad either. In the eighteen ships of the *Hawaiian Detachment,* there were probably no more than seven or eight thousand men, and fewer than two thousand or so of them would go ashore at any given time. When the ships were at sea, of course, there would be far less than that. Some of us came to enjoy the place.

Duty was light for the most part. We sailed on a schedule of tactical and battle drills which seldom kept us at sea for more than four or five days, a schedule which, in hindsight, made it simple for the Japanese to plan their attack for a time when the largest number of ships would be in port. Liberty was both often and generous. It was a good and comfortable life.[10]

Several times during the interwar period, the navy pressed to have the fleet move all the way to Manila Bay during its annual exercises, but the State Department consistently vetoed the idea so as not to unduly alarm Japan. Some of the more cautious officials at State wanted to prohibit all naval operations west of the 180th meridian.[11] But by the spring of 1940, Roosevelt was listening to Churchill as much as or more than to his diplomats.

The prime minister wanted the U.S. battle fleet at Singapore to tie down the Japanese, thus allowing the Royal Navy's heavy units to concentrate on their German opposites. Roosevelt recognized a fallacious plan when he saw one, but in May 1940 he did order the battle fleet to remain at Pearl Harbor after its coming summer exercises. Admiral James O. Richardson, the fleet commander, protested vigorously and at length. He saw that the Hawaiian garrison suffered a chronic insufficiency of long-range aircraft to properly scout the islands' approaches for an advancing enemy. Pearl Harbor itself was a death trap for big ships—a shallow, narrow, twisting anchorage that could bottle up a fleet of heavy vessels under attack. Richardson's anxieties ran as deep as John Jellicoe's at Scapa Flow a quarter century before, and their legitimacy was much greater. Eventually, Richardson's complaints—which in several instances were sent directly to the Oval Office—cost him Roosevelt's trust, and he was fired. Husband Kimmel, who had distinguished himself as fleet gunnery officer with the American battleship contingent in European waters in 1918, replaced him.[12]

Suddenly, Pearl Harbor and Honolulu were "swamped" by "thousands upon thousands of Battle Force sailors." Restaurants were jammed and movie theaters unbearably crowded, while bars, tattoo parlors, and locker clubs proliferated. "Long lines formed outside the doors of government inspected whore houses. A system of *rainchecks* was devised for those would-be lovers who could not perform with adequate speed. These *rainchecks* became acceptable currency in the settlement of shipboard gambling debts. No one," Floyd Beaver remembered, "had time to waste." Over on battleship *Arizona*, "Nobody ever locked their [personal] locker. But then when the war buildup started and everybody came in, you had to lock your locker."[13]

In October 1940, while Hitler's bombers pounded London and Japan continued to feed on Asia's carcass, *Life* magazine sent its reporters and cameramen to visit the fleet. "The U.S. Navy is good," the editors concluded when their people came back with the story from Pearl Harbor and Norfolk, a "great fighting creation of a people whose genius is . . . mechanical." The battleships incorporated "perhaps the greatest concentration of mechanical marvels and human skills ever assembled under one command," conveniently ignoring or forgetting the fact that the Axis navies were stocked with far more modern, fast, and powerful battleships.

Navy censors in these quiet days of peace when war remained oceans away permitted *Life* editors to make some astonishing admissions that were doubtless read with deep interest in admiralties from Berlin to Rome to Tokyo. Not only was the navy badly undermanned (15 percent below minimal peacetime complement), but "its anti-aircraft defenses are not up to scratch. It is strictly a one-ocean navy. It certainly cannot take on the world." Its battleships were "slow" and "heavy," and although its half-dozen aircraft carriers "are the finest afloat," its 1,812 "useful planes are not as modern as they might be," though the editors stoutly—and erroneously—insisted that "they are nevertheless better than those of any other power."[14]

Moreover, all evidence indicated that even at this late date, the navy remained firmly committed to outmoded traditions and perspectives. Despite the carrier,

the submarine, and the promises of amphibious warfare, "the training cycles of
the thirties reflected the expectation that naval wars of the future would be
decided primarily by clashes between opposing battlelines." The dozen ponderous twenty-one-knot battlewagons in the Pacific remained "the great hitting
might of the modern fleet," and despite the fact that their fourteen- or sixteen-
inch guns possessed an effective range of no more than twenty-three to twenty-
seven miles, the navy retained "complete faith" in these vessels. Along with such
monsters the navy could muster its six carriers together with eighteen heavy and
nineteen light cruisers and "upward of 80 destroyers and 40 long-range submarines." The fleet remained in the Pacific except for a few quick maneuvers in
the Caribbean that tested its ability to transit the Panama Canal quickly. There
was no Atlantic Fleet in 1940, only a motley collection of two or three battleships, one or two of the smallest and slowest carriers, and a handful of cruisers
and destroyers called the Atlantic Squadron.[15] *Life's* writers and editors did not
mention that at least a quarter of the cruiser flotilla and half the destroyers were
obsolete ships completed during or just after the Great War.

Nor did they emphasize the almost crippling weaknesses that beset a battle
fleet bewitched as late as November 1941 with the prospect of a "Pacific Jutland."[16] Service with the British Home Fleet in 1917–1918 had demonstrated
to the U.S. Navy's gunnery and armor specialists that "battleships could and
would engage each other at ranges of twenty thousand yards and beyond."
Moreover, Jutland had shown that massed firepower from concentrated squadrons of battleships laid on an enemy fleet was the surest guarantor of victory at
sea. "By 1917 British officers claimed that the massed fire power of one or two
battle divisions could break up an enemy line as Nelson had done" at Trafalgar.
Repeated references such as these to the climactic battle of the Age of Fighting
Sail reflected a naval mind-set on both sides of the Atlantic fatally wedded to
the past.

Mindful of the hitting power of big guns at sea, naval architects supplied the
dozen battleships of the *Nevada, Pennsylvania, New Mexico, California,* and *Colorado* classes commissioned between 1916 and 1922 with heavy "all or nothing"
armor protection over every important section of the hull. No other battleships
in the world were as well girded. Gunnery specialists, too, enthusiastically embraced the lessons learned during and as a result of their limited wartime deployments with the Royal Navy. The World War I–vintage American battleships
either displayed or were soon provided with advanced fire-control technologies
like the Ford Rangekeeper, an analogue predictor that "could solve the differ-

ential equation associated with the motion of two maneuvering ships." Unfortunately, the accuracy of such machines depended absolutely upon "relatively slow maneuvering for the development of a successful gunnery solution. Ensuring that one's own ships maneuvered deliberately was vital; otherwise the fire control solution would be incorrect and hitting would become a matter of pure chance." Slow maneuvering fitted in nicely with the felt need for heavy armor that so weighed down American battleship hulls that they could scarcely attain, much less maintain, their rated twenty-one-knot speed. At least three Japanese battle cruisers and some of Nippon's other battlewagons as well were known to be significantly faster and more maneuverable than the American leviathans. Admirals in Washington and the fleet fretted over the disparity, fully cognizant of the fact that their cumbersome behemoths were highly vulnerable to torpedo attacks from fast, nimble Japanese destroyers and cruisers as well as submerged, slow-moving submarines.

The eventual solution, worked on during the numerous fleet maneuvers of the twenties and thirties, was to seek a "reverse action," in which the U.S. battle fleet would steam on a parallel but opposite course down the enemy line. The rate of closure and passage—and thus the relative speed of the American battleships—would be nearly doubled, and the difficulties encountered by enemy light forces attempting to close for torpedo attacks would be correspondingly amplified. The problem, of course, was to maneuver in such a way as to entice wily enemy admirals into accepting a reverse action.

Moreover, a slow, ponderously moving battle line could never be risked in night action, which was rightly understood to be fraught with potential confusion. "Night battle plans focused on protecting the battle line from surface torpedo attack. Cruisers would fend off enemy destroyers while destroyers would attack the enemy battle line with torpedoes." Such tactics had not materialized at Jutland, nor were they likely to be successful against a Japanese enemy who had honed to perfection his own night combat tactics based on stealth, speed, and torpedo power.

By 1940–1941 battleship admirals could no longer deny or ignore the progressive elaboration of sea-based airpower. But they did not like it and fought savagely to restrict its scope. Years later Rear Admiral James Ramage remembered "a tremendous animosity against [naval] aviation at that time. We did have [torpedo] attacks from time to time upon the battle line," Ramage continued, "but the really decisive force was to be the battleships when they clashed with the enemy and slugged it out as Lord Nelson did." Fleet exercises during and after the midthirties usually included the three or four available carriers, which were assigned steaming positions in the middle of the battle formation, just behind the battleships. The exercises themselves were based on two theories. In the first instance, heavy gunfire would so damage and confuse the enemy battle line that torpedo planes or dive-bombers would enjoy a largely unobstructed chance to attack. Alternatively, aircraft attacking first could disrupt the enemy battle line sufficiently that concentrated fire from the U.S. battleships could finish it off. In nearly every fleet exercise, however, the umpires determined that the enemy battle fleet had been largely destroyed by the fourteen- and sixteen-inch guns of the battle fleet, not by aerial-launched torpedoes or bombs.

Such shortsighted tactical assumptions had tragic consequences for U.S. naval aviation. "They didn't have the carrier air strike as we knew it," Ramage told interviewers decades later. Advanced dive-bombers were available in 1941, but the best fighter plane, the F4F, was "simply too short-legged to do very much." The TBD Devastation Torpedo aircraft was four years old and at 206 miles per hour top speed simply too slow to avoid slashing attacks from enemy combat air patrols. On the eve of Pearl Harbor, the United States possessed "a pretty poor stable of aircraft." Moreover, "They weren't organized at all to do a coordinated strike. Really, until after the Battle of Midway they weren't capable of it, and they learned the hard way that you must form a strike group, and it must be escorted."[17]

Yet, within very narrow limits, the battleship admirals did try throughout the interwar years to forge as realistic a battle doctrine as possible. Their critics have seldom if ever recognized the dreadful dilemma they confronted: no American battleship sailor had ever experienced modern naval combat. The battle fleet never saw an enemy fleet unit during its North Sea sweeps with the Royal Navy during the Great War, now a quarter century in the past. Winfield S. Schley's brief brawl with the Spanish cruisers off Santiago in 1898 and Lieutenant George Dewey's systematic pulverization of the small, antiquated, and anchored Spanish squadron huddling in Manila Bay provided no compelling models. The Federal Navy spent the Civil War years either in riverine warfare in the West or on tedious blockade duty, with just a few skirmishes off the southern U.S. or European coasts.

In the 1920s and '30s obscure admirals named Schofield and Sellers, Cole, Pratt, Bostwick, and Reeves had to forge a feasible battle doctrine out of whole cloth, based on recent naval history, maneuver, deception, flexibility, and sound communications. Despite the assassination of their beloved battle line at Pearl Harbor, their bequest to the wartime admirals who followed them to command was substantial. They believed and acted upon the assumption that, as one of them stated, the average American naval officer was the intellectual superior of any seaman in the world and enjoyed an educational superiority as well. In annual and semiannual fleet training exercises these sea warriors developed ways to exercise "control" over "the pace of an engagement" between lines of battleships "through seizure of the tactical initiative." This required vigorous employment, "coordination of all arms," and a stress upon "tactical flexibility."[18]

Their negative reference point was Jutland, and the failure of John Jellicoe to bring Reinhard Scheer down in confrontational battle. Their solution—quintessentially American—was decentralization of command and control. Like Peter Drucker's later "concept of the corporation," which lauded General Motors for balancing the demands of the administrators committed to institutional preservation and the requirements of the doers "who define efficiency in terms of the aims and purposes for which the institution exists," the tactical philosophers of the U.S. Navy in the interwar years emphasized command flexibility and efficiency. Any tactic or program that achieved "decisive, positive, aggressive action" was accepted and lauded. Those that failed were discarded. Admiral Sellers, who "cast aside the battle plans in Fleet Problem XV (1934)," wrote that a prime idea "I have endeavored to emphasize is that of flexibility."

> . . . I commence a battle exercise with an entirely open mind. I have no set plan. The fleet commences searching for the enemy and making air attacks. The Battle Line and its attached forces are handled in accordance with the situation that develops, whatever this may be. By the use of general signals it is possible to operate the fleet in any way desired. Every situation is judged by its own merits. This is the only principle of naval tactics that is always applicable.

Sellers and other fleet commanders divided the battle line into squadrons of three or four big ships and their escorts, each under separate command, but all coordinated by an OTC—an "officer in tactical command." These squadrons would cruise together, then divide into an approach formation once the enemy was spotted, and finally maneuver as events and developments dictated, always with the objective of achieving the reverse action that would presumably confuse the enemy sufficiently to destroy him before he could recover. Such sophisticated seamanship required many elements for success, including superior long-range gunnery, effective aerial spotting, the employment of as many auxiliary weapons of disruption—dive-bombing and torpedo planes, submarines, and fast torpedo-carrying destroyers—as possible, and, finally but most important, reliable communications between the OTC and subordinate commanders. Such demands led in the thirties to the development not only of the Ford Rangekeeper but also of radar as an inestimable aid to gunnery, together with advanced scouting, dive-bombing, and torpedo aircraft designed to harass and further disrupt a confused enemy battle formation.

Broad "battle instructions" guided specific task forces who, in turn, issued their own often detailed directives to subordinate commands and commanders. A review of the 1935 fleet exercises noted that the OTC "gave no important orders to any of the detached forces, i.e., the [Naval] Air Force, the Submarine Force, and the Scouting Force. These forces conducted their operations entirely by means of the current Battle Instructions, thus proving the great progress made in the indoctrination of the Fleet. . . . In fact, these [instructions] are now becoming so well known, that they are required mostly of new units joining the Fleet."[19]

Sellers, Bostwick, Cole, Pratt, and the others thus forged, through repeated fleet exercises replicated and amplified on the war-gaming tables at the Naval War College at Newport, "a vehicle for shaping and disseminating a professional consensus on war fighting where it matters most—at sea." The knowledge that intelligent subordinates grasped both the strategic and the tactical demands placed upon them as battles developed defined the navy's the march from Tarawa to Okinawa and beyond in the latter stages of the Pacific war. Before the Battle of the Philippine Sea off the Marianas in June 1944, Fifth Fleet commander Raymond Spruance restlessly paced the fo'c'sle of his flagship *Indianapolis* as he grappled with what the Japanese enemy might be about. Once he decided and issued his battle plan, he replied to a query from carrier admiral Marc Mitscher regarding command arrangements: "Desire you proceed at your discretion selecting dispositions and movements best calculated to meet the enemy under most advantageous conditions. I shall issue general directives when necessary and leave details to you and [battleship commander] Admiral [Willis Augustus] Lee." In fact, the Japanese did not act as Spruance imagined they would, but once he had completed another round of pacing and issued a new, equally broad, battle plan, the Fifth Fleet commander went to the cruiser's flag bridge "to watch the action. Mitscher was in charge," and as enemy aircraft fell all around him, a few victims of antiaircraft fire, most felled by combat air patrols, "Spruance quietly read in his chair."[20]

The American doctrine of flexibility and decentralization in fleet control stood in marked contrast to that pertaining in the Royal Navy at the time of

Jutland and, indeed, well beyond. Three months after Scheer escaped Jellicoe's closing jaws, the British fleet commander issued an updated set of battle orders whose general instructions began, "The Commander-in-Chief controls the whole Battlefleet *before* deployment and on deployment except in case of low visibility.... He cannot be certain, *after* deployment, of being able to control the movements of three battle squadrons when steaming fast and making much funnel smoke; with the noise and smoke of battle added, the practicability of exercising general control will still be further reduced." At this point, and only at this point determined by the commander in chief, "*Flag officers* commanding battle squadrons have *at all times* discretionary power to maneuver their squadrons independently whilst conforming generally to the movements of the Commander-in-Chief, and complying with his known intentions." Here was a recipe not for flexibility but for chaos. Granted, fleet maneuvers in the often dim, murky North Sea were far different from those in the usually sunny Pacific. But British flag officers would, and were expected to, concentrate their attention not on the unfolding developments in front and to the sides of them but on the commander in chief's flagship. American flag officers would conform their actions to the developing battle scenario within the broad parameters of well-known battle instructions.

Jellicoe's post-Jutland battle orders of 1916 thus reflected an increasingly conservative and timid navy, American battle instructions a pugnacious, self-confident service out to do battle enthusiastically and without restraint against any potential enemy. This spirit not only guided America's naval strategists, tacticians, and seamen to victory in World War II but also carried over into the postwar world and the fashioning of an aggressive, forward "Maritime Strategy against the Soviet Union."[21]

Just a fortnight before the attack on Pearl Harbor forever ended the age of the battleship—and his own career—Husband Kimmel, fleet gunnery officer with the U.S. battleships at Scapa Flow twenty-three years before and now commander in chief of the Pacific Fleet, issued Plan 2M1 "for a medium range" fleet "engagement" with the Japanese battle line somewhere in the central Pacific. Trent Hone has argued that within the framework of experience, Kimmel's plan was sound, "extending beyond the battle line to encompass all aspects of a potential fleet engagement. It was designed to leverage U.S. Navy strengths while focusing on enemy weakness; it emphasized the coordination of all arms; it focused on tactical flexibility; and it was based on a decentralized command structure, relying heavily on individual initiative."[22]

But the context was obsolete. A new day was dawning in world sea power—indeed, had already dawned at Taranto and in the North Atlantic against *Bismarck*—in which speed and range (the airplane) together with detection and targeting (radar) had overwhelmed the blind, brute, short-range strength of the classic battle line that had obtained from before Nelson's time to Jellicoe. For all their striking efforts to think anew and act anew to save their fleet, America's naval leadership continued to stubbornly subordinate those new instruments of naval warfare that did not conform or did not fit into historic patterns of sea warfare. While Kimmel prepared for yesterday, his opposite, Isoroku Yamamoto, prepared to assassinate Kimmel's command with the weapons of today.

On the eve of Pearl Harbor, the U.S. fleet continued to be divided along historic lines: the Battle Force and a Scouting Force of heavy cruisers, destroyers, submarines, and aircraft carriers. *Life's* photography team accompanied the navy on its 1940 maneuvers and reported an exercise that could have been lifted whole cloth from a 1911 or 1913 version of War Plan Orange. The fleet sortied from Hawaiian waters, met the enemy in a massive fleet action between lines of battleships somewhere in the central or western Pacific, then retired, leaving carrier planes and a light cruiser-destroyer force to harry and destroy the last remnants of the opposing force. The editors insisted that their depiction "is a purely arbitrary invention, not bearing the O.K of the U.S. Navy."[23] Since the maneuvers were obviously aimed at Japan, it was only prudent to utter such a reservation. But given the fact that carrier dive-bombers and torpedo planes remained completely tied to a ponderous, short-range battle line, American naval planning remained tragically shortsighted and hidebound.

The navy suffered from other deficiencies as well. "There seemed to be little curiosity on the part of American officers about what people in other navies (and air forces) were thinking about or doing. A career in intelligence was not for the ambitious." In fact, as national security historian John Prados has recently demonstrated, the prewar United States Navy did possess a number of dedicated and capable intelligence officers; they were just not listened to. Stephen Jurika, a naval attaché in Tokyo from 1938 to 1941, remembered that the navy's handful of intelligence officers were concentrated on "the major staffs. Certainly they were not on CarDiv [Aircraft Carrier Division] staffs, they were not on battleship division staffs, they were not on cruiser division staffs." From 1930 on, American naval attachés at the embassy in Tokyo compiled and submitted to Washington often remarkably accurate and insightful reports on Japanese naval developments, including capital-ship construction and significant advances in Japanese naval aviation and ordnance. All such information was dismissed be-

cause it failed to conform to prevailing American racial stereotypes and prejudices regarding Japan. In 1942 Washington and the naval establishment would
profess astonishment at the appearance of the Zero fighter and the incredible
twenty-four-inch "long-lance" torpedo, both of which had been identified by
the naval attachés in Tokyo several years before. Indeed, when Jurika passed
through Pearl Harbor on his way home in June 1941, his head stuffed with
critical information on Japanese naval capabilities, "I didn't see anybody. It was
a weekend, a Saturday, and there was nobody around, not a soul. I did make an
attempt to find somebody connected with CinCPacFlt's intelligence outfit, but
nothing." The duty officer "wasn't much interested" in anything Jurika might
have to say. "He was, I think, over at the Officers' Club having lunch at the
time that I reported in. So that was useless."[24]

As the crude *Life* scenario for a showdown fight in the Pacific suggested, overall "American naval planning in the thirties was not unduly complex." While
War Plan Orange had rather timidly evolved in the late twenties and early thirties
to take into account airpower and amphibious operations, "planners shunned
alliances and expeditionary forces [to Europe] as unthinkable, lending an
artificial quality to their efforts."[25] In October 1940, Admiral Harold Stark's
"Plan Dog" to reverse American military and naval strategy from the Pacific to
Europe was still three months from fruition, and the fleet that would have to
defend the Pacific while the United States built and dispatched a major expeditionary force to Europe continued its peacetime routine in Hawaii.

Tactical abilities lagged as badly as strategic thought. Night flying from carriers
apparently languished in the late thirties, and the navy never seriously trained for
night surface action. A fleet based in the broad and sunny Pacific far from a new
generation of German U-boats was not particularly interested in antisubmarine
warfare, despite the fact that in the late thirties the nation's laboratories began
developing efficient sonar systems that complemented and soon exceeded the
British asdic detectors. The handful of exercises conducted by the destroyers of
the Atlantic squadron between 1937 and 1939 against their own submarines
revealed glaring deficiencies in locating, maintaining contact with, and effectively
attacking enemy underwater craft. As a cost-saving measure many of the excellent
new destroyers that began entering service after 1937 did not carry depth-charge
racks to save on weight, while many of the older four pipers had had their racks
removed.[26] A one-ocean navy, fixed upon the growing menace of Japan, simply
was not particularly interested in the cold, dark, and foggy North Atlantic.

But world war and the steadily rising challenge of Germany and Japan goaded
isolationist America into a massive naval construction program that was bound

to change the fleet—and the nation it served—forever. On July 19, 1940, Congress at last deferred to the realities it had resisted for a half century and enacted Roosevelt's request for a "Two Ocean Navy." It was to be a remarkably forward-looking and balanced fleet (which suggests that legislators deferred to innovators rather than traditionalists within the navy hierarchy) composed equally of the usual platforms (battleships, cruisers, destroyers) and what would become advanced, cutting-edge weapon systems (aircraft carriers). The two splendid battleships of the *North Carolina* class already nearing completion, the four follow-on *South Dakotas* and four fast forty-five thousand–ton *Iowas* had already been authorized. The two-ocean naval legislation provided for several more *Iowas*, four monster *Montana* class (twelve sixteen-inch main batteries) that were never built, no fewer than eleven new *Essex*-class fleet carriers, and a formidable submarine force, plus many cruisers and destroyers.[27]

Such a fleet could not be built in a year or even two. As late as the spring of 1941, the navy, its sister services, and the nation they served were tragically unprepared for war. Churchill's personal aide, Colonel Ian Jacobs, noted gloomily during the Argentia Conference that although the American military, air, and naval chiefs were undoubtedly decent chaps, "they appear to be living in a different world from ourselves." The U.S. Navy was marginally more prepared for war than the army, but "the Americans have a long way to go before they can play any decisive part in the war." Jacobs added, "The American Chiefs of Staff are quite clearly thinking in terms of the defense of the Western Hemisphere and have so far not formulated any joint strategy for the defeat of Germany in the event of their entry into the war."[28]

Pearl Harbor would prove the deadly accuracy of these impressions. To a nation steeped in isolationism, the attack was a sucker punch from a hostile world. Without it, the United States would probably have entered the second great global conflict much as it entered the first—as a consequence of unendurable German undersea warfare in the Atlantic. The country might well have fought once again as a somewhat detached associate of a renewed Allied cause against the villainous Hun, unwilling in the end to surrender its cherished isolationism from world affairs no matter how strongly Franklin Roosevelt yearned to do so. His chief speechwriter remembered that just days before Chuichi Nagumo's flyers struck Oahu, "as the limitless peril came closer and closer to the United States" in the Atlantic, "isolationist sentiment became even more strident in expression and aggressive in action." FDR "was relatively powerless to combat it. He had said everything 'short of war' that could be said. He had no more tricks left. The hat from which he had pulled so many rabbits was empty."[29] Then

Kido Butai reached across the Pacific to violently resolve all the president's problems and haunt the American memory ever after.

To the Japanese, the "surprise attack" on the U.S. Pacific Fleet was a brilliant act of power projection, an attempt both magnificent and desperate to arrest the racing scroll of history that Washington seemed to be unwinding to Nippon's utter detriment.[30] To the Americans, Pearl Harbor was nothing less than a slaughter of the innocents. As the dimensions of the incident emerged slowly out of the fog of wartime censorship and postwar preoccupations, its horror only grew. Young military couples picnicking on Waikiki the last Saturday afternoon of peace; dancing that evening to the strains of "Sweet Lailani" completely unaware of Nagumo's six plane-laden carriers plunging toward them through rough, rainy seas; the youngsters of the USS *Arizona's* band, many of them barely out of their teens, proudly holding their instruments after winning second place in the "battle of the battleship bands" the final peacetime night in Honolulu and eagerly looking forward to the reward of a late Sunday-morning sleep-in in the crew's quarters directly above the ship's magazine; all the clues of an impending attack that were discounted by sergeants and junior officers on Oahu who could have sent the fleet to general quarters in plenty of time to meet the enemy onslaught head-on.[31]

Sixty years later, the searing memories are readily summoned: Japanese warplanes coming over the lush, tropical mountains early on a quiet Sunday morning to fall viciously upon an unsuspecting anchorage and surrounding airfields; brief moments of stupefaction as the bombs started to fall, the torpedoes came slashing in through the water, and the bullets lashed decks and concrete; men rushing frantically to battle stations as ships rocked with bomb and torpedo explosions; the violent death of twenty-four hundred men and of a grand old battle line that down through the years, with Hollywood's help, had come to seem somehow part of the national character. Hours later, the carrier *Enterprise* and its cruiser-destroyer escorts cautiously nosed into the shattered harbor in the gathering dusk. As the big flattop nudged close by Hickam Air Field, a soldier called out: "You'd better get the hell out of here or the Japs will nail you too." Within moments, a grisly scene unfolded: sunken battlewagons, blasted buildings, oil-fouled waters, the entire scene framed in a lurid glare of fire and heavy clouds of acrid smoke. On the bridge, a hitherto obscure rear admiral named William Halsey—"Bull" to his friends—muttered words that would define a war effort culminating forty-four months later in two mushroom clouds over Hiroshima and Nagasaki: "Before we're through with 'em, the Japanese language will be spoken only in Hell!" Throughout the nighttime hours *Enterprise* and its escorts hastily refueled, rearmed, and reprovisioned. Before sunup, the small fleet was back at sea, seeking the enemy.[32]

Pearl Harbor became *the* defining event in twentieth-century American history. Never again must the country place itself in a position to be so victimized, so humiliated. If national security demanded that Americans go out into the world with guns and dollars to hold the line against aggression far from their shores, then they would do it, not from any desire for global dominance, but to make sure that there would never be a second Pearl Harbor. For good or ill, Korea, Lebanon, Vietnam, Grenada, Afghanistan, and Iraq together with the countless covert operations of the CIA and other American agencies around the world after 1945 were the products of a national mind-set created in one shocking instant on December 7, 1941. So were the Marshall Plan, Point Four, and the Alianza Para Progresso.

But mingled inextricably with resolve was suspicion. How could anyone in a position of authority have been so blind to Japanese intentions? *Were* they blind to Japanese intentions? Or had sinister men worked to ensure a successful enemy attack on Hawaii in order to draw the United States into World War II? Just eleven days after the last enemy warplane flew away from the burning fleet and blasted airfields on Oahu, the first congressional investigatory committee—a commission headed by Supreme Court Justice Owen J. Roberts—set to work to find the answers. Over the next four years, seven other army, navy, and congressional investigations were conducted into the disaster. The last inquiry, the Joint Congressional Committee on the Investigation of the Pearl Harbor Attack, began its hearings on November 15, 1945, and submitted its report the following July. This committee published not only its own hearings and supporting documentation but also records of the other investigations. The entire report came to thirty-nine volumes and in the end, like the Warren Commission Report on the Kennedy assassination, resolved nothing. The evidence gathered seemed so complex and contradictory that majority and minority reports were submitted. The majority report tended to absolve the administration in Washington and placed the blame on the Hawaiian base commanders, Kimmel and Lieutenant General Walter Short; the minority report apportioned blame and responsibility more generally between the White House and the Hawaiian commands.[33]

After the uncertain congressmen and generals came the cocksure historians. Charles Beard, perhaps the most eminent scholar of his generation, opened the attack in 1948, charging that FDR and his immediate entourage (Stimson,

Knox, Hull, Marshall, and Stark) deliberately maneuvered the Japanese into firing the first shots of a Pacific war that the White House was eager to instigate in order to join the Allied cause against Hitler. From August 1941 onward, Beard claimed, an informal American war cabinet progressively put the screws to the Japanese, making ever more impossible demands upon Nippon to bridle its expansive Far Eastern policy until at last Tokyo had no choice but to go to war. The Roosevelt cabal not only knew war was coming but actually provoked it by progressively withholding from Japan the raw materials of war—iron, steel, rubber, and, at last, petroleum, lubricants, and oil—that the island country desperately needed yet did not possess. Once having deliberately driven the warlords of Tokyo to desperation, a crafty president refused to adequately warn Kimmel and Short that the first shots of his engineered war would be aimed at them in order to ensure a national crusade of hatred and revenge against all of the Axis powers. Four years after Beard, Charles Tansill compiled essentially the same brief but added the melodramatic charge that Roosevelt had maneuvered Japan into war in order to save the empire of his good friend Winston Churchill, who had thoroughly bamboozled the president during their one and only meeting at Argentia, Newfoundland, the previous summer.[34]

Over the next forty years, culminating with the fiftieth anniversary of the attack, there appeared a steady trickle of literature about Pearl Harbor, much of it either specially pleading the case of Kimmel and Short or purporting to find new evidence to support the notion that Roosevelt knew of the impending attack and let it happen. Many titles were more appropriate to reading found in a supermarket checkout stand: *Betrayal at Pearl Harbor: How Churchill Lured Roosevelt into World War II; Infamy: Pearl Harbor and Its Aftermath; Scapegoats: A Defense of Kimmel and Short at Pearl Harbor; Days of Infamy: MacArthur, Roosevelt, and Churchill, the Shocking Truth Revealed;* and *How Their Secret Deals and Strategic Blunders Caused Disaster at Pearl Harbor and the Philippines.* Of the best-known books on the subject, only three, Roberta Wohlstetter's *Warning and Decision,* Gordon W. Prange's exhaustive *At Dawn We Slept,* and Walter Lord's gripping but unanalytic *Day of Infamy,* can be said to have approached the subject with any degree of scholarly detachment. Wohlstetter's argument remains the most compelling explanation for the debacle: that critical information on the Pearl Harbor attack *was* scattered throughout the hundreds of decrypts available to the handful of chronically overworked American code breakers in the last weeks of the peace but was surrounded by such a mountain of irrelevant information ("static") as to be unrecognizable.[35] Sixty years later,

9/11 would provide an almost perfect replication of the massive intelligence breakdown that led to Pearl Harbor.

Dispassionate scholarship, recently summarized by David M. Kennedy, has demonstrated beyond question that throughout 1941, FDR and most of his inner circle of hawks were squarely fixated on Hitler and the emerging quasi-naval war in the Atlantic. Thanks to "Magic" electronic intelligence intercepts, Roosevelt and his colleagues were aware of Japan's growing fixation on southern expansion into French Indochina, British Malaya, the Dutch East Indies, and even perhaps the Philippines. But as late as July, when he at last announced an immediate freeze on all Japanese assets in the United States, Roosevelt hoped that time might bring the Konoye government around. "The Japs are having a real drag-down and knock-out fight among themselves," he told Ickes, "trying to decide which way they are going to jump—attack Russia, attack the South Seas..., or whether they will sit on the fence and be more friendly with us." The president desperately hoped that Tokyo would sooner or later adopt the latter course. "No one knows what the decision will be, but as you know, it is terribly important for the control of the Atlantic for us to help keep the peace in the Pacific." The freeze on Japanese assets was designed, Kennedy has written, "to cultivate maximum uncertainty in Japan about future American intentions. More uncertainty in Tokyo meant more time for American shipyards and aircraft plants" to turn out the battleships, carriers, submarines, and planes that would make the Japanese warlords think twice, then thrice, about attacking such an industrial giant as the United States. "And more apprehension about the future of trade relations with America should breed a greater Japanese willingness to yield something at the negotiating table. Certainly Roosevelt did not envisage the freeze as a provocation to war." Indeed, Undersecretary of State Sumner Welles told his British opposite at the Anglo-American summit conference at Argentia, Newfoundland, several weeks later that the chief objective in the Pacific for the time being "was the avoidance of war with Japan." Alas, Tokyo refused to interpret matters as Washington wished and assumed. A step that FDR thought would lead to greater Japanese restraint and awareness in fact provoked Japanese fury and an almost immediate decision for war at Japan's time and place of choice.[36] Roosevelt's fatal blunder lay in believing that China meant less to Japan than it did to the United States—in fact, it meant more; it meant everything. Bogged down in a four-year stalemate there that apparently had no end, the warlords of Tokyo could never accept Washington's insistent demand that they abandon the entire project in humiliation and disgrace.

Having backed the Japanese into a corner, America's fledgling communication intelligence system, or COMINT, upon which an understanding of Japanese plans and intentions absolutely rested "more closely resembled a medieval feudal state" by December 1941 "than the empire it is today [1985]."

> The system was a hodgepodge. *No one was responsible for a continuous study of all material.* Recipients would read their portion of intercepts, and then it would be whisked away, never to be seen again. There was very little that could be done to put together all the pieces in a cohesive form, or to correlate them with information available from other sources. Though the technical side of COMINT, particularly in the breaking of the [Japanese] Purple [Code], had been performed with genius, *the analytical side had become lost in disorganization.*[37]

Beyond what Roosevelt, Kimmel, Short, and the others learned or were told in the final days before Pearl Harbor was what they knew, instinctively and implicitly. And what they knew was that the Imperial Japanese Navy—as a unit—had never once crossed the International Date Line. Neither, for that matter, had an American battle fleet moved into the western Pacific since Teddy Roosevelt's battleships had steamed there in 1908. Every revisionist argument, every defense or condemnation of Short and Kimmel, falls on this point. Thus, for example, the authors of *Betrayal at Pearl Harbor* state that "Churchill knew that the deadline of 1 p.m., when set against the 'Climb Niitakayama' decrypt of 2 December, must mean a dawn attack somewhere out in the Pacific, with the most likely target being Pearl Harbor."[38] But there is no evidence anywhere that anyone knew that *Pearl Harbor* was the "most likely target" of impending Japanese aggression. As Kimmel and Short explicitly reasoned, the base was simply too far from Japan's traditional area of naval operations to be considered a feasible target.

From its inception the Japanese fleet had perceived itself—and had been perceived—as an essentially *defensive* force dominating a *regional* area, the waters off East Asia and the western Pacific. This force would wait, lurking in the Carolines or Marianas, for an advancing American or Anglo-American fleet to come to it for the climactic battle of a great Pacific war. Japan had not fought a true naval war since 1905—thirty-six years earlier and long before airpower had become a factor at sea. Its power projection in that contest (and in the earlier war against China) had extended only some two to three hundred miles from its shores.

Immediate prewar activities in no way altered long-held perceptions. The Imperial Navy apparently conducted its last major peacetime exercises in the autumn of 1935 from the Kuriles southward to the northeastern coasts of the Home Islands. "The Japanese fleet," a contemporary report concluded, "like the American fleet last spring, will thus be in northern waters that have not hitherto witnessed extensive naval exercises, but its operations will be conducted many hundreds of miles westward of the area selected by the Americans." Not only were Japanese fleet commanders careful to avoid any implication of aggressive intent, but they were widely viewed in the West as rather bumbling fanatics who would risk often poorly built ships and vulnerable men in dangerous weather merely for the sake of proving how tough they were.[39] Japan apparently conducted no fleet maneuvers in 1936, or at least none that were publicized, and after 1937 much of the navy, including the carriers, was locked firmly into the "China Incident."

It is difficult in our age of astronauts spinning across the Pacific in thirty minutes and jumbo jets flying between Seattle and Tokyo in ten hours to cast our minds back to a time, sixty-five years ago, when the world was a far larger place. For the average person in 1941, New York remained three days from Los Angeles by train; Europe was five days from the East Coast by the fastest steamship (Pan-Am flying boats took almost twenty-four hours to hop the Atlantic from New York to Lisbon with several intermediate fueling stops); the Pacific took two weeks to cross by sea. The nearest Japanese possessions to Hawaii, the Marshall Island group, were two thousand miles away, roughly the distance between Washington, D.C., and Salt Lake City. In this context, the notion that the Japanese might cross three-quarters of a stormy early-winter ocean to launch an air strike against the American bastion at Pearl Harbor seemed beyond belief. Kimmel's justly remembered response to his intelligence people on December 2 when told that no one knew where the Japanese carriers were must be interpreted in this light:

> Captain Layton: As best I recall it, Admiral Kimmel said "What! You don't know where the [Japanese] Carrier Division I and Carrier Division 2 are?" and I replied, "No, sir, I do not. I think they are in home waters [around Japan] but I do not know where they are. The rest of the units I feel pretty confident of their location." Then Admiral Kimmel looked at me, as he sometimes would, with somewhat a stern countenance and said, "Do you mean to say that they could be rounding Diamond Head and you wouldn't know it?" or words to that effect. My reply was that "I hope they would be sighted before now," or words to that effect.[40]

As this exchange indicates, Kimmel—and Edward Layton—clearly believed that the very *notion* of a Japanese fleet anywhere near Pearl Harbor was preposterous. Joseph Rochefort, the Fourteenth Naval District's chief intelligence officer, felt the same way. The man who would become famous six months after the Hawaiian debacle for teasing the secret of the impending Midway invasion from Japanese codes was as disbelieving as anyone else. Yes, he told an interviewer years later, "we" knew that the Japanese changed their codes on December 1. Obviously, they were going to pounce "very shortly" somewhere in the Pacific.

> But I think our reasoning went something like this: if the Japanese moved against the United States, say, either at Manila or at Pearl Harbor, then this means war, as the Japanese are well aware of what's going to result here. If we become involved in a war with Japan, the Japanese cannot possibly win; therefore, the Japanese will not proceed against the United States directly but will rather reach their goals by, say, toward possibly Singapore, certainly Southeast Asia, maybe some of the islands, but not the Philippines, because this would probably bring them to war.[41]

The behavior of Roosevelt, Marshall, Stark, and the rest of the Washington political, military, and intelligence establishments clearly reflected the same assumption. In the end, the Pearl Harbor–as-conspiracy argument falls on its own internal illogic. By the night of December 6, 1941, it was clear to all in the know in Washington if not Hawaii that Roosevelt would have his war with Japan if that was in fact what he wanted. *If* FDR knew that the Japanese were about to attack Pearl Harbor, he also knew it was too late for Tokyo to call it off. The Hawaiian garrison could have been warned early on the morning of December 7 Washington time (around two in the morning in Hawaii) in order to defend itself and even to send the fleet to scatter at sea before the Japanese planes arrived (during World War I, the American battleship fleet, of which Kimmel had been a member, had often sortied from Scapa Flow after midnight). Several hundred Japanese fliers would have appeared over Pearl Harbor to find empty anchorages and fleet units steaming independently, guns at the ready, over several hundred square miles of ocean, with both navy and army air corps combat air patrols above. The brilliant, cunning, manipulative Roosevelt of revisionist fantasies could have thus had his war *and* allowed his navy the opportunity to fight back and suffer comparatively few casualties. That this in fact did not happen is the strongest indication that although war was widely expected, the idea that it could come first at Pearl Harbor was obviously beyond anyone's comprehension.

Chester Nimitz was later to remark that such a scenario would have been a disaster, "that the outcome would have been far worse if the fleet had been alerted and out to sea."[42] But would it? Nimitz may well have had in mind the fact that Yamamoto assaulted Pearl with both planes *and* an "advanced expeditionary force" of seven fleet submarines modified to carry and launch the "midget submarines" that would penetrate Pearl Harbor and aid in sinking the American battle line. The fleet boats themselves were to form two picket lines between Oahu and Molokai and Oahu and Kauai as the raid began, prepared to "torpedo any ships in sight after the air attack." Surely, at least some of the submarines would have picked up and picked off a battleship or two or three as the U.S. fleet hastily sortied from Pearl Harbor with its escorts in the tropical darkness. In fact, the Japanese submarine record at Pearl Harbor was deplorable. The midgets performed poorly, and all were lost. The fleet boats failed to intercept a single American warship, although the cruisers *Phoenix, St. Louis,* and *Detroit* rushed out of Pearl with several attendant destroyers in broad daylight shortly after the attack. That night the carrier *Enterprise* and its entire task force of cruisers and destroyers entered Pearl for hasty refueling and rearmament and were back at sea by dawn, wholly unmolested. There flyers from the *"Big E"* spotted and sank I-170 as it started on its way to the California coast for some commerce raiding and harassment. Five of the six remaining boats did reach the American West Coast and sank a few ships off California and Oregon before returning home in not a little disgrace.[43]

As for Japanese air strikes against the battle fleet, unlike *Repulse* and *Prince of Wales* several days later, each American capital ship would have had air cover immediately over it. The Japanese would have been forced to find each of the big units and to divide and scatter their compact formations to take care of each one, all the while under incessant attack from U.S. fighter planes. Not only were Nagumo's carrier pilots the best that Japan had, but they were *all* that Japan had. Had even one-third been shot down and killed or captured—and close to 50 percent might have been a more accurate figure—Japan could simply not have continued the war in any meaningful way. Tokyo might not have surrendered in 1942, but it surely would have been forced to by 1943.

Finally, those who argue that FDR deliberately maneuvered his country into war conveniently forget—totally—that Japan's objective from the outset was deception: to obscure its intentions, to fatally surprise the American Pacific Fleet.[44] In this, Yamamoto and his colleagues were brilliantly successful, and to deny them their success, however sinister it was, is to deny the reality of history.

Were Kimmel and Short then unjustly punished for simply *sharing* the sins and follies of their superiors? No. They were in command. Kimmel could have and presumably did read of the steady deterioration in Japanese-American relations in the "Professional Notes" section of nearly every issue of the *United States Naval Institute Proceedings* for the past decade. And, most important, despite its many follies, lapses, and failures, Washington *had* given Kimmel and Short a firm war warning as early as November 27, and Kimmel had been told to instigate patrol-plane flights around the islands for contingency purposes. He concluded that patrol planes earlier sent to Midway would adequately cover the only quadrant from which a Japanese attack could conceivably come, up from the Marshall Islands to the southwest.

The argument that the Hawaiian commanders had been sent the November 27 war warning for information purposes only rather than for action (as was the case with Douglas MacArthur and the Philippines) is not true and in any case in no way lessens their culpability. Washington *had* warned them explicitly. Granted, the "war message" emphasized the probability of Japanese aggression thousands of miles away, in Southeast Asia; it did not specifically preclude an enemy attack anywhere in the Pacific. Evidence has recently come to light that the Pacific Fleet reacted to the notion of an impending Japanese attack upon itself with a mixture of apprehension and incredulity. On the one hand, life went on as before, and the war remained far away. On weekends, Honolulu's bars and brothels hosted army and navy drinkers and brawlers, while the hotels staged more moderate parties for their officers. Very occasionally, a stray British ship, bombed and shot up in the far-away Mediterranean, with dead men still entombed in wrecked, unreachable compartments, would stagger briefly into Pearl on its way to a West Coast repair yard. Then it was gone. During the week, Kimmel worked his people hard. One would think from all the accounts of Pearl Harbor that the fleet had been there for weeks. It had not. The Battle Force was out most Monday mornings, occasionally for two or even three weeks of drill, then back on Friday afternoons. The bulk of the fleet returned to anchorage for the last time on December 5.

Junior officers aboard Kimmel's battleships "felt the noose tightening" during the increasingly somber autumn weeks of 1941. In November, while on maneuvers, the fleet was rousted in the middle of the night at its secondary anchorage in Lahaina Roadstead by news that "picket submarines and picket destroyers had detected a bunch of sonar contacts. Every man aboard knew that meant Japanese submarines. . . . There we were," an *Arizona* survivor recalled, "sitting anchored in open water. The Japs could've hit us there. They wouldn't have had to fly those planes in two weeks later."[45]

Yet neither Kimmel nor Short took appropriate action. Moreover, *on December 6,* Stark warned Kimmel that in view of the "grave" international situation, "and the exposed position of our outlying Pacific islands," Kimmel should authorize the destruction by appropriate personnel of all "secret and confidential documents." Only a fool would have failed to look to his defenses under such a prod. Yet Kimmel—and Short—did nothing. To take up the spurious arguments, as some in the United States Navy recently have, that Roosevelt or Marshall or Stark were somehow "responsible" for Pearl Harbor and that Kimmel and Short, who had received several explicit war warnings in the days and hours immediately preceding the attack, were not reflects a truly disturbing abandonment of the tradition of command responsibility and may reflect, as James Webb has recently asserted, a serious decline in accountability within the United States Navy.[46]

Finally, there is the matter of Kimmel's inexplicable and inexcusable behavior on the morning of December 7 itself. At dawn he was not asleep; he was preparing to play golf with General Short, and no mere submarine alarm was going to keep him from the links. Shortly after 0630, sailors aboard the USS *Antares,* nearing the Pearl Harbor channel, discovered that their old, slow target ship was being followed by a submarine. Sailors aboard the nearby destroyer *Ward* also saw the awash conning tower, and though no one could be absolutely certain of its nationality, *Ward's* commanding officer, Lieutenant Commander William Outerbridge, knew the sub was in an unauthorized area. With commendable initiative, he brought his old "four piper" roaring in to attack. Several shots were followed by depth charges, and the mysterious submarine disappeared, not to be rediscovered for decades. Within twenty minutes, around seven o'clock, nearly an hour before the first Japanese attack plane appeared over Pearl Harbor, Kimmel was notified of the incident. There had been numerous false sightings of submarines in recent weeks, so while continuing preparations for his outing, the admiral ordered that the incident be "verified. . . . Until that happened, he would not alert anyone." Regrettably, "the best intentions of all concerned strangled in telephone cord." Before the navy's sluggish chain of command could carry out Kimmel's order, the Japanese attack had begun.[47]

Writing sixty years after the event, Alan Schom laid out the Pearl Harbor scenario clearly:

> There certainly was a steady flow of information reaching army and navy
> headquarters on Constitution Avenue, but no one at the senior command
> level seemed unduly worried about the fact that such a large number of

carriers and subs had completely disappeared at a time when the rest of the Japanese Combined Fleet was loudly visible and apparently involved in a massive series of [preinvasion] operations [off Malaya and perhaps the Philippines]. That alone should have told Kimmel and Stark something, but they failed to comprehend the seriousness of the gap in information. Unlike King and Nimitz, Stark and Kimmel were representatives of the old navy, officers afraid of taking a chance or harming their careers by making errors. Lacking the ability and the mentality to make quick, important decisions when the moment required it, they instead followed, and depended entirely upon, written orders. Every "i" had to be dotted, every "t" crossed and sanctioned by the Navy Department or the Joint Chiefs of Staff [sic] before they would act. Individual initiative still had not been encouraged by the end of 1941, despite the grave situation worldwide.

Kimmel—and Short—had the watch that disastrous morning. As they enjoyed the many perquisites and privileges of command, so they also bore its burdens. Kimmel in particular had been warned—repeatedly. He failed miserably to fulfill his responsibility.[48]

The source of Kimmel's culpability is not difficult to uncover. He was a battleship man through and through. He had been a fleet gunnery officer with Hugh Rodman at Scapa Flow from December 7, 1917, through the end of the Great War and remained wedded to the big gun and the image of the Jutland battle lines as the model—the only pertinent model—of naval warfare. His thinking perfectly tracked U.S. naval doctrine of the time.[49] Peacetime exercises in which U.S. carrier planes successfully snuck up on Pearl Harbor had occurred before his watch. Moreover, Nagumo brought no fewer than a half-dozen big, modern fleet aircraft carriers with him across the North Pacific, all that Japan possessed. The United States Navy in December 1941 had never exercised with a half-dozen flattops. It possessed only seven in all to cover both oceans (the eighth carrier, *Hornet*, had not even begun its shakedown cruise). Thus, the notion of a mass enemy carrier attack against his battleships in the narrow, restricted confines of Pearl Harbor seems never to have seriously engaged Kimmel's mind or attention. Although his question to Layton suggests that he could entertain the notion in theory, his behavior indicates that in practical terms he thought such an assault beyond comprehension.

Pearl Harbor and the sinking of *Prince of Wales* and *Repulse* off Malaya three days later proved without further question that planes could kill battleships, not only at anchor in a supposedly secure harbor but also at sea when caught without air cover. Sea power must be based on airpower. No other navy, not even the Japanese, grasped that lesson as quickly, eagerly, or completely as the Americans, and none turned so swiftly or decisively to the aircraft carrier as the prime weapon of war at sea. After Pearl Harbor, with but a single exception (off Guadalcanal on the night of November 14–15, 1942), America's ten proud, powerful new fast battleships would be employed essentially as antiaircraft platforms for a rapidly accumulating carrier fleet.

The Hawaii attack transformed the American nation into a full-fledged arsenal, training ground, and garrison state. For the next forty-five months its people demonstrated to the world an unmatched mechanical and technical genius, thanks in large part to Henry Ford. Whereas in Europe and Japan custom-made and comparatively complex automobiles remained the province of the numerically small comfortable classes (though Hitler was seeking a change with his Volkswagen, or people's car), Ford and a handful of competitors had by 1929 responded to the public's demand for mass-produced industrial goods and put virtually every American behind the wheel of a simply constructed "car." (Two years later, humorist Will Rogers joked that the United States was the only economically depressed country in which the destitute drove to the poorhouse.) During the Depression decade, under the lash of a scarcity economy, nearly every American youngster became proficient at keeping these machines going. Whether they tinkered with jalopies, flivvers, or tin lizzies, millions of teenagers and young adults in the 1930s developed a routine but quite astounding ability to effectively fix or repair, somehow and in some way, any kind of automobile and its gasoline-driven motor.

There was another aspect to American technological genius that few in Europe, Asia, or even the Western Hemisphere recognized, and that was the propensity for massive engineering. Despite economic devastation, thirties America never lost its taste for projects of epic proportions that would somehow incorporate and express the national will. In the decade after 1931, planners, technicians, and builders conceived and completed New York City's Empire State Building (thirteen months, start to finish), the Golden Gate Bridge across San Francisco Bay, the Blue Ridge Parkway in Virginia and North Carolina, and Grand Coulee Dam in Washington State. A decade later, in the midst of world war, their talents and ambitions transformed into war making unleashed a cornucopia of products.

America's enemies at first dismissed its industrial potential. Göring assured Hitler that though the Yanks were "very good at refrigerators and razor blades," they could never build airplanes. In 1943 alone U.S. factories turned out eighty-six thousand. America's allies, on the other hand, soon came to understand and appreciate the country's mechanical genius. "In the United States the youth who cannot drive a car or has not operated a machine of some kind is a rarity," Canadian historian Chester Wilmot wrote several years after the war. American soldiers, sailors, and airmen confronting Europeans might appear unsure of themselves and betray feelings of inferiority by "gauche" and "juvenile" behavior, "but in the realm of machines, the Americans possess a self-confidence, indeed a sense of mastery, which European peoples do not know." Millions of women and men were rapidly trained to do highly technical work (the key was to assign a worker to labor that however crucial in the aggregate was individually repetitive), and with their mechanical aptitudes and background they often accomplished difficult tasks without much thought to the complexities involved. At midwar a young English-born journalist named Alistair Cooke wandered into industrialist Henry J. Kaiser's Richmond, California, shipyard. Before Pearl Harbor, Kaiser had never built a ship, and he always talked about the "front" and "back" ends of a vessel (upon hearing this, Roosevelt replied that he did not care what Kaiser called his ships as long as he delivered). Cooke found that Kaiser's yard

> was laid out like a gigantic chessboard, with cranes hovering overhead depositing parts, engines, and booms in alphabetically marked and numbered squares. Thirty thousand components came in this way, and it was like something out of Disney: trolleys whizzing, and hooters honking and buzzing, a whole deckhouse moving to the ways upside down. It would then be upended while the welders descended on it like an army of woodpeckers. You'd have a stem and a keel and then part of plate A-1 would be welded to A-2, and S-13 to S-14 and so on. The workers knew even less about shipbuilding than Kaiser. Only one in two hundred had ever been in a shipyard.

But it all worked, and Kaiser's Richmond yard was only one of many huge industrial plants—largely underwritten by federal money—that turned out planes, ships, guns, tanks, and vehicles at a prodigious rate.[50]

America's new navy was not born without struggle. Indeed, the entire national war effort between December 1941 and the summer of 1945 was characterized by chaotic planning, confused priorities, shortages, surpluses, and bottlenecks. Capitalist America, responding as much to profit as to emergency, got the job done the typical way: by bludgeoning, massive effort.[51] In the end, the Americans simply had more resources and laborers to squander than their Japanese and German enemies. Fortunately, they also possessed far more administrative geniuses than the enemy. Foremost among the American talents was navy undersecretary James V. Forrestal and his chief subordinate, Ferdinand Eberstadt, both of whom had come from Wall Street. Forrestal filled the undersecretary's post from its creation in the summer of 1940 to May 1944, when he succeeded Frank Knox as navy secretary. When he first came aboard, Forrestal discovered that the department possessed no overall mechanism to coordinate the purchases of the various bureaus. "Moreover, the Bureaus lacked sufficient men trained to handle the complex problems that developed in connection with research, design, purchasing, production, and transportation. There was no centralized general counsel's office staffed by lawyers competent to deal with the legal and commercial aspects of procurement contracts." If the navy was to fight and win the battle of production and training that was already getting under way before Pearl Harbor, Forrestal and his colleagues would have to take steps to remove the confusion of responsibilities that plagued the department. Over the next two years Forrestal found the men and fashioned the administrative instruments to ensure that the nation got the two-ocean fleet that Congress had begun authorizing in response to the fall of France. Shortly after Pearl Harbor he recommended to Knox that the Office of Procurement and Material be established. Created several weeks later, the OPM, directly responsible to Forrestal, began dealing intelligently and coherently with the numerous, varied, and complex problems of planning, statistics, procurement, production, and resources. In May 1942 Forrestal established another branch of OPM responsible for the vital inspection function. Forrestal was never entirely happy with his creation. Waste, duplication, and confusion continued to dog the massive wartime shipping buildup, as it did all other aspects of the mobilization effort. Moreover, the undersecretary inevitably found himself clashing time and again with Ernest King, who wanted to concentrate all aspects of the naval program from procurement to grand strategy in the Office of the Chief of Naval Operations. On several occasions, Knox and Forrestal had to go directly to President Roosevelt to curb or bridle King's zealous empire building. In retaliation, the embittered CNO did all he could to keep Forrestal ignorant of overall strategic and tactical planning. But thanks to the dedicated and talented bureaucrats and sailors of OPM, the ships were built, the required goods and supplies were produced and delivered to the fighting fronts, and America's war effort achieved an overall smoothness that it might not otherwise have achieved. Success lay in the statistics. On January 1, 1945, the U.S. military establishment as a whole totaled more than 12 million men and women out of a national population of around 150 million. On July 1, 1940, the U.S. fleet consisted of 1,058 vessels of all sorts, 383 of which were combat vessels. Uniformed personnel totaled 189,000 men. On November 1, 1944, the number of ships had increased to more than 4,000, including 9 new battleships; more than 70 new fleet, light, and escort carriers; 34,500 aircraft; 20 new cruisers; more than 500 new destroyers and destroyer escorts; more than 200 new submarines; and hundreds upon hundreds of landing craft with bewildering designations: LCI, LCT, LST, and so on. At one point near the end of hostilities, 11 combat vessels *per day* were coming from America's building yards on both coasts, ready for action and in immediate need of crews, while the total naval establishment had mushroomed to 3.6 million personnel, of whom 100,000 were women. The United States Navy was by far the largest sea service in the world—matching if not exceeding in size the prodigious British fleet of 1914–1918. Overseas, "supply depots, repair bases, and advance bases were mushrooming in a globe-wide expansion of the United States Navy."[52] The ability of the Construction Battalions, or "Seabees," to swiftly and routinely employ heavy machinery to build airstrips, wharves, warehouses, office buildings, and barracks almost overnight guaranteed that the American drive into the western Pacific in 1943–1945 would be accomplished with maximum efficiency.

With their limitless capacity for self-pity, America's defeated foes claimed that they never had a chance against such a flood of matériel. They were wrong. Weapons, like any other machines, are useless without men able to use them effectively and intelligently. By 1943 the Americans were proving that they could not only outproduce their enemies but outfight them and outthink them as well. Even before Pearl Harbor the United States Navy was beginning to abandon the "leisurely, careful, thoroughgoing" peacetime training regimen with its time for "theory, minute details and niceties of naval customs and traditions" in favor of a headlong rush into wartime conditions. After December 1941 training was "telescoped, concentrated, packed hard and delivered fast, taking advantage of every shortcut, cutting away every peacetime frill." Thrust abruptly into a war they neither wanted nor had trained for, America's emergency sailors behaved as they had in mastering technologies in civilian life: they learned by doing.

From a chronically undermanned peacetime establishment of roughly 400,000 men, the navy drew more than 3 million young American men and women from civilian life and transformed them rapidly into seamen, gunner's mates, aerial gunners, combat aircrewmen, firemen, armed guardsmen aboard merchant ships, signalmen, Seabees, bomb-disposal experts, radarmen, chemical-warfare experts, torpedo-men, amphibious-warfare specialists, ship repairmen, photo interpreters, ordnance men, sonarmen, damage-control experts, and 500 other specialties. "Aviation training presented such a tremendous undertaking that a separate program was created to fulfill the Navy's mission to become absolute masters of the air. To accomplish this task, the Navy trained 60,000 pilots, 360,000 air technicians, 3,000 air navigators and 45,000 combat air crewmen."[53]

The battle against Hitler's U-boats was far more than an "ensign's war," as Ladislas Farago has chosen to characterize it from the snobbish perspective of the wardroom. Several million youngsters from every layer of the American democracy were suddenly forced to adjust to complex battle. Many were hastily trained for antisubmarine warfare, "the most exacting and difficult job" in the fleet, requiring "innate aptitudes and physical and psychological conditioning well beyond the functions normally expected of the fighting sailor." In the earliest months of the war, outdated or inadequate weapons and unreliable radar and sonar equipment were all they had to train and work with. Moreover, their admirals had been as dilatory as those in Britain and Japan in developing effective antisubmarine strategies and doctrines. "Each of the four destroyer training centers of the Atlantic had a different set of attack instructions. And while the Atlantic Fleet's Anti-Submarine Warfare Unit in Boston counseled audacity, Vice Admiral Richard M. Brainard, USN, at Argentia [Newfoundland] urged caution." As in so many other aspects of war in 1942 and early 1943, American boys learned antisubmarine warfare by practicing it. Some failed to survive their natural mistakes. "A sonar man, for example, fresh from a brief course at Key West and never yet told about even the most common escape tactics of U-boats, had to discover (when it was too late) that the enemy he had on his sonar was forcing him to take ranges on his wake rather than his hull, or that the U-boat was fooling him with 'knuckles' in the water, conjured up by a sudden revving of the propellers."

The young naval flyers who began to hunt Dönitz's experienced U-boat sailors in 1943 from the short, narrow decks of escort carriers were burdened by their own "quickie training" and often gleefully bombed or strafed whales rather than submarines. Moreover, they had to learn in the crucible of battle the best means of approaching a surfaced, alert U-boat whose deck and bridge guns packed a hard wallop. They soon discovered that as in every other wartime endeavor, teamwork was the key to success. "After an initial period of hesitation and bungling," all of them, officers and seamen, sonarmen and pilots, began performing "with astounding competence."[54]

The first six months after Pearl Harbor were crucial. Boys who "only a few weeks before . . . had been living peacefully at home—most of them not yet able to vote—with the Friday-night dance, the new suit, the all-important question of money enough for that date" the dominant thoughts in their minds were now suddenly confronted with learning the intricacies of a modern steel and electronic warship on its way to deadly combat. In April 1942 the brand-new destroyer *O'Bannon,* bristling with the most modern five-inch guns, torpedoes, and electronic gear in the American fleet, slipped out of Boston Harbor for a hasty shakedown cruise. As the small ship bucked and pranced through North Atlantic swells, talk in the wardroom and chief's quarters, blue with cigarette smoke, was filled with the appalling ignorance of the youngsters on board. Lieutenant Carl Pfeifer, the engineering officer, told gunnery officer George Philip that he had asked one of his sailors to find the serial number on the turbine.

> There was no answer, so I asked him again. No answer. Finally he said, "I'm sorry sir, I don't know where the turbine is." The engineering officer paused for dramatic effect, then said, "And he's a machinist's mate, second class." The gunner waved his hand in an "I can top that" gesture and said that "one kid" walked up to a senior petty officer "and asked if we had any kitchens, 'because I'm very hungry.'" The petty officer asked if the boy had ever been aboard a ship before. Oh, yes, the sailor replied "'in the Brooklyn Navy Yard on Navy Day.'"

Down in the chief's quarters, Everett Padgett said he had had his young radiomen up until the small hours of the morning practicing Morse code. Toward the end the exhausted, frustrated chief asked a second-class radioman, "Tell me one thing, why did they ever put you in radio?" The boy grinned and replied that they had kept asking him in basic training if he had ever had anything to do with radio, "so I told them I did." Padgett's eyebrows shot skyward. "You were in radio before you joined up?" The radioman chuckled. "Yeah, I once built a crystal set." Jim Bess, the chief fire controlman, and his senior petty officer discovered that their crew "consisted of several schoolboys, an oil salesman, a miner from West Virginia, and a schoolboy who volunteered in order to save his father, who was head of the local draft board, from handing him his draft notice over the dinner table."

Toward the end of its normal schedule, the destroyer was suddenly ordered to join a convoy being badly hit by U-boats. For several days *O'Bannon* and several other escorts fruitlessly searched day and night for enemy submarines that attacked the merchantmen at will. Shocked youngsters saw several miles of floating debris, bodies without limbs or heads crushed inside shattered lifeboats, and corpses hanging head-down in the icy waters. Sailors belowdecks could not tell if thunderous explosions that pounded against the destroyer's thin sides were depth charges, torpedoes striking nearby merchantmen, or the death knell of their own ship. A few momentarily lost their heads, and on the night *O'Bannon* was ordered back to port, a teary-eyed young seaman approached the executive officer, Lieutenant Commander Donald J. MacDonald, on deck. "Please, sir, I want to be transferred. I don't want to be on a ship any more. I want to go ashore. I saw those bodies out there today. I saw the ships. . . . I'm afraid to die. . . . I have a wife." All MacDonald could do was remind the boy that several hundred shipmates devoutly wanted the same thing, but this was war and they would all have to carry on. The sailor waved his hand in a vague, exhausted salute and walked away.

But the chiefs and officers never lost faith in the youngsters under their command. They drilled and drilled and drilled them from dawn until late at night; once a piece of machinery was identified or a task mastered, the boys were blind-folded and told to do it ten more times—then ten or twenty times more after that. Slowly but unmistakably, *O'Bannon*'s crew jelled into a workmanlike, and ultimately deadly, team. Sent to the Pacific soon after Midway, the destroyer survived the dreadful battles around Guadalcanal in the autumn of 1942 to become one of the most experienced and decorated American "tin cans" of the war.[55]

Six months after *O'Bannon* left Boston, *Santee* departed Norfolk for the North African invasion. For some reason the new escort carrier flew off on only one antisubmarine patrol, and by the time it got to its support position off Safi, its pilots remained "definitely on the seedy side as fliers." Yet after a few mistakes and blunders, they performed superbly in supporting often hard-pressed ground forces, destroying enemy troop concentrations, vehicles, and guns and even shooting down an enemy bomber. Lieutenant Donald C. Rodeen was shot up while performing a ground-support mission and though wounded was able to crash-land his plane behind enemy lines: "Rodeen was typical of many of the *Santee* fliers, having only two and one half hours of flight time in the Avenger when 8 November dawned." *Bogue,* which would compile the greatest number of escort-carrier U-boat kills ever, was commissioned at Tacoma, Washington, on September 26, 1942, with a crew most of whom had never before seen blue water. The ship left Puget Sound after sea trials and further yard work on November 17, underwent a month's training off San Diego before moving through the Panama Canal to Norfolk, received a further six weeks' training there, and then was thrown into the Battle of the Atlantic on February 24, 1943. Within days, its fledgling pilots were finding U-boats lurking near the convoy routes, and they recorded their first of many kills.[56]

Daniel V. Gallery's *Guadalcanal* nearly matched *Bogue's* achievements. Of the twelve hundred men aboard,

> maybe a thousand were on their first ship. They were absolutely green.... In a way, having a completely inexperienced crew like that has some advantages. One of them was that I had very high ambitions for this ship. So I was proposing to the boys right from the start that we do some things that to an old-timer would sound a little far-fetched. In fact, an old-timer might say: "Well, this skipper is nuts. You just can't do this." But with a bunch of completely inexperienced kids, they said: "Well, if the old man says we can do it, we can." By God, they went out and did it.

And oftentimes they did it with a sense of awe at their own audacity. Film actor Douglas Fairbanks Jr. became an officer long before Pearl Harbor, and in April 1942 found himself censoring letters aboard battleship *Washington*. One evening he came across a hastily scrawled note from an enlisted man that read in its entirety: "Deer Mom—if only you knew where we was and what we was agoin to do you'd shit yerself—Love John."[57]

Finally, there was the American style of leadership. To a greater extent than any other participant, the United States fought a two-ocean, multidimensional war that, to succeed, demanded both centralized and decentralized decision making in an atmosphere of flexibility and rapid response to promising developments. In addition, the European theater of operations—preeminently an army and air corps "show" once men, equipment, and supplies ran the Atlantic gauntlet—required close coordination with often fractious allies. Leadership, goodwill, and staff work were thus at a premium, and theater commander Dwight Eisenhower and Army Chief of Staff George Marshall and their people provided both in necessary measure.

The Pacific was a different matter. There Douglas MacArthur and his often jealous, parochial staff not only exercised control over most of the army units in the Southwest Pacific theater but also had their own increasingly formidable navy, the Seventh Fleet. But MacArthur and his people were forced to share overall strategic and command responsibilities with the navy, led by "CinCPac" Chester Nimitz at Pearl Harbor, who directed the fast carriers and, by mid-1944, an enormous amphibious force of his own, including both marine and army units.

Conflict between the two commanders and their staffs, for men, goods, and operational opportunities, was predictably intense and occasionally had to be resolved by the Joint Chiefs in Washington, D.C., where Chief of Naval Operations Ernest J. King often expressed his own firm ideas about how to run the Pacific campaign. The result, according to one careful student, was a "quarrelsome but surprisingly successful system of divided command that drove the army and navy" both to distraction and to ultimate victory. The key to success lay in adherence by all to basic battle doctrines developed in the interwar years.

Effective implementation required frequent conferences among MacArthur, King, Halsey, and even Chester Nimitz and their staffs to ensure that everyone stayed on the same strategic and tactical pages. Throughout the war, King flew every other month to San Francisco where he met Nimitz coming over from Hawaii to apprise the Pacific Fleet commander of developments in Washington and gain his views on the war against Japan. Early on, MacArthur and Nimitz clashed over division of operational spheres in the Southwest Pacific–Solomon Islands area but resolved the issue without serious impairment to the war effort. By 1943 MacArthur was sending senior staff from his Southwest Pacific Command to Pearl Harbor to plan joint strategy. When at the end of that year Nimitz finally launched the central campaign through the Gilberts toward the Marshalls and Marianas as MacArthur drove deeper into New Guinea and the Southwest Pacific, operational imperatives and opportunities dictated temporary or permanent shuffles of amphibious units between the two commands, while Nimitz's carrier task forces raided enemy positions that lay within MacArthur's operational sphere.[58]

Aircraft carriers had delivered war to America's doorstep, and these ships, large and small, went on to shape and define the Pacific war, even as they contributed materially to the Allied victory in the Atlantic. But neither Japan nor the United States was responsible for the emergence of the aircraft carrier as the new queen of the seas. That task had already been accomplished by the British elsewhere—in the Mediterranean—during the early days of the war.

Britain's handful of aircraft carriers and their small air groups—brilliantly deployed by Andrew Cunningham at Alexandria and James Somerville at Gibraltar—dominated the early war in the Middle Sea. When Mussolini formally aligned his nation with Nazi aggression in June 1940, Britain seemed initially disinclined to challenge Italian air and naval power.[59] The Admiralty, concluding quite properly that "Britain's own survival as a European island in a death grapple with Germany constituted the supreme question," ordered Malta "virtually stripped" of all its offensive weaponry; divided the Mediterranean

Fleet between Gibraltar and Alexandria at the opposite "extreme corners of the Mediterranean," 2,150 statute miles apart; and shifted the imperial lifeline from the Gibraltar-Suez route to the infinitely longer passage around the Cape of Good Hope. But the Mediterranean could not be lightly abandoned. "Britain's traditional world-wide imperial position and obligations" east of Suez would not permit it. The transportation and communication route around South Africa to India and beyond was simply too cumbersome to keep the empire together for very long.[60] Somehow, the Gibraltar-Suez lifeline had to be maintained.

It would not be easy. The Regia Aeronautica was deployed all around the narrow, landlocked Mediterranean, in Sardinia, Sicily (only 60 miles from Malta), Libya, Albania, and the Dodecanese islands. By October 1940 the Italian fleet comprised six battleships (including two of the world's newest and most modern) together with a formidable collection of supporting heavy and light cruisers and destroyers.[61] Not only could this fleet pose a serious threat to British interests in the Mediterranean, but it could well help sweep Britain from the seas should it manage to steam out past Gibraltar and link up with Hitler's small but powerful surface navy. It therefore had to be confronted and beaten within the Mediterranean. There was also the strong, hostile squadron of French vessels at Oran in North Africa that included the splendid battle cruisers *Dunkerque* and *Strasbourg*. Having defeated the Third Republic, Hitler and his minions were busily engaged in the summer of 1940 creating a puppet government at Vichy under the popular old soldier Marshal Philippe Pétain. Only a comparative handful of French soldiers and airmen had escaped to London from the dreadful cauldron that the Wehrmacht had created in northwestern Europe. In such momentous and unsettling times, who could predict with certainty the loyalty of the French navy?

Certainly not Churchill. As the new Pétain regime prepared to surrender in early June 1940 with the disposition of the French fleet still in question, the British prime minister sent a long message to Roosevelt asking, in effect, for an American declaration of war to counterbalance the impending fall of France. Churchill was motivated entirely by naval considerations. Although his own government and he personally "would never fail" to send the Royal Navy across the Atlantic to Canada or the United States in the event of a successful Nazi invasion of England, he told the president the time might well come when "very easy terms could be obtained for the British islands by their becoming a vassal state of the Hitler empire." The prime minister was well aware that British opinion, particularly in the highest social and political circles, was balanced on a knife edge and that a "pro-German government would certainly be called into being to make peace and might present to a shattered or a starving nation an almost irresistible case for entire submission to the Nazi will." In that event, the British fleet might well be joined to those of Germany, Italy, and Japan. Given "the great resources of German industry, overwhelming sea power would be in Hitler's hands," and it was doubtful if he would use it "with a merciful moderation." Such a "revolution in sea power might happen very quickly and certainly long before the United States would be able to prepare against it."[62] Should the revolution occur, the large and modern French fleet then in North African waters could become the linchpin of a global naval menace to the United States. For the Royal Navy to ignore its malevolent potential and to evacuate the Middle Sea was simply unthinkable.

In a necessary but anguished act of assassination, Whitehall dispatched Somerville's newly formed Force H at Gibraltar (including several battleships and the carrier *Ark Royal*) to Oran in early July 1940 with the demand that Admiral Jean-François Darlan and his men either join the Royal Navy, scuttle or neutralize their ships, or face the dire consequences. Darlan, who considered himself the father of the modern French fleet, understandably refused to be bullied, and Somerville's main batteries and aircraft all but destroyed the French force. "And so that filthy job is over at last," Somerville wrote his wife. The captain of *Ark Royal* was so upset at firing upon ships and men that had been such recent allies that he asked to be reassigned, thereby effectively ending his naval career. But the French threat had been eradicated.[63]

Except for one memorable instance, Mussolini's sailors and airmen proved no real threat to either Somerville or Cunningham, though the Regia Aeronautica regularly undertook nerve-racking night raids against Cunningham's anchorage at Alexandria. The relative quietude of the Italian fleet was due as much or more to the steady and bold courage of the two British sea dogs as to the cowardice of their opponents. Still, cowardice was present in Italian naval circles. Mussolini ordered Admiral Domenico Cavagnari to mount "an all-out naval offensive" once Italy entered the war: Cavagnari replied that Italy would reach the postwar peace table "without a fleet." In early April 1940, two months before the duce sent his armed forces crashing into the hotel- and beach-clad French Riviera, Cavagnari "blurted out" to his fellow service chiefs that if one British fleet "will station itself at Gibraltar and another at Suez, we will strangle inside the Mediterranean." Nonetheless, Cavagnari sent his submariners out promptly against the Royal Navy once war came, only to discover that his "vaunted" boats were nothing but steel coffins. For all its stealth—and no little success—the Italian submarine campaign against Republic-bound shipping during the recent Spanish civil war had provided the Royal Navy with priceless information about enemy tactics and capabilities. In the twenty days following Mussolini's entry into the European war, the Italian navy lost ten U-boats. Their operations were "severely curtailed" from then until surrender three years later. Cavagnari consistently held his big ships back in the early days, either refusing to send them out or when pressured unendurably by Mussolini to do so ordering them back to port before contact with British forces was achieved. All in all, it was a shoddy performance.[64]

Somerville and Cunningham, on the other hand, were determined to use their fleets aggressively. Above all, they would expend every effort and resource to keep rapidly rebuilding Malta alive. As long as the island functioned, however minimally, the Axis could never hope to secure their southern flank in North Africa completely. Cunningham and Somerville soon hit upon the strategy of running often simultaneous convoys to Malta from both Gibraltar and Alexandria, coupling such efforts with periodic sweeps against Italian bases. The policy soon came to depend absolutely on airpower from the three British carriers in the area.

Throughout the latter half of 1940, the Italian fleet generally slept blissfully at its berths in Taranto, Naples, and elsewhere, leaving the molestation of British convoys and battle formations to the Regia Aeronautica. In August, Cunningham's fleet at Alexandria was bolstered by the arrival of battleship *Valiant* and the brand-new armored carrier *Illustrious,* both of which were equipped with air-search radar called Type 79Z. For the first time, incoming raids against either the convoys or the fleet could be spotted as far out as fifty miles, and the combat air patrols from *Illustrious* and the smaller old carrier *Eagle* could be vectored out to fight them.

British naval aircraft were still abominable, and the armored ships that carried them could handle only a few. The fifteen Fairey Fulmars aboard *Illustrious* had a top speed of less than 247 miles an hour (though they could reach nearly 400 miles per hour in a dive), and they struggled to reach 16,000 feet. The other eighteen aircraft aboard were the Swordfish biplane torpedo bombers, which for all their faults were at least stable, maneuverable craft that could carry fairly large missiles and had been fitted with extra fuel tanks to extend their range to 200 miles.

Between September 1940 and January 1941, *Ark Royal, Eagle,* and *Illustrious* ran wild in the central and eastern Mediterranean, not only protecting their respective convoys and fleet from attacks by the Regia Aeronautica but striking

Italian fleet and shore installations as well. The Swordfish bombed airfields, hit enemy convoys between Italy and North Africa, and mined enemy harbors. The first outstanding combination of radar with air defense occurred at the end of August during Operation "Hats," when a high-level Italian bombing raid against Cunningham's fleet was detected some 40 miles off and beaten back with bloody losses by Fulmars from *Illustrious* who had been given the time to climb to maximum altitude. No one cheered louder as the Italians tumbled from the blue skies than the weary antiaircraft crews on Cunningham's ships who had previously had to rely solely on the keen eyes of lookouts and their own questionable shooting to protect both warships and merchantmen from attack.[65]

Six weeks later *Illustrious* staged an effective night raid against Italian aviation facilities in the Dodecanese. By this time Cunningham was vividly remembering the desire of his former superior and mentor, Admiral William Fisher, at the time of the Abyssinian Crisis to strike the Italians in their lair as hard and as quickly as possible once war came. "We had not put away our idea of attacking the Italian fleet at Taranto." Even before the Dodecanese raid, Cunningham set Rear Admiral A. L. St. George Lyster aboard *Illustrious* to work making careful preparations and training his aircrews for an assault against the great Italian naval base. Taranto was probably the most heavily defended harbor in the world in 1940, with nearly a thousand antiaircraft guns ashore and on warships in the harbor, together with antitorpedo nets and sixty barrage balloons "whose steel [mooring] cables posed an almost unseeable menace to low flying planes at night."[66] Nonetheless, the British were determined to do to the Italians what Mussolini's flyers were attempting to do in their periodic nighttime attacks on Alexandria. In early November all was ready, and Cunningham's fleet put to sea. Originally, *Eagle* was to participate in the raid with *Illustrious,* but the obsolete little vessel developed engine trouble and its bitterly disappointed crew watched five of their planes take off and land on the bigger, newer carrier to augment that ship's modest-size air group.

Shortly before midnight on the eleventh, *Illustrious* reached its launch point roughly 40 miles west of Cephalonia and 120 miles from Taranto. It had left the main body of the fleet some hours before with Cunningham's modest message that success "may well have a most important bearing on the course of the war in the Mediterranean." A total of twenty-four Swordfish in two groups, each preceded by two flare-dropping "pathfinders," had been scheduled to take off from *Illustrious*'s moon-bathed flight deck. But the loss of *Eagle* together with various operational casualties reduced the final number to twenty-one.

Eleven of the aircraft carried eighteen-inch torpedoes, the others bombs or flares. The Italians were warned that the British were coming, and the aircraft batteries were manned and ready to meet the first wave of six Swordfish as they swept over the harbor. The antitorpedo nets, however, seem not to have been deployed. In the event, the flak was wild and poorly directed. As in the *Bismarck* episode six months later, the very slowness of the British torpedo planes apparently served to throw off enemy gunners while providing the pilots with an extraordinarily stable platform from which to launch their deadly "fish." Both waves of British aircraft were immeasurably assisted by the flares of the pathfinders and diversionary bombing that further divided and confused Italian gunfire and revealed the precise location of the balloon cables. As the second wave raced away, the results of the attack were beyond any Englishman's hopes.[67] Only two planes and four crewmen were lost, while at a stroke half the Italian battleship force had been torpedoed and was knocked out of the war for months; one of the three damaged ships, *Conte di Cavour,* eventually proved too smashed up to repair. The British also scored heavy hits on two cruisers. With this one raid, the aircraft carrier proved itself to be the supreme surface weapon in the war at sea. Its ability to project power scores of miles beyond that of any battleship's gun now was clearly established, though it would take Pearl Harbor and the sinking of *Prince of Wales* and *Repulse* to convince skeptics that planes could readily kill battleships.

Certainly, the Italians—and the Japanese—understood the import of Taranto far better than did many a stubborn British, German, or American battleship sailor. A fortnight afterward Force H was running a convoy into Malta when it encountered two Italian battleships and escorting forces off the cape at Spartivento. The British heavy ships were divided, and the Italians could have risked a major fleet action with promising results. But *Ark Royal* immediately flew off several torpedo-plane strikes to intimidate the enemy who raced away. In February 1941 battleships from Force H bombarded Genoa, while *Ark Royal's* squadrons added their own bombs to the assault, then struck the oil refinery at Livorno and mined the harbor at La Spezia. Force H sailed home unscathed to Gibraltar through fog and light haze despite formidable Italian air and sea forces sent to find it. Although few military objectives were hit (a battleship dry-docked at Genoa did not receive a scratch), Genoa itself was badly damaged, and "the psychological effect on the Italians was considerable." Their armies were retreating in North Africa, and now the navy and Regia Aeronautica could not even defend the homeland. As for the Japanese, Tokyo dispatched "a high level ... delegation" to Italy in May "with a long list of detailed questions about the Taranto raid." Isoroku Yamamoto and Minoru Genda were already deep into planning the attack against the U.S. Pacific Fleet at Pearl Harbor, and Taranto provided many promising leads and lessons.[68]

Winning control of the sea from the Italian navy was one thing. Keeping the seas in the face of land-based air attacks was something else. Churchill was almost pathologically keen in 1940–1941 to strike at the enemy wherever possible, and the Mediterranean provided ever growing opportunities. That sea consists of two basins, west and east, linked by a short middle passage—the Narrows— between the island of Sicily and the Tunisian coast. Britain had long-established naval bases and war fleets at both Gibraltar and Alexandria and had owned the island of Malta, just to the east of the Narrows, for exactly sixty years. The navy—together with whatever elements of the Royal Air Force Fighter and Bomber Commands could be spared from the United Kingdom and the Western Desert—was thus in a perfect position to interpose itself between Italy and its North Africa possessions and military forces. The prime minister was convinced that although Britain now stood alone, stand it must and not lie supinely awaiting the whims and initiatives of Hitler and his minions. Anyone willing to oppose either the Nazis or the Italians would instantly receive British support. At the end of May 1940, just before the fall of France brought Mussolini into the war, the Supreme (Anglo-French) War Council agreed that should Italy invade Greece, Britain and France would provide all possible support under the 1939 Anglo-Greek treaty. Six months later Churchill concluded that should Greece fall, the adjacent island of Crete must become "a permanent war fortress" and its superb harbor at Suda Bay a second Scapa Flow.[69]

The Mediterranean thus inevitably became a major battlefield when Mussolini's humiliating setbacks in Greece and North Africa in the autumn and winter of 1940–1941 enticed Hitler to dispatch mechanized and aerial formations into the Balkans and Tunisia. His decision had been buttressed by a rare agreement between Erich Raeder and Hermann Göring, both of whom recognized the "enormous advantages" accruing to German control of Suez and the Middle East.[70] Could that be effected, the Nazi war machine would forever have access to all the oil it needed, while depriving Britain of same. Moreover, control of Suez would cut the British lifeline to India and the Eastern empire. This was a prospect too tempting to ignore. In February 1941 Germany's finest field commander, Erwin Rommel, was ordered to Tripoli with a small but highly mobile army, charged with rescuing Mussolini's hapless soldiers, tying down the British Eighth Army, and eventually invading Egypt and seizing the canal. A month later German forces entered the Balkans, partly to retrieve the situation in Greece for Mussolini and partly to protect the Romanian oil fields seized in 1940 that were now threatened with aerial attack by small RAF forces staging from Greek airfields.[71]

The first Luftwaffe elements had arrived in Italy in January 1941 to support the Wehrmacht's incipient invasion of Greece. The primary targets for German aircraft would always be Malta and the pesky enemy convoys and fleets that were keeping the stubborn little island alive. Supplying Rommel's growing Afrika Korps from a few crowded Italian ports and even more unsatisfactory North African receiving wharfs would be extraordinarily difficult. The problem was compounded both by Hitler's decision that this front, like all others, should be marked by movement and action, not defense, and by Rommel's own dashing style of generalship that demanded frequent offensives with consequently heavy drawdowns on limited fuel stocks. Malta sat firmly astride the Italian–North African supply route. Planes, surface ships, and submarines operating from the island could not be allowed to cut that route, thus disrupting the always fragile but highly promising German offensives against Egypt and Suez. Malta had to be neutralized.[72]

But at least one source states that the German boys were told that their first objective was *Illustrious*. Knock that pest out of the war, and the whole British naval offensive in the narrow seas and eastern basin would be brought to a halt. The flyers hit upon a master plan. On January 10 several Italian torpedo planes and no fewer than three squadrons of Stukas caught Cunningham's fleet northwest of Malta escorting yet another convoy to the island. Its radar detecting two incoming Italian torpedo planes, *Illustrious* promptly flew off all the Fairey Fulmar fighters ready for combat, and the attacks were brushed off. Unfortunately, the fighter director aboard the carrier allowed his Fulmars to chase the Italians for twenty miles before he realized that another and far more deadly attack was gathering directly above. The Germans were about to do deliberately what the Americans would accomplish inadvertently at Midway little more than a year later. The Fulmars raced back, desperately clawing for altitude, but they failed to reach attack height before the German dive-bombers came screaming down. *Illustrious* was plastered with no fewer than six 1,000-pound bombs in about six minutes as the daring Stukas of Fliegerkorps X flattened out of their dives directly over the carrier's flight deck at funnel height and sped away. Only the 23,000-ton ship's stout construction kept it afloat. It limped into Malta where it was subjected to further determined bombing attacks, one of which blasted in some of its bottom plating from near misses in the shallow water of the harbor. Fortunately, at least one enemy attack was foiled by clouds of smoke and dust from ancillary raids. Cunningham realized that he had to get the ship away or it would be lost; the Admiralty concurred. *Illustrious* slipped out on the twelfth and eventually passed through the Suez Canal on its way to the big American shipyard at Norfolk where it remained under repair for the better part of a year. Taranto had been partially avenged, and the people of Malta would always recall January 1941 as "the *Illustrious* Blitz."[73] Meanwhile, the remainder of Cunningham's force, now bereft of air cover, was attacked unmercifully by enemy dive-bombers. Cruiser *Gloucester* was slightly damaged, while its sister, *Southhampton*, was struck in the engine room and had to be abandoned. Taranto had proved that used imaginatively and stealthily, carriers could kill battleships and thus win control of the high seas for their navy. But the fate of *Illustrious* suggested that the strategic role of carriers as both power projectors ashore and fleet-defense vessels was sharply circumscribed whenever confronted by land-based airpower. Carriers were apparently incapable of protecting either themselves or the ships around them from determined dive-bombing attacks.

Fortunately for Cunningham, *Illustrious*'s newest sister, *Formidable*, was available for service and arrived at Alexandria in March at just the moment when the eastern Mediterranean Fleet was about to undergo its first real ordeal. The admiral was by this time fully cognizant of the terrifying capabilities of airpower. Even with two carriers *(Eagle* and *Formidable)*, a few RAF squadrons scattered around North Africa and Greece, and *Ark Royal* occasionally on call from Gibraltar, British aircraft could not be everywhere. As the Eighth Army tried to clear Rommel and the Afrika Korps out of Tobruk in early 1941, the German and Italian air forces pummeled supporting British warships unmercifully. Cruiser *Terror* and destroyer *Dainty* went down together with several smaller ships. It was a foretaste of horrors to come.

But there was to be one last moment of glory for the Royal Navy, and carrier airpower would play a role here as earlier. As *Formidable* reached Alexandria, Hitler was clearly about to move into the Balkans to help his bumbling ally, Mussolini, retrieve the Grecian disaster of the previous autumn. Churchill scraped together fifty-eight thousand men (including an armored division) from the garrison in Egypt to stiffen the small British force already in Greece waiting to confront the looming Nazi offensive. Cunningham sent the reinforcements off to the Greek port of Piraeus in several convoys under light naval escort. Hanson Baldwin is properly despairing: "At this juncture, with the direct route through the Mediterranean at best a maritime Via Dolorosa for the

British, with shortages of all save courage, and the entire British Empire at bay, the gesture was politically and morally sublime—and militarily ridiculous. Like the charge of the Light Brigade at Balaclava, the British expedition to Greece was magnificent, but it was not war."[74]

With a large and active Japanese Embassy in Cairo to do Hitler's espionage work, British preparations could not be kept secret, and Berlin quickly learned of them. The führer was about to extend his own burgeoning empire to ridiculous and self-defeating proportions, but he was at least aware of how easily things might go wrong. Operation Barbarossa, the invasion of the Soviet Union, was but weeks away, and if it was to proceed with maximum force and on schedule, the Grecian adventure had to be completed quickly so that forces could be freed up to bolster the southern wing of the German advance eastward. Upon learning of the coming British reinforcement of Greece, German military and diplomatic circles promptly placed enormous pressure on Mussolini to get his fleet to sea to intercept and destroy the enemy troopships. The duce, now the laughingstock of Europe, had no choice but to comply, and Admiral Angelo Iachino was ordered out.

For the first of many times in the war, Enigma enabled the Royal Navy to win a stunning victory. Hitherto outmaneuvered by the superior work of their BDienst opponents in Berlin, the British intelligence team at Bletchley Park now scored its first major victory in the sea war. Decrypts of German signals indicated various moves by the Luftwaffe and Admiral Angelo Iachino's fleet units, suggesting a major aerial and naval assault against the Greek convoys. Within hours Cunningham had an Ultra dispatch in his hands warning him of probable enemy movements. But the clues were ambiguous and tantalizing, so Cunningham had to act in a fog of uncertainty. Not until an RAF flying boat out of Crete spotted elements of the Italian fleet steaming toward the southwestern Greek coast was Cunningham fully aware of the enemy's force and intentions. He ordered a returning convoy back to its Greek port, a northbound convoy to reverse course, and a British cruiser force under Admiral H. D. Pridham-Wippell in the Aegean to rendezvous next day with the main elements of the British fleet south of Crete. After spending the afternoon ashore golfing so as to throw off any enemy agents, Cunningham led his big ships out of harbor after dark and steered for precisely the point where he knew Iachino's force would be as it sailed to intercept the British convoy and its light escort force. The Enigma secret was kept for thirty years after the Second World War, and Cunningham maintained it in his 1951 memoirs by writing disingenuously that he did not believe the Italians would come after the British convoys until "we noticed some unusual Italian wireless traffic."[75]

Pridham-Wippell's cruiser force ahead of Cunningham first made contact with elements of the Italian fleet and, in the fashion of David Beatty at Jutland, sought to draw them back onto the main British force. This proved a difficult task. Cunningham's battleships—*Valiant, Warspite,* and *Barham*—were now of dubious quality. They still possessed their fifteen-inch guns, but the frisky twenty-five-knot colts of Beatty's column at Jutland had become tired and slow. As they retired toward Cunningham's slowly advancing column, Pridham-Wippell's handful of cruisers threatened to be overwhelmed by the big guns of the faster Italian cruisers and the splendid modern battleship *Vittorio Veneto.* In order to take the pressure off his subordinate, Cunningham launched a torpedo attack against the battleship from *Formidable.* It failed and, worse, tipped the Italians off to the fact that the main British force was undoubtedly at sea and certainly possessed of a carrier. Knowing what carrier torpedoes had done to his fleet in harbor scant months before, Iachino promptly turned tail for home.

A second attack from *Formidable* placed one torpedo in *Veneto's* stern, and the Italian flagship began to settle. However, its damage control proved adequate, and within an hour the ship had stanched the flood and was capable of making fifteen knots. Cunningham sent a third attack from *Formidable* at dusk that damaged and stopped the cruiser *Pola* not far off Cape Matapan at the southwestern tip of Greece. Thereafter, in what the admiring Correlli Barnett calls an exact reversal of Jutland, Cunningham decided to press a nighttime surface attack with his fast light forces against what he believed to be a badly damaged *Veneto* and its mass of escorts, with the main fleet to come up the next morning to finish the job. In the event, the Italian fleet had dispersed, and *Veneto* was in the process of escaping. But Iachino had sent two cruisers back to help *Pola,* and since none of the Italian ships possessed radar, they were sitting ducks for Cunningham, whose big ships stumbled across the Italians in the dark. The Italian sailors, their guns trained fore and aft and their attention focused wholly on saving *Pola,* were horrified when suddenly enemy battleships began pounding them at the point-blank range of three thousand yards. In four and a half minutes, it was all over. Three heavy cruisers, two destroyers, and 2,400 hundred men went to the bottom. "Next morning the [British] Fleet steamed for home through the sad wreck left behind by its victory, floating on a calm, sun-bright sea filmy with oil—boats, rafts, bits of debris, corpses."[76] The infuriated Italians countered with an aerial attack, but this time *Formidable's* combat air patrol easily broke it up. The battle off Cape Matapan was over, and with it any will on the part of the Italian navy to contest Britain's rule of the Mediterranean.

What the Axis could not achieve at sea, they would soon achieve from the air. German forces crushed the exhausted Greek army and swept the British from the Peloponnese with disheartening rapidity and ease. More than 12,000 men were lost together with 8,000 vehicles and 209 planes. But Cunningham's fleet managed to stage a little Dunkirk and snatched more than 50,000 men (figures vary slightly) from Nazi clutches. Since the Luftwaffe now completely controlled Grecian skies, Cunningham did not even consider bringing in the fleet's heavier ships to cover the evacuation; *Formidable,* with its scant complement of over-worked planes, would have been particularly vulnerable. This meant that evacuation could take place only at night. The operation turned out to be much like the successful withdrawals under enemy noses from Gallipoli twenty-six years before. The merchantmen and destroyers came in only after dark and were to leave no later than three in the morning. Those ships that somehow were unable to maintain this timetable were inevitably caught at sea at dawn and bombed. So disciplined were the British that they lost only six ships, most of them merchant-men, and Pridham-Wippell's destroyers and light cruisers worked magnificently. Just 14,000 troops were rescued directly from jetties or wharves, the remainder being snatched off open beaches by landing craft, small boats, "and any other craft that could be collected." Cunningham later paid tribute "to the inertness of the Italian fleet. Had they chosen to interfere, Operation 'Demon' would have been greatly slowed up" and possibly interrupted altogether.[77]

Crete, however, would be another matter. For the Luftwaffe and particularly General Karl Student, head of the German paratroop invasion force, Crete was simply a natural progression of the Grecian campaign that would culminate with German boys standing on the banks of the Suez Canal and walking the streets of Cairo. For Hitler, the conquest of Crete would complete an essential but unwelcome Balkan diversion. Crete would not be a springboard for an amphibious invasion of Egypt but rather the shield that would protect the comparatively weak Balkan flank of the imminent German invasion of Russia from any future Allied counterstroke. However mixed and varied their motives, the Germans wanted Crete, and the British knew it. This island fortress with its "second Scapa" at Suda Bay could not be allowed to fall.

Once again, however, enemy airpower proved irresistible, and this time it was employed on such a lavish and dramatic scale that Cunningham's navy was pulled into the fray and badly mauled. *Formidable*, Cunningham's only carrier, had been reduced to but four serviceable aircraft due to the continued wear and tear of recent operations, and Cunningham's only eight-inch-gun cruiser, *York*, had been completely disabled as the result of a daring attack by six fast Italian "explosive motor boats" on Suda Bay. Mussolini's fleet sailors may have displayed little stomach for fighting, but his small-boat men and underwater demolition teams were always feisty, daring, and resourceful.

The German airborne invasion of Crete began shortly after dawn on May 20, 1941, with reinforcements to come in by sea the following night. As the battle raged ashore during the next several days, British light forces north and east of the island found the enemy convoy with 2,300 German troops embarked and shot it to pieces; another small convoy with ammunition and food was also wiped out. For a time, the Australian–New Zealand defenders held the enemy at bay, inflicting terrible casualties. But the Germans proved up to the challenge. A last desperate gamble to land troop-laden JU-52s directly on the runway at Máleme paid off, despite heavy artillery and mortar fire. Now capable of being resupplied and reinforced by airlift, Student's determined paratroopers began a steady, grinding, irresistible offensive. Crete was doomed. Offshore, Stukas and Heinkels staging from fields in eastern Libya, Greece, and the Italian-held Dodecanese bombed the Royal Navy unmercifully, disrupting but not completely stifling British efforts to interdict enemy supply routes into Crete and maintain the flow of supplies to their own forces. The seas between Alexandria and Suda Bay came to be known to weary, desperate Jack Tar as "Bomb Alley." For a time, Cunningham's destroyers and cruisers beat back the Luftwaffe formations, but at a terrible cost in ammunition. As the enemy air raids continued (some ships were under continuous attack for up to three and a half hours), the toll began to mount. Hard-fighting cruisers and destroyers were wracked with bombs, then often heavily strafed as they broke up and went to the bottom. As early as the twenty-third, Cunningham replied to a rather hectoring cable from the Chiefs of Staff (read Churchill) in London with the observation that "the experience of three days in which two cruisers [including the gallant *Gloucester*] and four destroyers have been sunk and one battleship, two cruisers and four destroyers severely damaged shows what losses are likely to be" should the fleet be ordered to maintain control of the seas around Crete without the benefit of sufficient air cover. "Sea control in the Eastern Mediterranean," Cunningham concluded, "could not be retained after another such experience."[78]

Formidable's greatly reduced air group mounted one last successful night raid against the German air base at Kárpathos in the Dodecanese, but as the carrier and its escorts withdrew on May 27, both it and the battleship *Barham* were badly bombed by the vengeful Germans, and Cunningham promptly ordered all his big ships back to Alexandria. It was left to the antiaircraft cruisers and destroyers to undertake the last act of the campaign, yet another evacuation of friendly forces in the face of an aroused and determined enemy.

There are no more melancholy pages in Cunningham's splendid memoirs than those devoted to the evacuation of Crete on the nights of May 27–28 and 28–29, 1941. The "small boys" dedicated to the task were bombed repeatedly as they approached and withdrew from the island. Ammunition lockers were emptied and gun crews stupefied with fatigue as wave after wave of German and Italian aircraft roared down out of the skies. As ships heaved and rocked under the impact of bomb blasts aboard or near misses, several thousand sailors were pitched into the warm, salty waters, some to be rescued, many to perish along with their mates who went down with their ships. The final toll off Crete in the ten days after May 20 was three cruisers and six destroyers gone. Moreover, *Formidable,* the battleships *Warspite* and *Barham,* and four more cruisers were damaged beyond any hope of repair at Alexandria and had to be sent home (or to American yards) for months of rebuilding, while another nine cruisers and destroyers required several weeks or more of dockyard work at Alexandria.

Cunningham was aware of the peculiar strain of the operation. The ship's companies were not inspired to do battle with the enemy as they would have been had the Italian fleet or a German battleship appeared in their sights. "Instead they had the unceasing anxiety of the task of trying to bring away in safety, thousands of their own countrymen, many of whom were in an exhausted and dispirited condition in ships necessarily so overcrowded that even when there was opportunity to relax conditions made this impossible." And Cunningham concluded almost in despair, "There is rightly little credit or glory to be expected in these operations of retreat."[79]

But somehow the Tars and matelots who had been so contemptuously dismissed by their countrymen before and after Invergordon and never given the proper tools to do their jobs or save their lives stuck to their duty, inspiring the "hostilities-only" ratings and seamen in their charge. The Mediterranean Fleet bent badly off Greece and Crete, but under Cunningham's inspiring leadership it never broke. As a consequence, eighteen thousand now battle-hardened

Australian and New Zealand soldiers would live to fight once more against Erwin Rommel's legions.

With the seizure of Crete, Erich Raeder and his naval strategists came to view the Mediterranean, not Russia, as the pivot on which all of Germany's future aggressions should turn. The lure of Suez and the Middle East now took definite shape. "The appeal of a Mediterranean campaign lay not only in its objectives but in its economy of force." The critical Battle of the Atlantic could be sustained without interruption, and the continued raiding cruises by German armed merchantmen and battleships would periodically lure Force H away from Gibraltar out into the Atlantic, preventing reinforcement of Cunningham's meager fleet at Alexandria. German control of the eastern Mediterranean through Greece and Crete provided Hitler the opportunity to pressure Spain's fascist dictator, Francisco Franco, into allowing German troops and air force units to move through Iberia to seize Gibraltar. Spanish Morocco and the Canary Islands would be taken next, effectively flanking and neutralizing any rebel French forces in North and West Africa. At that point, Admiral Darlan at Algiers, without warships but with an army, might be tempted to throw in his lot with Berlin. "Russia, the timid giant, was to be offered concessions in . . . Iran, Afghanistan, and northwestern India as the Germans took the Dardenelles."

> Defense of that vast new area would be based on the Mediterranean—with the unassailable Sahara to the south, fringed by a few heavily fortified ports on the rugged and inhospitable western African shore. To the north an "Atlantic Wall" would be buttressed by mobile forces operating on interior lines in western Europe. Mussolini's "Mare Nostrum" would become an Axis military and commercial highway, and the lower North Atlantic a baseless and dangerous wasteland for the British.
>
> With Joseph Stalin's unwillingness to fight except defensively and with all the resources of western Europe concentrated against the British Isles and their supply lines, the chances for forcing British capitulation would have been quite good, especially if Hitler's demands had been moderate.[80]

It is clear now as it was to some then that had Hitler "wanted the Middle Sea as badly as he wanted Russia, he could have had it."[81] By the beginning of 1942, Axis forces occupied not only the entire northern shore but great stretches of the southern shore as well. All that stood between a successful German pincer movement into Palestine and on to the Persian Gulf was the Eighth Army in the Western Desert and Cunningham's units at Alexandria. For a brief moment

Hitler was tempted to grab the prize that was so nearly in his grasp. He and Mussolini together with their respective staffs seriously considered a combined air and sea assault to capture Malta that would have fairly isolated Cunningham at Alexandria from sufficient reinforcement.

By this time the Italian navy had thrown off its cloak of gloom and cowardice. The duce's sailors bestirred themselves to cooperate closely with the Regia Aeronautica in securing the vital convoy routes to the Italo-German North African front. Daring Italian "frogmen" penetrated Alexandria Harbor in December 1941 to blast and virtually sink the British battleships *Queen Elizabeth* and *Valiant* at their moorings, thereby crippling Cunningham's ability to project power and protect the Malta convoys.[82] They were still run, but by the spring of 1942 Malta was a desperate place to be, as it barely hung on.

Had Operation Herkules been carried out against the island successfully, it would have also precluded the Allied counteroffensive that began in North Africa the following November. American landings inside the Mediterranean would have been impossible given German and Italian air bases on nearby Malta, and the Atlantic beachhead at Casablanca might have been contained. Subsequent Anglo-American assaults on Sicily, Salerno, and Anzio could not have taken place; Italy would doubtless have remained in the war; and the Allies would have never gained the invaluable experiences in mounting combined operations that were an essential prelude to the landings in Normandy. In short, the seizure of Malta might have rendered Germany's position in the West impregnable.

But the perspective from Berlin between the late springs of 1941 and 1942 did not appear as promising as hindsight would suggest. Despite the marked improvement in his naval and air forces, Mussolini was at best an uncertain and increasingly costly partner. Above all, the British were getting just enough supplies through to Malta to keep the island free and functioning. Through much of its siege, the island remained home to the submarine Tenth Flotilla; its air defenses and bomber forces were never completely destroyed. In November 1941 the Admiralty dispatched to the island Force K—light cruisers *Arethusa* and *Penelope* and two destroyers—under the command of Captain W. G. Agnew. The small task force was soon reinforced by other light units and functioned effectively for nearly two months before blundering into the enemy minefield off the North African coast.[83]

Thus, although Malta approached collapse on several occasions—the last as late as the summer of 1942 when outright starvation faced the islanders due to the enemy's near suppression of convoys from Gibraltar and Alexandria—it never went under. As the crisis approached its climax that May, the Tenth Flotilla was withdrawn to Alexandria. But when the garrison had been strong in previous months, its handful of Wellingtons, Beauforts, Blenheims, Hurricanes, Swordfish, cruisers, destroyers, and submarines were able to massacre several enemy convoys supplying Rommel. In November 1941, "77 per cent of all Rommel's supplies had been sunk," and the Eighth Army promptly launched an offensive along the North African shore that drove the Germans back five hundred miles in six weeks. The German General Staff had already concluded after one slaughter the previous September that the situation in the western Mediterranean was "untenable. Italian naval and air forces are incapable of providing adequate cover for the convoys. . . . The Naval Staff considers radical changes and immediate measures to remedy the situation imperative, otherwise . . . the entire Italo-German position in North Africa will be lost."[84] It was this conclusion that prompted Hitler's disastrous decision to strip his still small but deadly Atlantic U-boat force of half its active strength in order to destroy the Malta supply convoys. But as desperate as was its eventual plight, Malta would undoubtedly have put up a very stiff and costly fight for survival should Axis forces have ever attempted to seize it.

Hitler's fatal adventure in Russia precluded such a step. To win the Mediterranean and thereby absolutely secure his southern flank, the führer would have had to postpone Operation Barbarossa indefinitely or, had the Russian campaign already begun, suspend virtually all operations on the vast arc from Leningrad to the Volga. This Hitler was never willing to do. Compared to the lure of the Ukraine and the distant Caucasian oil fields, the Mediterranean held little interest once the great Romanian oil fields at Ploieşti had been protected from British air attacks from Greece. The führer's essential uninterest and the always growing demands of the Russian front forced Rommel to operate on a shoestring. The Afrika Korps was always weaker and its supplies far less than Allied calculations supposed.

Even if the Russian front had not existed, it is doubtful that the führer would have moved against Malta in the winter or summer of 1942—or against the Canaries and Spanish Morocco the year before. The costly campaign in Crete (General Student's badly battered German paratroops never again played a major role in the war) reconfirmed Hitler's long-standing and profound fear of the sea, and Crete had been immediately preceded by the shattering loss of *Bismarck*. In some way the sea induced in Hitler a feeling he could not abide— the loss of control. Enterprises on and over water apparently possessed for him an inherent uncertainty and instability that did not accrue to land combat. He did make several "feeble" tries at securing his southern flank: strengthening the Luftwaffe in Italy and the Dodecanese in the autumn of 1941 when he believed Russia was on the ropes, ordering Dönitz to virtually close down the Battle of the Atlantic at roughly the same time in order to send German U-boats against both Force H and Cunningham's fleet, and occasionally devoting attention to getting convoys through to Rommel. But such fitful efforts proved a "no go. Signals inside hemmed him, made him uneasy, unsure," and he was thus instinctively receptive to Dönitz's complaints that the Mediterranean was not a decisive theater in which the U-boats could win the war for Germany.[85]

The early Mediterranean war taught Allies and Axis alike that airpower was the dominant factor at sea. What kind of airpower, however, was subject to violent debate. Obviously, battleships, cruisers, and destroyers were more or less helpless against it. Carriers, if used with daring and imagination, as at Genoa and Taranto, could be invaluable power projectors. But it seemed that they, too, in the end must bend to land-based airpower. Air forces could simply muster far more and perhaps better planes for assault than carriers could put up in their own and their fleet's defense. The rapid reduction of *Formidable*'s air group in operations off Greece and North Africa seemed to prove it. By the time of Crete, the ship, its crew, and its air group were exhausted. Shore-based pilots might or might not be better than flattop fliers, but in enclosed seas like the Mediterranean or off the coasts of Europe they had the inestimable advantage of being able to mount sudden, short-range attacks that demanded that a very large portion of the carrier's air group be concerned with round-the-clock defense.

Cunningham's bitter sailors properly asked where the Royal Air Force had been while they sweated and cursed, prayed and drowned off Crete. One evening in a Cairo street, Air Marshal Arthur Tedder, newly arrived deputy commander of the Royal Air Force–Middle East, was assailed "by a motley group of sailors and marines" who chanted in his face: "Roll out the *Nelson*, the *Rodney*, the *Hood*, / Since the whole fucking air force is no fucking good."[86]

A few naval theorists rejected the lessons of the Mediterranean campaign outright. Despite Taranto, they argued that the well-armored battleship was still the best power projector afloat, particularly given the comparative fragility of carriers, even those heavily armored ships that Cunningham and Somerville threw at the Axis. Isoroku Yamamoto and his colleagues in the Imperial Japanese Navy and Naval Ministry did grasp the implications of Taranto and the sinking of *Bismarck;* they understood the aircraft carrier's illimitable promise, particularly if such ships embarked a sufficiently large and varied air group and were able to operate in the open waters of midocean. After Pearl Harbor and the sinking of *Prince of Wales* and *Repulse,* the rest of the world understood also. The Hawaiian raid seemed to change everything, and carrier enthusiasts championed their weapon system with as much blind arrogance as the battleship sailors ever had. Look at what *Illustrious* had accomplished at Taranto and *Formidable* and *Ark Royal* in their own Mediterranean raids; remember how *Ark Royal* had "winged" *Bismarck* and what *Kido Butai* had done at Pearl Harbor and against British heavy cruisers and the small, obsolete carrier *Hermes* off Ceylon. "So far in this war," one carrier champion wrote in July 1942, "nine capital ships have been sunk, crippled, or capsized by aircraft," and six of them "met their fate from torpedo-planes and bombers launched from carriers. . . . In contrast, only one carrier has been reported sunk by battleships." Granted, carriers were in great jeopardy in enclosed waters like the Mediterranean or English Channel, but in comparison to these "front lawns," the Pacific resembled "the broad expanse of a big municipal airport" where carrier aviation could be displayed in all its power and variety. Japan's well-known strategy of employing naval airpower in the islands of the western Pacific to whittle down advancing American sea power would be defeated by the very nimbleness of the fast carrier fleets.

> To control absolutely the Western Pacific, Japan would have to concentrate huge fleets of planes at many island bases; she could not pick out one strategic base for the whole area, as the Germans have done at Sicily, in the comparatively small Mediterranean. In the vast Pacific fast ships, such as carriers, can literally hide and then, when ready, dart in and attack with impunity. As a result, carrier flyers claim, the Pacific is an ideal hunting ground and hide-out for their beloved ships.[87]

In the year after Pearl Harbor, off Ceylon and Japan, in the Coral Sea, at Midway, and in the violent waters surrounding Malta, carrier aviation became the center of naval warfare. On two occasions in the spring of 1942 Malta was literally saved by a sudden, eleventh-hour infusion of airpower brought in by *Eagle* and the American carrier *Wasp,* and in the following months *Eagle* and the new armored carrier *Indomitable* did what they could to protect the always savagely attacked convoys struggling to reach the island. In the process *Eagle* was lost to torpedoes, and *Indomitable* was bombed almost as terribly as had been its older sister *Illustrious.* But Malta hung on, and because it did the Axis failed to hold the Mediterranean, which was abruptly transformed after the November 1942 Allied landings in North Africa from an open British wound to an Anglo-American highway leading directly to the seizure of Italy and the eventual reconquest of southwestern Europe.

The Mediterranean campaigns of 1943–1945 required massive infusions of Allied airpower that Britain's handful of carriers simply could not provide. As Allen Andrews has rightly emphasized, Air Marshal Tedder gradually welded Allied land-based airpower into a single invincible instrument that first demonstrated its devastating capabilities during the battle for Tunisia in early 1943, "when a virtual air blockade of the Sicilian Narrows" by the RAF and units of the United States Army Air Corps "deprived the Germans of all extraneous support or means of retreat."[88] By the time of the invasion of Sicily several months later, Allied sea power, except in the crucial amphibious role, had been subordinated to land and land-based air forces throughout the European Theater of Operations. But sea-air power had held the Mediterranean line, however precariously, in the early stages of the war, discouraging Hitler and his generals from pursuing a strategy that could have prolonged the conflict indefinitely; winning the Battle of the Atlantic, providing the buildup and support for the invasion of Europe that doomed Nazism; and denying Japan the expansive Asian-Pacific empire that might conceivably have created an unbreakable stalemate. By the end of 1943 the Allies were on a march everywhere that the Axis proved unable to halt anywhere.

CHAPTER 11

Gem of the Ocean

THE REBIRTH OF American sea power in the Pacific began on the bright morning of June 1, 1943, when the splendid new 27,100-ton carrier *Essex* steamed majestically through the pale-green shoal waters off Pearl Harbor to tie up at Ford Island. The first in a class of twenty-four incomparable vessels each stretching nearly 900 feet, *Essex* could easily accommodate a ninety-plane air group. But as the great carrier entered harbor, it undoubtedly encountered one or two comparatively tiny vessels, decks almost awash, that had been carrying the war to Japan's empire, coasts, and even into its harbors for the past seventeen months.

Undersea war in the Pacific was far different, and in many ways far less dramatic, than the Battle of the Atlantic, but it was no less decisive. Nor was it waged with any greater restraint or pity. Within hours of the attack on Hawaii, the word went forth: "Execute unrestricted air and submarine warfare against Japan." Not only were there no neutrals in Pacific waters after December 1941, but the notion of "preserving" the "innocent" lives of women and children also went by the board.[1]

Whereas Germany's submariners concentrated on cutting the Allied lifeline between North America and the British Isles (disdaining, for example, to make concerted attacks upon the critical supply routes to the North African and Mediterranean fronts in late 1942 and early 1943), American submariners found that in order to whittle down the Japanese merchant marine and shrivel the Japanese Empire, they had to attack a profusion of enemy sea-lanes. But this problem reflected the much greater conundrum that confronted Tokyo. At the apex of its conquests in mid-1942, Japan possessed an oceanic empire to both supply and exploit that ran in a great arc from the Ryukyus to the Bonins, Marianas, Carolines, Marshalls, Gilberts, Solomons, and Admiralties on around to Java, Malaya, Borneo, Indochina, the Philippines, and the China coast. Tying such a huge empire together and maintaining it proved beyond the limited naval and merchant-marine capabilities of Japan when confronted by a determined enemy submarine offensive. The very size and diffusion of the "Greater East Asia Co-Prosperity Sphere" precluded use of the large, defensive convoy system that proved so effective in the North Atlantic in both world wars. In order to effectively feed and provision their numerous island garrisons and exploit the fabulous wealth of their sprawling new colonies, the Japanese were forced to fill the western Pacific with unescorted, independently sailing ships, much as the Allies had filled the western approaches and the Irish Sea in 1916–1917 before the imposition of the Atlantic convoy system. Small to medium-size escorted convoys were often employed when appropriate (that is, to supply the larger garrisons or to ensure the safe transportation home of strategically critical supplies like oil and lubricants), but here the Japanese ran into another problem of their own making.

The navy, with its samurai emphasis on offensive combat, had not been built or trained for the kind of tedious and intense defensive warfare that an effective antisubmarine campaign requires. The notion that an enemy should or would make war on "civilian" ships and cargo was beyond comprehension. As noted earlier, Japan's prewar antisubmarine capabilities were fatally hobbled by the offensive spirit that demanded precious naval tonnage be devoted to huge battleships like *Musashi* and *Yamato,* together with the modest carrier construction programs that produced *Hiryu, Soryu, Zuikaku,* and *Shokaku.* The substantial light forces that the Japanese navy was able to build and maintain were also conceived in wholly offensive terms. Its destroyers were not to be tied down to convoy-escort work; their job was to attack enemy fleet formations with torpedoes as well as gunfire and preferably at night. As the war progressed Japanese antisubmarine warfare did become more effective in some areas. Sailors and fliers laid often deadly minefields off their own and captured coasts, and the air patrols from the Home Islands and Philippines became ever more efficient. The United States lost a total of fifty-two boats in the forty-four months after Pearl Harbor, not a negligible number. Most of the submarines were listed as "overdue, presumed lost," so the precise circumstances of their demise were often unknown.

As the independently sailing Japanese merchantmen and small convoys spread out from the harbors and bays of Honshu and Kyūshū to resupply Saipan,

Kwajalein, or Truk, or as they set sail from Batavia, Balikpapan, Manila, Singapore, or Cam Ranh Bay with the precious loot of empire in their bellies to serve the Japanese war effort, they were wide open to American submariners whose only constraint in the first two years of the war was consistently faulty torpedoes that may well have induced aggressive, frustrated skippers to fatal risk by moving in too close to shore or to a target in order to ensure a kill.

The United States began the war with roughly seventy boats, more than half of which were the "old 'S' types" of 1916–1918. By early 1942, however, the first of what would amount to 228 *Gato-*, *Balao-*, and *Tench-*class boats were coming into service. From the outset each sub (excluding the "S" boats) carried radar, though the early SD sets were often "temperamental and unreliable," giving off such a powerful signal of their own that use was "tantamount to breaking radio silence." In July–August 1942, however, the first of the *Gato* boats went on patrol with an excellent new instrument, the SJ, a surface-search radar "designed specifically for picking up enemy shipping. It provided exact range and bearing, enabling the submarine to 'see' at night or in rain, fog or snow." When a PPI (plan position indicator) scope was later added, it enhanced capabilities for night surface torpedo attacks against what Japanese convoys there were.[2]

By 1943 the Americans were employing radar-equipped wolf packs to destroy enemy shipping day and night and were well on their way to solving the faulty torpedo problem. At the end of 1944 well over half of the Japanese merchant marine had been sent to the bottom, and the submarine service began aggressively attacking Japanese warships as well, especially when on surveillance duty off enemy harbors. Tokyo's desperate warlords had long since been reduced to transporting as much precious cargo as possible by junks and small coastal steamers. With most of their tankers at the bottom of the sea, the Japanese could no longer ensure the flow of precious fuel oil from Southeast Asia to the Home Islands. The bulk of the imperial fleet had no choice but to remain close to the oil fountains in Malaya and Borneo. But the unprocessed product that came out of the wellheads was at once highly volatile and contained impurities that damaged ships' boilers. There was no alternative but to use the dangerous fuel, which imposed critical operational constraints that contributed materially to the Japanese failures in the battles of the Philippine Sea and at Leyte Gulf. By the summer of 1945 U.S. submarines along with navy and air force fighters and bombers had imposed a tight blockade of the Home Islands.

The success of the United States Navy in denying Japan her vital oil supplies is told in one simple table of figures. Of what was produced in the southern oil-fields that Japan had conquered, the following amounts reached Japan: in 1942, 40 per cent; in 1943, 15 per cent; in 1944, 5 per cent; in 1945, none. This was what really defeated Japan. With or without the atom bomb, the Russian entry into the Pacific war, or the great naval battles, Japan was finished, because her ships, aircraft, tanks, and vehicles could not move. They had no fuel. This classic case of strategic warfare went unreported at the time because of a Navy Department directive that nothing should be written about submarines. Several correspondents wrote long and detailed stories on the daring achievements of American submarines against Japanese shipping, but the Navy Department refused to pass them.[3]

Whether the American submarine campaign alone defeated Japan is doubtful, and the author of the above paragraph is more than occasionally careless with his facts in pursuit of a good story. But the U.S. submarine campaign in the Pacific certainly had a substantial, if not decisive, impact on crippling the Imperial Navy, which almost never left its anchorages between the fall of Guadalcanal in February 1943 and the Battle of the Philippine Sea sixteen months later.

Japan's submarine campaign was defined by the same samurai spirit that hobbled its antisubmarine efforts: warriors did not fight and destroy civilians. From Pearl Harbor on, the Japanese undersea war concentrated almost exclusively on American fleet units, and Tokyo made no serious effort to sever the critical Allied transportation and communication routes between the American West Coast, Hawaii, and Australia. The few who have written on the imperial submarine service emphasize its offensive spirit. "The Japanese Navy expected much from its submarines," a former Japanese undersea commander has written, "and for this reason alone both officers and men were carefully selected and put through the most rigorous training. They considered themselves superior in technique in the field of submarine warfare to any in other navies." But on watery fields of battle, "the results were deplorable."[4]

As early as 1931 the Japanese had developed plans for employment of an eighty-five-boat submarine fleet designed for three purposes: first, to detect and follow the American battle fleet; second, to attack it in midocean; and, third, to assault it within and between the various Japanese-held island systems in the central and western Pacific. As plans to confront the United States matured and a direct attack upon Pearl Harbor became ever more attractive, a critical fourth use for the Japanese submarine fleet emerged: as a crucial adjunct to the air assault upon Hawaii. According to this scenario, the line of Japanese submarines stationed off Pearl Harbor during the attack would pick off any American fleet units that survived the assault and sought the open seas. The submarines were duly dispatched, some carrying "midget submarines" designed to penetrate the harbor and add to the chaos by torpedoing the enemy battleships under air attack. The entire operation failed, of course, which swiftly became a source of deep mortification to the navy.

It may well be, however, that historians have attributed a greater doctrinal and strategic coherence to the Japanese submarine warfare than in fact existed. If one looks at the construction program after 1920, there is little but chaos. The best doctrines, the finest strategies, depend upon use of a very few highly standardized, well-proven weapon systems for success. The Americans proved that point with their thousands of B-17s over Europe and B-29s over Japan. These weapons together with the 228 *Gato*-class submarines and 24 *Essex*-class carriers allowed the United States to fight a relatively efficient, coherent war with standard, interchangeable weaponry. The same might be said of the German U-boats that were simply overwhelmed by superior technology after pushing the Atlantic war to its limits. Such could not be said for the German Luftwaffe or the Japanese submarine service, which in both cases suffered from a plethora of designs and classes, resulting in the construction and combat operation of a comparative few of each. Japan's eighty-five-plus submarines were divided into nearly a score of separate or modified classes of boat, "with many types within classes." Though not necessarily designed for a wide variety of tasks, the boats were not focused on one or two mission responsibilities, either. A few were converted to small subsurface aircraft carriers. Others were used to supply the remotest garrisons bypassed in the Allied advance, and still others were used as mother ships for midget submarines and Kaiten suicide torpedoes that made attacks on enemy installations as far away—and far apart—as Diégo-Suarez (Antsiranana) and Sydney. All this was in addition to their principal function of supporting fleet operations and going after the enemy's capital ships.[5]

Japanese submarine operations may not have been poorly conceived, but they were almost invariably poorly implemented. The Pearl Harbor submarine force ordered on to the California coast after the Hawaiian assault failed to significantly affect coastal traffic at the time that their German allies were destroying East Coast shipping. The postwar U.S. Naval Technical Mission to Japan concluded "through conversations, interrogations and study that the percentage of overly discreet (submarine commanders) was large." The Americans found it "frankly impossible" to believe that the enemy submarine force off California spent weeks without making contact with a single ship, or that later, during the Guadalcanal campaign, Japanese submariners went forty days "running among the Solomons, 'without seeing any targets.'" This thinly veiled charge of cowardice needs to be modified somewhat. When Japanese submarine commanders were ordered against Allied merchantmen in largely undefended areas, such as the Indian Ocean after Pearl Harbor, they did rather well for the brief period they were on station. Moreover, in the first year of the war, they contributed substantially to Japanese fleet victories. I-168, lurking about Midway, polished off the damaged but still salvageable *Yorktown*. Other submarines heavily damaged *Saratoga* on two critical occasions in 1942 when American carrier strength was already weak. I-19 killed *Wasp* in spectacular fashion off Guadalcanal only five weeks into that campaign, and at the same time a sister sub ripped open the armored hull of the brand-new battleship *North Carolina,* sending it back to the repair yards for critical weeks. But after the early autumn of 1942, the Japanese submarine force failed utterly to mount any sustained, successful undersea warfare against the enemy. Its contribution to the national war effort proved insignificant, the tragic sinking of cruiser *Indianapolis* at the very end notwithstanding.[6]

Essex entered Pearl Harbor just six weeks before the new *Yorktown,* which was quickly followed by *Independence,* the lead ship of a nine-vessel class of fast light carriers built on cruiser hulls that carried roughly thirty-five fighter and attack planes. As *Yorktown* steamed out for its first operational mission on August 21, 1943 (against Marcus with the other two newcomers), the Ford Island tower sent it on its way with the heartfelt message "You look good out there honey."[7] Beneath the appreciative laughter on the carrier's bridge and flight deck was a profound sense of relief. For a year and a half the Pacific Fleet had absorbed every blow the Japanese could throw. Now the initiative was shifting decisively in America's favor.

Not only was the country gaining material and moral preponderance over the enemy, but it had gained strategic independence from its allies as well. At Casablanca the previous January, Winston Churchill and the British Chiefs of Staff formally acknowledged what had been reality since *Prince of Wales* and *Repulse* had gone down off Malaya thirteen months before: the Pacific belonged to the Americans. How they fought that campaign and how they would finish it was up to no one but themselves. The Japanese were about to be bounced out of Guadalcanal at that moment, giving U.S. armed forces their first offensive victory of the Pacific war, and a new battle fleet was rapidly forming that would have little impact on the European conflict but was ideally suited for the Pacific, where it would be the spear point driving the Japanese steadily back through their occupied islands toward home.

The Pacific war required far fewer men than Europe until that climactic moment (which would never come) when thousands of troops were expected to storm onto the beaches of Kyūshū and Honshu. Until mid-1944 the vast distances of the Pacific precluded the kind of massive, concentrated strategic bombing campaign against enemy cities and industrial facilities that character- ized the European war from its inception. So the European front received about two-thirds of American manpower, and that kept the Anglo-Soviet allies and their peoples reasonably satisfied. At Casablanca, Churchill began making noises that eventually rose to a crescendo about the imperative for a British Pacific fleet sailing and fighting side by side with the Americans against Japan, but that possibility lay in a future forever free of Nazism. His Chiefs of Staff complained, often bitterly, over allocation of resources, especially landing craft whose lack, they claimed, hobbled what would have been a far more promising Mediterra- nean approach to ending the war than an invasion of France. But in the end, both Europe and the Pacific got enough sinews of war to get the job done in remarkably short time without one being a drag on the other.[8]

Strategic independence, however, came at the price of internal division within the U.S. Pacific commands. The tides of war had swept away the neat postu- lates of prewar War Plan Orange, and the question had to be asked anew: what was the best way to defeat Japan? By mid-1943 two powerful warlords—a gen- eral and an admiral thousands of miles apart from each other—had developed conflicting answers. Douglas MacArthur sat in far-off Melbourne, Australia, as supreme Allied commander of the Southwest Pacific. The general had been a prominent public figure at home since World War I. A dedicated practitioner of leadership, control, and intimidation through mystique, MacArthur com- manded formidable ground, air, and sea forces that were in the process of clear- ing the enemy from the upper Solomons and neutralizing New Guinea in prepa- ration for breaking the Bismarck Archipelago barrier and a lunge toward the southern Philippine island of Mindanao. Largely immune from the immediate pressures and influence of wartime Washington, MacArthur was, by the same token, isolated from the decision-making process. He seethed with unsatisfied appetites. In retirement he had been ordered to defend the Philippines with meager forces and, in the view of some, criminally frittered away the best of what he had. His men were eventually defeated on Bataan and Corregidor, and he had fled to Australia, pledging as he left that he would return to the Filipinos whom he at once loved and condescended to. MacArthur's "creep-up" strategy for Pacific warfare focused wholly on retaking the Philippines. Only then could further moves toward Japan be contemplated.

At Pearl Harbor, Admiral Chester Nimitz and his people chafed to implement War Plan Orange at last. Strike the Gilberts, Marshalls, and Marianas. Then leap over to Formosa, bypassing the Philippines entirely. Next, invade the Chinese coast, and from bases there throw a tight blockade around Japan that would, they hoped, induce surrender or, if not, would provide the foundations for an invasion of the Home Islands. MacArthur pronounced such a policy anathema and sought every opportunity to oppose it. But whereas his navy opponents spoke with one voice all the way up the chain of command, Army Chief of Staff George Marshall treated MacArthur like the prima donna he was, a man who went so far in the summer of 1944 as to tacitly allow his name to be placed in nomination at the Republican National Convention, where it elicited much noise but little firm support. Marshall also understood and accepted the fact that the Pacific was largely a navy show. His own preoccupations remained fixed on Europe, and he could spare relatively little time to defend MacArthur's position to the Joint Chiefs of Staff, to whom Roosevelt generally deferred.

For the moment Nimitz and MacArthur continued to operate in distinctly separate spheres and cooperated smoothly, when and where necessary, as when MacArthur borrowed Nimitz's carriers for strikes against targets (for example, New Guinea in April 1944) well within the southwest Pacific sphere of responsibility.[9] But as the pace of offensive operations steadily gathered force in both the southwest and the central Pacific, a showdown over strategic priorities loomed ever larger.

However slow and costly the pace up the Solomons and through the Bismarck barrier, the southwest Pacific offensive was a successful war of attrition. Japan's naval and air resources by late 1943 were worn to the nub; so many planes and pilots had been lost that for many long months its precious, slowly rebuilding carrier fleet could not be provided with air groups. When at last enough planes were scraped together, their new young, hastily trained pilots would prove no match in the skies over the Philippine Sea and Marianas.[10]

By early November 1943, with the central-Pacific offensive about to commence in the Gilberts, *Bunker Hill* and the new *Lexington* had joined *Essex* and *Yorktown* together with *Saratoga* and *Enterprise,* while the light-carrier contingent had been stiffened by *Princeton, Belleau Wood,* and *Cowpens.* Moreover, the literal flood of escort carriers coming into commission had reached its crest, permitting a dozen and then twice that many of these most versatile ships to be used in the Pacific to provide tactical air support for the great amphibious operations. By January 1944 the United States Navy in the Pacific comprised no fewer than eight big fleet carriers and nearly a half-dozen light carriers with more of both classes on the way. The following summer the steadily expanding fleet stretched across forty square miles of ocean, and an enemy scout pilot who saw the concentration before being shot down informed his captors that when he glimpsed that armada he knew Japan had lost the war. For those who recalled the all too recent days of 1942 when three carriers and a half-dozen cruisers of any size were considered an extravagant luxury, it was a surfeit of riches.

The *Essex-* and *Independence*-class vessels were marvels of technology that allowed wide latitude for flexibility and innovation in carrier operations. This was reflected in the shifting composition of the ships' air groups. After the great carrier battles of 1942, strategists and planners in Washington and the fleet realized that, in Tom Hone's felicitous phrase, although carriers possessed "an awesome punch . . . they also had glass jaws." Carrier battles had been and would continue to be "quick and deadly." Even more to the point, assaulting Japan's outer and inner island-defense rings with their hordes of land-based naval aircraft whose pilots were skilled in attacking ships placed any advancing U.S. fleet in deadly peril. Radar and big, fast, tough new fighter aircraft, when combined with striking innovations in surface-to-air communications and shipboard command and control, allowed carrier crews to coordinate their own defense in a way hitherto impossible. "By 1945, strike aircraft composed only one-fourth of a carrier's air group."[11] Sea-based fighter squadrons provided the spear point of the American offensive across the Pacific, often swooping down unexpectedly on enemy island bastions to shoot up airfields and blast parked aircraft while knocking down whatever enemy planes got aloft before they could reach the fleet. On the few occasions when enemy strike aircraft did manage to approach fleet air-defense space, they met a solid wall of defending aircraft against which they dashed themselves to pieces. Only the mad kamikazes, often coming in low in groups of two or at most three "bogeys," managed to do significant damage to the U.S. fleet in the final stages of the war.

The great Pacific offensive that began at Tarawa and crunched its way into Tokyo Bay twenty-two months later was without doubt one of the two mightiest sustained acts of war ever undertaken.[12] America's three thousand–ship wartime fleet proved wonderfully efficient and durable. The products of wartime shipyards withstood heavy damage from kamikaze attacks and torpedoes while maintaining a high degree of fighting capability. They steamed the vast Pacific distances at consistently high speeds without requiring constant upkeep and overhaul. Bull Halsey, Marc Mitscher, and Raymond Spruance became the masters of sustained sea-air operations launched from a vast and nimble fleet that brought crushing and unrelenting power to bear against the enemy from all points on the compass. Chester Nimitz was the firm authority figure who carried them all with his calm assurance in their abilities. Carrier operations forced the art and science of seamanship into new dimensions and demanded a new kind of admiral and captain—sailors-turned-airmen who became sailors again.[13] Horatio Nelson and his captains, for all their dash and daring, never had to deal with four or even five integrated thirty-two-knot task groups, each composed of three or four immense carriers that demanded huge amounts of sea room whenever planes were launched or recovered or another kamikaze raid came winging in over the horizon. John Jellicoe, David Beatty, and Reinhard Scheer with their great blundering war castles of 1916 still employed and experienced sea power in a single dimension. The astounding competence of the American fleet admirals was matched only by their equally incredible confidence, which they effortlessly passed on to such key subordinates as Arthur Radford, C. A. Pownall, Jocko Clark, and Arleigh Burke.

To the officers of the Pacific Fleet, the march from the Gilberts to Tokyo Bay may have been grim, laden as it was with tedium, tension, exhaustion, frequent terror, and sadness at the loss of irreplaceable comrades, but it also possessed powerful elements of sheer fun. There was great excitement in handling a huge, modern, industrial sea-air fleet that fulfilled the Americans' love affair with big, complex machinery. The admirals and captains understood the weapons they had at their disposal—and they gloried in using them vigorously and effectively. "Haul ass with Halsey" was as much a term of respect—perhaps even affection—as it was of exasperation, for each mile at sea closer to Japan was a step nearer home.

Life was always tough aboard the destroyers that faithfully escorted the bigger ships through storm and sun, day and night, from Tarawa to Iwo and raced into the invasion beaches on D or A days to lay down withering covering fire under the mouths of enemy guns. For the men aboard the "small boys," months of alternate boredom and strain were transformed at Okinawa into long days of shock and horror under the deadly assaults of the kamikazes that rivaled the worst nighttime hours off Guadalcanal and Vella Lavella.

But one gains the impression from some memoirs that on the big ships like the carrier *Yorktown,* the Pacific campaign after November 1943 was waged with the kind of spice to be found in prewar Saturday-night southern fraternity houses from which many of the junior officers had come. Amid the growing fear of the Japanese suicide planes, the loss of aircrew and shipmates, the gruesome

damage to sister carriers, and the physical agony of rashes, scratches, itches, and
sleepless nights off enemy islands and coasts were the ceaseless pranks and horse-
play of lieutenants and commanders in wardrooms and flag plots. One day
Yorktown's gunnery officer, Pat Patterson, decided to relieve the mounting terror
of kamikaze attacks.

> A low bogey was coming in, and just before he opened fire, he pulled air
> plot's key on the squawk-box and yelled, "Southerners on yo' feet and
> Yankees under the table! The battle's about to begin!" He held the key
> down all during the firing, and I want to tell you, you never heard such a
> goddam racket in your life! It sounded like every gun on the ship had
> moved into air plot. The Exec came out of his chair like he'd sat on a tack.
> Telephones jumped out of their cradles. Pencils rolled off the desk. You
> couldn't hear yourself think, and my ears rang for ten minutes after they
> knocked off firing. That big Texas bastard's got the sign on all of us, and
> he knows it. But I'm just treating him polite till I can dream up a way to
> get back at him.

One evening in April 1945, off the coast of Japan, Arthur Radford came out on
the admiral's bridge aboard the carrier for a breather following eighteen hours
of steady enemy air attacks. J. Bryan III, a reserve lieutenant commander on his
staff who chronicled much of the high-spiritedness of the junior officers, asked
the admiral when he thought his tour might be over. "I don't know," Radford
replied. "I'd like to stay here another year, but I don't think its fair for me to
have this wonderful experience and not share it with others."[14]

Tarawa, Kwajalein, Saipan, Guam, Tinian, Peleliu, Leyte Gulf, Lingayen,
Iwo Jima, and Okinawa were essentially vast industrial operations involving
hundreds of thousands of men and hundreds of ships, landing craft, warplanes,
and vehicles thrown against stubborn enemy entrenchments on coral strips and
jungle or heavily wooded islands. Each campaign was longer than the last.
Tarawa took "76 stark and bitter hours" to secure,[15] Kwajalein a day longer;
Guam took twenty days, Saipan twenty-five, Iwo Jima a month, and Okinawa
more than two months. Each endeavor involved ever greater complexity, ever
more elaborate planning, and increasingly efficient tactical execution. The invasion of Leyte, for example, required the marshaling of a vast transport fleet
from three separate staging areas hundreds of miles away in New Guinea and
the Admiralty Islands. Sailing schedules and rendezvous points had to be carefully calculated; gunfire and aerial-support activities had to be measured to the
last shell, bomb, and bullet, and the battleships, cruisers, and destroyers had to

be assigned to precise anchorages or cruising areas within specific grids off the invasion beaches.

The plan for the invasion of Leyte was more than an inch thick. "It took four pages just to list who was to get copies. Six more pages told the many commanders of vessels and men where they fit into the organization, seven pages described their various tasks and functions, and twenty-five pages described the movement schedule for all units." But this was merely the master outline; each ship and unit had to develop their own internal plans to conform to the overall scheme. And plans were not confined to amphibious invasions. Each operation by the fast carrier task forces and groups was also planned with meticulous detail. Just before the anchors were weighed one morning in mid-April 1944 for the carrier strike against Hollandia (Jayapura) in northern New Guinea, "a fat-paged operations plan and its countless annexes, re-written for the last time," were brought aboard *Yorktown* and the other vessels of the fast carrier task force resting in the Marshall Islands by top-secret "guard mail." Within minutes on each of the hundred-odd ships in the force, intelligence officers and communicators began studying the provisions that applied to them. On the carriers, yeomen starting typing copies of the air annexes for each squadron, while the senior communications officers on all ships of the task force checked over the radio frequencies that had to be constantly monitored and assigned "guard watches" to their men. The ACIOs (air-combat intelligence officers) delved into their files for charts of the target area, while photo interpreters placed under intense stereoscopic scrutiny the high- and low-level reconnaissance pictures that had been rushed to the carriers from other Pacific commands, "picking out [enemy] ships, hangars, pillboxes, gun positions, all the things commentators lump together easily as ground installations." On *Yorktown* "a newly arrived specialist, Ensign Gibson, began building from clay and plaster an exact replica of the target as it would look from any angle to our approaching planes."[16] Jutland was less than twenty-eight years in the past; naval warfare had been thoroughly revolutionized once again, its pace and intensity almost beyond conception.

From Tarawa on, the essential pattern never varied. In the weeks before an amphibious assault, the fast carrier task forces roamed widely through the western Pacific, sometimes striking more than a thousand miles away from the designated target to keep the enemy guessing about American intentions, to disrupt his potential resupply routes, and to whittle down his island-based airpower. In the early stages, Rabaul, Marcus, and Truk were heavily attacked; later, as the

Philippine campaign loomed, Formosan airfields and naval installations were bombed and strafed. Finally, in anticipation of the landings on Iwo Jima and Okinawa, the American carriers began raiding Japan proper.

In the days immediately preceding an amphibious operation, with the invasion armada on its way to the objective, the fleet carriers and battleships turned to the target area itself to unleash devastating raids. On the eve of a D or an A day, the fleet steamed out two to three hundred miles beyond the invasion area to act as a shield against enemy air attacks or the Imperial Navy should it seek battle. A half-dozen or more of the slow prewar battleships (many raised from the mud of Pearl Harbor), together with perhaps a dozen cruisers, a score of destroyers, and two or three divisions of escort carriers, covered the landings themselves and provided close tactical fire- and airpower for as long as it took to secure the objective.

The goal of all this incredible activity was pure and "massive industrial destruction." Enemy shore installations were blasted, "plastered," and "pasted," as marines and soldiers stood nervously on the decks of their transports, bellies full of eggs and beefsteak, waiting to embark on their various landing craft and hit the beach. Ashore, Japanese boys in bunkers shaking under the naval gunfire grimly prepared to meet them, donning either *hachimaki*s, "the white headband that had symbolized defiance and acceptance of death for Japanese warriors down through the centuries," or *sennimbari*s, belts "of a thousand stitches made by families at home as a charm to ward off enemy bullets."[17] At Tarawa, several hours of intense preinvasion bombardment was deemed enough. It wasn't. Three months later Kwajalein received a "Spruance haircut"; a year after that, "softening-up" operations at Iwo Jima consumed days. According to one untraceable tale, a Japanese combat-infantry veteran was asked after the war who the best jungle fighters were, and he replied, "the Australians." Not the Americans? came the surprised reply. The Japanese looked at his interlocutors incredulously and said, "The Australians fought in the jungle; the Americans removed it."

The navy sought to do just that but never quite succeeded. Once the invasion began and the troops started pouring ashore from their landing craft, with the heavy naval bombardment and close-in air support right above them, the enemy opened up from still undiscovered concealment, often mowing down waves of invaders, filling surf and sand with bodies and blood. As the troops and vehicles determinedly came on, "beachmasters" working amid din and chaos on the bullet-lashed fringes of the island got reinforcements sorted out and sent to where they were needed most. Coral and sandy Pacific beaches were quickly transformed, as had been those at Normandy, into a massive, bloody junkyard.

From beginning to end the fighting ashore was grim, sickening, gruesome, macabre, and ultimately insane as the enemy was shot, blasted, burned, or buried in his underground bunkers by artillery fire, rifles, machine guns, and flame-throwers. Day upon day of endless, ceaseless combat in tropical heat or North Pacific rains produced an equal measure of heroism and terror, but no glory, even as it bred or reconfirmed "bone-deep racial hatred."[18]

In "the green quagmire" that was the island New Georgia in the Solomons, inexperienced draftees and National Guardsman being led down jungle trails by native guides were ambushed and massacred by well-concealed Japanese. "The operation proved to be on-the-job training" for the Americans. "No one seemed to know what to do" at first, "and indecision spread quickly." Nighttime was the worst; ghostly voices screamed in the "inky-black wetness that entombed the GI's." Japanese would creep right up to the defense perimeter, then yell in English "the code names of the battalion's companies" and "made references to the unit's training in Louisiana." With the cruel contempt of the combat veteran for the novice, veteran marine units that were mixed in with the army novices told horrific tales of "ape-men from Borneo who would swing down at night from the treetop dwellings and slay the unsuspecting in their [fox]holes." The green soldiers refused to sleep, throwing grenades and shooting their rifles at every sound. Wounding and even death from friendly fire grew. Men broke under the strain, stood up in their foxholes and screamed at the enemy to come get them. Going berserk, some would grab their buddy's weapons and start firing indiscriminately on anyone and everyone. Others hallucinated or developed paranoid schizophrenia. As time passed, their buddies, themselves clinging to sanity by a thread, ceased trying to cope. A rifle butt to the face solved a lot of problems. According to one participant, by the end of the New Georgia cam-paign, "shiploads of psychiatric casualties" were being sent back down The Slot to Guadalcanal, "shaken, disoriented, and with distorted faces. A ghastly scene."[19]

The longer the campaign, the greater the ordeal. Every instant could become a sudden horror. Eugene Sledge, who fought at Peleliu and again at Okinawa, told of one morning when a friend walked a short distance from the defense perimeter to relieve himself, only to step on a Japanese soldier playing possum. "Jay" raised his rifle and pulled the trigger, but the firing pin was broken. Throw-ing his weapon at the Japanese, who was pulling a grenade, the youngster turned and ran back to the perimeter, screaming, "Shoot him!" The Japanese threw his grenade, hitting Jay in the back, but it too was a dud, and the infuriated enemy, drunk with battle, drew his sword and came on. "Jay had spotted a BAR [Browning automatic rifle] man and fled in his direction yelling for him to shoot the enemy." The youngster just stood there until the last second when the enemy soldier was about to cleave Jay with his sword. Then the "BARman" ripped a short twenty-bullet burst into the enemy who "collapsed in a heap." Why hadn't the BARman fired sooner? the outraged Jay wanted to know. Well, the kid replied with a grin, he wanted to see if a twenty-round magazine at the closest range really could cut a man in half.

As the endless round of fighting days and sleepless nights went on and on, "the sun bore down" on marines and soldiers "like a giant heat lamp," and the stench of battle, blood, and fear became unbearable. "It is difficult to convey to anyone who has not experienced it the ghastly horror of having your sense of smell saturated constantly with the putrid odor of rotting human flesh day after day, night after night," Sledge later wrote. "Added to the awful stench of the dead of both sides was the repulsive odor of human excrement everywhere. It was all but impossible to practice simple, elemental field sanitation on most areas of Peleliu because of the rocky surface" that made burying urine and feces impossible. Added to that was dysentery, which many marines and soldiers developed during the first week or so of battle, together with "the odor of thousands of rotting, discarded Japanese and American rations. At every breath one inhaled hot, humid air heavy with countless repulsive odors." Sledge became convinced that he could never cleanse his lungs "of all those foul vapors." This was the environment in which men were shot, stabbed, or blown apart by shell or grenade to be hideously wounded or to die in further agony.[20]

When the firing at last died away and the pitiful handful of prisoners were marched to prison compounds by captors numbed by exhaustion, violence, and death, the devastated island was transformed into an advance base while the amphibious forces and fire-support ships sailed away to prepare for the next objective to the west or north. The fast carriers, after a quick stop for replenishment and recreation (two beers and a baseball game at Enewetak or later on Mogmog in the Ulithi atoll), began a new round of heavy raids against key installations deep within enemy-held territory.

Directly serving the vast war fleet and the advance island bases that supported it (and after the fall of 1944 the strategic air offensive against Japan as well) was an unglamorous and tiring task. But at least those who performed it believed that they were contributing immediately to the war effort. For the thousands of sailors like Thomas Heggen's "Mr. Roberts" who were stuck delivering essential supplies from point to point in the rear areas, life aboard the small cargo ships or transports involved endless steaming from one small, dreary island to another—from Tedium to Boredom, to Apathy and back again.

The American Pacific offensive conformed to long-standing Japanese defensive strategy. Although the midocean ribbon-defense line had been breached at nearly a dozen points from the Solomons to the Gilberts to the Aleutians, Japan in early 1944 still possessed the resources to construct an inner-defense line anchored on the great naval base at Truk in the Carolines, Malaya, the Philippines, Formosa, and the Ryukyus. From these bastions the Japanese planned to employ their forces as they had always intended, progressively whittling down the approaching American fleet and amphibious forces with island-based sea- and airpower.

But Japan's undersea fleet was proving woefully inadequate, while Midway should have demonstrated to the Japanese that carrier planes of sufficient capability could hold their own with any other aircraft, land or sea based. Their own combat air patrols certainly had done so for hours until they were overwhelmed by the unplanned, uncoordinated, near-simultaneous low-high-level attacks of American torpedo planes and dive-bombers. At Guadalcanal, American carrier aircraft had actually deployed to Henderson Field for a time as part of the Cactus Air Force, suggesting that American naval planes were good enough to be used interchangeably from both carriers and island airstrips.

To defend its outer island-defense ring properly, Japan desperately needed a next-generation fighter plane markedly superior to the excellent Zero. Such a task proved beyond its capabilities. Through prodigious effort, the Japanese reportedly managed to produce nearly ten thousand aircraft of all types between April 1943 and April 1944, but they were of existing types, and nearly sixty-five hundred were reportedly lost within a few weeks or months of coming off the production lines.[21] The Americans, meanwhile, had produced not only a flood of big new carriers but also a new generation of large, rugged, and increasingly maneuverable warplanes to fly from their decks. While the army air forces dealt the Japanese grievous blows with the P-38 and other high-performance aircraft, it was the navy's new Corsairs and especially the F6F Hellcats that swept all but a small handful of Japan's last good pilots from the skies over the South and central Pacific in the middle and later stages of the war.

The American veterans of the fighting over Truk, Marcus, the Philippine Sea, and Formosa will tell you that not all their colleagues were great or even good fliers. But the number of pilots coming out to the fleet was so large that after a few weeks of awful flying, the poorer ones among them were identified and weeded out, though mediocrities often remained.[22] The Japanese could afford no such luxury.

Many American carrier pilots never even saw an enemy aircraft in flight during all the weeks and months that they flew because as time went on and Japanese prowess steadily declined, the enemy chose not to tangle head-on with well-escorted incoming air raids. Old-fashioned "dogfights" of the World War I variety were thus very few. Most Japanese aircraft destroyed by carrier planes fell to the combat air patrols while making single-plane attacks against the fleet or were lost when American pilots, engaging in strafing attacks of enemy airfields, caught formations of Zeros on the ground or just after takeoff. The most candid among those who flew the Corsairs and Hellcats in the Pacific will admit that enemy (and U.S.) air losses were probably exaggerated by about 50 percent and that U.S. aircraft losses were due primarily to antiaircraft fire.[23]

Better ships, better men, and better aircraft did not exhaust the inventory of growing American superiority at sea during the last half of World War II. The proximity fuse in conjunction with radar-directed antiaircraft guns meant better fleet defense as well. Indeed, the fuse revolutionized the Allied war at sea.[24] By 1940–1941 time or contact fuses that had been in use during the prewar decades were becoming increasingly useless against fast-moving aircraft. Such fuses could be set by mechanical computers to obtain adequate bearing and altitude, but the range at which the fuse should be detonated was impossible to adequately determine. What was needed was "a device that . . . would detonate a projectile in the immediate vicinity of an enemy aircraft irrespective of timing errors." As one of the inventors of the proximity fuse later explained, "The fact of the matter was that the 5-inch 38s and the 3-inch 50s almost never hit an aircraft because of range error." Infinitesimal pointing errors also contributed to inaccuracy, James Van Allen continued, "but mostly [it was] the range error which was typically on the order of 500 feet—maybe 1000 feet—corresponding to a fraction of a second. And so for the most part, you made a lot of air bursts, but you didn't hit anything." Such inaccuracies were especially impermissible in navies hoping to operate successfully in enemy waters against efficient land-based aircraft. Developed in great secrecy in U.S., British, and German laboratories, the proximity fuse was essentially a tiny, hardened radio transmitter placed into the nose of an artillery or antiaircraft shell. The transmitter contained four electron tubes—an oscillator, amplifier, discriminator, and thyratron—each about the size of a ten-year-old child's little finger. Set for operation at heights up to twenty thousand feet and for comparable distances on a battlefield ashore, the fuse sent out an electrical impulse. When the reflected signal returning from the target reached a certain strength (within fifty to seventy-five feet of a target), the thyratron fired, activating a detonation switch and causing the shell to explode. Van Allen's inestimable contribution was to "harden" the tubes so that they "survived firing from a naval gun at about 20,000 g force. It's a real achievement, I think, to have a vacuum tube survive that." So it is. Radar-controlled guns permitting far more precise automatic tracking could guarantee the placement of an antiaircraft shell within the required distance to target, and the proximity fuse did the rest.[25]

The first successful American test of the fuse took place in January 1942, just weeks after Pearl Harbor. Full-scale production began almost immediately, but not until August 1942 was the first successful at-sea test achieved with a five-inch shell fired from the new cruiser *Cleveland* in Chesapeake Bay. Thereafter, the proximity fuse was spread broadly throughout the U.S. fleet, whose gunners quickly discovered that the combination of radar-controlled gunfire and proximity fuses permitted the creation of deadly curtains of fire around a carrier or battleship task force. Best of all, when proximity fuses failed (their success rate was consistently above 70 percent), the explosions took place beyond the barrel and burst forward, posing no danger to the gun crew.

All of Japan's steadily accumulating woes and infirmities came together in June 1944 when the Americans suddenly appeared off the Mariana Islands. This was one group of islands Imperial Headquarters simply could not let go by default. The inner-defense line had already been breached with the neutralization of Truk. Should the Marianas be lost, the enemy would be in a perfect position to strike west toward the Philippines or north-northwest toward Formosa, the Bonins, the Ryukyus, and even the Home Islands. Moreover, Guam's superb harbor would be a perfect staging area for the American submarine fleet, that would practically double in size since it would no longer have to stage out of distant Pearl Harbor or Brisbane on the western Australian coast. Tokyo might also have been aware that the newest American "VLR" (very long-range) bomber, the B-29, could reach Japan's big cities from airstrips on Saipan and Guam.

The Imperial Navy had hoped to fight the long-anticipated "decisive battle" off Yap or Truk (it should have fought it off Guadalcanal), but with the enemy about to invest Saipan, Japan's admirals had no choice but to come out immediately. In so doing, they intensified the growing strategic impasse between MacArthur and Nimitz.

Critics found the general's strategy for winning the Pacific war as flawed as the man. Not only was a New Guinea–Mindanao-Luzon campaign a "round-about" way of finishing the war, but it was too vague as well. What happened after the seizure of Luzon? A southwest Pacific advance would also be subject to withering flank attacks by Japanese air and naval units operating out of Malaya, Indochina, and the southern Philippines themselves, without promising that climactic air and sea battle against the Japanese navy that would leave the Home Islands wide open to either blockade or invasion.

But MacArthur held several trump cards, which he played masterfully and often. If reconquest of the Philippines was not a strategic necessity, he argued, it most certainly was a moral and political imperative. Leave the Filipinos and several thousand American prisoners of war (including a handful of women) at the mercy of fanatic, bypassed Japanese soldiers who had already marched Americans to death after Bataan, and no one could predict the results. All Asia, MacArthur preached, would never forget such a betrayal. Moreover, the navy's Formosa strategy assumed a further lunge onto the Chinese coast to seize base areas for the blockade or invasion of Japan. But early in 1944 Japanese forces began a major offensive in China aimed at isolating the Nationalist Government from the Allies, and it included a thick seeding of the Chinese coast with crack army units. At the very least, Formosa and the Chinese coast would pose formidable obstacles to invasion.

But so would Luzon, if not Mindanao. By 1944 enough ships, men, aircraft, and supplies were flooding into the Pacific to suggest that both MacArthur and Nimitz could be appeased, so long as allocation of resources for each operation was agreed upon in advance. Clearly unwilling to come down on one side or the other of the growing antagonism between Melbourne and Pearl Harbor, the Joint Chiefs early in March told the Pacific commanders that their "first major" strategic objective would be "the vital Luzon, Formosa, China Coast area." Formosa would be occupied on February 15, 1945, but Luzon might be also. This ambiguity prompted a rush of further staff work in Washington and a flood of communications among the Pentagon, Nimitz, and MacArthur. The general continued to categorically reject any notion of bypassing the Philippines and pronounced Nimitz's plan to assault Formosa by forces directly from Hawaii wholly impossible; Japanese land-based airpower would surely overcome the navy's carrier air groups. Only a prior occupation of Luzon and use of airfields there by the army air forces could guarantee a successful invasion of Formosa.[26] By June, with matters still unresolved and Nimitz preparing to strike at the Marianas, a decision over the Philippines-versus-Formosa strategy could no longer be delayed. The president himself traveled to Pearl Harbor to meet with his fractious commanders and cut the strategic knot.

The general prevailed. "I consider that from the strategical standpoint alone," MacArthur told the president and Nimitz, "the occupation of the Philippines is essential and it is my opinion that after that has been accomplished and bases have been established" cutting off the enemy's southern lifeline to Indonesia and Southeast Asia, "an assault upon Formosa will not be necessary. With Luzon properly organized it will be possible to bypass Formosa and strike deeper into enemy territory against objectives that can be obtained with less bloodshed and which will be of greater value, thus accelerating the time schedule of the [overall Pacific] campaign." Later, in a personal meeting with his president, MacArthur added a menacing coda. The Republican National Convention that would put forth MacArthur's name as a presidential candidate was only a few weeks away. If U.S. forces "bypassed" the Philippines, the general told his president, "I daresay that the American people would be so aroused that they would register the most complete resentment against you at the polls this fall."[27] FDR got the message, and MacArthur's dismissal of Formosa as an objective won Nimitz over as well. With neither Formosa nor the Chinese coast as a viable objective, and with MacArthur (and his own navy, the Seventh Fleet) prepared to be tied down for months in the Philippines, Nimitz's planners could get to work on an alternative scenario, the Bonins-Ryukyus route, that would take the navy right up to the Japanese doorstep. The only problem that a Philippine campaign would not resolve, of course, was the chief strategic preoccupation of the Pacific war: bringing the remaining Japanese fleet to battle in order to kill it. Tokyo soon resolved that dilemma.

In planning to destroy the Americans off the Marianas, Jisaburo Ozawa, commander of the newly reorganized Combined Fleet, clung to the hope that by infusing the Saipan and Guam garrisons with massive air reinforcements from the Palaus, Yap, and Rota, the enemy could be caught between the hammer of the Japanese carrier force and the anvil of the air forces ashore.[28] Japan still possessed the splendid *Zuikaku* and *Shokaku*, plus the new 29,300-ton fleet carrier *Taiho* and half a dozen light carriers of greater or lesser worth, all of which would be thrown into the fight. Ozawa's hopes were bolstered by the fact that his carrier aircraft possessed a range roughly two hundred miles greater than their American counterparts. If the five hundred planes to be mustered on Guam and Saipan could first soften up the American battle and invasion fleets, Ozawa's pilots would wing in for a follow-up blow on the way into Saipan and Guam, refuel, and hit the Americans again on the way back to the carriers. It was a good plan, but not realistic. The Americans now firmly controlled not only the surface of the Pacific but also the skies above and the depths below. Everything went awry for the Japanese.

The foundation of Japanese failure rested with Vice Admiral Kakuji Kakuta, commander of the Base Air Force of the Marianas, located on Tinian. Kakuta had no intention of denuding the Palaus, Yap, and Rota of all air cover to bolster Ozawa's attack. Should the Americans seize the Marianas, Peleliu or Yap would surely be next and would need all the air support they could muster. But Kakuta was unwilling to battle Ozawa over the issue. He chose to take refuge in evasion and outright fabrication. Spruance's carriers had hit Iwo Jima, Chichi-Jima, Rota, and Guam with heavy strikes in the weeks and days immediately preceding the invasion of Saipan. Thus, all of the potential staging and turn-around airfields that might have provided Kakuta and Ozawa with the land-based airpower required were heavily damaged, a fact that Kakuta did not see fit to pass on to his colleague.

Ozawa had gathered the Combined Fleet at Tawi-tawi, the westernmost island in the Sulu Archipelago, but even before it set out for the Marianas, American submarines began whittling down its strength. Ozawa lost four destroyers to enemy torpedoes or faulty seamanship before the Combined Fleet reached the battle area, and he could not help but be aware that his forces were being continually shadowed; the enemy knew he was coming and from which direction.

Nonetheless, Spruance was obsessed with the idea that Ozawa might somehow turn his flank and get among the Saipan invasion fleet, so he disposed Marc Mitscher's four-carrier task groups, comprising seven heavy and eight light fleet carriers, in an arc from northwest to southeast. Most important, he deployed a battleship-cruiser-destroyer barrage "line" under Admiral Willis Augustus Lee (who had led battleships *Washington* and *South Dakota* in the killing of *Kirishima* off Guadalcanal) some fifteen miles ahead of Task Group 58.3 in the direction from which Ozawa's planes would be most likely to come. To reach the invasion fleet, enemy aircraft would first have to break through the antiaircraft barrage put up by Lee's line and then face the combat air patrols from Mitscher's carriers. The finest pilots in the world could not escape severe casualties under those conditions, and Ozawa no longer possessed fine pilots. The flyers aboard the nine Japanese carriers comprised Japan's poorly trained and hastily assembled second team that had replaced the marvelous prewar airmen shot down or burned to death on carrier decks at Coral Sea, Midway, and Santa Cruz or killed over Guadalcanal, Rabaul, New Guinea, Truk, Marcus, and Rota. The novices never had a chance.

The Marianas "Turkey Shoot" was just that. Kakuta's small air force ashore was savaged by American carrier planes, but in response to Ozawa's queries, Kakuta replied that his boys were mauling the enemy carriers and the airfields on Guam were safe to use. Ozawa promptly launched a series of air strikes on the morning of June 19, and his young airmen soon dashed themselves to pieces against the battleship barrage; those who staggered through or evaded it were shot down in droves by the combat air patrols from Mitscher's carriers. The handful of planes that tried to reach Guam were destroyed on the fields or in the landing approaches. In all, Japan lost more than 450 planes and pilots in a single day.

While Kakuta's and Ozawa's airmen were falling to Lee's guns and Mitscher's air patrols, the Japanese fleet was being shattered by American submarines. Shortly after Ozawa had launched his second strike, *Albacore* torpedoed *Taiho* near its fuel tanks. Japanese damage control proved as inept as its air force. Despite the ruptured tanks and a damaged elevator that hampered air operations, *Taiho's* captain was determined to carry on and maintained twenty-six knots. Properly concerned that his hangar deck might fill with fumes, he ordered all passageways be kept open in the mistaken assumption that any fumes would be vented overboard. In fact, the fumes simply spread throughout the ship, and that afternoon it suddenly erupted in one huge explosion whose flames were so hot that rescue vessels could not approach. *Taiho* soon slipped burning and hissing beneath the waves carrying 1,650 of its 2,150-man crew with it. Meanwhile, *Cavalla* had slipped through the escort screen and sent four torpedoes crashing into *Shokaku*. That ship immediately burst into flames and lost all power. Shortly before *Taiho* erupted and sank, *Shokaku* did the same. Ozawa escaped the disaster by shifting his flag to a destroyer, then to *Zuikaku*.

The Battle of the Philippine Sea should have been over at this point. Japanese airpower had not only been devastated but been decisively proven to be completely inept. And two of Japan's last three fleet carriers had been brutally killed by American submarines. But late in the afternoon of June 19, with Ozawa reeling westward, Spruance and Mitscher made a fatal decision. The American carrier fliers would try to get one shot in at the enemy fleet. The distances were great, perhaps too great, and the day fading fast. But the airmen were keen, and so Mitscher sent them on their way.

Light carrier *Hiyo* was sunk, and its sister, *Junyo*, suffered moderate bomb damage, as did several other enemy ships in the ensuing attack, but the "mission beyond darkness" proved a foolhardy risk for the results achieved. Just twenty planes with most of their experienced pilots were lost in combat, but another

eighty were lost returning home (though most crewmen were saved) in water
landings when their fuel ran out or in crashes on darkened flight decks as desperate pilots sought to come aboard any carrier they could find as their gas
gauges fell below the empty mark. Perhaps another hundred or so more could
have gone down in the nighttime seas had the pilots not nursed their planes
back superbly, had not Mitscher turned on the lights of his task force, and had
not the airmen landed on the first available carrier deck they saw.[29] Landing-
signal officers and flight-deck crews were worked to total exhaustion to get the
men aboard.

Mitscher was simply following the disturbing pattern set by Frank Jack
Fletcher at the Coral Sea and subsequently repeated by Spruance at Midway: go
after the first enemy carrier you see with everything you have. Bull Halsey would
soon repeat the blunder off Luzon's Cape Engaño.

The boldness that Mitscher and Spruance displayed in the last stages of the
Battle of the Philippine Sea did not carry over into subsequent operations. The
Turkey Shoot should have convinced everyone in the fleet, at Nimitz's headquarters in Hawaii (which would soon move to Guam), and in Washington
that enemy sea-air power had all but disintegrated. The carrier air groups were
gone, along with nearly all their vessels, and the fatal vulnerability of battleships and cruisers to naval air was now a given. The autumn of 1944 was the
time to strike decisively northward, if not at the Bonins or Ryukyus at least
at Formosa. But here the American imprisonment to politics and perception
melded with the ongoing demands of the European theater of operations and
strategic timidity to create the worst possible situation.

MacArthur had used every dramatic and rhetorical weapon in his arsenal to
get his way with Roosevelt and Nimitz. But after the victory in the Philippine
Sea, he had another formidable opponent to beat down. Believing that Nimitz
was still on his side, Ernest King wanted to conduct just one landing in the
Philippines, apparently a token assault on either Mindanao or Leyte to pin down
enemy forces throughout the vast archipelago as prelude to a Formosa invasion.
But when the chief of naval operations visited Saipan in August, he discovered
that his Pacific commanders had turned against the scheme. Word had obviously
trickled down the chain of command, and that word was *Philippines.* Spruance
and Richmond Kelly Turner, the amphibious commander, insisted that the capture of Manila Bay was essential to further naval operations because it was the
only good anchorage in the Far East. Nimitz supported his subordinates, maintaining that the seizure of Luzon was a necessary prerequisite to an assault on

Formosa. King argued with all three. "If we get busy and set our minds to it," he told them, the rapidly accumulating supply facilities in Saipan and Guam and the magnificent fleet anchorage at the island of Enewetak were sufficient to maintain the navy's advanced position. Shortly thereafter, however, Pacific Fleet planners discovered serious "deficiencies" in both available army ground forces and transport shipping, "and it became clear that they could not be made good until early in 1945." Abandoned by his commander in chief and his subordinates, King caved in and on September 8, "with great reluctance," agreed to a major amphibious assault on Mindanao that inevitably focused American planning for the foreseeable future on the Philippines. When flyers from Halsey's Third Fleet struck at the central Philippines the following month and discovered negligible air opposition, the Mindanao invasion was hastily shifted to Leyte in the central Philippines.[30] MacArthur successfully pressed for another major amphibious assault at Lingayen Gulf in January 1945 to free Luzon. Apparently, earlier "deficiencies" were no longer a constraint. But the long, bloody campaign would pin down an entire American army to the last day of the war.

The Leyte and Luzon campaigns not only may have prolonged the Pacific war by at least several unnecessary months but also placed the American fleet at risk from the remnants of enemy naval power in a way and in a place where they did not have to be risked. Following the Battle of the Philippine Sea, the Japanese navy split fatally in two. While the bulk of what fleet remained returned to its anchorages in Borneo and Malaya to stay close to major fuel sources, the remaining carriers were forced to steam to the Home Islands in order to train a "third team" of combat pilots for whatever pitiful showdown might be left. Had the Americans moved against Formosa, the still powerful Japanese surface fleet would have had to steam between seven and eight hundred miles farther north to get at the U.S. Navy, exposing itself to at least another day or perhaps two of repeated air and submarine attack. But the Leyte operation placed the Japanese units in Borneo within thirty-six hours of the invasion beaches, cutting down substantially on American response time.

In the event, the battle for Leyte Gulf, however intrinsically fascinating as great naval combat, was a foregone conclusion.[31] American planes owned the skies above and submarines the depths beneath the waters through which Japanese forces had to pass. The enemy was spotted soon after he left harbor, stalked, and attacked early and often from both the air and under the sea. With the shocking exception of Kurita's force off Samar, Bull Halsey and Thomas Kinkaid, MacArthur's Seventh Fleet commander, generally knew where the advancing

Japanese were at any given moment. The situation was, ironically, exactly the reverse of Japanese prewar plans for a climactic Pacific battle fleet action in which an advancing U.S. fleet was progressively whittled down until it could no longer fight effectively.

By this time, the Imperial Navy high command was desperate. The carrier fleet was all but gone; only *Zuikaku* remained of the old *Kido Butai,* together with three operable light carriers. But there were few planes and no pilots now capable of standing up to American flyers. The surface fleet, however, still contained ten battleships, including the mighty *Yamato* and *Musashi,* together with two rebuilt hybrid "battleship–aircraft carriers," nearly twenty heavy cruisers, a few light cruisers, and more than thirty-five destroyers. All in all, a most formidable force. The plan for the Leyte Gulf action, Sho Ichi Go, or Victory Plan One, was typically elaborate. The most recent historian of the battle characterizes it as at once complex, realistic, and feasible, relying "heavily upon both timing and surprise for its success." Again, as at Midway, Japan would divide its fleet in the face of a formidable, and in this case overwhelmingly preponderant, foe. A "Central Force" of five battleships, ten heavy cruisers, and supporting vessels under the command of Admiral Takeo Kurita, and including *Yamato* and *Musashi,* would sail from Lingga Roads near Singapore; fuel up at Brunei, Borneo; cross the South China Sea to the north of the island of Palawan; pass into the Sibuyan Sea bounded by southern Luzon, Mindoro, Panay, and Masbate; then through the San Bernardino Strait, before swinging south past the east coast of Samar late at night to fall upon the American invasion beaches in Leyte Gulf from the north at dawn. Almost simultaneously, a "Southern Force" would set out in two columns from Brunei and from Chinese waters, respectively. The Brunei column, led by Admiral Shoji Nishimura, comprised two battleships, one heavy cruiser, and supporting vessels. Its task would be to cross the Sulu Sea from Borneo, steam through the narrow Surigao Strait at night, and fall upon the American invasion beaches from the south just as Kurita appeared from the north. The smaller force from Chinese waters, commanded by Admiral Kiyohide Shima and composed of three cruisers and four destroyers, would sail between Borneo and Palawan and across the Sulu Sea to pass through Surigao Strait right behind Nishimura and join him in the morning as Kurita and Nishimura placed the Leyte anchorages and invasion beaches in a vise of steel. Bull Halsey's American carrier-battleship fleet would be lured away by a fourth enemy column, the "Northern Force" coming down from the Home Islands and composed of Japan's four remaining carriers, with drastically reduced air groups of doubtful quality.

Japan's plans, together with its remaining sea power, began to unravel almost at once. As each of the three Central and Southern Force columns approached the Philippine archipelago, it was picked up and attacked by picket submarines, giving the Americans plenty of time to prepare a deadly ambush for Nishimura and Shima. Admiral Kinkaid seeded the shores of Surigao Strait with motor torpedo boats, destroyers, cruisers, and, at its narrow head where its waters flowed into Leyte Gulf, battleships. The battleship line was composed of the old warhorses that had made up the backbone of the prewar navy. Resurrected from the muddy shame of Pearl Harbor, *Tennessee, West Virginia, Maryland, California,* and *Pennsylvania* (along with *Mississippi,* which had been in the Atlantic in 1941) lay poised to deal a fearsome revenge. At around 2230 hours on the night of October 24, 1944, radar aboard the American ships picked up Nishimura's rapidly advancing battleship-cruiser-destroyer force. Destroyers and motor torpedo boats rushed in from the darkened near-shore flanks of the strait to launch torpedo after torpedo at the enemy. One torpedo hit battleship *Fuso,* which blew up thirty minutes later, the flames from her shattered hull lighting the scene for hours. Nishimura's people fired back with some effect, and, according to plan, the American "small boys" turned and retreated up the narrow waterway, luring the unsuspecting Japanese on to the guns of Jesse Oldendorf's big battlewagons. Aboard the OBBs (old battleships), radarmen and fire-control technicians sat by their plots, and gunners' mates in big, armor-sheathed turrets stood by their huge fourteen- and sixteen-inch naval rifles, as the battle moved closer and quiet voices in headphones methodically counted down the range. Torpedoes had already accounted for three Japanese destroyers when Nishimura sailed into the enemy battle line drawn up against him at the head of the strait in the classic T that brought every gun to bear on a Japanese line that could reply only with its forward batteries. The American line erupted in heavy sheets of flame, and aboard the enemy ships huge turrets exploded, superstructures collapsed, and hulls were pierced repeatedly by torpedoes from a new line of destroyers and motor torpedo boats that raced in through the blackness to launch "fish" after "fish" at the distracted, harassed, and soon de-moralized enemy. The waters of Surigao Strait shook and heaved with the force and incessant din of battle that reverberated across narrow waters from one low, jungle-clad hill to another.

It was the climax of the battleship age, a remorseless slugging match between big guns and big hulls whose outcome was foreordained. Reinhard Scheer steaming into the jaws of John Jellicoe's cleverly baited trap at Jutland never experienced such concentrated fury, such deadly accuracy. Off Guadalcanal, only one Japanese battle cruiser faced a single enemy battleship. Here, no fewer than eight mighty capital ships exchanged heavy gunfire until battleship *Yamashiro* was torn apart by shell and torpedo and went down, taking Nishimura with it.

Shima, coming up behind with his small cruiser-destroyer force, refused for some perverse reason to communicate with Nishimura (was it because the two men cordially detested each other?), and when destroyer *Shigure* staggered out of the cauldron and headed back down the strait, Shima did not make contact to find out what was happening. Pressing on in gathering smoke, his flagship, the big cruiser *Nachi*, collided with one of Nishimura's equally impressive cruisers, *Mogami*, which had been horribly beaten up and was in a semisinking condition, although it could still make eight knots. Convinced at last by subordinates that whatever had happened ahead had been disaster for the Japanese navy, Shima retreated. As dawn touched the littered, befouled waters of Surigao Strait, *Mogami*, whose sister *Mikuma* had been battered to pieces by American air off Midway before finally succumbing, now staggered like a prizefighter on his last legs. American destroyers and motor torpedo boats raced in for the kill, and yet another once-splendid Japanese warship slipped beneath the waves. *Nachi* followed ten days later and several hundred miles away under further American bombs and torpedoes. In the end, Japan's entire Southern Force with the exception of *Shigure* had been massacred.

Kurita's Central Force fared little better, but might have done more had the admiral kept his wits, though he cannot be wholly blamed for failure. The Central Force took the full brunt of American carrier airpower during its transit of the Sibuyan Sea, for Halsey had not yet learned of the small diversionary fleet of carriers and battleships steaming down from Formosa. He sent his flyers against the Japanese with all the force and fury at his command. *Musashi* and two heavy cruisers went down under a multitude of torpedo and bomb hits. Kurita pressed on, though his timetable had been irretrievably disrupted. He tried to warn Nishimura that he would be late at the Leyte Gulf rendezvous, but Nishimura insisted on pressing on through the night to his doom. At this point, Halsey was suddenly lured north with word of an enemy carrier fleet bearing down on Luzon. The glittering prospect of killing enemy carriers bewitched him as much as it had his predecessors. Believing that Kurita was finished, and learning from aerial reconnaissance that the Japanese fleet north of Luzon comprised several battleships in addition to the carriers, Halsey took his own fast, powerful battleships north with his carriers, whose flyers promptly sent all four enemy flattops, including *Zuikaku*, to the bottom. Along with Oldendorf's battlewagons, Pearl Harbor had at last been well and truly avenged.

But the invasion beaches and anchorages in Leyte Gulf and its environs were now wide open to Kurita, charging down off Samar with his remaining battleships, including *Yamato,* ready for the kill.

All he had to do to reach the invasion area and raise havoc was to brush aside a flotilla of small, slow enemy escort carriers and their destroyer and destroyer-escort screen. That would pose no problem. But it did. Horrified to see the tall pagoda masts of Japanese battleships suddenly appearing over the horizon at dawn on October 25, Admiral Ziggy Sprague, the escort-carrier commander, promptly ordered his little command into action. Rainsqualls hid the small American fleet from time to time, but as each passed, enemy eight-, sixteen-, and eighteen-inch-shell fire erupted all around and then aboard some of the little carriers and their escorting destroyers. Sprague had no choice but to send his destroyers and destroyer escorts against Kurita's behemoths. No one hesitated. The "small boys" raced in to attack the enemy at close range, emptying gun lockers and torpedo tubes. Then the survivors regrouped and went in again, some with empty torpedo tubes, and knocked-out five-inch main batteries. Kurita's gunners pounded two of the racing, twisting American destroyers *(Hoel* and *Johnson)* under the waves together with the destroyer escort *Samuel B. Roberts.* Meanwhile, desperate pilots gunned their aircraft off the flight decks of their "baby flattops," armed with the first ordnance that could be found: fragmentation bombs, depth charges, whatever. Some planes had sufficient ammunition in their guns; others had none or nearly none. But the flyers were as determined as their compatriots aboard the "small boys" and made strafing runs at mast level or below over Japanese decks in addition to conventional torpedo and bombing attacks. Somehow, incredibly, it all worked. After a short period of sparring that cost the Americans two escort carriers *(St. Lo* and *Gambier Bay),* Kurita lost his nerve under the incessant, if largely ineffectual, air and sea attacks. Who knew where Halsey was? No one could be certain what had happened to the Southern Force. The Americans were fully alerted. Time to turn back and fight another day, if possible. Behind him, beneath Philippine waters, Kurita left four carriers, three battleships, nine cruisers, twelve destroyers, at least two admirals, and many thousand officers and men rotting on the ocean floor. All too soon, the rest of the imperial Japanese fleet would die, too— *Yamato* in a suicide charge toward Okinawa the following April, the rest of the big ships (and many of the smaller ones) killed at their anchorages at home or in Malaya.

With the glaring exception of Halsey's race north (forever after known facetiously as "the Battle of Bull's Run"), the American admirals placed their numerically and qualitatively far-superior units in perfect positions to blast the enemy. For the last time, Japanese land-based airpower failed to play the kind of decisive role its authors had once hoped and assumed it would. Indeed, the four Japanese flattops off northern Luzon were half empty, largely because their already depleted air groups had been savaged on Formosa by American air raids in the days just proceeding the Leyte assault. Even had Kurita with his battleships and cruisers been able to slip past or destroy Sprague's escort carriers and destroyer escorts and shoot up the invasion beaches, American manpower and industrial might was such that it is doubtful that the timetable against Japan would have been set back more than four to six months at the most.

But the Japanese would never quit, and this fact imprinted itself indelibly on the American mind. The perception of the Japanese as bloodthirsty fanatics who would gladly give their lives to take one or more of the enemy with them was reconfirmed once again by the abrupt appearance of the kamikazes during the last nine months of the war. By the summer of 1945 the issue was not how to defeat Japan, but how to induce its leadership to surrender, and around this question furious debate revolved then and ever since.

A vigorous school of "revisionist" historians has argued since the 1960s with greater or lesser emphasis on one point or another that Japan could not have continued the war past the early autumn of 1945, that President Harry Truman and his advisers knew this, and so they employed the atomic bombs that came into their possession as diplomatic weapons against a Soviet Union perceived as the new danger to U.S. security and expansion in the world. Hiroshima and Nagasaki thus represented not the last shots of World War II but the first shots of the cold war.[32] At the heart of this thesis lies the assumption of immoral and unrestrained American use of power that seemed to many to be borne out in Vietnam at the time that the thesis first emerged.

Counterrevisionists have emphasized the remorseless fanaticism of the Japanese warlords who were determined to take their enemy and their country down in a final Götterdämmerung and who continued to impose a "crushing control" over the populace and armed forces.[33] The atomic raids (and, secondarily, the Soviet entry into the Pacific war) provided the only shocks capable of toppling these insane men. Hiroshima and Nagasaki at once gave the moderates the upper hand and the fanatics an excuse to submit at last to reality, though even then a pitiful remnant tried to storm the imperial palace and force the war to continue.

Beneath the seemingly endless historical debate over the purpose and morality of the atomic bombings lay a no-less-intense and fascinating contemporary debate during the summer of 1945 within the American armed services, a debate whose dimensions even now are not wholly understood.[34] A year before, at the height of the Marianas campaign, the U.S. military establishment reversed two decades of conventional wisdom about the conduct of a Pacific war. On July 14, 1944, General George C. Marshall told a meeting of the British and American Combined Chiefs of Staff that recent operations in the Pacific made it clear to the American leadership that "in order to finish the war with the Japanese quickly, it will be necessary to invade the industrial heart of Japan." The Roosevelt-Churchill summit at Quebec two months later confirmed that the final stage of the Pacific war involved "invading and seizing objectives in the heart of Japan" after "establishing a sea and air blockade, conducting intensive air bombardment, and destroying Japanese air and naval strength."[35] But the invasion and capture of Okinawa between April 1 and June 22, 1945, forced the American civil and military leadership to at last confront directly the least-costly and most expeditious means of defeating Japan. The army, army air forces, and navy all developed sharply differing recipes and agendas for victory, and each was convinced that its scenario was the only correct one.

Having seized Okinawa and sealed off all the sea approaches to Japan by submarine and aerial mining (from army air force B-29s), the United States Navy believed that the climactic stage of the war as outlined decades before in War Plan Orange had been reached. The strategies and tactics that had dominated the great central-Pacific offensive should simply be continued. Cut off from essential resources and food supplies on the Asian continent, Japan would soon "die on the vine" as so many of its garrisons from Hollandia to Truk to Formosa had done. Round-the-clock assaults on enemy coastal shipping by submarine and carrier aircraft would be complemented by tactical strafing and close-in bombing raids launched from the fleet offshore or staged by army air force fighter bombers flying out of the Ryukyus. Such a successful blockade of Japan would end the war, negating the need for a bloody invasion of the Home Islands.

The army air force agreed that invasion was unnecessary. But the air force argued that only the shock of massive high- and low-level "strategic" bombing of enemy population centers could bring Japan to its senses and force it to break the grip of its cornered but grimly determined leadership. Beginning in the spring of 1945, General Curtis LeMay's hordes of B-29s began subjecting Japanese cities to frightful firebombing raids that killed probably a million people and burned out the heart of Tokyo and six other major urban centers. The atomic bombs (whose full destructive capabilities were incapable of being fully appreciated in advance) were conceived as simply an extension and culmination of the strategic air war.

The army, however, insisted that both strategic bombing and blockade were too costly and time-consuming. They would require fully as many men and as much matériel as would be devoted to an armed invasion and would take longer to accomplish their mission. The only way to shock Japan into surrender and impose the American will was to storm Nippon's hitherto inviolable beaches. In support of that scenario, certain army officials apparently advanced a proposal that has only recently come to light, thanks to the research of naval analyst and historian Norman Polmar. A half century after the crucial White House meeting of June 18, 1945, that determined an invasion of Japan was the only feasible way to end the Pacific war, Polmar and his colleague Thomas B. Allen uncovered a twenty-nine-page memorandum "orchestrated" by Major General William N. Porter, chief of the army's Chemical Warfare Service, that urged the killing of "an estimated five million Japanese with poison gas." By the summer of 1945, Polmar and Allen state, the United States possessed "almost 51 million chemical artillery shells, more than 1,000,000 chemical bombs. More than 100,000 aircraft spray tanks" were available. Porter urged that B-29 and B-24 strategic bombers drop up to 56,583 tons of poison-gas bombs in the first fifteen days of a preinvasion "gas blitz." When the landings began on the island of Kyūshū in November 1945, "tactical fighters and attack planes were to drop another nine thousand tons of poison gas canisters, followed by 4,984 tons of bombs every 30 days. Other planes would swoop low, using spray tanks to spread thousands of tons of liquid gas over Japanese defenders." Polmar and Allen believe that Porter's proposal was discussed at White House meetings on June 14 and 18. On the former occasion Admiral Ernest King and Army Chief of Staff George Marshall discussed the use of gas, and Marshall subsequently wrote his naval counterpart, "Gas is the one single weapon hitherto unused which we can have readily available which assuredly can greatly decrease the cost in American lives and should materially shorten the war." Although the formal minutes of the June 18 White House meeting in which President Truman authorized the invasions of Kyūshū ("Olympic," November 1, 1945) and Honshu ("Coronet," March 1, 1946), respectively, are silent on both the poison-gas and atomic issues, they do refer to other, undisclosed, topics. We now know that one highly classified item that was discussed rather abruptly at the end of the meeting was use of the atom bomb. Polmar and Allen argue that Porter's memorandum urging a chemical blitz of Japan was surely the other undisclosed topic. If Truman and his top military and civilian advisers did consider the poison-gas alternative to nuclear warfare, the matter was apparently dismissed by the president, never to be raised again.[36] Truman subsequently acquiesced in the use of atomic bombs soon before his departure for the Potsdam summit conference with Stalin and Churchill on July 7.

Had Roosevelt ignored MacArthur's entreaties in the summer of 1944 and adopted Nimitz's argument to move directly from the Marianas against Formosa, or perhaps even Iwo Jima, the navy scenario of a decisive blockade might have had time to work. As it was, the U.S. fleet, army, and air forces reached the gateway to Japan in the early summer of 1945 filled with a profound war-weariness that was compounded by ever intensifying enemy fanaticism and ever larger casualty lists. There was thus great and mounting pressure to finish the war as expeditiously as possible. In the end, army assertions that a blockade would take too long and be too costly and air force assumptions that the mightiest weapon in the strategic air arsenal would be given a fair battlefield demonstration won the day.

The defeat of the navy's gradualist scenario in favor of the twin shocks of invasion and atomic bombing in fact hastened both the justification for and the use of nuclear weapons against Japan, for in July 1945—following the formal White House decision to invade Japan—U.S. signal intelligence began picking up rapidly accumulating evidence that the Japanese had determined not only the Kyūshū invasion site but also the specific beaches over which the invading forces would come and were reacting accordingly. Indeed, as early as April, "Magic" intercepts and decoding of high-level Japanese military traffic indicated not only that Tokyo was mining harbors and beaches all around Kyūshū but also that civilians were either being crudely armed or evacuated, local garrisons reinforced, and suicide aircraft stockpiled in the hundreds if not thousands in anticipation of an early American appearance. There were, intelligence analysts guessed, six divisions at or near the planned Kyūshū invasion sites. Of equal or greater weight was evidence from diplomatic as well as military traffic that the Japanese military was positively anticipating an invasion of Kyūshū, which it believed it could bloodily repulse, thereby achieving the long-cherished goal of a favorably negotiated peace.[37]

As the invasion of Japan loomed, Marshall and King forged a command agreement "in which Nimitz would turn over all army forces to MacArthur, who would, in turn, transfer to Nimitz command of the Seventh Fleet and those Marine divisions still in the South-West Pacific." King allowed Marshall to award supreme command to MacArthur; Marshall, in turn, "agreed that Nimitz, as the overall naval and amphibious commander, could appeal any of

MacArthur's decisions" to the Joint Chiefs of Staff. In the event, of course, the invasion never took place. But the elaborate wartime consultative system, together with the willingness of Washington officialdom and theater commanders to defer to the arguments and assessments of those on the spot when such arguments and assessments seemed compelling (as with Halsey and the Philippines), worked well when it had to. Once the war was won, however, the question of armed-forces unification uncovered long-simmering interservice antagonisms that nearly tore the U.S. defense establishment apart.[38]

By late June, as President Truman prepared to sail for Europe, "intercepted communications in this time period continued to show Japanese preparations for extensive use of suicide weapons and tactics." They also revealed that strong defensive positions at and near the prospective invasion beaches at Miyazaki, Ariake Bay, and the Satsuma peninsula were well advanced and being continually upgraded and elaborated. "Messages in late June describe additional bases for piloted suicide torpedoes *(kaiten)* and preparations for using oil and gasoline incendiary devices." Intercepted Magic messages in early July "dealt with the deployment of a flotilla of 940 suicide aircraft to 18 concealed bases on Kyūshū. . . . The same communications also showed training for night suicide attacks. It was becoming increasingly clear that Japanese naval air elements had been completely turned over to the suicide mission." On July 21,

> the Military Intelligence Service's daily summary on Japanese forces reported that three entirely new divisions had suddenly been discovered on Kyūshū. Another was discovered within the next few days, bringing the confirmed total [on the island] to ten combat divisions. . . . The MIS report of 2 August [as Truman was returning home from Potsdam and four days before Hiroshima] showed that estimated military manpower on Kyūshū had reached 534,000. As substantial as this increase was, it still did not include the full personnel of the recently confirmed eleventh combat division because analysts believed this division was not yet fully deployed. . . . These forces together represented the potential for another 40,000 troops.[39]

At least some of this shocking information had been conveyed to Truman at Potsdam. At the time of the June 18 White House conference that authorized invasion, the joint armed services War Plans Committee had estimated that the 766,700 American troops dedicated to the Kyūshū operation the following November would confront six Japanese combat divisions and two depot divisions totaling about 350,000 men. This estimate of Japanese strength had held steady since mid-1944. Now, however, with intelligence estimates calculating close to 600,000 enemy troops on Kyūshū (and MacArthur's headquarters now crediting the Imperial Navy with more than 2,600 suicide planes for the operation), it was evident that prospects for a successful American lodgment had diminished to the vanishing point—no modern invasion from the sea had been successfully mounted on a roughly one-to-one basis between invaders and defenders, no matter how great the disparity in firepower enjoyed by the assaulting forces. Truman later recalled that Marshall told him that an invasion—if mounted—would surely cost the United States a quarter-million casualties, and perhaps a million. Although Richard B. Frank, the most recent student of the last days of the Pacific war, expresses skepticism over the accuracy of Truman's recollections, he has also asserted that prior to late July, Marshall had withheld realistically high casualty estimates regarding Operation Olympic from his president.[40] Not only was the enemy not about to surrender, but he truly would fight to the death. *Moreover, the navy scenario of a successful air-sea blockade that would soon bring Japan to its knees at comparatively little cost was obviously failing dramatically.* Tokyo was experiencing little or no difficulty reinforcing the prospective Kyūshū front with suicide aircraft and troops, some of whom had been drawn from as far away as the garrisons on the Asian mainland.

Revisionist accounts of the atomic decision, suspect from the beginning because of their willful ignorance or dismissal of the military context and imperatives, become surreal in light of the newest information on intensifying Japanese military activities in the months and weeks preceding Hiroshima and Nagasaki. When American statesmen and planners compared these activities with what appeared to all to be a contemptuous Japanese dismissal of the Potsdam Declaration—which called only for the "unconditional surrender" of Japanese military units and not the Japanese political system as well—they had no choice but to continue to employ every weapon in the national arsenal to subdue a stubborn and savage foe. Every revisionist argument that has ever been advanced has been based on one or two highly questionable premises, and given the flood of immediately or marginally pertinent documentation relating to Hiroshima and the Potsdam Conference, one can construct almost whatever scenario one likes. But the only plausible and compelling scenario is that the bombings of Hiroshima and Nagasaki were meant to end a hideous war as quickly as possible by shocking a blindly fanatic enemy into capitulation. Once that war was over, "atomic diplomacy" inevitably and almost immediately emerged to bedevil East-West relations.

Certainly, the United States has always prosecuted its wars ruthlessly and totally; one need only ask the citizens of Georgia and South Carolina. Americans are magnanimous to the defeated only after the foe has, in effect, surrendered unconditionally. The American way of war has always revolved around the application of overwhelming force in which cunning and finesse are mere handmaidens. American soldiers, sailors, and airmen invariably arm themselves with devastating firepower. The Pacific war was no exception.

But American emotionalism and militarism are not the whole truth; indeed, they are not the most important truth, which is that the twentieth century spawned a new and terrifying kind of political system: the predatory state willing to engage in pitiless killing by the millions to advance and fulfill sinister agendas. Nazi and Japanese warlords could never understand that it was not just their aggression that so disturbed the world but the limitless way in which such aggression was carried out. The rape of Nanking, the destruction of the Jews, Pearl Harbor, and the Bataan Death March were horrifying events that gave the Allies a sense not only of justification but of necessity in waging war on the enemy's terms as well.[41]

The kamikazes sealed the conviction. To the men of the Third and Fifth Fleets who endured ever escalating suicide attacks from the air during the final ten months of the war, the enemy was barbaric. What country, a veteran of the kamikaze battles asked, "would resort to deliberate mass suicide as a national war tactic"? The first "horror stories about [war]ships being deliberately crashed into by bomb-laden aircraft sent shock waves to the fleet," he remembered. And the reality soon "came crashing in." Off the Philippines and Iwo Jima, the kamikazes were an increasingly worrisome presence. As the Americans crunched into Okinawa just four hundred miles south of the Japanese homeland on April 1, 1945, Japan's suicide squadrons defined the conflict that became, in Hanson Baldwin's words, the greatest sea-air battle in history.

"Imagine yourself down in the engine room" of a large fleet aircraft carrier when kamikazes attack, a veteran of that battle has recently written.

> You know it takes several minutes to wind your way through all the passageways and up the many ladders to reach a point where you could see daylight, but that would be the hangar deck, a huge open room filled with aircraft, gasoline bombs, and other ammunition! Now imagine you feel a shudder and hear a muffled thud. Your ship is hit. You are scared and want to leave, but you can't, your shipmates rely on you. Then your ship's communications go dead and she develops a severe list. You can't stand upright...without holding on. Now someone yells down the hatch "Abandon ship." As you leave the engine room panic and mass hysteria is everywhere. You struggle against gravity to find your way through smoke filled

passageways. Finally you reach the hangar deck—a maze of smoke and flames—and ammunition is exploding all around you. People on fire and running wild are everywhere.

Amid screams and cries for help, the young sailor (the great majority in their late teens to early twenties) finds himself in a quandary. Does he help his burned and bloodied buddies? If so, which ones? Or should he turn away from terror-stricken, pain-wracked shipmates to fight the fires? Should he grab a gun or join a gun crew to fight off ever more suicide planes who swarm about the ship like ravenous bees? Or does he jump over the side to save himself? These were the ghastly experiences and deadly choices that faced the three thousand–man crews of *Franklin,* of *Ticonderoga,* of *Bunker Hill* and *Randolph,* of *Essex* and *Hornet. Intrepid* was struck so severely on four separate occasions that it had to return to the States for major repairs, earning it the names *Dry I* and *The Decrepit.* More than seven hundred men perished aboard *Franklin* alone, and nearly that many aboard *Bunker Hill.* Although neither carrier was sunk, they never sailed in battle again.

For the several hundred men aboard each of the destroyers, the "small boys" on the "picket line" fifty to seventy-five miles ahead of the invasion-support fleet off Okinawa, conditions were, if possible, even grimmer. Jammed together in small, cramped spaces amid "massive machinery, equipment and ammunition," the youngsters of the tin-can fleet suffered hideously from even one hit by a bomb-laden plane. A single crashing airplane crushed, blew apart, and blasted overboard a score or a half-hundred men. The dazed survivors fought to save their ship. Often the first terrible crash would be followed by one or two others, sending the vessel to the bottom with men trapped helplessly belowdecks. For all hands at Okinawa, "it was not just an attack here or there, or a single engagement, those attacks were going on day and night for weeks. Japanese Kamikaze aircraft were almost always on a ship's radar screen somewhere, and more often than not the screen was filled with several flights." A destroyer sailor remembered an episode of the television series *Twilight Zone* in which the victim spends eternity endlessly "reliving his own nightmarish death . . . as if it happened for the first time." This was the fate of survivors of the kamikaze wars, he added. Grant the Japanese suicide pilots their heroism; they died only once. Years, decades, later, "for no apparent reason," their surviving enemies "break down in tears, many still have nightmares and suppressed memories. After more than 50 years—remembering still hurts!"[42] Yet if the situation had been reversed, would not desperate Americans have saluted *their* aviators and sailors for crashing the nation's dwindling supply of inferior planes and boats into an enemy fleet invading the beaches of New Jersey or California?

Decades later, bitter American sailors would charge that Washington kept the lid on the kamikazes because of their deadly effectiveness and that therefore the public never knew of their men's sacrifice and heroism. The charge was only half true. The public was told at the time, however guardedly, about the kamikazes, and early postwar histories and documentaries, most notably the wildly popular television series *Victory at Sea,* recounted the story in full. Certainly, enough was widely known in 1945 about the Japanese suicide planes both in Washington and in the country to reconfirm Japan as a nation of undying fanatics. Only the Pentagon and White House knew just how effective those fanatics were. Could the fleet keep the seas off Japan and support a prolonged invasion in the face of waves of suicide planes and boats attacking night and day? There may well have been doubt in many minds.[43]

In the broadest context, the necessity of the atomic raids on Japan to end mankind's most brutal total war was unquestionable. By the summer of 1945 the war had lasted far too long, tainting with immorality *all* who came within its boundaries. Japan continued to fight as it had fought for eight long years, savagely and unrestrainedly. That it was clearly beaten was beyond question; it had been for the past twelve months. That it would ever acknowledge the fact was far from obvious. As Ronald Schaffer has thoughtfully demonstrated, the forces of decency had themselves been soiled and corrupted by violence long before *Enola Gay* lifted off from its Tinian runway. Whatever justifications for mass aerial bombing may have existed before 1945, the incendiary raids that had wiped out most of Dresden in February and much of Tokyo the following month extended the limits of strategic terror bombing well past the point of *any* justification. It was time to end the bloodletting before the potential victors passed the threshold point from which the vanquished had begun their careers of unrestrained criminality.[44]

Historian Richard Frank raises a chilling point: could the United States have actually *lost* the war on the beaches and in the hills of Kyūshū? Of course, Washington would not have surrendered to the Japanese, but casualty figures could have become so horrific that the war-weariness gripping the American public and armed forces might have prevailed after weeks of savage, inconclusive battle. The eleven Japanese divisions on Kyūshū just might have gotten Tokyo what it was holding out for—a negotiated peace guaranteeing the continued sovereign independence of imperial Japan, free of enemy occupation and possessed of the same brutally aggressive military regime that had brought such widespread violence and woe to huge swaths of Asia and the Pacific. Frank has discovered evidence that between April and May 1945, Chester Nimitz reversed his endorsement of the Kyūshū invasion on the basis of casualty estimates worked up by his intelligence people. Ernest King kept this information from his president and colleagues on the Joint Chiefs of Staff until after the Hiroshima raid when he seems to have been prepared to reveal it and force a confrontation with Douglas MacArthur—and perhaps George Marshall—over their insistence that Olympic go forward if Tokyo failed to surrender. Only the Nagasaki bomb and Hirohito's decision to end hostilities forestalled a perhaps fatal paralysis in American strategic planning at the end of World War II.[45]

So the navy scenario for bringing the Pacific war to a close by blockade was confounded and discredited by Japan's ability to strongly reinforce the prospective Kyūshū front. The army scenario was unnecessary in the wake of the atomic raids. The bombs were used as the ultimate expression of the air force doctrine of strategic terror bombing. The Second World War passed away, and with it a salient chapter in the history of mankind and its dominion of the sea.

The massive bloodletting of 1939–1945 ushered in an age of world revolution. The peoples of Asia, Africa, and the Middle East either experienced or heard of the humiliation of the Western imperial democracies by German and Japanese boys, and they knew beyond doubt that they could throw off the now-palsied grip of their European masters. By midcentury the world would truly be turned upside down, as several hundred million people slowly, progressively, threw off the Western imperial yoke and began long, tortuous, still far from completed journeys to independence and dignity. Among the deserved casualties of the world revolution were two great maritime empires, those of Britain and Japan. The British Empire, the greatest ever known, born of and absolutely dependent upon the sea, died at the hands of two inferior sea powers. In the end it was the Japanese naval flyers off Malaya and Ceylon who destroyed the empire in the East and Dönitz's young U-boat sailors with their implacable trade and commerce war in the North Atlantic who destroyed the empire everywhere, and for good, by fatally undermining British economic strength and fatally weakening the British standard of living.

Churchill tried desperately to arrest his nation's decline. Following months of negotiation, he wrenched an agreement from his grudging, skeptical American allies that permitted a British fleet to be sent to the Pacific in the final stages of the war against Japan. Two British battleships and a total of five fleet carriers, together with supporting warships and a supply "train," made a brief appearance with the American armada off Okinawa in May 1945, then re-appeared in July to join the direct air assaults and sea bombardment of the Japanese homeland. In something of a replication of 1917–1918 at Scapa Flow, the British task force then steamed up Tokyo Bay in August with the Americans. Beneath Mount Fuji, *King George V* anchored next to *Missouri* in anticipation of the formal ceremony of Japanese surrender.

It was all hollow display. The year 1940 was long in the past, and there was no Somerville now, no Cunningham to lead dashing British carrier raids against unsuspecting foes. The ships themselves were slowly going to pieces from the strain of long-ago battles and, after mid-1942, prolonged exposure to tropical conditions in the comparative backwaters of the Indian Ocean where their air groups had had little chance to exercise their skills against the enemy. The fleet was commanded by Bruce Fraser, the stolid battleship man whose one moment of brilliance was in chasing down and killing *Scharnhorst* off North Cape eighteen months before. The carrier division was led by Philip Vian, who had won a deserved reputation as the gallant leader of the destroyer squadron that had kept the fatally crippled *Bismarck* pinned in its sights one long night until superior force appeared in the morning to end things. Vian had had little to do with carriers since.

Admirals, Tars, and pilots tried hard to keep up with the bustling Yanks, but it proved increasingly difficult. The latest official British naval history of the Pacific war is scathing in its assessment of the Royal Navy's brief appearances off Okinawa and Japan. Antiaircraft gunnery was generally poor, resulting in kamikaze hits to *Indefatigable* and *Illustrious.* The relatively small supply "train" proved inadequate to the demands of fleet replenishment. In particular, the fuel-pump rate of the tankers was insufficient. *Illustrious* and its sisters were smaller and slower than U.S. carriers, they embarked fewer aircraft, and observers at the time remarked that if a continually stiff breeze had not been blowing, the British ships would have been unable to launch and land aircraft since their speed was insufficient to generate enough wind across the flight deck. British flight decks themselves were comparatively short and narrow, and the armored-box arrangement for the hangar decks that permitted operations off European shores meant fewer onboard aircraft-repair facilities—machine shops and the like. Under the circumstances, it is perhaps not surprising that British pilots suffered an appallingly high accident rate in contrast to their American cousins. The kamikaze hits off Okinawa further weakened the structural integrity of *Illustrious,* which had been permanently compromised by damage from German Stukas at Malta. The carrier had to be withdrawn, but its replacement, the

equally battle-hardened *Formidable,* caught fire as the result of a hangar accident and was forced to sail all the way to the east coast of Australia to be hastily
patched for the climactic air-sea conflict off Honshu. Finally, the Royal Navy
simply did not know how to stay at sea for any length of time. According to
Samuel Eliot Morison, when Fraser and his ships left Okinawan waters for the
Leyte rest area after only thirty-two days of fitful action, they "set a record for
the Royal Navy in the days of steam" for consecutive days at sea.[46]

Not far in the background lay Britain's declining understanding of a world it
had once known well. By the midthirties, when matters should have been completely otherwise, the Royal Navy demonstrated a contempt for the Japanese
that was truly staggering. Britain's naval attaché in Tokyo wrote Whitehall in
February 1935 that the Imperial Japanese Navy was "inefficient" because "the
Japanese have peculiarly slow brains." The attaché attributed this ostensible
deficiency to the Japanese language, whose six thousand–plus characters broke
the brains of children forced to memorize them. The reason Japanese officers
could not improvise in a crisis, the foolish man added, was because they were
democratically recruited, and everyone knew that peasant boys lack the "power
of command." First Sea Lord Ernle Chatfield was sufficiently impressed with
the argument to wonder whether the Japanese might not be panicked in the
event of war by a demonstration of British light cruisers and destroyers somewhere off Singapore. Six years later, in those very waters, American reporter
Cecil Brown sat in the wardroom of HMS *Repulse* as it searched along with the
new battleship *Prince of Wales* for an enemy convoy said to be possibly heading
toward the city escorted by a *Kongo*-class battleship. The chaps in the battle
cruiser's wardroom were the same type that Lieutenant Commander Joseph
Wellings had run across aboard *Hood* just a year earlier—"charming, agreeable,
friendly" but perhaps too "nonchalant," neither indifferent nor phlegmatic,
just "casual." In more than two years of war they had steamed fifty-three thousand miles and never heard a shot fired in anger. Now they were facing the Japanese who, the consensus had it, were "bloody fools"—bloody fools who did
not know how to fly an airplane well, bloody fools who made "pinprick" landings and attacks rather than concentrating on Singapore, bloody fools who
could not shoot. Like all the men and boys in *Hood*'s wardroom, some of these
pleasant, decent chaps would be at the bottom of the sea before another sun-
down. Perhaps, in a way, the Germans had won after all in *both* wars, for when
Alfred von Tirpitz forced Jacky Fisher to bring the old Royal Navy back to home
waters to confront the High Seas Fleet more than a quarter century before, it
closed down whatever sophistication the British naval mind possessed, leaving

it prey to the kind of fatal, parochial thinking that cost the men of *Repulse* their ship and many their lives.[47]

The Americans had it all now: the huge fleet; the revolutionary strategic and tactical doctrines of naval air; the expertise in logistics and amphibious warfare; the enormous research, development, and productive capacities; the thrusting spirit of a new, young power anxious to play its own dominant role on the international stage. Above all, the United States Navy enjoyed the right to sail where it pleased and do as it wished on the world ocean, without let or hindrance, for by August 1945 there were no adversaries left. They had been destroyed. How it would all work out, no one could say on those quiet evenings beneath Fuji while everyone waited impatiently for the simple surrender ceremony that would at last send them home.

NOTES

Abbreviation

NIP   *U.S. Naval Institute Proceedings*

Chapter 1. The Containment of Sea Power: Washington, 1921–1922

1. The 1919 Peace Conference was held in Paris; the signing was at Versailles.

2. Frank H. Simonds, *Can Europe Keep the Peace?* 3.

3. Archibald Hurd, "Economy in the Fleet: Lord Fisher's Demand," 525.

4. Harold Sprout and Margaret Sprout, *Toward a New Order of Sea Power: American Naval Policy and the World Scene, 1918–1922,* 35.

5. Hurd, "Economy in the Fleet," 514, 523–26; italics in original. Fisher's first quote is on p. 514. His second quote is in Richard Hough, *Death of the Battleship: The Tragic Close of the Era of Sea Power,* 45. The comment on sacked Royal Navy officers is in Philip Gibbs, *Across the Frontiers,* 13.

6. James Neidpath, *The Singapore Naval Base and the Defence of Britain's Eastern Empire, 1919–1941,* 6–7.

7. "Memorandum by Planning Section: U.S. Naval Forces in European Waters October [?] 1918," in *Anglo-American Naval Relations, 1917–1919,* edited by Michael Simpson, 541–43.

8. "Memorandum by Rear-Admiral Sir Sydney Fremantle and Comments by U.S. Planning Section," October 1918, in ibid., 543–46.

9. "British Admiralty Draft of Naval Armistice Terms and Comments by United States Naval Advisory Staff," November 1918, in ibid., 554–58.

10. Stephen Howarth, *To Shining Sea: A History of the United States Navy, 1775–1991,* 325.

11. "'Strategic Conditions of Halifax and Esquimault' Memorandum by the Colonial Defense Committee for the Consideration of the Committee of Imperial Defence, Signed by J. E. Clausen, Secretary," May 4, 1905; "'Defence of Canada' Memorandum by the Admiralty for the Committee of Imperial Defense," February 24, 1905; "Na-

tional Policy—Memorandum by Hankey to the Committee of Imperial Defence," July 1919, in *The Collective Naval Defence of the Empire, 1900–1940,* edited by Nicholas Tracy, 37–39, 249–50. The Admiralty itself did not always accept the notion of British naval impuissance vis-à-vis the U.S. Navy. At the 1923 Spithead Naval Review, First Lord of the Admiralty Leopold Amery found himself standing with Mackenzie King gazing down on the British fleet. "It was the existence of these battle-lines," Amery remarked, that had made King "Premier of the Dominion of Canada and not, at best, the junior Senator from the American State of Ontario." A. P. Thornton, *The Imperial Idea and Its Enemies: A Study in British Power,* 147.

12. Hurd, "Economy in the Fleet," 527; see also Hurd, "Peace and a Naval Holiday."

13. See Archibald Hurd, "Shall We Suffer an Eclipse at Sea? American Progress." The superiority of American capital ships is mentioned in Phillips Payson O'Brien, "Politics, Arms Control, and U.S. Naval Development in the Interwar Period," in *Technology and Naval Combat in the Twentieth Century and Beyond,* edited by O'Brien, 148.

14. Sprout and Sprout, *Toward a New Order,* 51–53 (the General Board memorandum is quoted on p. 53); John Keegan, *The Price of Admiralty: The Evolution of Naval Warfare,* 170. The Navy Board Memorandum is summarized in Arthur S. Link, ed., *The Papers of Woodrow Wilson,* 53:312n. Wilson's press interview aboard ship moments before his departure for France is in "Diary of Dr. Grayson," in ibid., 313–15 (quote on pp. 314–15).

15. The following account is based on Sprout and Sprout, *Toward a New Order,* 61–64 (Wester-Wemyss is quoted on p. 61; Benson, Long, and Daniels are quoted on p. 62).

16. Daniels to Wilson, April 7, 1919, in *Papers of Wilson,* edited by Link, 57:91.

17. From William Shepherd Benson, with enclosure, April 9, 1919, in ibid., 180–88 (quotes on pp. 181, 182, 185, 187, 188).

18. Stephen Roskill, *Naval Policy between the Wars,* 1:91; Howarth, *To Shining Sea,* 326.

19. Simpson, *Anglo-American Naval Relations,* 610–12, 614.

20. Benson to Wilson, May 5, 1919; Wilson to Benson, May 6, 1919, in ibid., 612–13.

21. Charles M. Melhorn, *Two-Block Fox: The Rise of the Aircraft Carrier, 1911–1929,* 23–24; Norman Friedman, *U.S. Aircraft Carriers: An Illustrated Design History,* 32–33.

22. William Reynolds Braisted, *The United States Navy in the Pacific, 1909–1922,* 537; Sprout and Sprout, *Toward a New Order,* 88.

23. Kemp Tolley, *Yangtze Patrol: The U.S. Navy in China,* 82–83.

24. Braisted, *United States Navy in the Pacific,* 535–36.

25. Sprout and Sprout, *Toward a New Order,* 88–89.

26. Ibid., 92.

27. Howarth, *To Shining Sea,* 330. See also George F. Kennan, *Russia and the West under Lenin and Stalin,* 113.

28. Braisted, *United States Navy in the Pacific,* 541–43.

29. Ibid., 543–44.

30. Shizuo Fukui, *Naval Vessels, 1887–1945: Mitsubishi Zosen Built*, 22–25; Sadao Asada, "Japanese Admirals and the Politics of Naval Limitation: Katō Tomosaburō vs. Katō Kanji," in *Naval Warfare in the Twentieth Century, 1900–1945: Essays in Honor of Arthur Marder*, edited by Gerald Jordan, 145–46; Braisted, *United States Navy in the Pacific*, 538; Sprout and Sprout, *Toward a New Order*, 94.

31. Asada, "Japanese Admirals," in *Naval Warfare*, edited by Jordan, 147.

32. Braisted, *United States Navy in the Pacific*, 537–38.

33. Sprout and Sprout, *Toward a New Order*, 95–96; Howarth, *To Shining Sea*, 336; Roskill, *Naval Policy*, 1:106; Kenneth J. Hagan, *This People's Navy: The Making of American Sea Power*, 263.

34. Howarth, *To Shining Sea*, 332.

35. Keegan, *Price of Admiralty*, 171.

36. An argument could be made that the Aleutian chain in the far northern Pacific offers Japan (and Russia/Soviet Union) access to the North American continent and eventually the United States via Alaska and British Columbia. But in comparison to the coral-clad central-Pacific archipelagoes usually lapped in sunshine, distances in the Aleutians-to–British Columbia theater are immense, the mountain-fjord topography is hostile, and the weather is frequently abominable. Strategic geography will always condemn Japanese expansionism to the East and Southeast Asian–Western Pacific area.

37. The foremost Western historians of the Imperial Japanese Navy claim that the Sempill Naval Air Mission, designed to "provide a professional edge" to Japan's fledgling naval air arm, marked "the true beginning" of effective Japanese capabilities in this area. David C. Evans and Mark R. Peattie, *Kaigun: Strategy, Tactics, and Technology in the Imperial Japanese Navy, 1887–1941*, 181.

38. German successes at Ypres, Artois, and Champagne in 1915 provoked a storm of criticism against Britain in the officially inspired Japanese press. The alliance was declared unfair and one-sided, and Germany's apparent military invincibility was emphasized. Tokyo immediately placed a series of twenty-one demands on the Chinese government that, had they been carried out in toto, would have made the largest nation in Asia a virtual vassal state of Japan. Peking bowed to Tokyo's threat of force and granted sweeping concessions in both Manchuria and Shantung.

Germany promptly launched a quiet démarche in neutral European capitals, probing for either a formal alliance or an informal understanding with Tokyo. The Japanese apparently listened attentively for a time before prudently concluding that Germany was no more likely to win the war than were the Allies. Meanwhile, after some initially confusing signals caused by Wilson's preoccupation with the European war, Washington urged Japan to revoke its most extreme demands on China, which Tokyo grudgingly agreed to do. Fred W. Ikle, "Japanese-German Peace Negotiations during World War I"; John King Fairbank, *The United States and China*, 196; Warren I. Cohen, *America's Response to China: A History of Sino-American Relations*, 74–77. An interesting near contemporary account is Harold S. Quigley and George H. Blakeslee, *The Far East: An International Survey*, 10.

39. Morinosuke Kajima, *The Emergence of Japan as a World Power, 1895–1925,* 202.

40. Howarth, *To Shining Sea,* 338.

41. Braisted, *United States Navy in the Pacific,* 575–77; Neidpath, *Singapore Naval Base,* 39–41.

42. Roskill, *Naval Policy,* 1:279; Russell Grenfell, *Main Fleet to Singapore,* 46. Jellicoe is quoted in W. David McIntyre, *The Rise and Fall of the Singapore Naval Base, 1919–1942,* 22.

43. Sprout and Sprout, *Toward a New Order,* 244–45; Grenfell, *Main Fleet to Singapore,* 45; McIntyre, *Rise and Fall,* 21–22; Neidpath, *Singapore Naval Base,* 29–30.

44. Sprout and Sprout, *Toward a New Order,* 244–45; Neidpath, *Singapore Naval Base,* 31–32; Thornton, *Imperial Idea,* 217.

45. Evans and Peattie, *Kaigun,* 168–69.

46. Roger Dingman, *Power in the Pacific: The Origins of Naval Arms Limitation, 1914–1922,* 75.

47. Masanori Ito and Roger Pineau, *The End of the Imperial Japanese Navy,* 17.

48. Mark R. Peattie and David C. Evans, "Satō Tetsutarō and Japanese Strategy," 37–38.

49. Evans and Peattie, *Kaigun,* 171–75; Kenji is quoted in Asada, "Japanese Admirals," in *Naval Warfare,* edited by Jordan, 145, 147; Tomosaburō is quoted in Braisted, *United States Navy in the Pacific,* 540.

50. Tameichi Hara, Fred Saito, and Roger Pineau, *Japanese Destroyer Captain,* 19 (*Shimakaze* quote); Howarth, *To Shining Sea,* 336.

51. Oscar Parkes and Maurice Prendergast, eds., *Jane's Fighting Ships, 1919,* 3.

52. Antony Preston, *Battleships,* 120–21.

53. Ibid., 120; Howarth, *To Shining Sea,* 336.

54. H. P. Willmott, *Empires in the Balance: Japanese and Allied Pacific Strategies to April 1942,* 34.

55. Thornton, *Imperial Idea,* 217.

56. Howarth, *To Shining Sea,* 338–39.

57. Unless otherwise noted, the following assessment of the Washington Naval Conference is based on these sources: Braisted, *United States Navy in the Pacific,* 580–675; Dingman, *Power in the Pacific,* 196–219; Roskill, *Naval Policy,* 1:300–330; Simonds, *Can Europe Keep the Peace?* 286–89; Sprout and Sprout, *Toward a New Order,* 145–277; and F. C. D. Sturdee, "Naval Aspects of the Washington Conference," in *Brassey's Naval and Shipping Annual, 1923,* edited by Alexander Richardson and Archibald Hurd, 68–84.

58. This and the following quotations are from Fletcher Pratt, *Sea Power and Today's War,* 8–9.

59. Antony Preston, *Aircraft Carriers,* 32–33; J. F. Helweg, "Der Tag," *NIP* 48:5 (May 1922): 703–24. For a more sympathetic view of both Mitchell and the bombing tests, see Arthur Hezlet, *Aircraft and Sea Power,* 109–110.

60. Pratt, *Sea Power and Today's War,* 10. An excellent account of the background and consequences of the Billy Mitchell affair, including Mitchell's formidable abilities as a promoter of land-based airpower, is Hough, *Death of the Battleship,* 28–39, 53–56.

61. Pratt, *Sea Power and Today's War,* 10.

62. Ibid., 237 (quote), 63–116, 159–79.

63. Preston, *Battleships,* 129; Howarth, *To Shining Sea,* 341–42.

64. Pratt, *Sea Power and Today's War,* 7, 13.

65. Sprout and Sprout, *Toward a New Order,* 192–99.

66. Hezlet, *Aircraft and Sea Power,* 66–67, 77, 84, 111–12, 115, 116.

67. Clark G. Reynolds, *The Carrier War,* 32; Preston, *Aircraft Carriers,* 35.

68. Mark R. Peattie, *Sunburst: The Rise of Japanese Naval Air Power, 1909–1941,* 1–18 (quote on p. 16).

69. Ibid., 18–26; C. Ray Stokes and Ted Darling, "Yokosuka Naval Air Base and Japanese Naval Aviation," *NIP* 74:541 (March 1948): 339–42.

70. Robert F. Dunn, "The Spirit of *Saratoga,*" 17; Hezlet, *Aircraft and Sea Power,* 120–21.

71. Preston, *Aircraft Carriers,* 37; Friedman, *U.S. Aircraft Carriers,* 390.

72. Sprout and Sprout, *Toward a New Order,* 243.

73. The reaction of the Japanese "Fleet" faction to the Washington Conference and Jones's comment are in Asada, "Japanese Admirals," in *Naval Warfare,* edited by Jordan, 153. See also Ito and Pineau, *End of the Japanese Navy,* 9.

74. Akira Iriye, *The Origins of the Second World War in Asia and the Pacific,* 3.

75. Sprout and Sprout, *Toward a New Order,* 263–64; Melhorn, *Two-Block Fox,* 5. American naval planners had begun revising War Plan Orange well before the Washington Naval Conference based on the assumption that a major fleet engagement with Japan somewhere in the central Pacific would require capture of at least some of the enemy-held Marshall and Caroline islands as staging and support bases. Dirk A. Ballendorf and Merrill L. Bartlett, *Pete Ellis: An Amphibious Warfare Prophet, 1880–1923,* 113.

76. Viscount Cunningham of Hyndhope, *A Sailor's Odyssey: The Autobiography of Admiral of the Fleet Viscount Cunningham of Hyndhope,* 112, 114.

77. Donald S. Birn, "The Washington Naval Conference of 1921–22 in Anglo-French Relations," in *Naval History: The Sixth Symposium of the U.S. Naval Academy,* edited by Daniel M. Masterson, 176.

78. Sprout and Sprout, *Toward a New Order,* 260, 261 (quote).

79. Willmott, *Empires in the Balance,* 36; Asada, "Japanese Admirals," in *Naval Warfare,* edited by Jordan, 153–55.

80. William Henry Chamberlin, *Japan over Asia,* 147.

81. Hiroyuki Agawa, *The Reluctant Admiral: Yamamoto and the Imperial Navy,* 31–32.

82. Ito and Pineau, *End of the Japanese Navy,* 9; Hara, Saito, and Pineau, *Japanese Destroyer Captain,* 20; Agawa, *Reluctant Admiral,* 29–32.

83. U.S. national security historian John Prados has thoroughly examined—and refuted—popular allegations from the 1920s and early '30s that Japan was strongly

fortifying its mid-Pacific possessions (*Combined Fleet Decoded: The Secret History of American Intelligence and the Japanese Navy in World War II*, 95–98). The Singapore quote is from Thornton, *Imperial Idea*, 219.

84. Christopher M. Bell, "Thinking the Unthinkable: British and American Naval Strategies for an Anglo-American War, 1918–1931," 792–93.

85. Ibid., 794–95, 806–8.

86. Grenfell, *Main Fleet to Singapore*, 45–46.

Chapter 2. The Race Resumes

1. Mark R. Peattie, "Japanese Naval Construction, 1919–1941," in *Technology and Naval Combat*, edited by O'Brien, 93–95.

2. Mitsuo Fuchida and Masatake Okumiya, *Midway: The Battle That Doomed Japan*, 26.

3. Janusz Skulski, *The Heavy Cruiser Takao*, 7–10 (quote on p. 7).

4. Ibid. See also David C. Evans and Mark R. Peattie, "Ill Winds Blow," *NIP* 103: 10 (October 1997): 70–73. The authors have expanded their discussion of this matter in Evans and Peattie, *Kaigun*, 219–32.

5. Oscar Parkes, ed., *Jane's Fighting Ships, 1933*, 34–54, 311–29, 332.

6. Ito and Pineau, *End of the Japanese Navy*, 16.

7. This document is in folder FHR/12, William Wordsworth Fisher Papers, National Maritime Museum, Greenwich, England.

8. Norman Henry Gibbs, *Rearmament Policy*, 26–27.

9. Ibid., 27.

10. Fisher to Secretary of the Admiralty, September 27, 1933, folder FHR/16, Fisher Papers.

11. Henry L. Stimson and McGeorge Bundy, *On Active Service in Peace and War*, 166; Norman Friedman, *U.S. Cruisers: An Illustrated Design History*, 104, 164; Howarth, *To Shining Sea*, 349.

12. Keith W. Bird, *Weimar, the German Naval Officer Corps and the Rise of National Socialism*, 205.

13. Edward von der Porten, *The German Navy in World War II*, 2–4. Wegener's writings have been collected, translated, edited, and carefully analyzed by Holger H. Herwig as part of the Naval Institute Press series Classics of Sea Power. See also Wolfgang Wegener, *The Naval Strategy of the World War*.

14. Anthony Martienssen, *Hitler and His Admirals*, 7; Marlis G. Steinert, *23 Days: The Final Collapse of Nazi Germany*, 38–40. Doenitz is quoted in Steinert, *23 Days*, 39–40. Jochen Brennecke (*The Hunters and the Hunted*, 12–13) cogently discusses the character of German U-boat officers and the adoration in which Dönitz was held by his submarine crews after 1935.

These sources are in rather sharp exception to recent efforts by younger scholars with no personal ties to or memories of World War II who have sought to rehabilitate the reputations of the U-boat commanders of 1939–1945. Jordan Vause and to a somewhat lesser extent Eric Christian Rust have argued that with a few exceptions, the young German submarine officers of World War II were decent young chaps, not particularly politically motivated, who found themselves in a militarized world they never made and who simply and understandably went with the flow while doing their best to cling to and act upon their humane impulses. It is not a convincing argument. Vause, *Wolf: U-boat Commanders in World War II;* Rust, *Crew 34: German Naval Officers under and after Hitler,* 61–78.

15. Heinz Hohne, *Canaris,* 80, 81–82.

16. Martienssen, *Hitler and His Admirals,* 4–5; William L. Shirer, *The Rise and Fall of the Third Reich,* 33–34.

17. Unless otherwise cited, the following discussion is based on Eugene Davidson, *The Trial of the Germans: An Account of the Twenty-two Defendants before the International Military Tribunal at Nuremberg,* 370; Hohne, *Canaris,* 89; Antony Preston, *Submarines,* 92–93; and Dan van der Vat, *The Atlantic Campaign: World War II's Great Struggle at Sea,* 47–50.

18. Hohne, *Canaris,* 89–90; von der Porten, *German Navy,* 3.

19. Bird, *Weimar,* 219, 221; Tobias R. Philbin III, *The Lure of Neptune: German-Soviet Naval Collaboration and Ambitions, 1919–1941,* 9–21.

20. Holger H. Herwig, "The Failure of German Sea Power, 1914–1945: Mahan, Tirpitz, and Raeder Reconsidered," 90.

21. Von der Porten, *German Navy,* 5; Preston, *Battleships,* 132–33; Donald Macintyre, *The Naval War against Hitler,* 12–13; Gordon Landsborough, *The Battle of the River Plate,* 17–18; Theodor Krancke and H. J. Brennecke, *Pocket Battleship: The Story of the* Admiral Scheer, 5–6.

22. Stimson and Bundy, *On Active Service,* 165; Friedman, *U.S. Cruisers,* 164.

23. For Pratt's views, see William V. Pratt, "Naval Policy and Its Relation to World Politics," *NIP* 49:7 (July 1923): 1073–84.

24. Agawa, *Reluctant Admiral,* 22, 32–33.

25. Friedman, *U.S. Cruisers,* 164; Stimson and Bundy, *On Active Service,* 172; Howarth, *To Shining Sea,* 349–50.

26. Friedman, *U.S. Cruisers,* 164–66; Stimson and Bundy, *On Active Service,* 168; Howarth, *To Shining Sea,* 349.

27. Stimson and Bundy, *On Active Service,* 169–72.

28. Ibid., 169.

29. Quigley and Blakeslee, *Far East,* 239.

30. Agawa, *Reluctant Admiral,* 30; Ito and Pineau, *End of the Japanese Navy,* 18; Evans and Peattie, *Kaigun,* 237.

31. Hara, Saito, and Pineau, *Japanese Destroyer Captain,* 34.

32. The account of the American fleet visit to the South Pacific in 1925 and the

movement of British fleet units through the Panama Canal in February 1931 is from Edwin A. Falk, *From Perry to Pearl Harbor: The Struggle for Supremacy in the Pacific,* 279–80, 284–86 (quote on p. 280).

33. Quigley and Blakeslee, *Far East,* 239.

34. The *Herald Tribune* is quoted in "Professional Notes," *NIP* 58:3 (March 1932): 433.

35. Edna Lee Booker (*News Is My Job: A Correspondent in War-Torn China,* 248–52) made the claim about a giant Japanese carrier lying off the Bund launching planes. Mark Peattie's reconstruction of the short, sharp campaign in *Sunburst* (50–51) seems more persuasive. It is doubtful that Japanese naval officials would have risked such a huge prize in the very narrowly confined waters off the Bund. See also Saburo Ienaga, *The Pacific War: World War II and the Japanese,* 6; Christopher Thorne, *Limits of Foreign Policy: The West, the League, and the Far Eastern Crisis of 1931–1933,* 206–09; and Tolley, *Yangtze Patrol,* 199–201.

36. Herbert Hoover, *The Memoirs of Herbert Hoover: The Cabinet and the Presidency, 1920–1933,* 367–68.

37. Stimson and Bundy, *On Active Service,* 245–46.

38. Stephen E. Pelz, *Race to Pearl Harbor: The Failure of the Second London Naval Conference and the Onset of World War II,* 9–18 (quotes on pp. 11, 17).

39. Agawa, *Reluctant Admiral,* 193–94 (quote). See also Thomas C. Hone and Mark D. Mandeles, "Interwar Innovation in Three Navies: U.S. Navy, Royal Navy, Imperial Japanese Navy"; and Evans and Peattie, *Kaigun,* 333.

40. Agawa, *Reluctant Admiral,* 105; Peattie, *Sunburst,* 29.

41. Thorne, *Limits of Foreign Policy,* 214–20, 268.

42. Quoted in "Professional Notes," *NIP* 59:11 (November 1933): 1640. Vinson's nearly identical arguments are quoted in Pelz, *Race to Pearl Harbor,* 77–78.

43. *Washington Herald,* September 18, 1933; *Washington Evening Star,* September 19, 1933, quoted in "Professional Notes," *NIP* 59:11 (November 1933): 1639–40. The Roosevelt construction program to the end of 1933 is detailed in "Professional Notes," *NIP* 60:1 (January 1934): 117.

44. *Asahi,* April 16, 1933, quoted in "Professional Notes," *NIP* 59:7 (July 1933): 1071; Pelz, *Race to Pearl Harbor,* 19, 25.

45. Quigley and Blakeslee, *Far East,* 240; *New York Times,* May 28, 1933, and *Chicago Tribune,* May 27, 1933, as summarized in "Professional Notes," *NIP* 59:7 (July 1933): 1070. "A Treaty Navy," reprint of an undated article from the *San Francisco Examiner,* in "Professional Notes," *NIP* 59:11 (November 1933): 1650–51. See also reprint of Tokyo dispatch in *Washington Herald,* November 27, 1933, quoted in "Professional Notes," *NIP* 60:1 (January 1934): 131. Nye is quoted in Pelz, *Race to Pearl Harbor,* 81.

46. Pelz, *Race to Pearl Harbor,* 46–63 (quotes on pp. 46, 59); Joseph C. Grew, *Ten Years in Japan: A Contemporary Record Drawn from the Diaries and Private and Official Papers of Joseph C. Grew,* 147.

47. S. Takagi, "Japan and Her Navy: Influence of the London Naval Treaty," in *Brassey's Naval and Shipping Annual, 1935,* edited by Charles N. Robinson and H. M. Ross, 74, 84.

48. Evans and Peattie, *Kaigun,* 239; Allan Westcott, "Naval Problems: Japan Ends Washington Treaty," *NIP* 61:2 (February 1935): 253; "Professional Notes: Building Forecast," *NIP* 61:4 (April 1935): 579; "Professional Notes: Japan, Speech by C-in-C," *NIP* 61:8 (August 1935): 1179–80.

49. *Washington Herald,* November 7, 1933, quoted in "Professional Notes: Fleet Going Back to Pacific," *NIP* 60:1 (January 1934): 119–20 (quote on p. 119).

50. Ernest Hemingway, "Notes on the Next War: A Serious Topical Letter," *Esquire,* September 1935, in *By-Line: Ernest Hemingway; Selected Articles and Dispatches of Four Decades,* edited by William White, 178.

Chapter 3. A Lion in Winter

1. Parkes, *Jane's Fighting Ships, 1933,* v.

2. "Fleet Committee First Report, 7 December 1931," folder CHT/2/2, Ernle Chatfield Papers, National Maritime Museum, Greenwich, England.

3. Ibid.; "Lord Beatty's Motion, House of Lords, 1st July 1930," copy in folder FHR/11, Fisher Papers.

4. Archibald Hurd, "British Sea-Power, 1900–1930: Read at the Spring Meetings of the Seventy-second Session of the Institute of Naval Architects, March 25, 1931," copy in "Commonplace Book, Vol. VI," folder RIC/2/1, Herbert William Richmond Papers, National Maritime Museum, Greenwich, England; Parkes, *Jane's Fighting Ships, 1933,* v; Charles N. Robinson and H. M. Ross, eds., *Brassey's Naval and Shipping Annual, 1934,* viii.

5. Preston, *Aircraft Carriers,* 31; Richard B. Frank, *Downfall: The End of the Imperial Japanese Empire,* 38. See also Hezlet, *Aircraft and Sea Power,* 71; Hough, *Death of the Battleship,* 41–42; and Hone and Mandeles, "Interwar Innovation," 64–65.

6. "Extract from Admiralty Weekly Order 8886a of 14 March 1918, entitled 'R.N.A.S.—Transfer to Air Force,'" and "Letter . . . of 14 August 1918 from Admiral the Hon. Sir Stanley C. Colville, C-in-C Portsmouth to Admiralty. . . . Minutes Thereon by the Naval Staff," in *Documents Relating to the Naval Air Service,* edited by S. W. Roskill, 637–38, 705–9.

7. The Admiralty memorandum is in ibid., 711–12.

8. Allen Andrews, *The Air Marshals: The Air War in Western Europe,* 45. An excellent discussion of the postwar emergence of the RAF and the Royal Navy's unwitting assistance in that effort is in Hough, *Death of the Battleship,* 46–53. See also Hone and Mandeles, "Interwar Innovation," 64–65.

9. Hough, *Death of the Battleship,* 63–64. Knowledgeable people within the Royal Navy were, at least in the early thirties, more hopeful than convinced that modern anti-aircraft guns alone could bring down high-flying or fast-moving enemy torpedo bombers.

See "Address of the Commander-in-Chief, Mediterranean Station, 21st June 1930," folder CHT/2/1, Chatfield Papers.

10. Preston, *Aircraft Carriers*, 31; Cunningham, *Sailor's Odyssey*, 115.

11. For a devastating critique of British naval air policy in the early interwar period, see David Hamer, *Bombers versus Battleships: The Struggle between Ships and Aircraft for the Control of the Surface of the Sea*, 28–35. Preston (*Aircraft Carriers*, 54, 58–59) provides a coherent chronology.

12. Pratt, *Sea Power and Today's War*, 11.

13. Between 1919 and 1928 Britain's service chiefs were repeatedly informed by the highest cabinet officials, including, on occasion, the prime minister, that "they need not anticipate a major war within the next ten years." This "ten year rule" that, of course, crippled both military replenishment and expansion and strategic planning was at last revoked in 1932. A. J. P. Taylor, *English History, 1914–1945*, 228, 364.

14. The best account of the ongoing crisis on Britain's mess decks after the Great War is Anthony Carew, *The Lower Deck of the Royal Navy, 1900–39: The Invergordon Mutiny in Perspective*, 88–138. A less sympathetic contemporary study that emphasizes the ostensible communist leanings of the agitators and the basic loyalty of the British seaman to class and country is Kenneth Evans, *The Mutiny at Invergordon*, passim but see esp. 416–19.

15. Carew, *Lower Deck of the Royal Navy*, 116, 119.

16. Ibid., 128–29.

17. ibid., 124.

18. Ibid., 140–41.

19. Andrew Gordon, *The Rules of the Game: Jutland and British Naval Command*, 38, contains some biographical material. More may be found in the introduction to the Chatfield Papers and at various points within the papers.

20. Chatfield to the first sea lord from flagship *Queen Elizabeth* at Corfu, October 28, 1930, folder CHT/2/1, Chatfield Papers.

21. The best accounts of Invergordon are Carew, *Lower Deck of the Royal Navy*, 153–86 (quotes on p. 159); Evans, *The Mutiny at Invergordon*, passim; Roskill, *Naval Policy*, 2:95–132; and Len Wincott, *Invergordon Mutineer*, 85–151. A contemporary chronology of the crisis is in "The Board of Admiralty and the Mutiny in the Atlantic Fleet at Invergordon in September 1931," folder CHT/2/2, Chatfield Papers.

22. Roskill, *Naval Policy*, 2:97. A minor discrepancy exists with respect to dates. Roskill states that the supplementary Admiralty letter on the pay cuts was issued on September 10, but the Admiralty Chronology in the Chatfield Papers (folder CHT/2/2) notes that while the lord commissioners of the Admiralty directed on September 7 that a general announcement of impending pay cuts be released, the announcement was not actually made until September 13; thus, the supplementary letter would have had to have been issued sometime after the latter date, though it may well have been drafted earlier.

23. Wincott, *Invergordon Mutineer,* 85.

24. Cunningham, *Sailor's Odyssey,* 150–51.

25. Carew, *Lower Deck of the Royal Navy,* 161.

26. Wincott, *Invergordon Mutineer,* 150.

27. Carew, *Lower Deck of the Royal Navy,* 168, 170; Cunningham, *Sailor's Odyssey,* 151.

28. Lady Astor's complaint was forwarded by then first sea lord Chatfield to Sir Eric J. A. Fullerton, commander in chief of the Plymouth Station, in several letters in 1934. The flap was obviously not taken too seriously by the lords of the Admiralty since Fullerton continued to hold command until 1936. The letters are in folder FTN/4, Eric J. A. Fullerton Papers, National Maritime Museum, Greenwich, England. The modest improvement in seamen's leave and allotments is summarized in a memorandum of March 8, 1938, titled "1933–1938: Summary of Principal Developments Affecting Welfare and Conditions of Service of Ratings," folder CHT/3/1, Chatfield Papers.

29. Carew, *Lower Deck of the Royal Navy,* 184–85 (quotes); Evans, *The Mutiny at Invergordon,* 419.

30. "Address to the Mediterranean Fleet Issued from the [H.M.S.] *Queen Elizabeth* at Suda Bay on 21st October 1931," folder CHT/2/2, Chatfield Papers.

31. Chatfield to "DCNS" (penciled notation at head of document), from Admiralty House, Valetta, Malta, November 13, 1931, ibid.

32. Ibid.; "Mediterranean Letter no. 80/01101, January 14, 1932, to the Secretary of the Admiralty Responding to Admiralty Ltr n. 4144/31 of 30 November 1931," ibid.; Admiral Sir Edward R. G. R. Evans to Chatfield, October 10, 1937, and Chatfield's reply of October 13, 1937, ibid.

33. Fisher to "C-in-C Med," January 17, 1932, folder FHR/14/1, Fisher Papers. Fisher's various schemes for improving life and discipline within the Mediterranean Fleet once he succeeded Chatfield as commander in chief may be found in folders FHR/14/2 and FHR/15, ibid.

34. Admiral Sir John Kelly to F. L. Field, May 16, 1932, from Invergordon, folder CHT/4/6, Chatfield Papers.

35. Pound to Chatfield, August 7, 1937, folder CHT/4/10, ibid.

36. N. H. Gibbs, *Rearmament Policy,* 94.

37. G. A. H. Gordon, "The Admiralty and Appeasement," 44.

38. Chatfield to Fisher, June 4, 1934, folder CHT/3/1, Chatfield Papers.

39. Herwig, "Failure of German Sea Power," 88.

40. Germany's response to the British proposal for a new naval conference is in "Memorandum by the Office of the Chief of the German Naval Command, 31 October 1934," in *Documents on German Foreign Policy, 1918–1945,* 3:554–55. See also N. H. Gibbs, *Rearmament Policy,* 155, 325.

41. Unsigned memorandum, November 27, 1934, *Documents on German Foreign Policy,* 3:680–81; Holweg, "The Failure of German Sea Power," 89.

42. A. Taylor, *English History, 1914–1945*, 375–76; Winston S. Churchill, *The Second World War*, 1:117–19; Shirer, *Rise and Fall*, 283–88; Martin Gilbert, introduction to *The "Illustrated London News": Marching to War, 1933–1939*, 76.

43. Ambassador at London to the Foreign Ministry, March 19, 1935, *Documents on German Foreign Policy*, 3:1018–19.

44. Frederick T. Birchall, *The Storm Breaks: A Panorama of Europe and the Forces That Have Wrecked Its Peace*, 217.

45. Note by an officer of the naval command, March 27, 1935, *Documents on German Foreign Policy*, 3:1045. Hitler may have been a bit more ambiguous on this point than the German record would indicate. According to the official United Kingdom military history of the period, Hitler stated flatly that he wanted to avoid "an unlimited naval armaments race as had been the case before the war. Germany did not think it politically desirable nor had she the necessary financial resources for such a race" (N. H. Gibbs, *Rearmament Policy*, 158).

46. G. Gordon, "The Admiralty and Appeasement," 46.

47. Churchill, *The Second World War*, 1:119.

48. The first two quotes are from Shirer, *Rise and Fall*, 288; the final three quotes are from N. H. Gibbs, *Rearmament Policy*, 160. See also "Warships: Reich Demands Navy That Could Wipe Out Whole British Fleet."

49. Shirer, *Rise and Fall*, 289; this portion of the agreement is quoted in N. H. Gibbs, *Rearmament Policy*, 163.

50. Werner Rahn, "German Naval Strategy and Armament," in *Technology and Naval Combat*, edited by O'Brien, 119.

51. Quotes in Erich Raeder, *My Life*, 187.

52. Holweg, "Failure of German Sea Power," 90; Charles S. Thomas, *The German Navy in the Nazi Era*, 99.

53. C. Thomas, *German Navy*, 99–100.

54. Churchill, *The Second World War*, 1:124; Shirer, *Rise and Fall*, 289.

55. "Warships," 12–13.

56. G. M. Gilbert, *Nuremberg Diary*, 309.

57. The most recent and probably best account of the Abyssinian conflict is James Dugan and Laurence LaFore, *Days of Emperor and Clown: The Italo-Ethiopian War, 1935–1936*.

58. A distance of 8,957 miles by sea.

59. Ignatius Phayre, "Italy's Military Problems in Abyssinia," 270; Pratt, *Sea Power and Today's War*, 65.

60. Pratt, *Sea Power and Today's War*, 63, 66–67.

61. Philip Ziegler, *Mountbatten: A Biography*, 90.

62. Cunningham, *Sailor's Odyssey*, 162–73.

63. N. H. Gibbs, *Rearmament Policy*, 192–94, 213n; Reynolds M. Salerno, *Vital Crossroads: Mediterranean Origins of the Second World War, 1935–1940*, 10–14.

64. Cunningham, *Sailor's Odyssey,* 173–74.

65. Pratt, *Sea Power and Today's War,* 63; Cunningham, *Sailor's Odyssey,* 174–75.

66. Pratt (*Sea Power and Today's War,* 63) recounts the Italian admirals' fears; Brian R. Sullivan ("A Fleet in Being: The Rise and Fall of Italian Sea Power, 1861–1943," 117) records Mussolini's dismissive reply. The American journalist is quoted in Peter Padfield, *The Battleship Era,* 260.

67. Roskill, *Naval Policy,* 2:248.

68. Ibid., 253; Cunningham, *Sailor's Odyssey,* 175–76.

69. Roskill, *Naval Policy,* 2:255, 258–59.

70. Preston, *Aircraft Carriers,* 60. Following annual maneuvers in the early summer of 1935, the Admiralty concluded (as had the United States Navy somewhat earlier) that "it is the exception rather than the rule for fighters to succeed in interfering with [attacking] aircraft in Fleet exercises" (Hamer, *Bombers versus Battleships,* 33).

71. Quoted in Roskill, *Naval Policy,* 2:261.

72. Raymond J. Sontag, one of the most distinguished historians writing about the time, believes that Foreign Minister Laval probably gave Mussolini "tacit approval" to invade Abyssinia as early as January 1935 during a personal interview with the duce in Rome, well before Stresa (March) and the June naval agreement (*A Broken World, 1919–1939,* 287).

73. Roskill, *Naval Policy,* 2:262–63, 267; Ziegler, *Mountbatten: A Biography,* 90–91; N. H. Gibbs, *Rearmament Policy,* 207, 221.

74. Cunningham, *Sailor's Odyssey,* 174.

75. Charles Petrie, "Foreign Affairs," 737–39; P. Gibbs, *Across the Frontiers,* 140–43.

76. G. Gordon, "The Admiralty and Appeasement," 44–47.

77. Correlli Barnett, *Engage the Enemy More Closely: The Royal Navy in the Second World War,* 34.

78. "Notes by the First Sea Lord on Sir Robert Vansittart's Memorandum on the World Situation and Re-armament, and on the Comments Thereon by Sir Maurice Hankey Jan 5, 1937 Ernle Chatfield First Sea Lord," folder CHT/3/1, Chatfield Papers.

79. N. H. Gibbs, *Rearmament Policy,* 336–37; Gordon, "The Admiralty and Appeasement," 46; Barnett, *Engage the Enemy More Closely,* 37.

80. "Notes by the First Sea Lord," folder CHT/3/1, Chatfield Papers. Chatfield's condemnation of the League and British League policies had been prefigured in a memorandum he had written as chief of the naval staff just three weeks before. See "Memorandum by Chief of Naval Staff on League of Nations Reform, 11 Dec 1936," ibid.

81. Nathan Miller, *War at Sea: A Naval History of World War II,* 23. Churchill recalled his concern over the *KGV*s in *The Second World War,* 1:145–46. The structural weakness of the British battleships is mentioned in Russell Spurr, *A Glorious Way to Die: The Kamikaze Mission of the Battleship* Yamato, *April 1945,* 26, 273.

82. Barnett, *Engage the Enemy More Closely,* 45–46.

83. Ibid., 47–48.

84. Ibid., 48; Donald McLachlan, *Room 39: A Study in Naval Intelligence,* 12–13, 20–21. The quote is from Ronald Lewin, *Ultra Goes to War: The First Account of World War II's Greatest Secret Based on Official Documents,* 226.

85. W. S. Brancker, "Air Power and Sea Power," in *Brassey's Naval and Shipping Annual, 1921–2,* edited by Alexander Richardson and Archibald Hurd, 103–18 (quote on p. 118); William Mitchell, *Winged Defense: The Development and Possibilities of Modern Air Power—Economic and Military,* 125–26.

86. Documents bearing on the Fleet Air Arm while under RAF control and events leading to the formation of the Inskip Committee and its recommendations, including a detailed chronology, are in folder CHT/3/6, Chatfield Papers.

87. The talking points are in ibid. Chatfield to Churchill, May 5, 1936, commenting on the miserable state of the Fleet Air Arm, is in folder CHT/4/3, ibid.

88. Keyes's letters to Chatfield are in folder CHT/4/7, ibid.

89. The following discussion of British naval aviation and the Royal Navy's aircraft carrier force is based on Friedman, *U.S. Aircraft Carriers,* 129–30; Hamer, *Bombers versus Battleships,* 31–32; Hezlet, *Aircraft and Sea Power,* 126, 129, 136; and Preston, *Aircraft Carriers,* 54–61.

90. Gerald E. Miller, "Korea—the Carrier War," in *Into the Jet Age: Conflict and Change in Naval Aviation, 1945–1975,* edited by E. T. Wooldridge, 163.

91. Hamer, *Bombers versus Battleships,* 55.

92. Salerno, *Vital Crossroads,* 24–29, 114–11; N. H. Gibbs, *Rearmament Policy,* 391–92; B. Sullivan, "Fleet in Being," 119.

93. Pelz (*Race to Pearl Harbor,* 114–64) provides a good overview of the events leading up to and including the 1935–1936 London Conference. The quotes are on pp. 141, 164.

94. N. H. Gibbs, *Rearmament Policy,* 326–31 (quote on p. 328); Greg Kennedy, *Anglo-American Strategic Relations and the Far East, 1933–1939: Imperial Crossroads,* 30–35.

95. Chatfield to Pound, December 30, 1937, folder CHT/4/10, Chatfield Papers.

Chapter 4. Preparing for Armageddon: Germany

1. Walter Ansel, *Hitler and the Middle Sea,* 1.

2. Raeder, *My Life,* 187, 193; Martienssen, *Hitler and His Admirals,* 2–3. At the dock at Nuremberg, Raeder justified the violent seizures of Czechoslovakia and Poland in 1939 "as simply security measures" (G. Gilbert, *Nuremberg Diary,* 307).

3. Frank Clements, "Germany's Naval Aims," 277, 284.

4. Cajus Bekker, *Hitler's Naval War,* 146; Lewin, *Ultra Goes to War,* 8–10, 226; David Kahn, *Seizing the Enigma: The Race to Break the German U-boat Codes, 1939–1943,* 43.

5. Herwig, "Failure of German Sea Power," 88.

6. F. O. Ruge, "The New German Navy," in *Brassey's Naval Annual, 1937,* edited by H. G. Thursfield, 85.

7. Herwig, "Failure of German Sea Power," 91.

8. Clements, "Germany's Naval Aims," 278–79.

9. Raeder, *My Life,* 142–43.

10. William L. Shirer, *Berlin Diary: The Journal of a Foreign Correspondent, 1934–1941,* 267, 269. An illuminating study of the Nazi social revolution that produced the kind of atmosphere that Shirer found in the new Germany navy is David Schoenbaum, *Hitler's Social Revolution: Class and Status in Nazi Germany, 1933–1939.*

11. Davidson, *Trial of the Germans,* 372.

12. Von der Porten, *German Navy,* 9; Richard Grunberger, *The 12 Year Reich: A Social History of Nazi Germany,* 11–12.

13. Peter Padfield, "Grand Admiral Karl Dönitz," in *Men of War: Great Naval Leaders of World War II,* edited by Stephen Howarth, 179, 201; Davidson, *Trial of the Germans,* 371, 379.

14. Karl Dönitz, *Memoirs: Ten Years and Twenty Days,* 5.

15. P. Gibbs, *Across the Frontiers,* 199.

16. Ibid., 89, 91.

17. C. Thomas, *German Navy,* 160–61.

18. The following discussion of the makeup and training of the German officer corps and enlisted ranks is from Ruge, "The New German Navy," in *Brassey's Naval Annual, 1937,* edited by Thursfield, 91–94. Rust (*Crew 34,* 92–155) provides a detailed description of the background and training of the professional officer corps, which had not changed materially since Tirpitz's time.

19. Davidson, *Trial of the Germans,* 415. See also Andy Aitkin, series director, *Battlefield: The Battle of the Atlantic;* and van der Vat, *Atlantic Campaign,* 87.

20. G. Gilbert, *Nuremberg Diary,* 309; Brennecke, *Hunters and Hunted,* 11–12.

21. Wilhelm Deist, *The Wehrmacht and German Rearmament,* 73–78.

22. Carl-Axel Gemzell, *Organization, Conflict, and Innovation: A Study of German Naval Strategic Planning, 1888–1940,* 305–6.

23. Raeder, *My Life,* 193.

24. "Rivalry on the Seas," 17–18.

25. Wolfgang Frank, *The Sea Wolves,* 23.

26. Martienssen, *Hitler and His Admirals,* 10; von der Porten, *German Navy,* 3.

27. H. T. Lenton, *German Warships of the Second World War,* 22–23; von der Porten, *German Navy in World War II,* 20; Theodore Roscoe, *Tin Cans: The True Story of the Fighting Destroyers of World War II,* 10. This is a slight abridgement of Roscoe, *United States Destroyer Operations in World War II* (Annapolis: United States Naval Institute, 1953).

28. Herwig, "Failure of German Sea Power," 94.

29. Von der Porten, *German Navy,* 11–13; Lenton, *German Warships,* 21; Preston, *Aircraft Carriers,* 62–64.

30. Von der Porten, *German Navy*, 22; Cunningham, *Sailor's Odyssey*, 197–98.

31. Deist, *Wehrmacht and German Rearmament*, 79, 83; von der Porten, *German Navy*, 23; Lenton, *German Warships*, 19–25.

32. Deist, *Wehrmacht and German Rearmament*, 83–84.

33. Herwig, "Failure of German Sea Power," 93–94.

34. The quotes are all in Keith W. Bird, "Grand Admiral Erich Raeder," in *Men of War*, edited by Howarth, 43; Herwig, "Failure of German Sea Power," 95.

35. B. Sullivan, "Fleet in Being," 120.

36. Ibid.

37. See Paul G. Halpern, *A Naval History of World War I*, 151, 152, 166, 178, 394.

38. R. de Courten, "Italy's Naval Policy," in *Brassey's Naval and Shipping Annual, 1930*, edited by Charles N. Robinson and H. M. Ross, 89–97.

39. Cunningham, *Sailor's Odyssey*, 162–63.

40. David Miller and Chris Miller, *Modern Naval Combat*, 102.

41. David A. Thomas, *Crete 1941: The Battle at Sea*, 28–29.

Chapter 5. Preparing for Armageddon: Japan

1. Tokumyo Matsumoto, "'The Yellow Man's Burden,' Translated from the *Europaische Revue*, German National-Socialist (Non-party Monthly)," republished in *Living Age* (December 1935): 297–300.

2. Iruka Mikami, "Naval Policy Alone Can Bring Peace to All Sections of the World," *Nippon Hyoron*, February 1936, copy in "Commonplace Book, Vol. VI," folder RIC/2/1, Richmond Papers; Tadao Yanahara, "'Japan Looks South,' Translated from the *Kaito, Tokyo Topical Monthly*," reprinted in *Living Age* (August 1936): 491–93; Yonai quote in Ito and Pineau, *End of the Japanese Navy*, 11.

3. Pelz, *Race to Pearl Harbor*, 33–34; Spurr, *Glorious Way to Die*, 24; Yoshida Matsuru, *Requiem for Battleship* Yamato, xv; "apotheosis" is from Mark R. Peattie, "Japanese Naval Construction, 1919–1941," in *Technology and Naval Combat*, edited by O'Brien, 100.

4. Ito and Pineau, *End of the Japanese Navy*, 12; Spurr, *Glorious Way to Die*, 33; Evans and Peattie, "Ill Winds Blow," *NIP*, 103:10 (October 1997): 70–73. The "superhuman efforts" of Japanese naval architects are emphasized in Kitaro Matsumoto, *Design and Construction of the Battleships* Yamato *and* Musashi, 337.

5. The most authoritative discussion of the development of the two superbattleships is Matsumoto, *Design and Construction*, 337–50. Matsumoto states their light displacement as 69,100 tons (337). Apparently, no precise, agreed-upon figure exists.

6. Spurr, *Glorious Way to Die*, 25.

7. Preston, *Battleships*, 157.

8. Spurr, *Glorious Way to Die*, 43. The quote concerning *Yamato*'s comparative comfort is from Matsumoto, *Design and Construction*, 350. See also Akira Yoshimura, *Battleship* Musashi: *The Making and Sinking of the World's Greatest Battleship*, 125.

9. Masatake Okumiya, Jiro Horikoshi, and Martin Caidin, *Zero!* 14; Evans and Peattie, *Kaigun,* 308–14.

10. Evans and Peattie, *Kaigun,* 312–13; Saburo Sakai, Martin Caidin, and Fred Saito, *Samurai!* 18.

11. Peattie, *Sunburst,* 131.

12. Sakai, Saito, and Caiden, *Samurai!* 11–14. Peattie, a thorough researcher, quotes Sakai's figures in *Sunburst* (131). See also Agawa, *Reluctant Admiral,* 79.

13. Agawa, *Reluctant Admiral,* 79; Okumiya, Horikoshi, and Caidin, *Zero!* 13; Sakai, Caidin, and Saito, *Samurai!* 19–21. See also Peattie who minimizes as a long-term problem "the careless, daredevil elitism of the best of Japan's prospective naval aviators" (*Sunburst,* 32–33). Peattie also offers a detailed discussion of the growth of various skills and capabilities within the Japanese naval-aviation community in the decade after 1925 (33–50).

14. Hector C. Bywater, *The Great Pacific War: A Historic Prophecy Now Being Fulfilled,* 45; Turner is quoted in George Carroll Dyer, *The Amphibians Came to Conquer: The Story of Admiral Richmond Kelly Turner,* 1:203.

15. Hans G. Von Lehmann, "Japanese Landing Operations in World War II," translated by Michael C. Halbig, in *Assault from the Sea: Essays on the History of Amphibious Warfare,* edited by Merrill L. Bartlett, 195–201 (quotes on p. 199).

16. The quote is from Okumiya, Horikoshi, and Caidin, *Zero!* 12. The most recent and detailed account of Japan's naval air war in China between 1937 and 1941 is Peattie, *Sunburst,* 102–28.

17. Okumiya, Horikoshi, and Caidin, *Zero!* 13; James H. Belote and William M. Belote, *Titans of the Seas: The Development and Operations of the Japanese and American Carrier Task Forces during World War II,* 21.

18. Belote and Belote, *Titans of the Seas,* 21; Okumiya, Horikoshi, and Caidin, *Zero,* 12; Reynolds, *The Carrier War,* 40.

19. Okumiya, Horikoshi, and Caidin, *Zero* 18; Belote and Belote, *Titans of the Seas,* 23–24.

20. Okumiya, Horikoshi, and Caidin, *Zero!* 15.

21. Fuchida and Okumiya, *Midway,* 217; Evans and Peattie, *Kaigun,* 314–19.

22. Preston, *Aircraft Carriers,* 46, 50–52. Japanese naval authority Mark Peattie rates both the reconstructed *Akagi* and *Kaga* as capable of carrying a ninety-one-plane air group (*Sunburst,* 228–33). *Hiryu* and *Soryu* he rates at seventy-three and sixty-eight aircraft, respectively (237–41).

23. Preston, *Aircraft Carriers,* 52. Peattie pronounced *Shokaku* and *Zuikaku* the finest fleet carriers in the world prior to the appearance of the American *Essex* class in 1943 (*Sunburst,* 61).

24. Reynolds, *The Carrier War,* 39.

25. Evans and Peattie, *Kaigun,* 347, 349 ("box formation" quote on p. 347); Peattie, *Sunburst,* 73–75, 146–53 (quotes on pp. 75, 152).

26. Friedman, *U.S. Aircraft Carriers*, 130–31.

27. Willmott, *Empires in the Balance*, 89.

28. Evans and Peattie, *Kaigun*, 402–5.

29. W. D. Puleston, *The Influence of Sea Power in World War II*, 26.

30. Tolley, *Yangtze Patrol*, 199–286.

31. Quoted in Mark J. Gayn, *The Fight for the Pacific*, 119.

32. W. D. Puleston, *The Armed Forces of the Pacific: A Comparison of the Military and Naval Power of the United States and Japan*, 19–20. One example of the renewed fictional interest in a Pacific war in the late thirties is Gregory Bienstock, *The Struggle for the Pacific*, 242–69.

Chapter 6. American Revolution

1. The following discussion is based on Thomas Wildenberg, *Grey Steel and Black Oil: Fast Tankers and Replenishment at Sea in the U.S. Navy, 1912–1992*, 4–135.

2. Clark G. Reynolds, *The Carrier War*, 44.

3. Edward P. Stafford, *The Big E: The Story of the U.S.S.* Enterprise, 43–44.

4. Dyer, *Amphibians Came to Conquer*, 1:202–3, 21, 213, 214; U.S. Navy Bureau of Navigation, *Landing Force Manual: United States Navy, 1927*, iii.

5. The following discussion is based on Jeter A. Isely and Philip A. Crowl, *The U.S. Marines and Amphibious War: Its Theory and Its Practice in the Pacific*, 3–35; Allen R. Millet, *Semper Fidelis: The History of the United States Marine Corps*, 319–43; E. W. Broadbent, "The Fleet and the Marines," *NIP* 57:3 (March 1931): 369–72; Robert D. Heinl, "The U.S. Marine Corps: Author of Modern Amphibious Warfare," *NIP* 73:4 (November 1977): 1310–23; and Ballendorf and Bartlett, *Pete Ellis*, 18–19, 21–27.

6. Ballendorf and Bartlett, *Pete Ellis*, 58–59.

7. Ibid., 115–18.

8. Isely and Crowl, *U.S. Marines and Amphibious War*, 5; Millet, *Semper Fidelis*, 321.

9. Ballendorf and Bartlett, *Pete Ellis*, 118–22; Isely and Crowl, *U.S. Marines and Amphibious War*, 25.

10. The army studies are assessed and quoted in R. Frank, *Downfall*, 21–22.

11. Isely and Crowl, *U.S. Marines and Amphibious War*, 27.

12. Merrill L. Bartlett, "Ben Hebard Fuller and the Genesis of a Modern United States Marine Corps, 1891–1934," 85.

13. Isely and Crowl, *U.S. Marines and Amphibious War*, 33, 34, 37–44; Millet, *Semper Fidelis*, 331.

14. The following paragraphs on the development of Marine Corps aviation in the twenties and thirties is based on a memorandum titled "The Role of Aviation on the Marine Corps Team," dated April 22, 1948 (quotes on p. 2). The document was apparently prepared by Henry M. Dater of the Aviation History Unit (OP-05) of the Department of the Navy as one of a series of papers requested by Assistant Secretary of the

Navy for Air John Sullivan as part of the ongoing battle with the U.S. Air Force over postwar roles and missions. A copy is in box 10, folder "Aircraft Carriers," John Sullivan Papers, Harry S. Truman Library, Independence, Missouri.

15. Ibid., 2–3.

16. Ibid., 3; Isely and Crowl, *U.S. Marines and Amphibious War,* 33. MacArthur's comment to Truman is in "Substance of Statements Made at Wake Island Conference on 15 October 1950 Compiled by General of the Army Omar N. Bradley, Chairman of the Joint Chiefs of Staff, from Notes Kept by the Conferees from Washington," copy in Chairman's File, General Bradley, 1949–1953, box 2, folder "Wake Island," Record Group 218: Records of the Joint Chiefs of Staff, Military History Branch, National Archives, Washington, D.C. For a contrasting view in which the air force emphasized its effectiveness in close air support during the Korean War, see Conrad C. Crane, *American Air Power Strategy in Korea, 1950–1953,* 61–62.

17. Lynn Montross, *War through the Ages,* 782–83.

18. Bywater, *Great Pacific War,* 295–96.

19. The following discussion of U.S. naval aviation in the years 1918–1921 is based on Hone and Mandeles, "Interwar Innovation," 71–75; and Thomas Wildenberg, "In Support of the Battle Line: Gunnery's Influence on the Development of Carrier Aviation in the U.S. Navy."

20. Melhorn, *Two-Block Fox,* 9.

21. Chief of Naval Operations William S. Benson did not share the belief that aircraft were useful for fleet defense. He continued to argue that their only effective roles were reconnaissance and spotting the fall of shot during a battle. See Paolo E. Coletta, *Admiral Bradley A. Fiske and the American Navy,* 183.

22. Friedman, *U.S. Aircraft Carriers,* 11, 13, 33; Logan C. Ramsey, "Bombing versus Torpedo Planes, *NIP* 57:11 (November 1931): 1509–15.

23. Roy A. Grossnick et al., *United States Naval Aviation, 1910–1995,* 39.

24. Melhorn, *Two-Block Fox,* 3.

25. William Nelson, "Airships—or Not? *NIP* 59:9 (September 1933): 1327–28; Michael M. Mooney, *The Hindenburg,* 24–25, 39–40. See also Theodore Roscoe, *On the Seas and in the Skies: A History of the U.S. Navy's Air Power,* 175–204.

26. Mooney, *The Hindenburg,* 60–61.

27. Ibid., 62; Mark Sullivan, *Our Times: The United States, 1900–1925,* 6:620.

28. Mooney, *The Hindenburg,* 63–64; Guy Hartcup, *The Achievement of the Airship: A History of the Development of Rigid, Semi-rigid, and Non-rigid Airships,* 243.

29. Byrd's North Pole flight in particular came after a prolonged period of attempts at Arctic flight by dirigible. Admiral William Moffett, the U.S. Navy's first director of aviation, never lost his enthusiasm for the rigid airship until his death in 1933 aboard the dirigible *Akron.* Moffett eagerly pushed an Arctic dirigible flight as a means of testing and further expanding the technology. See John H. Bryant and Harold N. Cones, *Dangerous Crossings: The First Modern Polar Expedition, 1925,* 32–34, 189; Raimond E.

Goerler, *To the Pole: The Diary and Notebook of Richard E. Byrd, 1925–1927,* 18–20; and folders 4125, 4235, Admiral Richard E. Byrd Papers (RG 56.1), Ohio State University Archives and Polar Oral History Project.

30. Mooney, *The Hindenburg,* 64; Roscoe, *On the Seas,* 199–200; Hartcup, *Achievement of the Airship,* 216, 220–23.

31. Coletta, *Fiske and the American Navy,* 183–89; Roscoe, *On the Seas,* 33.

32. Melhorn, *Two-Block Fox,* 88.

33. Ibid., 89. See also Friedman, *U.S. Cruisers,* 168.

34. William F. Trimble, *Admiral William A. Moffett: Architect of Naval Aviation,* 171, 255.

35. Ibid., 89.

36. Melhorn, *Two-Block Fox,* 110–11; Friedman, *U.S. Aircraft Carriers,* 11.

37. Logan C. Ramsey, "Aircraft and the Naval Engagement," *NIP* 56:8 (August 1930): 679–87.

38. Melhorn, *Two-Block Fox,* 113–14; Preston, *Aircraft Carriers,* 38; Clark G. Reynolds, *The Carrier War,* 35–36; Alan Schom, *The Eagle and the Rising Sun: The Japanese-American War, 1941–1943, Pearl Harbor through Guadalcanal,* 35.

39. Preston, *Aircraft Carriers,* 38, 40; Hone and Mandeles, "Interwar Innovation," 78–79; Jan M. van Tol, "Military Innovation and Carrier Aviation: An Analysis."

40. David W. Kendall, "American Sea Power—1941 and Beyond," *NIP* 67:4 (April 1941): 474; Brent L. Gravatt, "On the Back of the Fleet," 18.

Chapter 7. Contours of Conflict

1. Duncan S. Ballantine, *U.S. Naval Logistics in the Second World War,* 3, 7.

2. Philip Pugh, "Military Need and Civil Necessity," in *The Battle of the Atlantic, 1939–1945: The 50th Anniversary International Naval Conference,* edited by Stephen Howarth and Derek Law, 32.

3. Atle Thowsen, "The Norwegian Merchant Navy in Allied War Transport," in ibid., 63.

4. Gary E. Weir, "A Truly Allied Undertaking," in ibid., 103.

5. Ibid., 103–12.

6. Dönitz's conception of German naval strategy is well summarized in Werner Rahn, "The Campaign: The German Perspective," in ibid., 538–40.

7. Hamer, *Bombers versus Battleships,* 366n6.

8. Chester W. Nimitz, "Your Navy as Peace Insurance," 705.

9. Francis Brown, *The War in Maps: An Atlas of "New York Times" Maps,* v.

10. Hans-Joachim Krug et al., *Reluctant Allies: German-Japanese Naval Relations in World War II,* 9–10, 133.

11. Peter Kemp, "Admiral of the Fleet Sir Dudley Pound," in *Men of War,* edited by Howarth, 26–27, 37–41.

12. Keith W. Bird, "Grand Admiral Erich Raeder," in ibid., 45–46.

13. Robert William Love Jr., "Fleet Admiral Ernest J. King," in ibid., 80–81.

14. Ikuhiko Hata, "Admiral Yamamoto's Surprise Attack and the Japanese Navy's War Strategy," in *From Pearl Harbor to Hiroshima: The Second World War in Asia and the Pacific, 1941–1945,* edited by Saki Dockrill, 69.

Chapter 8. The Axis: Lost Victories

1. "Churchill: War Cabinet Paper, 3 November 1939," in *The Churchill War Papers,* edited by Martin Gilbert, 326; Churchill to Pound quoted in Stephen Roskill, *Churchill and the Admirals,* 95; prime minister to first lord and first sea lord, August 4, 1940, in Churchill, *The Second World War,* 2:511.

2. The statistics are from John Keegan, ed., *The "Times" Atlas of the Second World War,* 48.

3. Raeder, *My Life,* 73; Bekker, *Hitler's Naval War,* 141, 143–45.

4. Ansel, *Hitler and the Middle Sea,* 484 (Hitler quote); Walter Warlimont, *Inside Hitler's Headquarters, 1939–45,* 60; Lewin, *Ultra Goes to War,* 226; McLachlan, *Room 39,* 83; John Hamilton, *War at Sea, 1939–1945,* 52.

5. Unless otherwise noted, the following discussion of German naval operations between September 1939 and the spring of 1941 are based on Barnett, *Engage the Enemy More Closely,* 57–139, 251–77; Bekker, *Hitler's Naval War,* 17–95; Churchill, *The Second World War,* 1:376–92, 435–73, 523–87, 2:342–56, 505–17; Dönitz, *Memoirs,* 64–65, 90–99; Hamilton, *War at Sea,* 16–37, 41–59; Macintyre, *Naval War against Hitler,* 11–109; Raeder, *My Life,* 349–50; Friedrich Ruge, *Der Seekrieg: The German Navy's Story, 1939–1945,* 49–183; Frank Uhlig Jr., *How Navies Fight: The U.S. Navy and Its Allies,* 101–12; van der Vat, *Atlantic Campaign,* 85–194; and von der Porten, *German Navy,* 39–93, 123–83.

6. Becker, *Hitler's Naval War,* 44–50.

7. The cruise and destruction of *Graf Spee* are well recounted in Dudley Pope, *Graf Spee,* and Landsborough, *Battle of the River Plate.* See also Bernd Stegemann, "The First Phase of the War at Sea up to the Spring of 1940," in *Germany and the Second World War,* by Research Institute for Military History, 2:166–67.

8. Hamilton, *War at Sea,* 34–37; von der Porten, *German Navy,* 123–38, 255; Ruge, *Der Seekrieg,* 174–83.

9. Hamilton, *War at Sea,* 34–37; Krancke and Brennecke, *Pocket Battleship;* Bekker, *Hitler's Naval War,* 37–52, 104, 207–15.

10. Macintyre, *Naval War against Hitler,* 83–85.

11. Keegan, *"Times" Atlas,* 48.

12. Peter C. Smith, *The Great Ships Pass: British Battleships at War, 1939–45,* 98.

13. Barnett, *Engage the Enemy More Closely,* 91–92; Dönitz, *Memoirs,* 64–65, 92; P. Smith, *Great Ships Pass,* 98.

14. Historian John Lukacs has recently written that at the outbreak of war, or very soon after, the British and French governments had "allowed themselves to be convinced

by experts to the effect that Hitler's Germany was desperately dependent on Swedish iron-ore imports; and that, especially for several months in the winter, that iron ore could not be shipped to Germany except southward along the coast of Norway. The economic experts were woefully wrong, as usual" (*The Duel: Hitler vs. Churchill: 10 May–31 July 1940*, 30).

15. Raeder, *My Life*, 302–3.

16. Ibid., 306–7; Warlimont, *Inside Hitler's Headquarters*, 67.

17. Warlimont, *Inside Hitler's Headquarters*, 67.

18. The most thorough and imaginative account of the Norwegian campaign is J. L. Moulton, *A Study of Warfare in Three Dimensions: The Norwegian Campaign of 1940*. See also Barnett, *Engage the Enemy More Closely*, 97–139; Bekker, *Hitler's Naval War*, 96–166; Donald Macintyre, *Narvik* and *Naval War against Hitler*, 17–40; Raeder, *My Life*, 300–311; Roskill, *Churchill and the Admirals*, 99–109; and von der Porten, *German Navy*, 63–80; Hamer, *Bombers versus Battleships*, 54–66; and Hezlet, *Aircraft and Sea Power*, 145–53, contain sketchy accounts of the Royal Navy's frustrating efforts to support the campaign in the face of superior German land-based airpower.

19. Barnett, *Engage the Enemy More Closely*, 93; Andrews, *Air Marshals*, 68.

20. "Lord Camrose: Note of Conversation with Oliver Stanley, 21 March 1940," in *The Churchill War Papers*, edited by M. Gilbert, 908; Roskill, *Churchill and the Admirals*, 95.

21. Roskill, *Churchill and the Admirals*, 101–2, 105; Andrews, *Air Marshals*, 71; Barnett, *Engage the Enemy More Closely*, 122.

22. D. Thomas, *Crete 1941*, i.

23. Montross, *War through the Ages*, 494.

24. Milton Shulman, *Defeat in the West*, 73–79.

25. Ibid., 79.

26. Ibid., 76–77.

27. Hezlet, *Aircraft and Sea Power*, 154–55.

28. John B. Hattendorf, ed., *On His Majesty's Service: Observations of the British Home Fleet from the Diary, Reports, and Letters of Joseph H. Wellings, Assistant U.S. Naval Attaché, London, 1940–41*, 78–85.

29. Lukacs has not argued such a possibility, but his detailed examination of these rather murky days in late May–early June 1940 suggests its plausibility (*Duel*, 89–91).

30. Hanson W. Baldwin, *Battles Lost and Won: Great Campaigns of World War II*, 82.

31. Howard W. French, "History of Japanese Raid on Oahu Rewritten," *New York Times*, republished in *Honolulu Star-Bulletin*, December 9, 1999.

32. Victor Davis Hanson has suggested that Nagumo's flyers could have ravaged the West Coast as well in the days immediately after Pearl Harbor (*Carnage and Culture: Landmark Battles in the Rise of Western Culture*, 364–65). This is not true. The Americans possessed the aircraft, and after December 7 the vigilance, to have dealt the Japanese a stinging if not fatal defeat.

33. Evans and Peattie, *Kaigun*, 488.

34. Puleston, *Influence of Sea Power*, 26.

35. Certainly, respected historian Richard Hough thinks so. His appreciation is in Hough, *The Longest Battle: The War at Sea, 1939–1945*, 146–55. The judgment is echoed by the anonymous authors of the [United Kingdom] MOD [Ministry of Defence] (NAVY), *War with Japan*, 2:130 ("one-third" quote). Condemnation of Nagumo including his alleged prewar neuroticism is in Kyoshi Ikeda, "Vice Admiral Chuichi Nagumo," translated by Richard Harrison, in *Men of War*, edited by Howarth, 264.

36. The most thorough recent accounts of the Anglo-Japanese naval confrontation in the Indian Ocean in April 1942 are Krug et al., *Reluctant Allies*, 43–57; and Hamer, *Bombers versus Battleships*, 150–64. A briefer account is [United Kingdom] MOD [Ministry of Defence] (NAVY), *War with Japan*, 2:127–30.

37. Hamer, *Bombers versus Battleships*, 134.

38. Churchill, *The Second World War*, 4:157, 196. See also Theodore Ropp, *War in the Modern World*, 365; and Uhlig, *How Navies Fight*, 202.

39. PT boat skipper Robert Bolling Kelly quoted in William L. White, *They Were Expendable*, 26.

40. H. P. Willmott, *The Barrier and the Javelin: Japanese and Allied Pacific Strategies, February to June 1942*, 36–47 (quotes on pp. 46–47); Krug et al., *Reluctant Allies*, 46–48. For Chandra Bose, see Louis L. Snyder, *The War: A Concise History, 1939–1945*, 254.

41. Führer naval conference, March 12, 1942, quoted in Churchill, *The Second World War*, 4:197.

42. Krug et al., *Reluctant Allies*, 73–74, 51–53.

43. Early in 1941 a British Commando raid on the Lofoten islands off northern Norway yielded the first, badly damaged German Enigma electromechanical coding machine on board an enemy trawler. If such a comparatively nondescript vessel used for weather reporting possessed such a machine, might not others? And U-boats as well? The Admiralty went hunting across the North Atlantic for other less damaged Enigmas, and the capture of U-110 in the North Atlantic on May 9 yielded not only the prized machine but also "a table of the daily alterations in settings to be used for the following month." Within days, British intelligence specialists were prizing out the Enigma secrets. Peter Kemp, "Admiral of the Fleet Sir Dudley Pound," in *Men of War*, edited by Howarth, 27.

44. Kahn, *Seizing the Enigma*, 214; Keegan, *"Times" Atlas*, 48, 88; Macintyre, *Naval War against Hitler*, 100; van der Vat, *Atlantic Campaign*, 175–76, 230–31.

45. Kahn, *Seizing the Enigma*, 211–12, 220–27 (quote on p. 227).

46. Keegan, *"Times" Atlas*, 88–89; Macintyre, *Naval War against Hitler*, 400.

47. Full details on immediate prewar and wartime construction and completion dates for British battleships and carriers is in *Jane's Fighting Ships, 1947–48* (a notation on the title page states that all details are accurate up to July 1948), edited by Francis E. McMurtrie, 22, 27–29.

48. Matome Ugaki, *Fading Victory: The Diary of Admiral Matome Ugaki, 1941–1945,* 93. The quote denigrating Nagumo's highly successful carrier thrust toward Ceylon in the spring of 1942 is from Krug et al., *Reluctant Allies,* 47.

49. Ibid., 68.

50. Willmott, *Barrier and Javelin,* 56–63 (quote on p. 63).

51. Raeder, *My Life,* 352.

52. Ibid., 353.

53. An excellent account of the crew's view and reaction to the visit is Burkard Baron von Müllenheim-Rechberg, *Battleship* Bismarck: *A Survivor's Story,* 96–98.

54. Raeder, *My Life,* 354.

55. The best accounts are Müllenheim-Rechberg, *Battleship* Bismarck; Ludovic Kennedy, *Pursuit: The Chase and Sinking of the* Bismarck; Russell Grenfell, *The* Bismarck *Episode;* and Robert D. Ballard and Rick Archbold, *The Discovery of the* Bismarck.

56. Raeder, *My Life,* 358.

57. Edwin Muller, "On Board the *Bismarck,*" 261, 263; Müllenheim-Rechberg, *Battleship* Bismarck, 182–83, 226, 235–40, 246.

58. The famous, or infamous, "Channel Dash" by the two battle cruisers and *Prinz Eugen* has most recently been told in Hamer, *Battleships versus Bombers,* 137–49. The German success was a melancholy tale of poor weather, incompetent British intelligence and flight crews, and plain bad luck. A fuller account is Terence Robertson, *Channel Dash.*

59. Dudley Pope, *73 North: The Defeat of Hitler's Navy.*

60. A contemporary account that imparts the distinct flavor of the battle without realizing or divulging the signal intelligence that gave it shape is Cecil Scott Forester, "How the British Sank the *Scharnhorst,*" 9–11, 66, 68, 70, 72. A more satisfactory overall account is in van der Vat, *Atlantic Campaign,* 358–62.

61. Patrick Abbazia, *Mr. Roosevelt's Navy: The Private War of the U.S. Atlantic Fleet, 1939–1942,* 91; Roscoe, *Tin Cans,* 11.

62. FDR's comments at his press conference on December 17, 1940, are in David M. Kennedy, *Freedom from Fear: The American People in Depression and War, 1929–1945,* 468. Kennedy (488–94) also discusses the implications of Lend-Lease for the Nazi U-boat campaign and the United States Navy. The summary of ABC-1 is in Werner Rahn, "War at Sea in the Atlantic and Arctic," in *Germany and the Second World War,* by Research Institute for Military History, 1:307. Samuel Eliot Morison, *Strategy and Compromise,* 20–21, summarizes the justifications for the Allied "Germany first" strategy.

63. Stimson and Stark are quoted in Joseph P. Lasch, *Roosevelt and Churchill, 1939–1941: The Partnership That Saved the West,* 265–66.

64. Robert E. Sherwood, *Roosevelt and Hopkins: An Intimate History,* 291; Roscoe, *Tin Cans,* 12–15. King and Operation Plan 3–41 are quoted in Jerome M. O'Connor, "FDR's Undeclared War," 25.

65. Sherwood, *Roosevelt and Hopkins,* 290. Morison (*Strategy and Compromise,* 23) acidly comments on Iceland's alleged foot-dragging. Raeder, *My Life,* 346.

66. Sherwood, *Roosevelt and Hopkins,* 294–95 (quote on p. 295). See also Abbazia, *Mr. Roosevelt's Navy,* 189; and William Stevenson, *A Man Called Intrepid: The Secret War,* 261.

67. The account in Stevenson, *Man Called Intrepid,* 259–65, is misleading regarding Smith's true role but substantially correct in other particulars. Abbazia, *Mr. Roosevelt's Navy,* 189, has the story right.

68. Roscoe, *Tin Cans,* 14; Michael Gannon, *Operation Drumbeat: The Dramatic True Story of Germany's First U-boat Attacks along the American Coast in World War II,* 87–88. FDR's letter to Admiral Stark is quoted in O'Connor, "FDR's Undeclared War," 27.

69. Jürgen Rohwer, "The Wireless War," in *Battle of the Atlantic,* edited by Howarth and Law, 411–12.

70. Lasch, *Roosevelt and Churchill,* 135, 142–43, 204, 208, 211 (quote).

71. Hanson W. Baldwin, "If England Falls—What of the British Fleet?" 1–5.

72. The "belligerency" quote is from William E. Leuchtenberg, *Franklin D. Roosevelt and the New Deal, 1932–1940,* 325. See also Roscoe, *Tin Cans,* 14–15; D. Kennedy, *Freedom from Fear,* 497–500 (the "rattlesnakes" quote is on p. 497); and Rahn, "War at Sea," in *Germany and the Second World War,* by Research Institute for Military History, 6:309–19 (FDR's warning is quoted on p. 319). The effect of Britain's Ultra capabilities on the Battle of the Atlantic at this time is in Rohwer, "The Wireless War," in *Battle of the Atlantic,* edited by Howarth and Law, 411.

73. The naval aspects and implications of the Doolittle raid are treated in Lisle A. Rose, *The Ship That Held the Line: The USS* Hornet *and the First Year of the Pacific War,* 49–76. The literature on the Japanese-American conflict is immense and growing steadily. Numerous attempts have been made to blend personal reminiscences, accounts of individual ships and battles, after-action reports, intelligence estimates, and other archival information into general histories of the conflict. Among the more recent efforts, Ronald H. Spector, *Eagle against the Sun: The American War with Japan,* remains in many ways the most authoritative account, together with David M. Kennedy's often masterful narrative in *Freedom from Fear,* 515–65, 610–14, 809–51. Other excellent studies are John Costello, *The Pacific War;* Henry A. Gailey, *The War in the Pacific: From Pearl Harbor to Tokyo Bay;* Nathan Miller, *War at Sea,* 201–90, 365–410, 435–532; and Dan van der Vat, *The Pacific Campaign, World War II: The U.S.-Japanese Naval War, 1941–1945.* Four of the six volumes of *Battle Report* by Walter Karig, Russell L. Harris, and Frank A. Manson cover the Pacific War: *Pearl Harbor to Coral Sea* (1944), *Pacific War: Middle Phase* (1946), *The End of an Empire* (1948), and *Victory in the Pacific* (1949). Together with ten of the fifteen volumes of Samuel Eliot Morison's *History of United States Naval Operations in World War II,* the projects provide essential baseline information and chronology. The Japanese side is well covered in Paul S. Dull, *A Battle History of the Imperial Japanese Navy, 1941–1945,* somewhat less so in Emanuel Marie Auguste Andrieu D'Albas, *Death of a Navy: Japanese Naval Action in World War II;* Ito and Pineau, *End of the Japanese Navy;* and, especially for the early stages of the

Pacific war, Krug et al., *Reluctant Allies*. Unless otherwise noted, the following accounts of the Pacific War are based on these sources.

74. Rose, *Ship That Held the Line*, 35–41.

75. The classic contemporary American account of the Battle of the Coral Sea is Stanley Johnston, *Queen of the Flat-tops: The U.S.S.* Lexington *and the Coral Sea.* Johnston, perhaps unwittingly, perhaps deliberately as part of a good story, gave away the fact that the Americans had broken and were reading the Japanese naval code. Calls were quietly made for his prosecution, but nothing happened. The best historical account remains Morison, *United States Naval Operations*, vol. 4, *Coral Sea, Midway, and Submarine Actions*, 3–64, but it must be supplemented by the intelligence perspective provided in Edwin T. Layton, Roger Pineau, and John Costello, *"And I Was There":* *Pearl Harbor and Midway—Breaking the Secrets*, 394–404 ("young man" quote on 397, "shot their bolt" on p. 399). A meticulous unraveling of the often confusing events of May 7 is John B. Lundstrom, "Sinking the *Shoho*," *Naval History* 20:2 (April 2006): 26–34 (faulty code-machine quote is on p. 30, as is "young man"). Howarth, *To Shining Sea*, 401–4 ("inverted triangle" quote on p. 401), is also worthwhile. Edwin P. Hoyt, *Blue Skies and Blood: The Battle of the Coral Sea*, is a competent popular history.

76. Midway is the most written-about naval battle of World War II. The earliest account appears to be Joseph Bryan III, "Never a Battle Like Midway." Others consulted by this writer, beyond the general histories of the Pacific war noted in footnote 75 above, include Walter Lord, *Incredible Victory;* Gordon W. Prange, Donald M. Goldstein, and Katherine V. Dillon, *Miracle at Midway;* and Thaddeus V. Tuleja, *Climax at Midway.* The most meticulous account of the air action is John B. Lundstrom, *The First Team: Pacific Naval Air Combat from Pearl Harbor to Midway*, 307–447. A brilliant and comprehensive account from the Japanese side is Fuchida and Okumiya, *Midway.* All three American carriers at Midway have been the subject of "biographies." For the *Hornet*, see Rose, *Ship That Held the Line*, 97–155; for *Yorktown*, see Pat Frank and Joseph D. Harrington, *Rendezvous at Midway: USS* Yorktown *and the Japanese Carrier Fleet;* and for *Enterprise*, Stafford, *Big E*, 82–106. Explorer Robert Ballard's 1998 discovery of the *Yorktown's* final resting place three miles down in the Pacific was the subject of yet another review of the battle by Thomas B. Allen and Robert D. Ballard, "Ghosts and Survivors: Return to the Battle of Midway." The confusing and controversial behavior of the *Hornet's* air group during the June 4 battle came to life again in 1999. See Bruce R. Linder, "Lost Letter of Midway," *NIP* (August 1999): 29–35; and the reply by Barrett Tillman in *NIP* (October 1999): 12, 14.

77. Fuchida and Okumiya, *Midway*, 73 (quote), 82–86. British historian Geoffrey Till has painted a superb picture of Captain Kameto Kuroshima, Yamamoto's "so-called 'God of Operations' who produced his plans after long sessions meditating naked in his cabin, drinking heavily, chain-smoking, and burning incense. His inspirational role was very much in the tradition of the medieval warrior-monk Muashi" who "never washed and perhaps unsurprisingly never married but exerted a tremendous mystic

influence over later generations of Japanese, including Yamamoto himself" ("Midway: The Decisive Battle?" 35).

78. Fuchida and Okumiya, *Midway,* 93.

79. Victor Davis Hanson (*Carnage and Culture,* 374) claims another element in Japan's defeat: criminal dilatoriness in repairing *Shokaku* following the Battle of the Coral Sea. The carrier steamed into Kure Naval Base ten days before the far more badly damaged *Yorktown* returned to Pearl Harbor. The Americans patched up their carrier in time for Midway, while Japanese authorities decided *Shokaku* would require a minimum of three months. But damage to *Shokaku's* flight deck proved a greater impediment to flight operations and repair than did *Yorktown's* internal damage.

80. In a recent article and a forthcoming book, Jonathan Parshall and Anthony Tully argue that all previous accounts of Japanese carrier activities at Midway (including, in passing, my biography of the U.S. carrier *Hornet*) are in error by presuming that the flight decks of *Kaga, Akagi, Soryu,* and *Hiryu* were filled with combat-loaded and fueled strike aircraft when the American dive-bombers appeared and blew them—and three of the four carriers—apart. In fact, they insist, few aircraft were on the decks; all the strike aircraft were below in enclosed hangars and could not have been brought up, spotted, and launched to strike the American task force for probably an hour after the final American attacks. Although this is an interesting addition, it directly contradicts the observations of two leading Japanese aviators who were on the scene and who state the flight decks were filled with fully armed planes ready to launch (Fuchida and Okumiya, *Midway,* 156–57). Moreover, if true, the position of the Japanese strike force (whether on flight decks or in carrier hangars) matters little to the overall result of the battle. Japanese carrier flight decks, like those of the American enemy of the time, were unarmored, and the bombs that struck either passed through into the ordnance- and aircraft-filled hangar decks before exploding or caused sufficient explosions on the flight decks to ignite the aircraft, fuel, and ordnance below. See Parshall and Tully, *Shattered Sword: The Untold Story of the Battle of Midway* (Potomac Books, forthcoming) and their Web site, http://www.combinedfleet.com, which contains a recent article summarizing their findings together with related materials.

81. Stafford, *Big E,* 88, 97.

82. Quoted in Rose, *Ship That Held the Line,* 271–72.

83. R. Frank, *Downfall,* 24.

84. Spector, *Eagle against the Sun,* 143–44; Robert William Love Jr., "Ernest Joseph King," in *The Chiefs of Naval Operations,* edited by Love, 148.

85. Grace Person Hayes, *The History of the Joint Chiefs of Staff in World War II,* 137–40 (quote on pp. 139–40).

86. Love, "Ernest Joseph King," in *Chiefs of Naval Operations,* edited by Love, 152.

87. Arthur M. Schlesinger, Jr., *The Crisis of the Old Order, 1919–1933,* 417–18.

88. E. B. Potter, "Fleet Admiral Chester William Nimitz," in *Men of War,* edited by Howarth, 141.

89. Charles Cook, *The Battle of Cape Esperance: Encounter at Guadalcanal,* 149.

90. Richard B. Frank, *Guadalcanal: The Definitive Account of the Landmark Battle,* 36–38, 46.

91. Mikawa failed to move on and destroy the unloading transports at their anchorage off Guadalcanal and was subsequently criticized bitterly for the "blunder." Japanese sources, however, have come to his defense, claiming that he had done what he had set out to accomplish, believing that the American assault team was small and could be easily brushed aside in the next few days or weeks. See Hara, Saito, and Pineau, *Japanese Destroyer Captain,* 104.

92. Archibald A. Vandegrift and Robert B. Asprey, *Once a Marine: The Memoirs of General A. A. Vandegrift, U.S.M.C.,* 132.

93. Ugaki, *Fading Victory,* 177, 178.

94. Ibid., 183.

95. Hara, Saito, and Pineau, *Japanese Destroyer Captain,* 104–6; Ugaki, *Fading Victory,* 193.

96. Of the numerous contemporary and later accounts of the Guadalcanal campaign, five stand out in terms of breadth and depth of study and exemplary storytelling: R. Frank, *Guadalcanal;* John B. Lundstrom, *The First Team and the Guadalcanal Campaign: Naval Fighter Combat from August to November 1942;* Thomas G. Miller Jr., *The Cactus Air Force;* and Morison, *United States Naval Operations,* vol. 5, *The Struggle for Guadalcanal.* Max Brand's *Fighter Squadron at Guadalcanal,* a long-lost gem of contemporary reportage, best captures the sweaty desperation of the early Solomons campaign in the air.

97. Cook, *Battle of Cape Esperance,* 149. Hara, Saito, and Pineau (*Japanese Destroyer Captain,* 112) observed that at the carrier battle of the eastern Solomons in late August 1942, only one of fourteen aircraft launched from the light carrier *Ryujo* carried a radio. Partly as a result of this deficiency, *Ryujo* was sent to the bottom by planes off the carrier *Saratoga.*

98. Peattie, *Sunburst,* 178, 193; Okumiya, Horikoshi, and Caidin, *Zero!* 149, quotes the Japanese source.

99. A month earlier, Nimitz admitted, "We are unable to control the sea. The situation is not hopeless, but it is certainly critical" (Schom, *Eagle and Rising Sun,* 386).

100. Mark Peattie (*Sunburst,* 174–76) has carefully sifted evidence accumulated over the past sixty years to argue that although Midway was indeed "a momentous reversal in the tide of Japanese conquest in the Pacific," it was "not 'The Battle That Doomed Japan'" (174). Replacement hulls for the four lost carriers were on Japanese building ways, and the loss of trained pilots and aircrew aboard the four doomed carriers was not nearly as great as generally imagined. "No more than a quarter of the carrier air crews the navy had at the start of the battle" perished, and most of them were from *Hiryu,* shot down while successfully attacking *Yorktown* (175). Moreover, the Japanese learned from Midway chiefly to shape their remaining carrier fleet exclusively for carrier war. American industrial might and crushing superiority in manpower that permitted

the construction and deployment of a brand-new, ultramodern navy after mid-1943 doomed Japan. Prior to that moment, it might still expect its sailors and flyers to gain the favorably negotiated peace it had set out to win at Pearl Harbor.

101. FDR and King are quoted in Love, "Fleet Admiral Ernest J. King," in *Men of War*, edited by Howarth, 87. Nothing better illustrates the criminal dilatoriness of the Japanese high command following Midway than the tale of *Musashi*, or "Battleship no. 2" as she was generally known before her formal entry into the imperial fleet. Following a very slow final construction process, *Musashi* was commissioned on August 5, 1942, then spent four leisurely months training and working up before cruising to the main Japanese naval base at Truk. (In contrast, new U.S. warships during World War II generally devoted two to five weeks maximum conducting "shakedown cruises" before heading to battle.) During the four months that *Musashi* spent in training, the Americans invaded Guadalcanal and victoriously completed the campaign. One is left to wonder how different the Pacific war might have been if Yamamoto had had *Shokaku* at Midway and *Musashi* available for nighttime action off Guadalcanal in November 1942. *Musashi's* career is recounted in Yoshimura, *Battleship* Musashi, esp. 132–33.

102. Roger Pineau, "Admiral Isoroku Yamamoto," in *The War Lords,* edited by Michael Carver, 400.

103. Morison, *United States Naval Operations,* 5:221.

104. The following account of Japan's industrial woes during World War II is based on *Japanese Naval Shipbuilding* (Washington, D.C.: U.S. Strategic Bombing Survey, Military Supplies Division, 1946), copy in Harry S. Truman Library, Independence, Missouri (quote on p. 10).

105. Ibid., 10, 11; Ugaki, *Fading Victory,* 512–13.

106. Ugaki, *Fading Victory,* 12, 31, 35, 38, 43, 51; Pineau, "Admiral Isoroku Yamamoto," *The War Lords,* edited by Carver, 390; Ikuhiko Hata, "Admiral Yamamoto's Surprise Attack and the Japanese Navy's War Strategy," in *Pearl Harbor to Hiroshima,* edited by Dockrill, 66; Ugaki, *Fading Victory,* 68.

107. Ugaki, *Fading Victory,* 253, 255, 293.

108. Hara, Saito, and Pineau, *Japanese Destroyer Captain,* 103; Hata, "Yamamoto's Surprise Attack," in *Pearl Harbor to Hiroshima,* edited by Dockrill, 67–68.

109. Ugaki, *Fading Victory,* 567.

110. See, for example, Stephen E. Ambrose, *D-Day, June 6, 1944: The Climactic Battle of World War II,* 90–177; Harry C. Butcher, *My Three Years with Eisenhower,* 420–570; Carlo D'Este, *Decision in Normandy,* 62–104; Frederick Morgan, *Overture to Overlord;* and Chester Wilmot, *The Struggle for Europe,* 191–243.

Chapter 9. Defending the Atlantic Lifeline

1. Clay Blair, *Hitler's U-boat Wars,* 1:xii–xiii.

2. Bernard Edwards, *The Twilight of the U-boats,* 2–14.

3. Rahn, "War at Sea," *Germany and the Second World War,* by Research Institute

452 NOTES

for Military History, 6:301, 303, 313, 323. R. H. S. Stolfi (*Hitler's Panzers East: World War II Reinterpreted*, 139–49) argues convincingly that Hitler's vacillation over strategic objectives that induced him to order Army Group Center to veer off into the Ukraine on August 11, 1941, gave Soviet forces just enough time—and him not enough time on the road to Moscow—to forever lose the initiative on the eastern front.

4. Rahn, "German Naval Strategy and Armament," in *Technology and Naval Combat*, in O'Brien, 119.

5. Blair, *Hitler's U-boat War*, 1:xiii; van der Vat, *Atlantic Campaign*, 183; Eberhard Rössler, "U-boat Development and Building," in *Battle of the Atlantic*, edited by Howarth and Law, 121–26; Edwards, *Twilight of the U-boats*, 15; David Syrett, *The Defeat of the German U-boats: The Battle of the Atlantic*, 3. Germany's essential replication of World War I naval technology in 1938–1942 applied to surface vessels as well. *Bismarck* and *Tirpitz*, "although large, fast and balanced," were "in fact a remarkably conventional design, being based on the *Baden* and *Bayern* of 1916" (Preston, *Battleships*, 134). Even Hitler was occasionally upset at what Raeder and Dönitz were willing to accept. "In 1938 the Fuehrer criticized the Navy's plans for shipbuilding in general and for the *Bismarck* and *Tirpitz* in particular, for their too weak armament and too low speed" (Davidson, *Trial of the Germans*, 387). Hitler spoke better than he knew. When marine archaeologist Robert D. Ballard discovered the wreck of *Bismarck* in 1989, he realized that the vessel's stern had collapsed under the weight of a torpedo hit in the propeller area and several subsequent shell hits. Combing German records, Ballard subsequently discovered that both pocket battleship *Lutzow* (ex-*Deutschland*) and cruiser *Prinz Eugen* had suffered similar collapses after being torpedoed near the stern. In short, the big German surface ships built after 1929 suffered from substantial structural weaknesses in the stern, due undoubtedly to the welding procedures used to join the hull together. Ballard and Archbold, *Discovery of the* Bismarck, 215.

6. E. J. Coates, introduction to *The U-boat Commander's Handbook*, 18. This publication is a verbatim reprint of a U.S. Navy translation of the document issued by the German high command of the navy, Torpedo Boat Command, titled *The Submarine Commander's Handbook; Incorporated in the Secret Archives under Heading IV, no. 4, Command 32, Submarine Flotilla, 1942, New Edition 1943*. Hereafter cited as *The U-boat Commander's Handbook*.

7. Blair, *Hitler's U-boat War*, 1:xiii; Morison, *United States Naval Operations*, vol. 10, *The Atlantic Battle Won*, 118.

8. Vause, *Wolf*; Timothy P. Mulligan, "Forcing a U-boat Ace to Surface: Source Materials in a Biography of Werner Henke," 250; Rust, *Crew 34*.

9. Erich Topp, "Manning and Training the U-boat Fleet," in *Battle of the Atlantic*, edited by Howarth and Law, 217–19.

10. Rust, *Crew 34*, 76.

11. *U-boat Commander's Handbook*, 23, 24, 45, 101, 88.

12. Ibid., 17, 18, 24.

13. Dönitz, *Memoirs*, 62–63.

14. Ibid., 63; *U-boat Commander's Handbook*, 23.

15. *U-boat Commander's Handbook*, 35–36.

16. Heinz Schaeffer, *U-boat 977*, 49.

17. Ibid., 49–50, 56.

18. Peter Kemp, "Admiral of the Fleet Sir Dudley Pound," in *Men of War*, edited by Howarth, 25. The conclusions of the British Naval Staff history are quoted in H. P. Willmott, "The Organizations: The Admiralty and the Western Approaches," in *Battle of the Atlantic*, edited by Howarth and Law, 180.

19. Edwyn Gray, *Submarine Warriors*, 179n, quoting B. Herzog, *U-boats in Action*; Terence Robertson, *Night Raider of the Atlantic: The Saga of the U-99*; Gannon, *Operation Drumbeat*, 29; Macintyre, *Naval War against Hitler*, photo captions between pp. 192 and 193; Bodo Herzog, "Admiral Otto Kretschmer," translated by Marianne Howarth, in *Men of War*, edited by Howarth, 384–85.

20. Preston, *Submarines*, 96.

21. Robertson, *Night Raider*, 157–58; van der Vat, *Atlantic Campaign*, 165; Gray, *Submarine Warriors*, 175, 179.

22. Churchill, *The Second World War*, 2:510, Herzog, "Admiral Otto Kretschmer," in *Men of War*, edited by Howarth, 388.

23. W. J. R. Gardner claims that only once during the entire war did the Germans state a tonnage-per-month-sunk requirement for winning the Battle of the Atlantic. "This was made in June 1941 by the German Naval Staff and cited a figure of 800,000 tons per month" (*Decoding History: The Battle of the Atlantic and Ultra*, 49). Six hundred thousand tons' sinkage rate had been widely cited after World War I as the point at which the U-boat war had reached a crisis, and the Allies used it often a quarter century later.

24. An excellent recent account of the incident is Gerald L. Duskin and Ralph Segman, *If the Gods Are Good: The Epic Sacrifice of HMS* Jervis Bay.

25. *U-boat Commander's Handbook*, 72.

26. Macintyre, *Naval War against Hitler*, 64–79. A gruesome but accurate fictive account is Nicholas Monsarrat, *The Cruel Sea*.

27. Terence Robertson, *Escort Commander: The Story of Captain Frederic John Walker*, xi–xii. See also von der Porten, *German Navy*, 176.

28. Churchill, *The Second World War*, 2:513–14. Churchill's lamentation regarding German naval aviation and figures on its effectiveness in the spring of 1941 are in Stephen Budiansky, *Air Power: The Men, Machines, and Ideas That Revolutionized War from Kitty Hawk to Gulf II*, 275.

29. Pugh, "Military Need and Civil Necessity," in *Battle of the Atlantic*, edited by Howarth and Law, 30–44 (quotes on pp. 30–31, 43).

30. Churchill, *The Second World War*, 2:515.

31. Tristan Jones, *Heart of Oak*, 129; Iain Ballantyne, *Warships of the Royal Navy: HMS* London, 72. Lest the reader think that contemporaries and I exaggerate the appalling conditions aboard British warships as late as World War II, a visit to HMS

Belfast anchored permanently in the Thames is encouraged. The wardroom and officers' quarters above decks and amidships are roomy and comfortable. A trip to the crew's "quarters" right up in the bow is close to a journey to hell.

32. T. Jones, *Heart of Oak,* 131.

33. Paul Kemp, *Convoy! Drama in Arctic Waters,* 128–29.

34. Monsarrat, *The Cruel Sea,* 262. Captain Fegen's leadership style is discussed in Duskin and Segman, *If the Gods Are Good,* 75, 78, 87, 90. By the end of the war, some of Britain's seamen served under truly deplorable conditions. Aboard the headquarters ship HMS *Lothian* on its way to the Pacific, enlisted men suffered from "over-intensive work in blazing temperatures; frustrations over lack of . . . shore leave; over discipline; poor supervision; bad food; lack of water; malcontent among the ratings; lack of belief in our mission. . . . One can only assume that by the end of summer 1944 it was being taken for granted that seamen would put up with anything, however desperate. Or had the Admiralty simply stopped caring?" Bill Glenton, a member of *Lothian's* crew wondered. "Were we any or much worse than many a ship's company? After five years of war there must have been quite a number of warships with similar misfits." Glenton, *Mutiny in Force X,* 228. The United States Navy could work its men brutally hard, but generally knew when human limits had been reached; the Royal Navy often seemed scarcely to care. Of course, there was one general exception to the rule: African Americans, especially those sailors who were used as stevedores in World War II and were on more than one occasion worked abominably, as their mutiny at Port Chicago in 1944 indicated. The men were absolutely right in protesting dangerously careless and life-threatening conditions by uncaring racist superiors. Their court-martial convictions were eventually overturned, but only after long years of injustice.

35. "A rough state of the sea restricts the use of submarines as a weapon of war," Dönitz told his men. German experts estimated that force 5 or 6 seas rendered it impossible for the smaller Type VII craft to effectively launch torpedoes from a submerged position, and force 6 or 7 seas created the same conditions for the later larger Type IX craft. Only "somewhat less rough" conditions would also disrupt surfaced torpedo fire. *U-boat Commander's Handbook,* 39; see also p. 45.

36. Von der Porten, *German Navy,* 171–76, 248; van der Vat, *Atlantic Campaign,* 165–66; Preston, *Submarines,* 93; Gannon, *Operation Drumbeat,* xvi.

37. Prien's death is recounted in van der Vat, *Atlantic Campaign,* 168. The explanation for the fires aboard the imploding U-boat come from Peter Huchthausen, Igor Kurdin, and R. Alan White, *Hostile Waters,* 87.

38. Schepke's gruesome end and Kretschmer's incredible survival are discussed in Robertson, *Night Raider,* 182–91.

39. Budiansky, *Air Power,* 275.

40. Peter Kemp, "Admiral of the Fleet Sir Dudley Pound," in *Men of War,* edited by Howarth, 31–32; Michael Wilson, "Admiral of the Fleet Sir Max Horton," in ibid., 436–37; Alan J. Scarth, "Liverpool as HQ and Base" in *Battle of the Atlantic,* edited by Howarth and Law, 245, 247.

41. Andrews, *Air Marshals,* 52; Hezlet, *Aircraft and Sea Power,* 136, 139; Hamer, *Bombers versus Battleships,* 33–34.

42. Van der Vat, *Atlantic Campaign,* 153–54, 176; Macintyre, *Naval War against Hitler,* 82; Preston, *Submarines,* 101.

43. Robertson, *Escort Commander,* 1–21. A good summary of Walker's career and achievements is David Hobbes, "Captain Frederic Walker," in *Men of War,* edited by Howarth, 421–27.

44. Robertson, *Escort Commander,* 22.

45. Ibid., 23.

46. Gannon, *Operation Drumbeat,* 49.

47. Robertson, *Escort Commander,* 55–56; Keegan, *"Times" Atlas,* 89.

48. Marc Milner, "The Battle of the Atlantic," 48.

49. Syrett, *Defeat of the U-boats,* 2. On February 1, 1942, the Germans began using a far more sophisticated Enigma coding machine called M-4 in which reflector rotor B, in use for more than four years, was divided into a smaller reflector and an additional "Greek" rotor called "Beta." Instead of a single period of nearly seventeen thousand digits, the new machine provided twenty-six different periods of that length. "Even when Bletchley Park solved the problem of the interior wiring of the new Beta rotor, analytical description remained impossible" because the Germans also introduced simultaneously a new indicator system and weather codebook, the most important source for breaking into the enemy system through cribbing. "The so-called 'big black-out' of U-boat signals began." Rohwer, "The Wireless War," in *Battle of the Atlantic,* edited by Howarth and Law, 412.

50. Sönke Neitzel, "The Deployment of the U-boats," in *Battle of the Atlantic,* edited by Howarth and Law, 282–84. Neitzel claims, "The permanent deployment of 15–20 boats in the Mediterranean during the decisive phase of the Battle of the Atlantic (that is, until April 1943) was the single most serious long-term consequence of Germany's Mediterranean campaign. From mid-September to early November 1941, "U-boat warfare in the North Atlantic was increasingly curtailed," and came to a dead halt in November and December (287). See also Gannon, *Operation Drumbeat,* 310; and P. Kemp, *Convoy!* 26.

51. Blair, *Hitler's U-boat War,* 1:630–37, 691–94. It may also be true that the British, resenting the presence of a rising naval power, tended to belittle and denigrate their often brash and insensitive cousins and so contributed to both the myths and legitimate criticism of American folly in first confronting the U-boat menace.

52. Homer H. Hickam Jr., *Torpedo Junction: U-boat War Off America's East Coast, 1942,* 1–4.

53. Gannon, *Operation Drumbeat,* 185.

54. Hickam, *Torpedo Junction,* 10, 291 (Dönitz quote); Gannon, *Operation Drumbeat,* 338–89 (Winn quoted on p. 340).

55. Syrett, *Defeat of the U-boats,* 3, 257–58; Roscoe, *Tin Cans,* 43–44.

56. Blair, *Hitler's U-boat War,* 2:47.

57. *U-boat Commander's Handbook,* 28–30, 74–78 (quote on p. 29).

58. Martin Middlebrook, *Convoy,* and Jürgen Rohwer, *The Critical Convoy Battles of March 1943: The Battle for HX 229/SC 122,* provide graphic descriptions of the wolf packs' last great successes. Rohwer (186–88) identifies the reasons Dönitz's promising offensive collapsed so quickly thereafter. Clay Blair discusses the miserable fate of another pack as it tried to penetrate and attack an Allied convoy bound for the Mediterranean and the invasion of Sicily (*Hitler's U-boat War,* 2:295–96). The lessons of that awful late-winter campaign are summarized in David Syrett, "Situation Extremely Dangerous: Three Atlantic Convoys in 1943," in *To Die Gallantly: The Battle of the Atlantic,* edited by Timothy J. Runyan and Jan M. Copes, 185.

59. Peter Cremer and Fritz Brustat-Naval, *U-boat Commander: A Periscope View of the Battle of the Atlantic,* 130; Robert Landauer, "O'Brien Is Just One of the Family," *Portland Oregonian,* July 14, 1996.

60. W. Frank, *The Sea Wolves,* 164–65.

61. Rahn, "Campaign," in *Battle of the Atlantic,* edited by Howarth and Law, 542.

62. Rohwer, "The Wireless War," in *Battle of the Atlantic,* edited by Howarth and Law, 413; James Bamford, *The Puzzle Palace: A Report on America's Most Secret Agency,* 396.

63. Daniel V. Gallery Jr., "U-boat War from Iceland to Murmansk and the Coasts of Africa," in *The Atlantic War Remembered: An Oral History Collection,* edited by John T. Mason Jr., 122–23.

64. See Gardner, *Decoding History,* 69–119. Gardner makes the point that Ultra's ultimate value lay in its ability to read advancing "German technology in a way that was not mirrored by the German intelligence system" (119).

65. Hamilton quoted in Ballantyne, *Warships of the Royal Navy,* 94–95. At nearly that same moment, Admiral Sir John Tovey, commander in chief of the Home Fleet, wrote the Admiralty, "It was difficult to believe that the population of Cologne would notice much difference between a raid of 1,000 bombers and one of 750" (Budiansky, *Air Power,* 277).

66. Robertson, *Escort Commander,* 27–49.

67. Kenneth Poolman, *Allied Escort Carriers of World War II in Action,* 16; David Brown, *Carrier Operations in World War II,* 48.

68. Middlebrook, *Convoy,* 310–33 (quotes on pp. 311, 322).

69. Peter Gretton, *Crisis Convoy: The Story of HX-231,* 173.

70. D. Brown, *Carrier Operations in World War II,* 48–49; William T. Y'Blood, *Hunter-Killer: U.S. Escort Carriers in the Battle of the Atlantic,* 298.

71. Y'Blood, *Hunter-Killer,* 66–158.

72. Van der Vat, *Atlantic Campaign,* 329, 349–51.

73. Edwards, *Twilight of the U-boats,* 127.

74. W. Frank, *The Sea Wolves,* 164; Blair, *Hitler's U-boat War,* 2:276; van der Vat, *Atlantic Campaign,* 275.

75. Dönitz, *Memoirs,* 406–7.

76. Edwards, *Twilight of the U-boats,* 169–83.

77. Morison, *United States Naval Operations,* 10:325–38 (quote on p. 327). The May 1944 statistics are from Edwards, *Twilight of the U-boats,* 185.

78. One commander later related that the short-outs created a vacuum that "took our breath away and made us feel as if our heads were exploding" (Herbert A. Werner, *Iron Coffins: A Personal Account of the German U-boat Battles of World War II,* 330).

79. Blair, *Hitler's U-boat War,* 2:480.

80. Edwards, *Twilight of the U-boats,* 186 (Dönitz quote); Morison, *United States Naval Operations,* 10:327–28; Preston, *Submarines,* 117–20; Blair, *Hitler's U-boat War* 1:ix–xi.

81. Ballantine, *U.S. Naval Logistics,* 44–45.

82. The depth of the German shock upon seeing the Allied invasion fleet abruptly materializing out of the dawn mists of D Day is admirably recaptured in Paul Carell, *Invasion—They're Coming! The German Account of the Allied Landings and the 80 Days' Battle for France,* 75–77.

83. D. Kennedy, *Freedom from Fear,* 598; Morison, *United States Naval Operations,* vol. 11, *The Invasion of France and Germany, 1944–1945,* 142–43.

84. Adrian R. Lewis, "The Navy Falls Short at Normandy."

85. For the German reaction to the Allied bombardment and assault, see Carell, *Invasion—They're Coming!* 52–57; for the influence of naval gunfire on the development of the campaign, including von Rundstedt's quotes, see D'Este, *Decision in Normandy,* 151–53; and Morison, *United States Naval Operations,* 11:195–212.

86. Roland G. Ruppenthal, "Logistic Planning for Overlord in Retrospect," in Eisenhower Foundation, *D-Day: The Normandy Invasion in Retrospect,* 87–103.

87. Martin Walker column, *Seattle Times-Post Intelligencer,* June 5, 1994.

Chapter 10. The Allies: Foundations of Conquest

1. John D. Alden, *Flush Decks and Four Pipes,* 5.

2. Among the excellent accounts of enlisted life in the prewar United States Navy, Jonathan G. Utley's *An American Battleship at Peace and War: The U.S.S.* Tennessee is outstanding. I have also drawn on numerous stories and tales heard from senior people while serving as an enlisted sailor between 1954 and 1957.

3. Ibid., 62; Abbazia, *Mr. Roosevelt's Navy,* 9.

4. *The Bluejacket's Manual, United States Navy, 1940,* 3.

5. Utley, *American Battleship,* 46; Arthur A. Ageton, *The Naval Officer's Guide,* 144–45.

6. Joy Waldron Jasper, James P. Delgado, and Jim Adams, *The U.S.S.* Arizona: *The Ship, the Men, the Pearl Harbor Attack, and the Symbol That Aroused America,* 73.

7. "The U.S. Navy," 89; Abbazia, *Mr. Roosevelt's Navy,* 9.

8. Jasper, Delgado, and Adams, *U.S.S.* Arizona, 50–62 (quotes on pp. 52, 60).

9. Ibid., 51, 68–69.

10. Floyd Beaver, "American Cruisers in the Twilight of Peace," 26.

11. Puleston, *Influence of Sea Power*, 28.

12. James O. Richardson, *On the Treadmill to Pearl Harbor: The Memoirs of Admiral J. O. Richardson;* Hagan, *This People's Navy*, 291–92, 305; Spector, *Eagle against the Sun*, 1–2.

13. Beaver, "American Cruisers," 27; Jasper, Delgado, and Adams, *U.S.S.* Arizona, 65.

14. "The U.S. Navy," 23, 70.

15. Ibid., 9, 25; Uhlig, *How Navies Fight*, 137; Abbazia, *Mr. Roosevelt's Navy*, 20.

16. The following paragraphs rely heavily on the excellent study by Trent Hone, "Evolution of Fleet Tactical Doctrine in the U.S. Navy, 1922–41." The quotes are on pp. 1112, 1113, 1115, 1123.

17. James D. Ramage, interview, U.S. Naval Institute Oral History Collection, Annapolis, Maryland, 1:33–34.

18. Trent Hone, "Building a Doctrine: U.S. Naval Tactics and Battle Plans in the Interwar Period," 2, 27.

19. Ibid., 9–30 (quotes on pp. 27, 28); Peter F. Drucker, *The Concept of the Corporation*, 44–45.

20. Thomas B. Buell, *The Quiet Warrior: A Biography of Admiral Raymond A. Spruance*, 265, 274.

21. Jellicoe's post-Jutland "Grand Fleet Battle Orders" dated September 11, 1916, are reprinted in A. Temple Patterson, *The Jellicoe Papers: Selections from the Private and Official Correspondence of Admiral of the Fleet Earl Jellicoe* 2:47–57 (quote on p. 46); Michael A. Palmer, *Origins of the Maritime Strategy: American Naval Strategy in the First Postwar Decade*, xviii

22. Hone, "Fleet Tactical Doctrine," 1143.

23. "The U.S. Navy," 9.

24. Prados, *Combined Fleet Decoded*, 24–39; Stephen Jurika Jr., interview, U.S. Naval Institute Oral History Collection, Annapolis, Maryland, 453.

25. Uhlig, *How Navies Fight*, 137; Abbazia, *Mr. Roosevelt's Navy*, 29.

26. Abbazia, *Mr. Roosevelt's Navy*, 18–20; Uhlig, *How Navies Fight*, 138.

27. See James C. Fahey, *The Ships and Aircraft of the U.S. Fleet*, vol. 1.

28. Schom, *Eagle and Rising Sun*, 110, 114.

29. Sherwood, *Roosevelt and Hopkins*, 382–83.

30. The question as to who was ultimately "responsible" for the great Pacific war of 1941–1945 will last as long as there are historians to debate it. A good recent summary emphasizing Japan's inability to build a viable coalition of partners in the world community to support its aggression while the Roosevelt administration was able to create such a coalition to contest it is Michael A. Barnhart, "The Origins of the Second World War in Asia and the Pacific: Synthesis Impossible?" The matter seems clear enough: Japan's unappeasably aggressive spirit and horrific means of waging war threatened not only the destruction of China but also the safety of all East Asia and much of Oceania. To forestall such a prospect, the Roosevelt administration in 1940–1941 sought to

progressively cut off Tokyo's war-making capabilities through an embargo on essential resources. This policy reached a climax in the summer of 1941 with an embargo on oil. Japan had no choice but to find alternative war-making resources in the mineral-rich Western colonial holdings in Southeast Asia, which would draw it inevitably into war with the United States, Britain, and the Dutch government in exile in London. The only way such a war could be won was to strike the only enemy fleet in the Pacific capable of contesting Japanese expansion. And so the air raid on Pearl Harbor was ordered and carried out.

31. The fiftieth anniversary of the attack brought out much of the poignancy that had been obscured by wartime fury. A number of television retrospectives were devoted to the subject of which American Broadcasting Corporation and NHK Japan, *Pearl Harbor: Two Hours That Changed the World,* was far and away the best.

32. Stafford, *Big E,* 32–34 (quote on p. 33).

33. A. Russell Buchanan, *The United States and World War II,* 2:77n.

34. Charles A. Beard, *President Roosevelt and the Coming of the War, 1941,* 526–57; Charles Callan Tansill, *Back Door to War: The Roosevelt Foreign Policy, 1933–1941,* 640–52.

35. James Rusbridger and Eric Nave, *Betrayal at Pearl Harbor: How Churchill Lured Roosevelt into World War I;* John Toland, *Infamy: Pearl Harbor and Its Aftermath;* Edward L. Beach, *Scapegoats: A Defense of Kimmel and Short at Pearl Harbor;* John Costello, *Days of Infamy: MacArthur, Roosevelt, Churchill; The Shocking Truth Revealed: How Their Secret Deals and Strategic Blunders Caused Disaster at Pearl Harbor and the Philippines;* Roberta Wohlstetter, *Pearl Harbor: Warning and Decision;* Gordon W. Prange, Donald M. Goldstein, and Katherine V. Dillon, *At Dawn We Slept: The Untold Story of Pearl Harbor;* Walter Lord, *Day of Infamy.* Husband E. Kimmel, *Admiral Kimmel's Story,* though understandably bitter, at least strove to avoid the appearance of sensationalism.

36. D. Kennedy, *Freedom from Fear,* 510–11.

37. Bamford, *Puzzle Palace,* 58; italics added. See also Spector, *Eagle against the Sun,* 91.

38. Rusbridger and Nave, *Betrayal at Pearl Harbor,* 14.

39. "Professional Notes: 'Speech by C-in-C,' " *NIP* 61:8 (August 1935): 1180; "Professional Notes, 'Japan Naval Maneuvers' and 'Fifty-three Lives Lost,' " *NIP* 61:11 (November 1935): 1715–16.

40. Henry C. Lee and Bruce Lee. *Pearl Harbor: Final Judgement,* 243. Kimmel's chief intelligence officer, Edwin T. Layton, quotes the same conversation in Layton, Pineau, and Costello, *"And I Was There,"* 18.

41. "The Reminiscences of Captain Joseph J. Rochefort, U.S. Navy," interview, U.S. Naval Institute Oral History Collection, Annapolis, Maryland, 168–69.

42. Paul Stilwell, "Looking Back: Pearl Harbor at 60—an Enduring Legacy."

43. Prange, Goldstein, and Dillon, *At Dawn We Slept,* 94, 203–204, 338–43;

Mochitsura Hashimoto, *Sunk! The Story of the Japanese Submarine Fleet, 1941–1945,* 155–56.

44. See Donald M. Goldstein and Katherine V. Dillard, *The Pearl Harbor Papers: Inside the Japanese Plans,* for the impressive documentation on elaborate Japanese ruses and deceptions.

45. Jasper, Delgado, and Adams, *U.S.S.* Arizona, 74–83 (quote on p. 83).

46. Schom, *Eagle and Rising Sun,* 131; James Webb, "Defending the Navy's Culture," *NIP* 122:7 (July 1996): 91–93.

47. Schom, *Eagle and Rising Sun,* 134; Prange, Goldstein, and Dillon, *At Dawn We Slept,* 497.

48. Schom, *Eagle and Rising Sun,* 128. Historian John Costello (*Days of Infamy,* 41–42) has argued that if anyone should have been sacked after the events of December 7, it was MacArthur, not Kimmel and Short. According to Costello, Roosevelt and Churchill had agreed at Argentia that the U.S. Far Eastern Air Force—which by December 1941 comprised several score B-17 bombers and several squadrons of fighter planes based at Clark Field, some sixty-five miles north of Manila—would guarantee the security of the entire Allied position in East Asia. Just hours after Pearl Harbor, the bulk of this air force was caught on the ground at Clark by attacking Japanese fighters and bombers and was virtually wiped out. Costello makes a compelling case for MacArthur's dismissal, but it in no way vitiates the arguments against Kimmel and Short. Alan Schom (*Eagle and Rising Sun,* 219–32) has recently revived and amplified Costello's contention, now widely accepted among scholars, including MacArthur's most recent biographer, that the general—and his chief of staff, Richard Sutherland—deserved to be fired for dereliction of duty.

49. Hone and Mandeles, "Interwar Innovation."

50. Wilmot, *The Struggle for Europe,* 491; Alistair Cooke, *America,* 342, 345.

51. A balanced, full-fledged account of the American economy in World War II remains to be written. The best extant account is still Eliot Janeway, *The Struggle for Survival: A Chronicle of Economic Mobilization in World War II.*

52. Arnold Rogow, *James Forrestal: A Study of Personality, Politics, and Policy,* 94, 95n, 100–103.

53. Louis Denfeld, "The Navy Trains for War," in *Battle Stations: Your Navy in Action; A Photographic Epic of the Naval Operations of World War II Told by the Great Admirals Who Sailed the Fleet from Norfolk to Normandy and from the Golden Gate to the Inland Sea,* 42.

54. Ladislas Farago, *The Tenth Fleet,* 109–110.

55. James D. Horan, *Action Tonight: The Story of the Destroyer* O'Bannon *in the Pacific,* 7, 12, 13, 21.

56. Y'Blood, *Hunter-Killer,* 21, 29, 39–50.

57. Daniel V. Gallery Jr., "U-boat War from Iceland to Murmansk and the Coasts of Africa," in *Atlantic War Remembered,* edited by Mason, 121; Douglas Fairbanks Jr., *A Hell of a War,* 107.

58. Love, "Fleet Admiral Ernest J. King," in *Men of War*, edited by Howarth, 100–106; E. B. Potter, "Fleet Admiral Chester William Nimitz," in ibid., 149–50.

59. For the war in the Mediterranean Basin between 1940 and 1942 I have relied primarily on Ansel, *Hitler and the Middle Sea;* Barnett, *Engage the Enemy More Closely,* 207–50, 317–77; Churchill, *The Second World War,* 2:357–88, 453–69, 3:48–65, 79–92, 184–257, 335–53; Cunningham, *Sailor's Odyssey,* 227–460; James Holland, *Fortress Malta: An Island under Siege, 1940–1943;* Macintyre, *Naval War against Hitler,* 146–263; Preston, *Aircraft Carriers,* 72–77; Roskill, *Churchill and the Admirals;* Bernd Stegemann, "The Italo-German Conduct of the War in the Mediterranean and North Africa," in *Germany and the Second World War,* by Research Institute for Military History, 3:641–707; D. Thomas, *Crete 1941;* Warren Tute, *The Deadly Stroke;* and Uhlig, *How Navies Fight,* 119–31. Unless otherwise cited, information in the following pages is from these sources.

60. Barnett, *Engage the Enemy More Closely,* 211; B. Sullivan, "Fleet in Being," 120.

61. B. Sullivan, "Fleet in Being," 120–21.

62. The message has been widely reprinted in whole or in part. See, for example, Churchill, *The Second World War,* 2:162–63; Lukacs, *Duel,* 137; and Lasch, *Roosevelt and Churchill,* 159–60.

63. Tute, *The Deadly Stroke,* 202–3.

64. B. Sullivan, "Fleet in Being," 121–22.

65. Cunningham, *Sailor's Odyssey,* 272, 283.

66. Ibid., 283. An excellent brief summary of Taranto is Thomas P. Lowry and John W. G. Wellham, *The Attack on Taranto: Blueprint for Pearl Harbor.* See also Budiansky, *Air Power,* 259–61.

67. Cunningham, *Sailor's Odyssey,* 285. As so often in war, Cunningham had no idea how successful his flyers had been until an RAF reconnaissance flight from Malta the next day brought back irrefutable pictorial proof. See Holland, *Fortress Malta,* 68.

68. Budiansky, *Air Power,* 257–58; Stegemann, "Italo-German Conduct," in *Germany and the Second World War,* by Research Institute for Military History, 3:663.

69. Churchill, *The Second World War,* 2:110; Baldwin, *Battles Lost and Won,* 94.

70. Holland, *Fortress Malta,* 77.

71. Baldwin, *Battles Lost and Won,* 95. Greece and the subsequent campaigns in Crete and North Africa gravely strained the historic ties of loyalty and affection that bound Britain to its great Pacific dominions, Australia and New Zealand. London, Canberra, and Wellington reached an agreement in 1940 that if Australian and New Zealand troops and warships were again dispatched to the Mediterranean and Middle East, as in 1914–1918 to stem the enemy tide, Britain would, when and if necessary, reinforce Singapore with sufficient air, ground, and naval units to stop any Japanese drive into the South Pacific. The Australian and New Zealand armies and navies promptly sailed for Suez and beyond where they were immediately incorporated into the British war machine so tightly as to be inextricable. But when Japan began spreading inexorably

southward soon thereafter, London was in no position to substantially reinforce its position in the East. There would be no "Main Fleet to Singapore" beyond the doomed *Prince of Wales* and *Repulse,* no significant increase in the pitifully small and obsolete air force based on the great island bastion. The Singapore army garrison was large, and its artillery batteries, dutifully covering the seaward approaches, were powerful. This was all the assistance and intimidation that London could provide. When Japan swept over Malaya and the East Indies barrier, Australia and New Zealand were forced to look elsewhere for salvation. They turned naturally to the nation whose Great White Fleet thirty-four years earlier had suggested to them where their true source of national security lay. See David Day, *The Great Betrayal: Britain, Australia, and the Onset of the Pacific War, 1939–42.*

72. Stegemann, "Italo-German Conduct," in *Germany and the Second World War,* by Research Institute for Military History, 3:659–61.

73. Preston, *Aircraft Carriers,* 76–77; Holland, *Fortress Malta,* 78–91.

74. Baldwin, *Battles Lost and Won,* 92–93.

75. Cunningham, *Sailor's Odyssey,* 326; Lewin, *Ultra Goes to War,* 276–77; Barnett, *Engage the Enemy More Closely,* 333–34.

76. Barnett, *Engage the Enemy More Closely,* 344.

77. Cunningham, *Sailor's Odyssey,* 356, 357.

78. Ibid., 376.

79. Ibid., 390.

80. Von der Porten, *German Navy,* 100–101.

81. Ansel, *Hitler and the Middle Sea,* 484.

82. B. Sullivan, "A Fleet in Being," 123.

83. John Cresswell, *Sea Warfare, 1939–1945,* 104–107.

84. Macintyre, *The Naval War against Hitler,* 204. Statistics on Axis losses, the continuing importance of Malta as a naval and air bastion in 1941–1942, and its decline to near "starvation" status by June–July 1942 that prompted the move of the Tenth Submarine Flotilla to Alexandria are in Holland, *Fortress Malta,* 197–323.

85. Ansel, *Hitler and the Middle Sea,* 484–85.

86. Andrews, *Air Marshals,* 258.

87. Melville Bell Grosvenor, "The New Queen of the Seas," 3, 5.

88. Andrews, *Air Marshals,* 258–60 (quote on p. 258).

Chapter 11. Gem of the Ocean

1. The standard account of the American submarine war in the Pacific is Clair Blair Jr., *Silent Victory: The U.S. Submarine War against Japan.* See also Charles A. Lockwood, *Sink 'Em All,* and Admiral I. J. Galantin's introduction to Corwin Mendenhall, *Submarine Diary.* A classic account based on the unit histories of eleven boats is Edward L. Beach, *Submarine!*

2. Blair, *Silent Victory,* 90–91, 296–97; Mendenhall, *Submarine Diary,* x; Fahey, *Ships and Aircraft,* Two-Ocean Fleet Edition, 18–20.

3. Phillip Knightley, *The First Casualty: From the Crimea to Vietnam; The War Correspondent as Hero, Propagandist, and Myth Maker,* 299, quoting statistics from the fifth and final volume of the British history of the war against Japan, *The Surrender of Japan* (London: Her Majesty's Stationery Office, 1969), n.p.

4. Hashimoto, *Sunk!* 160.

5. Krug et al., *Reluctant Allies,* 28–29. Carl Boyd and Akihiko Yoshida, *The Japanese Submarine Force and World War II,* 16–35, provides an excellent summary of the various submarine classes Japan produced during the interwar years and World War II. See also [United Kingdom] MOD [Ministry of Defense] (NAVY), *War with Japan,* 1:77.

6. [United Kingdom] MOD [Ministry of Defense] (NAVY), *War with Japan,* 1:77.

7. Oliver Jensen, *Carrier War,* 47.

8. Morison, *Strategy and Compromise,* 79–81. It is well to recall that most of us alive at the time (I was a schoolboy) thought until at least the end of 1944 that World War II would last well into the late forties. "Golden Gate in '48" seemed reasonable until the defeat of Germany; thereafter, "I'll be in heaven in '47" summed up hopes about ending the war against Japan.

9. Jensen, *Carrier War,* 3–19.

10. Love, "Fleet Admiral Ernest J. King," in *Men of War,* edited by Howarth, 99.

11. Tom Hone, "The Navy's Dilemma," *NIP* 127:4 (April 2001): 75. See also Paul Nagy, "Network-Centric Warfare Isn't New," *NIP* 127:9 (September 2001): 44–46.

12. The Russo-German war of 1941–1945 was the other. In addition to sources listed in footnotes above, readers should consult a number of excellent contemporary and later works dealing specifically with sea-air operations in the Pacific during the latter stages of the war. These include Belote and Belote, *Titans of the Seas;* Joseph Bryan III, *Aircraft Carrier;* Kenneth M. Glass and Harold L. Buell, *The Hornets and Their Heroic Men;* Morris Markey, *Well Done! An Aircraft Carrier in Battle Action;* and Clark G. Reynolds, *The Fast Carriers: The Forging of an Air Navy* and *The Carrier War.* For those who wish to delve even more deeply, the Library of Congress possesses literally dozens of individual ship "cruise books" from the latter stages of the war. The Nimitz Library at the United States Naval Academy in Annapolis has a more limited sample. Copies of the 1945 color MGM film *The Fighting Lady* dealing with the birth and life of the second *Yorktown* can be obtained from a number of film-supply sources.

13. Years ago my late brother told me of an incident on the new fleet carrier *Philippine Sea* shortly after the war. The ship was slowly steaming up Narragansett Bay in a fog toward the pier at Quonset Point. As the 888-foot vessel inched slowly along, Captain Delbert H. Cornwell, an aviator who had recently commanded an escort carrier in the Pacific, became more and more agitated. The bridge Fathometer, eight decks up from the waterline, consistently registered sufficient water under the keel, but Cornwell kept asking for readings. Finally, the officer at the Fathometer called out, "Still 12 fathoms,

captain; it's OK." Cornwell spun around on him: "No, goddamn it! It's not!" Turning to the engine telegraph-order operator, he bellowed, "All back full!" A later reading of the charts indicated the carrier was within a hundred yards of grounding. My brother, who had the helm, later asked Cornwell how he knew the huge ship was in potential trouble. "The water didn't feel right," Cornwell replied.

14. The Pat Patterson story and Arthur Radford quote are in Bryan, *Aircraft Carrier*, 114–15, 184.

15. Julian C. Smith, "The Battle for Tarawa," in *Battle Stations*, 222.

16. Thomas J. Cutler, *The Battle of Leyte Gulf, 23–26 October 1944*, 54–55; Jensen, *Carrier War*, 6.

17. Richard Wheeler, *A Special Valor: The U.S. Marines and the Pacific War*, 172; Craig M. Cameron, "Race and Identity: The Culture of Combat in the Pacific War," 564.

18. Cameron, "Race and Identity," 565.

19. Brian Altobello, *Into the Shadows Furious: The Brutal Battle for New Georgia*, 206–13.

20. E. B. Sledge, *With the Old Breed at Peleliu and Okinawa*, 132–33, 142–43.

21. D'Albas, *Death of a Navy*, 294.

22. Harold L. Buell, *Dauntless Helldivers: A Dive-Bomber Pilot's Epic Story of the Carrier Battles*, 73–74, 262–63, 272–73.

23. Comment by Wilton Hutt to the author, April 2006. Hutt flew combat missions from the Gilberts in November 1943 to the kamikaze attack on *Bunker Hill* in May 1945.

24. Unless otherwise noted, the following discussion is based on Maurice Jacobson, producer, *The Deadly Fuze: The Story of World War II's Best-Kept Secret*; Cameron D. Collier, "Tiny Miracle: The Proximity Fuze," 43–45; and Brian Shoemaker interview with Dr. James Van Allen, November 18, 1997, as part of the Polar Oral History Project conducted by the American Polar Society and the Byrd Archival Program of the Ohio State University.

25. Van Allen interview, 9; R. O. Holbrook, commentary on "Tiny Miracle: The Proximity Fuze"; H. Buell, *Dauntless Helldivers*, 241.

26. Hayes, *Joint Chiefs of Staff*, 604–6.

27. MacArthur's briefing to FDR and Nimitz is quoted in ibid., 611; his aside to the president is in Cutler, *Battle of Leyte Gulf*, 34.

28. The best and most complete descriptions of the Battle of the Philippine Sea or "the Marianas Turkey Shoot" are in Dull, *Battle History*, 209–310; Morison, *United States Naval Operations*, 8:213–321, 412–17; and William T. Y'Blood's excellent *Red Sun Setting: The Battle of the Philippine Sea*.

29. A contemporary account of the June 19 American long-range attack against Ozawa's fleet is Joseph Bryan III and Philip Reed, *Mission beyond Darkness*. A later personal account is H. Buell, *Dauntless Helldivers*, 295–311. Belote and Belote (*Titans of the Seas*, 357) offer a devastating critique of Mitscher's decision.

30. Love, "Ernest Joseph King," in *Chiefs of Naval Operations*, edited by Love, 173–74.

31. Leyte Gulf exceeds Midway and may rival Jutland as the most written-about naval battle of the twentieth century. The first serious effort to tackle a battle that was at once complex in conception but brutally simple in outcome was undertaken in 1947 by a young U.S. Navy veteran who later became one of the country's most distinguished historians. Nearly sixty years on, C. Vann Woodward's *Battle for Leyte Gulf* remains a vital source, well researched and clearly written, whose assertions have stood up over time and the onslaught of new research. The floodgates of histories and memoirs opened thereafter, and the best bibliography is in Thomas J. Cutler's recently completed *Battle for Leyte Gulf.* Textual quotes are taken from this source, pp. 75, 77, 224–25, 226. See also Trent Hone, "Triumph of U.S. Navy Night Fighting," *Naval History* 20:5 (October 2006): 54–59.

32. The classic statement of this thesis is Gar Alperovitz, *Atomic Diplomacy: Hiroshima and Potsdam; The Use of the Atomic Bomb and the American Confrontation with Soviet Power.* Over the past thirty-odd years it has been restated, elaborated, or assumed in at least half a hundred historical studies. In 1995 Alperovitz in a massive book, *The Decision to Use the Atomic Bomb and the Architecture of an American Myth,* updated, but did not revise, his argument incorporating all of the revisionist (and some counterrevisionist) discussion of the issue. A broader recent sampling of the various revisionist arguments is Kai Bird and Lawrence Lifschultz, *Hiroshima's Shadow.*

33. Japan's leadership readily acknowledged that the nation was in ever increasing peril. Following the debacle in the Philippine Sea, Prime Minister Tōjō and his cabinet were dismissed to be replaced by General Kuniaki Koiso who had to continue fighting "a war which he personally feared was lost." Admiral Matome Ugaki, who had been Yamamoto's chief of staff and after the admiral's assassination by American warplanes in April 1943 moved on to command of a battleship division, wrote sadly of "the prospect of a victory...fading out gradually" as the remnants of the imperial fleet fled from the Marianas. But the warlords also knew that they might well be held accountable for the inexcusable undeclared war against China, the invasion of French Indochina, Pearl Harbor, and the onslaught against Western holdings in Asia. Beyond personal considerations lay their not unfounded conviction that the Allied call for unconditional surrender would "result in the 'destruction' of the national polity and the 'ruin' of the Japanese race." So they continued to play on the same sentiments that had brought Nippon abruptly out of agrarian isolation and into the midst of the modern industrial world eight decades before. *Nippon sieshin*—the mind, the soul, the spirit of Japan—would prevail in the end. "Japan may be weak in resources, but she is strong in spirit. This will lead the nation to victory." Paradoxically, the closer the Americans came, the more certain was victory ordained. "Like the inveterate gambler who always knows he is going to turn his luck with the next bet, so too did Imperial Headquarters proclaim that the 'decisive battle' to be fought on Japan's shores would bring the nation its long-sought victory." Out in the islands of the Pacific and in the fleet anchorages off Borneo and in the Inland Sea, the steadily dwindling number of colonels, captains, lieutenants, soldiers, sailors, and airmen believed such nonsense and fought on stubbornly, often with growing

rather than diminishing confidence, refusing to submit to the facts of war. All the above quotes, except Ugaki's, are from Robert J. C. Butow, *Japan's Decision to Surrender,* 1967 ed., 12, 37, 73; Ugaki, *Fading Victory,* 416. The most recent, and in the main strikingly successful, effort to demonstrate that Japan was ready to fight to the death in the summer and autumn of 1945 is R. Frank, *Downfall.* The study does suffer, however, from an unwillingness to view the impending atomic bombs as an important factor in U.S. military and especially diplomatic calculations from the spring of 1945 onward. The fact that the bombs did not constitute the decisive factor in no way lessens their importance in the bureaucratic and political equations of the time.

34. The following discussion is based on three authoritative sources: George W. Baer, *One Hundred Years of Sea Power: The U.S. Navy, 1890–1990,* 267–70; R. Frank, *Downfall,* 68–360; and Douglas J. MacEachin, *The Final Months of the War with Japan: Signals Intelligence, U.S. Invasion Planning, and the A-Bomb Decision.*

35. Marshall is quoted in R. Frank, *Downfall,* 30. The Quebec decision is quoted in MacEachin, *Final Months,* 1.

36. Norman Polmar and Thomas B. Allen, "The Most Deadly Plan," *NIP* 124:1 (January 1998): 79–81. As early as 1988, Ronald Schaffer published a very brief account of America's wartime chemical and biological weapons stockpiling that indicated that by 1944 the nation had produced anthrax and botulism bombs. "Air Force staff officers started to develop a contingency plan for gas attack on Japanese cities" (*Wings of Judgment: American Bombing in World War II,* 164).

37. R. Frank, *Downfall,* 103–96; MacEachin, *Final Months,* 6.

38. Love, "Fleet Admiral Ernest J. King," in *Men of War,* edited by Howarth, 100–106; Potter, "Fleet Admiral Chester William Nimitz," in ibid., 149–50; Hone, "Building a Doctrine."

39. MacEachin, *Final Months,* 17, 19; R. Frank, *Downfall,* 170–77.

40. MacEachin, *Final Months,* 12, 17, 26; R. Frank, *Downfall,* 144–46, 190, 201–8.

41. At Nuremberg, Dönitz was delighted to receive a message from Nimitz acknowledging that the United States had conducted unrestricted submarine warfare from the first day of the Pacific War. Dönitz told American psychiatrist G. M. Gilbert that Nimitz's cable "is a wonderful document!"

> In the next room Ribbentrop and Raeder were also taking great comfort from the document which Doenitz had shown them. "You see," said Raeder, "unrestricted warfare—anything is permitted as long as you win! The only thing you mustn't do is lose."
>
> Ribbentrop sought to use this even to justify the the breaking of the Munich Pact. "There you are—unrestricted warfare in the whole Pacific Ocean where America really doesn't belong! And when we make a Protectorate of Bohemia and Moravia which belonged to Germany for a thousand years it is considered aggression!"

"But there is still a difference between the two situations," I pointed out. "You had signed a pact in Munich not to take more than the Sudetenland, while we were attacked without warning in the Pacific in the midst of negotiations. There is a clear difference there between aggression and defense."

Ribbentrop refused to concede the point. G. Gilbert, *Nuremberg Diary,* 316.

42. For a survivor's account of the kamikaze campaign and its horrors, see Bill Sholin, *"Truman's Decision": Kamikaze's the Unknown Factor,* 32, 65, 106, 109. See also Baldwin, *Battles Lost and Won,* 461–78.

43. Sholin, *Truman's Decision,* 22.

44. Schaffer, *Wings of Judgment,* 103–6, 149–89.

45. See R. Frank, *Downfall,* 274–77.

46. Douglas Ford, "British Naval Policy and the War against Japan, 1937–1945: Distorted Doctrine, Insufficient Resources, or Inadequate Intelligence?"; [United Kingdom] MOD [Ministry of Defense] (NAVY), *War with Japan,* 6:11–19, 201–17, esp. 214–15. Morison, *United States Naval Operations,* 14:249–50, 316–18, recounts the actual operations (quote on record British steaming time on p. 250). Preston, *Aircraft Carriers,* 161.

47. The British naval attaché is quoted in Pelz, *Race to Pearl Harbor,* 182–83. The contempt displayed for the Japanese aboard *Repulse* (which admittedly was general throughout the Anglo-American military at the time) is in Cecil Brown, *Suez to Singapore,* 299, 307.

SELECTED BIBLIOGRAPHY

THE FOLLOWING BIBLIOGRAPHY is highly selective, listing only those works that immediately and directly influenced my thinking on the course of early-twentieth-century sea power in the context of international politics and economic, social, and technological development. Citations of the numerous articles from the *U.S. Naval Institute Proceedings* have been excluded for space reasons. Sufficient citations may be found in the appropriate endnotes.

Manuscript Collections

Harry S. Truman Library, Independence, Missouri
Japanese Naval Shipbuilding
John Sullivan Papers

National Archives, Washington, D.C.

Record Group 218: Records of the Joint Chiefs of Staff,
Military History Branch

National Maritime Museum, Greenwich, England

Ernle Chatfield Papers
William Wordsworth Fisher Papers
Eric J. A. Fullerton Papers
Thomas Jerram Papers
Charles Madden Papers
Herbert William Richmond Papers

Ohio State University Archives and Polar Oral History Project

James Van Allen Interview
Admiral Richard E. Byrd Papers (RG 56.1)

Interviews, U.S. Naval Institute Oral History Collection, Annapolis, Maryland

Stephen Jurika Jr.
James D. Ramage
Joseph J. Rochefort

Other Sources

Abbazia, Patrick. *Mr. Roosevelt's Navy: The Private War of the U.S. Atlantic Fleet, 1939–1942.* Annapolis: Naval Institute Press, 1975.

Adams, Henry H. *1942: The Year That Doomed the Axis.* New York: David McKay, 1967.

Agawa, Hiroyuki. *The Reluctant Admiral: Yamamoto and the Imperial Navy.* Translated by John Bester. Tokyo: Kodansha International, 1979.

Ageton, Arthur A. *The Naval Officer's Guide.* New York: McGraw-Hill, 1943.

Aitkin, Andy, series director. *Battlefield: The Battle of the Atlantic.* Polygram Video International, 1996.

Alden, John D. *The American Steel Navy: A Photographic History of the U.S. Navy from the Introduction of the Steel Hull in 1883 to the Cruise of the Great White Fleet, 1907–1909.* Rev. ed. Annapolis: Naval Institute Press, 1989.

———. *Flush Decks and Four Pipes.* 1965. Reprint, Annapolis: Naval Institute Press, 1990.

Alford, Jonathan, ed. *Sea Power and Influence: Old Issues and New Challenges.* Osmun, Sweden: Gower and Allenheld, 1980.

Allen, Thomas B., and Robert D. Ballard. "Ghosts and Survivors: Return to the Battle of Midway." *National Geographic* 195:4 (April 1999): 81–103.

Alperovitz, Gar. *Atomic Diplomacy: Hiroshima and Potsdam; The Use of the Atomic Bomb and the American Confrontation with Soviet Power.* New York: Random House, 1965.

———. *The Decision to Use the Atomic Bomb and the Architecture of an American Myth.* New York: Alfred A. Knopf, 1995.

Altobello, Brian. *Into the Shadows Furious: The Brutal Battle for New Georgia.* Novato, Calif.: Presidio Press, 2002.

Ambrose, Stephen E. *D-Day, June 6, 1944: The Climactic Battle of World War II.* New York: Simon and Schuster, 1994.

American Broadcasting Corporation News and NHK Japan. *Pearl Harbor: Two Hours That Changed the World.* December 1991.

Anderson, Orvil A. "Air Warfare and Morality." *Air University Quarterly Review* 3:3 (winter 1949).

Andrews, Allen. *The Air Marshals: The Air War in Western Europe.* New York: William Morrow, 1970.

Ansel, Walter, *Hitler and the Middle Sea.* Durham: Duke University Press, 1972.

Argyle, C. J. *Japan at War, 1937–1945.* London: Arthur Barker, 1976.

Baer, George W. *One Hundred Years of Sea Power: The U.S. Navy, 1890–1990.* Stanford: Stanford University Press, 1994.

———. "U.S. Naval Strategy, 1890–1945." *Naval War College Review* 44:1 (winter 1991): 6–31.

Baker, Ray Stannard, and William E. Dodd. *The Public Papers of Woodrow Wilson: The New Democracy; Presidential Messages, Addresses, and Other Papers (1913–1917).* 2 vols. New York: Harper and Brothers, 1926.

Balano, Randy C. "U.S. Navy Owes T. B. M. Mason." *Naval History* 19:3 (June 2005): 26–31.

Baldwin, Hanson W. *Battles Lost and Won: Great Campaigns of World War II.* New York: Avon Books, 1968.

———. "If England Falls—What of the British Fleet?" *Reader's Digest* 39:232 (August 1941): 1–5.

Ballantine, Duncan S. *U.S. Naval Logistics in the Second World War.* Princeton: Princeton University Press, 1947.

Ballantyne, Iain. *Warships of the Royal Navy: HMS London.* Barnsely, South Yorkshire: Leo Cooper, 2003.

Ballard, Robert D., and Rick Archbold. *The Discovery of the Bismarck.* New York: Warner, Madison Press, 1990.

Ballendorf, Dirk A., and Merrill L. Bartlett. *Pete Ellis: An Amphibious Warfare Prophet, 1880–1923.* Annapolis: Naval Institute Press, 1997.

Bamford, James. *The Puzzle Palace: A Report on America's Most Secret Agency.* New York: Penguin, 1985.

Banning, Kendall. *Annapolis Today.* New York: Funk and Wagnalls, 1938.

Barlow, Jeffrey C. *Revolt of the Admirals: The Fight for Naval Aviation, 1945–1950.* Washington, D.C.: Department of the Navy, Navy Historical Center, 1994.

Barnett, Correlli. *Engage the Enemy More Closely: The Royal Navy in the Second World War.* New York: W. W. Norton, 1991.

Barnhart, Michael A. "The Origins of the Second World War in Asia and the Pacific: Synthesis Impossible?" *Diplomatic History* 20:2 (spring 1996): 241–60.

Barone, Michael. *Our Country: The Shaping of America from Roosevelt to Reagan.* New York: Free Press, 1990.

Bartlett, Merrill L. *Assault from the Sea: Essays on the History of Amphibious Warfare.* Annapolis: Naval Institute Press, 1983.

———. "Ben Hebard Fuller and the Genesis of a Modern United States Marine Corps, 1891–1934." *Journal of Military History* 69:1 (January 2005): 73–91.

Battle Stations: Your Navy in Action; A Photographic Epic of the Naval Operations of World War II Told by the Great Admirals Who Sailed the Fleet from Norfolk to Normandy and from the Golden Gate to the Inland Sea. New York: William H. Wise, 1946.

Beach, Edward L., Jr. *Scapegoats: A Defense of Kimmel and Short at Pearl Harbor.* Annapolis: Naval Institute Press, 1996.

———. *Submarine!* New York: Signet Books, 1953.

———. *The United States Navy: 200 Years.* New York: Henry Holt, 1986.

Beard, Charles A. *President Roosevelt and the Coming of the War, 1941.* New Haven: Yale University Press, 1948.

Beaver, Floyd. "American Cruisers in the Twilight of Peace." Pts. 1 and 2. *U.S. Navy Cruiser Sailors Association Journal* 14:2 (spring 2005).

Bekker, Cajus. *Hitler's Naval War.* New York: Kensington Publishing, 1977.

Bell, Christopher M. "Thinking the Unthinkable: British and American Naval Strategies for an Anglo-American War, 1918–1931." *International History Review* 19:4 (November 1997): 789–808.

Belote, James H., and William M. Belote. *Titans of the Seas: The Development and Operations of Japanese and American Carrier Task Forces during World War II.* New York: Harper and Row, 1975.

The Best from "Yank," the Army Weekly. Washington, D.C.: Council on Books in Wartime, 1945.

Bienstock, Gregory. *The Struggle for the Pacific.* New York: Macmillan, 1937.

Birchall, Frederick T. *The Storm Breaks: A Panorama of Europe and the Forces That Have Wrecked Its Peace.* New York: Viking Press, 1940.

Bird, Kai, and Lawrence Lifschultz. *Hiroshima's Shadow.* Stony Creek, Conn.: Pamphleteer's Press, 1998.

Bird, Keith W. *Weimar: The German Naval Officer Corps and the Rise of National Socialism.* Amsterdam: B. R. Gruner, 1977.

Blair, Clay, Jr. *Hitler's U-boat War.* 2 vols. New York: Random House, 1996, 1998.

———. *Silent Victory: The U.S. Submarine War against Japan.* 2 vols. Philadelphia: J. B. Lippincott, 1975.

The Bluejacket's Manual, United States Navy, 1940. 10th ed. Annapolis: Naval Institute Press, 1940.

Booker, Edna Lee. *News Is My Job: A Correspondent in War-Torn China.* New York: Macmillan, 1941.

Bosworth, R. J. B. *Explaining Auschwitz and Hiroshima: History Writing and the Second World War, 1945–1990.* London: Routledge, 1993.

Boyd, Carl, and Akihiko Yoshida. *The Japanese Submarine Force and World War II.* Annapolis: Naval Institute Press, 1995.

Boyne, Walter J. *Clash of Titans: World War II at Sea.* New York: Simon and Schuster, 1995.

Braeman, John, Robert H. Bremner, and Everett Walters, eds. *Change and Continuity in Twentieth-Century America.* New York: Harper Colophon Books, 1966.

Braisted, William Reynolds. *The United States Navy in the Pacific, 1909–1922.* Austin: University of Texas Press, 1971.

Brand, Max. *Fighter Squadron at Guadalcanal.* Annapolis: Naval Institute Press, 1996.

Brennecke, Jochen. *The Hunters and the Hunted.* Translated by R. H. Stevens. New York: W. W. Norton, 1957.

Brown, Cecil. *Suez to Singapore.* Garden City, N.Y.: Halcyon House, 1942.

Brown, David. *Carrier Operations in World War II.* 2d ed. Annapolis: Naval Institute Press, 1974.

Brown, Francis. *The War in Maps: An Atlas of "New York Times" Maps.* New York: Oxford University Press, 1943.

Bryan, Joseph, III. *Aircraft Carrier.* New York: Ballantine Books, 1954.

———. "Never a Battle Like Midway." *Saturday Evening Post* 221:39 (March 26, 1949).

Bryan, Joseph, III, and Philip Reed. *Mission beyond Darkness.* New York: Duell, Sloan, and Pearce, 1945.

Bryant, John H., and Harold N. Cones. *Dangerous Crossings: The First Modern Polar Expedition, 1925.* Annapolis: Naval Institute Press, 2000.

Buchanan, A. Russell. *The United States and World War II.* 2 vols. New York: Harper and Row, 1964.

Budiansky, Stephen. *Air Power: The Men, Machines, and Ideas That Revolutionized War from Kitty Hawk to Gulf II.* New York: Viking Press, 2004.

Buell, Harold L. *Dauntless Helldivers: A Dive-Bomber Pilot's Epic Story of the Carrier Battles*. New York: Dell Books, 1991.

Buell, Thomas B. *The Quiet Warrior: A Biography of Admiral Raymond A. Spruance*. Boston: Little, Brown, 1974.

Butcher, Harry C. *My Three Years with Eisenhower*. New York: Simon and Schuster, 1946.

Butow, Robert J. C. *Japan's Decision to Surrender*. 1954. Reprint, Stanford: Stanford University Press, 1967.

Bywater, Hector C. *The Great Pacific War: A Historic Prophecy Now Being Fulfilled*. 1925. Reprint, Boston: Houghton Mifflin, 1942.

Cameron, Craig M. "Race and Identity: The Culture of Combat in the Pacific War." *International History Review* 27:3 (September 2005): 550–66.

Cant, Gilbert. *The War at Sea*. New York: John Day, 1942.

———, ed. *This Is the Navy: An Anthology*. New York: Penguin Books, 1944.

Carell, Paul. *Invasion—They're Coming! The German Account of the Allied Landings and the 80 Days' Battle for France*. Translated by E. Osers. New York: Bantam Books, 1964.

Carew, Anthony. *The Lower Deck of the Royal Navy, 1900–39: The Invergordon Mutiny in Perspective*. Manchester, England: Manchester University Press, 1981.

Carse, Robert. *A Cold Corner of Hell: The Story of the Murmansk Convoys*. Garden City, N.Y.: Doubleday, 1969.

Carter, Worrall Read. *Beans, Bullets, and Black Oil: The Story of Fleet Logistics Afloat in the Pacific during World War II*. Washington, D.C.: Department of the Navy, 1953.

Carver, Michael, ed. *The War Lords*. London: Wiedenfeld and Nicholson, 1976.

Casey, Robert J. *Torpedo Junction: With the Pacific Fleet from Pearl Harbor to Midway*. Indianapolis: Bobbs-Merrill, 1942.

Chamberlin, William Henry. *Japan over Asia*. Garden City, N.Y.: Blue Ribbon Books, 1939.

Chant, Christopher. *Warfare of the 20th Century: Armed Conflicts Outside the Two World Wars*. Secaucus, N.J.: Chartwell Books, 1988.

Churchill, Winston S. *The Second World War*. 6 vols. New York: Bantam Books, 1961–1962.

Clausen, Henry C., and Bruce Lee. *Pearl Harbor: Final Judgement*. New York: Crown Publishers, 1992.

Clements, Frank. "Germany's Naval Aims." *Fortnightly Review* (March 1939): 277–84.

Coates, E. J. Introduction to *The U-boat Commander's Handbook*. Gettysburg, Pa.: Thomas Publications, 1989.

Coats, Wendell J. *Armed Force as Power: The Theory of War Reconsidered*. New York: Exposition Press, 1966.

Cohen, Warren I. *America's Response to China: A History of Sino-American Relations*. 3d ed. New York: Columbia University Press, 1990.

Coletta, Paolo A. *Admiral Bradley A. Fiske and the American Navy*. Lawrence: Regents Press of Kansas, 1979.

———. *The United States Navy and Defense Unification, 1947–1953*. Newark: University of Delaware Press, 1981.

Collier, Cameron D. "Tiny Miracle: The Proximity Fuze." *Naval History* 13:4 (August 1999): 43–45.

Condit, Kenneth W. *The History of the Joint Chiefs of Staff: The Joint Chiefs of Staff and National Policy*. Vol. 2, *1947–1949*. Wilmington, Del.: Michael Glazier, 1979.

Congdon, Don, ed. *Combat Pacific Theater: World War II*. New York: Dell Books, 1958.

Cook, Charles. *The Battle of Cape Esperance: Encounter at Guadalcanal*. New York: Thomas Y. Crowell, 1968.

Cooke, Alastair. *America*. New York: Alfred A. Knopf, 1973.

Costello, John. *Days of Infamy: MacArthur, Roosevelt, Churchill; The Shocking Truth Revealed: How Their Secret Deals and Strategic Blunders Caused Disaster at Pearl Harbor and the Philippines*. New York: Pocket Books, 1994.

———. *The Pacific War*. New York: Rawson, Wade Publishers, 1981.

Crane, Conrad C. *American Air Power Strategy in Korea, 1950–1953*. Lawrence: University Press of Kansas, 2000.

Cremer, Peter, and Fritz Brustat-Naval. *U-boat Commander: A Periscope View of the Battle of the Atlantic*. Translated by Lawrence Wilson. Annapolis: Naval Institute Press, 1984.

Creswell, John. *Sea Warfare, 1939–1945*. Berkeley and Los Angeles: University of California Press, 1967.

Cunningham, Viscount, of Hyndhope. *A Sailor's Odyssey: The Autobiography of Admiral of the Fleet Viscount Cunningham of Hyndhope*. New York: E. P. Dutton, 1951.

Cutler, Thomas J. *The Battle of Leyte Gulf, 23–26 October 1944*. New York: Harper Collins, 1994.

D'Albas, Emanuel Marie Auguste Andrieu. *Death of a Navy: Japanese Naval Action in World War II*. New York: Devin-Adair, 1957.

Davidson, Eugene. *The Trial of the Germans: An Account of the Twenty-two Defendants before the International Military Tribunal at Nuremberg.* New York: Macmillan, 1966.

Day, David. *The Great Betrayal: Britain, Australia, and the Onset of the Pacific War, 1939–42.* New York: W. W. Norton, 1988.

Dehio, Ludwig. *The Precarious Balance: Four Centuries of the European Power Struggle.* Translated by Charles Fullman. 1948. Reprint, New York: Vintage Books, 1962.

Deist, Wilhelm. *The Wehrmacht and German Rearmament.* Oxford: St. Anthony, 1981.

D'Este, Carlo. *Decision in Normandy.* New York: E. P. Dutton, 1983.

Dictionary of American Fighting Ships. 8 vols. Washington, D.C.: Navy Department, Naval History Division, 1959–1981.

Dillon, Katherine V., and Donald R. Goldstein, eds. *Fading Victory: The Diary of Admiral Matome Ugaki, 1941–1945.* Translated by Masataka Chihaya. Pittsburgh: University of Pittsburgh Press, 1991.

Dingman, Roger. *Power in the Pacific: The Origin of Naval Arms Limitation, 1914–1922.* Chicago: University of Chicago Press, 1976.

Dockrill, Saki, ed. *From Pearl Harbor to Hiroshima: The Second World War in Asia and the Pacific, 1941–1945.* New York: St. Martin's Press, 1994.

Documents on British Foreign Policy, 1919–1939. 2d ser. 21 vols. London: His [Her] Majesty's Stationery Office, 1946–1984.

Documents on British Foreign Policy, 1919–1939. 3d ser. 10 vols. London: His [Her] Majesty's Stationery Office, 1949–1961.

Documents on German Foreign Policy, 1918–1945. Ser. C, *The Third Reich: First Phase.* 5 vols. Washington, D.C.: U.S. Government Printing Office, 1957–1966.

Dönitz, Karl. *Memoirs: Ten Years and Twenty Days.* Translated by R. H. Stevens. Cleveland: World Publishing, 1959.

Dower, John W. *War without Mercy: Race and Power in the Pacific War.* New York: Pantheon, 1986.

Drucker, Peter F. *The Concept of the Corporation.* New York: Mentor Books, 1964.

Dugan, James, and Laurence LaFore. *Days of Emperor and Clown: The Italo-Ethiopian War, 1935–1936.* New York: Doubleday, 1973.

Dull, Paul S. *A Battle History of the Imperial Japanese Navy, 1941–1945.* Annapolis: Naval Institute Press, 1978.

Dunn, Robert F. "The Spirit of *Saratoga*." *Naval History* 11:6 (December 1997): 16–20.

Duskin, Gerald L., and Ralph Segman. *If the Gods Are Good: The Epic Sacrifice of HMS* Jervis Bay. Annapolis: Naval Institute Press, 2004.

Dyer, George Carroll. *The Amphibians Came to Conquer: The Story of Admiral Richmond Kelly Turner.* 2 vols. Washington, D.C.: U.S. Government Printing Office, 1972.

Edwards, Bernard. *Doenitz and the Wolfpacks.* London: Brockhampton Press, 1996.

———. *The Twilight of the U-boats.* Annapolis: Naval Institute Press, 2004.

Eisenhower, Dwight D. *Crusade in Europe.* Garden City, N.Y.: Permabooks, 1952.

———. *The White House Years: A Personal Account.* 2 vols. Garden City, N.Y.: Doubleday, 1963, 1965.

Eisenhower Foundation. *D-Day: The Normandy Invasion in Retrospect.* Lawrence: University Press of Kansas, 1971.

Evans, David C., and Mark R. Peattie. *Kaigun: Strategy, Tactics, and Technology in the Imperial Japanese Navy, 1887–1941.* Annapolis: Naval Institute Press, 1997.

Evans, Kenneth. *The Mutiny at Invergordon.* London: Putnam, 1937.

Fahey, James C. *The Ships and Aircraft of the U.S. Fleet.* Vols. 1–8 (1939–1965). Annapolis: U.S. Naval Institute Press, 1994–1996.

Fairbank, John King. *The United States and China.* 3d ed. Cambridge: Harvard University Press, 1971.

Fairbank, John King, Edwin O. Reischauer, and Albert M. Craig. *East Asia: The Modern Transformation.* Boston: Houghton Mifflin, 1965.

Fairbanks, Douglas, Jr. *A Hell of a War.* New York: St. Martin's Press, 1993.

Falk, Edwin A. *From Perry to Pearl Harbor: The Struggle for Supremacy in the Pacific.* New York: Doubleday, Doran, 1943.

Faltum, Andrew. *The Essex Aircraft Carriers.* Baltimore: Nautical and Aviation Publishing Company of America, 1996.

Farago, Ladislas. *The Tenth Fleet.* New York: Paperback Library, 1964.

Ferguson, Niall. *Empire: The Rise and Demise of the British World Order and the Lessons for Global Power.* New York: Basic Books, 2002.

Ford, Douglas. "British Naval Policy and the War against Japan, 1937–1945: Distorted Doctrine, Insufficient Resources, or Inadequate Intelligence?" *International Journal of Naval History* 4:1 (April 2005). Available online at http://www.ijnhonline.org.

Forester, Cecil Scott. "How the British Sank the *Scharnhorst.*" *Saturday Evening Post* 216:9 (March 25, 1944): 9–11, 66, 68, 70, 72.

Frank, Pat, and Joseph D. Harrington. *Rendezvous at Midway: U.S.S. Yorktown and the Japanese Carrier Fleet.* New York: John Day, 1967.

Frank, Richard B. *Downfall: The End of the Imperial Japanese Empire.* New York: Random House, 1999.

———. *Guadalcanal: The Definitive Account of the Landmark Battle.* New York: Penguin Books, 1990.

Frank, Wolfgang. *The Sea Wolves.* Translated by R. O. B. Long. New York: Ballantine Books, 1958.

Friedman, Norman. *Seapower as Strategy: Navies and National Interests.* Annapolis: Naval Institute Press, 2001.

———. *U.S. Aircraft Carriers: An Illustrated Design History.* Annapolis: Naval Institute Press, 1983.

———. *U.S. Cruisers: An Illustrated Design History.* Annapolis: Naval Institute Press, 1984.

Fuchida, Mitsuo, and Masatake Okumiya. *Midway: The Battle That Doomed Japan.* Edited by Clarke H. Kawakami and Roger Pineau. New York: Ballantine Books, 1955.

Fukui, Shizuo. *Naval Vessels, 1887–1945: Mitsubishi Zosen Built.* Nagasaki: Mitsubishi Shipbuilding and Engineering, n.d.

Fuller, J. F. C. *The Decisive Battles of the Western World and Their Influence upon History.* Vol. 2, *1792–1944.* Edited by John Terraine. London: Grenada Publishing, 1970.

Gailey, Henry A. *The War in the Pacific: From Pearl Harbor to Tokyo Bay.* Novato, Calif.: Presidio Press, 1995.

Galantin, I. J. *Submarine Admiral: From Battleships to Ballistic Missiles.* Urbana: University of Illinois Press, 1995.

Gannon, Michael. *Operation Drumbeat: The Dramatic True Story of Germany's First U-boat Attacks along the American Coast in World War II.* New York: Harper and Row, 1990.

Gardner, W. J. R. *Decoding History: The Battle of the Atlantic and Ultra.* Annapolis: Naval Institute Press, 1999.

Gayn, Mark J. *The Fight for the Pacific.* New York: William Morrow, 1941.

Gemzell, Carl-Axel. *Organization, Conflict, and Innovation: A Study of German Naval Strategic Planning, 1888–1940.* Stockholm: Esselte Studium, 1973.

Gibbs, Norman Henry. *Rearmament Policy.* Vol. 1 of *Grand Strategy,* edited by

J. R. M. Butler. United Kingdom Military Series History of the Second World War. 6 vols. London: Her Majesty's Stationery Office, 1956–1976.

Gibbs, Philip. *Across the Frontiers.* Garden City, N.Y.: Doubleday, 1938.

Gilbert, G. M. *Nuremberg Diary.* New York: Signet Books, 1961.

Gilbert, Martin. *The "Illustrated London News": Marching to War, 1933–1939.* New York: Military Heritage Press, 1989.

———, ed. *The Churchill War Papers.* Vol. 1, *At the Admiralty, September 1939–May 1940.* New York: W. W. Norton, 1993.

Glass, Kenneth M., and Harold L. Buell. *The Hornets and Their Heroic Men.* North Port, Fla.: U.S.S. Hornet Club, 1992.

Glenton, Bill. *Mutiny in Force X.* New York: Hodder and Stoughton, 1986.

Goerler, Raimond E. *To the Pole: The Diary and Notebook of Richard E. Byrd, 1925–1927.* Columbus: Ohio State University Press, 1998.

Goldhagen, Daniel Jonah. *Hitler's Willing Executioners: Ordinary Germans and the Holocaust.* New York: Alfred A. Knopf, 1996.

Goldstein, Donald M., and Katherine V. Dillard. *The Pearl Harbor Papers: Inside the Japanese Plans.* Dulles, Va.: Brassey's, 1993.

Gordon, Andrew. *The Rules of the Game: Jutland and British Naval Command.* London: John Murray, 1996.

Gordon, Charles S. *The German Navy in the Nazi Era.* Annapolis: Naval Institute Press, 1990.

Gordon, G. A. H. "The Admiralty and Appeasement." *Naval History* 5:2 (summer 1991).

Gravatt, Brent L. "On the Back of the Fleet." *Naval History* 4:2 (spring 1990).

Gray, Edwyn. *Submarine Warriors.* New York: Bantam Books, 1990.

Grenfell, Russell. *The* Bismarck *Episode.* New York: Macmillan, 1949.

———. *Main Fleet to Singapore.* New York: Macmillan, 1952.

Gretton, Peter. *Crisis Convoy: The Story of HX-231.* London: Peter Davis, 1974.

Grew, Joseph C. *Ten Years in Japan: A Contemporary Record Drawn from the Diaries and Private and Official Papers of Joseph C. Grew.* New York: Simon and Schuster, 1944.

Grossnick, Roy A., William J. Armstrong, W. Todd Baker, John M. Elliott, Gwendolyn J. Rich, and Judith A. Walters. *United States Naval Aviation, 1910–1995.* Washington, D.C.: Department of the Navy, Naval Historical Center, 1997.

Grosvenor, Melville Bell. "The New Queen of the Seas." *National Geographic* 87:1 (June 1942): 1–30.

Grunberger, Richard. *The 12 Year Reich: A Social History of Nazi Germany.* New York: Ballantine Books, 1972.

Gunther, John. *Inside Asia.* New York: Harper and Brothers, 1939.

Haffner, Craig, and Donna E. Lusitana, producers. *Sink the* Bismarck*!* Greystone Productions: Arts and Entertainment Network, 1996.

Hagan, Kenneth J. *This People's Navy: The Making of American Sea Power.* New York: Free Press, 1991.

Halpern, Paul G. *A Naval History of World War I.* Annapolis: Naval Institute Press, 1994.

———, ed. *The Keyes Papers: Selections from the Private and Official Correspondence of Admiral of the Fleet Baron Keyes of Zeebrugge.* 3 vols. Boston: George Allen and Unwin, 1972–1981.

Halsey, William F., and J. Bryan III. *Admiral Halsey's Story.* New York: McGraw-Hill, 1947.

Hamer, David. *Bombers versus Battleships: The Struggle between Ships and Aircraft for the Control of the Surface of the Sea.* Annapolis: Naval Institute Press, 1998.

Hamilton, John. *War at Sea, 1939–1945.* Poole, England: Blandford Press, 1986.

Hanson, Victor Davis. *Carnage and Culture: Landmark Battles in the Rise of Western Culture.* New York: Anchor Books, 2002.

Hara, Tameichi, Fred Saito, and Roger Pineau. *Japanese Destroyer Captain.* New York: Ballantine Books, 1961.

Harrod, Frederick S. *Manning the New Navy: The Development of a Modern Naval Enlisted Force, 1899–1940.* Westport, Conn.: Greenwood Press, 1978.

Hartcup, Guy. *The Achievement of the Airship: A History of the Development of Rigid, Semi-rigid, and Non-rigid Airships.* London: David and Charles, 1974.

Hashimoto, Mochitsura. *Sunk! The Story of the Japanese Submarine Fleet, 1941–1945.* New York: Avon Publications.

Hastings, Max. *Overlord: D-Day and the Battle for Normandy.* New York: Simon and Schuster, 1984.

Hattendorf, John B. *Doing Naval History: Essays toward Improvement.* Newport, R.I.: Naval War College Press, 1995.

———. *Naval History and Maritime Strategy: Collected Essays.* Malabar, Fla.: Krieger Publishing, 2000.

———, ed. *On His Majesty's Service: Observations of the British Home Fleet from the Diary, Reports, and Letters of Joseph H. Wellings, Assistant U.S. Naval Attaché, London, 1940–41.* Newport, R.I.: Naval War College Press, 1983.

Hattendorf, John B., R. J. B. Knight, A. W. H. Pearsall, N. A. M. Rodger, and Geoffrey Till. *British Naval Documents, 1204–1960.* London: Scolar Press, 1993.

Hayes, Grace Person. *The History of the Joint Chiefs of Staff in World War II.* Vol. 2, *The War against Japan.* Annapolis: Naval Institute Press, 1982.

Herwig, Holger H. "The Failure of German Sea Power, 1914–1945: Mahan, Tirpitz, and Raeder Reconsidered." *International History Review* 10:1 (February 1988): 68–105.

Hezlet, Arthur. *Aircraft and Sea Power.* New York: Stein and Day, 1970.

Hickam, Homer H., Jr. *Torpedo Junction: U-boat War Off America's East Coast, 1942.* Bluejacket Edition. Annapolis: Naval Institute Press, 1999.

Hohne, Heinz. *Canaris.* Translated by J. Maxwell Brownjohn. London: Secker and Warburg, 1979.

Holbrook, R. O. Commentary on "Tiny Miracle: The Proximity Fuze," by Cameron D. Collier. *Naval History* 13:6 (December 1999): 12.

Holland, James. *Fortress Malta: An Island under Siege, 1940–1943.* New York: Miramax Books, 2003.

Homan, William H. "Kamikazes, Turtle Backs, and Torpedoes That Made U-turns." *Naval History* 4 (summer 1990): 22–23.

———. "Nightmare at Port Arthur." *Naval History* 4 (summer 1990): 21–27.

Hone, Thomas C., and Mark D. Mandeles. "Interwar Innovation in Three Navies: U.S. Navy, Royal Navy, Imperial Japanese Navy." *Naval War College Review* 40:2 (spring 1987): 63–83.

Hone, Trent. "Building a Doctrine: U.S. Naval Tactics and Battle Plans in the Interwar Period." *International Journal of Naval History* 1:2 (October 2002). Available online at http://www.ijnhonline.org/index_oct_02.html.

———. "Evolution of Fleet Tactical Doctrine in the U.S. Navy, 1922–41." *Journal of Military History* 67:4 (October 2003): 1107–48.

Hoover, Herbert. *The Memoirs of Herbert Hoover: The Cabinet and the Presidency, 1920–1933.* New York: Macmillan, 1952.

Horan, James D. *Action Tonight: The Story of the Destroyer* O'Bannon *in the Pacific.* New York: G. P. Putnam's Sons, 1945.

Hough, Richard. *Death of the Battleship: The Tragic Close of the Era of Sea Power.* New York: McFadden, 1965.

———. *The Longest Battle: The War at Sea, 1939–45.* 1986. Reprint, London: Cassell, 2001.

Howarth, Stephen. *To Shining Sea: A History of the United States Navy, 1775–1991*. New York: Random House, 1991.

———, ed. *Men of War: Great Naval Leaders of World War II*. New York: St. Martin's Press, 1992.

Howarth, Stephen, and Derek Law, eds. *The Battle of the Atlantic, 1939–1945: The 50th Anniversary International Naval Conference*. Annapolis: Naval Institute Press, 1994.

Hoyt, Edwin P. *Blue Skies and Blood: The Battle of the Coral Sea*. New York: P. S. Eriksson, 1975.

———. *Japan's War: The Great Pacific Conflict, 1853 to 1952*. New York: McGraw-Hill, 1986.

Huchthausen, Peter, Igor Kurdin, and R. Alan White. *Hostile Waters*. New York: St. Martin's Press, 1997.

Hugill, Peter J. *World Trade since 1431: Geography, Technology, and Capitalism*. Baltimore: Johns Hopkins University Press, 1993.

Hurd, Archibald. "Economy in the Fleet: Lord Fisher's Demand." *Fortnightly Review*, n.s., 634 (October 1, 1919): 514–28.

———. "Peace and a Naval Holiday." *Fortnightly Review*, n.s., 630 (June 2, 1919): 879–93.

———. "Shall We Suffer an Eclipse at Sea? American Progress." *Fortnightly Review*, n.s., 642 (June 1, 1920): 849–63.

Hyatt, A. M. J., ed. *Dreadnought to Polaris: Maritime Strategy since Mahan; Papers from the Conference on Strategic Studies at the University of Western Ontario, March 1972*. Annapolis: Naval Institute Press, 1973.

Ienaga, Saburo. *The Pacific War: World War II and the Japanese*. Translated by Frank Baldwin. 1956. Reprint, New York: Pantheon, 1965.

Ikle, Fred W. "Japanese-German Peace Negotiations during World War I." *American Historical Review* 71:1 (October 1965): 62–76.

Ingersoll, Ralph. *The Battle Is the Pay-Off*. New York: Harcourt, Brace, 1943.

Iriye, Akira. *The Origins of the Second World War in Asia and the Pacific*. London: Longman, 1987.

Isely, Jeter A., and Philip A. Crowl. *The U.S. Marines and Amphibious War: Its Theory and Its Practice in the Pacific*. Princeton: Princeton University Press, 1951.

Ito, Masanori, and Roger Pineau. *The End of the Imperial Japanese Navy*. Translated by Andrew Y. Kuroda and Roger Pineau. 1956. Reprint, New York: MacFadden Books, 1965.

Jacobson, Maurice, producer. *The Deadly Fuze: The Story of World War II's Best-Kept Secret.* Grand Valley, Mich.: Grand Valley State University, WGVU, WGVK, 1995.

Jane, Fred T. *The Imperial Japanese Navy.* London: W. Thacker, 1904.

Janeway, Eliot. *The Struggle for Survival: A Chronicle of Economic Mobilization in World War II.* New Haven: Yale University Press, 1951.

Jasper, Joy Waldron, James P. Delgado, and Jim Adams. *The U.S.S.* Arizona: *The Ship, the Men, the Pearl Harbor Attack, and the Symbol That Aroused America.* New York: St. Martin's Press, 2001.

Jensen, Oliver. *Carrier War.* New York: Simon and Schuster, 1945.

Jentschura, Hansgeorg, Dieter Jung, and Peter Mikel. *Warships of the Imperial Japanese Navy, 1869–1945.* London: Arms and Armour Press, 1977.

Johnson, Paul. *Modern Times: The World from the Twenties to the Eighties.* New York: Harper Colophon, 1985.

Johnston, Stanley. *Queen of the Flat-tops: The U.S.S.* Lexington *and the Coral Sea.* New York: E. P. Dutton, 1942.

Jones, Geoffrey P. *Defeat of the Wolf Packs.* London: William Kimber, 1986.

Jones, James. *WWII: A Chronicle of Soldiering.* New York: Ballantine Books, 1976.

Jones, Tristan. *Heart of Oak.* Toronto: Bantam Books, 1984.

Jordan, Gerald. *Naval Warfare in the Twentieth Century, 1900–1945: Essays in Honor of Arthur J. Marder.* London: Croom Helm, 1977.

Kahn, David. *Seizing the Enigma: The Race to Break the German U-boat Codes, 1939–1943.* Boston: Houghton Mifflin, 1991.

Kajima, Morinosuke. *The Emergence of Japan as a World Power, 1895–1925.* Rutland, Vt.: C. E. Tuttle, 1968.

Karig, Walter, Russell L. Harris, and Frank Manson. *Battle Report* [World War II]. 6 vols. New York: Rinehart, 1944–1952.

Keegan, John. *The Price of Admiralty: The Evolution of Naval Warfare.* New York: Viking, 1988.

———, ed. *The "Times" Atlas of the Second World War.* New York: Harper and Row, 1989.

Kemp, Paul. *Convoy! Drama in Arctic Waters.* London: Brockhampton Press, 1999.

———. *U-boats Destroyed: German Submarine Losses in the World Wars.* London: Arms and Armour, 1997.

Kennan, George F. *American Diplomacy, 1900–1950.* New York: Mentor Books, 1952.

————. *Russia and the West under Lenin and Stalin.* New York: Mentor Books, 1961.

Kennedy, David M. *Freedom from Fear: The American People in Depression and War, 1929–1945.* New York: Oxford University Press, 1999.

Kennedy, Greg. *Anglo-American Strategic Relations and the Far East, 1933–1939: Imperial Crossroads.* London: Frank Cass, 2002.

Kennedy, Ludovic. *Pursuit: The Chase and Sinking of the* Bismarck. London: Collins, 1974.

Kennedy, Paul M. *The Rise and Fall of British Naval Mastery.* 1976. Reprint, London: Ashfield Press, 1987.

————. *The Rise and Fall of the Great Powers: Economic Change and Military Conflict from 1500 to 2000.* New York: Random House, 1987.

Kimmel, Husband E. *Admiral Kimmel's Story.* Chicago: Henry Regnery, 1955.

King, Ernest J. Introduction to *Battle Stations: Your Navy in Action; A Photographic Epic of the Naval Operations of World War II Told by the Great Admirals Who Sailed the Fleet from Norfolk to Normandy and from the Golden Gate to the Inland Sea.* New York: William H. Wise, 1946.

Knightley, Phillip. *The First Casualty: From the Crimea to Vietnam; The War Correspondent as Hero, Propagandist, and Myth Maker.* New York: Harcourt Brace Jovanovich, 1975.

Krancke, Theodor, and H. J. Brennecke. *Pocket Battleship: The Story of the Admiral Scheer.* New York: Berkley Publishing, 1958.

Krug, Hans-Joachim, Yoichi Hirama, Berthold J. Sander-Nagashima, and Axel Niestlé. *Reluctant Allies: German-Japanese Naval Relations in World War II.* Annapolis: Naval Institute Press, 2001.

Landsborough, Gordon. *The Battle of the River Plate.* London: Panther Books, 1956.

Lasch, Joseph P. *Roosevelt and Churchill, 1939–1941: The Partnership That Saved the West.* New York: Harper and Row, 1976.

Lawson, Ted W. *Thirty Seconds over Tokyo.* New York: Random House, 1943.

Layton, Edwin T., Roger Pineau, and John Costello. *And I Was There: Pearl Harbor and Midway—Breaking the Secrets.* New York: William Morrow, 1985.

Lech, Raymond B. *All the Drowned Sailors: The Story of the U.S.S.* Indianapolis. New York: Stein and Day, 1982.

LeCompte, Malcolm A. "Radar and the Air Battle of Midway." *Naval History* 6:2 (spring 1992).

Lee, Henry C., and Bruce Lee. *Pearl Harbor: Final Judgement.* New York: Crown Publishers, 1992.

Lehman, John F., Jr. *Command of the Sea.* New York: Scribner's, 1988.

——. *On Seas of Glory: Heroic Men, Great Ships, and the Epic Battles of the American Navy.* New York: Free Press, 2001.

Lenton, H. T. *German Warships of the Second World War.* New York: Arco Publishing, 1976.

Leuchtenburg, William E. *Franklin D. Roosevelt and the New Deal, 1932–1940.* New York: Harper and Brothers, 1963.

Lewin, Ronald. *Ultra Goes to War: The First Account of World War II's Greatest Secret Based on Official Documents.* New York: Pocket Books, 1980.

Lewis, Adrian R. "The Navy Falls Short at Normandy." *Naval History* 12:6 (November–December 1998): 34–38.

Link, Arthur S. *The Papers of Woodrow Wilson.* 69 vols. Princeton: Princeton University Press, 1966–1994.

Lockwood, Charles A. *Sink 'Em All.* New York: Dutton, 1951.

Lockwood, Charles A., and Hans Christian Adamson. *Hellcats of the Sea.* New York: Greenberg, 1955.

Lord, Walter. *Day of Infamy.* Austin, Tex.: Holt, Rinehart, Winston, 1957.

——. *Incredible Victory.* New York: Harper and Row, 1967.

Love, Robert William, Jr. *History of the U.S. Navy, 1775–1991.* 2 vols. Harrisburg, Pa.: Stackpole Books, 1992.

——, ed. *The Chiefs of Naval Operations.* Annapolis: Naval Institute Press, 1980.

Lowry, Thomas P., and John W. G. Wellham. *The Attack on Taranto: Blueprint for Pearl Harbor.* Mechanicsburg, Pa.: Stackpole Books, 2000.

Lukacs, John. *The Duel: Hitler vs. Churchill, 10 May–31 July 1940.* London: Phoenix Books, 1990.

Lundstrom, John B. *The First Team: Pacific Naval Air Combat from Pearl Harbor to Midway.* Annapolis: Naval Institute Press, 1984.

——. *The First Team and the Guadalcanal Campaign: Naval Fighter Combat from August to November 1942.* Annapolis: Naval Institute Press, 1994.

MacEachin, Douglas J. *The Final Months of the War with Japan: Signals Intelligence, U.S. Invasion Planning, and the A-Bomb Decision.* Washington, D.C.: Central Intelligence Agency, Center for the Study of Intelligence, 1998.

Macintyre, Donald. *Narvik.* New York: W. W. Norton, 1959.

——. *The Naval War against Hitler.* New York: Scribner's, 1971.

Maiolo, Joseph A. *The Royal Navy and Nazi Germany, 1933–39: A Study in Appeasement and the Origins of the Second World War.* London: Macmillan, 1998.

Manchester, William. *The Glory and the Dream: A Narrative History of America, 1932–1972.* Boston: Little, Brown, 1974.

Marder, Arthur J. *Portrait of an Admiral: The Life and Papers of Sir Herbert Richmond.* London: Jonathan Cape, 1952.

Markey, Morris. *Well Done! An Aircraft Carrier in Battle Action.* New York: Appleton-Century, 1945.

Martienssen, Anthony. *Hitler and His Admirals.* New York: Dutton, 1949.

Mason, John T., Jr., ed. *The Atlantic War Remembered: An Oral History Collection.* Annapolis: Naval Institute Press, 1990.

———. *The Pacific War Remembered: An Oral History Collection.* Annapolis: Naval Institute Press, 1986.

Masterson, Daniel M., ed. *Naval History: The Sixth Symposium of the U.S. Naval Academy.* Wilmington, Del.: Scholarly Resources, 1987.

Matsumoto, Kitaro. *Design and Construction of the Battleships* Yamato *and* Musashi. Tokyo: Haga Publishing, 1961.

Matsuru, Yoshida. *Requiem for Battleship* Yamato. Translated by Richard H. Minear. Seattle: University of Washington Press, 1985.

McIntyre, W. David. *The Rise and Fall of the Singapore Naval Base, 1919–1942.* London: Macmillan, 1979.

McKee, Christopher. *Sober Men and True: Sailor Lives in the Royal Navy, 1900–1945.* Cambridge: Harvard University Press, 2002.

McLachlan, Donald. *Room 39: A Study in Naval Intelligence.* New York: Atheneum, 1968.

Mears, Frederick. *Carrier Combat.* Garden City, N.Y.: Doubleday, Doran, 1944.

Melhorn, Charles M. *Two-Block Fox: The Rise of the Aircraft Carrier, 1911–1929.* Annapolis: Naval Institute Press, 1974.

Mendenhall, Corwin. *Submarine Diary.* Annapolis: Naval Institute Press, 1995.

Middlebrook, Martin. *Convoy.* New York: Morrow, 1977.

Miller, Bill. *Ocean Liners.* New York: Mallard Press, 1990.

Miller, David, and Chris Miller. *Modern Naval Combat.* New York: Crescent Books, 1986.

Miller, Edward S. *War Plan Orange: The U.S. Strategy to Defeat Japan, 1897–1945.* Annapolis: Naval Institute Press, 1991.

Miller, Nathan. *War at Sea: A Naval History of World War II.* New York: Scribner's, 1995.

Miller, Thomas G., Jr. *The Cactus Air Force.* New York: Harper and Row, 1969.

Millet, Allen R. *Semper Fidelis: The History of the United States Marine Corps.* New York: Macmillan, 1980.

Millis, Walter, ed. *The Forrestal Diaries.* New York: Viking Press, 1951.

Milner, Marc. "The Battle of the Atlantic." *Journal of Strategic Studies* 13:1 (March 1990): 48.

Mitchell, William. *Winged Defense: The Development and Possibilties of Modern Air Power—Economic and Military.* New York: G. P. Putnam's Sons, 1925.

Modelski, George, and William R. Thompson. *Seapower in Global Politics, 1494–1993.* Seattle: University of Washington Press, 1988.

Monsarrat, Nicholas. *The Cruel Sea.* 1951. Reprint, Toronto: Bantam Books, 1970.

Montross, Lynn. *War through the Ages.* New York: Harper and Row, 1960.

Mooney, Michael M. *The Hindenburg.* New York: Bantam Books, 1973.

Morgan, Frederick. *Overture to Overlord.* Garden City, N.Y.: Doubleday, 1950.

Morgan, Kenneth O. *The Oxford History of Britain.* New York: Oxford University Press, 1988.

Morison, Samuel Eliot. *History of United States Naval Operations in World War II.* 15 vols. Boston: Little, Brown, 1947–1962.

———. *Strategy and Compromise.* Boston: Little, Brown, 1958.

Morris, James. *Farewell the Trumpets: An Imperial Retreat.* San Diego: Harcourt Brace Jovanovich, 1978.

Moulton, J. L. *A Study of Warfare in Three Dimensions: The Norwegian Campaign of 1940.* Athens: Ohio University Press, 1967.

Müllenheim-Rechberg, Burkard Baron von. *Battleship* Bismarck: *A Survivor's Story.* Translated by Jack Sweetman. 2d ed. Annapolis: Naval Institute Press, 1990.

Muller, Edwin. "On Board the *Bismarck.*" *Harper's Magazine,* February 1942, 258–63.

Mulligan, Timothy P. "Forcing a U-boat Ace to Surface: Source Materials in a Biography of Werner Henke." *Prologue: Quarterly of the National Archives* 27:3 (fall 1995): 249–57.

Musicant, Ivan. *Battleship at War: The Epic Story of the U.S.S.* Washington. San Diego: Harcourt Brace Jovanovich, 1986.

Nalty, Bernard C. *Long Passage to Korea: Black Sailors and the Integration of the U.S. Navy.* Washington, D.C.: Department of the Navy, Naval Historical Center, 2003.

Neidpath, James. *The Singapore Naval Base and the Defence of Britain's Eastern Empire, 1919–1941.* Oxford: Clarendon Press, 1981.

Nichols, John B., and Barrett Tillman. *On Yankee Station.* Annapolis: Naval Institute Press, 1987.

Nihon Kaigun. Http://www.combinedfleet.com/. Kaigun: Imperial Japanese Navy page. A surprisingly professional and trustworthy Internet site.

Nimitz, Chester W. "Your Navy as Peace Insurance." *National Geographic* 89:6 (June 1946): 681–720.

O'Brien, Phillips Payson. *Technology and Naval Combat in the Twentieth Century and Beyond.* London: Frank Cass, 2001.

O'Connell, Robert L. *Sacred Vessels: The Cult of the Battleship and the Rise of the U.S. Navy.* Boulder: Westview Press, 1991.

O'Connor, Jerome M. "FDR's Undeclared War." *Naval History* 18:1 (February 2004): 24–29.

Okumiya, Masatake, Jiro Horikoshi, and Martin Caidin. *Zero!* New York: Ballantine Books, 1956.

O'Neill, Gearoid. "One Final Ordeal." *Naval History* 18:5 (October 2004): 27.

Overy, Richard. *Why the Allies Won.* New York: W. W. Norton, 1996.

Padfield, Peter. *The Battleship Era.* London: Rupert Hart-Davis, 1972.

Palmer, Michael A. *Origins of the Maritime Strategy: American Naval Strategy in the First Postwar Decade.* Washington, D.C.: Department of the Navy, Navy Historical Center, 1988.

Parkes, Oscar. *British Battleships,* Warrior *1860 to* Vanguard *1950: A History of Design, Construction, and Armament.* Annapolis: Naval Institute Press, 1990.

———, ed. *Jane's Fighting Ships, 1933.* London: Sampson, Low, Marston, 1933.

Parkes, Oscar, and Maurice Prendergast, eds. *Jane's Fighting Ships, 1919.* London: Sampson, Low, Marston, 1919.

Parrish, Thomas. *The Submarine: A History.* New York: Viking, 2004.

Patterson, A. Temple. *The Jellicoe Papers: Selections from the Private and Official Correspondence of Admiral of the Fleet Earl Jellicoe.* 2 vols. London: Spottiswoode, Ballantyne. 1968.

Peattie, Mark R. *Sunburst: The Rise of Japanese Naval Air Power, 1909–1941.* Annapolis: Naval Institute Press, 2001.

Peattie, Mark R., and David C. Evans. "Satō Tetsutarō and Japanese Strategy." *Naval History* 4:4 (fall 1990): 34–39.

Pelz, Stephen E. *Race to Pearl Harbor: The Failure of the Second London Naval Conference and the Onset of World War II.* Cambridge: Harvard University Press, 1974.

Petrie, Charles. "Foreign Affairs." *English Review* (December 1935): 737–39.

Peyton, Green. *5,000 Miles towards Tokyo.* Norman: University of Oklahoma Press, 1945.

Phayre, Ignatius. "Italy's Military Problems in Abyssinia." *English Review* (September 1935).

Philbin, Tobias R., III. *The Lure of Neptune: German-Soviet Naval Collaboration and Ambitions, 1919–1941*. Columbia: University of South Carolina Press, 1994.

Polenberg, Richard. *War and Society: The United States, 1941–1945*. Philadelphia: J. B. Lippincott, 1972.

Poole, S. L. *Cruiser: A History of British Cruisers from 1889 to 1960*. London: Robert Hale, 1970.

Poolman, Kenneth. *Allied Escort Carriers of World War II in Action*. Annapolis: Naval Institute Press, 1988.

———. *The Winning Edge: Naval Technology in Action, 1939–1945*. Annapolis: Naval Institute Press, 1997.

Pope, Dudley. *Graf Spee*. Philadelphia: J. B. Lippincott, 1957.

———. *73 North: The Defeat of Hitler's Navy*. Philadelphia: J. B. Lippincott, 1958.

Potter, E. B. *Bull Halsey*. Annapolis: Naval Institute Press, 1985.

———, ed. *Seapower: A Naval History*. Englewood Cliffs, N.J.: Prentice Hall, 1960.

Prados, John. *Combined Fleet Decoded: The Secret History of American Intelligence and the Japanese Navy in World War II*. New York: Random House, 1995.

Prange, Gordon W., Donald M. Goldstein, and Katherine V. Dillon. *At Dawn We Slept: The Untold Story of Pearl Harbor*. New York: McGraw-Hill, 1981.

———. *Miracle at Midway*. New York: McGraw-Hill, 1982.

———. *Pearl Harbor: The Verdict of History*. New York: McGraw-Hill, 1986.

Pratt, Fletcher. *Sea Power and Today's War*. New York: Harrison-Hilton Books, 1939.

Pratt, Fletcher, and Harley E. Howe. *The Compact History of the United States Navy*. Rev. ed. New York: Hawthorn Books, 1962.

Preston, Antony. *Aircraft Carriers*. New York: Gallery Books, 1979.

———. *Battleships*. New York: Gallery Books, 1981.

———. *Submarines*. New York: Gallery Books, 1982.

Puleston, W. D. *The Armed Forces of the Pacific: A Comparison of the Military and Naval Power of the United States and Japan*. New Haven: Yale University Press, 1941.

———. *The Influence of Sea Power in World War II*. New Haven: Yale University Press, 1947.

Quigley, Harold S., and George H. Blakeslee. *The Far East: An International Survey.* Boston: World Peace Foundation, 1938.

Raeder, Erich. *My Life.* Translated by Henry W. Drexel. Annapolis: Naval Institute Press, 1960.

Research Institute for Military History [Freiburg im Breisgau, Germany]. *Germany and the Second World War.* 6 vols. Oxford: Clarendon Press, 1991–2001.

Reynolds, Clark G. *The Carrier War.* Alexandria, Va.: Time-Life Books, 1982.

———. "Cherokee Jocko Fights the Cold War." *Naval History* 19:3 (June 2005): 18–22.

———. *The Fast Carriers: The Forging of an Air Navy.* New York: McGraw-Hill, 1968.

Richardson, Alexander, and Archibald Hurd, eds. *Brassey's Naval and Shipping Annual, 1921–2.* London: William Clowes and Sons, n.d.

———. *Brassey's Naval and Shipping Annual, 1923.* London: William Clowes and Sons, 1923.

Richardson, James O. *On the Treadmill to Pearl Harbor: The Memoirs of Admiral J. O. Richardson.* Washington, D.C.: U.S. Government Printing Office, 1973.

"Rivalry on the Seas." *Newsweek,* September 19, 1938, 17–18.

Robertson, Terence. *Channel Dash.* London: Evans Brothers, 1958.

———. *Escort Commander: The Story of Captain Frederic John Walker.* Toronto: Bantam Books, 1979.

———. *Night Raider of the Atlantic: The Saga of the U-99.* New York: Ace Books, 1955.

Robinson, Charles N., and H. M. Ross, eds. *Brassey's Naval and Shipping Annual, 1930.* London: William Clowes and Sons, n.d.

———. *Brassey's Naval and Shipping Annual, 1934.* London: William Clowes and Sons, 1934.

———. *Brassey's Naval and Shipping Annual, 1935.* London: William Clowes and Sons, 1935.

Rogow, Arnold. *James Forrestal: A Study of Personality, Politics, and Policy.* New York: Macmillan, 1963.

Rohwer, Jürgen. *The Critical Convoy Battles of March 1943: The Battle for HX 229/SC 122.* London: Ian Allen, 1977.

Ropp, Theodore. *War in the Modern World.* 2d ed. New York: Collier Books, 1971.

Roscoe, Theodore. *On the Seas and in the Skies: A History of the U.S. Navy's Air Power.* New York: Hawthorn Books, 1970.

———. *Tin Cans: The True Story of the Fighting Destroyers of World War II.* New York: Bantam Books, 1960.

Rose, Lisle A. *Dubious Victory: The United States and the End of World War II.* Kent: Kent State University Press, 1973.

———. *The Ship That Held the Line: The U.S.S.* Hornet *and the First Year of the Pacific War.* Annapolis: Naval Institute Press, 1995.

Roskill, Stephen. *Churchill and the Admirals.* London: Collins, 1977.

———. *Naval Policy between the Wars.* 2 vols. New York: Walker, 1968, 1976.

———, ed. *Documents Relating to the Naval Air Service.* Vol. 1, *1908–1918.* London: Scolar Press, 1969.

Ruge, Friedrich. *Der Seekrieg: The German Navy's Story, 1939–1945.* Translated by M. G. Saunders. Annapolis: Naval Institute Press, 1957.

Runyan, Timothy J., and Jan M. Copes, eds. *To Die Gallantly: The Battle of the Atlantic.* Boulder: Westview Press, 1994.

Rusbridger, James, and Eric Nave. *Betrayal at Pearl Harbor: How Churchill Lured Roosevelt into World War II.* New York: Summit Books, 1991.

Russell, Richard A. *Project Hula: Secret Soviet-American Cooperation in the War against Japan.* Washington, D.C.: Department of the Navy, Naval Historical Center, 1997.

Rust, Eric Christian. *Crew 34: German Naval Officers under and after Hitler.* Ann Arbor: UMI, 1987.

Sakai, Saburo, Martin Caidin, and Fred Saito. *Samurai!* Toronto: Bantam Books, 1978.

Salerno, Reynolds M. *Vital Crossroads: Mediterranean Origins of the Second World War, 1935–1940.* Ithaca: Cornell University Press, 2002.

Schaeffer, Heinz. *U-boat 977.* Toronto: Bantam Books, 1981.

Schaffer, Ronald. *Wings of Judgment: American Bombing in World War II.* New York: Oxford University Press, 1988.

Schlesinger, Arthur M., Jr. *The Crisis of the Old Order, 1919–1933.* Sentry Edition. Boston: Houghton Mifflin, 1965.

Schoenbaum, David. *Hitler's Social Revolution: Class and Status in Nazi Germany, 1933–1939.* Garden City, N.Y.: Doubleday Anchor Books, 1967.

Schom, Alan. *The Eagle and the Rising Sun: The Japanese-American War, 1941–1943, Pearl Harbor through Guadalcanal.* New York: W. W. Norton, 2004.

Sherwood, Robert E. *Roosevelt and Hopkins: An Intimate History.* New York: Harper and Brothers, 1948.

Shirer, William L. *Berlin Diary: The Journal of a Foreign Correspondent, 1934–1941.* New York: Alfred A. Knopf, 1941.

———. *The Rise and Fall of the Third Reich.* New York: Simon and Schuster, 1960.

Sholin, Bill. *"Truman's Decision": Kamikaze's the Unknown Factor.* Bonney Lake, Wash.: Mountain View Publishing, 1996.

Shulman, Milton. *Defeat in the West.* 1947. Reprint, New York: Ballantine Books, 1968.

Simonds, Frank H. *Can Europe Keep the Peace?* New York: Harper and Brothers, 1931.

Simpson, Michael, ed. *Anglo-American Naval Relations, 1917–1919.* London: Scolar Press, 1991.

Skulski, Janusz. *The Heavy Cruiser* Takao. Annapolis: Naval Institute Press, 1994.

Sledge, E. B. *With the Old Breed at Peleliu and Okinawa.* Novato, Calif.: Presidio Press, 1981.

Smith, Peter C. *The Great Ships Pass: British Battleships at War, 1939–45.* London: William Kimber, 1977.

Smith, Rex Alan, and Gerald A. Meehl. *Pacific Legacy: Images and Memory from World War II in the Pacific.* New York: Abbeville Press, 2002.

Smith, William Ward. *Midway: Turning Point of the Pacific.* New York: Thomas Y. Crowell, 1966.

Snyder, Louis L. *The War: A Concise History, 1939–1945.* New York: Julian Messner, 1960.

Sontag, Raymond J. *A Broken World, 1919–1939.* New York: Harper and Row, 1971.

Spector, Ronald H. *At War at Sea: Sailors and Naval Warfare in the Twentieth Century.* New York: Viking, 2001.

———. *Eagle against the Sun: The American War with Japan.* New York: Free Press, 1985.

Speer, Albert. *Inside the Third Reich: Memoirs by Albert Speer.* New York: Macmillan, 1970.

Spence, Jonathan D. *The Search for Modern China.* New York: W. W. Norton, 1990.

Sprout, Harold, and Margaret Sprout. *Toward a New Order of Sea Power: American Naval Policy and the World Scene, 1918–1922.* Princeton: Princeton University Press, 1940.

Spurr, Russell. *A Glorious Way to Die: The Kamikaze Mission of the Battleship Yamato, April 1945.* New York: Newmarket Press, 1981.

Stafford, Edward P. *The* Big E: *The Story of the U.S.S. Enterprise.* New York: Ballantine Books, 1974.

Steinert, Marlis G. *23 Days: The Final Collapse of Nazi Germany.* Translated by Richard Barry. New York: Walker, 1969.

Stern, Robert C. *The* Lexington *Class Carriers.* London: Arms and Armour Press, 1993.

Stevens, William Oliver, and Allan Westcott. *A History of Sea Power.* New York: Doubleday, Doran, 1942.

Stevenson, William. *A Man Called Intrepid: The Secret War.* New York: Ballantine Books, 1976.

Stilwell, Paul. "Looking Back: Pearl Harbor at 60—an Enduring Legacy." *Naval History* 16:2 (April 2002): 4.

Stimson, Henry L., and McGeorge Bundy. *On Active Service in Peace and War.* New York: Harper and Brothers, 1947.

Stolfi, R. H. S. *Hitler's Panzers East: World War II Reinterpreted.* Norman: University of Oklahoma Press, 1992.

Straboli, Joseph Montague Kenworthy. *Sea Power in the Second World War.* London: Hutchinson, 1943.

Sullivan, Brian R. "A Fleet in Being: The Rise and Fall of Italian Sea Power, 1861–1943." *International History Review* 10:1 (February 1988): 106–24.

Sullivan, Mark. *Our Times: The United States, 1900–1925.* 6 vols. New York: Scribner's, 1926–1935.

Sumrall, Robert F., ed. *Warship's Battle Damage Report No. 1: U.S.S.* Hornet *(CV-8) Loss in Action in the Battle of Santa Cruz, 27 October 1942.* Missoula: Pictorial Histories Publishing, 1985.

Sweetman, Jack. *The Great Admirals: Command at Sea, 1587–1945.* Annapolis: Naval Institute Press, 1997.

Syrett, David. *The Defeat of the German U-boats: The Battle of the Atlantic.* Columbia: University of South Carolina Press, 1994.

Tansill, Charles Callan. *Back Door to War: The Roosevelt Foreign Policy, 1933–1941.* Chicago: Henry Regnery, 1952.

Taylor, A. J. P. *English History, 1914–1945.* New York: Oxford University Press, 1965.

Taylor, Theodore. *The Magnificent Mitscher.* New York: W. W. Norton, 1954.

Thomas, Charles S. *The German Navy in the Nazi Era.* Annapolis: Naval Institute Press, 1990.

Thomas, David A. *Crete 1941: The Battle at Sea.* London: Andre Deutsch, 1972.

Thorne, Christopher. *Limits of Foreign Policy: The West, the League, and the Far Eastern Crisis of 1931–1933.* London: Hamish, Hamilton, 1972.

Thornton, A. P. *The Imperial Idea and Its Enemies: A Study in British Power.* 1959. Reprint, Garden City, N.Y.: Doubleday Anchor Books, 1968.

Thursfield, H. G., eds. *Brassey's Naval Annual, 1937.* London: William Clowes, 1937.

Till, Geoffrey. "Midway: The Decisive Battle?" *Naval History* 19:5 (October 2005): 32–36.

Toland, John. *But Not in Shame: The Six Months after Pearl Harbor.* New York: Signet Books, 1962.

———. *Infamy: Pearl Harbor and Its Aftermath.* Garden City, N.Y.: Doubleday, 1982.

Tolley, Kemp. *Yangtze Patrol: The U.S. Navy in China.* Annapolis: Naval Institute Press, 1971.

Tracy, Nicholas. *The Collective Naval Defense of the Empire, 1900–1940.* London: Ashgate Press, 1997.

Trimble, William F. *Admiral William A. Moffett: Architect of Naval Aviation.* Washington, D.C.: Smithsonian Institution Press, 1994.

Tuleja, Thaddeus V. *Climax at Midway.* New York: W. W. Norton, 1960.

Tute, Warren. *The Deadly Stroke.* London: Collins, 1973.

Tyushkevich, S. A. *The Soviet Armed Forces: A History of Their Organizational Development, a Soviet View.* Translated by the CIS Multilingual Section, Translation Bureau, Secretary of State Department, Ottawa, Canada. Published under the Auspices of the United States Air Force. Moscow: n.p., 1978.

Ugaki, Matome. *Fading Victory: The Diary of Admiral Matome Ugaki, 1941–1945.* Translated by Masataka Chihaya. Pittsburgh: University of Pittsburgh Press, 1991.

Uhlig, Frank, Jr. *How Navies Fight: The U.S. Navy and Its Allies.* Annapolis: Naval Institute Press, 1994.

[United Kingdom] MOD [Ministry of Defence] (NAVY). *War with Japan.* 6 vols. London: Her Majesty's Stationery Office, 1995.

"The U.S. Navy." *Life,* October 28, 1940, pp. 9–89.

U.S. Navy, Bureau of Navigation. *Landing Force Manual: United States Navy, 1927.* Washington, D.C.: U.S. Government Printing Office, 1927.

Utley, Jonathan G. *An American Battleship at Peace and War: The U.S.S. Tennessee.* Lawrence: University Press of Kansas, 1991.

Vandegrift, Archibald A., and Robert B. Aspery. *Once a Marine: The Memoirs of General A. A. Vandegrift, U.S.M.C.* New York: W. W. Norton, 1964.

van der Vat, Dan. *The Atlantic Campaign: World War II's Great Struggle at Sea.* New York: Harper and Row, 1988.

———. *The Pacific Campaign, World War II: The U.S.-Japanese Naval War, 1941–1945.* New York: Simon and Schuster, 1991.

van Tol, Jan M. "Military Innovation and Carrier Aviation: An Analysis." *Joint Force Quarterly* (autumn–winter 1997–1998): 97–109.

Vause, Jordan. *Wolf: U-boat Commanders in World War II.* Annapolis: Naval Institute Press, 1997.

von der Porton, Edward. *The German Navy in World War II.* New York: Thomas Y. Crowell, 1969.

Warlimont, Walter. *Inside Hitler's Headquarters, 1939–45.* Translated by R. H. Barry. New York: Praeger, 1964.

"Warships: Reich Demands Navy That Could Wipe Out Whole British Fleet." *Newsweek,* June 15, 1935, 12–13.

Wegener, Wolfgang. *The Naval Strategy of the World War.* Translated by Holger H. Herwig. Annapolis: Naval Institute Press, 1989.

Werner, Herbert A. *Iron Coffins: A Personal Account of the German U-boat Battles of World War II.* New York: Bantam, 1969.

Wheeler, Richard. *A Special Valor: The U.S. Marines and the Pacific War.* Edison, N.J.: Castle Books, 1983.

White, Theodore H. *In Search of History: A Personal Adventure.* New York: Warner Books, 1978.

White, William, ed. *By-Line: Ernest Hemingway; Selected Articles and Dispatches of Four Decades.* New York: Bantam, 1968.

White, William L. *They Were Expendable.* Washington, D.C.: Infantry Journal, Penguin Books, 1944.

Whitehouse, Arch. *Fighting Ships.* New York: Curtis Books, 1967.

Wildenberg, Thomas. *Grey Steel and Black Oil: Fast Tankers and Replenishment at Sea in the U.S. Navy, 1912–1992.* Annapolis: Naval Institute Press, 1996.

———. "In Support of the Battle Line: Gunnery's Influence on the Development of Carrier Aviation in the U.S. Navy." *Journal of Military History* 65: 3 (July 2001): 697–711.

Williamson, Murray, and Allen Millett. *A War to Be Won: Fighting the Second World War.* Cambridge: Harvard University Press, 2000.

Willmott, H. P. *The Barrier and the Javelin: Japanese and Allied Pacific Strategies, February to June 1942.* Annapolis: Naval Institute Press, 1983.

———. *Empires in the Balance: Japanese and Allied Pacific Strategies to April 1942.* Annapolis: Naval Institute Press, 1982.

Wilmot, Chester. *The Struggle for Europe.* 1952. Reprint, London: Fontana Books, 1959.

Wincott, Len. *Invergordon Mutineer.* London: Weidenfeld and Nicolson, 1974.

Winslow, W. G. *The Fleet the Gods Forgot: The U.S. Asiatic Fleet in World War II*. Annapolis: Naval Institute Press, 1982.

Winter, C. W. R. *The* Queen Mary: *Her Early Years Recalled*. New York: W. W. Norton, 1986.

Wohlstetter, Roberta. *Pearl Harbor: Warning and Decision*. Stanford: Stanford University Press, 1962.

Woodward, C. Vann. *The Battle for Leyte Gulf*. New York: Macmillan, 1947.

Wooldridge, E. T., ed. *Into the Jet Age: Conflict and Change in Naval Aviation, 1945–1975*. Annapolis: Naval Institute Press, 1995.

Y'Blood, William T. *Hunter-Killer: U.S. Escort Carriers in the Battle of the Atlantic*. New York: Bantam Books, 1992.

———. *Red Sun Setting: The Battle of the Philippine Sea*. Annapolis: Naval Institute Press, 1981.

Yoshimura, Akira. *Battleship* Musashi: *The Making and Sinking of the World's Greatest Battleship*. 1991. Reprint, Tokyo: Kodansha International, 1999.

Ziegler, Philip. *Mountbatten: A Biography*. New York: Alfred A. Knopf, 1985.

INDEX

Note: Numbers in italics refer to illustrations

—U.S.: *Albacore,* 403; *Antares,* 352; *Arizona,* 333; *Augusta*-class, 50; *Balao*-class, 384; *Belleau Woods,* 389; *Bogue,* 319, 360–61; *Bunker Hill, 165,* 389, 417; *California,* 407; *California*-class, 334; *Cavalla,* 403; *Cimarron,* 169; *City of Flint,* 206; *Cleveland,* 399; *Colorado*-class, 334; *Cowpens,* 389; *Detroit,* 350; *Eagle*-class, 311; *Enterprise, 159,* 187, 237, 251, 258–59, 261–62, 268–69, 272, 343–44, 350, 389; *Essex,* 382, 387, 389, 417; *Essex*-class, 342, 382, 386, 390, 439n23; *Florida,* 29–30; *Franklin,* 417; *Gambier Bay,* 409; *Gato*-class, 384, 386; *George Washington,* 11; *Greer, 160;* *Guadalcanal,* 361; *Hoel,* 409; *Hornet, 159,* 225, 251, 258–59, 261–62, 265–66, 269, 274, 417; *Huntington,* 179; *Independence,* 387; *Independence*-class, 390; *Indianapolis,* 331, 387; *Intrepid,* 417; *Iowa*-class, 50, 137, 342; *Johnson,* 409; *Jupiter,* 185; *Langley, 31,* 185–87; *Lexington, 31, 34, 158,* 168–69, 186–87, 237, 252–56, 389; *Liscome Bay,* 318; *Makin Island, 164;* *Maryland,* 24, 407; *Maryland*-class, 24, 29; *Massachusetts,* 235; *Maumee,* 168; *Mississippi,* 407; *Missouri,* 420; *Modoc,* 247; *Montana*-class, 137, 342; *Neosho,* 169, 255; *Nevada*-class, 334; *New Mexico,* 8; *New Mexico*-class, 334; *North Carolina,* 235, 272, 387; *North Carolina*-class, 137, 272, 342; *O'Bannon,* 359–60; *Omaha*-class, 54, 184; *Panay,* 110, 147; *Pennsylvania, 9, 149,* 179, 407; *Pennsylvania*-class, 334; *Philippine Sea,* 463n13; *Phoenix,* 350; *Princeton,* 389; *Randolph,* 417; *Ranger,* 143, 187, 235; *Reuben James,* 250; *Robert C. Tuttle, 159;* *St. Lo,* 409; *St. Louis,* 350; *Samuel B. Roberts,* 409; *Santee,* 360; *Saratoga, 31, 34,* 186–87, 265–66, 387, 389, 450n97; *Seattle,* 179; *Sims,* 255; *South Dakota, 14,* 235, 272–73, 402; *South Dakota*-class, 50, 137, 272, 342; *Tench*-class, 384; *Tennessee, 158, 164,* 407; *Texas,* 57, 248–49; *Ticonderoga,* 417; *Utah,* 29–30; *Ward,* 352; *Washington,* 235, 273, 402; *Wasp,* 225, 265–66, 269, 272, 380, 387; *West Virginia, 158,* 407; *William D. Porter,* *166; Wyoming,* 29–30; *York,* 261–62; *Yorktown,* 143, 187, 225, 237, 252–56, 259, 387, 389, 391–93, 449n79, 450n100; *Yorktown*-class, 50

Shirer, William L., 120
Short, Walter, 344–45, 347, 350–53, 460n48
Sicilian Narrows, 381
Simon, John, 62, 83, 112; Anglo-German Naval Agreement and, 86–88, 91, 92, 99
Sims, William Sowden, 172, 183–84
Singapore: Britain and, 20–21, 84, 96, 461n71; concession over fortification of, 35, 38; Japan and, 147, 421; Japanese conquest of, 227, 231, 384
Sino-Japanese War of 1894–1895, 140
Sledge, Eugene, 395–96
Slot, The, 266, 268–69, 272, 395
Smith, Leonard, 247
Smuts, Jan, 68–69, 71
Solomon Islands, 267, 388; eastern, 268, 450n97; Japan and, 236, 279; in Japan's defense line, 194, 225, 227, 257, 397; New Georgia, 395; Rabaul, 266, 268, 270–71; Santa Cruz, 253–54, 262, 269, 272, 278; Savo, 266–67, 278; Tulagi, 227, 252–53, 257, 263, 267; upper, 270. *See also* Battles and campaigns: World War II
Somerville, James, 229–30, 362, 364–65
Southeast Asia: Japan needing resources from, 384, 458n30; Japanese expansion through, 226–27, 231; lack of Japanese strategy for, 274, 276–77
South Sea Islands, 60
Spain, 5, 110–11
Spanish Civil War, 110–11, 365; Guernica, 105
Spector, Ronald, 263
Spee, Maximilian Graf von, 21
Sperry, Charles S., 168
Sprague, Ziggy, 409–10
Sprout, Harold, 17
Sprout, Margaret, 17
Spruance, Raymond A., *155,* 195, 390–91, 402; at Midway, 259, 261; Philippines and, 338, 404
Spurr, Russell, 136
Stalin, Joseph, 48–49, 110
Stanley, Oliver, 212
Stark, Harold, 243–44, 341, 352–53

LISLE A. ROSE is the author of eight previous books, including *The Ship That Held the Line: U.S.S.* Hornet *and the First Half of the Pacific War* and *The Cold War Comes to Main Street: America in 1950*. He served in the U.S. Navy from 1954 to 1957 and in the U.S. Department of State's Bureau of Oceans and International Environmental and Scientific Affairs from 1978 to 1989. He lives in Edmonds, Washington.